Unified social science
A SYSTEM-BASED
INTRODUCTION

Unified social science

A SYSTEM-BASED INTRODUCTION

ALFRED KUHN
University of Cincinnati

 1975

THE DORSEY PRESS   Homewood, Illinois   60430
Irwin-Dorsey International, London, England   WC2H 9NJ
Irwin-Dorsey Limited, Georgetown, Ontario   L7G 4B3

© THE DORSEY PRESS, 1975

First Printing, January 1975

ISBN 0-256-01444-2
Library of Congress Catalog Card No. 74–12930
Printed in the United States of America

PREFACE

For perhaps half a century people have debated how best to introduce college freshmen to social science. The historical or philosophical survey of civilizations, the "problems" approach, and a little-bit-of-each discipline are among the most widely used attempts at broad coverage in a single course. In addition are found a variety of multi-discipline, multi-instructor courses. Many others insist—perhaps properly under the present state of affairs—that only a solid introduction to a single discipline is academically sound.

The difficulty is, of course, that as presently conceived and taught there is no conceptual unity among the social sciences. Sociology, economics, political science, anthropology, human geography, history, and psychology—depending on where one draws his boundary of the social sciences—each has a vocabulary and conceptual structure of its own. There is also a sense in which the social sciences themselves fall into a dichotomy, even if the dividing line is fuzzy and often breached. Sociology, economics, and political science are sometimes viewed as "core" ("basic" or nomothetic) disciplines, seeking generalizations independent of time and place. Anthropology, geography, and history are more likely to be oriented to particular cultures, places, and times, respectively —even in the process of comparing cultures, places, and times. Our language also identifies a difference, as when we speak, for example, of political anthropology, economic geography, or social history; but not of anthropological politics, geographic economics, or historical sociology. Any one of the first three social sciences fits comfortably as an adjective for any of the latter three, but not the reverse—though we may, of course, speak of the history of any line of thought. For reasons that will become

v

clearer as we proceed, this volume concentrates mainly on the subject matter of the first three (core) disciplines, though with significant attention to some aspects of anthropology. Given the relative exclusivity of the disciplines and the jealousy with which some devotees guard their ramparts it might seem to those who want broad-gauged introductory courses that little more can be done than to keep trying new variations on the pedagogic themes already developed.

In contrast, this volume is premised on a conceptual unity of social science, which social scientists should identify and use. Each need not reinvent the wheel for itself! Now the function of any introductory text is to organize, systematize, synthesize, and clarify the central ideas and information from its field. The task requires selection from a large body of material and some simplification of conceptual structure. In that sense the objective of this volume is the same as that of any other introduction. The difference is that its "field" is traditionally viewed as several disciplines, not one. Its technique, however, is merely to extend the normal function of a text. This text identifies some concepts the disciplines have in common, but whose identity has been hidden by the fact that the specialists use different languages for them, accord them different emphasis, and read too little of one another's literature to recognize the similarities.

Unless such similarities of concept and logic are identified, fears of Mickey Mousism and intellectual sterility legitimately haunt teachers of "integrated" courses. However, if there *is* a bona fide set of common concepts, there is no reason why an introduction based on them need be less rigorous than a good introduction to any standard discipline. And it might be much more useful. In this vein I have tried to produce a comprehensive introductory social science that is intellectually honest, intelligible to freshmen, both broad gauged and "real" enough for a good terminal course, while also providing a solid base for higher level courses in the separate disciplines with minimal conceptual retooling.

To be more specific, this volume uses a conceptual structure which sees the *basic* social science disciplines, not as sociology, economics, and political science, but as communication, transaction, and organization, approached through a base in system analysis. Although each of these four may be a substantial discipline in its own right, the main concepts and principles of any one can be introduced with rigor and simplicity within several chapters. This approach encompasses both social processes and social structures, the latter mainly in connection with organization—though there are more variations than we can even hint at in a preface.

As a science matures it normally shifts from descriptive material to concepts, generalizations, and relationships. "It is the essence of theory that it organizes and simplifies the profusion of facts in the world" (Morrissett, 1966: 5). In that spirit the small proportion of descriptive material herein more nearly resembles that of economics than of the other social sciences. Unlike much traditional economics, however, most of it will seem direct and real to students.

There are many different ways the book can be taught, and I would strongly urge only that the instuctor be familiar with the whole before teaching any of its parts.

Although the general contours and many details of this volume are my own, the whole obviously rests on the presently developed state of the social and behavioral sciences, and on system analysis. The thinking that went into this volume depends far more on that of Kenneth Boulding than on any other person, but also on the encouragement of the many persons who responded favorably to my initial efforts in unified social science of a decade ago. Special thanks are due to Robert Beam who, as student assistant, helped greatly with finding detailed information. Also to students in my classes who provided much critical comment, and whose refusal to stop pounding at me until the chapter on the family achieved a reasonably contemporary, unchauvinist tone is greatly appreciated. Many constructive changes, some quite large, were made in consequence of suggestions and criticisms from Dodd Bogart, Dana Hiller, Charles A. Berry, and Wesley Allinsmith, all of the University of Cincinnati. Important readers from other campuses were John Curtin, California State University at San Francisco; Thomas E. Drabek, University of Denver; Leonard W. Moss, Wayne State University; and Robin M. Williams, Jr., Cornell; their sometimes pungent comments led to many useful changes. Miriam Tucker and Janet Schaible typed most of the manuscript and Nina Kuhn prepared the index.

December 1974   ALFRED KUHN

CONTENTS

recreation. A short note on love and hate. Authority and decisions in the family. Some trends.

plines. Society and a science of society. What can we do about social systems?
The internals of complex formal organization. Broad-scale social planning.
Conclusion.

1

INTRODUCTION

POTENTIALITIES AND LIMITATIONS

Your rich uncle has just died. He has left you exactly what you wanted—a low-slung sports car and enough money for a comprehensive tour of the United States. With a stack of maps in front of you, you beam and say, "Now I can drive anywhere in the country that I like." "Anywhere there are roads!" murmurs your friend.

As you drive you gradually observe from both the countryside and the maps that you can actually drive your sports car into only a tiny fraction of all the territory of this country. Particularly in much of that vast region between the Great Plains and the West Coast you find that the map shows remarkably few roads. What is more, when you actually get there you find to your surprise (if you come from more populated areas) that in many sparse areas there *are* no roads that are *not* shown on the map. Not even winding little roads of scraped dirt.

You will find, that is, that there is a *structure* of roads. You can travel easily where roads have already been built. But you can travel only with difficulty, if at all, where there are no roads. You also know that you cannot drive sideways or vertically, over logs, or through water. You cannot stop quickly on ice, and the car is not geared to go backward as fast as forward. Thus your freedom to do what you like with the car is limited, not only by the structure of the highway network, but also by the kinds of *functions* your car is able to perform.

All human societies similarly have structures and functions. Their structures allow you to "go" some places within them with relative ease, while they also make it difficult or impossible to "go" other places.

The structures and functions of both highway systems and social systems are determined partly by the natural environment and partly by what man has deliberately or inadvertently done within it. Nature makes highways easy to build in the flat spaces of New Jersey, Kansas, or Arizona, and difficult to build in the mountains of West Virginia, Colorado, or Alaska. And to humans it seems sensible to build cars that will climb a three-inch curb but not a ten-inch one, or that will easily climb a grade of 10 percent but not 50 percent. In social systems nature similarly prescribes that a couple can have three children but not three hundred, and that the society must be structured to provide each person with a food intake of about two thousand calories per day, not three or three million.

By contrast, that a person may have only one spouse, who may not be a close blood relative, is determined by the society, not by biological nature. So is the fact that in the United States private individuals may legally form a corporation to produce bubble gum or electricity but not to establish an army or (in most states) a house of prostitution. Within wide limits allowed by natural forces, much of what human beings can and will do together is determined by the structures and functions of their societies. These structures and functions differ from time to time and from society to society.

Where the necessary structures and functions are available, people will find their ability to do certain things greatly enhanced. Where such structures and functions are not available, people will face obstacles— sometimes insurmountable—to doing what they want. Moreover, what is perhaps society's greatest impact on the individual lies in molding what he wants and how he sees things. Even the person who resists and resents society's prescriptions actually accepts much more than he knows—as we shall see.

A WORD ABOUT SCIENCE

This book is entitled SOCIAL SCIENCE. The purpose of science is to help us understand how things work. The purpose of social science is to help us understand how societies work. Societies involve interactions (functions or behaviors) and patterns of relationships (structures) of two or more people. In the broadest sense a society can consist of as few as two people or as many as all on earth. One person cannot be a society.

Social science is not usually viewed as a single field. Just as the "natural" sciences are divided into such areas (disciplines) as physics, chemistry, biology, geology, and astronomy—to mention only the main headings—so are the social sciences also divided. We typically think of six social sciences: sociology, economics, political science, history, anthropology, and human geography. (We will discuss psychology later below.) The first three are sometimes described as "core" disciplines. Each studies a particular aspect of social systems. For example, political science focuses mainly on government, and economics focuses on the production and distribution of marketable goods. Sociology might be said to deal with all of the many human interactions and structures not explicitly dealt with by the other two core social sciences.

The three core disciplines seek principles that are independent of time or place. Let us look at one example of each. "Most of the behavior of any individual is determined by the culture in which he grows up." "The price and quantity of a good will be determined by the interaction of supply and demand." "A successful ruler must possess and know how to exercise power." These statements are intended to apply, respectively, to any social system, any economic market, or any government, regardless of when, where, or by whom it has been established.

By contrast, history gives attention to explicit times, places, and persons, usually with an emphasis on time sequence, and may be thought of as a social science or a humanity, depending on how one goes about it. Geography gives attention to particular places, and to the relationships of things in space. Anthropology focuses on particular societies, and on how the patterns of living differ, for example, as among the Japanese, the Eskimos, the Hopi Indians, and the Trobriand Islanders. In addition to having certain kinds of science in their own right, each of these three disciplines also leans to some extent on the "core" disciplines, as in economic history, political geography, or social anthropology. Psychology, strictly viewed, studies the individual. In that sense it is not a social science. Many psychologists, however, feel that individual behavior cannot be understood except as one human being relates to others. To the extent that psychology studies such relationships it, too, is a social science. The term *behavioral science* is sometimes used to encompass both psychology and the social sciences, with emphasis within the social sciences on the explanations of why particular persons or social units behave as they do. In that sense this volume may be viewed as broad-based behavioral science.

More specifically, the main purpose of this volume is to introduce the kinds of things studied by sociology, economics, political science, and to a lesser degree, anthropology—though many of the concepts herein should also be useful in *all* social science. We will not try to summarize each of the separate disciplines, nor to "relate" them in their present forms. Instead we will focus on some ingredients that all have in common. These should provide the basis both for understanding real societies and for more advanced study of the specialized social science disciplines.

An analogy may help. All complex mechanical machines are made up of different combinations of such basic mechanical units as gears, wheels, pulleys, levers, etc. Understanding these mechanical basics will not itself make you a competent designer or repairman of either watches or sewing machines. But you certainly will not go very far as a specialist in watches or sewing machines if you do not understand levers, gears, etc. Furthermore, if you *do* understand these basics you should be able to learn rather quickly how any *particular* machine works. Similarly, in electronics an understanding of resistors, capacitors, transformers, and transistors is not in itself an understanding of amplifiers or radio. But your understanding of amplifiers and radio will be primitive if you do *not* understand these things.

This book is about the "basic mechanics" of societies. It suggests that social analysis deals with three basic ways of interacting, which we call communication, transaction, and organization. *Communication* deals with the process of transferring information between parties—whether the information is true or false, and whether or not it is valued. (Do not quibble over whether it could be "information" if it is false. If I say, "It is raining hard," you understand my statement even if the sky is cloudless. In fact, you could not conclude that my statement is false unless it first is clear *as a communication*.) *Transaction* deals with the transfer or exchange of valued things between parties. The things exchanged may be tangible and impersonal, like tires or coffee. Or they may be intangible and personal, like affection and respect. *Organization* is any relationship between two or more persons for producing some joint effect. It includes governments, corporations, families, PTAs, and two people carrying a table.

The way any two or more persons interact is molded by the nature of the persons. The interactions also have certain effects on the persons, who may be changed as a result. In studying the individual person, we will focus on his information, his motives or goals, and his skills and abilities—all as they relate to his interactions. Because these aspects of the individual deal respectively with information, with values, and with producing or performing effects—just as do communication, transaction, and organization, respectively—in this volume the three kinds of interactions *between* persons are tied directly to the three kinds of states or conditions *within* persons. This arrangement brings a much closer relationship between the psychological and social levels of human behavior than do other approaches to social science. The system language names for information, motives, and performance abilities are, respectively, detector, selector, and effector functions, and will be detailed later. The individual and social levels are intimately related: we cannot understand man without society or society without man.

A difference between this book and the "standard" social sciences is simple and fundamental. By analogy, the existing disciplines introduce the student to transmissions and differentials, but never get around very clearly to the basic principles of gears. They introduce the student to radios and amplifiers, but without telling him much about transformers and capacitors. This book reverses things. It introduces the student first to the fundamentals. After he is familiar with these basics he is shown how they can be put together into particular combinations: to make watches or sewing machines, radios or amplifiers. That is, after the student is introduced to communications, transactions, and organizations he is shown how they can be used to help understand such things as authority, dominance and submission, family, government, legislature, status, class structure, market, corporation, or culture. We deal with the simplest situations before going to the more complex.

Since the units that make up a society are individual human beings, we will look at the human creature—his potentialities and his limitations—before we examine interactions between two or more. Since every human being and every organization of human beings is also a system, and since system analysis runs through much of this volume, we will precede our discussion of the individual human with an introduction to systems.

Most of this book will deal with principles that many situations have in common—respects in which they are *similar*. Toward the end we will discuss unique situations—the respects in which each situation is *different* from others. Also, most of the volume will be concerned with how a particular social interaction or structure works, given its ingredients. Near the end we will discuss how and why those ingredients change over time. Again by analogy, we will study mostly how a radio or a sewing machine works—if it is built of a particular set of components. Later we will study how and why radios and sewing machines have been changed over the years.

This arrangement is seen in the Table of Contents. The first parts of the book do not deal with sociology, economics, and political science. Instead—and following chapters on general and human systems—the book deals with communications, transactions, and organizations. Only after the reader is grounded in these basics do we move to particular types of social systems, such as governments, economies, and families. We trust that the reader will understand those particular "social machines" better because he first understands their components.

Among other things I harbor the hope that the discussions of models, detector processes, and communications will provide an understandable introduction to that too-often esoteric field known as the philosophy of science.

© 1972 United Feature Syndicate, Inc.

part I
Systems in general

2

THE GENERAL NOTION OF SYSTEMS AND TYPES OF SYSTEMS

"All systems are go," says the voice, before the space vehicle is launched. "Systems analysts wanted," says the employment page. "The economic system is basically healthy," says the financial page. "The ecological system is strangling in pollution." "Will the educational system survive the 70s?"

Such is the language of our times. Is "system" a real thing we can examine, touch, and study? Is it a good word to use so as to sound up-to-date? Are systems enough alike so that "when you've seen one you've seen 'em all"? Or are they so different that you might know a great deal about one kind of system and still know nothing about some other kind?

The word *system* has been around for centuries. The idea that it can be a precisely defined scientific concept, rather than a loose layman's term, dates mainly from about World War II, and most conspicuously from the mid-1950s. The study of systems, viewed as a science, is thus about as old as the present college generation. (And about as accepted by many of that generation's elders.) Although the study of systems is clearly a fledgling science, relatively inexperienced, the sense of this book is that the science is now able to take on some serious responsibilities. Some devotees insist it can do most jobs better than its intellectual parents. This book does not make that particular claim, at least not very loudly. It does insist that a systems view can do many jobs as well as its forebears, a few better, some perhaps not as well, but that it makes far more sense of the total reality than does any other way of looking at things.

9

WHAT IS A SYSTEM?

The word *system* is often used in a way that apparently means nothing more than "systematic." It is often useful, of course, to do things systematically. But that statement could just as well have been made by Moses or Galileo as by a present-day system analyst. I also get the impression that many people think "system analysis" merely involves drawing some boxes or circles to represent some things, and putting labels and arrows on them. Visual aids are obviously helpful, and we could perhaps use more of them. But they are hardly a startling addition to scientific knowledge. There are also scores of articles headed something like "A Systems Approach to Transcendental Malarkey." But beyond the title there is no reference to systems or a systems approach. The malarkey is unchanged.

It is the point of this book that system analysis, which is used interchangeably with systems analysis, is distinct both as a *body of knowledge* and as a *particular way of organizing knowledge.* As to the latter, it is a way of looking at many different kinds of things so that their similarities are more readily apparent. If successful, it enables us to understand a wider variety of things with a smaller bundle of basic principles. As a body of knowledge, it does seem to have some principles of its own, as we shall see.

A *system* is any set of interrelated or interacting components. "Set" means merely a collection of two or more, not a mathematically defined concept. To say that two components "interact" means that a change in one component brings about or induces some change in the other. The term *system* is sometimes applied to relationships that are not actions, as when one speaks of a system of philosophy or religion, a mathematical system, or a logical system. These may be referred to as *pattern systems,* to distinguish them from the kind of *acting systems* just discussed. To illustrate, a corporation is an acting system, but its structure or organization chart is a pattern system. For reasons to be seen when we get to the chapters on those subjects, a person is an acting system while his personality is a pattern system, and the same distinction is made between a society and its culture. The American economy is an acting system while the economic theory that describes its operation is a pattern system—the difference between behaviors and explanations of behaviors. Furthermore, a person may act very differently if he adheres to one system of religion rather than another, as in the way he prays or conducts a wedding. But it is the person (or the church) that acts, not the religion or the ritual. To return to the opening of Chapter 1, the structure of roads in the United States, which structure is a pattern system, does quite as much as you or your car, which are acting systems, to determine where you will drive. The patterns do not act, but can be tremendously important in constraining and controlling the actions of the acting systems. This statement is valid for patterns both inside and outside the system—the internal and the environmental—and there is no point in debating which is the more crucial. For reasons we will not go into here, I think the distinction between acting and pattern systems is also the basis for a more sensible approach to an old problem—the dualism between matter and mind. In studying acting systems we are concerned mainly with the way one part acts on another. Regarding pattern systems our main concern is whether their parts are consistent or inconsistent with one another, according to some kind of standards or criteria of some acting system.

BOUNDARIES OF SYSTEMS

Every system has a *boundary,* which is some kind of division or listing that separates what is inside the system from what is outside—that is, that separates the system from its environment. The first and easiest kind of boundary to visualize is physical, or *spatial.* A fence around a property separates what is inside the system from what is outside it. Your body is bounded by the surface of your skin, hair, and nails. The state of Ohio is bounded by Lake Erie, the Ohio River, and some surveyor's lines. All the people who live in a one-family house are inside a given family system, and all who do not live in it are outside that system.

Second, systems are sometimes bounded *functionally.* In that case all the components that perform a given function are included in the system boundary and all others are outside of it. In a given family the father and grown daughter may hold jobs and earn money, while the mother and two small sons do not. In that case the father and daughter are included in the "income-earning system" and the other three are outside of it. All five, however, are presumably in the "income-using system."

The digestive system of your body includes teeth, saliva, stomach, and intestines, but excludes the heart, sense organs, and the kidneys. The propulsion system of a car includes the engine and drive train, but excludes lights, brakes, and radio.

A functional boundary often includes only certain aspects or behaviors of a particular part. For example, the power provided by an automobile engine is included in the propulsion system of the car. But the engine's function of slowing down the car (as in going down a steep hill in low gear) is part of the braking system. In social science we can, for example, view the child-rearing function of a family as part of a social system, its voting function as part of a political system, its earning and spending functions as part of an economic system, and all of these as part of a cultural system. In a university the functions of teaching and maintaining buildings are both spread spatially across nearly the whole organization. But since they perform different functions, we say that the teaching system and the maintenance system are functionally bounded to exclude each other.

The third kind of boundary is *analytical.* Here we include within a system all those components and interactions that can be analyzed and understood by using a particular kind of science, or a given kind of analysis. The bones, tendons, and muscles are parts of the body's "mechanical" system; the nerves and the brain are the main parts of its electrical system. A kitchen stove may have electric heating units, an electric timer, and an electric light—all performing very different functions. The hydraulic system of a car includes braking, cooling, automatic transmission, forced lubrication, windshield wiper, and possibly other components—which are also very different functions. We may bound a governmental unit differently depending on whether we are analyzing it economically or politically, and we will later distinguish (bound) certain communications and transactions systems on the basis of which kind of analysis we apply.

Functional and analytic boundaries sometimes merge or overlap, as when we apply economic *analysis* to the earning *functions* of a family and political *analysis* to its voting *functions.* The two kinds of boundaries are nevertheless distinct types.

To bound a system we may also sometimes need to identify its level, and its relation to other levels of systems. Except for the universe at one end of the scale and elemental subatomic particles at the other end, any system can be a subsystem of some larger system, while it also has subsystems of its own. You are a system of your own. But you are also a subsystem of a family, school, or city. At the same time you have subsystems within you, such as your digestive, circulatory, and respiratory systems. Any such set of two or more levels is called a "hierarchy of systems," or simply a *hierarchy.* In fact, the very definition of system implies hierarchy, since the components are "lower in level" than is the whole system that includes them. Among other things, this means that an interaction between, say, you and your brother is *intra*system with respect to your family, since it occurs *within* the family. But it is *inter*system with respect to the persons, since it is an interaction *between* you and your brother.

Nature's vs. the investigator's boundaries

Nature has provided a hierarchy of some kinds of systems. Particles are organized into atoms, atoms into molecules, molecules into cells, cells into tissues and organs, tissues and organs into organisms, and organisms into communities or societies. In many of these cases nature has provided rather clear boundaries. The earth is rather clearly bounded, and so are the solar system and many galaxies.

For most of this book we will be interested in boundaries set by the observer (which often means by his culture), not by nature. We will decide as we go along whether we want to focus on the individual, the family, the corporation, the church, or the nation. We will also decide whether we want to focus on the learning function or the digestive function of the individual, on his income-earning function or his voting function, and so on. We will also decide whether we want to examine a corporation or a government as a whole or whether we want to look at its subsystems, such as departments, divisions, or individual members. Thus, although nature provides relatively clear boundaries for a few kinds of systems, in most cases even the boundaries of natural systems are not determined by nature. They are determined by the investigator, on the basis of what he wants to know or look at. Boundaries may also be determined by the state of knowledge in a science or a culture. As we know from the maps of ancient times the "boundaries" of the earth were then much smaller than they are now, and for years physicists did not deal with subsystems of atoms because they did not know they were there.

Similarly, there is rarely any point to arguing whether something is or is not a system. The question is rather whether the investigator is interested in viewing it as one. To the auto mechanic your car is a complicated system, with numerous subsystems and sub-subsystems. But to the traffic policeman it is just one more "lump" going through the intersection. To a physician your body is an extremely complex system, but to the Census Bureau it is just one more unit to be counted. To the ecologist or the geologist the earth is a fantastically complicated system, but to the astronomer it is simply a chunk of matter orbiting the sun.

To summarize both points, for all purposes of interest to this volume, *the investigator, not the thing investigated, determines whether or not he will view a given unit as a system, and if so, how he will bound it.* The investigator will, of course, find some boundaries more useful than others, in the sense that he will probably be able to understand an automobile better if he divides it into such subsystems as the propulsion system and the steering system rather than into, say, the left-hand system and the right-hand system. It nevertheless remains the investigator (or his culture) that makes the choice.

SIMPLE ACTION VS. FEEDBACK SYSTEMS

System interactions can be of two types. The first is a simple, one-way action of one component on another. The second is mutual interaction, in which A acts on B and B acts in turn on A. The second are feedback systems. The first are one-way, or nonfeedback, systems.

To illustrate the former, in the system that washes gullies in a field, the main components are rain, runoff, and erosion. Here the rainfall affects the runoff and the erosion, but the erosion has no effect on the subsequent rainfall. The light reflected from a landscape affects the film in a camera, but taking the picture has no reverse effect on the landscape. In doubtful cases the question again is not whether there *is* a reverse action but whether the observer wishes to take it into account.

Without being so named, nonfeedback systems have been the central concern of science for centuries. They are crucial to traditional cause-effect relationships, which we now see as highly inadequate in many respects. In them, if A is the cause of B, then B cannot also be the cause of A. Feedback systems, by contrast, deal with the cases where A is a cause of B while B is also a cause of A. One-way causation is often diagramed as $A \rightarrow B$, whereas mutual causation, or a feedback relation, is diagramed as $A \rightleftarrows B$. System analysis enables us to deal with the complicated interactions we face, with much more insight than is possible without it.

CONTROLLED VS. UNCONTROLLED SYSTEMS

Controlled systems

In layman's language, the controlled system has a goal, and is a goal-oriented or goal-seeking system. It prefers some state or condition to some other one. (I prefer food to wasp bites, and seek the former and avoid the latter.) For nonliving things and plants we will put "goal" and "preference" in quotes, while for humans (and for higher animals, if one likes) we will not. "Preferences" in plants are known as tropisms, with heliotropism and hydrotropism as the "preference" of the plant to grow toward light and water. The idea that an inanimate system, such as an automatic pilot or an electric refrigerator, can have a "goal" or "preference" has helped bridge a previously enormous gap in our thinking. Obviously a different kind of enormous gap still remains between the complexity and freedom of action of the human and the very limited range of response of the mechanical or electrical system, with computers perhaps occupying an interesting middle ground.

In more technical language that applies to the coldly mechanical as well as the warmly human system, a *controlled system* is one that maintains at least one variable within some specified range, and so acts as to bring it back within that range if it happens to go beyond it.[1] The biological human contains many controlled subsystems, as do all other animals. The temperature-regulating mechanism that keeps all of us close to 98.6 degrees is probably the best known. Other subsystems regulate the pulse rate, the blood sugar level, the red cell count, the breathing rate, fatigue levels, the metabolic rate, and a host of other things.

Among controlled mechanical systems the household thermostat is perhaps the best known. In a cold climate, with the thermostat set for 72, when the temperature falls below that level the thermostat turns the furnace on, and when the temperature rises above that level the thermostat turns the furnace off. Similarly, the toilet tank is designed to keep the water at a point marked "water level." When this "desired" level is disturbed by flushing, the system reacts, first by closing the outlet, and then by allowing more water to flow in. The inflow is stopped by a float valve when the desired level is reached. The governor on a steam engine, the pressure regulator on the air tank in a gasoline station, and the temperature regulators in an oven or refrigerator are other examples of controlled systems. The automatic pilot in a plane and the guidance system in a guided missile are very complicated kinds of controlled systems.

Industry now incorporates thousands of mechanical, hydraulic, electronic, and other controlled systems, which are also sometimes called servomechanisms. The computer-operated inventory system in a department store that automatically reorders when the stock falls below a specified level is also a controlled system.

Any controlled system can be called a *cybernetic* system, and the study of controlled systems is known as *cybernetics*. Norbert Wiener introduced the term (Wiener 1948) and is regarded as the "father" of this aspect of systems science. Uncontrolled systems cannot be cybernetic. A

---

[1] This definition will do for the time being. For reasons that will be elaborated in connection with informal organization, in doubtful cases the distinction may have to be made on the basis of whether or not the observer can identify a control mechanism. This problem is discussed in more detail in connection with ecosystems, in Chapter 17.

cybernetic system can also be thought of as one that is able to discern and narrow the gap between what *is* and what is *desired,* or between what *is* and what *ought* to be—as reflected in its goals.

A controlled (cybernetic) system that holds a single variable within a given range, like the governor on a steam engine and the temperature-regulating mechanism in a refrigerator or a human being, is known as a *homeostatic* system. The process of maintaining a given level is called *homeostasis.* A firm that tries to maintain a constant rather than a maximum level of profit is behaving homeostatically with respect to profit. It might also seek a homeostatic rate of growth, of, say, five percent per year. "Don't rock the boat" is a cruder type of homeostatic regulator in many situations.

The controls of a controlled system operate within the system itself, with respect to its own goals, and are not to be confused with constraints from outside. A child who of his own accord takes off his coat when he is warm and puts it on when he is cold is operating as a controlled system. If he is forced into these acts by parents he is "controlled," but in a different sense. Since the controls are those of the parents, not those inside the child, this aspect of his behavior is not "controlled" in the sense that we are using the term. We are speaking only of this one aspect as "not controlled." As a biological creature the child is, of course, a controlled system in many other respects.

To avoid confusion, such outside forces will be called *constraints* instead of controls. An ordinary clock is highly constrained, in that it is constructed and set to run at one unvarying speed. But if something causes its speed to change (if it is dirty or has run down), the clock has no inner mechanism to restore its previous speed. The solar system is similarly highly constrained, but has no means of restoring a planet to its previous orbit if some force should push it out. The clock and the solar system are therefore highly constrained systems, but not controlled systems. In driving, you are constrained by the location of highways. But the highways are not a *control* in the present sense of the term. Neither control nor constraint means there is no room for choice. You can drive off the highway if you like. And although hunger pangs are part of your biological controls, you can choose not to eat even when you are very hungry. Many systems are uncontrolled, but none are unconstrained.

Thus far all living things (organisms) and two types of man-made systems are the only clear cases of controlled systems we know of. The two types of man-made controlled systems are mechanical systems (in the broad sense) and formal organizations. The basic difference is that the components of mechanical systems are nonliving (like gears or pumps), while the components of formal organizations are individual human beings.[2]

---

[2] The status of the social insects is not clear. For example, the tightly organized societies of ants or bees may well qualify as controlled systems. So might some social relationships among the more intelligent mammals, such as chimpanzees or dolphins. The nature of the question will be somewhat clearer after the discussion of ecological systems in Chapter 17. Fortunately, uncertainty about these cases need not muddy our discussion about the general meaning of the terms. The

Uncontrolled systems

An uncontrolled system is any system that does not meet the conditions of being a controlled system. It has no goal or preference, and does not maintain any variable within given limits. A furnace that burned at the same rate regardless of temperature would be an uncontrolled system. Though the house would at all times be warmer with the furnace than without it, the temperature of the house would rise and fall with the outside temperature, rather than act in such a way as to compensate for changes in the outside temperature. If a careful tenant were to turn the furnace on and off by hand often enough to maintain an even temperature, the furnace system itself would still not qualify as controlled. However, we could consider the *whole* system as controlled if we expanded its boundaries to include the tenant, who is a human being acting in place of the thermostat.

In contrast to the toilet tank, a natural lake or river is uncontrolled. The height of the water is whatever level it happens to take in light of the amount of inflow, outflow, evaporation, leakage, etc. If there is a long-term increase in rainfall, the height of the water will rise and stay up indefinitely. If there is a long-term decrease, it will stay down indefinitely. Given a change in level, the uncontrolled river or lake has no reaction that will restore its previous level. Man can, of course, convert it into a controlled system by installing dams and gates to keep the water at a nearly constant level.

Other than living things, all known natural systems are uncontrolled. "Natural" in this context means not man-made. The weather, glaciers, erosion, earthquakes, and other geological processes; the solar system and the tides—to mention only a few—are all uncontrolled in the sense that we are using the term. Just as a control is not the same as a constraint, so uncontrolled does not mean the absence of constraint. The state of the weather at any given moment is constrained (determined, or caused) by such factors as temperature, moisture in the air, wind velocity, north or south origin of the air, and so on. But whereas the thermostatically controlled heating system can maintain a constant temperature *despite changes in causal factors* outside, the weather just does whatever its causal factors determine that it shall do. A humidity control device in a house can keep the moisture level constant whether the conditions outside are dry or drenched. By contrast, the weather itself is as wet or as dry as the determining conditions make it; it has no "preference" and no device for effectuating one. Later in the volume we will deal with *ecological* systems, which we define as uncontrolled systems, at least some of whose components are controlled systems. Further clarification of the difference between controlled and uncontrolled systems will be made there.

"broad sense" of "mechanical" is intended to cover essentially all nonliving systems, including chemical, astronomical, hydraulic, and electrical systems. As we will detail in the next chapter, except for organizations, all systems will be treated as either controlled or uncontrolled, with no middle ground.

SYSTEMS OF MULTIPLE HUMANS—ORGANIZATIONS

Whether or not man is some very special class of creature, hard-nosed observation makes clear that man does many things no other systems can do. Or at least he does them at so different a level of complexity that some of our study of human behavior must differ from our study of other systems, even those of the most closely similar apes. Two such differences are necessary to our classification of systems.

First, humans are the only systems (other than man-made computers and related types of systems) that exchange information to any significant degree by language, in *semantic* communication that uses words and other signs or symbols.

Second, exchanges of materials and energy are going on constantly in nature, as in the way water is exchanged among soils, streams, oceans, plants, animals, and atmosphere. Matter and energy are also widely exchanged among humans. In part the quantities exchanged are determined by technical factors, as when ore, coal, and limestone are purchased in a particular ratio to make iron. Those technical factors are not the subject matter of social science.

As a *social* problem the important aspect of such exchanges is the ratios of their *values*. A ton of limestone chips does not exchange equally for a ton of diamond chips, nor a gallon of milk for a gallon of gin.

Because humans transfer information by means of language and transfer commodities and services on the basis of their prices or other measures of value, and because no other systems do these two things to any significant extent, interactions among humans must be studied on a different basis from interactions among all other kinds of systems. For the same reason, systems that have two or more human beings as subsystems, such as families and corporations, must be studied very differently from those whose subsystems are lions, roaches, rivers, or electrical switches. We will give the name *organizations* to systems that consist of multiple humans, and simply apply the term *system* to all others.

If an organization is a controlled system in the sense that it has some goal or goals as a unit and behaves in such a way as to achieve those goals, we will call it a *formal organization*—as with a corporation or a government. If people simply interact for their individual purposes, without any centralized controls, the system is uncontrolled. Such an uncontrolled system of two or more persons we will call an *informal organization*. A completely free market economic system, and some of the individually oriented interactions we call the "social" system, illustrate informal organization. There are also many intermediate situations, some of which will be called *semiformal organization*.

SUMMARY OF KINDS OF SYSTEMS

You ask, "How many different kinds of living things are there?" I reply, "Two. Plants and animals." In suggesting this division, I have implicitly distinguished nuts from nuthatches and man from mangoes, since in each pair one is a plant and one an animal. But I have not at all distinguished snails from quails, palms from plums, or worms from germs. In short, I have distinguished types of living things only at a very general level, leaving vast detail to be filled in. It is nevertheless true that if you can know only one thing about a particular living specimen, for most purposes the most important thing to know is whether it is plant or animal. What is more, except at very elemental levels of life, where it is hard to distinguish, as soon as you do know that something is a plant or an animal you already know quite a bit about it—at least if you are a biologist.

Similarly, the kinds of classifications of systems we have suggested in this chapter are very broad and general. They nevertheless do identify the most basic differences among systems, and it is well to know which of these broad types something belongs to before we try to learn more about it. For convenience we will group these into a chart, in Figure 2–1. The chart includes only acting systems, since there does not seem to be any simple way of categorizing pattern systems.

Since no convenient name covers all systems that are not organizations, we have simply headed the right-hand column "Other systems." It includes individual human beings as well as all other living things. It also includes systems in which humans are just a part, such as the earth's ecological system or a moon rocket, in both of which people are only one of the many important parts of the system. By contrast, in social systems human beings are the only components of direct interest to the investigator. Mammals, insects, and other animals have social systems, but we will not deal with them in this volume.

In this chapter we have introduced the general idea of systems, and of different kinds of systems. In the next chapter we will introduce some general ideas about how systems behave.

Figure 2–1
TYPES OF ACTING SYSTEMS

	Social systems (components are multiple humans or other animals)	Other systems (main components are not humans)
Uncontrolled	Informal organizations (and many degrees in between)	Ecosystems and uncontrolled mechanical systems
Controlled	Formal organizations	Living organisms and servomechanisms

3

BEHAVIORS OF SYSTEMS

EQUILIBRIUM

An occasional ailment of toilet tanks is that the bulb does not fit tightly over the outlet pipe. The water then flows out as fast as it flows in, and the tank never refills. Under these circumstances the tank ceases to act as a system, and behaves simply like a trough or a pipe through which water runs. On the other hand, if the tank were fastened, without a lid, at the bottom of Niagara Falls, many times as much water would flow into it as could be discharged through its outlet pipe, and it would be perpetually full. Again it would not be functioning as a system, but simply as a tiny obstacle to the mammoth flow that so attracts newlyweds. A system is a system only within a given range. Beyond that range it either ceases to be a system at all, or changes into a different kind of system.

By contrast, in normal operation the tank maintains an equilibrium level of water that is high enough to perform its flushing function when released, but not so high as to overflow. Perhaps the single most crucial concept about systems is *equilibrium,* which is a relatively stable balance between two or more forces. In some systems the "balance" may be a cycle rather than an unchanging state, as with the alternations of night and day.[1]

---

[1] In some usages "equilibrium" means a state in which nothing is happening—a static state—as with three balls nesting in the bottom of a bowl, or a pendulum at rest. This contrasts with a steady state, or dynamic equilibrium. There something is happening, but two or more forces are in balance, as in the case of a lake whose level remains steady when outflow equals inflow. Social

Literally or figuratively, equilibrium can be thought of as a relation between stocks and flows, in what economist and system analyst Kenneth Boulding calls the "bathtub principle." We will illustrate the relation first in an uncontrolled system. Figure 3–1 represents a cross section of a pond, with a small stream running in at the left and the overflow going out over a narrow dam at the right.

If the inflow is small, the water will rise only a short distance above the top of the dam—perhaps only half an inch. That slight increase in height will not push the water over the dam very fast, so the outflow will also be small. But if a heavy rain sends a large volume of water into the pond, the height of the pond will rise, to perhaps four or five inches above the dam. This increased height will push the water out much faster. For any particular amount of inflow, there will be some level that will push the water out just as fast as it comes in. If a given rate of inflow continues unchanged, the water in the pond will remain indefinitely at a level that just balances the outflow with the inflow. That is the equilibrium level.

Figure 3–1
UNCONTROLLED SYSTEM

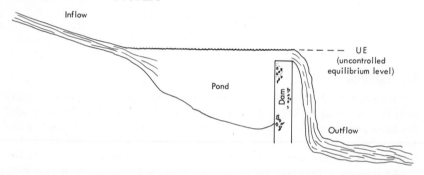

The distinguishing feature of this uncontrolled system is that no "preference" has been built into it. We have shown the uncontrolled equilibrium level in Figure 3–1 as occurring at UE. If the inflow were larger, the level would have been higher. If the inflow were smaller, the level would have been lower. There is no mechanism to keep the water at any *particular* level. The actual level will rise or fall with the amount of the inflow.

Suppose, however, that the owner of the pond wants to keep the water level from rising very far above the top of the dam. He might do this by installing an outlet pipe near the bottom of the dam. When little or no water is flowing into the pond, a metal disk will cover the opening of the pipe, and no water will flow out through it, as in Figure 3–2a. But the disk is attached to a hollow float on top of the water. When the water starts

equilibriums are nearly all of the dynamic, or steady state, variety. Unless the contrary is indicated, in this volume "equilibrium" used alone will always refer to this type.

Figure 3–2
CONTROLLED SYSTEM

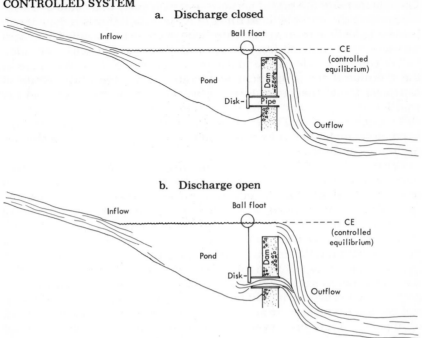

a. Discharge closed

b. Discharge open

to rise, the float rises with it, lifting the metal disk and allowing water to flow out through the pipe, as in Figure 3–2b. The higher the water, the farther open will be the opening to the outlet pipe, and the greater will be the flow of water out through it. If the water starts to flow out through the pipe faster than new water flows into the pond, the float goes down and partly or completely covers the outlet pipe. Although such an arrangement cannot keep the water level completely constant (since there must be *some* change in order to activate the control mechanism), if it is built to accommodate such changes of inflow as can be expected in this pond the height of the water can be kept much more uniform with the control than without it.

Like any other controlled system, this one will operate only within a certain range. If the inflow greatly exceeds the capacity of the outlet pipe, the level of the pond will keep rising, even if the outlet is all the way open. And if there is no inflow at all, evaporation or seepage into the soil will allow the water level to drop below the top of the dam, even if the outlet pipe is completely closed.

The principles are the same regardless of the size of the system, and of whether or not there is a man-made dam at the outlet end. After several years of unusual rainfall the level of the Great Lakes, especially Lake Erie, had risen in 1972 to about two feet above normal. Because the higher level led to increased damage from storms, there was talk of enlarging the outlets of the lake at the Niagara River and the Welland Canal to increase the rate of outflow—but with gates that could be closed to maintain the water level in times of low rainfall. If this is done it will convert Lake Erie from an uncontrolled system to a controlled one, with its water level changed from an uncontrolled to a controlled variable.

The equilibrium level of a controlled system can change. We can reset the thermostat for a different temperature. The equilibrium rate of heartbeat is not the same during work as it is during sleep, and the equilibrium supply and demand for automobiles is not the same in the 1970s as it was in 1910. There is no simple rule about the causes of change in equilibrium level. But we must know that an equilibrium *can* change, even in a controlled system.

Organizations of human beings occupy a complete spectrum from pure controlled to pure uncontrolled, and perhaps the same could be said of some animal societies. All other types of systems are considered either controlled or uncontrolled, with no middle ground. All living things are controlled systems. No nonliving things are controlled systems except those man-made systems into which the necessary controls have been built—as with the thermostat or the automatic volume control on some radios. If a man-made mechanism is controlled, then unless the control mechanism stops working entirely (a broken thermostat) it is still considered controlled even if it does not work very well—as when the thermostat keeps the temperature at 70 degrees plus or minus 15 degrees instead of 70 plus or minus one degree. The question is not how *well* the control mechanism works, but whether there *is* one. We also consider the system controlled even if the controls operate only within a narrow range—as with a poor thermostat that is not sensitive to temperature changes above 75 or below 65 degrees.

The principles of equilibrium: In uncontrolled systems

To discover the underlying principles of equilibrium let us look again at Figure 3–1. As the water level rises, the rate of outflow also rises. That is, the rate of outflow varies *directly* with the height of the water. But an increased rate of outflow, other things equal, will lower the level of water. That is, the level of the water varies *inversely* with the rate of outflow.

Here is a basic condition for equilibrium. If *A* varies *directly* with a change in *B,* but *B* varies *inversely* with a change in *A,* the situation tends toward an equilibrium. This relation is also known as *negative feedback.* Since this term is often misunderstood, let it be clear that "negative" does not necessarily mean "bad" or "minus." It merely means that two things are related in such a way that a change in one induces an opposite, or "corrective," change in the other. If the water for some reason starts flowing out too fast, the faster outflow lowers the water level. This lower level then slows—i.e., "corrects"—the rate of outflow. If the water level for some reason rises, the ensuing increased outflow tends to offset, or "correct," the raised level.

The opposite of negative feedback is, of course, *positive feedback.* As before, this does not mean either "good" or more-than-zero. It merely means that the action set off by a change is not opposite and "corrective," but is in the same direction and aggravating. By the same token, positive feedback is also known as deviation-amplification—the "vicious circle." To illustrate, when a house catches fire, the hotter it gets the faster it burns and the faster it burns the hotter it gets. The job of the firemen is not to eliminate the positive feedback relation, which cannot be eliminated, since it is inherent in the situation. Their job instead is to get it moving downward instead of upward. If they succeed, the relation is then that the cooler it gets the slower it burns and the slower it burns the cooler it gets. The squeal that often develops in public address systems is a very direct example of positive, deviation-amplifying feedback.

The relation is called *positive* feedback whenever both changes are moving in the *same direction,* whether that direction is upward or downward. Whether the relation in the burning building is hotter-hotter or cooler-cooler, it is still positive. Arguments sometimes behave this way. In the upward direction, the angrier two people get the more illogical they become and the more illogical they become the angrier they get. In the downward direction, the calmer they become the more rational are their arguments and the more rational their arguments the calmer they become. We are not suggesting that people are *always* that way, but merely that *when* they are the relation is one of positive feedback. An important aspect of positive feedback relations is the question of how, when, and whether the movement can be stopped or reversed.

The population "explosion" arises from positive, or nonequilibrating, feedback. Other things equal, the larger the population the larger the number of births and the larger the number of births the larger the population. Modern medicine and technology have reversed the prior situation of negative, or equilibrating, feedback, when a larger population led eventually to a smaller number of births by first bringing on a higher death rate. For obvious reasons, positive feedback situations are disequilibrating, unstable, explosive, or destructive, depending on which is the more appropriate term. In contrast to negative feedback, positive feedback is also a major source of social dynamics and developmental change—as noted in Maruyama (1963).

Positive feedback, though self-aggravating and disequilibrating, is not necessarily bad. For example, within wide limits the easier it is to learn the more one learns and the more he learns the easier it is to learn still more. In economic development, the more capital a nation has accumulated the more efficiently it can produce and the more efficiently it can produce the more capital it can accumulate. In personal development, the more self-reliant the child becomes the less parental supervision he normally receives and the less supervision he receives the more self-reliant he becomes.

Positive feedback can also reach a stable equilibrium if there is a limit or constraint on at least one of the two items. When a candle is first lighted it follows the same principle as the burning house: the hotter it gets the faster it burns and the faster it burns the hotter it gets. But there is a limit to the rate at which melted wax will rise in the wick. As soon as the flame reaches the point at which the wax burns as fast as the wick supplies it, a steady state equilibrium can continue, and the flame will remain constant in size.

If two things happen to vary oppositely with some third thing, the result is the same as if they varied oppositely with each other. A well-known example is supply and demand. Here the quantity consumers will buy varies inversely with the price, and the quantity producers will offer varies directly with the price. An equilibrium occurs when the quantity supplied (inflow to the market) at a given price just equals the quantity demanded (outflow) at that price.

Equilibrium in controlled systems

The general conditions of equilibrium are the same for both controlled and uncontrolled systems. Negative feedback is equilibrating for both. Positive feedback is disequilibrating for both—until and unless one or more of the interacting elements reaches a limit, at which point an equilibrium may be reached. The important difference is that the controlled system maintains a *particular* equilibrium, rather than just any equilibrium it happens to reach.

Although equilibrium may be reached under positive feedback, and although a limit may deliberately be placed on one of its elements as a means of *constraining* it to a given equilibrium level, only negative feedback can, by definition, be used as a compensating mechanism to correct deviations from an equilibrium. Hence equilibrium in controlled systems (or homeostasis) must be viewed as being achieved solely by negative, compensating feedback. And just as positive feedback and disequilibrium are not necessarily bad, neither are negative feedback and equilibrium necessarily good. It all depends.

In the thermostatic system, the lower the temperature in the room the more the furnace runs (inverse relation) and the more the furnace runs the higher the temperature (direct relation). In the carbon dioxide mechanism for the blood, the higher the carbon dioxide level in the blood the faster one breathes (direct relation) and the faster one breathes the lower the level of carbon dioxide in the blood (inverse relation). In the plant, the less water it gets the farther it will send out its roots (inverse relation) and the farther it sends out its roots the more water it will get (direct relation).

Diagrams and further discussion

A simple diagram indicates these relationships, whether in a controlled or an uncontrolled situation. Here a sloping arrow indicates both the direction of action (*A* to *B*, or *B* to *A*) and its direct or inverse nature. To keep the diagrams simple and uniform we will always assume that the left-hand item of each pair moves upward, or increases. The slope of the arrow then indicates whether the right-hand item increases (direct relation) or decreases (inverse relation) as a result. For example, line *a* of Case 1 can be read as *"B* varies directly with *A,"* which is the same

	Negative feedback		Positive feedback	
	Case 1	Case 2	Case 3	Case 4
a.	$A \nearrow B$	$A \searrow B$	$A \nearrow B$	$A \searrow B$
b.	$B \searrow A$	$B \nearrow A$	$B \nearrow A$	$B \searrow A$

as saying that "the greater A is the greater B will be." Line b of Case 1 can be read as "A varies inversely with B" or as "the greater B is the smaller A will be." The meaning of the arrows is the same for all cases.

In Cases 1 and 2 the fact that the arrows slope in opposite directions immediately identifies the feedback as negative. In Cases 3 and 4 the parallel slope of the two arrows identifies the feedback as positive. We can apply the same device to "real" cases by using words instead of letters, as follows.

<table>
<tr><td align="center">Case 5
Negative feedback</td><td align="center">Case 6
Positive feedback</td></tr>
<tr><td align="center">Hunger → Eating
Eating ↘ Hunger</td><td align="center">Burning → Temperature
Temperature → Burning</td></tr>
</table>

An upward-sloping arrow means "more" of some magnitude. Depending on the situation, this might be larger, higher, faster, thicker, denser, wetter, etc. It does not matter how a given change is expressed (e.g., "greater thinness" or "less thickness") so long as it is consistent throughout and the direct or inverse relation is stated consistently with those words.

Sometimes the simple verbal statement is easier than the diagram. A difficulty often faced by students is: the greater the tension the worse the grades and the worse the grades the greater the tension. Since we have used a form of diagram which always shows the left-hand item (or independent variable) as going up, we have to invert the second half (line b). Instead of saying "the worse the grades the greater the tension," we state the logical equivalent: "the better the grades the less the tension." The diagram then appears as:

Case 7
Postive feedback
a. Tension → Grades
b. Grades ↘ Tension

The cure does not lie in achieving negative feedback, since that presumably is not the nature of the situation. It lies rather in reversing the direction from downward to upward, so that: the better the grades the less the tension and the less the tension the better the grades. The trick, of course, is to reduce the tension by a technique that does not also adversely affect grades (confidence, not drugs), or to raise grades by techniques that do not increase tension—study-as-you-go instead of last-minute cramming. (P.S. Up to a certain point increased tension increases learning.)

Once we understand and accept this principle, it also tells us what to look for when we are observing systems we do not yet understand. If the system shows a consistent tendency to return to some particular state or condition after being disturbed, our first task is to discover the two items whose relationship is direct one way and inverse the other. The second is to find the nature of the connections by which *A* acts on *B* and *B* acts back on *A*. To know this is not the whole story. But it is the key to the central question of how the system maintains itself as a continuing functioning unit. By the same token, if we examine such a steady state situation and cannot find the two oppositely paired elements, we do not understand the nature of the control or of the equilibrium. In the language of science, if a principle tells us what to look for, it assists the process of *discovery*. Once we have found the ingredients we are looking for, the same principle will help us to understand their probable consequences, in the process of *explanation* and *prediction*.

More than two elements. For simplicity we have spoken thus far only of pairs of elements. An equilibrium, controlled or uncontrolled, is possible with any number of elements, so long as the prescribed conditions occur somewhere. To illustrate negative feedback in a chain, if *B* varies directly with *A*, *C* directly with *B*, *D* directly with *C*, and *A* inversely with *D*, an equilibrium is possible among the set of elements, since the fourth interaction "corrects" the three previous ones. To take another example, eating varies directly with the level of hunger pangs, chewing varies directly with eating, swallowing varies directly with chewing, the quantity of food in the stomach varies directly with swallowing, and hunger pangs vary inversely with food in the stomach. The final inverse item alone is sufficient to provide the negative feedback for a chain of positive ones. The length of the chain, or even the number of items at a given step, does not matter, so long as there is at least one positive and one inverse relation. If the chain contains more than one negative (inverse) relation, the net effect will be negative if the number of negative elements is odd and positive if it is even.

Direction vs. magnitude of "correction." Negative feedback is a necessary but not a sufficient condition for control. Control cannot exist without it. But the corrective action may not be large enough or fast enough to make the control effective. Or it may be too large—an overcorrection. Despite this reservation, a vast strength of this kind of control is that it can, and often does, work successfully and precisely by detecting only the *direction* of needed change without having to measure its *magnitude*. For example, a thermostatic control detects only whether the temperature in a room is above or below a certain level, and turns the furnace off or on accordingly. It has no device for detecting *how* warm or cold the room is. (The thermometer on the front is solely to inform you. It is not connected into the control system.) If the detecting element is sensitive and the heating system's response is rapid, the room may be maintained within a narrow range of temperatures. Many of the fantastically intricate and sensitive controls put into our biological systems by our genes operate by *direction* of deviation only, though some corrective actions are at least roughly proportional to the magnitude of the deviation.

OSCILLATION

To speak of deviations and corrections implies that a system is perpetually straying from the straight and narrow path of equilibrium, and then pulling itself back. This is the case with all open systems in a varying environment, in contrast to the still pendulum or the orange resting in a bowl. The succession of movements on either side of some position is known as *oscillation*. Oscillation can rarely be avoided entirely in an environment of change, since there must be *some* deviation, or corrective action cannot be set off. And no matter how fast the correction, there is *some* time lag before it is effective. If there is an increased flow of water into the pond, the water level must rise *some* distance before water will start flowing out faster, whether over the top of the dam or through the outlet pipe.

Furthermore, unless the correction is of precisely the right amount it will either produce an opposite deviation or leave some deviation still to be corrected. In general, however, the faster and the more sensitive the offsetting actions the smaller will be the oscillations. Depending on the system, the sources of oscillations may be regular, like the tides and the Christmas rush, or irregular, like the weather and the stock market. In theory, at least, if a variation is precisely predictable in both timing and amount, a system can execute compensatory actions that will exactly offset it. If so, that particular oscillation could be eliminated entirely. Anything that reduces the size of oscillatory swings is called *damping*, even if it is as mundane as putting cushions beside you to keep from sliding from side to side when the car goes around corners.

OPEN AND CLOSED SYSTEMS

No real system is immune to influences *from* or *on* its environment. Any system that affects or is affected by its environment is said to be *open*. Thus, all real systems are open to a greater or lesser degree. They receive some kind of inputs from and release some kind of outputs to their environment in greater or lesser amounts.

Sometimes the inputs and outputs are so small, slow, or unimportant that we ignore them. For example, the solar system constantly receives and emits radiation in interactions with outer space. Meteorites and other particles also enter and leave it. Yet we can predict the velocity and orbits of planets as if the solar system has no connections at all with any other parts of the universe. To back away slightly from this statement, any effect from outer space on planetary movements is so tiny that for all *practical* purposes, and with respect to *that problem,* we can treat the solar system *as if* it were closed.

No social systems are that well insulated, which means that all social systems are relatively more open than the solar system. We have nevertheless indicated that the boundaries of a system are set by the investigator, not by nature. Hence for certain purposes an economist may examine internal supply and demand in the American economy and ignore all imports and exports. Similarly, at least for a first approximation a demographer might estimate future population from internal birth rates and death rates and ignore immigration and emigration. In such cases we say either that the observer is *treating* the system as closed, or that it is *analytically* closed. Actually, the system is not closed. The observer's mind is closed to certain aspects of it. His purpose is to keep the system under study simple enough to understand. After he understands its internal interactions he may open it analytically to study its relations with its environment.

SYSTEM UNITS VS. SYSTEM STATES

We have talked about systems as entities, or things. We have also talked about their subsystems, as well as about their supersystems, in a similar way. The reader may have noted, however, that whenever we talked about relationships, and particularly about equilibrium, we did not talk about the entities themselves, but about their states or conditions. We did not talk about the interaction of room and furnace, but about the temperature in the room and the on-or-off condition of the furnace. We did not talk about the interactions of dam, pond, and pipes, but about water level, position of the float, and rates of flow. Similarly, we did not talk about the interaction of student and tests, but about the degree of tension and the level of grades.

These distinctions are fundamental in a systems approach. Although we must identify the entities so as to know what we are talking about, our statements of principle or of science deal with the relationships of *system states,* not system entities. We are not interested in the interaction of gasoline and piston, but in the expansion of the burning gasoline and the position of the piston—nor in the interaction between John and Mary, but in the interaction between John's love and Mary's indifference. We are interested in the relationships of variables, not entities, a *variable* being any state or condition that is able to take at least two different positions.

In contrast to a variable is a parameter. As the term will be used here, a *parameter* is some state or condition that is relevant to a given problem, but that does not change (or is assumed not to change) during the period of study. Among the illustrations we have used, such things as the size of the discharge pipe in the pond and the heating capacity of the furnace are relevant to the operations of their respective systems. But since they did not change during the course of the relationships discussed, they are considered parameters, not variables. Mathematically, a parameter is like a constant in a formula.

CONCLUSION

In the preceding chapter we examined the basic *types* of systems. In this chapter we have examined their major *behaviors.* Of these the most interesting characteristic is equilibrium and the conditions that produce or allow it.

The reasons are not hard to find. Any system that is not subject to equilibrating effects will presumably continue to grow larger or smaller indefinitely in some respect, until it either explodes or shrinks out of existence. In either case it behaves more like a passing event than like a *thing,* and we are not likely to think of it as a system at all.

Without debating whether this is always or necessarily the case, we can nevertheless state that unless a system does have the capacity to maintain at least some aspect of itself more or less unchanged in the face of changes going on around it, we are not likely to attend to it as an entity in its own right. For all practical purposes we can therefore say that some reasonably persistent and reliable equilibrium tendency is a necessary condition for anything to be considered a system.

A complex system, such as the human being, can show strong and precise equilibrium mechanisms in some of its subsystems, such as internal temperature or even basic life-style, while showing growth or developmental change in other respects. It may even be that the more dependable the equilibrium processes in many of the subsystems the greater is the margin for tolerance of disequilibrium in other subsystems. The idea of *no* equilibrium, however, seems flatly at odds with the very notion of systemness. Hence we can say that *some* equilibrium tendency will be found in all continuing systems, controlled or uncontrolled.

part II

The model of man: Intrasystem view of humans

4

MAN AS SYSTEM: UNLEARNED COMPONENTS

INTRASYSTEM VS. INTERSYSTEM

A society is a system that consists of two or more persons in some kind of relationship, that is, in groups. But before we examine the characteristics of groups, it is important to know what they are groups *of.* Groupness among humans is very different from groupness among trees, fish, ants, or birds.

Social science also deals with interactions of people. But except very superficially we cannot study the interactions between two systems without knowing the nature of both systems. It is pointless to study the interactions between two ants, two computers, or two governments without having some idea of what an ant, a computer, or a government is like. Nor can we deal sensibly with the relation between man and dog, boy and girl, or bee and flower without knowing something about the units of each pair.

Much of what man thinks and does is determined by his environment, particularly his culture, not by inherent "human nature." This is meant in the same sense that much of the "behavior" of an automobile—such as where, how often, and how fast it goes—is determined by the driver, not by the nature of the automobile itself. But the act of driving does not determine the horsepower of the car, its gear ratio, or the fact that it has four wheels instead of two or three. The human similarly has some traits that do not depend on his environment, such as his height, rate of growth, and the fact that his IQ will be somewhere in the neighborhood of 100, not 5 or 500, and that even with the best of luck he is unlikely to live to a hundred. So even if much of man's behavior is learned, he starts with equipment and capacity that are not learned and that his environment cannot change very much.

In this book's nearest approach to identifying a "human nature," this chapter and the next will sketch some of the main characteristics of the human system—where it came from, its main parts, and how those parts operate, in the *intra*system view. Where a person goes, what he actually does, and how he interacts and lives with other human beings are matters for later chapters. Some nonbiological items thought of elsewhere as "basic human needs" or "human nature" (for example, Etzioni 1968) are here viewed in later chapters as socially developed, not inborn.

A MODEL OF SOCIAL MAN

Our introduction to the individual human is not a summary of psychology, but rather a brief statement of those traits of humans that seem useful for social science. It is couched partly in psychological language and partly in systems language, and its purpose is as follows.

Economists use a model known as "economic man." When an economic man is the owner of a business he is assumed to have only one goal—to make the largest possible profit. If he is a consumer he is assumed to know his wants, and to spend his income for those things that will best satisfy them. If he is a worker he will seek the job that will pay him the highest wage for his level of skill and energy. If he is an investor he will put his money where it will pay him the highest rate of return for a given amount of risk.

We know that real people, even businessmen, do not behave exactly like economic man, but sometimes act from friendship, hatred, ignorance, or sheer impulse. In some respects these exceptions nevertheless tend to average out, and at least in their *business* relations people generally prefer more money to less, and are more likely to do things they think will improve their material welfare than those they think will worsen it.

In broad terms, the ensuing science is like a road map of, say, California. Vast detail is left out—such as the ridges of bark on that huge redwood just off highway 101. Yet as a general guide to finding your way around, or to recognizing where you are, the road map may be a very useful picture of reality. Similarly, the assumption of economic man, and the science built upon it, leaves out vast detail. But as a rough guide to the lay of the economic land it is enormously better than no guide at all.

This book is about many more aspects of society than are dealt with by economics. Its rough mapping of society needs more than economic man, which model tells us nothing about the human as parent, brother or sister, artist, friend, supervisor, or political candidate. It needs a model of *social* man—more than economic man, but much less than the whole of psychological man.

Our concept of social man parallels that of economic man in that it represents what the person *brings into* society, not what he takes from it or how he is molded by it. It is an *intrasystem* view of man. The remainder of this chapter will describe our model of social man. Since it is couched in system language, we will need to say a few more things about systems in general before we detail the human system.

MAN: A COMPLEX ADAPTIVE SYSTEM

We will not debate the essentially theological question of whether man has a soul. What he unquestionably does have is the ability to think about a soul, and to worry over whether he has one. This is presumably something no other animal can do. When we fully comprehend what it means for a structured complex of protoplasm merely to ponder the question, perhaps man's sheer ability to wonder about whether he has a soul dwarfs the question of whether he actually *has* one. Some humanists might argue that the ability to wonder about it, and to wonder about wondering, *is* the soul.

In contemporary scientific language, man is a highly developed self-preserving system, with a self-organizing, high-capacity information processing center in the brain. A *self-preserving system* is one that so adapts to its environment as to increase significantly its chances of surviving. The *high-capacity information processing* means that man can engage in complex, varied, and sometimes highly roundabout adaptations, which we can also describe as creative and imaginative. The ability to give highly varied responses leads us to call man *adaptive* rather than *adapted* (Dunn 1971), the latter being the ability to give just one or a few responses that are highly appropriate for some particular situation. Adaptivity is also much more than the dogged toughness to survive under widely different environmental conditions—a kind of well-adapted behavior found in the cockroach and the virus.

The components of adaptive (i.e., controlled) systems

Man is highly adaptive. But before going into the complexities of his high adaptivity, we will first examine what traits or components a system must have to be adaptive at all. Since an adaptive system is necessarily and by definition a controlled system, we can say that this section is about the conditions required for a controlled system. Controlled (cybernetic) systems are also sometimes known as self-regulating or self-stabilizing.

Adaptive behavior, which to some extent is engaged in by all living things, means basically responding differently to different circumstances. "Adaptive" alone normally means "successfully adaptive," which means leaving the organism (system) in some way better off. The plant grows toward light and water, not toward darkness and dryness. The dog eats beef but not sawdust. Systems that are adaptive in general may nevertheless engage in some particular behaviors that are unadaptive. These behaviors can also be referred to as unsuccessfully adaptive, or dysfunctional. They leave the system worse off or, at best, no better off. To engage in adaptive behavior a system must meet the following minimum requirements.

First, if an organism is to respond differently to two different states of its environment it must be able to tell which is which. If the plant is to grow toward light it must have some device or process for detecting where light is. The dog must similarly be able to tell beef from sawdust. We will call this process "detecting the state of the environment"—in the language of psychology, this is the process of *receiving and identifying the stimulus*—and we will call the subsystem of the organism that performs this process or function its *detector*. Systems at the level of complexity of the human being often need to detect information about their own inner states, and to respond to them. We will return to that problem later, but continue for the moment to deal with the simpler and more universal ability to detect the state of the environment. ·

Second, adaptive behavior requires that the organism select one response rather than another. For the moment we will talk about these alternatives in the simplest terms—to approach or avoid, accept or reject. Having detected which side is the lighter, the plant must be able to "select" growth toward the light, not away from it. Having discerned the difference between meat and sawdust, the dog must accept the former and reject the latter. The subsystem that performs this selective function or process will be called the *selector*. In psychological language the selector reflects the *nature and state of the organism*.

The third and remaining ingredient of adaptive behavior is actually to carry out the selected behavior, and the subsystem that does so will be called the *effector*. In the language of psychology it represents the *response*.

There are thus three necessary ingredients of adaptive behavior: a *system*, giving a *response*, in and to its *environment*. To put the three in the simplest order of occurrence, (1) the *environment* (2) acts on the *system*, (3) which engages in *adaptive behavior*. In the language of the psychologist the three represent respectively the *Stimulus*, the state of the *Organism*, and the *Response*, diagramed as S → O → R. In the language of the controlled, or adaptive, system these functions are performed respectively by the *detector*, the *selector*, and the *effector*. For convenience we will hereinafter refer to them collectively as DSE.

We say that these three ingredients are *necessary* because we cannot imagine how a system could adaptively respond to its environment if we were to omit any one of them. (The perceptive student may have noted that all three are inescapably implied by the statement of the problem.) The three DSE components, or subsystems, are functionally defined and bounded. That is, we do not define them by where they are (spatially) in the body or brain, or by what kind of science we apply to them (analytically), but by what they *do*.

Figure 4–1 shows the DSE subsystems in their simplest form. Information about the environment enters the system through its detector. It then goes to the selector, which chooses the appropriate course of behavior. The selection is communicated to the effector, which carries it out. The carrying out of behavior has some effect on the environment or on the system's relation to it. "Behavior," as we use the term, includes doing nothing at all, in which case the output would be zero.

We have shown a broken arrow labeled "Feedback" going from the output of behavior back to the detector. This means that the system

Figure 4–1
DIAGRAM OF THE DSE SUBSYSTEMS OF ANY
CONTROLLED SYSTEM

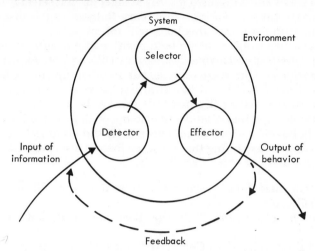

detects the change produced by its behavior, and may or may not then do something else about it. Details about that relationship—including the fact that a cycle of behavior may start with the selector or effector rather than the detector—will be taken up later in connection with decisions.

In more humanly oriented language, the detector function provides the individual with information about the condition(s) in which he exists. His selector function can be described variously as involving his goals, motives, preferences, values, aspirations, or likes and dislikes. The effector function uses the muscles and other parts of the body to execute, or carry out, the behavior that has been selected.[1]

In most studies of human behavior we are interested mainly in the detector and selector—learning whether the tire *is* flat versus whether we *like* it that way—and in how and why one chooses his behavior in consequence. We are relatively little interested in which nerves, muscles,

---

[1] To use the psychological language again, if the detector represents the *perceptual and cognitive* aspects of the person, the selector represents the *affective* aspects, and the effector the *motor* aspects. In psychiatric language the detector represents the *reality principle* and the selector the *pleasure principle*. For some purposes the difference might be thought of as that between the actual and the ideal. In philosophical language the detector represents *factual or scientific judgments* and the selector represents *value judgments*. In language to be used later in connection with decisions, the detector informs one of what is possible, or the *opportunity function*, while the selector constitutes the *preference function*.

The many different terms from different disciplines that distinguish these same basics seem to me convincing evidence that the time is long past due for adopting a common language that will serve all the disciplines involved. I have added more detail elsewhere (Kuhn 1961) about the similarity of concepts in this particular area.

or bones he uses in fixing the tire, or in what happens to his breathing and pulse rates in the process. Hence the attention of both psychologists and social scientists is directed mainly at detector and selector functions, and relatively little at effector functions. Subject to the discussion in connection with decisions, this book will follow suit.

If we take "wanting" to mean both positive and negative wants—that is, likes and dislikes—in layman's language DSE become *knowing, wanting,* and *doing.* The three are represented, incidentally, in the Camp Fire Girls' trio of *head, heart,* and *hands,* and somewhat less obviously in the Scouts' physically strong (E), mentally awake (D), and morally straight (S). The same three ingredients are also necessary for the logical explanation of behavior—which is not necessarily the same as logical behavior. For example (assuming that no other factors are involved), in deciding on a purchase of shirt X or shirt Y:

First premise (detector): If George perceives that shirt X is blue and shirt Y is purple, and
Second premise (selector): if George likes blue shirts but hates purple ones,
Conclusion (effector): then George will accept X and reject Y.

More generally, if we want to "explain" the behavior of any controlled system (i.e., give a "behavioral" explanation) we need to know the nature and state of its detector, selector, and effector, and the possible interactions among them. For very simple controlled systems, such as thermostats, we *can* explain their behavior if we know the states of their DSE subsystems. More explicitly, the nature and states of the DSE subsystems are the "causes" of the behavior performed by the systems. Because of the complexity of the human being we will not presume to "explain" his behavior fully in this way.

BASICS OF THE MODEL OF MAN

The biological base—the maintenance system

In stating that the components of man we will be interested in are the detector, selector, and effector, we have conspicuously omitted such things as the heart, lungs, torso, and limbs. The reason is simple and clear. Social science, like psychology, is interested in behavior. Behavior obviously requires a functioning biological body, since we are not dealing with ghosts. Eating, drinking, sleeping, procreating, excreting, and other activities are necessary to keep the human body and the human race going, and a society must provide for these activities. In the language of Berrien (1968: 25) this biological system receives maintenance inputs; hence the name *maintenance system.*

As noted, for social science we are interested in *why* people do what they do, not in which muscles they use or how many calories they consume. In contrast to the maintenance system, the *control* system, or guidance system, is of great interest to us. This is the subsystem that does the actual guiding, controlling, or directing of the controlled system. As diagramed in Figure 4–1, it receives inputs of signals, or information (Kuhn

1963: 55; Berrien 1968: 25), not inputs of food, water, and air. We will assume that the body and its processes are there and that they work; but we will not explicitly attend to them. When we later come to the study of organizations we will similarly take for granted that they have buildings, machines, materials, and fuel, but for social science we will disregard those things. For certain purposes, including a desire to avoid confusion between the "controlled system" and the "control system," we will often call the control system the *behavioral system*.

The behavioral system: Basics

The behavioral (control) system in man consists of the brain, the attached nerves and sense organs, and certain processes inside the human but outside the nervous system that are involved in emotions. The behavioral system's inputs consist of information, and its outputs consist of *directed behavior*, which we will define below.

Perhaps the best simple way to describe man's behavioral system is to say that it is similar to those of other higher mammals, such as the ape or the dog, except that man shows distinctly less unlearned behavior and vastly greater capacity for learned behavior. Not only *can* man learn more than other animals. He *must* learn more because there are far fewer things he can do without learning. But more of that later.

Our model of man's behavioral system is summarized in Figure 6–2. A full understanding of that summary is adequate for most of the social science in this book. Unfortunately, for the summary to be understood, considerable explanation and background are necessary—as in the next two chapters and the remainder of this one. The reader may nevertheless find it useful to look ahead to that chart from time to time to help see how the various parts fit together.

The behavioral system: Inborn components

By "inborn" ("genetically inherited" or "unlearned") we mean those aspects of the human being that are present at birth or that reliably develop irrespective of experience as the healthy individual grows older. For example, at birth the infant has arms, legs, eyes, and the ability to cry, breathe, and kick. With time he will get bigger, grow two sets of teeth, and develop the sex characteristics necessary to produce offspring. Although he will have learned relatively little before birth, he will be born with an active brain that functions in a certain way, and is capable of learning. The unlearned, inborn components of the human system, both behavioral and maintenance, are "blueprinted" in the genes.

The evolutionary process. The unlearned components of man were derived through a long evolutionary process, which, according to recent (1972) estimates, had developed essentially human creatures perhaps as long as 2.5 to 3 million years ago. Among contemporary scientists a proposal that man did not arrive on earth by an evolutionary development is about as acceptable as a proposal that the earth is flat. We will therefore pause momentarily to put the human system into an evolutionary context by noting two main things.

First, no directed behavior of significance for social science is inborn in human beings. By "directed behavior" we mean behavior controlled by the voluntary muscles, as contrasted to that controlled by the autonomic nervous system, such as the heartbeat, peristaltic movements of food through the digestive system, most breathing, and the like. "Directed behavior" excludes reflexes, such as eyeblinks, knee jerks, withdrawing from contact with a hot stove, or the infant's sucking on a nipple between its lips. It also excludes certain facial expressions or body postures that reflect inner states, such as laughing, crying, frowning, shivering, or tensing—although one can learn to consciously direct or redirect these responses very substantially.

In this absence of inborn directed behavior, humans stand in marked contrast to virtually all other animals, which do many complicated things—such as walking, flying, eating, mating, and nest building —largely on an inborn, unlearned basis. Man has to learn such things by instruction, imitation, or individual experience. Although some details of eating and mating are performed reflexively, the overall, total patterns even of these apparently have to be learned. Since directed behavior is the only kind of interest to social science, this means that *all social behavior* that we will examine in this volume *is learned behavior.*

Second, instead of inheriting patterns of *explicit behavior,* as do other animals, humans inherit *behavior-selecting* mechanisms, mainly in the form of preferences. The difference is simple. But it is often badly confused, and we will use some examples to get it straight.

If there is one compelling principle in evolution it is survival. Any species whose members do not to some extent engage in survival-favoring behavior and avoid survival-threatening behavior will not last long. As noted, most species inherit some very explicit behaviors that produce this effect, but man does not. However, most things that are painful also contain a threat to health or safety if they are not avoided. If one can successfully avoid pain by avoiding its causes (rather than by killing the pain with drugs) he will also avoid many threats to his survival. To do this he need not have an "urge to survive," only an urge to avoid pain. In general, things that create unpleasant sensations are detrimental to survival, and survival is enhanced if they are avoided. Witness the unpleasant odor of excrement or rotten food, the bad taste of many things that cannot safely be eaten or drunk, the unpleasant smell of poisonous gases, the unpleasant sensation from inhaling water or choking, the pain of excessive heat or cold, or the displeasure of sharp hunger or overfull bowel or bladder.

To use pain as an example of the relation between behavior-selectors and evolutionary survival, at least until after considerable learning the individual does not avoid pain so he will survive, but because it is unpleasant. Evolution, however, has made it unpleasant so he will avoid it. In short, the evolutionary process has so designed the human system that survival-threatening things will be avoided. The human gives the proper responses to them long before he has any notion of what life and death, survival and nonsurvival, are. He will continue to give them even if he should never understand survival. Furthermore, in addition to their instinctive behaviors most other animals also have behavior-selectors of this sort. That is, lower animals also engage in actions that avoid unpleasant sensations, and thereby enhance their chances of surviving, even though we are reasonably sure that they have at most an extremely vague notion of what life and death are.

To illustrate the positive, eating and procreating are essential to the survival of the individual and the species, respectively. Again, the individual does not eat to survive, but because eating is pleasant and hunger unpleasant. He similarly engages in sexual activity for the most part because it is pleasant, not to produce offspring, and although he sometimes wants children he often takes great trouble to avoid producing them. In the logic of evolution, however, these things are pleasant so that humans will do them. (In fact, till rather recently—in the long view of history—man did not know the connection between intercourse and pregnancy.)

In short, aside from a few reflexive details, the human being does not inherit specific behavior patterns that will save him from physical harm, put food in his stomach, shelter him, or produce offspring. Instead he inherits inborn connections that give him pleasant and unpleasant sensations—urges or impulses, if you like. As he gradually learns *how* to achieve the pleasant and avoid the unpleasant sensations he thereby contributes to survival. This is the meaning of an inherited behavior-selecting mechanism, as contrasted to inherited behavior. The complications will come later, particularly in connection with the detector.

Three things should be kept in mind about evolution. First, although "genetic drift" may have changed some superficial characteristics, such as physical size, eye color, and skin pigmentation, and although there are obvious differences between races in such traits, the kinds of traits we are interested in here have apparently not changed significantly since well before the earliest civilizations. In fact, what is inherently pleasant and unpleasant is not very different for the human than for the dog or the chimpanzee. If civilization has brought pleasant sensations that are dangerous, and unpleasant ones that are healthful, these were not the conditions under which man acquired his inherited mechanisms.

Second, behavior need favor survival only on the average, not in every case. In practically every species the number of seeds, eggs, or new individuals vastly exceeds the number needed to continue the species. There is room for much individual error and accident.

Third, except for the very young, everyone you know has already learned a great deal. This learning starts early and is deeply entrenched. As a result many of us tend to consider as instinctive, and as unchangeable "human nature," many learned behaviors that are found only in our own society. We will note these in a later chapter on culture.

THE EVOLUTIONARY PRODUCT

We have just discussed the evolutionary *process.* What is its *product?* What is the actual unlearned content of the human behavioral system? As before, we are not attempting to be comprehensive, but merely to identify the things we need in a model of social man. Although the social scientist is interested in learned behavior, all learning must be built on and with the help of an unlearned base, which base determines a great deal about what can be learned, and how quickly.

Detector

As to the detector, the sense organs and nerves are all built into the human—eyes, ears, nose, and taste buds. Also built in are a variety of skin senses—sensitivity to heat, pressure, cold, tickle, and tension—all normally set off by conditions outside the individual. In addition, conditions inside the biological (maintenance) system set off such sensations as hunger, thirst, bladder pressure, nausea, and dizziness. Each of the above senses is connected on a point-to-point basis with some spot in the brain; together they provide the brain with its primary, or unlearned, level of information (which we will later call uncoded information) about the environment. Without any prior experience or learning by the individual, his salt-sensitive taste buds and nerves are activated by salt in the mouth, his sound-sensitive nerves are set off by sound in the ear, his heat-sensitive nerves are set off by heat on the skin, and so on. *Sensation* refers to primary information of this kind, which takes the form of activation of any sensory nerves. Such sensations go on whether or not the individual is conscious of them. For example, how could one be awakened by a noise or a slap if he did not have the sensations before he became consciously aware of them?

There is a quite precise inborn relationship between certain simple states of one's environment and the kind of information received by his brain. Salt in the mouth activates different brain cells than does sugar. Green light activates different cells than does red light, and green light in the left of the visual field activates different nerves than does green light in the right. Similar things are true of the other senses. Thus with no prior learning the human acquires certain kinds of information about his environment because different inputs "select their own channels" —as will be clarified later. This is the inborn aspect of the detector on which and with which all learned information is built.

Selector

The inborn, unlearned aspects of the selector have already been identified in a general way in our discussion of behavior selectors—certain sensations are inherently pleasant, others unpleasant, and still others neutral. The logically simplest explanation is that some sensory nerves feed into "pleasure centers" in the brain, some into "displeasure centers," and some into neither (Olds 1955). The main evidence is that when electrodes are placed in certain areas of its brain a rat will repeatedly press a bar that electrically activates those areas. Stimulation of some areas is so rewarding that the rat will bar-press to exhaustion. Other areas are punishing, and the rat quickly learns not to stimulate them. Similar areas have been found in the human brain—though less well tested. Whether or not this is the central explanation of the nature of inborn preference, any such sense of pleasantness or unpleasantness constitutes a *valence*—positive if pleasant and negative if unpleasant.

The main neutral sensations are those of light (sight) and sound (hearing). Except at intense levels sound and light are neither pleasant nor unpleasant in themselves: they provide information but have no valence. The same is true of moderate changes of temperature or pressure on the skin.

Emotions are more complicated. The valences discussed above are within the nervous system, primarily in the brain, and hence within the control system. The sweetness of candy or the hurt of a bruise may *seem* to be in the mouth or the flesh. But it actually occurs in the brain, as we know from the fact that we taste or feel nothing if the nerves to the brain are cut or anesthetized. By contrast, the emotions involve the maintenance system as well. They are reflected in such observable forms as a pain-racked face, sweating palms, or a goose-pimply skin; and in such less observable forms as changes in pulse rate, blood pressure, or blood chemistry. Sensory nerves from the maintenance system feed information about these bodily states back into the brain, which is how we can know they are happening.

More than fifty years ago psychologists reported three apparently inborn emotions: love, fear, and rage (anger). (Watson and Morgan 1917). We will accept these for our model, and add frustration, which is often reflected in anger. Each of these emotions has a different effect on relationships among people. Love leads to approaching and helping others; fear leads to avoiding others; and anger leads to attacking or hurting them. Frustration typically leads to vigorous, more or less random responses that just might produce a result when more rationally controlled responses have failed. It often leads to abandoning some task. Frustration may lead to an abrupt change in almost any aspect of social relationships. These emotions are also valenced, love being basically pleasant and the other three unpleasant—subject to some observations below about a self-actualizing pleasure in simply using *any* of our faculties.

This list of emotions is adequate for our social science. We can view other so-called emotions either as combinations of these emotions or as special situations under which they occur. Jealousy, for example, may combine love, fear that some third person will steal that love, anger at that person, and frustration over the possible loss. Grief has elements of massive frustration, as when the death of a loved one ends a rewarding relationship.

We probably have built-in priorities among these emotions. Many conditions that bring unpleasant sensations could shortly injure or kill, as with the pain of extreme temperatures, the feeling of asphyxiation when air is cut off, or the nausea of spoiled food in the stomach. The emotion tied to intensely unpleasant sensations is fear, leading to avoidance. By contrast, many pleasant sensations can be postponed for hours, days, or indefinitely without serious harm. Hence survival-favoring controls can be expected to give a priority to fear: when fear is aroused it will tend to displace and dominate pleasanter valences and emotions. If fear does not lead to successful escape, and counterattack is necessary, anger must then dominate fear. We will incorporate these priorities into our model.

Just as the sensations are primary levels of information in the detector, so the *primary motives* in the selector are the inborn feelings (valences) of pleasantness and unpleasantness attached to various sensations or emotions. Note that "feeling" is defined more precisely here than in "I have a feeling it will rain" or "What is your feeling about Jim's progress?" These looser everyday usages often include information (detector), whereas the present usage refers to valences (selector) only.

Effector

The main inborn aspect of the effector is that each muscle is controlled ("instructed") through an inborn point-to-point connection into the brain. It is thus possible to activate any particular muscle by electrically stimulating the appropriate nerve endings in the brain. (This does not mean, incidentally, that electrodes can control anything more than the simplest kinds of overt behavior.) Conversely, muscles are "paralyzed" when the nerves leading to them are cut or deactivated: there is nothing wrong with the muscles; they simply are not receiving "instructions."

LEARNING

In the newborn infant the relation between sensory inputs and behavioral outputs is essentially random. A blinking light may lead to bending the knee, flexing the wrist, turning the head, crying, laughing, curling the toes—or to no response at all. And so might the sound of a voice or a stroking of the head. In an overall sense the learning process is one in which behavioral outputs gradually become more ordered with respect to informational inputs. Since any pattern of overt behavior merely reflects some pattern already existing inside the brain, and since informational inputs reflect situations in external reality, learning can also be described as a process through which inner patterns are formed that in some way correspond to external patterns. More accurately, we might say that initial behavior is ordered solely with respect to inner states of the organism, and that an important part of learning is the process of converting behavior from inner-oriented to outer-oriented. The process is never completed. Indeed it is hard to imagine what we would mean by behavior that was completely ordered with respect to outer reality.

Conditioning

All learning of interest to social science takes place in the brain. *Conditioning* is a process of making connections inside the brain as a result of which we come to connect or associate two or more things. It is the most basic learning process, to which we will confine our attention in this section. Some processes of more highly organized learning will be discussed later.

By conditioning we can connect inputs with inputs, as in associating the appearance of lemon with its sour taste or the sight of the sun disappearing below the horizon with the advent of darkness. We can connect behavioral outputs with other outputs, as in combining a jumping motion with a throwing motion in playing basketball or a smile on the face with pleasant words issuing from the mouth. Or we can connect inputs with outputs, as in learning to stop when we see a red light or not to touch red-hot steel.

Thoughts show similar connections. If you have repeatedly had picnics on the beach, then the thought of picnics may activate thoughts of the beach, and vice versa. Even if you have had only one picnic on the beach, but have recalled it repeatedly, the conditioned connection will be made. In fact, you need not have had *any* picnics on the beach to make the connection, if you have repeatedly heard about picnics and beaches together. The ability to create a conditioned connection between two things you have merely thought about, without ever overtly experiencing either, is a kind of ability apparently possessed only by humans. It presumably accounts for man's ability to formulate scientific theories, write poetry, design houses, and communicate by language—among many other things. It is a necessary basis for any but the most elementary society and culture.

A simple example of learning, and of the importance of a behavior-selecting valence, is this. As an inborn, reflexive action the human can withdraw his hand from a hot stove after he has touched it. Because the sensation is unpleasant, he can learn to avoid touching the stove in the first place. And we sometimes even learn sensible behaviors just by being told—like not using a match to check the gas tank!

Higher-order conditioning, and imagination

The important ability to make connections inside our heads either consists of, or is related to, *higher-order conditioning.* To illustrate, if a rat has repeatedly been exposed to the flashing of a green light, followed shortly by the sound of a buzzer, it will come to "expect" the buzzer shortly after seeing the light. If, independently and without any green light at all, the rat is repeatedly shocked through an electric grid soon after the buzzer sounds, it will learn to get off the grid promptly after the buzzer is sounded. Having independently established both conditioned connections, if the rat then sees the green light it will get off the grid. Since the buzzer has become associated with the green light, the light now brings the same behavior previously associated only with the buzzer. Two things connected with the same thing become connected with each other in the brain, even though the two have never been directly connected in experience.

Unlike lower animals, human beings have the ability to make indefinitely long chains, connecting event A to event Z through successively connecting each separate pair in between. These connections can have various logical qualities. In mathematics we say that two things equal to the same thing are equal to each other. In everyday life we say that if Jim is taller than Jane and Jane is taller than Joe, then Jim is taller than Joe. In logic we use the middle term of a syllogism to connect the other two, as in: All blonds have pink ears; Elsie is a blond; therefore Elsie has pink ears. Second-order conditioning in the rat, stated in logical form, would be: green lights are followed by buzzers; buzzers are followed by shock; therefore green lights are followed by shock.[1]

There is no particular limit to either the kinds or number of connections that humans can thus make inside the head. A central question, however, is whether the connections made inside the head correspond to those outside it. For example, if the green light will, in fact, be followed by an electric shock, the connection is "real," and the rat's behavior is "logically sound" and "appropriately adaptive" if he gets off the grid on seeing the green light. But suppose the buzzer that follows the green light has no connection with the one that precedes the shock, even though both buzzers sound alike and are in about the same place. In that case the green light will not, in fact, be followed by shock. The connection inside the rat's head is "imaginary," and his getting off the grid is therefore "unsound," "illogical," "unadaptive," or "superstitious."

If the connections made inside the human head are used only for daydreaming, fiction, or casual conversation, it makes little difference whether the inner connections correspond to outer ones. But if the inner connections lead to action, the action will be sensible if the inner connections correspond to outer ones, and unsensible if they do not. The logic is the same for all animals capable of higher-order conditioning. The problem is far greater for man, however, because of his vastly greater ability to make inner connections not directly based on outer ones.

This greater capacity of man is a double-edged sword. It is the essential basis for science, art, and other advanced learning. But it also permits fantastic departures from reality, as with the insane, or with (some would insist) the proponents of certain "far-out" religious sects or political ideologies, and with all of us in dreams. This ability is either closely related to or the same as imagination, and is also a prerequisite for the ability to lie. As a result of his greater ability to make inner connections man's capacity for both sensible and nonsensical behavior is far greater than that of any other animals. Which it will be depends largely on the amount and quality of checking with external reality.

Some effects of positive and negative motives

Whether with first- or with higher-order conditioning, conditioned connections that reflect fear and avoidance can be extremely stubborn. Let us suppose that the charged grid is not, in fact, related to the green light, but that the rat has made a second-order conditioned connection between them. (This is a kind of connection that in the human we would call a superstition—which can also arise from irrelevant stimuli in reward situations.) Every time the light flashes, he gets off the grid, and

---

[1] Although I would agree that as a field of study logic is not dependent on psychology, I nevertheless think we might profit if logicians would investigate in more detail some parallelisms between logic and learning processes.

the neural connection is strengthened by being used. Because he gets off the grid he never experiences the fact that he will *not* get shocked follow-ing the green light. Hence he never learns that his conditioned inner connection is "false." In humans this aspect of conditioning almost cer-tainly helps explain some stubborn irrational fears and superstitions. It could also have much to do with the continuance of fears and suspicions between nations, races, and cultures, particularly if supplemented by the priorities attached to fear.

Positively motivated behavior does not show this effect. Suppose that instead of shock, pellets of food had appeared five seconds after the buzzer sounded, and that the expectation of food had similarly been connected by second-order conditioning with the green light. When the light flashed, the rat would have gone to the spot where the food-that-follows-buzzer had appeared. If food had been forthcoming, the inner connection would have been strengthened by having been checked against external reality. The strengthening of a conditioned connection when two things are connected in reality is called *reinforcement.* But if no food had appeared, the rat would have quickly discovered its absence. The inner connection would not have been confirmed and strengthened by outer reality, but would have been weakened. The gradual weakening of an inner connection when it is tried and not confirmed by reality is called *extinction.*[2]

More accurately, the inner connection is not wiped out, but rather is suppressed, and a substitute response is established in its place. This substitute could be described as a positive connection between green-light and empty-food-box.

SUMMARY

Virtually all human behavior of interest for social science is learned. But it is built with and on a base that is inborn and unlearned. While the human clay can be molded into many forms, clay is still not marble, steel, or putty, and has its own potentialities and limitations. It has been the purpose of this chapter to describe briefly the nature of the human clay.

The term "human nature" has been mentioned only in passing, and for good reason. Many persons tend to attribute much human behavior to "inevitable" or "compelling" human nature, when in fact it merely reflects deeply ingrained habits or customs. The model of man in this and the next chapter is this book's nearest substitute for a description of "human nature."

As a controlled, adaptive system, man must possess detector (informa-tion), selector (goals or motives), and effector (muscular) functions.

---

[2] The terms reinforcement and extinction are used primarily in connection with behaviorist psychology, which focuses on external stimuli and overt re-sponses and ignores as irrelevant what goes on inside the brain. In a larger per-spective, however, we must assume that *something* happens inside the brain that brings about the changed relation between outer stimulus and outer response. Our attention here to these internals differs from the psychologist's emphasis but presumably not from his logic.

Knowledge of all three is necessary for an understanding of any controlled system, including the human. All three are part of the behavioral (or control) system of the human, and we simply take for granted his biological, or maintenance, system.

Beyond the level of the reflex, the human being inherits no specific, preprogrammed responses to his environment. He inherits instead a behavior-selecting system, or selector, in which survival-favoring behaviors produce pleasant results and survival-threatening behaviors produce unpleasant results—at least in general and on the average. These inborn selectors are called primary motives, and secondary motives can be built on them—as we will see.

In his detector the human inherits primary information processes, in that different kinds or forms of information in the environment activate different nerve channels. In the next chapter we will see how the detector function organizes these primary nerve impulses into complex levels of information.

The effector function does not seem to show a distinction between primary and secondary levels in this same sense. Particular muscles are connected to particular points in the brain. But all organized activity directed toward a particular result must be learned. The newborn infant is able to perform only uncoordinated and undirected gross bodily movements, such as bending the arms and legs and turning the head.

The human inherits *channels* through which inputs of information go *to* the brain and through which outputs in the form of instructions go to the muscles *from* the brain. "Inherited channels" means that what flows through those channels is *not* inherited. We inherit the capacity for learning a great variety of things; we do not inherit the specifics.

Learning is mainly a process of connecting things into patterns, which, at its simplest level, is known as *conditioning*. At more complicated levels the brain sorts and reassembles things into new and different patterns: it "organizes" inputs and outputs through processes described in the next chapter.

The social scientist is interested in emphasizing the smallness of the unlearned components in human behavior, since it is the society that determines most of the learned components. He is also interested in a scientific model, not a religious, mystical, poetic, or folk model. That model turns out to be considerably more Western than Oriental in flavor.

5

MODEL OF MAN: LEARNED COMPONENTS OF DETECTOR

The preceding chapter briefly identified the human being's unlearned equipment. This chapter shifts to the learned equipment. For this purpose we will try to identify the major forms that learning takes in the human, while showing how those learned forms are based on the unlearned ingredients already discussed. Here we will examine *how* people learn, rather than *what* they learn.

The conspicuous difference between man and other animals lies in the vastly greater capacity of man's detector function to sort, store, organize, and use information. But as we shall see, important differences between man and other animals with respect to motives and goals, skills and overt activities, also depend on this greater information capacity. As summarized in Figure 6–2, all learned aspects of DSE will be viewed as either pattern learning or pattern using.

In using detector, selector, and effector as nouns, we run the danger of thinking of them as *things,* and the reader should keep in mind that they are *functions*—knowing, wanting, doing. We use the DSE language because it applies to many different kinds of systems and because other language is much clumsier.

DETECTOR

How does one *know*—about his physical environment, about other people, about himself? To the psychologist these are problems of perception and cognition, which we deal with here under the heading detector. The detector function deals with knowing what *is,* as contrasted to what is *preferred*—the reality principle as contrasted to the pleasure principle.

Knowing and wanting are complexly intertwined. Among other things one often cannot satisfy *wants* unless he first *knows how* (he must *know* where a concert is being played to achieve the *pleasure* of hearing it). Hence the instrumental desire to know is often tied closely to the main desire itself. Other motives are also attached to learning, which is sometimes fun and sometimes frustrating. Although it is probably safe to say that all learning is motivated in some way, or it would not occur, certain aspects of learning can be analyzed without regard to why one wants to know. Despite complications, *wanting* to hear the concert is a very different question from *knowing* how to get to it. Knowing involves the detector.

Models: Tools of knowledge

We are describing a model of man. An important ingredient in it is his detector function. Since an important part of the detector function consists of using models, the fact that man uses models in his thinking is part of our model of man. Hence in this section we describe part of our model of man by describing how man uses models. We think so highly of our model that we *use* it as a means of *describing* it!

A carpenter uses saws and hammers; a house painter uses brushes and ladders; an earth mover uses bulldozers. Many of us are not aware that thinking also requires tools. A *model* is an important tool for thinking.

"Model" in ordinary language means several things. One meaning is ideal or unusually good, as in model behavior or a model city. A second is a representation, as in a model railroad or a clay mock-up of next year's automobiles. Such models often omit much detail. In science, a model incorporates some of both ideas: both an idealized and a simplified representation. "Idealized" is used here in an analytic or scientific sense, not a moral or ethical one. For those familiar with them, Plato's "ideas" and Max Weber's "ideal types" are different ways of describing a model.

More broadly, a model is a mental image we think with. Suppose I shout, "Let's go to the beach next Sunday!" and the shout is enthusiastically accepted. Consciously or not, each member of the family has a model in his head, a model for most purposes being a set of assumptions. We will go to the beach—assuming that the car does not break down, the house does not burn, nobody gets sick or injured, Aunt Tedius and Uncle Portly do not come for an unannounced visit, an oil slick does not wash up on the beach, we do not have snow (it being the 18th of July)—and so on.

There are differences between models used by scientists and those used in ordinary life. Those of the scientists are usually more explicit, are typically designed to cover a wider variety of cases, are systematically tested against reality, and much knowledge can often be derived from them. Decision makers in government, business, engineering, social planning, and other areas often use models (sometimes called "simulations") more consciously than we use our model about going to the beach. Their purpose is usually to describe complex situations simply enough to be understood.

Models are also used by scientists for explaining. When a scientist says, "I propose that reality is like my model" (or "My model is like reality"), his model becomes a theory. More particularly, he manipulates his model in certain ways, and certain results follow. He then predicts that if reality were similarly manipulated, the corresponding real consequences would follow. These "manipulations" may be logical, mechanical, graphic, or of other types.

The weatherman uses a model. He says, "The temperature is now 25 degrees in Rabbit Hash. This cold front is moving eastward at 19 miles per hour. It will reach Shoulder Blade by nine o'clock, and it will then be 25 degrees there." If reality turns out to be like his model, his prediction will be correct. If reality is not like the model (or if the model does not match reality, which is perhaps a better way of putting it), the prediction will not be correct, except by chance. (West Virginia residents will later find the same cold front arriving at Left Hand, Looneyville, Leather Bark, and Burnt House.)

A road map is also a model. If it matches reality closely it will accurately predict where you will get by taking a given road. A road map is also a theory about where various roads go, albeit a theory so well tested that confidence in it can be very high.

Models involve potential difficulties, of which we will mention two. First, we have all seen maps drawn by early explorers that would lead us a merry chase if we tried to follow them. This is the problem already mentioned, where the model does not match reality very well. Second, suppose we come to an intersection where we think we should turn, but there are no road markings at all. We turn in the hope that we are right, and shortly come to another intersection where there are also no markers. We look at the map and scratch our heads. This problem is known in science as that of *identification*. How can we tell whether a particular piece of reality corresponds to a particular piece of the map? With accurate maps and well-marked roads the problem is simple. But if we are not sure the map is right *and* if the roads are not well marked, we may make mistakes.

Any map (or model) corresponds with reality in some ways but not others. A simple road map has no information about the contours of the earth, and a pure contour map shows mountains and plains but no highways. Maps of highways in mountainous areas, as in Mexico, sometimes show vertical directions but not horizontal ones—how far a driver will go up and down but not whether the road is winding or straight.

For like reasons we would not ask whether a highway map is "right" or a contour map "wrong," but merely whether we can learn from the map what we want to learn. Our models of man will be handled similarly.

The two main problems of science, as of navigating through ordinary life, are thus (1) to build models that correspond in useful ways with some aspects of reality and (2) to learn rules of identification by which one can tell reliably which parts of reality correspond to which parts of the model. The two problems are interdependent, in a positive feedback relationship. As we improve our models we improve our ability to identify the pieces of reality that correspond to them, and as we improve our ability to identify pieces of reality we are better able to improve our models. Sometimes, however, what seemed a promising model is thrown out entirely in favor of another (T. S. Kuhn 1970). If a change of this kind is large it can take such forms as a scientific, religious, or ideological revolution, in either a society or an individual. If smaller, it may change the way of looking at only one thing.

Another aspect of models can be clarified by an example. The simple model of the lever as we study it in eighth-grade general science states that the weight times the distance on one side of the fulcrum equals the weight times the distance on the other side. Whether or not the teacher identifies it as such, this is a "perfect" model. The fulcrum has no width and is perfectly hard—that is, it will support the lever without squashing under the weight it supports. The arms of the lever are weightless—what is it made of?—all the weight being at the two ends. The arms are also perfectly rigid, and do not bend.

It is, of course, possible to produce real levers that come close enough to these conditions so that their actual behavior is very similar to that of the model. But suppose we have a slab of rather mushy ice resting on top of an irregular mound of compact snow. On one end of the ice sits a seal. When a polar bear climbs onto the other end, what will happen? The slab of ice may act like a lever, in which case the polar bear's end will go down and the seal's end will go up. Or the ice may bend or break, and the bear will go down without the seal's going up. Or the snow might compress further and both ends go down. Or any combination of these things may happen, and the law of levers will not tell us which. We will refer to this occasionally as the "mushy ice" problem.

In short, models are not frighteningly abstract. Everyone uses them every day, even if less formally and consciously than does the scientist or the policymaker. We will later call them images, concepts, or patterns.

Images vs. reality

We have just described how *in general* man uses models in his thinking. We now turn from models in general to the particular model of man we will use in this book. But first a digression.

What is reality? Do I exist? I think, therefore I am. The only reality is the inner reality; all else is uncertain.

The question of what reality *is* is philosophical, theological, mystical, and in some areas of science intensely practical. Man has been grappling with the question explicitly for at least two to four thousand years. In some form it may go back the more than two million years man has been on earth. We will not settle the question here, but will make explicit the approach used in this book.

I focus a camera on a tulip and click the shutter. Light strikes the film. I pull a paper tab, and chemicals develop the picture. Until I remove it, a picture of the tulip is there inside the camera.

The camera is an information processing system. Relative to that system, the tulip is external reality and the picture is an internal image of it. The tulip is an external pattern, and this internal pattern corresponds to it in some ways but not others—as was also true of the map. The internal pattern corresponds to the outer one in general color and contour. But the image is two-dimensional, while the reality has three dimensions. The inner pattern provides no information about the cell structure of the flower, its moisture content, its chemical makeup, the arrangement of atoms within it, or its growth. In fact, considering the millions of cells and billions of protons and electrons in constant motion in the tulip, we can confidently say that there *is no such thing as a complete image* of the tulip.

Any image of it is a vast oversimplification, and the same can be said for any other object man knows about. We will leave till later the way the brain actively organizes information, rather than merely record it the way the camera does. Our point here is simply to distinguish "outer reality" from "inner image" (or simply "reality" and "image"), and to note that the two can never correspond perfectly. The conclusion is as valid for images in the human head as for images created by cameras—which is to say that we can never know precisely what reality is like and that all our images are to some degree false. Although we have spoken above of visual images, the conclusion also applies to images based on taste, sound, smell, or touch.

With the camera the relation between reality and the image is determined by the lens, focus, kind of film, development, and so on. The relation between images in human heads and outer reality is determined by the characteristics of our ears, eyes, brain processes, and the like. Somewhat parallel to the sensitivity of the film, the strength of an image in the human brain depends on how recently, frequently, and intensely a given input of information has been received. Images in the head can be strengthened simply by thinking about them over and over—in a sort of parallel with the length or intensity of development of a film. More important, however, images in the brain depend on its information-organizing activities, which do not appear in the camera at all, and to which we turn next.

The brain's images are organized

Suppose you had been born blind, with a congenital cataract. You learned Braille, could find your way around rather well, and did honors-level work in school. As a graduation present your family scraped together the money for an operation, which the doctors thought would now work because some earlier complications had cleared up. The bandages are eventually removed, and amid shouts and tears of joy the doctors announce that your vision is now perfectly normal. After all the years of cautious and inhibited movement, now you will suddenly be able to run down the corridors and among the trees, play tennis, read books, and—joy of joys—watch television!

No you won't. Not for a long time. Even though you have been able to do it easily by feel, it will take you weeks before you will be able to tell a circle from a triangle by sight. You will have to count the corners to make sure it is a triangle, and if the color of the light is changed, you will not be sure you are still seeing the same thing. It will take you months to recognize your family by sight, and perhaps several years before you learn to sort out a larger number of faces (Hebb 1949: 81, 114). Looking at a page of print would give you no more information than looking at a plot of grass. Looking at anything at all would at first give you no more information than "snow" on a television screen.

For some time you will have to close your eyes to get your bearings. As with seeing someone on television after knowing only his voice over radio, you may have to close your eyes to recognize a voice.

The cataract operation can give you normal visual equipment. What it cannot give you, and what you must acquire for yourself, is the ability to use it. The inborn equipment does include some ability to distinguish colors, and probably the ability to recognize horizontality.

Most of us wrongly believe in what Whitehead calls "naive realism"— that we "see" something because it is there and we are looking at it. The problem is easier to understand with perceptions that are not immediately clear. Suppose you say, "What's that smell?" and then, "I hear a noise in the basement, but I haven't the vaguest idea what it is." In each case sensations have entered your nervous system. But you cannot identify what kind of external reality set them off. You have received sense data but have not perceived.

For the new infant everything is like that—a big buzzing confusion of sensations, but with no idea of what they represent. You at least know that there *is* an external reality, whereas the infant presumably does not know even that. We tend to be naive realists because by the time we are old enough to think about the problem we perceive most things so efficiently, especially by sight, that we jump to identifying external things without being aware of the intervening sensations.

Suppose that an old refrigerator in use in your basement had sprung a leak. The leaking refrigerant was what you smelled. It hissed as it escaped, and banged a metal flap against the motor, which you also heard. If you did not know how refrigerators work you would have had sensations but no image of the event as you sniffed and listened from upstairs.

You next go to the basement. You observe what is happening, while someone tells you about the cooling liquid. You get the refrigerator repaired, but a month later it happens again. This time you do not say, "What's that smell?" and "What's that noise?" You say, "That blasted refrigerator is leaking again." You now have an *image* of this event. You not only receive sensations. In addition those sensations serve as *cues* which trigger the image you previously learned. The image is the *organized* grouping of impressions received through nose, ear, and eye, along with the verbal explanation you received. We know very little about how the brain performs this information-organizing job. But we are sure that it *is* done, and that this organizing ability is vastly greater for humans than for other animals. That inborn ability is vastly increased by the fact that we *name* things, and then organize images by the proxy method of organizing words. A difficulty (and a weakness of much formal education) is that some people learn only the words and not the images. The parallel complaint from students is that they are expected only to memorize and regurgitate the words, and then forget them.

Pattern learning vs. pattern using

Let us turn to an identification by sight, which is the kind we most often think of as perception. To make sure I beat the mailman I often put letters into my rural mailbox at night. Often the only thing I "see," literally, is a vague blob of light about chest-high to my right at the bottom of the driveway. I nevertheless confidently walk up to it, grasp the handle, pull down the front flap, put in the letter, close the flap, and put up the flag. If I had to depend on the light then entering my eyes I could do none of these things, since there is not enough light to reveal the handle or the flag, or to show me where and how each is hinged. There is barely enough light for me to find the box itself. How, then, are these detailed movements possible?

The answer is that we mostly do not respond to information entering our senses at the moment. We respond to a previously learned and stored image. What I perceive is not a vague blob of light, but the whole mailbox, with hinge, flag, front flap, post, name and street number painted on the sides, and even the cocoon in the far right corner. I also perceive the same mailbox whether I look at it from right, left, front, back, or any odd angle—a kind of response often discussed as the "constancy" problem. The light actually coming into my eyes at a given moment merely serves as cues, a *cue* being some part of a pattern that helps identify a whole pattern, and *sufficient cues* being enough parts of the pattern to identify the whole pattern with a level of confidence that is good enough for the purpose at hand. After you had learned the image, the sound and odor were sufficient cues for you to identify the event "leaking refrigerator." You could not make the identification the first time, not because the cues were insufficient, but because you had not yet formed the image and learned the relationship of cues to the image. Whether cues are sufficient may also depend on how many similar things are going on in the environment—an involved matter that we will not detail here (but see Figures 29–1 and 29–2).

The process is presumably universal for things you are familiar with. You perceive a whole person, though less thàn half of him is ever visible at any one time, and often much less. In fact, unless someone is playing a trick, you can reliably perceive a whole person from the cue of a moving eye or finger. You perceive a moving car as having four wheels, even if only one or two or even none, are in your line of sight. In fact, you never "see" the whole of anything. The question is how much of a cue you need to know what it is.

In brief, to perceive a given thing in your environment you must complete two steps, one past and one present. In the past you must have formed the image by organizing earlier sensations. The sensations are primary, or unlearned, information. The image is secondary, a learned pattern. In language we will use later, the primary information is *un-*

coded; the secondary is *coded.* In the present, having previously organized and stored the pattern, you use incoming sensations as cues to identify it. The first stage is often referred to by psychologists as concept learning or cognition, and the second as perception.

Pattern (image) learning.   We learn patterns (images, or concepts) of objects and events in essentially the same way, an *object* in the broadest sense being a static pattern of relationships at a given moment in time and an *event* being a change in pattern of relationships over a period of time. In its simplest terms pattern learning is a process of grouping things by their similarities and separating things by their differences. We can learn to group things together for ourselves from our own experience, in *concept formation.* Or we can learn the groupings already developed by others, in *concept attainment.* For example, if a child is given a pile of shapes, and if he separates them without guidance or previous instruction into piles of triangles, squares, and circles, the child has himself noted the difference and *formed* the concepts, even if he does not know names for them. By contrast, if someone else sorts them, and the child learns the difference from the already sorted piles, he has *attained* the three concepts by learning them from others. Before the infant learns language, much of his learning is necessarily concept formation. After he learns language, it shifts heavily to concept attainment, when people tell him the difference between things. Much of our formal education would probably be more successful and interesting if we used more concept formation and less concept attainment. Concept learning is also a form of information storage—we store much of our information in the form of learned concepts (the image of my mailbox in my head).

Learned patterns are indispensable for dealing with reality. The number of patterns around us is for all practical purposes infinite. Entomologists report nearly a million species of insects, and there are thousands of varieties of reasonably large plants. What is more, no two trees or insects of the same species are exactly alike, nor are any two houses or hills. Despite man's large brain we would be overwhelmed if we had to deal with each individual specimen on its own terms. We have no choice but to learn the group pattern "fly" or "mosquito," and then act mostly as if every fly or mosquito were like every other fly or mosquito. Despite their differences it is generally satisfactory to act one way toward every chair, a very different way toward every telephone, and a still different way toward every dollar bill. When we face many specimens of essentially the same thing we do not respond to the individual specimen, as such. We identify what type of thing it is, and respond to our *image* of that *type.*

It is as if we sorted our information into bins. We have one binful of information about mice, one about birds, and other bins about automobiles, oceans, governments, copper, weddings, and floods. How we do this sorting (or "slice up reality") depends partly on the nature of things and partly on our interest and convenience. Whether we group deer with lions under the heading of mammals, or deer with inchworms as things that eat leaves, is determined by the focus of our interest as well as by the nature of the animals involved. Whether we group a newspaper firm with other profit-making corporations or with other transmitters of information is not determined by the nature of the newspaper firm alone, but also by whether we are interested in the firm as a place to invest our savings or as a source of information. And whether we consider the dolphin a fish or a mammal depends on whether we focus on where it lives (land or water) or on the way it breathes and reproduces.

IMAGES OF EVENTS

"I don't get it. When you're freezing it comes and goes very fast, but when you're hot and sweating it just hangs around and hangs around."

Drawing by W. Miller; © 1971 The New Yorker Magazine, Inc.

We said earlier that whether or not something is to be considered a system, and where it is to be bounded, depends largely on the interest and convenience of the observer. Our grouping of things into different conceptual bins similarly depends on our interest and convenience. The nature of things will make some groupings more convenient than others. But man, not nature, does the grouping.

To tie in this discussion with previous materials, concepts are our models, our images, and our cognitive maps of reality. They are the tools we think and perceive with. They are *meanings*. The philosophically minded may note that concept formation is *inductive,* in that a concept is a generalization about the traits a number of things have in common.

Pattern (image) using. If pattern learning is the process of information storage, or of putting information into bins, pattern using is the process of information retrieval, or of taking it out of bins. (Information, of course, differs from matter-energy in that it can be "taken out" without ceasing to be there.) *Using* information stored in the brain consists of *activating* it.

A basic use of stored images is for perception, though they are also used in thinking and in communicating by language. We will deal here mainly with perception—the process of identifying or activating stored images by the use of cues. In the language of communications theory, perception involves *scanning* and *channel selection.* By analogy, you *scan* the coins from your pocket and *select* the nickel to feed the parking meter. If a circular disk is randomly moved over a surface that has some circular depressions into which it will fit and some triangular depressions into which it will not fit, the disk might be said to be *scanning* the openings. It *selects* one that it *matches* when it drops into it. In a figurative sense it has *identified* the pattern to which it corresponds,[1] and the identification corresponds to its *meaning.*

Figure 5–1 diagrams this process. The *signal inputs* from the environment consist of sound waves entering the ear, light waves entering the eye, and so on. When these received signals activate sensory receptors and the attached sensory nerves they have been *detected.* At this stage they are merely *sensations,* without meaning. The *transmission* process (electrical impulses traveling through neurons) carries the sensations to the brain. There they enter a *"scanner,"* in which they serve as cues. The scanner compares the patterns in the sensations with the patterns already in the brain in the form of stored images. If the sensations contain sufficient cues, then on the basis of some kind of match or fit[2] they select a channel that activates one of the stored images. The stored image that is selected by the pattern of sensations is the *meaning* of those sensations, and of the signals. The combined processes of scanning and channel selection are also called *decoding,* or extracting the meaning. Decoding is also an act of identifying a stored pattern from the incoming cues.

If we assume that the patterns have already been formed and stored, and if for convenience we ignore the transmission process, we can say that *perception* consists of detection plus decoding, of sensation plus channel selection, or of sensation plus identification—whichever language we happen to prefer. Except at the primary level, where we are

---

[1] "Selection" in this usage is a straightforward information, pattern-matching process. It should not be confused with the value selection performed in the selector, and it is unfortunate that both usages of the term are so well established. The analogy of the disk should clarify that it is possible to have a "selection" that does not involve a "preference" of the type that appears in the selector. "Selection" in the scanning process of the detector is a matter of *same* or *different;* that in the selector is a matter of *liked* or *disliked.* To relate these terms to others used earlier, a preference of the sort in the selector function of DSE is found only in controlled systems. By contrast, the disk is just a "lump"; it is not even a system (if we do not drop to the molecular level), much less a controlled one. This problem is discussed in more detail in Kuhn (1974: 98–99).

[2] The meaning of "match" or "fit" in this connection is a long and complicated philosophical problem. There is no such thing as a "perfect fit," and the main question is how much mismatch there can be between the two patterns while we nevertheless consider them a match. We will not attempt to answer the question. We also know woefully little about how the brain actually performs this process.

Figure 5-1
A SCHEMATIC DIAGRAM OF PERCEPTION (details of human detector system)

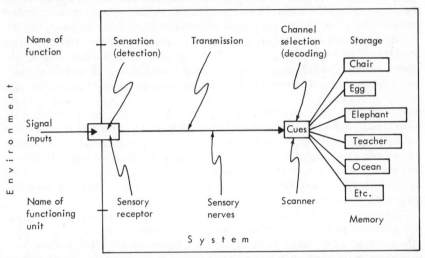

As with much else in the model, this schematic is a vast oversimplification, particularly in suggesting that scanning is a single-step process. If nothing else, we should at least allow for the identification of cues from subcues, which are identified from sub-subcues. Although we have much information about many details of perceptual processes we have remarkably little basic theory of the overall process, and later findings might call for a very different model than this one. If we keep in mind that this model is not made by psychologists for psychology but by a social scientist for social science, we may make good use of it meanwhile, and with a clear conscience.

interested in the sensation as sensation (warmth, tickle, sweet taste, erogenous sensation) without regard to the kind of external thing that sets it off, we say that a stimulus is not a stimulus until it is identified. It is not the sensations to which we respond, but the identification that tells us whether the sensations were activated by (and therefore represent) a shirt, an automobile, or a snowstorm. As related to consciousness, at the level of sensation alone we may be conscious *that* we are receiving sensations, but we do not know *what* is activating them.

In contrast to pattern learning, which we said is inductive, pattern using in perception is *deductive.* It joins the primary information in the incoming sensations with the secondary information in the stored image to infer information about presently experienced reality that is not present in either the primary or secondary information alone (Bruner 1956: 17; Kuhn 1961: 104–7).

Summary and complications. Two steps are required for perception: learning images and using them. We have now added that the pattern-using step itself involves two steps. The first is the receipt of primary information in the form of *sensations,* and the second is the use of this primary information as cues to *identify* or activate secondary information in the form of the previously stored images. To use an overt parallel, suppose you put the recipe for sponge cake on a red file card, for bean soup on a green card, and for pot roast on a yellow card. If you knew the cues, the signal "yellow" would identify and "release" to you the pot roast recipe stored on the card. In recent years pattern formation and pattern recognition by scanning and matching have been done by computers.

The importance of these processes for social science is simple and fundamental. With exceptions or reservations unimportant enough to ignore in this model, *you cannot perceive something in your environment* (in contrast to merely receiving sensations from it) *unless an image of it has already been learned and stored in your head.* A vast majority of images in people's heads, and particularly images about relationships of people, are learned from society. This means that for the most part you can perceive only those aspects or conditions of society that the society has taught you to perceive. Though imaginative individuals and groups may break those boundaries, it is still true that most of us most of the time are not able to see, know, or think about things not taught us by society.

For discussion we have separated image learning from image using. In fact, both go on more or less constantly. A perception may be inaccurate because the image is faulty, and a nasty brush with reality may cause the child to modify its image of wasps to include the fact that they sting. Images may be revised when reality changes, as when a street is relocated or your house is painted a different color. You may think that size alone is a sufficient cue to tell a lemon from a grapefruit. But when you discover the very large lemons you will have to add shape, odor, taste, or color as additional cues if you are to tell which is which.

Whereas the brain is relatively slow at forming distinctly new images it can join existing ones into new combinations very quickly. If you have already formed one image of tree and another of truck, you can almost instantly combine the two to perceive a tree on a truck, even if you have never seen that combination before. As we will state it in connection with language, you *intersect* your existing concepts of "tree," "on," and "truck" to perceive tree-on-truck.

We will later use the term *intuition* for essentially unconscious thinking. You can coordinate a complex set of muscles when you walk or jump, without conscious thought about *which* muscles you are using. You can similarly coordinate a set of concepts to reach a new concept or conclusion without being conscious of *what* concepts you are using or *how* you are relating them. Sometimes it is also fast thinking. Intuition can be sound or unsound, just as jumping can be well coordinated or clumsy.

6

MODEL OF MAN: LEARNED COMPONENTS OF SELECTOR AND EFFECTOR
(AND SUMMARY OF MODEL)

In Chapter 4 we discussed the general nature of the human system and identified its inborn components. In Chapter 5 we discussed the learned aspects of the detector. It is the large information processing capacity of man's detector that sets him so far apart from other animals. In this chapter we will see that man's large learning capacity in selector and effector also relies mainly on that of the detector. Following discussion of the learned components of selector and effector we will look at the many possible interrelations among the DSE subsystems, introduce the concept of personal power as related to the magnitude (rather than merely the nature) of behavior, and close with a summary of the model of man.

SELECTOR

We indicated that the inborn components of the selector, or primary motives, consist (in our model) of pleasant or unpleasant valences that are activated by certain sensations and emotions. Some neutral sensations are not part of the selector. This section deals with the learned components of the selector, or secondary motives. As with the detector, we will deal with these learned components under the headings of pattern learning and pattern using.

Pattern learning in the selector

The simplest kind of learning of new patterns in the selector is that of making new connections on the basis of experience. By biological inheritance moderately sweet and salty tastes are pleasant, while sour and bitter tastes are unpleasant. Beer is somewhat bitter, and dill pickles and lemon are definitely sour. Yet through repeated use we may come to like all three. An unpleasant association can make a person dislike almost any food that was initially liked, as when eating chocolate candy till one gets very sick makes the taste of chocolate nauseating. Like most children, I found orange juice originally pleasant. But after it was used several times as a cover for castor oil, I disliked orange juice for years because it seemed to taste like castor oil. One can similarly learn to like or dislike particular odors, colors, sounds, or skin sensations through their conditioned association with something else.

Learned valences of this sort are also found in other animals, such as household pets. By contrast, the more subtle and complex likes and dislikes of man depend on images formed in his detector. To deal first with exceptions, in such things as loud rock music or certain colors one may learn to like or dislike the sensations themselves. More commonly, however, our secondary motives consist of a conditioned connection between a valence and a concept—the learned motive is a concept (image) with a valence attached. You cannot "like steak" (in contrast to liking the sensations it produces in your mouth) until you have formed the concept of steak. You cannot like photography, travel, or the theater without having concepts of these things; none of them produces any distinctive sensations. Many people form images of ethnic groups (blacks, whites, Orientals, Poles, Jews, Irish) and attach assorted positive or negative valences to each. In all the above cases pattern learning involves both (1) learning the image in the detector and (2) attaching a valence to it in the selector. Often both occur at the same time.

Images and valences can change. One can first get interested in music through rock and later expand his liking to symphony—or the reverse. One can start with an impression that some ethnic group is weird or bad and later conclude that "they're just like us." Both the original learning and later modification of images and valences are part of "pattern learning."

This relation of images and valences seems very clear with emotions. Fear can be aroused directly by a sensation—the pain of a knife pressed into your chest, even if you do not know what is causing the pain. But fear can also be aroused by seeing someone poised to thrust the knife, even though it is not touching you and there is no sensation of pain at all. Fear in this second case depends on perception—your previously learned concept of "being knifed." After all, the visual sensations of seeing a person threaten you with a knife have no more or different valence than those activated by a waiter offering you pie: the visual sensations themselves are neutral in both cases. It is your *concepts* of pie and of knifing to which your valences are attached. Otherwise you could not feel fear or say yes to the waiter until you had actually felt the knife or tasted the pie. The idea of a valence attached to a concept is also very clear when we say, "It nauseates me just to think of eating that stuff" or "I don't see how the astronauts can stand being cooped up in such a small space." For abstract things like education, nationalism, or freedom it is hard even to imagine having a like or dislike (approval or disapproval) except in relation to the concepts.

Valences about beer and pickles can be modified through sensory experience alone. Valences of sensations can also be altered through conceptual learning. For example, pain is an unpleasant sensation. The approval of others is widely liked—a valenced concept. In some cultures the ability to endure pain brings strong approval as a sign of bravery. By a conditioned connection to the concepts of bravery and approval a substantial amount of pain can come to be liked. Up to a certain point almost *any* input can feed into and strengthen a feeling that is dominant at the moment—as when some people find erotic response strengthened by pain or a feeling of guilt. Relatedly, a pain often hurts worse if we add the valenced *thought* of hurting to the sensation itself.

Pattern using in the selector

We use learned patterns of likes and dislikes whenever we make choices that reflect them. You like rock but dislike symphony, so you choose tickets to the former. If you have learned to like the approval of fellow students but don't care about approval by the dean, you "use" that preference when you choose behaviors applauded by students even if those behaviors are frowned on by the dean. If you like corporations and dislike unions, voting Republican "uses" that preference. Conflicts often occur (you disapprove the Republican views on abortion), but we will not deal with those complications here.

EFFECTOR

With the above background the effector can be described very simply. Pattern learning in the effector lies in learning the muscular coordinations (patterns) with which we walk, jump, sit, sew, throw, write, or pole-vault—the learning of motor skills, including the ability to make the sounds (as contrasted with learning the meanings) of speech. Pattern using is actual performance of these learned skills—actual walking, talking, throwing, and so on.

As with the selector, the more complex motor behaviors are tied to the detector, in at least two ways. First (and at least after a certain stage of maturity), we use a conscious concept of how a task is to be performed to guide our practice until the motor skill becomes largely automatic. This sequence is clear when someone instructs us, "Grasp the racket as if you are shaking hands"; "Swing in a horizontal plane." The motor skill is fully learned (is wholly in the effector) when it can be executed without thinking.

Second, all the more complicated motor responses of the effector need guidance from the detector. Although we may throw a stone smoothly using the motor skill alone, if we are to hit something we must add visual perceptions to guide the throw. The skier may have adequate motor skills in his effector. But he also needs complicated detector judgments about where to turn, the texture of the snow, and the movements of other skiers.

To the actual motor skills of making a dress or repairing a car must be added conceptual knowledge about tools, materials, and steps of the process. For related reasons, the cases where we run into difficulty carrying out behaviors are likely to take us back to detector or selector to deal with the complications—which is a reason for our relatively little attention to the effector.

Again, it is the inability of other animals to develop the highly organized (detector) concepts that guide the practice and performance of complex motor skills which prevents their doing the many complicated things that humans can do. Except for the apes, the absence of fingers and the opposable thumb with which to grasp things, and the inability to walk on two limbs so that the other two are free to manipulate things, are also monumental obstacles. The physical and mental factors may have worked in a positive feedback evolutionary relation: a bigger brain did not develop because the body could not execute the more complicated behaviors, and the physical equipment of the body did not develop because the brain was unable to use it.

Tools, technology, and science are additional results of the high-capacity detector that put man far beyond all other animals. The ability to make tools (which implies the concept of the tool and conceptual guidance of the tool-forming actions) has long been considered the feature that distinguishes early humans from their apelike ancestors. Language is another distinguishing feature, perhaps more crucial than tool-making. But we have only tools to tell us whether some early creatures should be considered human, since their tools remain but their speech does not. We now know that some apes, particularly chimpanzees, can make simple tools, as by stripping a twig or stem of grass to put into an ant hole to retrieve ants for food. Recent experiments also indicate that chimpanzees and dolphins may be able to use simple messages (Chapter 12). However, even if we cannot draw an absolute line between man and other animals, the *degree* of difference is huge.

THE DSE PACKAGE

Interrelations among DSE

We have talked mainly thus far of the separate DSE subsystems, and also of the way the more complex learned components of selector and effector depend on organized images in the detector. As with models in general, this one is a simplified picture. The actual complications and interactions among the three, and even within any one of them, can be fantastically complex. We will illustrate how those complications are dealt with in this model.

First are interrelations among the three, and we have already indicated that learned aspects of selector and effector depend on the detector. But the three also modify one another. An example is modification (distortion?) of detector by selector. We often see what we want to see, hear what we want to hear, and believe what we want to believe, despite evidence to the contrary. The conservative Republican may read about and remember all of Nixon's virtues and ignore his faults, while the liberal Democrat may do the reverse. We selectively remember our successes and forget our failures (though the emotionally disturbed sometimes do the opposite), thus providing a rosy distortion of our own capacities and performances.

The reverse interaction is modification of selector by detector. Perhaps in reflection of the "sour grapes" principle we tend actively to want things that are possible and not actively to want things we perceive as not possible. We may daydream about the impossible, but the desire does not ordinarily guide overt behavior. For example, if we have actually been working toward something, and later conclude that it is not possible to attain it, after the initial disappointment the desire itself subsides. In reverse, I have observed a mild background interest turn overnight into a burning desire in each of my sons when some turn of events made it suddenly seem possible for him to have his own car. Psychologists call this reaction the "expansion and contraction of aspirations." It probably assists adaptive behavior, since it prevents us both from being perpetually frustrated and from sitting idle while great opportunities pass by.

A note on objectivity

In this connection the notion of *"objectivity"* is interesting. We typically say that we are "nonobjective" or "biased" when our detector is modified by the selector: a researcher opposed to abortion may be more likely to find it medically unsafe than one who approves it. The two researchers may focus on different facts, give different weight to the same facts, or both. It is nevertheless *possible* for a trained and conscientious researcher to avoid such bias. An important part of scientific and academic training is directed toward designing research whose conclusions are not affected by such attitudes, and are not affected by personal attitudes and values. Perhaps more realistically, the scholar is expected to substitute the values of the scientific community for his own when he does scientific work. Among other possible forms of discipline, the subculture of scientists can undercut the credibility of a researcher whose conclusions show such bias.

By contrast, there is no escape from the bias in one's conceptual set. Different conceptual sets involve more than different conclusions from the same facts. The "facts" are different. To the ancients it was a *fact* that all heavenly bodies moved around the earth. Anyone with eyes could see it, as he could also see that the earth is flat! The contemporary person sees it as *fact* that the earth is round and that all heavenly bodies (except the moon) only *seem* to move because the earth turns.

The sensations (i.e., primary information) received by modern man looking at the skies are no different than those of ancient man. It is the stored images, or models, that are different. We tend to assume that our model is "correct" and that theirs was "wrong." Perhaps so, though later years may find our view faulty.

Different images as well as different goals are involved in ideological battles. What the American conservative *sees* in the capitalist economy is healthy expansion in productivity and rising human welfare as new products, new techniques, and new geographic areas are developed. What the Marxist *sees* is capitalism's desperate dying struggle, through imperialism, to avoid drowning in the surplus it generates by monopolistic exploitation. The Marxist also sees a *working class* in the United States, even if it is less active and cohesive than he might like. The capitalist sees employees, unions, and welfare chiselers, but no *class* of working people. The two could *see* the same thing only if one adopted the other's images or both adopted some third set. Both also see what they want to see—but that is a different problem.

Self-actualization

Almost any system seems to have some optimum level of operation. Below that level it is relatively inefficient: it uses more inputs per unit of output. Above that level it seems to strain, and to tire or wear out faster. At the optimum level the system seems to operate smoothly, effectively, easily. Living things are apparently no exception. We also assume (as generally appears to be the case) that an individual finds affirmative satisfaction from operating at or near that optimum level, and dissatisfaction at levels much above or below it. Although other authors do not use the term with this same meaning, we will define *self-actualization* as the sense of satisfaction from optimal operation, while boredom and overload are respectively the dissatisfactions from operating below or above optimum. More broadly, there is some satisfaction in simple functioning of the system, in contrast to its being unused.

In this model the functions of the behavioral system consist of forming and using patterns in all three DSE subsystems. As to pattern forming in the detector, much play activity of children is directed toward learning images of the reality around them, and toward identifying things. The child of one or two often squeals with delight when it learns a new pattern or successfully identifies one. In learning to put square pegs into square holes the child is learning the image of squareness. When the child can later repeat the operation with several shapes with little or no error he is giving overt evidence that he has correctly formed and identified (used) the patterns. If left to his own devices, the child will avoid activities too complicated for his level of achievement, which would constitute overload and frustration. The child also loses interest after such activity is so thoroughly learned that further attention to it would constitute underload, and be boring. The squeals may disappear as we get older, but we all know the frustration of struggling to get some idea straight, and the marvelous "Aha!" or "Eureka!" feeling when the idea falls into place. (I still squeal occasionally!)

In the selector we receive satisfaction from learning to like new things, and possibly from learning to dislike some. The former gives double satisfaction—that from the process of learning the new like *plus* that from the new thing itself. The latter is mixed. It involves the pleasure of learning the dislike *minus* the dissatisfaction from the thing itself. The pleasure from pattern using in the selector is that of actually making or expressing choices. One of the pleasures of either real or window shopping is that of exercising preferences. "Isn't that beautiful?" or "I wouldn't be caught dead in *that!*" are expressions of learned preferences, and are typically rewarding.

In the effector it is fun (if it goes at the proper pace) to learn to drive a car, drive a straight nail, sew a straight seam, or play basketball or tennis, or, for the infant, to learn to walk, stoop, or run—all pattern learning. Having learned the skills, one also finds it fun to exercise them —actually to do these things. There is double satisfaction in the combination—to do what one does well, and in the doing to learn to do it even better. As the coach puts it, "That was fine. Now let's see you do it better next time." This motive is widely evident in the young of many animals, such as bears, otters, cats, and apes. They go through all sorts of mock fighting, biting, chasing, sliding, and other actions through which they learn the muscular coordinations they will need later.

Experiments have been conducted in which human subjects were suspended in warm water in space suits that completely cut off all outside sensations—no sounds, no sights, no feel of weight, no temperature changes, no odors, and no tastes. Although some might think this an idyllic state, it is highly unpleasant, disorganizing, and disorienting. There is affirmative satisfaction in the more or less continuous stimulation of at least some of the senses. There is also satisfaction from simply using the body and muscles.

The optimum level of activity differs from person to person, and with each person's age, health, rest, and other factors. The level is also influenced by learning. If an individual has generally been successful in learning and using patterns, his optimal level will be high. If he has often failed or been criticized, his satisfaction from trying new patterns will be low. McClelland (1951) refers to this general urge as NAch, or the Need-Achievement level—important in determining how well someone will do in class, on the job, with the guitar, or at basketball. The self-motivated desire to learn new patterns, especially in the detector, is a more explicit description of curiosity.

Self-actualization and feedback learning

All overt behavior is based upon and reflects some inner pattern. To pick up and play a guitar reflects one's detector state of knowing what a guitar is and perceiving it; it reflects his selector state of liking to play (at least at the moment); and it reflects the required motor skills in his effector. In broad terms of self-actualization, the simple desire to *use* our abilities and faculties includes satisfaction in externalizing, or *symboling,* inner patterns. This often means doing for the sake of doing: making for the sake of making, decorating for the sake of decorating, playing for the sake of playing, learning for the sake of learning, collecting for the sake of collecting, talking for the sake of talking, even working for the sake of working. In short, many activities are self-motivated. Otherwise there seems to be no explanation why all peoples engage in such a steady barrage of activity that makes no instrumental contribution toward any discernible objective goal.

An important consequence of externalizing (symboling) inner pat-

SELF-ACTUALIZATION

© 1972 United Features Syndicate, Inc.

terns is that we can then observe and modify them. A relatively vague idea of a house or a table can be externalized in a rough sketch. By studying it, one can modify and refine his idea, next make an improved sketch, then further refine the image by examining the improved sketch. The process can continue until a satisfactory level of refinement has been reached. An important reason why college teachers are asked to write for publication, and why students are asked to write themes or examinations, is that there is no better means to refine and clarify one's thinking than to externalize it in a form that can be examined at length.

Motor skills behave similarly. If we repeatedly throw the ball too high we have external evidence of a faulty inner pattern, and can use this evidence to revise the inner pattern that controls the throwing. Though we often correct such errors unconsciously, the correction will probably come sooner if we consciously direct it.

Figure 6–2 includes frustration alongside self-actualization. When the system is functioning well, and within optimal range, we have the good feeling here referred to as self-actualization, or as self-expression. When things go badly, and we cannot seem to form or use patterns successfully in detector, selector, or effector, the result is frustration. (Whereas we discussed frustration in Chapter 4 we deferred self-actualization to this chapter because it cannot be described satisfactorily until details of pattern learning and using have been spelled out.)

INTRODUCING A MORE COMPLETE MODEL

The reader may often have the feeling, "But the human is really much more complicated than this model." Of course. The model is deliberately simplified. It is possible, however, to handle much additional complexity with another level of subsystems. Assume that the DSEs discussed thus far are *main level,* and that each of the three has a subdetector, subselector, and subeffector of its own. An outline example shows the meaning of each. The capitalized main headings are the *Main-Level DSEs,* and the subheadings are the *Sub-DSEs.*

DETECTOR—Information
Subdetector: Information about information.
      "I don't understand this stuff about systems."
Subselector: Motives about information.
      "I wish I did understand about systems."

Subeffector: Actions about information.
              "I will study harder about systems."

SELECTOR—Motives
Subdetector: Information about motives.
              "I know that I dislike country music."
Subselector: Motives about motives.
              "I wish I liked it."
Subeffector: Actions about motives.
              "I will listen to more of it, and perhaps
              I will learn to like it."

EFFECTOR—Actions or skills
Subdetector: Information about skills.
              "I know that I can't ski."
Subselector: Motives about skills.
              "I wish I could ski."
Subeffector: Actions about skills.
              "I will practice skiing."

The three subdetectors represent "consciousness" in this model—but, of course, do not explain what it is any more than does any other model. Since the detector can be said to consist of images, the subdetector of the main detector can similarly be said to consist of our images of our images, the study of which has been called "iconics" (Boulding 1956). Anyone who likes may try another level of sub-sub-DSEs—though I see no need for them.

Just as we said that the main-level DSEs can interact with one an-

Figure 6–1
THE BEHAVIORAL SYSTEM IN AN
ENVIRONMENT (including DSE subsystems)

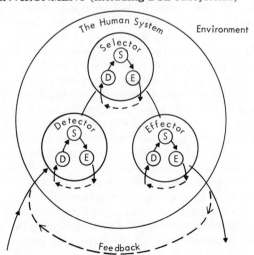

other, so could any of the nine sub-DSEs interact with any of the other nine, or with any of the three main-level ones. We will not trace these, since that much complexity is not needed here. This section merely indicates that the model *can* handle considerable complexity if so desired. For those who want a diagram, Figure 6–1 adds the above detail to Figure 4–1.

POWER AT THE INDIVIDUAL LEVEL

In studying DSE thus far, we have paid attention to *what* behavior is selected—the *nature and direction* of the effect. But it is also important to know *how much* effect is produced, or its *magnitude.* How much can the system actually accomplish? How fully and satisfactorily does it adapt? The effectiveness of the whole system can be analyzed in terms of the effectiveness of its three subsystems, taken separately and jointly.

As to the detector, the better one's information the more likely he is to respond effectively. The deaf man may not know the boulder is rolling toward him from behind, and one who knows about wheelbarrows can move more sand than one who knows only about buckets. Education is a broad-gauged process of raising power by improving the detector.

As to the selector, the strongly motivated person accomplishes more than the weakly motivated one, and anyone accomplishes more when he is strongly motivated than when he is not. As to the effector, the more strength and motor skill one has the more he will accomplish.

The environment must also provide something to work with, since one cannot build a stone house of straw or grow corn in Arctic snows. To the extent that the environment is the way one wants it, he can satisfy wants from it by doing little or nothing. To the extent that it is not, he can satisfy his wants only by transforming the environment, as by growing corn or building a house. He may also change his relation to the environment, as by moving into the shade in hot weather or by migrating to fertile areas when he finds that corn will not grow in the desert. "Transforming the environment" includes changing one's relation to it.

Later chapters pay much attention to *power,* which we define as one's ability to satisfy his wants. For social science we are interested mainly in satisfying wants through others. But even then, *some*one must make the desired transformations. Hence we deal with this ability at the level of the individual before trying to understand power in a society. For the lone individual (Robinson Crusoe) power rests in the ability to make desired transformations, and the larger the quantity and quality of such transformations he can make the greater is his power. This ability can also be described as productive capacity, which depends on one's DSE states taken in conjunction with the state of the environment. The "state of the environment" can be described as the amount, quality, and accessibility of natural resources. *For the individual acting alone, power is his ability to produce.* We will call this intrasystem or intrapersonal power, in contrast with intersystem or interpersonal power, to be dealt with later. For some interpersonal purposes power also lies in destructive capacity—as we shall see.

MODEL OF MAN: SUMMARY

Figure 6–2 summarizes the model of man. Like any other controlled system, man has detector, selector, and effector processes—knowing, wanting, and doing. Each process has inborn, or primary, aspects, mainly in the form of inborn connections of certain sensory processes (detector), of certain valences of pleasure or displeasure (selector), and of certain muscles (effector). By associating and organizing the patterns of incoming sensations, the individual forms mental patterns, or images, that correspond to outer reality in some ways but not in others. By attaching some of those images (which are secondary information) to primary valences, the individual acquires secondary, or learned, motives. By organizing the patterns of outgoing "instructions" to muscles, the individual learns motor skills.

Except at the level of reflexes, which are of no direct concern to social science, humans have no inborn connections between inputs of sensory information and outputs of muscular behavior. All such connections are learned. As a result of learning, patterns in all three DSE functions that were initially random with respect to the environment gradually become ordered toward the environment. Some relations remain random, and one cannot even imagine a human being who is "wholly ordered" toward his environment—which itself is not wholly ordered. The environment toward which we become ordered is both natural and social, though much of our ordering toward nature is also social, in that it is copied from others around us—by attainment, as contrasted to independent formation, of patterns.

Our primary motives are oriented toward survival, and in a simple sense assist us to learn particular behaviors that favor survival. But our learning capacity is so large and many of our learned likes and dislikes are so far removed from their primary base that it would be nonsensical to try to relate them either to survival or to a simple pleasure-pain formula. The ability to abstract from reality, which depends upon higher-order conditioning, enables us to be inventive and imaginative—to form and report "untrue" images (including lies).

Once we have formed patterns we use them. Patterns in the detector, or images, are used whenever we perceive. Patterns in the selector are used whenever we make learned choices. Patterns in the effector are used every time we engage in learned muscular movement.

In addition to the inborn valences about specific sensations, the human gets a distinct satisfaction from simply using any of these faculties: from both forming and using patterns in detector, selector, and effector, and particularly from improving the patterns through using them. (He also often gets satisfaction from observing others exercising *their* skills.) This kind of satisfaction, along with the activities we engage in to achieve it, are known as self-expression, self-actualization, or self-reali-

Figure 6-2
OUTLINE OF THE MODEL OF MAN

	Unlearned, inborn components	Learned components	
		Pattern learning	Pattern using
Detector	*Sensations (primary information)* On an inborn basis, light, sound, odors, tastes, pressure, heat, etc. actuate different nerves and enter the brain through different channels.	*Concept formation and attainment (learning secondary information) (induction)* The brain organizes sensory inputs into patterns and patterns of patterns. Image learning and testing.	*Perception (deduction)* Sensations currently received serve as cues which identify already learned patterns. Image using and identification (detecting plus decoding).
Selector	*Valences (primary motives)* On an inborn basis certain tastes, odors, and other sensations are pleasant, others unpleasant. These sensations, along with some emotions, guide the learning of more complex approach or avoidance behaviors.	*Secondary motives* The brain connects the inborn valences to new or different sensory inputs, and to concepts.	*Making choices* Choices are made on the basis of secondary motives, which are mostly valenced concepts.
Effector	*Motor connections* Each muscle has an inborn connection to a particular point in the brain, so that different muscles are actuated by different channels from the brain.	*Motor skills* Through practice the brain connects muscle responses into groups and sequences that constitute performance skills.	*Motor performance* Motor skills already learned are executed.

In addition, two valences, one positive and one negative, operate across all of the above:

Self-actualization: There is a certain satisfaction from actually performing or using any or all of the above nine items. This satisfaction is greatest at some optimum level, below which there is boredom and above which there is overload, both of which seem related to frustration.

Frustration: There is a certain dissatisfaction from blockages in the use of any of the above items. Frustration is often, if not always, marked by a nonmatch of patterns, including a mismatch between a pattern of expectation and one of achievement.

zation. The level of such activity that produces satisfaction varies with such factors as the person, age, state of health, state of rest, and the amount of previous success in similar activities. Rates of use above the satisfactory level constitute overload and frustration. Lower rates constitute boredom and restlessness.

All of the above aspects of the model deal with the nature or direction of behavior. But we are also interested in the magnitude of its effect, which we call power. The amount of one's power depends on how well he sizes up the situations he must deal with (detector), how strongly he is motivated (selector), and how skilled he is at producing results (effector), along with the conditions in the environment that assist or provide obstacles to achievement. Although we are interested mainly in one's power in relation to others (interpersonal power), all such power must be based somewhere in someone's intrapersonal power. Hence we introduce the latter concept here.

Like other models, this one is a very rough mapping of the terrain, leaving out most of the detail. But it is enough for most social science. We have had to invent our own model of man for social science, since psychologists have not produced a usable, brief one for us.

7

SELECTING BEHAVIOR: DECISIONS

"Man is the missing link between
the ape and the human being."
Konrad Lorenz

"No one in his senses would want his daughter
to marry an economic man."
Kenneth Boulding

Our model describes man as having inherited a behavior-selecting system but not behavior. The main ingredients in that behavior-selecting system are the primary and secondary levels of both information and motives in the detector and the selector. But thus far we have not even hinted about how the behavior-selecting system actually goes about selecting a behavior—to which we now turn.

As presented in previous chapters, the model of man was made by simplifying, tightening, and narrowing a wide variety of materials from psychology, sociology, and system theory. By contrast, economics and decision theory have already developed extraordinarily tight and systematic models of behavior selections. Reversing the methods of the previous chapters, we will modify those materials for our purposes by widening and loosening them.

Strictly speaking, decision theory does not describe how people *do* make decisions, but how they *would* if they were to act rationally. The somewhat expanded concept of rationality used here nevertheless brings those alternatives (*do* and *would*) closer together than one might anticipate, and makes our decision model a sensible conclusion to our treatment of the intrasystem aspects of the human units of a society.

ON RATIONALITY

We will apply the term *rational* to a relationship between means and ends, and say that behavior is rational if it is instrumentally directed toward some goal. We could also say that rational behavior is *advantageous*—or that it is *successfully adaptive.* In language to be developed shortly, rational behavior is behavior whose expected benefits equal or exceed its expected costs.

But let us ask some questions. If you are fed up with your idiotic boss, is it "rational" to punch him in the nose, even if it will cost you a good job? Is it "rational" to buy an expensive sports car because of people's admiring looks when you zoom past, even though a car at a third the cost would be more "sensible"? Is it "rational" to "trip" on drugs because you like it, even if you thereby risk injury or imprisonment?

Values taken as given

There is no easy answer to these questions. In explaining why, we will clarify the present model. First, *all motives* (which for this purpose will mean all satisfactions or dissatisfactions currently experienced or expected in the future) *are in the final analysis subjective.* Furthermore, we will take them as given. I think kidneys taste horrible. But if you like kidneys, I cannot conclude that you are irrational if you eat them. I may think someone strange if he prefers poverty to affluence. But if he gets moᵣₑ pleasure from helping others than from having things for himself, I cannot therefore deem him irrational. If you assure me it is worth losing your job to punch your boss, I cannot conclude that to you the benefits are less than the costs.

In the present model, what you like or dislike, and how intensely, is your business: matters of taste are not subject to dispute *(de gustibus non est disputandum)*. The question of rationality cannot be asked of goals (selector states), but only of means as related to them. In later chapters we will see that most of one's goals and preferences are acquired from his society, though also reflecting individual differences. In studying decisions, however, we are concerned with the consequences of preferences, not with their origins. That is what we mean by "taking them as given."

A set of likes and dislikes is a *value structure.* It encompasses both minor preferences (food, dress, vacations) and larger, longer-run preferences (freedom, education, religion, patriotism). We are interested in one's *real* value structure, as reflected in his actual choices. These may or may not coincide with his *verbalized* value structure. To say that one's preferences about beer and education are both parts of his value structure does not mean that they are of the same importance. It merely means that they have parallel kinds of effects on his choices.

In any one decision only a few likes and dislikes are apt to be involved —you need not consider your views on freedom and education to decide on today's lunch. The subset of values involved in a particular decision is the *preference function* for that decision. As noted, our model of decisions takes the preference function as given, not as something to be questioned or examined.

Information images taken as given

The second half of the problem of rationality concerns information— the state of the detector. Suppose you are driving north on Wobbly Street and want to turn west on Senile. You come to an intersection marked "Senile," and turn left. It shortly turns out that you are on Cursory instead of Senile, because some prankster moved the signs. Did you behave irrationally when you turned?

We will say that you acted on incorrect information, and therefore made an error. But your behavior was "directed toward" your objective, and was rational in light of your actual information. We will even consider your behavior rational, though mistaken, if the street sign was correct but you read it wrong.

There are many reasons for faulty information. In fact, we have said that *all* information about reality is to some degree faulty or distorted— which problem involves two steps. First is the question of whether a person bases his behavior on his image. Second is the question of whether his image is in accord with reality. We will attend solely to the first question, and consider one's behavior rational if it is instrumentally directed toward his goals *within the context of the situation as he sees it*—i.e., if it is based on his images. Whether his images are "correct" is a problem of the detector, not of the logic of decisions. Thus, to examine the logic of decision making, as such, we need not know whether a rain dance is more likely to produce rain than is cloud seeding.[1] We assume that you already possess certain information and that you act on it. Later we will deal with costs of information in decisions.

One's perception or image of the situation he is facing is his perceived *opportunity function.* Whereas the preference function reflects what is wanted, the opportunity function reflects what is possible. What is possible depends in turn on (1) what the situation *is* and (2) what he is able to *do about it.* For the thief who has ducked into a blind alley to escape the police, the perceived situation *is* that the only ways to escape are to climb a ten-foot wall, crawl through a sewer, or shoot his way back past the police. These things he discerns through his detector.

What he is able to *do about it* will depend on his strength and skill in climbing walls, his flexibility in sewer slithering, and his facility with guns. What one can *do* is determined by a complicated mixture of his capacities and the overt circumstances, and it is often pointless to ask whether one's ability to accomplish something is limited by his personal capacities or by the environmental situation within which he must work. The latter often involves scientific principles, as when a decision to pry a window open depends on certain scientific principles of levers, and you may or may not think about them explicitly. The environmental limitations sometimes reflect social actions or the DSE states of others, as with laws or the relative desires of the police to catch the thief and avoid danger. In short, your perceived opportunity function is the set of things you think possible, in the light of both your capacities and the obstacles. For this introduction to decisions we also take your perceived oppor-

---

[1] A decision is sometimes said to be "subjectively rational" if it is consistent with one's inner system states, and "objectively rational" if those system states correspond adequately with external reality. The present decision model does not need these additional terms.

tunity function as given. The opportunity function may also be thought of as the set of *constraints* within which one operates.

As to rationality, *if* you believe a particular line of action to be possible (or acceptably probable), *and if* it is your preferred alternative, *then* we will accept your behavior as rational if you make that choice—even if you are mistaken about your opportunities and unorthodox in your preferences.

Then what can be irrational?

It is always possible, of course, that you will later reassess the situation. After you punch the boss you may decide it wasn't worth it, and following a shift in motivation conclude that you behaved irrationally. (A friend might have told you the same in advance.) Now to the main point. If we do not question the motives (and include those of emotion and passion), and if we accept one's perception of his opportunity function as of the moment he acts, then behavior can be judged irrational only by a different person, or by the person himself after his opportunity and/or preference functions have changed. This statement does not change our meaning of "rational" and "advantageous." It merely means that a course of action that seemed advantageous under one set of detec-

Drawing by Modell; © 1971 The New Yorker Magazine, Inc.

tor and selector states no longer seems so after those states have changed.

Two other kinds of situations can be clarified, as follows. We all know of cases where we want to do something and "decide" to do it. But emotions or other inner states keep us from doing it—we decide to speak but get flustered and the words won't come. We will view this as a failure of the effector, not as an irrational decision to speak. Some persons resolve over and over to look for a job. But an unconscious fear of failing always brings excuses for putting it off. In this case we might say that the fear itself is irrational—a selector state out of touch with reality. But we will not say that the decision to avoid job-hunting is irrational if the fear is, in fact, the really dominating motive. Fortunately, we can get on with decision theory without having to resolve such vexing questions in individual cases.

Scope of the model

This model of the decision, it is hoped, is able to encompass at least some of the kind of behavior selection dealt with by the psychiatrist and clinical psychologist on the one hand and by the economist on the other. The economist deals initially with so-called objective rationality, in which the decision maker has both an explicit, consciously formulated goal, and adequate information about all the circumstances relevant to his decision. In theory, his decision is as simple as deciding whether to turn east or west to get from St. Louis to Denver. If alternative X provides a million dollars' profit and Y only a half million, he chooses X.

As soon as we go beyond the initial economic model, however, we find a continuous gradation of cases between the formally explicit and the subjectively vague. We have spoken of the impulsive nose-punching as bringing a possible sudden shift in motivation. But external factors can bring equally sudden shifts. Five minutes after an executive dedicates an expensive new ore-processing plant he may learn that a competitor's discovery of a fabulously rich new ore deposit makes his new plant obsolete. What five minutes before was a lovely dream is now a potentially bankrupting nightmare. For our model it does not matter whether the motive is instrumental to tangible external realities or fleeting internal urges. In either case the decision can be analyzed only with reference to the preferences at the moment the decision is made. Nor do we have to assume that the executive holds only the single-minded goal of profit maximization. He may want to bolster his ego, cement his reputation with the chairman of the board, or brag to his son that he signed a 200 million dollar check. Perhaps his really dominant motive is to impress a wife who thinks him mousy and ineffectual. Our model assumes that there *is* content to the decision. But the model is indifferent to *what* it is.

Why study decisions?

Sociologists tend to focus on behavior determined by habit, norms, and culture. While accepting the importance of those forces, we nevertheless note that many choices are neither habitual nor culturally prescribed, but are made by individuals who see one behavior as more advantageous than another. Even to say that something is habitual is not to deny that it is advantageous. For despite silly exceptions many habits are simple repetitions of behavior that was originally chosen because it was sensible. In any case, sociologists emphasize the frequency of role conflict —any such conflict being the occasion for a decision. Furthermore, if I perceive that a glass is filled with varnish instead of Scotch and soda I do not avoid drinking it out of habit. For how can I have a habitual response to a choice I never made before? Nor do I avoid it because my culture frowns on drinking varnish, though I suppose it does, but because I expect an unpleasant result. When I see tempting vistas across field and stream, it is not only habit or rules that keep my car on the road, but also a rational awareness of how easy it is to get stuck.

The meaning of "decision"

There is no easy way of knowing what fraction of people's actions are open to meaningful choice, and we will simply analyze the process of choice when it is available and used. We are not interested in responses that are casual or automatic, such as stopping for a red light or dressing in the morning, but in the more complicated and difficult choices that we call problems. In this vein we will define a *decision* as the process of making a choice when we face a problem, a *problem* being a situation in which there is significant uncertainty about the opportunity function, the preference function, or both. Perhaps the occasion for a decision is a condition the psychologist calls "dissonance"—and the sociologist "conflict"—though we will not argue the point. Furthermore, we will focus on *decision theory,* which deals with the decision process in humans when opportunity and preference functions are both explicit and conscious.

We do not mean that decision makers are in fact consciously aware of all their opportunities and preferences, but merely that in decision theory we focus on those components of decisions that *are* conscious. We might also say that decision theory deals with choices made in those problem situations in which the decision maker has in mind an explicit model of the situation he is dealing with.

THE DECISION MODEL

We have said that any controlled system must have detector, selector, and effector (see Figure 4–1), and that we can understand and diagnose its behavior only (if at all) when we know all three. A decision involves the same three steps. But when a decision is carried out it usually has consequences. Often the decision maker becomes aware of such consequences and modifies his subsequent behavior accordingly. The modified behavior is then carried out, *its* consequences are observed, and so on through potentially endless cycles. Each successive cycle nevertheless utilizes the same three steps. To illustrate this we will show only a single pair of cycles. Since the stages are the same for unconscious behavior as for conscious decisions, we will refer to these as the stages of adaptive behavior rather than merely of decisions.

The stages of adaptive behavior

A. Performance Stage.
1. Detector: Identifying the stimulus situation, or formulating the opportunity function.
2. Selector: Selecting the response—choosing the preferred alternative on the basis of the preference function. In complex decisions the preference function may need to be formulated as explicitly as the opportunity function.
3. Effector: Performing the response.
B. Learning Stage.
4. Detector: Identifying the feedback stimulus—discerning the new state of affairs following the behavior effectuated at step 4.
5. Selector: Evaluating the feedback.
6. Effector: Reinforcing, extinguishing, or modifying appropriate aspects of any of the preceding five steps, and executing appropriate new behavior.

Let us clarify a learning stage as contrasted to a performance stage. The household thermostat turns a furnace on or off, using the three steps of the performance stage. In due time it detects the resulting change in temperature. Detection of that change constitutes feedback. To compare the new temperature with the temperature setting of the thermostat is an evaluation of the feedback, and to reverse the prior instruction to the furnace is an execution of appropriate new behavior.

The system, however, does not learn. No matter how often the furnace repeats the cycle, it performs no differently the thousandth time than it did the first—if we ignore wear and tear.

But with the human each cycle may change the system. In the course of the initial or the feedback detection (steps 1 or 4) the individual may modify his concepts. As to the sub-DSEs of his detector, (D) he may discern that he possesses or needs new information, (S) he may alter his desires for information, and (E) he may improve his information-gathering or information processing techniques. In layman's language, he may now know more or think more clearly.

At the selector one may learn from feedback that his goals are easier or harder to achieve than he had thought, and expand or contract his aspirations accordingly. At the effector he may improve his skills, or recognize that he needs to improve them to accomplish his goals.

The important difference between you and the thermostat is that you may never again perform the cycle as you did before. Although you *may* recycle routine activities with little or no learning, in many activities one or more of your DSE states may be altered so that thereafter the same stimulus elicits a different response, a different stimulus elicits the same response, or both. Such learning is one base for developmental change (detailed in Chapter 27).

Courtesy of King Features Syndicate, Inc., by Bud Blake, January 29, 1973.

Costs and benefits

A *good* is any wanted thing. It can be material, like a nail or a battleship. Or it can be nonmaterial, like the scratching of an itch, the repairing of a roof, a lovely sunset, someone's love, or the services of a government. A good can be called a goal, a goal object, or a desired thing. It can also be thought of as an external thing or situation that is positively reinforcing, or toward which one gives an approach response. Although "good" is borrowed from economics (referring mainly to material things exchangeable for money), its meaning is much broader here.

Utility is the ability of something to satisfy a want—the quality or property that makes it a good. The utility of a nail is its ability to hold things together, and the utility of a battleship is its ability to blow things apart. The utility of scratching is that the itch feels better, and the utility of being loved is that it provides a wonderful sense of well-being. Utility may also be thought of as the satisfaction flowing from the use of a good.

Disutility (negative utility) is the quality of something which one wants to avoid. By extension, a *bad (negative good)* is anything that has negative utility, and generates an avoidance response. Utility is not a trait of the thing or of the person but a relation between the two. The battleship has utility to the navy, disutility to those receiving its salvos, and neither to an Eskimo not affected by it.

To simplify, we will focus only on the eventual subjective satisfaction one can get from a good, not on the good itself. One rarely wants a nail for itself, but only for its instrumental use of fastening things. We will disregard the intermediate instrumental value of something and go directly to the *subjective* utility it provides.

As noted, in making a decision we rely on our images of the situation, not on the whole reality, which is never totally knowable. We similarly cannot know when we decide in favor of something whether it will, in fact, provide the satisfaction we expect. Hence we focus on the decision maker's image of the utility he will receive, or his *subjective expected utility*—which is what "utility" means hereinafter when used in connection with a decision.

Any alternative in any opportunity function has some degree of utility: positive, negative, or zero. We do not mean that its utility can necessarily be accurately measured, like dozens of dollars or millions of melons, but merely that the decision maker values some things more highly than others.[2] The positive utility received from any one alternative will be called the *benefit* of that alternative. But to choose any one alternative means to deny or do without some other. The utility denied by selecting a given alternative is the *cost* of that alternative. Defined internally and more broadly, *cost* is the satisfaction or utility denied in the course of receiving other satisfaction or utility. Defined externally, *cost* is the goods that must be sacrificed in the course of acquiring other goods. Satisfaction may arise from a positive utility received or a negative one avoided. The decision process formulates the opportunity function and then assesses the benefits and costs of each alternative in one's preference function. It is also a sort of one-person exchange of a cost for a benefit.

Costs and the necessity of choice

It is difficult to imagine anything that has no cost. Even to lie face down on the beach has the cost that you cannot simultaneously lie face up, and to be lying on the beach has the cost of not being in the water or playing tennis. If you have a low desire for other alternatives, that is another way of saying that the cost is low for the one you have chosen— which is fine. In that case the selection of alternatives is probably so simple as not to qualify as a "problem" or a decision. To say that everything has a cost is nevertheless valid for the vast majority of situations.

Costs arise from many sources, which we will group under two main headings. *Opportunity costs* are those that require us to forfeit what we would like to have—to avoid what we want to approach. *Disutility* costs require us to accept what we do not want—to approach or accept what we want to avoid. Opportunity costs can arise in turn from either *incompatibility* or *scarcity.*

Incompatibility reflects the fact that in some cases two things are not both possible, because of the nature of the things. You cannot have your house painted white with green trim and also blue with pink trim. If you are afraid of flying you cannot get from New York to San Francisco in one day without leaving the ground. You cannot tell lies regularly and maintain a reputation for scrupulous honesty. Idleness is incompatible with accomplishing very much in most pursuits. Strict incompatibility reflects a relation of things to things, without regard to the wants of the decision maker.

Scarcity costs, by contrast, reflect a relation between the wants of the decision maker and the external availability of the things he wants. Here both of two things are possible, but the decision maker lacks sufficient resources to acquire both. There is nothing incompatible about having both a new car and a trip to Europe. But if you do not have enough money for both you must forfeit one to have the other. Time is often a severe

---

[2] We accept here a proposition widely found in welfare economics, decision theory, and philosophy, that except under very narrowly defined conditions utility cannot be measured cardinally, only ordinally. It resides ultimately in a state of the nervous system, and is "private." See, for example, Rothenberg (1961), Boulding (1952), Little (1949), Arrow (1951), and others.

constraint, and you cannot do all the things you would like, simply because there is not enough time. Intangibles can also be scarce, as with beautiful sunsets, affection, or friendship.

Scarcity is not a condition of the things themselves nor of human wants, but a relation between the two. There might be only one ounce of some chemical on earth. But if no one wants it, it is not scarce. By contrast, four billion gallons of water may be available to a city daily. But if the city wants five billion, the water is scarce. For this chapter we will attend only to those things that are scarce for the decision maker himself. Scarcity for a whole people is a different problem.

Whereas opportunity costs (both incompatibility and scarcity) require us to do without what we want, disutility costs require us to accept what we do not want. You cannot lie in the sun the whole of your first day on the beach without the disutility of sunburn, do outdoor work in hot weather without the disutility of sweating, ski at certain times without the disutility of biting winds, or have the earnings of the typical job without the disutilities of getting out of bed and taking orders. Disutility costs can also be viewed as negative ways of stating incompatibility costs—lying in the sun is incompatible with *not* sunburning, skiing at certain times is incompatible with *not* being cold, and so on.

In all cases we are speaking of what the economist calls *real* costs, not *money* costs. The money cost of buying a car is, of course, the money spent. The real cost is that of doing without all the other things that could have been bought with the same money—the sacrifice of alternatives.

Costs of particular things may rise or fall over time. As oil and coal are used up, their scarcity costs rise. Air conditioning reduces the incompatibility between being in the South and being cool, and if one learns to enjoy cold wind the disutility cost of skiing goes down.

Free goods are those that have no cost. Nothing else has to be sacrificed to have them, and there is no disutility in using them. Free goods are easier to define than to find, and the air we breathe is perhaps the only clear example. Breathing is normally not incompatible with anything else we do, it is not scarce, and it has no disutility. In the age of smog *clean* air is nevertheless becoming more costly, and breathing may have some disutility if one has a broken rib.

Some other terms about decisions

Several additional terms are useful in speaking about decisions.

A *preference ordering* is a listing of alternative goods or lines of action in the order of their desiredness—for either an individual or a group.

Value is the position of an item in a preference ordering. The higher its position the greater is its value.

Cooperation (or a cooperative relation) is a situation in which two or more wants can be satisfied by the same good or action. In this volume we never use "cooperate" as a verb. It is not something people do, but a relationship among their wants. Two wants can stand in a cooperative relation within a person (bathing both cleanses and cools) or between persons (cutting your grass pleases both you and your neighbor, or the new highway raises the value of your property and provides others with faster transportation). A cooperative relation is the kind of thing economists call "external economies."

Conflict is a situation in which one satisfaction can be achieved only by denying some other satisfaction—the same as costs, but with a different emphasis. "Conflict" is predecisional, and "costs" are postdecisional. For example, before the fact we would say that going to a party Sunday night conflicts with your studying for a Monday exam. But once you make the choice, missing the party is the cost of studying, and vice versa.

Like cooperation, conflict can occur between or within parties. Your desire to play your hi-fi at 3:00 A.M. conflicts with your roommate's desire for quiet, and one city's desire to dump its sewage in a river conflicts with a downstream city's desire for clean water. Again, conflict is a relation between system states, not persons: the *desires* of your roommate and you conflict, not the persons. A conflict relation between parties is essentially the same as an "external diseconomy."

SOME GENERALIZATIONS ABOUT DECISIONS

If benefit is the satisfaction received from choosing an alternative and cost is the satisfaction sacrificed or denied by it, it follows that satisfaction will be increased if, starting from some point, an alternative is selected whose benefit exceeds its cost.[3] The "point" is the moment at which the decision becomes effective. If in April you try to decide whether to take a job starting July 1, the costs and benefits of that job are assessed as you expect them to be on and after July 1, not as they are meanwhile. For simplicity we will focus on decisions that are effective immediately after they are made.

Some details of costs and benefits are as follows. If one set of tableware is made of silver and another of stainless steel, the material can be a basis for a choice between them. But if both are of identical stainless steel, then some other trait (such as price or shape) must be used as a basis for choice. More broadly, any trait or aspect that is identical for two alternatives cannot be the basis for a choice between them. This conclusion is self-evident, but its repercussions may be overlooked.

If you are making a decision *now* between alternatives X and Y, then anything that has happened before this moment will be the same regardless of which you choose, and hence cannot be a basis for the choice. It is a past that is identical for both. Now this is a tricky point, so we will say it carefully.

Obviously the present *you* is a product of your whole past. And what constitutes a sensible course of action from here on depends on the present you. But it is your *present* condition, not the process of reaching it, that counts.

For example, with $300 in your pocket you have decided to drive for

---

[3] This principle of decisions can be viewed in the stock-flow model. If total satisfaction is viewed as a stock, benefits as inflow, and costs as outflow, the stock will increase when the inflow exceeds the outflow.

a ten-day vacation from New York City to Denver. Two days and $50 later you run into an old friend in Chicago. He is hitchhiking for a vacation in the mountains, and urges you to join him (via your car) in the Catskills. "But," you respond, "I've just driven 800 miles *from* the Catskills." He replies, "So what?"

So what? We will jump to a conclusion, then return to details. The time and money you spent getting from New York to Chicago are sunk costs, a sunk cost being any cost already incurred that cannot be recovered. According to a basic principle of decision making, the magnitude of sunk costs incurred up to a given point cannot be the basis for a decision effective after that point. (As with the two sets of stainless tableware, the size of the sunk costs is the same regardless of which alternative you choose, and hence cannot be a basis for preferring one to the other.)

You are now in Chicago. And you have eight days and $250 left. These facts *are* important to your decision. But it makes no difference to your choice *why* you are in Chicago, or *why* you have eight days and $250. You might have started from New York with $250 and picked up a hitchhiker who paid all your expenses. Or you might have started with $400, paid $50 in expenses, and dropped $100 on a horse at Saratoga. You might also have left New York with 9 days available and driven to Chicago in one, or had 15 to begin with and taken 7 getting to Chicago.

Your present opportunity function is the outcome of all your past—which includes the first leg of this trip. But it is the *present content* of that opportunity function on which the decision is based, not the antecedents that made it what it is.

The logic is the same for your preference function. Your whole past life may be involved in forming your present preference for Denver or the Catskills. Part of that past life is the just-completed trek from New York, and some of your attitudes toward either Denver or the Catskills may have changed during that jaunt. But the only thing to consider is that you *have* those preferences *now,* without regard to when, why, or how you got them.

To return to your opportunity function, you are still free to decide how you will use the eight days and $250 still remaining, but you have no discretion at all about the time and money already gone. The way we will say it henceforth is that you have a choice with respect to those things still in the future; these can rationally enter your calculation. But since you have no choice regarding things already past, these cannot rationally enter your calculation. We can now join this with our previous conclusion for the following generalization.

General Rule of rational decisions

A statement we will call the General Rule is that *a rational decision selects that alternative whose future benefit exceeds its future cost.* As noted, "future" is measured from the time the decision is effective, which may or may not be later than when it is made. The "time the decision is effective" is that at which behavior starts to be different because of it. If on April 1 you decide to take a job starting July 1, and on May 1 you must start moves that are different from what they would be if you had not accepted the job, your decision is "effective" as of May 1.

But you are still sitting in Chicago wondering what to do. We will not tell you, but merely indicate the rationale. The General Rule tells you to disregard the time and money spent getting to Chicago, and to decide solely on the basis of the best use of what you have left—by going on to Denver or backtracking to the Catskills.

"Well," you say, "I would really prefer to go back. But if I do I will throw away the two days and $50 I spent getting here, whereas if I go on to Denver I will be using them." To which the General Rule replies, "The two days and $50 are already thrown away ('sunk'). You have already made a mistake by coming to Chicago, albeit one you could not have known about in advance. But having made that much of a mistake, do not compound it by piling another on top of it." In short, having arrived in Chicago, you must decide how to get maximum satisfaction from the time and money still remaining. If you will really get more satisfaction by going back to the Catskills with your friend, then you would be accepting a lesser satisfaction, not achieving a greater one, if you refused to "throw away" the first leg of the trip.

This, however, is not necessarily the end. Suppose your parents have been belaboring you lately for vacillation—for never making up your mind and carrying out your decision. You have been tending to agree, and to wonder whether you really *can* carry through a planned course of action. In fact, you started this trip partly in the hope of demonstrating your firmness of purpose, your resolute steadfastness, to your parents and yourself. The conflict then starts inside you.

"I must go on to Denver, because I said I would."

"But no. The sacred General Rule says I must go back East with my friend."

"I won't be able to face myself or my parents if I go wishy-washy again."

"I must be rational. There is nothing more rational than being rational, so I must turn back. Surely I cannot be condemned for being rational."

"There is no way. There is no choice but suicide. Or maybe a beer. Yes, that's it."

Despite everything, you are still in Chicago, albeit more relaxed. Will the General Rule relax too, and let you go on developing your character and reputation? Yes, if you consult it in private session. All the General Rule says is that only those costs and benefits still in the future should be included in the calculation. Your character and reputation are still in the future. If putting on blinders and heading straight west will give more satisfaction in the form of improved self-image than would the extra satisfactions from going to the Catskills, it is wholly rational to hit the westward trail. As noted, *all costs and all benefits are in the final analysis subjective.* Only you can decide whether the value of an improved image is worth more than the other satisfactions sacrificed by continuing to Denver.

"Don't cry over spilt milk," "Let bygones be bygones," and "Don't throw good money after bad" are layman's language for not counting sunk costs. Unless something can be learned from it of use to future behavior, delving into a bad situation to find out "whose fault" it was is a fruitless preoccupation with sunk costs. So is the pursuit of revenge —unless this will make something in the future more advantageous to the person seeking it. We might suggest that it is always irrational to count sunk costs, but would then face the question of the person who increases his satisfaction (a rational move) by deliberately being irrational! (Some further complications about sunk costs are discussed in Chapter 28 in connection with personality.)

It is often useful, particularly in considering goals reached by successive steps, to think of a decision ladder or pyramid with the goal at the top. Each step climbed constitutes a cost already expended and sunk. Unless there is some change in costs or in the value of the goal, each step completed raises the relative desirability of completing the remaining steps—not because of the costs already spent but because of the smaller costs still remaining.

The ingredients of a decision

The terms *costs* and *benefits* can be made more explicit, in terms of a possible choice between the mutually exclusive alternatives X and Y. The *gross benefit of X* means the amount of satisfaction to be derived from having X, but without subtracting any of its costs. It is the satisfaction from the thing acquired, but without counting the time, effort, or money spent in getting it—like the benefit from a pure gift. For something you do or make for yourself, it is the satisfaction received from the waxed floor, but without subtracting the dissatisfactions in effort or frustration or the costs of materials.

But X normally has costs. One cost is that we must do without Y. This we call the Y *cost of X*. For example, if we must choose between the mountains (X) and the beach (Y), to go to the mountains involves the cost of not going to the beach, which is the Y cost of X. But the mountains involve their own special costs of tent, sleeping bag, and climbing effort. These are non-Y costs of X. The beach might similarly involve costs of its own (as for surfboard or blowing sand). These are non-X costs of Y.

Since there is no problem (and no need for a decision) unless there are costs, no decision can be made on the basis of gross benefits alone. We therefore add two terms to help keep costs and benefits straight. The *net benefit of Y* is the gross benefit of Y minus the non-X costs of Y. Similarly the net benefit of X is the gross benefit of X minus the non-Y costs of X. Satisfaction will be greater from the alternative with the larger net benefit. This means that the overall satisfaction from the mountain will be greater than that from the beach if the satisfaction from the mountain minus the cost of the tent, etc. is greater than the satisfaction from the beach minus the cost of surfboard, etc.

As between two things, it is sufficient to say that satisfaction will be greater if we select the alternative with the higher net benefit. But for choices among three or more alternatives, we introduce the *final net benefit.* This is the net benefit of one alternative minus the net benefit of the alternative to which it is being compared.

Before going to three alternatives, let us see how final net benefit behaves with two. If X has a higher net benefit than Y, and we subtract the net benefit of Y from that of X, X will have a positive final net benefit. The final net benefit of Y is the net benefit of Y minus the net benefit of X—in this case a negative sum. Thus the final net benefit of one, but only one, alternative can be positive. Since the final net benefit is the only type of benefit that has been charged with all its costs, unless otherwise indicated "benefit" hereinafter means "final net benefit."

We now move to three mutually exclusive alternatives, X, Y, and Z, and start by comparing Y and Z in the manner described above. If Y turns out to have a positive final net benefit (and Z a negative) we can next compare X and Y. Now, to select either X or Y means to do without Z. But if we were to charge the net benefit of Z against both X and Y in computing *their* final net benefits, we would not affect the relative desirability of X and Y, since the charge would be equal against both. The comparison between X and Y can therefore ignore Z. In this comparison, if X shows a positive final net benefit it will provide more satisfaction than Y, which has already been seen to have more than Z—and the search is ended. However, if Y shows the positive final net benefit, then *it* is the best alternative.

By extension, among any number of alternatives one, and only one— the one that will provide the most satisfaction, or utility—can have a positive final net benefit.

Note that in this discussion we have not indicated what people *do* —only the alternative that would give them the most satisfaction *if they choose it.* Decision theory is a theory for maximizing utility, or satisfaction, not a theory of behavior. To make it a theory of behavior we need the additional assumption that people actually do what the theory says. But that is a matter for later, and we will tie various aspects of decision making together at the end of the next chapter.

8

MORE ON DECISIONS

THE TIME RANGE OF DECISIONS

Assuming no complications, your decision whether to drink white or chocolate milk has little or no consequences beyond the emptying of your glass. A decision to go to college has direct effects for four years and indirect effects for the rest of your life. Other decisions have intermediate time ranges. Decisions of large organizations, particularly governments, might alter events for centuries.

In the preceding chapter we discussed your Crisis in Chicago as if the direct costs and benefits lasted only for the duration of the vacation. We did nevertheless introduce possible effects of the decision on your self-image, which effects would presumably outlast the vacation, and the decision could also have longer-run effects on your friendship. Since a decision may be quite different if you consider long-term consequences as well as immediate ones, an important aspect of any decision is the expected time range of its costs, its benefits, or both.

Satisfactions in the present and the near future are generally more strongly motivating than those more distant. This fact may partly reflect the principles of *recency* in conditioning: things closely connected in time become more strongly and more promptly conditioned than things more widely separated. It may also reflect the fact that our images of the present and immediate future are clearer than those of the more distant future, if only because we have more information about them. These explanations are speculative only. But the fact seems clear—people generally do give more weight to satisfactions fairly close at hand than to those long delayed.

Time preference is the name given to this difference. It is called *positive time preference* when it appears in the form just stated, which seems to occur most frequently. Its opposite, negative time preference, is perhaps easiest to understand (and perhaps most likely to occur) for a recycled desire subject to satiation. When you have just completed a large meal, your desire for food in the future may be greater than your desire for it now. "Time preference" is a term borrowed from economics, and deals with the same kind of thing the psychologist calls "delayed gratification." A high positive time preference is sometimes about the same thing as weak willpower, seeking present satisfaction even at disproportionately high future costs.

One of the first things to do in making a decision is to set our time range, even if unconsciously. Are we concerned with the next five minutes, years, or decades?

Whenever we make a decision with any significant time dimension, we are allocating costs and benefits as between present and future. If I take some peppermint creams with me onto the plane and eat them immediately I am receiving the benefit of an immediate satisfaction at the cost of having to do without them later. If I save them I receive a satisfaction later at the cost of denying one now.

Things do not always work out as expected, and I may not actually get the later satisfaction if I inadvertently leave the peppermints in my hip pocket for two hours. As before, because we cannot know how things will actually turn out, we deal only with the decision maker's expectations, or images. For our analysis of decisions we are also interested solely in deliberate actions, not accidental or casual ones—as noted.

Sometimes costs and benefits occur concurrently, or nearly so. At the cost now of using time, lemon, and sugar I can make some lemonade to satisfy my thirst now. A present cost incurred to achieve present satisfaction is a *variable cost*.

A lag between costs and benefits can occur in either direction: costs first and benefits later, or the reverse, subject to some reservations that will be made below. Simple waiting involves only straight-time preference. But if I plant tomatoes in May I expect my satisfactions in August to be larger than the present cost. The same is true if I invest money in securities (at the present cost of not spending it and of risking its loss) in the hope that I will later get back more than I put in now.

In these cases my present ratio of benefits to costs is low, possibly zero, since I incur the costs now but the benefits do not come till later. At the later point the ratio is much higher, since then the benefits are accruing but the costs are not being incurred. For convenience we refer to this ratio of benefits to costs as the *B/C ratio,* and define *investment* as any current costs, over and above those incurred to provide current benefits, which are designed to improve the future *B/C* ratio.

Although "investment" is borrowed from economics, its essential meaning is the same in many areas. If I incur the present cost of telling the truth when it hurts so that I will later achieve that valued thing called integrity and credibility, the truthtelling is an investment. It is also investment if I now renounce worldly goods to assure myself a better seat in heaven. If I go out of my way to be friendly in the hope of building a rewarding friendship, that too is investment. (If I get present satisfaction from being helpful, the costs are variable, not investment.)

When things deteriorate, their B/C ratios typically decline. To deal first with exceptions. With the help of time and friendly neighborhood microbes, a pile of grass clippings will deteriorate into compost, which is much more valued. With increasing age antiques often gain more in value than they lose from physical deterioration.

But now to the cases that are not exceptions. If your body is not to deteriorate, you must stoke it regularly with food and drink. If your skill at algebra, crossword puzzles, or guitar playing is not to deteriorate, you must continue to practice. A house needs occasional paint and repair, a continuing reputation as an actor may require new performances, and a friendship may deteriorate without contacts. Such deterioration can be described as a drop in the B/C ratio and we will define *fixed costs* as current costs over and above those required for current satisfactions which are incurred to prevent a drop in the B/C ratio. If you do any of these things because you like to, they are, of course, not costs, fixed or otherwise.

The general logic is the same for both investment and fixed costs. The difference is that investment is intended to raise the B/C ratio, and fixed costs are intended to keep it from going down. To join the two, you pay the investment costs of arduous practice to develop skill at the guitar and then must incur the fixed costs of continued practice to keep it from slipping. The movie hopeful invests a brawl and two divorces to draw public attention, and then is faced with the fixed costs of additional divorces to maintain it. Fixed costs, incidentally, need not be paid if one is willing to accept the loss of B/C ratio that results. In business affairs it is sometimes carelessly thought that fixed costs are unavoidable. But "unavoidable" merely means that the B/C loss would be so large relative to the fixed costs of avoiding it that one would not ordinarily contemplate omitting them—as by failure to pay taxes, rent, or fire insurance.

Disinvestment, the opposite of investment, is the receipt of current benefit at the cost of a deterioration of the B/C ratio. Simple cases are withdrawing invested money to make current purchases, or chopping good furniture for firewood. Telling a lie or smearing a friend's reputation for immediate advantage may also be disinvestment. Just as investment is "something like" paying fixed costs, disinvestment is "something like" not paying fixed costs. On the negative side it does not seem worthwhile to distinguish the two. Hence we will use "disinvestment" to mean either an active drain upon a given B/C ratio or a simple passive failure to pay fixed costs, or both.

We suggested earlier that benefits may sometimes be taken in the present and costs paid later—subject to qualification. The qualification is that in an overall sense benefits cannot be achieved without first paying their costs—I cannot have the tomatoes unless I first plant and cultivate. For any particular, limited decision, however, one can have benefits before costs if he can draw on an accumulated pool and pay the costs later by replacing the withdrawals. He can also borrow from others and repay later.[1]

The principles about time range are simple. One decides in favor of an investment if the amount of increase in net benefit produced by the investment is greater than the dissatisfaction of having to delay the receipt of satisfaction—that is, if the increase in B/C ratio is greater than the time preference during the intervening period. Otherwise he decides against it. One similarly decides in favor of incurring a fixed cost if the loss avoided by it is greater than the time preference for the relevant period. The practical difficulties lie in estimating consequences and knowing one's time preferences. In decisions involving money alone it is at least theoretically possible to make an exact count of benefits and costs. But since part of the information needed for the time-range decision is always about a future event, it is subject to possible error. The difficulties are even greater with subjective and complex items. What are the chances that a lie will be discovered, and how much will one's reputation suffer if it is? When outcomes depend on so many imponderables, the simplest approach may be some simple rule: "Honesty is the best policy."

THE COST OF MAKING DECISIONS

We have discussed decisions thus far as if the decision process itself had no costs or benefits—though we did allow you to agonize a while in Chicago. We now take decision costs into account.

Some costs of making a decision are explicit and objective, as when a corporation pays a consultant for information or advice. Others may be largely subjective, such as the anguish of uncertainty. Objective costs are typically involved in learning the opportunity function, while subjective costs more often involve uncertainty about preference function. A mixed case would be frustration over contradictory information, such as conflicting predictions about another person's response to an action.

When decision costs are large they may be treated as components of the decision itself. There is no point spending 15 minutes to learn the correct turn at an intersection if the wrong one means only a five-minute delay. There is no point in paying a consultant $50,000 to tell you whether A or B is the better choice if you would lose only $5,000 by a wrong decision. Let us look at three situations.

---

[1] A distinction is widely recognized between economic costs and accounting costs, and the same could be said for revenues. Economic costs are further subdivided into real and money costs. For example, actual wear and tear on a building is a real cost, whereas expenditures for repairing or replacing deterioration are money costs. The concept of costs used here resembles the economist's real costs, but extended to include social and psychological items the economist normally does not deal with. The central themes of other related concepts—such as fixed and variable costs, and investment and disinvestment—are similarly taken from economics. Although their definitions look somewhat different from the customary ones in economics, I do not think they would cause significant difficulty if applied to economic phenomena.

First, if you are reasonably sure in advance that the difference in net benefit between two alternatives will be greater than the cost of assuring the correct decision, you will get maximum satisfaction if you incur the decision costs. Second, if you are reasonably sure in advance that the difference in net benefit will be smaller than the cost of assuring the correct decision, you are better off to make the choice on some random, intuitive, or arbitrary basis—like coin tossing, hunch, or alphabetic order. Third, if you cannot be reasonably sure in advance whether the difference between the alternatives will be greater or less than the cost of making the correct decision, you cannot know whether to study the problem thoroughly or to toss a coin at the outset. Here, too, you may as well toss a coin or follow your impulse.

You could, of course, go about the task in steps. You could first expend a small cost for a preliminary decision as to whether the decision is worth incurring a larger decision cost. On that basis you could decide whether to study the problem further or toss a coin. Or you could make a pre-preliminary survey to find out whether the preliminary survey is worth *its* cost. In fact you could spend ten years deciding whether to make a decision!

The point is simple, yet often not recognized. Certain problems are worth high decision costs to help assure the best decision. In other cases it is utterly rational to decide arbitrarily or impulsively. These latter decisions, incidentally, are not necessarily unimportant. They could occur either when decision costs are very high or when the difference in net benefit between alternatives is small. Sometimes the necessary information is simply not available at any cost, and again there may be no choice but to decide by impulse or intuition. March and Simon (1958: Chap. 7) emphasize the limit on man's ability to know, calling it "bounded rationality," which leads to the suggestion that "the beginning of wisdom for decision makers is to recognize that they can deal with only a tiny fraction of what is possibly relevant—even with electronic computers" (Kuhn 1963: 272). Sometimes the most difficult and important part of a decision is deciding whether or not a decision is needed.

The decision process sometimes provides benefits, as when decision making is a game or puzzle enjoyed in its own right. Some persons enjoy making shopping decisions or deciding how to remodel the house, and choosing a vacation can be half the fun. If the decision process provides benefits, the logical effect is the same as a reduction in decision costs. If the benefits are great enough, it could even be rational to spend great effort choosing between equally satisfactory alternatives.

Formulating the opportunity function

We have talked thus far as if the decision maker knew the basic alternatives but needed more information about them. In addition, however, one often has a gnawing fear that he has completely overlooked the obviously best alternative. Unfortunately, decision theory provides no very useful advice on this score except "search." That is, the general process of knowing the available alternatives to some decisional problem is no different from the process of knowing anything else—and includes experience, intelligence, imagination, intuition, and good search techniques.

A particularly thorny question is the preliminary decision about how far to open a decision. For example, suppose you are not doing well in a course in your major field. A relatively narrow opening of the decision would be whether to buy a study guide. A slightly wider opening would be whether you should drop dramatics and study harder. Successively wider questions would be whether you should drop the course, drop the major, or drop out of college. People must sometimes decide whether to drop out of life, and psychiatrists suggest that misuse of drugs and alcohol often represents partial or symbolic suicide. Circumstances (such as probation) may, of course, force you to open the question wider than you would like. But to the extent that you have discretion, there are no very useful rules about how wide you should open the decision.

The scope of a decision is one aspect of formulating the opportunity function, sometimes also called the decision set. You could say, for example, "My alternatives are to study harder, to drop dramatics, to drop the course, etc." In setting up that kind of set of alternatives, there are, in a sense, no holds barred in advance. The opportunity function can be drawn up, however, with certain constraints. For example, "Assuming that I want to stay in this course and finish it, what are the possible ways of doing it?" Slightly more broadly, "Assuming that I want to continue majoring in Psychedelics, what can I do about this course?"

Often the question of scope involves time range, in that the wider the question is opened the longer is the relevant time span: the wider question of whether to drop out of college normally has longer-run repercussions than the question of whether to drop dramatics and study harder.

Formulating the preference function—and deciding

At some point before a decision is made, the preference function must be brought to bear on the perceived opportunities. How or when this will be done may vary greatly with the circumstances, the person, and the complexity of the problem.

Although the selector function is listed as the second item of the DSE trio, you may approach a problem by first formulating your goals. Without having studied the problem at all, you might be able to say, "I hope that I can achieve goals B, C, and A, in that order of preference." You might then study the problem to discover what lines of action are, in fact, possible—the opportunity function. These could then be compared with your preferences. You might find that C is impossible, in which case you restate your preferences as B and A, in that order. Or, if A was assigned a low initial priority on the assumption that C would be accomplished, A might seem more important after C is ruled out, and now take precedence over B. In short, although we have talked as if opportunity and preference functions were independent, they sometimes affect one another.

Under other circumstances you may know nothing at the outset except that things are unsatisfactory. You can then survey all possible avenues of change without yet thinking about which you prefer. You might next list the benefits and costs (often called advantages and disadvantages) of each, and then select the preferred one. Without listing the benefits and costs of each explicitly, you might simply say, "Among these three, I like *B* best, *C* next, and *A* least."

Concepts and motives are often arranged hierarchically. Hence a goal may be broken into subgoals, each with sub-subgoals of its own. This hierarchy is a more complex kind of preference function, and would presumably have to be accompanied by an opportunity function arranged according to the same hierarchical structure. A decision about going on a vacation, for example, must be broken into such subdecisions as how to finance it, what kind of transportation to use, where to stay, what to wear, and what equipment to take. These hierarchies appear very clearly in organizations, because the functions are divided among departments, each of which has its departmental goals. Even a family may divide duties and decisions among its members. Any such arrangement, of course, requires coordinating the various subdecisions toward the overall objective.

"MORE OR LESS" DECISIONS: MARGINAL ANALYSIS

The discussion thus far has dealt with decisions among mutually exclusive alternatives, in which selecting one alternative means denying another. Multiple attacks are also possible, as in buying a study guide *and* dropping dramatics. These things must be mentioned, but there is little else we can say without going into great detail.

By contrast, in many decisions we do not choose between all *A* and no *B,* but between more *A* and less *B.* Such decisions take their clearest form when the units of cost and benefit do not come in chunks, like automobiles or marriages, but in divisible quantities, like time, money, or granulated sugar. More time for dramatics means less for study; more money for books leaves less for baubles.

As with some other aspects of decisions, the underlying logic is simple, though the details of application may be very complex. Two principles are involved, both derived from economics but apparently universal.

The first is the law of diminishing utility, considered universal because no one, apparently, can think of an exception. The law states that as any party acquires more and more units of the same thing, after some point additional units will provide less additional benefit. This approach focuses mainly on the additional benefit provided by one additional unit, as more and more units are received.

The second principle is increasing cost. This states that as more and more units of any given thing are acquired, after some point the cost of additional units will rise. Here, too, we focus on one additional unit as more and more units are acquired.

The law of increasing cost is based partly on the law of diminishing productivity and partly on a broader principle. The law of diminishing productivity, like that of diminishing utility, is also accepted as universal because no one can think of an exception. To illustrate the law before stating it, if you keep putting more and more bags of fertilizer on a given field, the output of crops will rise for a time. But as still more fertilizer is added, the amount of *additional* output of crops brought by an *additional* bag of fertilizer will decline. As more and more people are added to the work force of any office, field, or factory, beyond a certain point the additional contribution of an additional worker will decline. Sometimes productivity drops dramatically after just one unit: the second driver of a bus, for example, would add little or nothing to the effectiveness of driving, and might diminish it if he actually tried to do anything.

Diminishing productivity is an aspect of the opportunity function, dealing with externals and not with human attitudes. The general statement of the law is: in any system of production, if more and more identical units of one kind of input are added (the variable input) while all other inputs remain constant (fixed inputs), and if there is no change in the technique of production, then after some point the amount of additional output per additional unit of input will decline. There may or may not be a period of rising output before that point is reached.[2]

If the output per unit of input goes down, this is another way of saying that the amount of input per unit of output goes up, which is also another way of describing an increase in cost per unit of output. Diminishing productivity is thus an important source of increasing cost of additional units of the same thing. Diminishing returns, however, often set in only "after a point" of increasing returns. Up to that point there will be falling costs, not rising ones.

Whether or not increasing cost is experienced because of diminishing productivity, diminishing utility has broader effects. We stated earlier that in the final analysis all benefits and all costs are subjective. We also said that one cost of anything is the opportunity cost of the alternatives forgone. But the alternatives are also subject to diminishing utility. Now if an additional unit of something *received* provides *less* benefit than the preceding one, then in the reverse direction each successive unit of the thing *forfeited* means giving up a *greater* benefit than has been given up for the previous one forfeited. An illustration and a diagram will help clarify this matter.

You have been hiking through a sparsely inhabited area and are very hungry when you happen upon a small stand that sells only hamburgers and milkshakes. Both cost the same, and you can spare enough money to buy a total of eight items. Should you get eight hamburgers and no milkshakes, eight milkshakes and no hamburgers, or some combination of the two? To sharpen the illustration, let us assume (contrary to fact) that we can count units of satisfaction, often called *utils*. The first hamburger, we will assume, provides you with 100 utils of satisfaction, the second 90 utils, the third 80, the fourth 70, and so on. The milkshakes

---

[2] An economist once suggested that knowledge is the only kind of input not subject to diminishing returns (Clark in Samuelson 1970: 513). The suggestion is not pertinent, however. Since no two units of knowledge are identical, the suggestion violates that requirement of the law.

provide identical amounts of satisfaction, at 100, 90, etc., respectively.

Since we said we would examine such situations one unit at a time, let us assume that you start with one hamburger, which provides you with 100 utils. Should your next item be a second hamburger or a first milkshake? A second hamburger would provide 90 utils, whereas a first milkshake would provide 100. Hence you would receive greater satisfaction from the milkshake. Had you been so unwise as to take a second

Figure 8–1
COSTS AND BENEFITS OF VARIOUS COMBINATIONS OF
HAMBURGERS AND MILKSHAKES

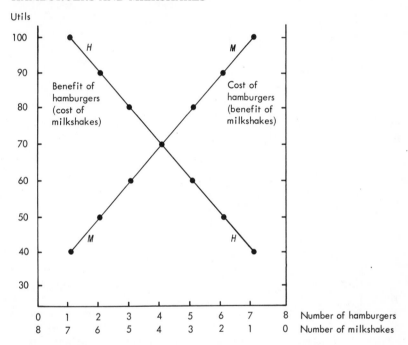

hamburger, your next choice would have been between a third hamburger and a first milkshake. Here the former would have provided you with only 80 utils, while to get it you would be doing without the latter at 100 utils—an abominably stupid decision.

Let us jump to the other end and work back. As a point of reference we will assume an initial choice of four each. In that case the fourth hamburger would provide 70 utils and so would the fourth milkshake. But if you had chosen instead five hamburgers and three milkshakes, how would your total satisfaction compare with four each? By getting the fifth hamburger, you would be receiving 60 utils, but at the cost of going without the fourth milkshake, which would have provided 70. A sixth hamburger would provide 50 utils, but would require sacrificing the third milkshake at 80—and so on. The situation is diagramed in Figure 8–1.

The scale across the bottom shows alternative combinations of hamburgers and milkshakes, with all pairs adding up to eight items. The line HH represents the utility of successive hamburgers, at 100 for the first and 30 for the eighth.

An important point is reflected in the labels. Line HH is labeled both benefit of hamburgers *and* cost of milkshakes. Line MM is both benefit

Figure 8–2
COSTS AND BENEFITS OF VARIOUS COMBINATIONS OF
HAMBURGERS AND MILKSHAKES—STEPWISE DIAGRAM

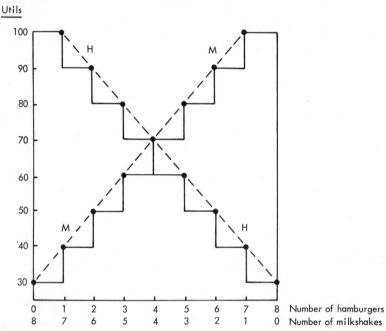

NOTE: For strict accuracy the steps should be centered on the dotted lines, with half of each step above and half below the line. This refinement would complicate the illustration, but not alter its logic.

of milkshakes *and* cost of hamburgers. One can get an additional hamburger, starting from any prior number, only by giving up a milkshake, and vice versa. The 100 utils of the first hamburger is thus both the satisfaction received from that hamburger if purchased *and* the satisfaction denied if a milkshake were taken instead. Thus the curve of diminishing utility for one item is the curve of increasing cost for the other, and illustrates why additional units of one thing can be acquired only at increasing cost.

If hamburgers and milkshakes were perfectly divisible, the two lines of Figure 8–1 would suffice—that is, if you could get half a hamburger, or a tenth, or a hundredth, and the same were true for the milkshakes. To simplify the illustration we spoke only of whole hamburgers and whole milkshakes. These are partially "chunky" rather than "continuous" quantities. If they are to be graphed accurately they must be shown as steps. To enable us to use the numbers already given, rather than fractions, we will rediagram this relation in Figure 8–2 to show the rates of utility received as flat across the whole units already indicated. They will then move stepwise from level to level and remain flat at each level till the next unit is started. We can then read the graph literally in the sense already indicated. That is, where line HH lies between zero and one hamburger it shows a satisfaction of 100 utils. Over the same distance, which is between eight and seven on the milkshake scale, the line MM shows 30 utils. The two together mean either that (1) the 100-util benefit of the first hamburger is achieved at the 30-util cost of denying the eighth milkshake, or that (2) the 30-util benefit of the eighth milkshake is achieved at the 100-util cost of the first hamburger.

Continuous vs. either-or decisions

Let us return for a moment to the original discussion of decisions between mutually exclusive alternatives. There we stated that satisfaction will be increased by any choice whose benefit exceeds its cost. Does our discussion of multiple units agree or disagree? Obviously it agrees. If the benefit of the first hamburger is 100 utils and its cost is the 30 utils of the eighth milkshake denied, then the choice is for the former and against the latter. Proceeding with the same logic, we can see that for each hamburger up to and including the fourth the benefit exceeds the cost. Graphically this is seen in that through all of that distance the benefit line lies above the cost line. But when we move from the fourth to the fifth hamburger, the benefit line falls below the cost line. This means that total utility will be reduced, not increased, if the fifth hamburger is purchased at the sacrifice of the fourth milkshake.

In summary, the largest total satisfaction will be achieved at the point where the cost and benefit lines cross—which is where they are equal.[3] If we move left from that point we forfeit a possible gain. If we move right we take an unnecessary loss.

Decision as equilibrium

Chapter 3 noted two things about equilibrium. First, it is one of the most important characteristics of continuing systems. Man is very much a continuing system. Hence it is important to a systems analysis of man to see whether his actions conform to the equilibrium model. Second, it was seen that the major condition that produces equilibrium is that of oppositely paired variation: if A varies directly with B, then B must vary inversely with A. By extension, we saw that equilibrium is also possible if A and B vary oppositely with some third thing, C. That is the case here, C being the quantity of hamburgers. We see that line HH represents the

---

[3] It does not matter whether we shift focus and consider the milkshake line as the benefits and the hamburger line as the costs, and "ride down" the milkshake line till we meet the hamburgers, so long as we then read from right to left.

benefit from successive units of hamburgers. This line falls from left to right, which means that the benefit from successive hamburgers varies inversely with the quantity. MM (the cost of successive hamburgers) rises, which means that the cost of successive hamburgers varies directly with the quantity. With benefits varying inversely and costs directly with quantity, we thus have the conditions necessary for equilibrium. Thus a central feature of human activity, the selection of behavior, can be couched as equilibrium. In fact, this kind of equilibrium analysis was being used by economists for about a century before system analysis appeared.

The principle of marginality

The thinking described above is *marginal analysis.* "Margin" has the same meaning here as in common usage—the boundary or edge that separates one thing from another. We did not attend above to total utility received, but merely to the additional, or "marginal," unit, and the difference, if any, between its benefits and costs. Whatever the prior total, if benefits from an additional unit exceed its costs, the total utility will rise. If its costs exceed its benefits, the total will fall. Hence without ever measuring the total, we know that it will be largest when marginal benefits and marginal costs are equal.

The principle is the same for three or more alternatives, but we will not pursue it further here.

In Chapter 3, we also spoke of equilibrium as a relationship between stocks and flows. If we are willing to think of total utility as a stock of satisfaction, and of costs and benefits as flows, we can describe the decision process in terms of this "bathtub principle." Benefits are seen as inflows and costs as outflows of satisfactions. Any unit of a good that produces a greater inflow than outflow raises the level of the stock, and any unit that produces a greater outflow than inflow reduces its level.

To detour to the main purpose of this book, it is important to note that decision making among humans can be couched, in sound analytical terms with a long history in economics, in language that can also be applied to biological, mechanical, hydraulic, astronomical, electrical, and a variety of other kinds of systems. True, "satisfaction" is not a "stock" in the literal sense that water or money is. Yet every reader knows what is meant by "more satisfaction" or "less satisfaction," and has a pretty good idea much of the time whether his level of it is rising or falling.

Diagraming decision making in a graph may suggest only cold, calculating decisions. Not so. Even if you are a warm and impulsive individual who never makes a "calculated" decision, you inescapably make marginal decisions day in and day out. You put two teaspoons of sugar in your coffee. Why? "By habit," you answer. But why is your habit not one or six? Because two is the quantity you like best. And how did you find this out? Because sometimes you put in less and found you wanted more, while at other times you put in more and found you wanted less. Let us assume that you did not count the cost of the sugar—you acted as if the cost were zero, graphed as a horizontal cost line. As you added more units of sugar up to two spoonfuls per cup, the benefit exceeded the cost, while beyond two the benefit was less than the cost. Hence your equilibrium occurred at two spoonfuls, which is where you stop thus exemplifying marginal decision making.

You go to the beach. On impulse you later leave when you feel like leaving. What is the impulse? You are tired of the beach and want to do something else. If you have stayed five hours, then up to that point the marginal benefit has exceeded the marginal cost in the form of other activities forgone. To say that you are "tired of the beach" is layman's language for saying that after that point the marginal cost exceeded the marginal benefit. Hence you leave.

When your alarm goes off in the morning, the benefit of a few more minutes in bed is deliciously high and the cost low. As the minutes speed by and you gradually wake, the benefit of additional minutes in bed gradually goes down, while the cost in added rush, tension, bolted break- fast, and risk of being late goes precipitously up. When the cost and benefit curves cross, you get up. If you did not get to bed till four and are headed for a dull class in unified social science, the benefit curve of staying in bed may be so high and the cost curve so low that they will not cross till hours later—unless you have an intolerable instructor who penalizes cuts to keep your cost curve high.

SUMMARY AND CONCLUSION

Why a discussion of decisions in a book on social science? First, be- cause this is unified social science, which includes economics, and deci- sion theory is central to economics. Political scientists are also interested in how decisions are made, albeit more in certain organizational settings than within individuals. But since a group decision in some way reflects the separate decisions of its members, we say something about decisions for the political scientists. Although sociologists pay little attention to decisions as such, they do refer at times to adaptive behavior, and a decision is central to the process of adapting. Decision making is also important to organization theory, which should perhaps be considered a basic social science instead of a subdivision of the business administra- tion curriculum.

Meanwhile we can observe that in every society from the most primi- tive to the most industrialized every individual inescapably allocates his time, effort, attention, affection, hate, strength, thought, money, materi- als, and a thousand other things. At any given moment habit or custom is important. But it is only a stopgap explanation, since it gives no hint as to why the habit or custom was established in the first place, why it continues, or why it shows so many variations. Furthermore, to say that a response is habitual is another way of saying that its decision cost is near zero. It is one form of arbitrary selection, which is thoroughly ra- tional in many common situations.

Although rational and impulsive or intuitive behavior are readily dis- tinguishable at the extremes, in the present model there is no sharp dividing line between them. There are only differing degrees of explicit and conscious formulations of opportunity and preference functions, and the present model explicitly encompasses emotions and "gut reactions." The model does not itself suggest that emotionally based behavior is either rational or irrational, though most observers would conclude that an impulsive dive into a lake fully clothed to save oneself from 500 pursuing hornets is rational but that a dive over Niagara Falls for the same reason is not.

"Careful calculation" is itself frustrating to some, which is another way of saying that to them decision costs are high. Since all costs and benefits are ultimately subjective, it is no less rational for such persons to make a decision on impulse because "cold calculations" are frustrating than for an executive to make decisions by intuition when the cost of information exceeds its benefit. For other persons or under different circumstances it may be eminently worthwhile to incur large decision costs to avoid a mistake.

Even impulsive behavior nevertheless involves detector and selector —opportunity and preference functions. The hornet-ridden chap must perceive the lake and expect that the hornets will not follow him underwater. He may or may not recall that he cannot swim. And without some kind of preference he would stand there and let the hornets sting.

We have nevertheless defined a "decision" as requiring more thought than an impulsive jump in the lake. We then say that one will be best off if he selects the alternative whose final net benefit is positive, when he considers only costs and benefits that are still in the future. We can also add that he will maximize his satisfaction if he manages his fixed costs, variable costs, investments, and disinvestments to reflect his time preferences.

When we shift from either-or to more-or-less we move to marginal decision making, which is important for several reasons. One is its universality, for it is otherwise hard to understand vast numbers of allocations of time and effort by most people much of the time. Second, because marginal decision making is analyzable as an equilibrium, this important aspect of human behavior falls into place in the broadly based systems analysis. Third, marginal analysis is central to some well-developed theory in economics. Finally, marginal reasoning is also the basis for analyzing some social interactions in later chapters.

Perhaps more with regard to decisions than elsewhere in this book, we are using the language of the analyst, not of the ordinary decision maker—the theorist's model, not the practitioner's. Practitioners do not need to know the model in order to behave in accordance with it any more than rats need to study psychology in order to learn a maze. However, many people in organizations now make decisions in close conformity with this or some much more detailed model for the simple reason that that is what they have been hired to do. (This raises an interesting question about the status of a science that accurately describes the behavior of certain units for the simple reason that the units are consciously practicing the theory.)

This chapter does not prescribe what people *ought* to do. Any reader who decides (!) to base his behavior on it may praise or curse the author (and decision theory) at leisure.

part III

Social interactions: Intersystem analysis of humans

From systems in general and the intrasystem analysis of humans we now move to interactions of humans. Since an interaction involves two persons in a relationship it is also a system in its own right. Throughout Part III, however, we will examine only the interaction as such, and wait till Part IV (organizations) to look at the higher-level system itself.

In Part III (and in the rest of this volume) we classify all interactions as communications or transactions, or some combination of the two. In communication we examine the transfer of information (pattern) between parties, and in transaction we examine the transfer of value (goods, broadly defined). The question is not whether an interaction *is* a communication or a transaction. Any real interaction is inescapably both. The question is merely whether we focus on its informational or valuational components. That is, we bound the system analytically, on the basis of whether we use communicational or transactional analysis to understand it. We will look first at models of pure communications and transactions and then at their interesting combinations.

We are concerned with interactions between parties. A *party* is any person or organization of persons (a corporation, club, government) acting as a unit. For convenience we will talk of parties as persons. In a sense communication is the more basic glue in holding a society together —people must communicate to work together. But even if they are able to communicate, there is still no point in interacting unless people sense some value in it—the transactional aspect. Both kinds of interactions are indispensable for a society.

9

VALUE-BASED
INTERACTIONS:
TRANSACTIONAL BASICS

THE NATURE OF TRANSACTION

Introduction

Your car has thrown a rod, and you wander into a used car lot wondering
whether you should replace it. A reasonably clean Python 6 marked $600
would be fine. You don't want to spend over $400, but figure you might
go to $600 as an absolute limit if you can't argue the price down. The
proprietor comes over, and you start talking.

The marked price probably means he thinks he could accept as much
as $600 without looking like a crook, and might get it. But considering
the state of the car, the market, his bank account, and what he paid for
the car, he would let it go for $400 if necessary.

The proprietor, who has some bargaining sense, does not start by
telling you he would accept $400, but tries to convince you it is worth
every cent of $600. You say hesitantly that it will be tough to go over $350.
He points out the warning light that flashes automatically if you drive
through more than three feet of water, and the reclining seats. You live
in dry country and ignore the lights, but the reclining seats could be
worthwhile. You point out the rusted rocker panels and bald tires, while
mumbling that your friend just got a similar Python with good tires and
no visible rust for $550. He replies, as he coughs, that he just turned down
$550 for this one. After further jockeying, you agree on $500.

If you had wanted the car more intensely than you did, or your money
less, you might have paid $550, $600, or even more (if the car hadn't been
marked $600 to begin with). You would have been surer of getting it if
you had been willing to pay more. On the other hand, if you had wanted

"If everyone saved one gallon a day, there wouldn't be a gas shortage, and with this baby, you can save a gallon in less time."

© 1973 *Sentinel Star.* Reprinted by permission of Publishers-Hall Syndicate.

the car less, or your money more, you would not have paid over $450, $400, or even $300. Also, you would have been less likely to get the car. If the lot owner had wanted your money more intensely than he did, and the car less so, he might have let you have it for $400 or less. He would also have been surer of making the sale and of getting money from you. If he had wanted the money less and the car more, he would have refused to sell for less than $600, or even $700. He would then have got more for it *if* he had sold it, but would have been less likely to sell it.

This exchange is objective and tangible. But similar kinds of things can be said about more subjective and intangible circumstances. If you are lonely, or need a sympathetic ear to hear about your antediluvian parents or boring professors, you will give more of your own time, favors, or a reciprocally sympathetic ear to some fellow student than if you are self-contained and pleased with your parents and teachers. If your time, patience, and ability to do favors are in short supply and painful to give up, you will be willing to give less of them in order to get a given amount of sympathetic attention from someone else.

These general effects are not confined to individuals. A corporation will give an inventor more for a patent if it has lots of money and an intense desire for the patent than if it has little money and a mild desire. But in the latter case it will be less likely to get the patent. The United States will make more concessions in negotiations with Japan for a mutual defense treaty if we think that that country is indispensable to our line of defense than if Japan is seen as unimportant; but in the latter case we will be less likely to get the treaty.

There is a certain intuitive validity to the above examples, which will tend to make you agree with them. But you may also think of exceptions. We will clarify our initial model first, and deal with seeming exceptions later.

Some definitions

To generalize we will call you A and the car dealer B. We will give the name X to the thing initially possessed by A (money) and Y to the thing initially possessed by B (the car). The action we are examining is one in which A gives up X to B in exchange for Y.

This action is an exchange. But because some other actions follow similar principles, even though we would hardly want to call them exchanges, we will call this transfer a *transaction,* defined as (1) a transfer of valued things between parties, or (2) an interaction between parties analyzed with respect to the values of the things transferred. For either definition the values may be either positive or negative. If you are A and your money is X, AX will represent your desire for your money—that is, your desire to keep it, or not to give it up. If X is a service, rather than a commodity or money, AX is your desire *not* to perform it—the logical equivalent of keeping it. The more intense this desire the larger is AX. Your desire to get the car will similarly be called AY. In a parallel manner, BX is B's desire to get what A has, money, and BY is B's desire to keep what he already has, the car. The *terms* of the transaction are measured in how much X is exchanged for how much Y—in the illustration, \$500 for one automobile. In situations where the things exchanged are relatively personal and subjective, as with affection or respect, AY and BX may be thought of as the "emotional investment" of each party in the other person or in what he can provide, or as one's "dependence" on the other party (Emerson 1962).

Your ability to *get* the car we will call your *power.* To distinguish it from some other kinds of power, we will sometimes call this "plain" power or "particular" power. Unlike the intrapersonal power discussed in Chapter 6, this power is interpersonal, involving one party's ability to get something from another party rather than produce it for himself. The second question is how much you will have to give in return for it, or the terms on which you get it. Your ability to get Y on *good terms,* by giving relatively little in return for relatively much, we will call your *bargaining power.* The main questions we will ask about any transaction are how much power and bargaining power each party has, and why.

How much you would be willing to give at the most for the car we will call your *effective preference* for Y, or $EP.Y$. How much you would give reflects both your desire, indicated by the word "preference," and your ability to come up with the necessary money, indicated by the word "effective." An *EP* is the desire to get something along with the ability to provide something in exchange, a one-person parallel of what the economist calls effective demand.

Interpersonal power and bargaining power thus can be seen to depend partly on individual (intrapersonal) power, as described in Chapter 6, and on the particular relationship between the two parties. As to the intrapersonal aspect, if *A* does not already have *X* he has no power to get *Y*, since he has nothing to offer *B* in return, and his already having *X* does not depend (in our model) on his relationship with *B*. And as to the interpersonal aspect, if *B* does not want *X*, then *A* has little or no power to get *Y*, since *B* will then have no inducement to give it up. *A*, of course, must not only have *X* but also be willing to give it up. He must be both *willing* and *able* to provide *B* with the inducement to part with *Y* (Thibaut and Kelley 1959). The interpersonal "plain" power and bargaining power of *A* thus depend both on his personal condition and on his particular relationship with a particular *B*. It should be noted that we speak of *"A's power to get Y from B,"* never of *"A's power over B,"* because a clearer understanding seems to be possible with the former way of viewing it.

Tactics and strategy

In the illustration the dealer did not tell you straight off that he would sell for as little as $400, but instead tried at first to make you believe that somewhere in the neighborhood of $600 was the least he would accept. Meantime he was trying to discover the maximum you would give. Similarly, you did not blurt out that you would give as much as $600, but tried at first to leave the impression that $350 or $400 was your maximum. Only after some bargaining did he reveal that he would accept less than $600, and did you reveal that you would pay more than $400. The processes or acts of trying to find out the other party's *EP* while concealing or understating (i.e., misrepresenting) your own we call *tactics*. Tactics deal with beliefs and information about *EPs*—that is, with the detector aspects of the transaction.

Something else also happened. The dealer pointed out the high-water warning and reclining seats in the hope that he would thus increase or extend your *EP*, perhaps to $700. You pointed out the rust and bad tires in the hope of extending his *EP*, perhaps by making him think he would have a hard time selling the car. Any attempt to change *EPs* themselves will be called *strategy*, or strategic moves, in contrast to tactics, which merely try to influence beliefs about *EPs*. Because they deal with the values of the parties, strategic moves can be said to involve their selector states in the transaction.

The principles (and diagrams)

To diagram this situation, in Figure 9–1 the top bar, labeled *A's EP. Y*, covers all the terms on which you would be willing to trade—namely, to

Figure 9–1

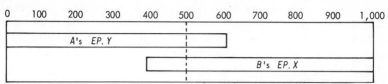

Diagram adapted from Boulding (1962: 18).

give $600 or any smaller amount. Actually, your *EP* extends an indefinite distance to the left beyond the diagram. For example, to extend it to minus $100 would mean that you would be willing to accept the car plus $100 while giving nothing in return. But this event is unlikely enough to ignore. The bar labeled *B's EP.X* extends from the right side to $400, but presumably extends indefinitely to the right.

Between $400 and $600 there is an *overlap of EPs*, and the broken line at $500 represents the terms actually settled upon, which in this case fall at the *midpoint of the overlap.* If two *EPs* extend to the same point, as in Figure 9–2, we will say arbitrarily that they "overlap" at that point.

Figure 9–2

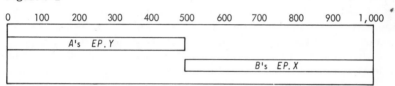

With these definitions we can generalize the statements above and for reference add some others that follow from them.

1.1 If the *EPs* of *A* and *B* overlap, an exchange is possible, and terms anywhere within the overlap will be acceptable to both parties.

1.2 If the *EPs* overlap only at a point, an exchange is possible only on the terms represented by that point. At any higher price *A* would not buy, and at any lower price *B* would not sell.

1.3 If there is an overlap, *A* has enough power to get *Y* and *B* has enough power to get *X*.

1.4 If the *EPs* do not overlap, the transaction cannot go through. *A* lacks sufficient power to get *Y*, and *B* lacks sufficient power to get *X*.

1.5 *A*'s power varies directly with his own *EP*. In Figure 9–1, if *A*'s *EP* extended only to $400 it would be just barely enough to get the car. But since it extends to $600, he has enough power to get the car, with some to spare. Expressed as a likelihood, with *B*'s *EP* at $400 *A* is much surer of getting *Y* if his own *EP* extends to $600 than if it extends to only $400. This point is clearer if we assume that *B*'s *EP* is not known exactly. If we know nothing more than that it is probably somewhere between $400 and $600, then we can certainly say that the longer *A*'s *EP* the more likely he is to reach *B*'s *EP*, and therefore to get the car.

1.6 *A*'s power varies directly with *B*'s *EP*. *A* is more likely, or more "able," to get the car if *B*'s *EP* is long enough to extend to $400 than if it extends only to $600 or $800. To avoid possible confusion, let us note that *B*'s *EP* is "larger" when it extends to smaller numbers. Being willing to give a certain amount of car, namely one, for a smaller amount of money is logically equivalent to being willing to give a larger amount of car for a given amount of money.

1.7 *A*'s bargaining power (*BP*) varies inversely with his own *EP*, large bargaining power for the buyer being the ability to get a low price and for the seller the ability to get a high price. To clarify, let us assume that *A* and *B* are equally good tacticians, so that any negotiations over terms will be settled at the midpoint of the overlap. For any given length of *B*'s *EP*, the longer *A*'s *EP* the farther to the right will be the midpoint of the overlap, and the higher the price paid by *A*. As can readily be seen by trying it, the midpoint of the overlap will shift by one half the amount of change in one *EP*.

1.8 It follows from 1.7 that *A*'s bargaining power varies directly with *B*'s *EP*.

1.9 The amount of overlap represents the total amount of gain in subjective utility as between the parties if the transaction is completed. In Figure 9–1, for example, *A*'s *EP.Y* extends to $600. This means that at any price below $600 he would prefer the car to the money and that at any price above $600 he would prefer the money to the car. At exactly $600 he is indifferent, and would be equally pleased to get the car or to keep the money. If he actually gets the car for $500 he has made a subjective gain of $100, the difference between what he was willing to pay and what he actually paid. This is the one-person equivalent of what economists call "consumer surplus." Similarly, if the dealer was willing to sell for $400 but got $500, he too gained by the amount of difference. Both parties are better off after the transaction than before, with a total subjective gain equal to the amount of overlap. Had the transaction taken place at $400, *A* would have gained $200 of subjective value, while *B* would have gained none. At $600, *B* would have gained $200, and *A* none. Other prices between $400 and $600 would divide the subjective gain differently, but it would always total $200.

For this reason the transaction is often called a "positive sum game," in which the "players" are collectively better off subjectively after the game than before. Although mistakes in judgment are possible, clearly neither party would complete the transaction if he did not at least break even on his expected subjective utility. In short, in any voluntary transaction neither party loses in expected subjective utility. If there is an overlap, at least one party gains, and both will gain unless the settlement falls exactly at an end of the overlap.

We can now see an important social aspect of the transaction, namely, that it contains both conflict and cooperation. The *fact* of the transaction is cooperative, in that it normally produces a net gain for both parties. But its *terms* are conflictual, since the better the terms for one party the worse they are for the other. Since the transaction itself produces a net gain, normally to both parties, while it also contains an inescapable element of conflict, the reader should avoid any value judgment that conflict is either good or bad in itself.

1.10 Within the overlap the terms of settlement are indeterminate. Although the illustration arbitrarily assumed a midpoint settlement, that does not necessarily occur. The only firm conclusion is that the settlement must fall within the overlap, and that its exact location depends on tactics. (Some authors use "bargaining power" in connection with settlement *within* the overlap. That usage is never employed in this volume.)

Strategies are also essentially indeterminate. Either A or B may or may not succeed in lengthening the other's EP, and if he is careless (or honest) he may shorten it. Thus for both tactics and strategy we can only say, "It all depends."

1.11 All of the above statements about power and bargaining power are reciprocal, and so will be all others below. Every statement remains valid if we interchange the parties (A for B and B for A), the goods (X for Y and Y for X), or both.

We can now summarize. For A an increase in B's EP is all to the good. It increases both A's power to get Y (as in 1.6) and his bargaining power (as in 1.8). A's own EP is a mixed bag, however. The larger it is the greater is A's power to get Y, as in 1.5, but the worse will be the terms on which he will get it, as in 1.7.

This last point is important. Many social scientists see power as a central idea, as in references to community power structure, the power of union or company, the power elite, power centers, the great powers, or the corrupting influence of power. Yet the concept of power has remained elusive (March 1966). An apparent reason is the failure to distinguish sharply between plain power and bargaining power. Since one varies directly and the other inversely with one's own EP, many statements valid for one are not valid for the other. If the two are sharply separated, this confusion disappears, and definite statements can be made about each. To put the statements in layman's language, the more you want something the more likely you are to get it because you will be willing to provide another person with more and bigger inducements to give it to you. But the more you are willing to give the more he is likely to get from you, and hence the more it will cost you.

The reader should note that in this model we never use the phrases "A has more bargaining power than B" or "A has power over B." The reasons are amplified in Kuhn (1974, especially pages 182 and 186).

A formula for bargaining power

The statements about power and bargaining power thus far are related to EPs. They are satisfactory in that form for most cases we will deal with later. However, each EP depends on two components. To say that you are willing to pay up to $600 for the car reflects your relative desire for the car, or AY, as compared to your desire to keep your money, or AX. B's willingness to sell it for as little as $400 similarly reflects his desire for money, or *BX,* as compared to his desire to hold on to the car, or *BY.*

Let us look at these four items. As to *AX,* the more intensely you want to keep your money the more you will insist on getting before you will give it up, and the more *B* will have to give you to get it from you. Either way of stating it means that the greater the size of *AX,* other things equal, the more you will insist on receiving before you will give up *X,* and the greater will be that part of your bargaining power based on this factor. As to *BX,* the more intensely *B* wants *X* the more he will be willing to give you for it and the more you will be able to get for *X.* Hence the greater *BX* the greater will be that part of your bargaining power based on *BX.* We can join the two and say that your bargaining power varies directly with both *AX* and *BX.* We can also say that your bargaining power varies directly with the value of what you already have, *X,* both in its value to you as reflected in your desire to keep it and in its value to *B* as reflected in his desire to get it.

By the same logic, the greater *AY* and *BY* the smaller will be your bargaining power. That is, *A*'s bargaining power varies inversely with *AY* and *BY,* and the larger the value of what *B* already has, to either *A* or *B,* the smaller will be *A*'s bargaining power to get it.

1.12 If we group the two positive and the two negative factors in *A*'s bargaining power, they appear as follows:

$$BP_A = (AX + BX) - (AY + BY)$$

1.13 Since we have already indicated that all statements are reciprocal, *B*'s bargaining power goes up as *A*'s goes down. Hence in a simple reversal of the two halves of 1.12:

$$BP_B = (AY + BY) - (AX + BX)$$

1.14 Given the components of the *EP*s, we can now add that:

$$A\text{'s } EP.Y = AY - AX$$

In the illustration, *A*'s desire for the car is such that, after we subtract from it his desire to keep his money, he will still be willing to give up $600.

We should note in passing a possible misuse of the symbols. We can, as the terms are defined, properly speak of *AX, AY,* or *A*'s *EP.Y.* But we cannot properly speak of *A*'s *EP* for *AX* or for *AY,* as this would mean "his desire for his desire" for *X* or for *Y.* Though a desire for a desire is not beyond the ken of this psychedelic age, we do not include it in our symbols. We may also note that *X* and *Y* are externals, the commodities or services that change hands. By contrast *AX, AY, BX,* and *BY* are system states, or subjective attitudes of *A* and *B* toward *X* and *Y.*

By putting these items into a formula, we do *not* imply that we can compute a numerical measure of bargaining power. All we mean is that *AX* and *BX* enhance *A*'s bargaining power while *AY* and *BY* detract from it. Although it seems doubtful that we will ever be able to put exact numbers into the formulas, they are by no means useless. It is often important to know in which *direction* a force is pushing, even if we cannot know precisely *how hard*—as we saw in connection with negative feedback.

On gaining power and bargaining power

If A wants power or bargaining power in some transaction, we can now make certain recommendations. One is to try to increase B's $EP.X$, since to do this will raise both A's plain power and his bargaining power. To break it into its parts, this means to increase BX, to decrease BY, or both, as by trying to make X seem the answer to B's prayers and Y fit stuff only for his nightmares. Commercial advertising typically tries to do both. If we view the seller as B and the potential buyer as A, B tries to make A believe that his product, Y, is the key to immediate and perpetual happiness, while money, X, is painless to part with under the easy payment plan. The seller tries to keep from view that his product may be junk and that the installments may be a do-it-yourself design for easy bankruptcy. If you are trying to woo an employer or a mate you try to create the impression that his life will be miserable indeed without you.

Molding your own wants is more a psychological problem than a social one, but it is clear what you must do to accomplish this. One method is to decrease your desire for what the other person has, AY, as by repeating twenty times a day that true happiness comes from making things for yourself, or from doing without. "I can live without him (her)" is one statement of a lowered AY. Another method is to increase your desire to keep what you already have, or AX, as by reminding yourself how much you like X.

The above prescriptions deal with strategy—with molding the actual magnitudes of AX, AY, BX, and BY, which means molding the EPs. The appropriate tactics can also be derived from the propositions. If A wants to get the best terms *within* given EPs, his appropriate tactics are to try to learn the true length of B's EP and then to represent his own EP as just barely meeting it. Car dealers are usually better at this than are their customers.

The fact that one's bargaining power varies in the opposite direction from his plain power can create a practical difficulty. So long as the EPs overlap, A's shorter $EP.Y$ raises his bargaining power while leaving him enough plain power to get Y. But if his EP falls short of meeting B's $EP.X$, A cannot get Y at all, since he does not have enough (plain) power. This pair of opposite effects can present puzzling problems in tactics, especially if A cannot find out even approximately where B's EP really is. For purposes of bargaining power A will want to represent his own EP as short. But if he represents it as so short that it does not meet B's, B may give up the negotiations as pointless. This is the tricky game of "hard to get but not too hard," which is perhaps the most obvious of the many complex details of actual negotiations.

HOW VALID IS THIS KNOWLEDGE?

We observed earlier that the reader might have reservations regarding the above statements about power and bargaining power.

"The book is only talking about a cold, calculating relationship. What about warm, impulsive ones?"

"Tactics are schemes and lies, and I don't like either."

"What if the car dealer is your well-heeled brother who knows you are hard up? He may sell you the car for 200 even though it cost him 5."

"Suppose the salesman is only an employee who has no authority to sell for less than the posted price?"

"What if the salesman thinks you are an effete snob and hikes the price to $800 just to keep you from getting what you want?"

"Anyway, what has all this got to do with all those purchases where the price is what it says on the tag? You buy or you don't buy, but you don't haggle."

"I would feel ashamed to try to talk a person down from the price he asked."

These are all valid objections, and others could be added. If so, is there any validity to the conclusions? Few readers would throw them out entirely. The real world contains *some* situations like those detailed above, and for those situations the above conclusions about power and bargaining power seem valid. After all, many people do bargain, including husbands and wives, parents and children, job applicants and employers, unions and management, political candidates and party bosses, wooer and wooed, nations, and even students and teachers. Even though fixed-price purchases like those in most stores loom large when we first think of exchanges, it is probable that the vast majority of all transactional relations are not completed on a predetermined amount of X for a predetermined amount of Y. A fuller understanding of these many bargainable exchanges will come as we examine more examples.

Having said this, let us return to the question of whether it is possible to make valid, "scientific" statements about transactions when we can apparently state so many exceptions. The answer is, "Yes, if we carefully state the conditions we are talking about." Let us therefore examine the case of the used car to see what conditions must exist if the propositions are to be valid.

To begin with, we assumed a vast amount of context—that you wanted a car, that you had money, that you had got to the used car lot, that the car was there and for sale, and that you talked the same language as the salesman. We also assumed many other things about you, the salesman, and the relation between the two of you. We assumed that you preferred a low price to a high price, that the salesman preferred a high price to a low one, that the price was bargainable, that you were offering money for the car rather than marijuana or turnip greens, that the salesman was not angry with you nor you with him, that the salesman was not in love with you, that you did not threaten to poison his wife if he asked more than $450, and that you were willing to use at least some mild evasions about your own *EP*.

Perhaps unfortunately, to make statements that are valid and unchallengeable we must specify numerous conditions, also known as assumptions. The set of assumptions used for any particular purpose is often called a *model,* as discussed in Chapter 5. With such a model we can then say, to put it in its most general form: "If conditions *a, b, c* . . . prevail, then conclusions *x, y, z* . . . follow." If we change the assumptions, or model, the conclusions will also change. For example, "If conditions *a, b, d* . . . prevail, then conclusions *p, q, x* . . . will follow." The first set of conditions can be called the *initial model,* and later changes can be called *modifications* or *relaxations* of the model.

THE INITIAL MODEL OF THE TRANSACTION

We will now state the particular set of conditions under which all the propositions numbered 1.1 through 1.11 would be valid. This list is included in full to show what is meant by a good model and logical thinking in social science, to settle the reader's possible reservations about previous conclusions, and to serve as a base from which some subsequent changes in the model will lead to different conclusions about different situations. The assumptions are as follows.

a. Only two parties are involved, *A* and *B.*

b. Only two exchangeable things (goods) are involved, *X* and *Y,* which are held at the outset by *A* and *B* respectively.

c. Each party tries to maximize his benefit in the transaction, which means to give as little and receive as much as he can. But each will conclude the transaction if the expected value to him of the thing received exceeds the value to him of the thing given up. This condition is called *selfish.*

d. Each party is indifferent to the welfare of the other, and wishes neither to help nor to hurt him. That is, neither has any feelings about the other party that would cause him to modify his *EP* from the position taken by his own self-interest. Items *c* and *d* together will be known as the *selfish-indifferent* situation.

e. Each party knows his own effective preference. This does not mean that it is carefully calculated, but merely that each knows the worst terms he will accept. The effects of norms and other social forces in molding his preferences will be discussed in later chapters.

f. Both *X* and *Y* are positive goods. They are affirmatively wanted, like meat or money, not something to be avoided, like pain or incarceration. They generate approach rather than avoidance responses.

g. *X* and *Y* are already possessed by *A* and *B,* and it is irrelevant how they got them.

h. Neither party has any desires relevant to the transaction except those for *X* and *Y.* Among other possible things, there is no satisfaction or dissatisfaction from the transaction process itself, such as cost of time consumed, pleasure in or distaste for bargaining, or pleasure in each other's company.

i. The transaction is unique, and stands solely on its own merits. Neither party considers its possible effect on any other transaction with anybody over anything, or considers the possible alternative of dealing with someone else.

j. *AX, AY, BX,* and *BY* are all independent variables. That is, a change in any one does not in itself bring a change in any of the others.

k. Both *A* and *B* are principals acting in their own interest, not agents acting in the interest of others.

l. No question of delivery is involved. Either *X* and *Y* change hands simultaneously, or there is full confidence that delivery will be made as agreed.

m. Each party can withhold from the other the thing he already has. This assumption excludes, for example, theft or removal of privacy without one's consent.

n. Each party can give the good in question to the other. To illustrate this condition by its opposite, one may not be able to give love or respect if he feels contempt.

o. The necessary communications can be carried on. For example, A and B can both talk and understand each other clearly.

This may seem a discouragingly long list. But if we leave out any of these items, someone might properly claim that some statements above about power and bargaining power are not necessarily valid—that he has thought of an exception. By contrast, if this list has been properly drawn, then if all these conditions stated in the model prevail, the conclusions in propositions 1.1 to 1.11 are *necessarily valid*. If someone can find a loophole, another assumption can presumably be added to close it.

By focusing on a single relationship between two parties, this initial model of the transaction classifies as *segmental*—in the language of the sociologist. Continuing relationships that involve repeated communications and transactions between the same two parties (a *dyad*) over a period of time will be discussed later.

Not all approaches to power are framed in the same way. For example, power is sometimes defined as one's ability to get another party to do something against his will, or despite his resistance (Weber 1947: 152). One can also speak of A's exerting power over B, or getting B to do A's bidding. Those ideas are all incorporated here, but in different language. For example, we have said that either X or Y can be a service as well as a commodity. Hence when we say that "B gives Y to A," this means, if Y is a service, that B is "doing something for A," or that B is "doing A's bidding."

Our model also assumes that B has some cost in performing the service, Y, such as time, effort, or disutility. BY is B's desire not to perform the service, which is the same as his costs of performing it. As we describe it, B will not be willing to perform Y unless his desire for X (BX) is greater than his desire not to perform Y (BY). Thus we say that B performs the service for A, not "against his will" or because A "has power over him," but because the benefit to B of performing the service is greater than the cost of doing so, considering all the circumstances. B's "resistance" is overcome by providing him an X which is more valuable to him than the Y he gives up. For transactions in bads the content of X is different, but not the logic or the language.

CONCLUSION

A transaction is an interaction between two persons. Hence it is *social*, not individual. In one or another of its many forms, it is a kind of interaction you have engaged in thousands of times, possibly starting shortly after birth. With so much experience, you already know quite a lot about transactions. But you have probably never thought about the process very explicitly, or clearly formulated your thoughts. Besides, your own experience has perhaps not been varied enough to give you the broad range of types required to extract basic generalizations—in the same sense that though everyone learns a great deal about the nature of gravity from his own experience, it was not until Newton formulated it that we had the scientifically usable statement of the law of gravity. In any case, systematic knowledge of this kind generally arises from the accumulated pooling of experience of many people over many years, and it is only recently, as human history goes, that this particular kind of interaction has been distinguished from other kinds, and that a systematic science of it has been attempted. So the thing to do is to see whether the statements of this chapter square with your experience, and to see whether they help you understand it.

If some real experience does not behave like the model, then either or both of two conditions must exist: either the real situation is not like the model in some significant respect, or there is some error in logic or assumptions in the model, or both. Patient thought and investigation may be required to tell which.

Although the kind of relation involved in bargaining over the price of a used car is only *one type* of transactional relation, and a fairly specialized type, it is *not unreal.* Vast numbers of real transactions meet the conditions of the model. For each of them the materials of this chapter should constitute valid science, enabling the observer both to understand the process and, if he can know the *EP*s involved, predict the consequences.

It should be clear from this chapter that social science is not all remote from the everyday experience of ordinary mortals, but is an intimate part of what goes on all the time in your own life. The important thing is that if you get a clear understanding of these things close to home you will have a solid base for understanding many things more remote, such as the relations between giant corporations or nations. The basic logic of those relations is not different, only their content.

A DETOUR ABOUT MODELS

The long list of assumptions in the initial model of transactions raises a crucial point about the nature of science. Our desire is to have reliable social *science,* and that requires that the conditions one is talking about be made explicit, for otherwise the conclusions are not valid. The physical sciences, especially physics, seem to have such nice simple principles that something like the above model of a transaction seems clumsy and complicated by comparison. But the difference is not as great as it seems. For just as some readers may have taken for granted the conditions that make sense of the transaction about buying a car, they may also take for granted the conditions that are necessary to make certain "simple" physical principles valid. This is an important and touchy point, and we must deal with it head on.

Archimedes' principle is a "simple" statement that when a solid is placed in a liquid it will lose weight equal to the weight of the liquid displaced. Those familiar with the principle are likely to conclude unthinkingly that it is always and universally true, and does not need qualifications. Let us look a little closer.

Is granulated sugar a "solid" for purposes of Archimedes' principle? It is certainly not a liquid or a gas. But if it dissolves, how much weight does it lose and how does one measure it? Does the principle hold if the solid is a sponge? Or, suppose the liquid is water and the solid is a small piece of sodium metal. It will bounce around on the surface, spit fire, combine chemically with the water, and possibly not displace any significant amount. What if the liquid is molten steel and the solid a wooden shingle, in which case the solid will promptly disappear in smoke? The principle also says nothing about the shape of the container. Suppose it is a smooth, hollow cylinder, and the solid is a piston that fits so snugly that no liquid can move past it. The piston will lose all its weight, and no water will be displaced at all. Or what if the liquid is gasoline and the solid is red-hot steel? And what about the principle if the solid is dropped from 50 feet and splashes liquid out of the container? This list of exceptions to Archimedes' principle has been drawn up by a social scientist. A physicist presumably could think of more.

A strict statement of Archimedes' principle, like a strict statement about transactions, requires a list of assumed conditions. Without them the statement is not valid. Archimedes' principle thus requires a model just as much as do the principles about transactions. That model would have to read something like this. "Assuming that:

1. the solid does not combine chemically with the liquid,
2. the solid does not dissolve in the liquid,
3. the solid does not burn,
4. the liquid does not burn,
5. the solid does not absorb the liquid,
6. the shape of the container and the solid are such as to allow the liquid to flow out of the container,
7. the solid is placed gently so as not to splash liquid out of the container,
8. there is no evaporation of liquid or solid during the period under observation,
9. et cetera,

then (and only then) will a solid placed in a liquid lose weight equal to the weight of the liquid displaced." The simple statement we usually study in eighth-grade general science is not so innocently simple as it looks. If the model of the transaction contains a longer list of assumptions, it is only because the transaction is a more complicated situation.

Any other scientific statement, to be strictly valid, must also be accompanied by a list of the assumptions, or conditions, that make it acceptable. Even that science of kingly precision, astronomy, includes assumptions when it predicts the positions of the planets a century hence. Some are: that the sun will not explode meanwhile, that the planets will not explode or burn up, that a large body from outer space will not exert a gravitational pull within the solar system, that no cosmic cloud will enter the solar system and exert friction on planetary movements, etc., etc., etc.

10

VALUE-BASED
INTERACTIONS:
SOME GORY DETAILS

We noted in Chapter 7 that a rational decision is the selection of an alternative whose benefit exceeds its cost. A transaction also involves decision. For example, for A the benefit is the satisfaction from the Y he gets from B, and the cost is the sacrifice of giving up X. The important new ingredient is that transaction requires *two mutually contingent decisions.* ("Contingent" is defined more fully in Chapter 13.)

It is valid to say that A and B have *agreed* to make the transaction. But they did not literally agree to the *same thing*—they did not make the *same decision. A* decided to give up X for Y, B to give up Y for X, and these are very different decisions. In fact, in one sense A and B must disagree (A must prefer Y to X, and B must prefer X to Y), and this important interaction works only when people differ in their values. As in Figure 9–1, the greater the difference in those preferences the greater the overlap of EPs and the greater the potential benefit from the transaction. Furthermore, the area of overlap represents the degree to which the transaction is cooperative—an act that provides satisfaction to both parties. Interestingly, the overlap also represents the degree of conflict within which the benefit of better terms for one party can be achieved only at the cost of worse terms for the other. As we shall see, differences in preferences with respect to transactions are an integrative bond that helps hold a society together.

MULTIPLE MOTIVES

Near the end of Chapter 9 we noted that the introductory model of the transaction is a particular case, and that many assumptions are needed

119

to make its conclusions valid. Most of this chapter and the next looks at other transactional situations. However, in these new cases we do not start over. We merely change one or two assumptions at a time while leaving everything else unchanged.

The generous transaction

The initial model assumed that each party was indifferent to the other, and wished neither to help nor to hurt him (assumption *d*). Many transactions are like that, particularly purchases and sales by businesses.

But many transactions are different. Aunt Clerestory may get a positive joy from stuffing cookies into her nephew. The missionary may delight in saving the heathen. The spouse may want to give a satisfying sexual experience, even when it is not mutual. No infant could survive if someone did not provide for him without overt return. The con artist may soften you up with generosity so he can "take" you later.

In each case one party wants to give without the explicit contingency of receiving in return. We will not probe his "true" or "ultimate" reasons, but (as with decisions) accept his preferences as given. Since generosity between customer and used car dealer is improbable, we will shift examples.

You are *A*, and do not know or care about *B*. A mutual acquaintance, *C*, to whom neither of you feels any obligation, learns that both of you want to go to Sioux City—you because a fine heirloom desk is waiting there for you. But it is a long trip, you are nearly broke, and it does not seem quite worth the trouble. *B* has no car, and has a heavy box to take along. At *C*'s suggestion *B* calls you. After some talk you agree that you will drive him and his box to Sioux City and that he will pay for your gasoline and meals. However, each of you is barely willing to go through with the arrangement on these terms—your *EP*s just meet, as diagramed in Figure 10–1(*a*). (Note that our diagrams of transactions involving money used only a single scale, indicating the amount of money given for a single good. More complicated cases need two scales, the top one representing the *X* that *A* will give and the bottom one representing the *Y* that *B* will give.)

With the *EP*s just meeting under mutual indifference, suppose *C* now tells you that *B* has been through a very rough time. You are willing to go out of your way to help him, though not without limit. The amount of this willingness is shown as the dotted area of your *EP* in Figure 10–1(*b*). With this area added, your *EP* is obviously longer than under indifference, and we will call this dotted area a generous extension of an *EP*. We have shown it as extending to where you would accept *B*'s offer to provide your food but not your gas.

In a selfish transaction the terms are indeterminate within the overlap, and depend on tactics. Before predicting the outcome in this case, we must consider *B*'s attitude. If he takes a selfish stance and you a generous one, the answer is clear. You will drive him in return for food only, and he will accept—though he might first try to get you to drive him for nothing. However, if *B* also takes a generous stance, he may offer to

Figure 10–1

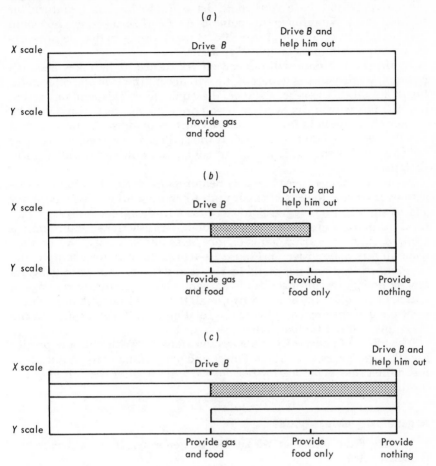

provide both gas and food. As before, the outcome within the overlap depends on tactics. But under generosity the tactics are reversed. Instead of pretending that the *EP*s are shorter than they are, each will reveal the full *EP* to begin with. In fact, if each is sure the other is also bargaining generously, the *EP*s may be overstated. For example, you would not say, "I don't feel like giving up the time and money to get that crummy old desk, but I might be willing to get it if someone would help out on the costs"—as you might in a selfish stance. Instead you might say, "I can hardly wait to get that fabulous antique," and he might say, "I just got some unexpected cash, so let me pay for the gas too." If you are equally good at generous tactics, the outcome will be somewhere between the limits of the two *EP*s—perhaps that he will provide the food and pay for half the gas.

Let us move now to Figure 10–1(*c*). Suppose *B*'s rough experience distresses you greatly and you are feeling great sympathy. Now we extend your *EP* to where you would drive *B* and his box in return for nothing at all. We refer to this point as *B*'s *EP* of zero—where he would give nothing in return for *X*. An *EP* of *A* that extends to that point represents your willingness to give *X* as a gift.

Again the outcome will depend on *B*'s stance. If he takes a selfish position, while yours is generous, he will accept the ride and offer nothing. If he takes a generous stance, the outcome will depend on tactics, but will fall within the overlap. If you are a master tactician, while he is inept (has "shellout falter"—phrase courtesy of Myron Tribus), he will pay for neither gas nor your food. If the skills are reversed, he will pay for both; and if the skills are about equal, you will end somewhere in between.[1]

Money exchanges are obviously neater to diagram. Nonmoney transactions involve different *kinds* of units—bringing lunch *and* paying for gas, or signing a nonaggression pact *plus* a trade agreement *plus* a cultural exchange agreement. Whereas dollar transactions require only a scale of quantity, varied items cannot be scaled so easily. Nor do they come in any fixed order. In Figure 10–1(*b*) or 10–1(*c*), for example, the positions of food and gas could be reversed with no change in logic. As among nonaggression pact, trade agreement, and cultural exchange, a nation might offer any one, any two, or all three in some exchange. These multiple dimensions complicate the relationship, the analysis, and the diagrams, but not the basic logic.

The effect of generosity is always to extend *EP*s, whether the parties are siblings, lovers, or nations. Power and bargaining power continue to mean the same as before, for reasons we will see after we introduce the hostile transaction.

Is generosity always good?

We are often told that we should be generous. If so, what are the consequences?

We have already noted the increase in power of both parties, and the increase in bargaining power of one of them, under generosity. Although we venture no judgment as to whether power or bargaining power is good or bad, more power gets people more of what they want than does less power, and is presumably advantageous.

Simple logic agrees. If I can get satisfaction either from having a particular Picasso painting for myself or from knowing that you have it (whether or not I ever see it in your house), the overall likelihood that I will get satisfaction from that painting is greater than if I could get satisfaction only from owning it. The principle can be generalized for almost anything that might be given as a gift. As we will see, generosity is also an important integrating factor in any organization or society.

But there are reservations. If your grandmother gives you a pink-and-purple platter heirloom for Christmas, you may feel obliged to admire

---

[1] The selfish transaction (present language) is often referred to elsewhere as "economic," while the generous is called "social." The unfortunate implication is that you must study two different disciplines to understand them.

it, even though it nauseates you. Having observed your appreciation, she later gives you a large vase to match. Since she often visits unexpectedly, you feel that the items must be on your mantel at all times. Because she likes them, the two items were costly for her to give up. Because you dislike them, they are costly to you to accept and keep visible. To make you more willing to accept them, she may even have said she had no room for them, even though she would have liked to keep them but mistakenly thought you craved them.

Whereas in the selfish-indifferent transaction both parties normally gain, the generous transaction may bring a loss to both. This can occur, however, only under tactical misrepresentations—if you pretend you like the platter when you don't or your grandmother pretends she doesn't want to keep it when she does.

Whereas in a selfish-indifferent transaction, each party need know only his own preferences for the transaction to bring a net gain, in the generous one the other party's preferences must also be known. Generosity assuredly brings a gain only when the giver assuredly knows the receiver's preferences. Some cases leave little doubt, as with food for the starving or gasoline for the stranded motorist. For less obvious items, gifts work best among those who know each other's preferences.

We are talking only about a generous transaction taken alone and on its own merits. That generosity might undermine character, cement friendship, or do a thousand other things are matters we will not take up here.

The hostile transaction

In contrast to the generous transaction, a hostile transaction is a transaction in which one or both parties want to hurt the other—to reduce his satisfaction. Again we will not try to ascertain the "real" motives, which might be dislike, anger, getting even, or discipline by a loving parent. At this point we will deal with hurting the other only by withholding goods. Later we will deal with the imposing of bads.

Hostile transactions may be as varied and important as generous ones, and the brevity of this discussion is not intended to downgrade their significance. But once we understand the selfish-indifferent transaction and the way it is modified by generosity, we already have the key to hostile ones. Whereas generosity extends EPs, hostility shrinks them. Hence all the consequences of hostile shrinkages are the opposite of generous extensions. If A's hostility to B shrinks his EP, the result is to reduce A's plain power, B's plain power, and B's bargaining power. The only advantage to either party is to increase A's bargaining power. If A's EP shrinks to a point where it no longer overlaps, the effect is a one-party boycott, in which A imposes the cost on B of having to go without X, but at the cost to A of having to go without Y.

Miscellaneous motives in transactions

Once this general scheme of transactions is understood, the effects of other motives can easily be traced. Any positive attitudes by A toward B

tend to extend A's EP and improve B's position. These attitudes include love, affection, liking, friendship, respect, consideration, sympathy, empathy, pity, and the like. The effect is reversed by negative attitudes, which include anger, hatred, dislike, disrespect, contempt, disapproval, enmity, and pique.

Still other motives, some of which are not attitudes toward the other party, also affect EPs, power, and bargaining power. For example, suppose you, A, enjoy the act of bargaining, quite apart from the things you acquire. Your total satisfaction is now AY_1, the satisfaction from getting Y itself, plus AY_2, the satisfaction from the transactional process. The results of this longer EP are a decline in your bargaining power, an increase in B's, and an increase in the plain power of both. If you dislike bargaining, the results are reversed. Or perhaps you find transactions an excuse for chatting, the enjoyment of which will also extend your EP.

By contrast, suppose you enjoy driving a hard bargain. Even though you might otherwise be willing to give much in the exchange, to do so would destroy some of your satisfaction. Your EP would therefore shrink by the amount of your displeasure in "being soft." On the other hand, if you want to be thought generous, your EP may extend so as to make you look that way. Thus if you know the nature of any additional transactional ingredient you can figure out its consequences for yourself.

ON SOCIAL PRESSURES AND SOCIAL COHESION

We have now come far enough to observe some important social processes. The ordinary selfish transaction brings a gain to both parties, and the desire for such gains is a motive for people to be in contact and to interact. Hence the advantages of interacting are "ties that bind" people together—cohesive forces that keep people integrated into a society instead of leaving them a batch of separate individuals. Selfish transactions are not the only such integrating force, as we shall see. But they are an important one.

We have seen that affection and liking bring a generous extension of EPs. We have also seen that B's longer EP raises A's bargaining power and the plain power of both A and B. Dislike of A by B leads to a hostile shortening of B's EP, with a decline in A's bargaining power and the plain power of both. There are thus clear transactional benefits from being liked and from not being disliked. Furthermore, most of us learn these things early. At only a few months the infant is likely to start learning that things are pleasanter when there is a smile rather than a frown on mother's face. By the age of one or two he observes what kinds of behavior bring smiles and what kinds bring frowns, and by conditioning he learns to engage in more of the former and less of the latter. In due time he also undergoes generous extensions and hostile contractions of his own EPs, with results already seen.

However intuitive and unconscious one's learning of these things, they are likely to be learned firmly from repeated experience. Given frequent reinforcement, they are also likely to acquire early and strong intrinsic reward value, which will almost certainly receive additional reinforcement many times through life. The result is a strong general tendency to do and say things that will make others like and approve of us, and to avoid doing and saying things that will generate dislike and disapproval.

At least two important social consequences follow. First, among people who like one another *EP*s will overlap much oftener and farther than among those who are indifferent or hostile. If transactions in general are cohesive and integrative forces they are even more so if people like one another. Conversely, dislike and hostility are loosening and disintegrative forces. Thus do the emotions in our model of man translate into definite social effects.

Second, expressions of approval and disapproval, of liking and disliking, themselves often constitute rewards and punishments. Hence they are ways by which one can influence others. Although we do not say these things, since saying them might destroy their effect, we engage in many implicit transactions of the sort: "If you do something nice for me, I will express approval of you. If you don't, or if you do something nasty, I will express disapproval." Expressions of approval or disapproval can thus constitute *sanctions* and provide power with others. Implementing such approval or disapproval overtly in transactions is, of course, a stronger sanction than merely expressing it. The sociologist calls such sanctions "social controls"—though they are by no means the only ones.

Implicit and open-end transactions

Life is full of transactions that are conducted implicitly rather than explicitly. You live in Florida but have a summer cottage in Maine. A Maine neighbor ties back shutters loosened by the wind, waters your perennials during late dry spells, and generally keeps an eye on the place in your absence. Every December you send him a crate of oranges. Each act is, overtly, a generous, friendly gift. Yet the acts probably are contingent, and the chances are that if either party discontinued his half of the arrangement, the other would eventually drop his. To acknowledge the mutual contingency, however, would "downgrade" the relation from generous to selfish—from "social" to "economic." Even within your respective families you may soften the language and say, "Since the Ipswiches were so good about looking after our cottage, I'd like to show our appreciation by sending them some oranges." Or you may be more straightforward and say, "If we don't send them something, I don't think they are likely to keep looking after our place so conscientiously." Continued firsthand relations inescapably contain many generous acts that are not explicitly contingent on a return favor, but are nevertheless done in the expectation that some obligation to reciprocate will, in fact, be felt. We will call these acts that depend on "norms of reciprocity" open-end transactions.

Completely open end are transactions in which we do someone a favor, even though we have no expectation of ever seeing him again, perhaps without even knowing who he is. We may do such things, of course, because they make us feel good or because we have been trained to do

THE NORM OF RECIPROCITY

"Whaddaya mean, 'Well, goodbye'? I just spent forty cents on you and you say goodbye?"

Copyright © 1973. Reprinted by permission of *Saturday Review/World* and Bill Hoest.

them—which may be two versions of the same thing. But in general we expect that if each of us does favors for others as needed, each in the long run will receive a helping hand as often as he gives it. Some see these as transactions with the Deity—to help one's fellows is to grow in favor with God.

For reasons already stated, implicit and open-end transactions are also highly "integrative." It is hard to imagine anything but the most primitive, ineffective, and unsatisfactory society without them.

TRANSACTIONS USING BADS AS STRATEGIES

Thus far we have dealt with transactions in things people want, or goods. But transactions can also be based on bads—things people want to avoid or get rid of. Bads include criticism or insult, fear, pain, stench, destruction, frustration, insecurity, disease, noise, distraction, ugliness, and invasion of privacy. A bad can also be the withdrawal, cessation, or reduction of a good, such as reducing an allowance or a vacation. Although some kinds of preferences are reasonably universal, what is good or bad often depends on the individual's tastes and value structure.

Bads may be inflicted directly on an individual or indirectly on someone he cares about. The importance of a bad for transactions is that one may be willing to pay to have it prevented, removed, or stopped. In dealing with bads, we withdraw assumption *f* of our original model—that both *X* and *Y* are goods. We replace it first with the assumption that *X* is a bad while *Y* remains a good. That is, *A* tries to get something he wants from *B* through the leverage of doing something unpleasant to *B,* as in blackmail.

We also modify assumption *g*—that *X* and *Y* are already possessed by *A* and *B,* respectively, and that it is irrelevant how they got them. To look first at the transactions in goods, in a potential exchange of my snake oil for your bowie knife it does not matter where, how, or when I got my snake oil, or whether I had you in mind when I got it. It is enough that I have it and am willing to part with it.

Whereas a good can be a material thing, a bad is normally a "service." To make a material thing a bad I must pour it on your rug, release it into the air you breathe, or otherwise impose it on you. Even so, it is not the material thing, but what I have have done with it—the "service"—that is bad. Unlike the good, which I can simply produce or buy in the hope that I will sometime be able to exchange it for something from somebody, if I want a good from you in return for a bad, the bad must be directed explicitly at you.

The heading of this section refers to the use of bads as a strategy, which is an attempt by one party to alter one or both *EP*s, but particularly that of the other party, in his own favor. That is the purpose of bads used in transactions.

Bads can be used in either stress or threat transactions. In the first I apply some stress to you and then promise to relieve it if you will give me some *Y.* I apply the stress as a unilateral act: we do not negotiate over it. It is pretransactional. Only after I have applied the stress do we negotiate about my relieving it.

The threat reverses things. In it I merely state that I will do something nasty to you if you do not do what I want. The negotiations come first. If you do not do as I ask, the bad is applied unilaterally after the negotiations—or rather, after the *failure* of negotiations. In the threat the bad is also unilateral. But it is posttransactional, not pretransactional. We will look first at stress.

Stress as strategy

I spring a bear trap on your leg (or twist your arm, stand on your cat's tail, lay you on pointed bamboo shoots—choose your favorite torture). This is the pretransaction stage of applying stress. We then start talking. "Will you tell me your secret formula for gardenia fertilizer if I unspring the bear trap?" This is the transaction stage.

We will note three important comparisons between transactions in goods and bads. First, and perhaps surprisingly, the power and bargaining power ingredients of transactions in bads behave exactly as in the original model. My bargaining power is $(AX + BX) - (AY + BY)$, and yours reverses the two halves of the formula. As in any service by A, AX is the desire not to perform it—that is, my desire not to relieve the stress, or not to let you out of the trap. BX is B's desire to have the stress removed —your desire that I let you loose. AY is A's desire for Y, which is my desire for your formula. BY is B's desire to hold on to Y, which is your desire to keep your formula to yourself.

Second, all ingredients in the transaction stage are positive. True, putting you in the trap was a bad for you. But letting you out is a good, and that is what you bargain for. Third, since bads must be directed explicitly at the party from whom something is wanted, he is apt to resist. Hence the stress often cannot be imposed by A unless he has more productive (or destructive) power than B to begin with. Thus for transactions in bads the relative abilities of the two parties to "produce" bads must be considered directly in each interaction, whereas for transactions in goods it could remain in the background. Transactional power in bads therefore presupposes the necessary "muscle," even if certain kinds of bads require muscles no more powerful than those of the tongue or the trigger finger. We will illustrate the more obvious forms that produce pain, injury, or destruction.

Such bads are often thought of as *coercive,* and we will use the term as applied to them. There is nothing absolute about coercion, however: the term does not imply that one has no choice. Some accept fantastic tortures or death without conceding (is coercion coercive if it does not coerce?), while others give in to a mild hair pulling. Those who find certain positive inducements too strong to resist (love or money) are also essentially "coerced." Coercion is not a new ingredient in transactions. It merely refers to an EP to avoid bads that is so strong as to leave little doubt of the outcome.

Consequences of stress

The main generalizations about stress transactions are as follows. First, if it is costly to A to impose stress on B, this fact will reduce A's power and bargaining power, much as if, in a positive goods transaction, A had very little X. Second, the greater B's desire to have the stress relieved the greater will be BX and hence the greater A's bargaining power and plain power.

Third, if A must undergo a cost in removing the stress, this is the same as an increase in AX. It shortens A's EP and increases his bargaining power. For example, if the stress A has imposed on B is to put him on a raft in a lake full of crocodiles, and if someone has then stolen A's boat, A may find it very costly to release B. B will then have to give A not only enough to induce him to be willing to release B, but must add enough more to pay the costs of enabling A to release B. Any generous impulse by A toward B makes A more willing to relieve the stress and reduces his bargaining power. Chickenheartedness in the use of bads does not pay!

Fourth, we must distinguish physical blockage from stress. If you have me locked up or tied down, I cannot prevent you from doing anything you like. Physical blockage is not a transactional relation: it takes one party out of the transactional relation. A transaction involves consent, even if coerced. (Note that we say "*A* coerced *B*'s consent," not that *A* coerced *B* to act without his consent.) Even when *A* has complete physical control over *B*, consent may still be necessary for getting such things as promises, permissions, or information.

Fifth, stress can be mutual. We need not detail it, since your stress on me has the same kind of effect as my stress on you. Sixth, as with positive goods, *A*'s promise to relieve the stress provides no bargaining power if *B* does not believe it. If the college president believes students will stay in the administration building even if he grants their demands, their sit-in holds no power. Seventh, the stress must be relievable. A burned building is distressing, but holds no power because those who burned it cannot relieve the stress.

Finally, the effect of stress may be ambiguous. If it is costly to *A* to continue the stress, he might relieve part of it in one case because it has worked (*B* has conceded some part of *Y*). In a different case he may relieve part of it because it has not worked (*B* has not conceded much, and does not seem likely to). Such cases leave *B* in a quandary as to whether his further concessions would end the stress or have the appeasement effect of inducing *A* to increase his demands. Thus *B* might concede when he ought to hold out (type 1 error) or hold out when he ought to concede (type 2 error). Critics of Western foreign policy say, in effect, that Great Britain made a type 1 error with Hitler and that the United States made a type 2 error with North Vietnam. Supporters of American policy say that Britain made a type 1 error with Hitler and that the United States dared not repeat it in Vietnam. Unfortunately, one cannot know the opponent's intent, and he usually won't tell. This "double edge of concession" (Cartter 1959: 122) is what makes negotiations so confoundedly tricky, and fear of a type 1 error is what makes negotiators so stubborn about seemingly trivial details. One also senses a mystique, under which a type 2 error somehow seems "safer" than a type 1, and wonders how many wars or divorces might have been avoided if the parties were not more afraid of type 1. As the reader may have guessed, this double edge can appear in transactions over goods as well as bads.

Threat as strategy

Stress was seen as a bad applied pretransactionally, after which the transaction about relieving it takes place. Threat reverses things. It starts with the transaction stage, which is accompanied by *A*'s "promise" that unless *B* does as he asks, *A* will do something nasty to him.

However, we have already said that all bargaining power resides in the ability to do something wanted. We can see that logic if we merely change the language. It is not the bad *A* threatens to apply that may bring a concession from *B*, but the promise, express or implied, that *A* will *not* carry out his threat if *B* concedes.

To clarify with a contrasting case, suppose I say to you, "Tell me the combination to the safe or I'll clobber you." In this transaction I will get the combination if you value unclobberedness more than withholding the combination. But suppose I say instead, "Your beady green eyes remind me of my uncle who used to beat me, so I'll clobber you anyway after you tell me the combination." My bargaining power now evaporates—not because I have withdrawn my threat, but because I have withdrawn my promise *not* to execute it. The bargaining is not over executing the threat, but over *not* executing it.

To hold power a threat must be credible. That is, *B* must be convinced that *A* is willing and able to execute it. But since *B* will presumably stop *A* from executing it if he can, *A*'s threat will not be credible if *B* believes he can prevent *A* from executing it. Hence *A* may display his weapons, flex his muscles, or clobber some third party to impress *B*. Furthermore, a threat may not be credible if *B* is sure that *A* will be worse off if he executes it than if he does not. A pistol against *B*'s head may not get a concession if *B* can confidently say, "You wouldn't shoot. I'm worth much more to you alive."

Not only must a threat be credible, but the *EP*s must overlap. "Give me a dime or I'll let the air out of your tires" may bring an overlap and a dime. But "Give me a thousand dollars or I'll let the air out of your tires" ordinarily would not.

If *B* does not respond to *A*'s threat, the transaction, strictly speaking, is finished. That is, there was a negotiation, which failed because the *EP*s did not overlap. *A* must then decide whether to execute his threat, the execution being a posttransactional, unilateral act by *A*. *A* cannot logically make this decision on the basis of the transaction just past, which ended in failure. The only reason to execute a threat is to make or keep the next threat credible. In weighing this decision the transaction that has failed is logically disregarded—a sunk cost. *A* must focus instead on such questions as when, about what, and to whom he is likely to make subsequent threats. If he does not expect to make future threats he has no reason to execute this one.

Union-management and international relations are two conspicuous cases in which the parties have continued contacts, and in which any one negotiation is almost certain to be followed by others. Hence in both areas the execution or nonexecution of a threat produces an inescapable impact on the credibility of future threats. The results are two. First, the parties may suffer a serious loss of "face" (which in this context means reduced credibility of subsequent threats) if they do not execute a threat that failed. Second, they recognize (if they understand these things) that they had better not make a threat unless (*a*) they are reasonably sure it will produce a satisfactory concession or (*b*) they are prepared to execute it. Thus if not handled with care, a threat may end by hurting the threatener more than the threatened.

We have mentioned only the bare beginnings of the possible complications, one of which is that the threat may generate hostility. If so, the threatener, *A*, must overcome not only *B*'s normal reluctance to give up *Y* but also the effect of the hostile shortening of *B*'s *EP* for *X*. All of which suggests that parents as well as nations can get into awkward positions if they are not careful about whom they threaten with what.

Instability of threat relationships. Continuing relationships built on threats tend to be unstable, for several reasons. First, each party may be unsure why the other is behaving as he does, or what he will do in response to a given move by his opponent. Second, a party who does not execute a threat from time to time may lose credibility. In international politics and union-management relations the temptation to get tough from time to time, just to convince the other party, sometimes leads to fights that are not worth it on their merits. As one author puts it (Hein, 1966: 39):

> The noble art of losing face
> May one day save the human race
> And turn into eternal merit
> What weaker minds would call disgrace.

The confoundedly difficult thing is that one cannot be sure the other party will reciprocate, or how serious the situation will be if he does not.

Perhaps the main instability in threat relationships is their tendency toward positive feedback if A's threat leads B to make a counterthreat. The arms race is a conspicuous case, in which nation A increases its armaments to make its threat posture credible, whereupon nation B increases its armaments to impress A, and so on. Many a divorce has resulted from escalating threats, as each partner responds with a larger counterthreat instead of conceding. With nations or marriages, giving in might often be sensible on its merits, but might seem to invite still bigger demands—in the appeasement effect. Uncertainty whether concession would end the problem or make it worse aggravates the instability. In friendships and marriages, escalating generosity is also possible, though it is hardly likely among nations.

Stress-threat combinations, and nonviolent bads

We have dealt with relatively pure cases of stress and threat. Several mixed cases deserve attention. For example, if I threaten to twist your arm and you do not give in, I could actually twist it and use the twist as a stress. However, I could not convert a threat to burn your house into a stress, since that is not relievable.

Second, merely to live under a continuing threat is stressful, and you might make concessions merely to get out from under it. Third, a stress may itself be an implicit threat. The mild stress of your knife gently resting against my chest is an implicit threat that you may push harder if I do not give in.

Our illustrations of bads have been confined thus far to pain, injury, or destruction—i.e., force or coercion—and to explicit transactions. But something need not involve force or be blatantly bad to be a bad, and the transaction could be implicit. To illustrate both conditions, if your neighbor's dog seems to get into your flower bed every time you turn your hi-fi above 80 decibels, but always stays tied up if you keep the volume down, you may suspect a strategic stress from your neighbor. Your suspicion is confirmed when you keep the volume down for a week and your roses go unmolested, while the next time you turn the decibels up, the dog reappears.

Among intimates a continuing mutual stress may be cleared by an explicit transaction: "OK, I'll stop squeezing the toothpaste in the middle if you stop banging the door when you come in late." Bads need not always represent hostility or transactional strategies, as when a parent punishes for the sake of the child.

The social disadvantages of bads

People generally feel that power based on bads is bad, and try to restrain it. We will try to spell out why, and will speak of such force as injury, pain, or destruction. We can summarize the most obvious points here.

a.   In contrast to transactions in goods, those in bads are normally negative sum "games." They reduce rather than increase total utility among the parties.

b.   Whereas a party's power based on goods is limited by his ability to produce, there is no similar limit to power based on bads.

c.   Power relations based on threats are highly unstable—as seen, and as amplified in Chapter 21. Power based on stress can also shift suddenly and dramatically, as when a prisoner snatches a gun from a careless guard.

d.   The results are often highly unpredictable. One may give his all if his life is threatened, or refuse to give a nickel.

e.   Bads can be highly destructive of health, comfort, security, and property.

f.   By virtue of e, bads can disastrously undercut motivation by depriving people of the assurance that they will enjoy the fruits of their labors.

g.   Since stress or threat can be imposed unilaterally by A, the fact of the transaction is not voluntary for B, even though he consents to the eventual terms (as we have defined "consent").

h.   Because at a very small cost A can destroy B's life, his health, or many years of his productive effort, the use of bads that produce such results will normally dwarf the value of goods. When used by only one side, bads bring highly one-sided transactions.

The last point is, of course, precisely why force is so attractive to some parties if they can get away with it. Given its high payoff for some but its severe disadvantages for others, we can expect any sensible society to limit such transactions.

* * *

The next chapter is also about transactions and we will summarize our discussion of transactions at that point.

11

VALUE-BASED INTERACTIONS: TRANSACTIONAL EXTENSIONS

The two preceding chapters introduced the transaction in its simplest form, and then added some modifications. The focus nevertheless remained on single transactions, unrelated to others. This chapter shifts to transactions that *are* related to other transactions.

MORE THAN TWO PARTIES

Our discussion of transactions thus far has dealt with only two parties, *A* and *B*. But many transactions involve more than two parties. Your relations with your father on some matter may hinge on your mother's position on it. Your relations with one used car salesman may depend on what you have been offered by another. Your relations with a potential robber will hinge on the presence or absence of a policeman. Though organizations, including governments, can also be parties to transactions, for convenience we will continue to talk only of persons.

We will not deal with transactions involving three or more persons, as such. Rather, among *A, B,* and *C* we will speak about the way in which one paired relation affects or is affected by another paired relation. For example, the interaction between *A* and *B* may be affected by a relation between *A* and *C, B* and *C,* or both. If *A* and *B* act jointly in dealing with *C,* we have a two-party relation between *A–B* and *C,* but one which is also subject to intraparty relations between *A* and *B.* We will discuss multiparty transactional relations under such headings as agents, competition, coalition, and collective bargaining.

Agents, and some dynamics of bargaining

Union members do not negotiate directly with their employer, but through union officers and a union negotiating team. Parties to a court action are normally represented by lawyers, children by parents, stockholders by a board of directors, citizens by legislators, and presidents by ambassadors. These representatives are *agents,* and the parties represented are *principals.* Long before Priscilla Mullins responded to John Alden's courtship speech on behalf of Myles Standish with, "Why don't you speak for yourself, John?" people knew that transactions conducted through agents might turn out differently than those conducted by the principals.

For one thing, since the agent is not the same person as his principal, he may differ from the principal in age, sex, race, creed, ability, stamina, or legal status. For another, even an agent who is very much like his principal may nevertheless have goals of his own, which may lead him to bargain better or worse than would the principal on his own behalf. We will designate A's agent as a and B's agent as b, and will illustrate a relation in which A and B are both represented by agents. The reader can contract this logic for the case in which only one party uses an agent, or extend it to multiple levels of agency—as when the company negotiator is an agent of the president, who is an agent of the board, who are agents of the stockholders.

A common case occurs between unions and management, with A the union membership, a their chief negotiator, B the company management, and b the chief company negotiator. The underlying relationship is between A and B, while a and b perform the actual negotiations. If a and b cannot make any agreement not authorized by A and B, respectively, we thus see a minimum of three relationships: A–a, a–b, and b–B, as in Figure 11–1.

Figure 11–1

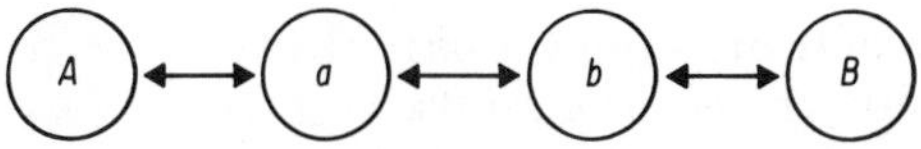

The total set of relations here can be very complicated, and we will examine only a few of its elements. A wants a to be a good negotiator, while a wants A to provide him with more pay and prestige. Concessions are wanted by a from b so that a will seem to A to be worth his salary. If a is an elected official in the union, large concessions from b will help assure his reelection. Similarly, b wants a to soften his demands and make concessions so that b will look good to B. B, of course, wants b to get concessions from a so as to save him (B) money. But these only start the complications. If we add arrows for all possible interactions among the four parties, instead of the previous three arrows we now have six, as in Figure 11–2.

A direct A–B relation would occur if the management polled the employees about their attitudes toward items being negotiated between a

Figure 11–2

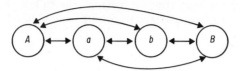

and b. An A–b interaction would occur if b had informal conversation with some union members in a bar. An off-the-cuff conversation between a and B might clarify the real problems on both sides, and facilitate a mutually acceptable settlement.

But all parties also have other relationships. One negotiator's wife may be skeptical that bargaining sessions really last till 5:00 A.M., and a concession that will get him home by midnight might help maintain domestic tranquillity. The company president may have heard that the Council of Economic Advisers urged a courageous stand against inflation, and take a harder line on wages. The children of a and b may attend the same school and be good friends.

Figure 11–3 adds only a few of these possible other connections. What is more, each of the four main "parties" is potentially an internally conflicting group rather than an individual.[1]

Agents may be more ruthless or more softhearted than their principals. The tycoon's agent may foreclose mortgages, bribe competitors, and use other raw power plays that his boss would not personally authorize, while the boss leaves the impression that he would rather not be asked.

Figure 11–3

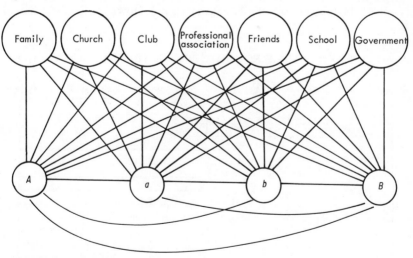

---

[1] Perhaps the most detailed analysis of the union-management relation, on which the above analysis leans, is Walton and McKersie (1965).

In reverse, the principal may instruct his agents to be tough. But the agents who see the misery they create may not follow through, and may perhaps return with fictionalized accounts of how hard they tried. They may also be lazy.

Competition

In everyday usage *competition* refers to a vague assortment of situations in which individuals have conflicting objectives. We will define it more precisely as a situation in which two or more parties seek to complete the same transaction, and in which success for one means failure for the other. If A and B both try to sell the same orphan an encyclopedia, marry the same girl, get elected to the same office, or win the same golf trophy, they are competitors.

In competition we remove assumption i of the original model, which specifies that neither party consider the possibility of dealing with someone else. We assume instead that A surveys the scene and tries to complete a transaction for a given good, Y, with that B from whom he can get the best terms. We will start with one A but multiple Bs, all competitors.

To illustrate, A is shopping for a particular model of new car, which several dealers (Bs) are offering. A's effective preference (EP) extends to $3,200, while those of the dealers range from $3,000 for B_1 to $3,400 for B_5, as shown in Figure 11–4.

It is clear at the outset that A must write off B_4 and B_5, since, competition or not, A would not pay their prices. A purchase from B_3 is possible, but only if better terms cannot be received from B_1 or B_2. Assuming that all the EPs shown for B_2 through B_5 are their final offers, and that A has learned them all, he will next examine his transaction with B_1. B_1 would accept $3,000, but is tentatively asking $3,150. However, since A has al-

Figure 11–4
DIAGRAM OF MULTIPLE BS COMPETING IN TRANSACTION WITH A
SINGLE A

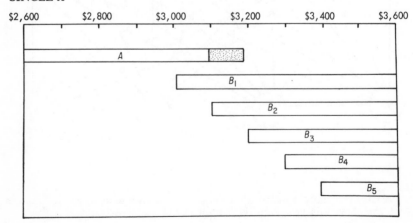

ready been offered a prize of $3,100 by B_2, he will not pay more than $3,100 to B_1. We can represent this by shortening A's EP to $3,100, as by subtracting the shaded area. The power factors now leave the terms indeterminate between $3,000 and $3,100, and the precise terms will depend on tactics.

This illustration shows two important principles of competitive transactions. First, in any transaction between A and B *the floor under A's bargaining power and the ceiling over B's is the best alternative available to A.*[2] In a parallel manner, the best alternative available to B is the floor under his bargaining power and the ceiling on A's.

If there are multiple As as well as multiple Bs, with every A aware of the price asked by every B and every B aware of the amount offered by every A, in due time things will shake down to a single price asked by all Bs and the *same* amount offered by all As. Since all have "agreed" on the same terms, we will call this a consensus by transaction. And since this kind of relationship among multiple buyers and sellers is known as a market, it can also be called a *market consensus.* In a market consensus multiple persons face the same overt alternatives, even if they have different subjective preferences.

Second, *the strongest competitor is the one with the least bargaining power.* To review, we have said that one's bargaining power varies inversely with his own EP. In Figure 11-4, B_1 is the B with the longest EP, hence the least bargaining power. Among all the Bs, he will accept objectively worse terms than any other B. But precisely because he will accept worse terms he is the B who will complete the transaction with A.

We have also said that one's plain power varies directly with his own EP. Hence we conclude that B_1 has the most power among all the Bs, since he has the longest EP. B_1 is the one who is the most likely to get the desired thing, A's money. For an understanding of competition the distinction between power, the ability to get something, and bargaining power, the ability to get it on good terms, is crucial.

These principles also apply to less obvious cases. The floor on the citizen's bargaining power in deciding whether to vote for candidate B_1 is the best alternative candidate, B_2. In choosing a marriage partner, the floor under Mary's bargaining power with John, and the ceiling on John's bargaining power with Mary, is the availability of Joe and what he can offer Mary. As to plain power, the B with the most intense desire for what A has will be the most likely to get it. He has the most power, even though he has the least bargaining power.

Competitive contests can be described with two simple modifications of this analysis, viewing the As as the competitors for the prize and B as the one who bestows it. The first modification is that the thing "given" in the contest—such as chess playing prowess, low golf scores, or beauty —are merely acknowledged or recognized by B, rather than literally "re-

---

[2] A floor under bargaining power is the same as a ceiling on the terms one can be induced to give. Either party's movement toward the other's baseline in the diagram represents his lowered bargaining power, and his "floor" is the point beyond which he cannot be pulled in that direction.

ceived" by him. The second modification is that the prize will be given to the competitor with the longest *EP,* without regard to *how* long it is. The "longest *EP"* means essentially the same as before—namely, the giving of the largest amount of the particular good in question. In such contests the length of the *EP* depends mainly on its effective component, which is usually skill, rather than its preference component.

Bargaining coalitions

A bargaining coalition is an agreement among two or more competitors that none will conclude a particular kind of transaction on terms less favorable than those agreed upon. In Figure 11–4, for example, B_1, B_2, and B_3 might agree that none would sell for less than $3,200. India and Bangladesh may agree that neither will release Pakistani prisoners until Pakistan recognizes Bangladesh's independence.

In Figure 11–4 it is clear why B_3 would want such a coalition. With it he stands an equal chance with B_1 and B_2, whereas without it he has no chance at all—assuming that A surveys the field. The payoff is mixed for B_1 and B_2. By joining the coalition, B_1, for example, forfeits a virtually assured sale at or slightly above $3,000 in return for a one-in-three chance of selling at $3,200. He undergoes a loss in plain power and a gain in bargaining power. We would need further information to tell whether he is helped or hurt by joining the coalition. If there were many As instead of just one, B_1 would have a choice between larger volume with a smaller return per unit (without the coalition) and smaller volume with a higher return per unit (with the coalition).

Stronger competitors are typically restive under a bargaining coalition, since it deprives them of an advantage they may have worked mightily to achieve—the ability to undersell the competition. Strong competitors sometimes flatly withdraw, make secret price concessions, or give superior quality or service. "Fair trade" legislation has helped bargaining coalitions to maintain prices, but has not fared well in the courts. Fair-trade prices are typically set at a level at which the weaker competitors (e.g., B_4 and B_5) could sell without a loss, since it is normally the weaker competitors who most actively support fair-trade pricing.

The bargaining coalition is all loss and no gain to A—unless we accept the tongue-in-cheek assertions of coalition members that they save A the trouble of shopping around!

The bargaining coalition as social control. Implicit or explicit coalitions are found widely. If mother would lend Sam her car in exchange for two hours' work, while father would insist on five, a coalition of parents could set the minimum at three, and Sam is stuck with it. A coalition of professors (e.g., a faculty vote) might set minimum amounts of work required for credit to prevent students from shopping around for "snap" courses. A coalition of customs inspectors might keep tourists from getting through a checkpoint for a tip smaller than $5, and a coalition of priests might prevent parishioners from getting forgiveness without repentance. Some societies establish broad coalitions, such as no food without work or no sex without marriage.

Since a shorter *EP* by *B* reduces both the plain and the bargaining power of *A*, a hostile shrinkage of *B*'s *EP* can exert pressure on *A*. If several *B*s feel hostile toward *A* and stick together they can make it very difficult for him. In fact, if the *EP*s of all *B*s shrink to the point where none overlap *A*s, *A* cannot get *Y* at all—if *Y* is something he cannot create for himself. If *A* is disapproved so widely that he is boycotted on virtually all his transactions, it will be almost impossible for him to live in the society. Although we will deal with this kind of social pressure in more detail in Chapter 17 we note in advance that hostility added to the bargaining coalition is a potent technique for keeping people in line.

Collective bargaining

Whereas a coalition is an agreement among competitors, collective bargaining is joint bargaining among multiple parties, *all* of whom transact with the same other party. Whereas under a coalition *A* completes the transaction with B_1 *or* B_2, etc., under collective bargaining *A* completes the transaction with B_1 *and* B_2, etc. The *B*s in a coalition are *substitutes* who compete with one another, whereas in collective bargaining they are *supplements* or *complements* to one another. The best-known example of collective bargaining is that between a union of employees and their employer.

Another difference between collective bargaining and coalitions is that the terms of the former are explicitly negotiated with and accepted by the other party. For example, a union negotiates with an employer and signs an agreement covering all its members. By contrast, in a coalition of oil companies to fix the price of gasoline the price is set unilaterally by sellers. Generally speaking, collective bargains are legal in the United States, while coalitions in the sale of goods are illegal.

OTHER INTERRELATIONS AMONG TRANSACTIONS

In this section we will note two additional ways in which transactions tend to affect one another. Transactions can be interrelated by connections between goods, connections between persons, or both. As to the former, in many cases one wants or is allowed a single unit of a good: one copy of a newspaper, one furnace, one passport, one spouse. To complete a transaction for one unit thus shortens to zero the *EP* for additional units. By contrast, if successive units show only slowly diminishing utility, the *EP* may be almost as long for the second unit as for the first. In addition, if two goods are *substitutes,* like pork and beef, to acquire one decreases the *EP* for the other. On the other hand, if the two are *complements,* like film and camera, to acquire one increases the *EP* for the other. In these and other ways the completion of one transaction affects the terms on which one will be willing to complete other transactions.

Transactions are also interrelated by connections between people. For example, an interesting story is a good. So is the attentive interest of other persons. The first time your roommate tells you about his exciting encounter with caribou in Canada, you reward him with rapt attention. The second time you are less attentive, and his beginning of the fifth repetition finds your *EP* so short that you boycott him with the excuse that the student health service wants to examine your ingrown toenails. In contrast to such diminishing returns, other persons may "grow" on you, so that each successive contact extends your *EP* for their company.

The above illustrations involve strategic changes from one transaction to the next—the *EP*s themselves are altered. There are also tactical changes as two people engage in successive interchanges. For example, in one transaction you may learn whether the other person is a tough or an easy bargainer, and whether he adamantly sticks to an initial position or later backs down great distances. You may also learn whether he typically takes an indifferent, a generous, or a hostile stance.

More important for continued intimate relationships, as two persons repeatedly deal with one another they come to know each other's likes, dislikes, and past histories, with several consequences. First, it becomes harder and less useful for either to use tactical misrepresentations as the other learns to spot them. The result is to reduce the time spent in jockeying for position, as the two "level" with one another and eliminate the "games." This result is not universal, however, and some couples reach their golden wedding anniversaries with their original bargaining postures intact.

Generally, however, as two persons come to state their positions more and more candidly they also come to trust each other. Each can do something generous in the confidence that the other will reciprocate. If not—well, nobody's counting. Even persons who never drop their guard show a certain kind of "reliability," which can serve as a partial equivalent of "trust."

One goal of planned group interactions, known variously as encounter groups, sensitivity groups, or T-groups, is to get people to drop their tactical bargaining postures and get on with their business, since such postures are often used where they perform no useful function. On the other hand, there is often sound sense in reticence until you know who can be trusted not to betray you. To the extent that trust develops, however, it greatly simplifies and facilitates transactions, and therefore is a tremendously important "tie that binds" a society together. It is integrative and cohesive.

Hierarchical sets

Like ideas and systems, transactions sometimes come in hierarchical sets, as in an agreement that two parties will enter into some continuing relationship with subrelationships within it. The top-level, continuing agreement will be called the *main* or *major* bargain, and lower-level agreements pursuant to it will be called *subsidiary* bargains. Contracts of employment, marriage vows, and international treaties are examples of explicit major bargains. At least when it is instituted, a constitution can be a major bargain between citizens and their government, a corporation charter a major bargain between stockholders and an enterprise, and bylaws the major bargain of a club.

Many important major bargains are implicit only. Although two people sometimes put into words an agreement that "we will be friends," the agreement is usually left implicit. Two superpowers, such as the United States and Russia, may develop a tacit understanding that neither will seriously undermine the power position of the other without the most severe provocation.

Any such major bargain entails subagreements to effectuate it, and these may or may not precede the major bargain. A marriage is a major bargain. A subagreement under it might determine whether the wife will take a full-time job. If she does, there may be a sub-subagreement about who will do the housework. At still lower levels relatively unique transactions can arise, such as "Will you do the clothes this week if I do the cooking?" These follow the general principles of power and bargaining power, and may or may not contain generous or hostile elements.

In a hierarchical arrangement of transactions the more strongly one values the continued relationship (i.e., the longer his EP for continuing the major bargain), the less his bargaining power will be in subsidiary transactions. For example, if the employee desperately needs his job but the employer could easily replace him, the employee has little bargaining power over details and the employer has much. Conversely, if the employee has unique skills and several good job offers elsewhere, the employee has high bargaining power over details and the employer little. Similarly, if a husband is highly dependent on his wife, whereas she is self-sufficient and would readily divorce him, her bargaining power on details will be high and his low. Regarding a commitment to peaceful settlements, the nation or person more willing to use violence or "make a scene" has the bargaining advantage in details.

A "shared" value is something that is the same for all members of some group, whether any particular individual wants it or not. If the living room is clean and orderly, and its windows are clean, they are that way for everyone in the family. On a larger scale unpolluted air and water are shared values, as is the continuance of a free society. As with the major bargain, those who have the greater desire for the shared value have lower bargaining power in the transactions necessary to achieve it, and will make more than their proportional contribution toward it. The one who most wants an orderly house may complain, but will probably do more picking up and straightening than those who don't care.

Those with the more intense desire to continue the major bargain or achieve the shared value are often characterized as the more "responsible." Perhaps an important reason for the frequent slowness of social improvement is the weak bargaining position of those who want it most.

POWER AND FREEDOM

We have defined A's interpersonal power as his ability to get Y from B. This he can do whenever there is an overlap of effective preferences. Another way to say it is that, regardless of where the two EPs touch or overlap, A has the power to get Y whenever the sum of the two EPs spans the whole length of the diagram, as in Figure 11–5.

This means that the longer B's EP the shorter A's can be and still give

Figure 11–5

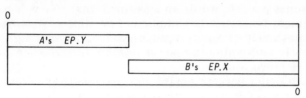

A enough power to get Y. Similarly the longer A's EP the shorter B's can be. Let us think for the moment of B's EP as his resistance to giving Y to X, in which case a long EP represents little resistance and a short one great resistance. If A wants to get Y he must overcome B's resistance by having an EP of his own long enough to meet B's EP. If B's EP extends all the way to the left of the diagram, there is no resistance to be overcome, and A can receive Y as a gift. If B's EP is zero, A cannot get Y by offering X. Either he cannot get it at all, or he will have to offer more than X in return for it. The resistance to getting Y is very large.

Note that it is the shortness, or relative absence, of B's EP that constitutes the resistance, not its length, or relative presence. This somewhat clumsy language can be made more convenient if we think of the absence of resistance as *freedom* (Russell 1940: 251). With this wording we can say that the greater B's EP the greater is A's freedom to get Y. If we also think of A's own EP as the strength of his "push" to get Y, we can then say that A's ability to get Y consists of of his push plus his freedom. If the sum of the two spans the distance, he has the power to get Y. Otherwise not. We can now join the two and say that the more push he has the less freedom he needs, and that the more freedom he has the less push he needs.[3]

In this context we can also think figuratively of nature as having an EP toward humans. If man is A and nature is B, then (at least when both people and pollution were scarce) nature's EP extended figuratively to A's EP of zero with respect to air and water. They were gifts of nature, free for the taking. For other necessities of life, particularly food, nature's EP is long in the tropics, moderate in the temperate zones, short at the edges of the Arctic zones, and virtually zero at the poles. This leads to the observation that the "free" in "freedom" is logically the same thing as the "free" in "free goods." Whether B is nature or another person, Y is free, and A has complete freedom to have it, if B has no costs to overcome in providing Y, and his (its) EP extends to A's EP of zero. It is thus easy to see why freedom is so popular. Under freedom one does not have to overcome much cost to get what he wants.

---

[3] If we had not already defined power to include the effect of *both* EPs we could formulate a more intuitively appealing version—the more power one has the less freedom he needs, and the more freedom he has the less power he needs. I considered redefining power to make the latter version possible, but found the analytical costs in other areas too high. The latter version nevertheless has a certain rule-of-thumb validity if one does not try to base detailed analysis on it.

Free things also have a certain egalitarian spirit. If something is free to everyone, no one demonstrates superiority by having it. Anyone who does not have it does not look inferior; he just doesn't want it. Relatedly, one person can have more without requiring anyone else to have less; he can rise without pushing someone else down. To be able to increase one's own satisfaction without reducing anyone else's is also an absence of conflict, by definition. Freedom is thus generous, egalitarian, and non-conflictual—a generally appealing situation.

But if the *EP*s all of us face are short, and present great resistance to our getting what we want, things are much less pleasant. Then only those with great push (long *EP*s) get what they want. This requires an intense desire, considerable resources, or both—the preference and effective aspects of *EP*. If much of the effective part of an *EP* is inherited, as with money or land, the long *EP* is likely to be resented by those who inherit less.

Legal prohibitions and restrictions are limitations on freedom, since they are forms of cost. To perform a prohibited act involves such additional costs as risking imprisonment, bribing officials, avoiding detection, or restricting what you can say to whom. Prohibited things are generally not unavailable; they are just more costly—less free. The so-called lack of freedom of a child or a colonial nation, incidentally, is really more a lack of power (Chapters 14 and 15).

Freedom and interpersonal costs

We often talk of *freedom from* and *freedom to*. Both involve allocations of costs and benefits among parties. Because I live in the country I can play my hi-fi late at night and bother no neighbors. But if I had near neighbors I would have *freedom to* receive the benefit of doing this only by imposing on them the cost of destroying their *freedom from* noise. A downstream town can have *freedom from* pollutants in its water only by denying the upstream town its *freedom to* pollute. One party has *freedom to* impose costs on a second only by destroying the other's *freedom from* those costs. A law that prohibits the upstream town from dumping sewage into the stream imposes the cost of a sewage treatment plant on that town while simultaneously relieving the downstream town of the cost of either polluted water or water treatment.

Many social conflicts and the attempts to deal with them by legislation are of this sort. The freedom of whites to discriminate long destroyed the freedom of blacks from discriminatory practices, and civil rights legislation since World War II has sought to provide blacks with freedom from discrimination by prohibiting the freedom of whites to discriminate. Without pretending to settle the thorny question of whether the unborn are "persons" or have rights, we can state that in most of the United States prior to to the Supreme Court decision of 1972 the freedom of the fetus to be born was protected by denying the mother's freedom to have an abortion. The court decision reversed the freedoms.

Although there is a general feeling that freedom is good, it is thus obvious that in many situations one person's freedom can be increased only by decreasing someone else's. Only in those cases where freedom for some can be increased without imposing additional costs on someone else—that is, without decreasing *their* freedom—is it an unalloyed good. The problem is also eased if the values of a society clearly consider one freedom more important than another, as in seeking to protect freedom from burglary at the expense of freedom to burglarize. Within the past three decades most Americans have concluded that freedom from discrimination is more worthy of protection than freedom to discriminate, though outside the legislative halls the dispute is not yet over.

The sense of freedom

We typically have a sense of increased freedom when the cost of something declines and of decreased freedom when it goes up, particularly in regard to things that do not have money prices. As a driver I have a sense of increased freedom when I find that a narrow, crooked highway has been replaced with a superhighway, or if the inspector waves me through customs when I had expected to wait an hour. In both cases my costs in time were less than anticipated. Reverse experiences would give me a sense of decreased freedom.

Once I am used to a particular situation I no longer think of it as a problem in freedom: it is the discrepancy between reality and expectation that elicits a sense of increased or decreased freedom. For me to spread my arms and fly to work like Superman would be quick, scenic, and low in fuel and maintenance costs. But I do not feel deprived of freedom without this technique, since I never seriously contemplated its possibility. Here, too, freedom is amenable to logical analysis.

SUMMARY AND COMMENT ON TRANSACTIONS

In connection with decisions we defined a good as any wanted thing, from affection to bridges and clean air. There are three ways to get goods. One is to produce what you want for yourself. A second is to produce what someone else wants and to give it to him in exchange for what you want. The third is to produce jointly with someone else. For things you cannot produce for yourself, such as affection and airline transportation, only the second and third methods will work.

Adaptive behavior is a process of achieving more-wanted rather than less-wanted conditions, which is another way of saying that it is a process of getting goods—always keeping in mind our very broad definition of "goods." In our first statement about power at the end of the chapters on decisions we introduced the first method—producing for oneself. In our discussion of the transaction we have presented the second method. We will later deal with the third, as organization.

The ability to get what one wants we have called power, intrapersonal for the first method and interpersonal for the second. Since social science is concerned with relationships among persons, we gave only passing mention to the first type of power but gave detailed attention to the second. Since most human wants must be satisfied directly or indirectly through others, power exercised by and through transactions is a crucial feature in any society.

To understand power we must distinguish (plain) power from bargaining power. The first involves the ability to *get* something valued from someone else; the second involves the *terms* on which it is gotten—how much must be given in return. Clear understanding requires us to separate the two, since, other things equal, the more you want something from someone else, the greater your power, but the less your bargaining power, will be. Of central importance, except for transactions involving generosity or bads, all power and bargaining power with others reside in being or having something wanted by them, and in being willing and able to give it in exchange. Even with bads, however, power and bargaining power grow from their positive side, the removal of the bad. And with gifts the giver presumably wants the gift to induce in the recipient some change that the giver desires.

Selfish-indifferent transactions are the norm for the many impersonal interactions of the workaday world, especially in large industrial societies. Generous transactions occur mainly in the close personal circle of family and friends and in small tribal societies. Although they are one-sided at the moment they occur they tend to even out over time, and under the "norm of reciprocity" there is a general expectation that in the long run each person will give in gifts and favors about as much as he receives. Thus whereas there is mutual contingency for each separate selfish-indifferent transaction, with generous transactions the mutual contingency is spread over a series of transactions and often is not very explicit. Because they reflect feelings and emotions, and have rough counterparts in the interactions of many animals, generous and hostile transactions are more "elemental" than selfish-indifferent ones, which require rational decisions at a level only humans are capable of. The larger and more complex the society the greater will be its use of selfish transactions relative to generous and hostile ones. Except through error the selfish transaction will always increase the satisfaction of the parties, or at least not reduce it. The generous one may increase it, decrease it, or leave it unchanged, depending on how well the parties estimate one another's desires. Hostile transactions are also unpredictable on this score, but transactions in bads will normally reduce net satisfaction.

Our analysis of transactions thus far has been "pure," in that it has paid attention solely to the valuational aspects of interactions. We will next look at the "pure" communication, which attends solely to the informational aspects, after which we will examine mixtures of communications and transactions.

As we shall see later (pages 350–52) in connection with markets, when numerous As and Bs competitively transact the same Xs and Ys, they tend to produce a single ratio of exchange of Xs and Ys. This "agreed" ratio constitutes a *market consensus,* or a *consensus by transaction.* This kind of consensus supplements and contrasts with the consensus by communication discussed below (page 174).

12

INFORMATION-BASED INTERACTIONS: COMMUNICATIONAL BASICS

Having completed our main discussion of transactions, we now move to communication. Communication is the second of the two basic interactions that make a society out of a multiplicity of persons, a supersystem out of a collection of otherwise separate systems. In parallel with our definition of transactions we define *communication* as (1) a transfer of information between parties or (2) any interaction between parties analyzed with respect to its information content. (For certain broader purposes one can substitute *pattern* for *information* and *systems* for *parties*.) In this chapter and the next we will focus largely on the nature of the communicational process, and we will reserve to later chapters the more strictly social causes and consequences of communication, including the many combinations of communications with transactions.

Let us return to your Chapter 9 encounter with the used car salesman. You discussed the price. You also discussed tires, rust, seats, and warning lights. Perhaps you also talked about insurance, title, license plates, test-driving, guarantee, and mode of payment. Although the central feature of the interaction was the transfer of car and money, it is impossible to imagine that the exchange could be made without some communication. Whether by talking, notes, sign language, third party, or some other technique, transfers of information are indispensable to virtually all human interactions.

To exchange *particular* information about this situation the two of you assembled the words of a common language into particular sentences. Although your ideas may have seemed pretty much your own, neither you nor the salesman invented the language or the car, building, lights, paving, check, money, title, receipt, insurance, gasoline, and numerous other things that entered directly or indirectly into the transaction. Without all those other things in the background you would have been as helpless as without language.

In this chapter we will examine how such patterns are transmitted, reserving for later chapters the question of where they came from originally.

CULTURE AS COMMUNICATION: THE CULTURAL PROCESS

The figure labeled R represents a plaster cast. We will be concerned only with the shape of its left side. Someone makes a plaster cast of it, the right side of which will look like L. A cast of L is then made, which looks like R: a cast of R is made, which looks like L; and so on. If the technique of making plaster casts were perfect, the thousandth R would be shaped exactly like the original. Similarly, if the copying process were

"Simpkins fell into the duplicating machine."

perfect, a photograph of a photograph of a photograph, or a Xerox of a Xerox of a Xerox, would be just like the original, no matter how many times the copying process was repeated.

If the total set of ideas of one generation were passed flawlessly to the next generation, which passed them flawlessly to the third, and so on, a thousand years later people would still have exactly the same set of ideas. We will call such a situation a "perfectly transmitted culture." Such perfect duplication is not actually possible for photographs, plaster casts, or Xeroxes, much less for human beings. For the moment, however, perfect reproduction is nevertheless a useful idea, since some *tradi-*

Figure 12–1

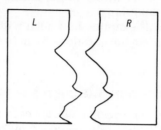

tional, or *closed,* societies change so slowly that the observer gets the impression of nearly perfect duplication.

This process has been stated very simply, because some specialists tend to give it a mystical aura. Whereas we say that each generation copies the patterns of its forebears, or that parents communicate patterns to their children, some are inclined to say that the patterns "reproduce themselves" or that the whole set of ideas thus transmitted has "a life of its own" (White 1949: Chap. 5). There is nothing wrong with such language if it does not obscure the communicational, pattern-duplicating nature of the process. This simplified statement does not prejudice the questions of *what* patterns are or ought to be transmitted, or *how* —both of which are of interest to contemporary education. Some additional interesting traits of patternness, as such, are discussed in connection with ecology and culture in Chapters 17 and 29.

Nonlinguistic transmissions

In discussing the transaction over the automobile we noted the many things directly or indirectly involved. And in Chapter 5 we noted that any overt activity is an external reproduction of an internal pattern. We can now put these things together into what is perhaps the most important single ingredient of human society, *communication,* which we will discuss at first without referring to such obvious forms of communication as speech and writing.

Suppose I have patterns in my head of a bow and arrow, and of how to use them. Suppose also that my son has never seen or heard of these things. While he watches me, I make a bow and some arrows, and shoot the arrows. If he watches and practices, he may be able by imitation to duplicate my actions. He may learn faster (or slower) if I also try to instruct him, but such instruction is irrelevant to our main point.

I started with certain patterns inside my head. I reproduced them externally, partly in the form of the muscular movements of shooting and partly in the form of objects, the bow and arrow. Once my inner patterns were thus reproduced, their external form could be observed by my son. In the philosopher's language, my private patterns were made public. In that overt form my son observed and imitated them, and he now has patterns in his head that correspond to mine. The evidence is that he now performs actions that correspond to mine. It is true, of course, that children may eventually come to question and dislike the patterns they learned from their elders. But they cannot even do that until they have first learned them. The likelihood that they will have the opportunity or ingenuity to develop their own independent patterns is a matter we will take up later.

This process goes on not only between parents and children, but between all who already have certain patterns and those who have not. It occurs when this year's batch of six-year-olds teaches games to next year's batch. It occurs among those who try to avoid the "straight" society, as when each new arrival in a hippie community learns patterns from those already there. It also occurs when successive generations observe and continue the patterns of governmental structures and voting, of going to symphonies or discotheques, of vacationing, of setting off fireworks on the Fourth of July, or of eating cattle and hogs but not horses and dogs.

The relationship is diagrammed in Figure 12–2. On the left we show individuals, and their inner patterns in the form of DSE states. The arrow that goes out from the top represents outputs of behavior. These are shown on the right as external things, labeled "The Content of Culture." In this "public" form they are observed, thus becoming inputs to

Figure 12–2
CULTURE AS COMMUNICATION

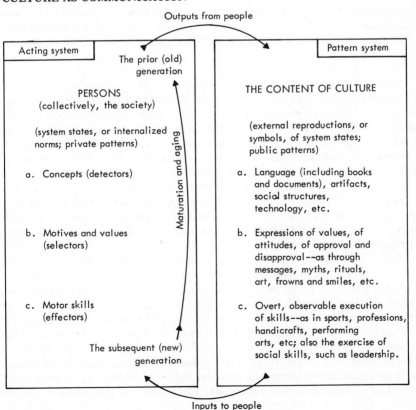

other individuals, as shown by the arrow at the bottom. The diagram shows the outputs going from the older generation and the inputs flowing to the new generation. An arrow inside the left-hand box indicates that each new generation gradually becomes the old one. A particular younger person may, of course, learn certain things before an older one, in which case the patterns might be passed "upward" instead of "downward." The main movement is necessarily downward, however, as the old generation dies and the new one is born.

Figure 12–2, it will be noted, includes more detail than Figure 12–1, but represents the same fundamental logic. Incidentally, the fact that L and R in Figure 12–1 show opposite contours is coincidental to the attempt to provide a simple, visual picture.

The notion of culture

The total of such transmitted patterns constitutes the *culture* of a people, and the process of transmitting a pattern from one person to another through the intervening external form constitutes a *communication*. Since a society would not need to transmit patterns if its members were born with them, we are interested only in the transmission of *learned* patterns. We are not interested in patterns learned by one person but never passed on to anyone else. We therefore define *culture* as *communicated, learned patterns.* Mack calls it shared, learned behavior (Mack 1969: 58). We are also interested for the most part in those patterns that are common to a whole society or a substantial part of it. But the process is the same for only two persons, and we therefore do not specify number of persons in the definition.

The patterns that are thus transmitted constitute the *body* or *content* of culture, and the transfer of those patterns from one generation to the next constitutes the *process* of culture. The process might also be thought of as one aspect of a *theory* of culture—that is, as an explanation of why each generation, despite variations, behaves for the most part like the generations that preceded it. Another important aspect of a theory of culture concerns where a culture comes from and how it changes over time. This is a problem in developmental change, which will be discussed mainly in Chapter 27. For those who like to view them that way, the body of culture can be thought of as the *stock* of patterns available to a given society, and the process of culture as the *flow* of those patterns through time and space.

Some parts of the body of culture spend most of their time, so to speak, in the internal form, especially in societies that use little or no writing. Folk songs are often passed from generation to generation without ever being written down. Those that are sung only at some annual festival are thus externalized only briefly once a year, and remain in internal form the rest of the year. Ditties used with children's games behave much the same way. By contrast, buildings, tools, social structures, works of art, and printed communications exist continuously in external form. In fact, artifacts of ancient peoples are often found after having existed thousands of years in external form only. The pattern of the neolithic ax you see in the museum has been transmitted from its maker's head to yours across many centuries during which it existed in no one's head.

Culture as symbols

The term *symbol* indicates the relation between an external pattern and an internal one. We will follow White (1949) in using it as a verb, but will expand his meaning from language to include all examples of the process. *To symbol* is thus a short way of describing the process of reproducing internal patterns externally, discussed in Chapter 6. (In this sense projective tests are techniques for interpreting symbols.) Used as a noun, a *symbol* is an external pattern thus produced in correspondence with an internal one.

The process of culture can now be redescribed by saying that one generation symbols (verb) its inner patterns, which symbols (noun) are observed by the next generation and become inner patterns in *it*. An internal pattern molds an external one, which then molds an internal one, which then molds an external one, and so on indefinitely.

CULTURE AND SOCIETY—PATTERN AND ACTING SYSTEMS

Figure 12–2 contains two boxes. The one at the left represents persons, and the one at the right represents external patterns. Both a person and a society of persons are acting systems. The patterns that constitute the body of culture are a pattern system. People *do* things. Patterns do not, but are things "done" by people. Patterns, however, like the structure of roads discussed in the opening of Chapter 1 and the DSE states of each individual, are the main determinants of *what* the acting system actually does.

We define a *society* as any group of people having the same body and process of culture. Since both the body and the process of culture are elements of communication, this is a communicational definition of society. By sharing the same body of culture, the people in a society have generally similar internalized system states, which they externalize in similar behavior.

To say that the members of a society share the same process of culture means that they are in communicational interaction. But since two or more interacting components constitute a new and higher level system, a society is an emergent supersystem relative to its members. We will deal with the pattern-transmission process here and with the content of culture later.

Our definition of society does not specify its size. Depending on the circumstances, as few as two and as many as the human race could be a society. We tend to think of a nation as a starting point, with subsocieties and sub-subsocieties, which have subcultures and sub-subcultures. Any set of people who tend to develop some degree of consensus by communication (Chapter 13) can be viewed and analyzed as a society, including a family, the employees in a department, sociologists, and the inhabitants of the Warsaw ghetto.

LANGUAGE AND CULTURE

Of all the patterns in a human culture, language is probably the most important. The ability to communicate by language depends on the large information capacity of man's brain. Language is certainly the most important trait distinguishing human beings from all other animals (White 1949), and as a society we would be helpless without it. We noted in connection with the purchase of the car that two distinct levels of ideas were transmitted. The first comprised the particular ideas that you and the car dealer exchanged, and the second the total set of cultural patterns among which you lived. The first type we will call *messages,* which are the particular patterns transmitted by language or other signs. But language is itself a part of cultural content as well as the means by which messages are purveyed. We will deal with this second aspect first.

Language as cultural content

As a child you are introduced to the word *cheese.* You learn the sound of the word when you hear it, and you learn to say it. You also taste cheese, smell it, see pictures of it, squeeze it, and throw it on the floor. From all these experiences you form a pattern in your head corresponding to the substance "cheese."

As you learn additional words you form a mental pattern corresponding to the object or event that each represents. For things you can experience directly and repeatedly for yourself, such as cheese, chair, mother, or running, your mental pattern is rather clear. For things you cannot experience directly, and for which your information comes solely through words or pictures, such as politics, patriotism, transcendentalism, osmosis, or social science, your mental image may be rather fuzzy. For each person there are many degrees of clarity of different patterns, and what is clear to one may be fuzzy to another. You may also learn wholly imaginary images associated with various words, such as goblin or unicorn.

A large proportion of the patterns within any given culture have names. Hence when you learn the meanings of words in a language you learn much of the content of the culture. Even if they have different languages, two similar cultures, such as those of the French and the English, have similar sets of patterns represented by different sets of words. Two very different cultures, such as those of the urban American and the Sioux Indian, not only have different words for some patterns they hold in common, such as horse or water, but also have many unshared patterns which are not directly translatable into each other's languages. The Sioux culture, for example, does not include such things as gin rummy, typewriter, or Benzedrine—at least it didn't till the Sioux picked them up from the surrounding society. The Sioux in turn have names for many concepts for which no terms exist in urban English. These concern such things as plants and animals, tribal behavior, utensils, weapons, and gods. We cannot name them in English because we have no terms for them, and we would not know the concepts merely by being told the Indian names.

The patterns of a culture can be learned in several ways. One is by simple observation, use, or imitation. Second, for those patterns that have names, which is probably most of them, the learning is reinforced when the words for the pattern are learned. Third is learning by messages, as when you are told that it is sinful to waste food, that you should always tell the whole truth but not be a tattletale, or that tides are caused by the gravitational pull of the moon. A pattern may be learned by one, two, or all three techniques, and most of us are unaware of how we learned any particular pattern. For patterns that are approved or disapproved, other members of the society may apply rewards and punishments (*sanctions*), to see that they are properly learned.

The transmission of culture is part of *pattern maintenance* in a society (Parsons 1966: 28–29), and is widely referred to as the *socialization*

"It is my wish that this be the most educated country in the world, and toward that end I hereby ordain that each and every one of my people be given a diploma."

Drawing by Handelsman; © 1972 The New Yorker Magazine, Inc.

process. The *group,* as the agent of transmission, helps keep the patterns uniform, as individual variations are averaged out and corrected by imitation. In addition, the whole of a culture ordinarily contains more patterns than any one individual or any few individuals can learn. A dozen or so persons in an interstellar spaceship, for example, would probably be grossly inadequate to transmit a large body of culture. If subgroups specialize—as is the case for priests, lawyers, rulers, artisans, and farmers—a given generation can encompass the totality of patterns and pass them on to the totality of the next generation. Hence with larger groups the patterns will change less rapidly and more patterns can be transmitted.

None of the above implies that we symbol inner patterns *in order to* pass them on. We produce them mainly for our own purposes, practical or mystical, and the fact that they are communicated is often unintentional. Once a pattern is internalized in an individual, he may symbol it any number of times, in much the same sense that a printing press can run off any number of copies from a page of type. In fact, whereas the pattern of type eventually becomes weaker with use, repetition strengthens and clarifies the pattern in a human brain.

An advantage of viewing culture as communication is to reveal its parallelism with the genetic transmission of biological traits. In genetic transmission one set of DNA material transfers its pattern more or less by contact to another set of matter. The second set transfers its pattern to a third set, and so on through the generations. This sequence parallels the successive transmission of cultural patterns by communication. The crucial difference is that genetically acquired patterns are inborn in the individual, whereas cultural patterns are learned. A Japanese infant brought up in a Spanish family may or may not continue to look Japanese, and his genes will not change one iota. But he will speak and behave like a Spaniard.

THE BASICS OF COMMUNICATION, AND OF MESSAGES

All knowledge and information that we are concerned about for a study of human societies takes the form of patterns in human heads, and communication is the process by which these patterns get from one head to another. Having examined the broad form of cultural transmission, we now move to the more explicit communications of messages. However, we will first examine some simpler forms of pattern transmission or transfer, which are communication in its broadest sense.

The basics of pattern transfer

The simplest form is pattern transfer by direct contact, as from plaster cast to plaster cast, or boot to bootprint. To use the language of communications theory, when the pattern of one thing, *A,* has been imposed on a second thing, *B,* we can say that *B* has been *modulated* by *A,* or that *B contains information* about *A.* Ripples on the water contain information about the presence of wind or a swishing fish. Light reflected from a building contains information about the building that was not in the light before it bounced off the building. An exposed film contains information about the scene in front of the camera. Vibrations in the air contain information about the slamming door.

The next simplest form is transfer by mediated contact. If A is the source, or starting point, of a pattern and B the ultimate receiver of it, in the mediated contact A imposes its pattern on M, a medium, which then imposes its pattern on B. Two steps of the pattern transfer described in connection with Figure 12–1 would be an example. A bootprint in the mud from which a plaster cast is made is another. In black-and-white photography the transfer of pattern—first from the scene to the negative, then from the negative to a positive print—is mediated. The principle allows many intervening steps, but a mediated transfer must have at least one.

Since as far as is known at present, it is not possible for one brain to put information into another brain by direct physical contact, all communication between humans is mediated. It seems convenient to divide a mediated communication into five steps, which we will state first in connection with simple physical contact—as with boot to mud to plaster cast. These five steps are:

1. The pattern exists in A.
2. The pattern is transferred from A to M.
3. M moves from A to B.
4. The pattern is transferred from M to B.
5. The pattern exists in B.

In simplified form we can talk of getting an idea from one person to another by spoken words by the same steps, as follows:

1. An idea (mental pattern) exists in A.
2. By speaking words that represent his idea, A transfers his mental pattern into patterns of sound waves in the air.
3. The sound waves travel from A to B.
4. The pattern of sound waves in the air is transferred into a pattern of vibrations in B's ear, which he is able to interpret.
5. The idea exists in B.

If the message is in writing, A's pattern is first put into visual patterns on paper, which are transmitted by light waves to B's eyes. Visual sign language, like that of the deaf, first becomes patterns of muscular movements that are transmitted by light. Tactile sign language, like that of persons both deaf *and* blind, is transmitted by patterns of pressure (touch).

Two complications must be added if we are to understand communication by language. One is that any communication between real human beings involves more than these five steps. Taken alone, this is a pure quantitative difference—like going through five doors instead of one. The second is that ideas transferred by words or other signs undergo a qualitative change. We will deal with the quantitative problem first.

Starting with an idea, A must first choose the words to convey his message, which at first are still in his head. The words next become patterns of nerve currents from his central cortex to the motor control centers of his brain. From there they become nerve currents to various muscles. After that they become patterns of muscular movements in diaphragm, tongue, larynx, jaw, and lips. Only then do they become patterns of airwaves, which are the medium that moves from A to B.

When heard by B the patterns become first a set of ear vibrations, then a set of nerve currents. Only after several more transformations do they end as patterns of recognized words in B. Having made clear that it actually takes A many steps to transform his idea into a pattern of airwaves, and B many steps to transform it back to an idea, we will henceforth ignore these processes inside A and B. The essentials still remain that A imposes a pattern on a medium, that the medium moves from A to B, and that the pattern is then transferred to B.

The qualitative difference is quite another matter. The transformations of pattern we have talked about thus far—from word pattern to nerve pattern, to muscle pattern, to airwave pattern, to ear pattern, and so on—are all "mechanical" in the broad sense. As in the transfer from finger to fingerprint or from reality to film, no question of *meaning* is involved. Despite inaccuracies there is a general one-to-one correspondence from step to step. For each detail of neural impulse there is a corresponding detail of muscle movement. For each detail of the finger there is a corresponding detail in the fingerprint, and so on. Such one-to-one correspondence is known as an *isomorphic* relation, or transformation.

The special problems of coded transfers

In Chapter 5 we differentiated sensation from perception. The former is characterized by a general one-to-one, or isomorphic, correspondence between the patterns of energy that impinge on the boundaries of the human system and the patterns of sensory nerves that are activated. But when perception occurs, a pattern already stored in the head is identified, after which thought and action are based on the stored pattern, not on the incoming sensations. Returning to the example of Chapter 5, I do not respond merely to the vague blob of light that I see in the dark, but to the whole of my mailbox, including the parts that are not even in my line of sight.

The relation between perception and linguistic communication is simple and fundamental. Once the concept of mailbox is stored in my head, it can be tapped by a wide variety of cues. These include a top view of the mailbox in full daylight, the vague blob of light reflected from its side in the darkness, its photograph, a simple line drawing—or the word *mailbox*. Once we understand the use of cues to identify stored patterns, the main thing we must do to understand language is to substitute verbal cues for perceptual ones. In Figure 5–1 we think of word patterns entering the senses, instead of patterns coming directly from objects in such forms as sound, light, or odor.

The steps of a linguistic communication between humans must reflect this distinction between (1) receipt of the sensations of the sounds of spoken words or the sight of written words and (2) the extraction of their meaning by identifying a stored pattern. The first step is *detection,* or simple isomorphic receipt of the sensory patterns. The second is *decoding,* since it selects or identifies the coded image already in the head, which is to be activated by the sensory patterns. The same distinction could be made (in reverse order) in the source of a message, in that he must (1) select the words and then (2) externalize them as sound waves. However, it is convenient to use the word *encoding* to include all steps involved in putting an idea into externalized words.

With a modest modification to reflect the preceding paragraph we now restate the steps of a coded, or linguistic, communication in the language of communications theory, emphasizing the key word at each step.

1. *Source* has the pattern
2. *Encoding* of the pattern into a medium
3. *Medium* moves the pattern to receiver
4. *Detection* of the pattern in the medium by the receiver
5. *Decoding* of detected pattern, which pattern is now in the head of the receiver

Although we do not need it for the above five-step sequence, the term *recoding* is available for any essentially isomorphic transformation of information. In electronic sound equipment the transformation from wiggly grooves in records to electrical impulses in the amplifier and then to sound waves in air are all recodings. The transformations of motor nerve currents into muscular actions, and of those muscular actions into sound waves, are also recodings, as is the detection of sound waves in the ear of a listener. We give the special names *encoding* and *detection* to the recodings at the output boundaries of the source and the input boundaries of the receiver, respectively.

Signs: Semantic and syntactic

We have noted that a verbal cue can substitute for a perceptual one. A verbal cue is called a *sign,* which is an external pattern, or symbol, used to represent and serve as a sufficient cue for some internal concept or image.

Most signs consist of a single word, such as *beet.* A single sign may consist of more than one word, as with *sugar beet.* In that case there is only a single image, but we happen not to have a single word for it. A sign may also consist of only part of a word, as when the *pre-* in *precolonial* has a meaning of its own just as clearly as if the separate word *before* had been used.

The image represented by a sign is called its *referent.* It is important to keep in mind that the referent of a sign is the image, or concept, in the head, of the sender or the receiver; it is *not* the definition as it appears in a dictionary. More important, it is *not* a piece of external reality. An understanding of language, of communication in general, and of some related philosophical problems can be abominably confused if we think of the referents of signs as anything except the stored images in human heads.

Linguistic signs are mostly arbitrary, as is illustrated if we note that *house, maison,* and *casa* all mean the same thing, with no cue at all in either the spoken or written form of the word that suggests its meaning. Onomatapoeic words, such as *whoosh,* are not wholly arbitrary, since the word sounds something like the image it represents. However, *wish* has much the same sound, but a different meaning. Some written forms of language are not wholly arbitrary, as in hieroglyphics, in that the written form is a simplified picture of the referent. To take a hypothetical case, ⌂ could stand for *house* and 𝘟 for *man.* But by the time such picture languages develop to a point where they can represent a wide variety of concepts, they too become highly arbitrary. Otherwise one could make fair sense out of Japanese or Chinese character writing without ever studying it.

Signs that have concepts or images as direct referents, like those above, are *semantic* signs. Some other signs deal only with communicative process, and make no sense at all except in connection with it. These are called *syntactic* signs, which indicate the relation among the semantic signs. The most common syntactic sign is word order, which makes a dramatic difference between "Lion eats Leon" and "Leon eats lion." Forms of words are also syntactic signs, as in the difference between "balls bounce" and "ball bounces," or between "eater" and "eaten." Punctuation and speed and tone of voice also perform syntactic functions, as in the difference between "crybaby" and "Cry, baby!" To sharpen the difference between semantic and syntactic signs, the image of "house" is valid and useful in its own right, whether or not the idea is ever communicated. But the idea of "comma" or "the" is nonsensical except as a device to help clarify a communication.

A set of semantic signs and their referents, along with the related syntactic signs and the rules for using them, constitute a *linguistic code* or language. Together they could be compiled into a dictionary plus a grammar—though strictly speaking the code is in the head, not on paper. We need not attend to transmission codes, such as Morse code or wigwag flag signals, since they are merely special ways of spelling out letters or words.

The message

Communication between humans is a transfer of pattern from one head to another, and a message is a particular communication couched in language. How is a message conveyed?

Suppose I say, "Cows eat grass." We will ignore that you already know what I am telling you, and examine whether you *could* learn something from this message if you did not already know it. We will also try to find out what you needed to know beforehand in order to understand my message.

Suppose I say instead, "Pids lun manders." Knowing English, you suspect that the three words are subject, verb, and object, in that order. But you do not know the meaning of any of the words (I hope), and hence have no idea what I am trying to say. However, your uncertainty helps identify what you need to know before you can understand my message. You must know the meaning of each word, and also recognize the syntactic signs that indicate the relations among the semantic ones. As to the latter, even if you get no meaning you nevertheless know that "Pids lun manders" means something different from "Manders lun pids." That may not seem like much. But if you did not know that much you also could not tell the difference between "Lion eats Leon" and "Leon eats lion."

To say that you know the meaning of each word is another way of saying that you have already formed mental patterns or images corresponding to "cows," "eat," and "grass."

Can a message consist of a single word? More strictly, can a pattern be transferred by one sign? No. Suppose I say "Cow." The pattern already stored in your head will presumably be activated, and you might start thinking about a cow lying under a tree or jumping over the moon. But the one word could not have started you thinking about cows if the pattern of cows were not already *in* your head. The word cannot *put* the pattern there. It can only activate a pattern that is already there. Hence we say that a single sign cannot constitute a message; it cannot transfer into a head a pattern that is not already there.

This is not to ignore the occasional usefulness of activating an existing pattern, like *danger*. But we will reserve that discussion till later, and look first at some additional aspects of communicating a new pattern by a message, and note how *communicating* a pattern is related to the process of *learning* a pattern.

Messages as intersections. We noted in Chapter 5 that knowledge (in this model) is hierarchically structured. From a given level of pattern, superpatterns may be developed by the abstraction of similarities, or subpatterns may be separated out by intersection. We noted that separating subpatterns by intersection proceeds rather rapidly, whereas abstracting superpatterns is relatively slow. Although much more study might be needed to discover whether this is always or necessarily so, it seems that in general messages consist of intersections. That is, they particularize, not generalize—though we must note carefully that this statement refers to the *technique* of transferring a pattern, not to its *content*.

Let us start with "cows eat." Following the logic of Chapter 5, out of all the possible aspects of cows we focus on only one—eating. Similarly, out of all the possible aspects of eating we focus on only one, that done by cows. We see the relation between these aspects in Figure 12–3. If you are the receiver of the message, the whole of your concept of cows, their nature and behavior, is included in the left-hand circle. And the whole of your concept of eating, of anything by anything, is included in the right-hand circle. The message that cows eat is a particular subpattern made by the intersection of the two concepts.

Figure 12–3

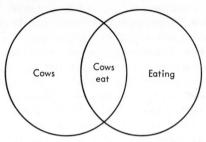

The three words of "cows eat grass" can be indicated similarly by three circles, as in Figure 12–4. Longer and more complex sentences do not change the logic, but they do complicate the problem of diagraming at a distressing rate.

To illustrate further from a recent newspaper item: "A Louisville, Ky., management consultant Tuesday went on record as opposing the miniskirt because it is detrimental to office efficiency." (The article failed to explain why the consultant did not instead oppose office efficiency on the ground that it is detrimental to enjoyment of miniskirts.) To begin with, Louisville, Ky., is a subset of towns named Louisville. A management consultant is a subset of all kinds of consultants, and "management consultant[s] from Louisville, Ky.," are further sub-subsets. Each additional word narrows the category by intersecting it with another category. Such a management consultant "going on record" is a subset of other management consultants, while going on record Tuesday is a further narrowing of all goings on record. A miniskirt is a subset of skirts, office efficiency is a subset of types of efficiency, and so on. There is probably no "correct" hierarchy of concepts in such a sentence, but the technique of linguistic communication is clear. In short, a linguistic message can inform someone of a pattern he does not already know if it is a new combination of concepts he already *does* know.

Since we cannot have a combination or intersection of one concept,

Figure 12–4

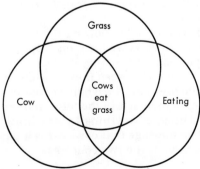

a message must contain at least two concepts, each represented by a semantic sign. And since it makes a difference *how* they are intersected ("Hit Jack" vs. "Jack hits"), we need at least one syntactic sign to identify that relationship. Hence the general conclusion that a message must contain at least three signs, two semantic and one syntactic.

The process logically parallels that of perception. If you are already familiar with green, plastic, and beach balls you can readily perceive a green plastic beach ball, even if none of the green things you ever saw before were plastic or beach balls, if none of the plastic you ever saw was green or a beach ball, and if none of the beach balls you ever saw were green or plastic. The main differences between this perception and the receipt of a verbal communication are (1) that in the latter the cues consist of words rather than visual sensations, and (2) that the words require a syntactic relation to clarify the relationship which the reality itself provides in the perception.

We can often reciprocally describe each of two things in terms of the other. For example: "A building is sort of a big box that people live or work in, made of durable materials that keep out wind and rain." Conversely: "A box is a sort of small, portable building without doors or windows, for putting things like shoes and candy in, and it doesn't have to be weatherproof." Given enough concepts, it may be possible to describe almost any of them as intersections of others. The result is not a single hierarchy, but a vast network of hierarchies of great flexibility.

If any particular message of, say, sentence length is communicated by intersections, how do we communicate abstractions? Here we are less sure of our ground and will speak more cautiously. Often it is obvious that we do not directly transmit the concept of a particular abstraction, but communicate the information that helps the receiver to make the abstraction for himself, as in "This is green; that is green; and that over there is green. Now do you know what green is?" For abstractions that are not directly observable, such as diminishing productivity, the usual technique is to try to state the idea in words, to follow the statement with examples, and to hope that the receiver will get the idea. Things are simplified because of the complex flexibility described in the previous paragraph. In one hierarchical structure "culture" is abstracted from the set of common properties of such diverse things as vases, automobiles, family structures, rituals, and attitudes—namely, that all were created by man and are transmitted. Yet once someone has made the abstraction, the idea itself can be communicated by intersecting "communicated," "learned," and "patterns," as in our definition in this chapter.

Named vs. unnamed concepts

A message identifies concepts that do not have names by intersecting concepts that do have names. Named concepts may have many real members, like tree or author; one member, like George Washington or the Renaissance; or no members, like centaur or elf. In general we give names to those concepts that more or less everybody knows and use messages for those *particular* pieces of information that some people know and want to communicate to others.

The service station manager instructs the mechanic: "Install new brake linings; check and, if necessary, repair and replace wheel cylinders, master cylinder, and brake lines; and bleed and refill brake fluid. Oh, and don't forget to check the brake drum and have it turned if it's scored." Once this set of details is standardized in the heads of both boss and mechanic it is given a name, "brake job." Thereafter those two words (which are only one sign) can be substituted for the previous forty, for a saving of 95 percent. A message is still required for a *particular* piece of information, as in "Do a brake job on that blue Ford."

The logic of adding or not adding a particular new term to the language would seem to be that of benefit versus cost. The benefit is the saving of time and effort. The main cost is that everyone involved must learn both the name and the whole concept (brake job), since the latter is no longer communicated in messages. There would probably also be many misunderstandings till everyone is familiar with the term, as illustrated by a case I ran into in remodeling. I asked my contractor to replace a flight of badly worn poplar stairs with oak. What I got was oak treads and fir plywood risers. Too late did I learn that to this contractor "oak stairs" meant oak treads only.

The larger the group the greater will be the cost of introducing a new term and the longer it will be until everyone knows it. Among family or friends a new term may be introduced in minutes and become "standard usage" within days. Hence the vocabulary of large societies tends to change slowly, though such mass communication media as radio and television speed the change.

Mixtures of messages and perceptions

In Chapter 5 we dealt with pure perception, in which none of the information comes from another person's brain. Just above we have dealt with pure messages, all of whose information comes from another head, and which require at least three signs. We next deal with mixtures. A shout of "Halt!" seems to violate the requirement of at least two semantic signs. However, "Halt" is not spoken in a flat voice by a stranger sitting across from you at lunch. It is shouted to marching men by the sergeant on the drill field. Not only do sergeant and rank and file soldier both perceive the same context, but each knows that the other also perceives it. This mutually recognized perception constitutes a second semantic element, or context, which intersects with the spoken word to produce a message.

If the context is not mutually clear, neither is the message. Suppose I am sitting at the table loudly munching celery, writing on a white tablecloth with indelible ink, and scuffing the wall by swinging my foot when my wife says, "Stop!" I have no idea which of my actions she has in mind, and it is obviously beyond reason to stop all three. Since the contextual half of the message is missing, I get no message. Context can be deliberately manipulated to provide nonlinguistic signs, as by putting a pained look on one's face while waving his thumb to say, "My thumb hurts."

Paul Revere seems to have received a message from his informant (a usually reliable source in a high post in Old North Church) by the use of only one sign. Actually the relevant messages were communicated in advance in the forms of "The British are coming by land" (one lantern) and "The British are coming by sea" (two lanterns). The only function of the lanterns was to activate a pattern already stored in Paul Revere's head. (Incidentally, the two lanterns were one sign, in the same sense that two dots in Morse code stand for *i*, not two *e*'s.) Even so, the sign appeared in a prearranged context. It was not just any old lantern on some wharf or in some Boston dive, but a lantern aloft in Old North Church.

As noted by Ashby (1958), even actuating a pattern that already exists in the receiver requires at least two possible signs, only one of which is transmitted. The two signs in Paul Revere's case were one light or two. They could also have been one or none, though none may provide low confidence. The absence of a light *might* have meant that the British were coming by land. But it might also have meant that the signaler had got soused in a local grogshop and never made it to the church. Incidentally, although things turned out all right, I sometimes marvel at the high confidence that the British *would* arrive. The local lookouts apparently did not think it necessary to anticipate such alternatives as "Relax, the British aren't coming at all" or "They've got ten thousand moles tunneling under the Charles River."

COMMUNICATION AND SOCIETY

In the three preceding chapters we dealt with transactions, which are interactions between humans analyzed with respect to their value content. We have now shifted to communicational interactions analyzed with respect to their information (or pattern) content. Transactions reflect and affect selector states; communications reflect and affect detector states. Importantly, none of the generalizations or principles about transactions were used in discussing communications, or vice versa. The two are different and independent sciences.

The broad kind of pattern communication from generation to generation that we call culture is essential for any society at or above the level of the apes, and perhaps for some below that level. Any one generation could learn for itself only a tiny fraction of the knowledge possessed by even a primitive civilization, and the kind of behavior we think of as "human" rather than "animal" reflects many thousands of years' accumulation and modification of communicated patterns. Humans also use language which is both the vehicle for particular messages and the vehicle that transmits much of the body of culture. While bowls and family structures may be communicated by observing them, many beliefs and concepts can be transferred only by language. In addition, language and the concepts represented in its vocabulary are important parts of the culture itself. Thus the linguistic code is both a vehicle for transmission and something that is itself transmitted.

Because most important concepts in any society have names, to learn the language and its semantic referents also means to learn much of the culture. Learning the language is thus an important part of the socialization process, by which the new member learns to conceptualize things the same way as do other members of the society. Learning the nonlinguistic patterns of the culture constitutes another important part of socialization.

All these things become system states of the individual—they are internalized. Since overt behavior is an outward manifestation of system states, and since the individual has acquired system states mainly from prior generations, his overt behavior must resemble theirs in many ways. The process does not rule out individuality or deviance. But except in extreme cases, even the obvious deviant follows many patterns of the main society, and may be very comformist within his own subsociety. And while he can be deviant about the way he values things, the things about which he has deviant values are mainly learned from his culture.

13

INFORMATION-BASED INTERACTIONS: NORMS AND OTHER PATTERN TRANSMISSIONS

In the preceding chapter we introduced the main concepts about communication, described how a pattern can be transmitted from one brain to another, and identified culture as an aspect of communication. In this chapter we look more at the social aspects of communication: who, mainly, transmits culture and what are the social causes and effects of communications? How does communication help hold a society together? We will also look at certain aspects of communication as an equilibrium, and close with some similarities and differences between communications and transactions.

SOME HOWS AND WHOS OF CULTURAL TRANSMISSION

The family as transmitter of culture

From the simplest to the most complex societies, the family is the basic transmitter of culture—though the family may vary from dozens of members, as in some tribal societies, to as few as two, as when there is only one child and one parent is missing. It is within the family that the child learns his preferences among foods, and how to eat them. Here he learns to stand, walk, sit, dress, sleep on bed or straw, keep warm, and bathe. Depending on the society, here is where the maturing child learns to cook, sew, hunt, grow crops or animals, weave, and perform scores of other skills. Most important, perhaps, it is mainly within the family that the child learns to talk, and therewith learns the vocabulary that represents much of the culture of the society, or at least that part of the culture that his family shares. For the most part it is also the family that molds his attitudes and broad values toward honesty, religion, work, learning, love and hate, family life, and nature. Even though the child may learn to like some things his parents dislike, and vice versa, for the most part and for most of the human race each individual learns to perceive and to value the world around him much as his parents do. However, this relation is much diluted in a cosmopolitan society with mass communication, such as present-day America.

If these things are deeply learned at home, they are usually carried over without much change through subsequent life. This effect is most important, and provides a cultural parallel to genetic inheritance, especially in slow-moving traditional societies. In genetic inheritance a person receives his genes from his parents. Although radiation or certain drugs or diseases might alter his genes, but rarely do, experience and learning cannot. With rare exceptions the adult therefore passes on to his children the same genetic patterns he received from his parents, regardless of what has happened during his own lifetime. There is thus continuity and stability in the patterns of biological inheritance, since the genes remain unchanged for many generations despite starvation, disease, or other adverse conditions.

In parallel, when cultural patterns learned during childhood are carried over unscathed through later life, they too are passed from one generation to the next unaffected by events that have taken place during the lifetime of the parents. We need not debate *how much* of childhood learning behaves this way, but merely note that *to the extent* that it does, cultural transmission can have an almost-genetic continuity. Since the family is the major transmitter of culture to the child, it thus maintains cultural stability across many generations—though other agencies for training the young could have the same effect. By the same token, cultural change could be effected most rapidly if such agencies take over training of the young. Given the persistence of patterns learned in early childhood, the family is a fundamentally conservative force. Hence revolutionaries see it as the link they must break if they are to create a different society.

To the extent that television-as-baby-sitter has already broken the parent-child link in cultural transmission it has become a major cultural factor in its own right. It is probably a significant factor in the "generation gap," though by no means the only one. It is easy to note this change in cultural process but hard to know what change in content it has brought.

If a person marries someone with cultural patterns very different from his own, or if later experiences alter his patterns substantially, the pattern is modified before transmission. However, through most of human history relatively unchanged transmission from one generation to the next has been the usual situation.

The church, the school, and other agencies

Church and school are potent transmitters of culture. Despite marked differences around the world, organized religion typically deals with two things. One is the nature and origins of the universe and of man, with or without god or gods as part of the explanation. The second is man's behaviors and attitudes—the moral or ethical aspect which identifies behaviors as right or wrong. The influence of the church is probably secondary to that of the family, in the following sense. Even if a child is in close contact with the church, the degree to which he accepts it will probably depend on his family. If the parents accept some church teachings and disregard others, the child will probably do the same.

The general formal function of the school is to transmit specialized skills that the family is not equipped to teach. It deals relatively more with detector than selector functions, and hence is less potent than the family in molding goals and attitudes. Further, it typically does not meet the child till after many basic attitudes have been well formed. However, the peer groups (informal and semiformal organization) within schools are potent transmitters of values and attitudes—as toward drugs and sex in recent years.

Whereas most people become parents, relatively few become teachers. Furthermore, much of what teachers teach they themselves learned outside the home. The school is thus more open than the family to new ideas, despite a continuity of its own due partly to societal pressures. For example, many parents are upset if they learn that a history course has stopped teaching about George Washington and the Cherry Tree. The reason, of course, is that they do not really want schools to teach the "truth," but rather to produce duplicates of themselves, by repeating the same folklore *they* learned.

The cultural transmission process is also assisted by other organizations, such as unions, chambers of commerce, and trade business, and professional associations. Their influence is usually more limited and specialized.

Rituals, myths, folklore and folk wisdom, and media

In the preceding chapter we described the two main forms of pattern transmission as (1) the observation and imitation of symboled inner patterns and (2) messages couched in language. Rituals typically combine the two. External symbols include such things as totems and statues, body motions (dances, salutes, bowing, marching), flags, and sounds (tom-toms, martial and religious music, firecrackers, shouts, and songs). Messages in language include religious liturgy and sermons, patriotic speeches, pledges of allegiance and solidarity, prayers, and blessings to the faithful and curses to the unfaithful. Rituals are useful in transmitting a sense of solidarity under circumstances in which logic or enlightened self-interest might not command it.

Myths and folklore, including songs and poems, bolster confidence and pride in the society and enhance the egos of its members, usually by depicting its wise, heroic, and possibly divine origins. Myths and folklore typically suggest that the people and the culture are special or superior. A frequent theme recounts how the group won its freedom from prior subservience to some (supposedly) morally or intellectually inferior oppressors—as the Jews from Egyptian bondage, the American colonials from British tyranny, or the blacks from American slaveholders and discriminatory whites. If it is premature for the folklore to describe how the people *did* win their freedom, it may describe how they *will,* as in "We Shall Overcome." It is essentially irrelevant to its function whether this folklore is true or imaginary, so long as it provides a sense of identity, superiority, power, unity, and importance.

Folk wisdom provides verbalizations that enable one to dispose of troublesome problems, whether or not he has any assured evidence in the case ("God will make everything right"), whether or not the sayings are applicable to the case at hand ("Everything that goes up must come down, so prices will come down someday"), and even if two pieces of the folk wisdom conflict ("Out of sight out of mind" versus "Absence makes the heart grow fonder").

In addition to communicating particular messages, the mass media in an advanced society hold the society together by simultaneously putting a common set of images into a large number of heads. Not only do many people become aware of the same things; they also have a mutual awareness of that awareness. This is a powerful glue in holding a society together. The media can also help disintegrate a society if they focus on conflict, confrontation, and differences.

Collections of art and artifacts in a museum perform the same sort of function for those who view them. In the performing arts, such as dance, music, and the theater, everyone is directly aware that everyone else in the audience is simultaneously receiving the same message, which is thereby magnified in effect. What is more, if others laugh or cry when you do, you are confirmed in your interpretation of what you are seeing. Although without the explicit interaction of the theater, the viewer of television also knows that thousands or millions of others are simultaneously receiving the same inputs, in what McLuhan calls the "retribalizing" of society.

To summarize this section, cultural transmission does two important things. One is to transmit patterns throughout a society and from one generation to the next. The second is to create a mutual awareness among a people that others share the same patterns. The two together are highly cohesive.

THE ACCURACY OF COMMUNICATION
(as prelude to viewing its consequences)

In Chapter 5 we noted that any real object or event is incredibly complex. We can perceive only those aspects of it for which we have formed inner images, which are gross simplifications of reality. Although by careful observation we can add detail and rigor to our images, all perceptions are in some degree false. Many are nevertheless quite good enough to enable us to navigate successfully through our environment.

Much the same can be said of communications, with a notable exception. To dispose of the exception first, certain communications are devoid of real content. They are essentially syntactic only, not semantic, in that their signs have no real referents. Mathematics and formal logic are examples, as in "$a = x + y$" and "A implies B; B implies C; therefore A implies C." In a certain sense such "statements" are completely accurate. Incidentally, we must not confuse accuracy of communication with truth. A message can be accurately transferred even if wholly false. "The car wasn't damaged at all" is perfectly clear as a communication, even if the car is a total wreck.

To move from the exceptions to the main cases, we can now spell out the conditions for accurate communication for each step of pattern transfer.

1. *Source:* A clear image of the pattern to be transmitted exists in the head of the source.
2. *Encoding:* The pattern is accurately encoded into words.
3. *Medium:* The sounds, or written form, of the words are transmitted accurately to the receiver.
4. *Detecting:* The receiver accurately detects all the sounds or written forms, and extracts from them the same words as were transmitted.
5. *Decoding:* The detected words select the proper channels, or tap the proper existing concepts, in the receiver.

Some technical aspects

The third step above is essentially technical, and errors are remediable in principle, as by having the source speak louder or write more legibly, or by developing better telephone or mail service. Furthermore, ordinary language has much redundancy, and unless there is very bad transmission the excess information will fill gaps and correct errors. For example, if a typing error spells "wind,w," you can have no difficulty substituting an *o* for the comma. If a noise blanks out the missing sounds in "I had cof . . . . fast this morning," there is enough contextual redundancy for you to fill in "-fee for break-." By contrast, there is no such redundancy in numbers. If I type in error, "Paul lives at 8,3 Surrey Road," the message itself contains no excess information that will identify the number that belongs in the place of the comma.

If detection is faulty at step 4, it may be remedied by more careful reading or listening. As to encoding at step 2 and decoding at step 5 some persons are skillful and others are not. All we can recommend is increased competence.

Differences in codes

One detail dominates all others as a contributor to faulty communication. This is the question of whether the words of a message mean the same to the source as to the receiver. Do A and B have the same code—the same list of signs and referents?

The signs give little trouble. They are public and observable, like the shape or sound of "hypochondriac." The problem is with the referents. These are the images in people's heads, not the definitions in the diction-

ary. They are private—observable only to the person who owns them.
What is more, no concept is the same in the heads of any two people, since
to each person the concept is the product of his own experience. Hence
no two persons have identical referents for any word, and no pattern can
be transferred precisely from one head to another. This is the communicational parallel of the statement that no perception can be precisely
accurate, with the addition that we must now consider two persons instead of one.

There is also a communicational parallel for our earlier statement
that many perceptions are nevertheless quite good enough for the purpose at hand. Suppose I say, "Would you throw down my gloves from the
top of my bureau?" Now the gloves may be more jettisoned than thrown,
they may travel farther than I had anticipated, and the act may take 20
seconds instead of my intuitively anticipated 10. The response nevertheless falls well within my notion of what I intended, which is to say that
the communication was accurate enough for the purpose—and that is all
we need or expect. If the above words suggest annoyance on my part, the
annoyance was toward the attitude or aim of the receiver of my message.
The explicit content of the message was obviously understood.

To take a more ambiguous case, suppose Jack says to you, "Joe spent
a week in Paris last spring." Insofar as this means merely that Joe was
in Paris, not selling bicycle pumps back home in Teaneck, the communication means the same to you as to Jack. But suppose that to Jack "Paris"
means nightclubs and wild wenches, while to you it means museums and
cathedrals. If so, "week in Paris" triggers different images in you than
exist in the source. At that level the message becomes highly inaccurate.

It is common to distinguish the denotative meaning of a word or message from its connotative meaning. The general assumption is that the
denotative meaning is that which refers to some mutually observable
external, which is public information. The connotative meaning, by contrast, conjures up many mental associations that are individual and private. Such a distinction, unfortunately, will not hold up under scrutiny,
since there does not, in fact, exist any truly common denotative meaning
of any word. There exists a "true, denotative meaning" only under the
same circumstances and to the same extent that we can say that a communication is accurate enough for the purpose at hand. Hence we will
use only the latter kind of wording to describe the problem.

A common difficulty with gossip arises when the receiver of an ambiguous message repeats it to a third party. Typically he does not repeat the
words, but redescribes the image *he* received, in different language. Suppose that you and Jack have the respective images of Paris described
above, but we now reverse the sender and receiver of the message. You
say, "Joe spent a week in Paris," knowing that paintings and cathedrals
occupied his time. Jack's image on hearing the message, however, is Joe's
week with a bevy of wanton women. Jack's restatement to Valerie is, "I
hear Joe spent a real wild week in Paris." What Valerie later says to
Veronica we will leave to the reader. The point is not that people are
dishonest or malign when they do things like this, but merely that com-

munication is distorted whenever the image referents of words differ markedly in sender and receiver.

Sometimes the images are so different that a message is more confusing than no communication at all. "Students want change." To one hearer these words evoke images of beaded, bearded, barefoot, bug-eyed youths of uncertain sex, financed from Moscow, Peking, and Havana, planting bombs under science buildings, and wanting to poison water supplies with fluorides. To another the image is one of crew-cut, business-suited boys and demure girls sitting around a table politely discussing ways to improve the Junior Chamber of Commerce. Little wonder there is so much "failure to communicate" and so much complaint that "they don't understand, even though we really try to tell them."

All of this does not mean that reasonably accurate communication is not possible. It does mean, however, that persons with such discrepant images may require hours, weeks, or even years of patient discussion until their images converge reasonably well. However, if their self-images are threatened or their minds are otherwise closed, even years may bring no significant change. In fact the differences may harden.

It should now be clear why we say that interactions both reflect and affect system states. An encoded message is an outer reproduction that reflects the source's detector state, and the decoded message affects the receiver's detector state—at least if it contains new information. An inaccurate message does not leave the the receiver's detector unaffected. It merely affects it in ways not in line with the image in the source.

The quantification of information

It is sometimes useful to measure quantity of information. The most common unit of measure is the *bit,* a shortened term for *binary digit,* which is the amount of information required to make an unequivocal selection between two equally probable alternatives. For example, assume that the only two possible answers in a given case are yes and no. Then *yes* selects one answer and rejects the other, and is said to contain or to constitute one bit of information. A similar selection between on and off, black and white, open and closed, or left and right also constitutes one bit. The game of Twenty Questions involves an attempt to identify some person with twenty bits of information—i.e., with twenty successive yes-or-no answers.

One bit of information is also said to halve doubt. If you must select one item from among eight, these could be arranged in a row:

A B C D E F G H

You ask, "Is it in the right half or the left half of the row?" I reply, "Left." You then know that the correct answer is A, B, C, or D, not E, F, G, or H. You then divide the left half in two, and ask, "Is it in the right or the left half?" I indicate the right. You now know that it is C or D, not A or B. You then divide *that* segment in two and repeat your question. I say, "Right," and thereby unequivocally identify that the item is D, not C. We thus say that unequivocally to identify or select one item from among eight equally probable ones requires three bits of information—that is, three successive selections between two alternatives.

The number of bits can also be stated as the power to which 2 must be raised in order to equal the number of items in the list. For example, it requires 5 bits of information to select one item from among 32, as reflected in $2^5 = 32$. The number of bits of information per sign can be expressed as $log_2.N$, where N is the number of signs in the list (vocabulary or code). If we let n represent the number of signs in a message, the number of bits of information in the whole message is then $n.log_2.N$.[1]

It is now possible to make precise counts of the information content of messages in their external stages, and in the neural transmission of their internal stages. We can count the number of bits per letter or per word of a message, or in the activation or nonactivation of neurons. To quantify information in a digital computer is simple and basic, as all information in it is processed as an on-or-off state of some circuit.

By contrast, there is no way to quantify the amount of information contained in the referent of a given sign. To illustrate, it requires only one bit of information to distinguish A from B. But A and B may be coded letters for two complex plans of action, each of which requires a thousand pages to spell out. "Astronomy" is only one sign. But to the astronomer its meaning—i.e., its referent—is a vast amount of detailed knowledge. Thus, although the information theorist can count the bits in the *signs* of a message, no one can measure the quantity of *meaning* represented by a sign. For those who care to express it that way, we can quantify the isomorphically transformable stages of pattern transmission. It is important to know that some aspects of communication can be quantified and that others cannot.

ISOMORPHIC TRANSFER OF PATTERN

By permission of John Hart and Field Enterprises Inc.

---

[1] This brief statement is accurate so far as it goes. Bit counts are introduced here to indicate that there *is* such a thing as precise measurement of some aspects of communication, mainly as a foil for clarifying the aspects which are not quantifiable.

SOME SOCIAL ASPECTS AND CONSEQUENCES
OF COMMUNICATION

Mutual contingency and social interaction

We have seen in Chapter 9 that a transaction involves two mutually contingent decisions. We have discussed communication thus far without raising the question of contingency, which can be defined by saying that an action of A is *contingent* on B if it is designed or modified to affect B, or A's relation to B. Since the effect to be produced is still in the future, only expected future states or actions of B, not past ones, are relevant to contingency. As with decisions, the past influences the base from which a present action is taken. But the past cannot itself be influenced by the present action.

CONTINGENCY

By permission of John Hart and Field Enterprises Inc.

If I observe a caveman's stone ax in a museum, a pattern has been transferred from his head to mine via its externalized form. But he certainly did not form the ax with the intent of having an effect on me. Nor do I observe it with the intent of having an effect on him. This transfer of pattern from him to me therefore involves no contingency. We therefore say that, although this relation fulfills the definition of communication, and hence of interaction, it is not a *social interaction*, which we define as an interaction involving mutual contingency.

A normal conversation involves mutual contingency. My talking is contingent on your listening, which is contingent on your expectation of responding. Even if you only pretend to listen so as not to offend me, the pretense is a form of contingency.

Written communication between far-removed individuals is often not contingent. I have read Plato's *Republic*. But when he wrote it he had no intent of affecting me, personally, and in reading it I certainly have no expectation of affecting him. (Any reader inclined to say "But your reading of Plato is certainly contingent on the fact that he wrote" had better review our definition of "contingency.") Messages broadcast to some undefined audience, as by radio or billboards, and without expectation of specific answers, involve a partial one-sided contingency. The sending of such messages is contingent on the expectation that someone will receive it, but the behavior of the receiver is not contingent on his expectation of affecting the sender. We need not explore all possible variations so long as the basic meaning of "contingency" is clear.

Contingency is related to feedback, or the response to a message, which indicates whether or not the message was received and understood. If the gloves come flying down the stairs, I know my message got through. On the other hand the response "There aren't any bulbs on your bureau" indicates a partly inaccurate communication. Absence of response can constitute feedback of sorts, even if ambiguous. It might mean either that the message was not received or that the recipient did not care to respond.

The direct effects of messages

A communication, according to Ackoff (1960), can be used to inform, to motivate, or to instruct. In our present language, it can affect detector, selector, or effector, respectively, of the receiver.

The communication may be nonlinguistic, like the imitative copying of a bowl or the arousal of emotions in witnessing a ritual dance. In such cases the recipient may reproduce detector, selector, or effector patterns relatively directly from the source.

However, if the communication is a linguistic message it *must* initially be a transmission of information. "There's free beer at the student union tonight" will motivate behavior. But it must first communicate the image, by being correctly detected and decoded. Similarly, "Push down the clutch pedal before shifting into low" must be understood as information before it can be executed as instruction. Any portion of activity that is subject to verbal instruction is executed under the direction of the detector, not by effector-contained skills alone. This is the communicational parallel of that kind of behavior described in Chapter 6 as being guided by perceptions. As in many other respects, receipt of a message can be viewed here as a perception decoded from verbal instead of from direct sensory cues.

Consensus by communication—and collective concept formation

Chapter 11 noted the process of achieving consensus by transaction. Since transactions are interactions based on valuations, which are selector functions, consensus by transaction brings a set of common valuations, reflected in a common set of ratios of exchange of valued things among some set of interacting parties. A different kind of consensus can be achieved by communication. Since communications are informational interactions, which are detector functions, a consensus achieved by communication brings a common set of conceptual patterns, at least at first. But since a communication can indirectly affect selector and effector it can also bring similarities of values and skills. We will deal first with similarities of concepts.

The process is that of Chapter 6 extended to multiple persons. There we observed that a person can symbol an inner pattern externally, as by making a rough sketch of his plans for a house. Because either his sketch or his ideas are rough, the sketch does not match his initial image. By observing the sketch, he refines his image, whereupon he is able to make a revised sketch. From this he further revises his image, from which he makes an improved sketch, and so on.

Let us return to you, Jack, and Paris. Both of you have been there, and had experiences that led to the different images described earlier. For convenience we will call these saint and sinner views, respectively (without implied aspersions on either of you). To sharpen the illustration, we also assume that neither of you knows much about Paris except what you learned from your own experiences. Starting with these very different images, you get together and talk.

At first you think you must be talking about different cities, as he describes the hot spots of the sinners and you describe the colder ones of the saints. But as you talk, his image is gradually modified by yours and yours by his. Given enough time and talk, your previously very different images will become more similar. For this purpose it does not matter whether either image is accurate; the two are more nearly alike. The process of achieving this similarity between two or more views by communicating observations is what we mean by *collective concept formation,* or *conceptual consensus by communication.*

In a much more formal way scientists do the same thing. Each makes certain observations and reports them to other scientists, while the group try among them to fill in gaps in the total set of images. The result is an enlarged body of conceptual consensus. Disagreement often looks greater than it actually is, because scientific journals give little space to things on which scientists agree. Those things go into the textbooks.

Most communicational consensus lies between the type done informally by two people and the type done formally by scientists. It is done informally, but by essentially the whole of a society or subsociety instead of by pairs, and is an important part of the cultural process. Other things equal, the collectively formed concept would tend to be more accurate than concepts formed by individuals ones for the same kind of reason that the average of a dozen measurements of the length of a room should be more accurate than a single measurement. Other things often are not equal, however, and the consensus may perpetuate systematic biases.

Consensus as equilibrium.   Consensus by communication can be viewed as an equilibrium process. We have just seen that between you and Jack, the more you communicated the more similar became your concepts of Paris—and the same kind of result can normally be expected of almost any continuing communications. We have already noted in connection with accuracy of communication that the more similar your concepts the more accurate will be your subsequent communication. We have now added that the more accurate and adequate your communication the more similar will your concepts become. If more accurate communication increases the similarity of your concepts, and the increased similarity of your concepts increases the accuracy of your communications, we have a positive feedback relation between the two ingredients. Its obvious equilibrium limit is reached when the concepts are identical and communication is completely accurate—though for reasons stated earlier complete identity and accuracy will probably not be reached.

Parallel statements can be made without referring to accuracy: The more people communicate the more similar become their conceptual sets (codes) and the more similar their conceptual sets the more they communicate. Again, the potential equilibrium is at identity, even if it is impossible to reach.

Consensus and norms. Since communication can have effects on detector, selector, and effector, the process of culture (which is communicational) produces increased similarity of concepts, values, and behaviors among any group who interact regularly. Sociologists call these similarities *norms,* which are brought about by the *normative process.* The normative process is basically communicational, but is strongly assisted by transactional sanctions (Chapter 14).

"Norm" refers to a kind of behavior or belief that is expected, right, or proper, and that society tends to enforce. But in addition uniformity has certain benefits and costs of its own, as follows.

Social benefits of norms

Tension and frustration reduction. In Chapter 4 we spoke of frustration and tension as pattern mismatch. In many ways such mismatch is reduced or avoided if people hold similar patterns. An important result is that one can often predict the behavior of others, because (given similarity) it is the same as one's own. If you extend your hand following an introduction you can be confident that the other person will shake it, not slap you or scream.

Despite the many frustrations that nevertheless occur, they are far fewer and life is much smoother under reliable normative behavior than it would otherwise be. Incidentally, we have talked as if we expected uniformity across a whole population, whereas some behavior may actually be expected only within a given role (Chapters 15 and 16). Thus you can go to a barbershop confident that the man with the razor and shears will cut your hair, not your clothes or your throat. This fact adds to the number of patterns to be learned, but does not detract from the benefits of uniformity within any one role.

In addition to producing reliability, similarity among persons reduces the number of patterns one must learn if he is to deal with all the different persons he meets. Uniformity thus keeps down the information cost of living among others.

Reliability is also an important ingredient of *trust.* Purely aside from questions of integrity, anyone whose behavior is highly predictable can be "trusted" to behave as expected. Uniformity thus helps produce the "trust" without which a society could hardly operate. Aspects of trust related to honesty and promises will be dealt with later.

Norms and good communication. We have already noted that the more nearly similar the patterns in people's heads the more accurate their communication will be. The vocabulary of a language reflects most of the patterns of thought and behavior that are widely found in a society. To join the two points, the more nearly similar the thoughts and behaviors of a people—i.e., the more narrowly normative they are—the more accurate will be their communications. For the same reason, members of the same society, who, by definition, share the same culture, communicate more accurately than do members of different societies. For the same reason, the more different the cultures the less accurate the cross-cultural communication.

Cross-cultural communication could nevertheless be accurate for things found in both cultures, such as tree or sky.

Norms and the boundaries of a society. We have earlier defined a society as a collectivity of people who have the same body and process of culture. As we can now see, that is much the same as saying that a society is a set of interacting people who share the same norms. By the same token a particular set of norms may be a good criterion for the bounding of a given society, and for determining who is in it and who is outside.

A society, however, does not have neat, clearly defined boundaries like a corporation or a nation, since it is relatively easy to tell who is or is not a member of these entities, and the nation also has clear-cut geographic boundaries. In a rough way we can talk of the people of the United States as one society and those of England as another. But their cultures have a great deal in common, they read one another's literature, their legal structures and traditions are very similar, and their mutual language undergoes similar changes. In those respects they are both parts of the "same" society. On the other hand, the Maine fisherman, the Harlem Puerto Rican, the Chicago inner-city black, and the Texan rancher are far more different from one another in the way they think, talk, act, and live than are the middle-class urban Englishman from his American counterpart. Occupations also make people very different, and the banker, dirt farmer, actor, professor, engineer, and assembly line worker move in such "different worlds" that in a very real sense we can say that they have different cultures and belong to different societies. For convenience we call them subcultures and subsocieties. Furthermore, no two persons within the same subculture are precisely alike, while others are versatile enough to be at home in several quite different cultures. Hence our statements about the boundaries of societies and cultures, and about communications within cultures versus communications between cultures, though valid, do not refer to neatly bounded and packaged groups of people or cultural traits.

Boundaries, mass media, and mass merchandising. We have indicated that the many subcultures within a nation can be very different, but also that increased communication is a way of making people more similar in beliefs and behaviors. The obvious conclusion is that mass communication helps reduce cultural differences. From the northern tip of Maine to the southern tip of California, even if the people are not communicating with one another they are receiving the same communications from common sources. They see and hear the same soap operas, the same TV commercials, and the same national newscasters. Although they may not themselves adopt the "standard" accent of the national announcers, they can all understand it. Even if their views on these matters differ, they all have a common awareness of such highly visible occurrences as the Vietnam war or Watergate. And although there will be differences by educational level within each section of the country, in all sections those who take the trouble to listen are simultaneously aware that the Supreme Court has handed down a new ruling on abortion and that the dollar has been devalued abroad. Newspapers have the same effect since they use the same national wire services, though they differ widely in their local coloration.

The national retailing chains may have even greater homogenizing effects than radio and TV. Across the country, in large cities and small towns, one sees the same company names on five-and-tens, drug stores, hamburger joints, gas stations, motels, and shoe stores, identical ads for the products of these companies in the newspapers, and the same or similar merchandise for sale. Even if a local name appears on the sign outside the store, the same merchandise under the same brand names can be bought in Montana or Florida. Hence in many respects the patterns of behavior and the corresponding patterns inside men's heads are similar because they have all been put there by the same source—a pattern transmission that is communicational in the broad sense.

The similarities created by mass media help hold a people together, in a sense of oneness, while similarities in what they buy and use vastly simplify the process of producing, transporting, and selling merchandise.

Social costs of norms

Despite their high uses (and their inevitability), norms also have costs. The most conspicuous, and the only one we will mention, is the limitation they place on variety—since greater similarity means less variety. Less variety means less choice, less individualization, less freedom of expression, and a smaller range of options. Some options not available in a society might be the best solutions for its problems. For example, if the norms provide only for severe punishment of illegal behavior they may prevent therapeutic treatment in many cases in which it would be less expensive and more effective. A norm that the captain must go down with his ship may waste trained manpower, and a norm that subordinates are not paid to think may consign many useful ideas to oblivion.

The above cases illustrate behaviors that are not available because they are prohibited or discouraged. The normative tendency may even more effectively exclude certain ideas by making people unaware of them—they simply do not come to people's minds. Since progress is related to variety (Chapter 27), norms can also inhibit change.

Although norms may reduce tension and frustration directly, by reducing the range of options norms can nevertheless increase tension and frustration indirectly. If one is angry at his mother, but the norms allow only polite language toward her, the consequence is frustration. If the norms allow only a demure glance at the creature one wants passionately to embrace, frustration again results. Smaller frustrations arise when one may not drink soup from the bowl, or when his creative ideas bring frowns from all listeners. Norms can be especially irksome if they have no justification except "that's the way it's always been done!" The young who are not yet used to them often find such norms frustrating and try to avoid or change them.

FLOWS, STOCKS, AND EQUILIBRIUM IN THE CONTENT OF CULTURE

Norms and other aspects of culture, like almost anything else, can be examined either statically or dynamically. The static approach deals with the parts of a culture as they exist at a given moment, and the dynamic approach deals with changes in parts over time. At the risk of partial misrepresentation, it is nevertheless useful to think of the static and dynamic views of culture in terms of stocks and flows, respectively. If the inflows of something regularly equal the outflows, the result is a stable equilibrium in that thing. In several respects the concept of equilibrium as an equalization of inflows and outflows is applicable to culture.

To deal first with nonapplicable aspects, transfers of pattern are unlike transfers of matter-energy in a fundamental respect. Whereas matter or energy ceases to be at A after it is transferred to B, pattern does not, which is another way of saying that the laws of conservation of matter and energy do not apply to pattern in general or to information in particular. For example, the pattern in the tire tread does not cease to be on the tire after it has impressed itself on mud. Nor do the patterns of the letters cease to be in your typewriter after you have typed a theme with it. An idea does not leave one person's head when he tells it to someone else; in fact, it may be strengthened in the telling. In consequence we can think of a "stock" of cultural patterns in only a figurative sense. For two million persons to know something is not really "more information" than for one person to know it, in the same sense that there is no more information in two million copies of a book than in one copy. Yet a single new idea adds to the total, even if it occurs in only one head.

Second, ideas or patterns are not additive in the same way as is water or sand. Apples and oranges cannot be added if we think of them as different patterns, though they can be if we look at a common ingredient, such as sugar content, or a common dimension, such as weight. They can also be added if they are subsumed under a more general pattern, such as "pieces of fruit." Putting two patterns together, however, usually pro-

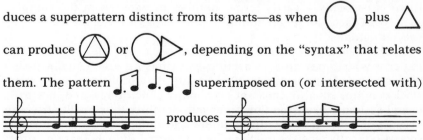

which is quite different from either pattern taken alone or the two patterns simply added. Furthermore, new patterns often merely substitute for old ones, and it would be extremely difficult to say whether the "quantity" has changed at all. Is the idea of one God larger or smaller than the idea of a separate god in every tree or bush? How does the "quantity" of the idea of tent compare with that of hut or house?

Despite these reservations, there is nevertheless a real sense in which we can say that one culture contains more patterns than another, or that the quantity of patterns changes over time in a given culture. Vocabulary is a rough measure of the number of concepts in a society. On this basis we would have to note total vocabularies of not much over five to ten

By permission of John Hart and Field Enterprises Inc.

thousand words in some primitive societies (Taylor, 1973: 134), as compared to about half a million in an unabridged English dictionary. Now the latter includes multiple words with the same basic meaning, though such duplications are also found in languages with smaller vocabularies. The main difference is the many words dealing with medical, technical, and scientific concepts in an advanced industrial culture. "Technical" includes words familiar to the layman in an advanced society but completely unknown to the simpler society, such as *pulley, tire, plastic, refrigerator, molecule, corporation, jail, mathematics, jet stream,* and *labor union.* However loose the notion of "quantity" as applied to patterns, there is certainly a vastly larger number of patterns in the complex society. In fact, the larger number is perhaps the best measure of its greater complexity.

In this sense, then, there is real meaning to the idea of a stock of patterns which may grow or decline over time. An excellent discussion of this view is found in Meier (1965: 84–101). In a traditional society that stock remains roughly constant over many generations, and in a truly closed system there is no flow in or out. Stability thus results from an absence of flow, not an equality of inflow and outflow. By contrast an open society typically receives inflows of new patterns. But whereas an import of ideas increases the stock, an export does not decrease it—since we have seen that a pattern does not leave *A* when it is transferred to *B*. A decrease nevertheless could arise from disuse.

INDIVIDUAL MOTIVES FOR COMMUNICATION

We have spoken of benefits and costs of communication in a society. But as we shall see (Chapter 15), motivation is fundamentally individual. We will therefore examine how and why individuals need and desire communication. The basics have already been stated; we now move them into this new context.

First, each individual needs much information accumulated by prior generations if he is to deal with his natural, technical, and social environment. Since he cannot possibly learn through his own experience all it might be useful to know, he must learn many things from his society's culture.

Second, he wants particular information from others through messages, as to be told that his goats have got loose, that his car lights are on, or that he has been invited out for Sunday dinner. He also needs to tell things to others.

Third, consensus concepts are likely to be more accurate than perceptions by one person alone, particularly if the thing observed is not well known or is complex. One may therefore want to check his observations with others.

Fourth, it is useful to know things about ourselves, and our best mirror is the way others respond to us.

Fifth, communication is self-expression, and merely to talk about our likes and dislikes, hopes, fears, and perceptions is an important avenue for self-expression. Artworks, decorations, handicrafts, and patterns of personal relationships are similarly self-expression by externalizing inner patterns. If others appreciate them, our satisfaction is enhanced.

Finally, we have also seen that an externalized pattern can be observed, and from that observation the internal pattern can be modified. The responses of others to our externalizations supplement and assist this process. Furthermore, the interaction process may itself be enjoyable (Chapter 14), amplifying the satisfaction.

In short, communication is a behavior. As such, it will not occur unless it is motivated. To explain *why* people communicate, rather than merely *how,* we have therefore identified some motives for communicating.

SUMMARY, AND COMPARISON OF COMMUNICATIONS WITH TRANSACTIONS

Transactions and communications both reflect and affect the system states of the parties to them. That is, either type of interaction is both cause and effect of the related system state—detector states for communications and selector states for transactions. But there is also an important difference in the relation between system states and interactions. With transactions, the greater the *difference* in *A*'s and *B*'s valuations of the items to be exchanged, the greater is the overlap of *EP*s and the more successful their transaction. By contrast, the greater the *similarity* in communicational codes between *A* and *B* the more successful will be the communication.

It is thus basic to transaction and communication that the degree of satisfaction is roughly proportional to the degree of difference and similarity, respectively. We are now speaking solely of the satisfaction from *accuracy* of communication, and will deal later with its truth or usefulness.

The kind of code similarity that brings accurate communication is found most clearly among persons who share the same culture. Hence one who wants to communicate clearly will prefer communications with other members of his own society or subsociety. For communicational purposes it can therefore be expected that people will tend to associate with others who share their culture. They tend to form cultural clusters, with relatively much communication within clusters and relatively little between them. The more adventuresome and creative members, however, can have interesting new experiences by making contacts with cultures other than their own.

Communications differ from transactions in another important respect, which assists clustering. All selfish transactions, even those with generous components, contain potential conflict, since the more for one party the less for the other. Hence for tactical reasons people may hesitate to be truthful about their attitudes toward things that may enter into future transactions. Pure communication calls for no such reticence. Hence persons who expect to interact only through communication can relax and enjoy the interaction. Nor need they hesitate to cultivate others whose values differ from their own. In conversations about the subtleties of life, however, the payoffs are generally highest with home folk, whose codes are like one's own.

Having observed the effects of system states on interactions, we now reverse the field and look at the effects of interactions on system states. Here the effects of transaction and communication are parallel. The more people interact through transactions, the more nearly similar do their valuations become, in a consensus by transaction. Also, the more people interact through communication, the more nearly similar do their conceptual codes become, in a consensus by communication. Either interaction thus tends to reduce individual difference—which is perhaps the most important single effect of interaction.

14

COMBINATIONS AND MIXTURES OF COMMUNICATIONS AND TRANSACTIONS

Thus far we have dealt with models of relatively pure transactions and communications. But most real interactions are much more complicated than the models. This chapter will show how the models can be used in different combinations to help understand the complexities of real interactions. We will deal with those combinations first under the headings of *communication as transaction* and *transaction as communication,* then look at some other patterns of social behavior that can be understood in those contexts.

This chapter continues to examine interactions as such, leaving to later chapters discussion of an interaction as a system in its own right. We will nevertheless hint at such systemness, as a prelude to later analysis. For as soon as people get even a vague feeling that they are part of a larger system, each behaves somewhat differently than he would if he were wholly independent. And that is a fundamental difference between a society and a batch of interacting individuals.

COMMUNICATION AS TRANSACTION

Information is often valuable. Which turn do I take for Attleboro? What diet will prevent soft bones? In any given communication if we shift attention from the process or accuracy of the information transfer to the *value* of the information transferred we also shift from communicational to transactional analysis of the interaction.

As Bennis (1970: 607) has noted, in the present age information about things often comes to be worth more than the things themselves.

Whether something exists, how to make it, who can supply it, who will buy it, how to get rid of it, who will vote for it, what effects it will have—these and dozens of other kinds of information about goods are often more valuable than the goods themselves. One indication is that people who can provide information are often paid more than those who can provide material goods.

Since man's arrival on earth he has been concerned mainly with harnessing matter and energy. With sophisticated technologies the limitations on man's accomplishments lie increasingly in the area of his ability to process information. The crucial importance of the computer in many contemporary organizations reflects this change.

But man has always needed information, and there have always been occasions for someone to command values in exchange for it—as with the spy, the pollster, the gossipmonger, the expert, and the "usually reliable source." If X is the valued information A can provide to B, the more valuable that information is to B the greater is the value of the Y that A can command in return for it, and the greater are A's power and bargaining power.

An exchange or purchase of information can be as straightforwardly transactional as the purchase of a used car, with A and B haggling over how much or what kind of information A will give in return for what. To hire a consultant, subscribe to a reporting service, or buy a book is also a straightforward purchase of information. Among friends many exchanges of information are open-end transactions, as in the tacit agreement that "I'll tell you what I hear if you tell me what you hear."

It is often advantageous that some other party *not* know something. In that case the promise or willingness to withhold information can be the X or Y in a transaction. For reasons that are obvious from our model, it may be advantageous for someone not to release information that bears on tactics or strategies in transactions to which he is a party. In fact, we might ask whether there is a rational reason for keeping *any* information secret unless it bears on some actual or potential transaction. That question certainly seems to apply for blackmail. Relatedly, any information about a person taken without his consent, often thought of as an invasion of privacy, is a form of theft.

Communication as adjunct to transaction

The logic of transactional strategies extends in many directions. We will mention just two, one affecting personality and the other affecting the broad contours of a society. As to the first, some persons may have had experiences early in life in which information about them was used to their disadvantage. Perhaps without knowing why, they developed ingrained habits of reticence, and regularly hide information about themselves even when there is no sound transactional reason to do so. They never "let down their guard" or "level" with anyone. Others with different early experiences remain free and open about their feelings. This, of course, is only one of many possible explanations of such differences in personality. Much fascinating detail is provided by Jourard (1971a and 1971b).

On a much larger scale, to get people to believe in a particular ideology is to extend their *EP*s for it, and to make them more willing to sacrifice time, money, effort, and other things to support it. Hence, increased support for a given ideology raises the power and bargaining power of those who benefit from that ideology. Relatedly, any social system gives power to some and keeps it from others. Those in power normally use it to generate strong *EP*s among the public for that system. When they use the mass media to say, "Ours is a great system, and you ought to support it (and thereby keep us powerful and affluent)," their approach is essentially the same as that of the job seeker who says "I am a very capable fellow, and you should be happy to hire me at a large salary." Commercial advertising similarly attempts to generate longer *EP*s for particular products or firms. In a dictatorship virtually the whole of the mass communication system may be used as a tactical device in the transactional relation between rulers and ruled.

In short, communication as a strategy for generating longer *EP*s can be used at levels from the smallest transaction to attempts to maintain or change a whole society.

On confirming and disconfirming messages

Would you rather receive a message that confirms your beliefs or one that contradicts them? Perhaps you say that it is best to receive truthful messages. If they support your beliefs, fine. If not, you ought to examine your beliefs. But things are not that simple.

If you consider yourself basically sensible and considerate you will probably be displeased to receive a message that depicts you as unsensible and insensitive. If your close friend seems honest and generous, you will probably be displeased to hear someone say he is plotting to do you in. By contrast, you will probably be pleased if someone gives you or your friend a sincere compliment.

Such messages have a value to you, positive or negative. But unlike the earlier examples, this is not simple instrumental value—like knowing which road to take. Of the many subtler values that might be involved, we will illustrate two, and a mixture. One involves self-images, which we are pleased to have enhanced and displeased to have reduced. And since we are judged in part by the company we keep, we are similarly affected by information that enhances or reduces the images of our friends. Second, even if some image is not pleasant or unpleasant in itself, new information that is inconsistent with it involves the costs of inner dissonance and possibly of revising the image. As to the mixture, criticism of you may involve both the costs of changing the self-image and the lowered value of the image itself.

If a message from *B* pleases you for any of the above reasons it is a good, and its transactional effect on the relationship parallels that of his giving you a scarf or a book that pleases you, by making you willing to give something in return. It also tends to make you like *B*. A displeasing message produces the opposite effects.

There is often substantial overlap of *EP*s in communicational transactions, even when the goods are only a "stroke," such as a nod, a smile, or "Nice job." The only requirement for a transaction is that each party want what the other can give more than he wants to keep what he already has. In the exchange of compliments or smiles the cost of giving is typically smaller than the benefit of receiving, and the *EP*s clearly overlap.

A complication of messages as transactions is that the receiver must believe the message or its value declines. If you think I praise you just to make you feel good or to get you to do me a favor, the praise has little value. Hence, to keep praise valuable I must give it only when it seems deserved. (Incidentally, affection has wider currency than praise, and is therefore more integrative. It is appropriate to feel affection for someone during both his failures and his successes, whereas praise is oriented more toward success.) Another aspect of credibility is that, unlike a chair or an ashtray (matter-energy), an unpleasant message already received cannot be "returned," and the nearest equivalent is to ignore or disbelieve it—detector influenced by selector. A variation is to conclude that its source is a knave (who deliberately misrepresents the information in his detector) or a fool (whose detector works badly to begin with). Either version allows the receiver to conclude that he knows better than the source of the message. True or not, this is a comforting thought. Since many of us need comforting thoughts, we probably see others as knaves or fools oftener than they really are.

Disconfirming messages as pattern mismatch (dissonance)

Our model of man includes a negative valence attached to dissonance, or mismatch of patterns. That part of the model is directly applicable to disconfirming messages. It does not depend on the threat to self-image described above—though it can add to or substitute for it. For example, suppose you think Swedish modern a magnificent style of furniture, and also consider yourself to have good taste. You then discover that your friend Phillips, whose taste and judgment you respect, also considers it magnificent. Consonance and harmony prevail! You have good taste, so has Phillips, and Swedish modern is great. But what if Phillips considers Swedish modern atrocious? You then undergo dissonance, since your concept of yourself is inconsistent with your image of Phillips as a person of good taste.

If dissonance is unpleasant and you seek to eliminate it, something must give.

One of you could change his views about furniture. Or you could change your views of him or of yourself. Any one of the four changes would eliminate the dissonance.

Another common situation occurs when a person (rather than furniture) is the object of conflicting attitudes. Suppose you have independently met Fillister and Phillips. Because you like both of them you tend to assume that they would like each other. You then learn that Phillips and Fillister have a deep mutual hatred. Again, something must give.

This kind of problem has been detailed by Festinger (1957), Pepitone (1964), and Brehm and Cohen (1962). The consequences can be deduced from the previous materials. First is the cognitive (detector) dissonance, in which two things you previously viewed as "the same" now must be viewed as "different." You must readjust your concepts of Phillips, Fillister, or both. You will probably also have dissonance in your selector, in that your liking both people seems inconsistent with their hating each other. Such dissonances can be strictly intrasystem: you could feel them even if they brought no change in your actual relationships.

But there probably are intersystem consequences as well. As to communications, you may now hesitate to mention either to the other, whereas you would have felt free to before. At the transactional level, mentioning Fillister to Phillips might bring unpleasant thoughts to Phillips, thus constituting a bad imposed on Phillips by you. That bad would generate a psychological tendency in Phillips to avoid you and a transactional tendency to give you less goods than before.

Among the possible outcomes, you might manage to reconcile your two friends, drop one of them, or continue to see both but not talk about it. For these and many other reasons, people generally prefer communications that confirm rather than disconfirm their existing images. In consequence they tend to associate with others whose detector and selector states resemble their own.

Costs and benefits of the communicational process

Like the transaction, the communication has side benefits and costs. Some are intrasystem, as in talking for the sake of talking. If the talking is done *to* someone (which some folk think makes sense) it is also a communication. Communicating for its own sake can thus be positively motivated for the same reason symboling is. Without this motive it is hard to account for the amount of talk that goes on among humans. It can also provide the intrasystem satisfaction of simply doing something well. However, for those who do not do it easily, talking may be a painful reminder of inadequacy.

If a listener responds he adds to the above effect by allowing the talker to refine and modify the images he has put into words. Further, for B to listen and respond provides A with a valued service, and his providing it can be analyzed as a transaction. If B also enjoys responding, there will be a long overlap of EPs, whereas if B finds A a bore, his EP for A's conversation will be short. Even if B listens merely to avoid A's whining—"Nobody cares about me"—his behavior is still transactional: it avoids this verbal stress by A.

TRANSACTION AS COMMUNICATION

Your car will not run smoothly if a tire is flat. If it *is* running smoothly, then without even looking you can safely conclude by deduction that no tire is flat. More broadly, information about effect can often be deduced from knowledge of cause, and vice versa.

We have said that system interactions both reflect and affect system states. To say that an interaction "reflects" a system state means that the system state in some sense "causes" the interaction. If your seven-year-old neighbor eagerly offers to swap his magnificent roast beef sandwich for your peanut butter sandwich, you will normally deduce that his selector prefers peanut butter to roast beef. Whenever A's overt behavior reflects his inner states (as it must), and B observes that behavior, B may be able to figure out something about A's inner states—though he may be wrong. Our problem is: How reliably does a given system state of A lead to a given overt behavior, and how much can B learn about A by observing his behavior?

Among the many such situations, several need mention. Although other motives are sometimes involved, one is generous mainly with those he likes. Hence, any transaction in which A is obviously generous to B can say, "I like and care about you." Since the receipt of a gift is normally a good, and generates an approach response toward its source, A's gift can also say, "I want you to like me." The gift can be a material object, comfort or advice, a tidbit of gossip, or even just listening to B. Since gifts are normally given between friends, a gift can say, "We are friends," or "I hope we will stay friends." If A and B have a common enemy, the gift can say, "We're sticking together." It can also communicate power and status, as we shall see.

"Gifts" of bads (insults or stink bombs), or other transactions with obvious hostile components, can similarly say, "I dislike you," "I don't care if you dislike me," or "We're through." In this connection bads include not returning a smile or being conspicuously inattentive. Because such behaviors symbolize inner states they are often called *symbolic behavior.*

A's transactions can also show his attitude toward the things exchanged, or toward the transactional process. Normally, for A knowingly to pay a ridiculously high price for something symbolizes his strong desire for it—although it might mean that he doesn't know it is cheaper elsewhere, or that he doesn't like to haggle. And if you actually watch him bargain you may learn something about his bargaining tactics and strategies. Perhaps the most important thing we all seem to learn intuitively from a series of transactions is that all interpersonal power and bargaining power (except that of bads) lies in being or having something wanted by others.

As we trace things further, they become complicated apace. We have noted that a generous transaction can say, "I like you," and that the advantages of being liked are learned early in life. "A likes me" is therefore not only a communication implied by A's generous transaction. It is also a communication whose content has value to B, subject to the earlier analysis of communication as transaction.

Many interactions are even more complex, as with: "I am doing this favor for you (transaction) so you will know I care about you (communication) and will then feel less lonely (transactional result)"—a transactional result couched as a communication which is itself couched as a transaction. If I told you about all this before I actually did it, and if the content of the message were itself valued, *that* message would be a communicational transaction. The whole package would then be a communicational transaction about a transactionally communicational transaction! Laing (1970) has caught beautifully the spirit of such relationships.

THE JOINTNESS AND SEPARABILITY OF COMMUNICATIONS AND TRANSACTIONS

Our point above is intended neither to frighten the reader nor to make him an expert at such things, but merely to indicate that even subtle or complex interactions can be diagnosed as communication, as transaction, or as some combination of the two. All real interactions are *both,* and we cannot imagine any interaction totally devoid of either element.

The fabric of any real interaction must have both warp and woof to hold it together. However, warp and woof are not the same thing, and the fabric would disintegrate if they were. To use another figure, although every physical force must have both magnitude and direction, these are very different things, and a "pure theory" of one provides no understanding of the other. Yet real magnitudes affect real directions (the direction of a five-ounce force can be seriously deflected by a rosebush but that of a five-ton force cannot), and real directions affect real magnitudes (the force of a baseball will change very differently if the ball is thrown upward rather than downward). The question is not whether a particular interaction *is* a communication or a transaction (it is always both), but whether we are interested in the information or in the values transferred, or in both. That is, communications and transactions are analytically bounded.

In a larger version of the same question, economists concentrate their attention on transactional relationships in markets. They know that communications are also part of any real market system, but pay little attention to them. By contrast, sociologists and social psychologists do give much attention to interactions here described as transactional. But many of them, along with some anthropologists, insist that all interactions are exchanges of "meanings"—"symbolic behavior" or "symbolic interactions." The economic axis thus acknowledges both communications and transactions but confines attention to transactions, while the sociological axis actually attends to both but widely insists that it is dealing with only one. (Interestingly, one of the people who reviewed the manuscript of this book suggested that I offer transactional analysis as one means of conceptualizing communication! I obviously see it as having an independent role.)

The present approach insists on separating those interactions that reflect and affect detector states from those that reflect and affect selector states. In the hope of pinning down that distinction, we will try the following. You repeatedly dated a visitor from France who, after returning home, has written, "Je t'aime, et je reviendrai bientôt pour me marier avec toi." If you understand French, there has been a communication and a transfer of meaning. If you know no French and get no translation you will know that a message has been sent to you. But you will have no idea whether the letter describes the trip home, asks for money, contains gossip, or expresses love or hate. Whether or not you *understand* the message is a pure communicational problem.

Let us assume that you understand the letter, and know from it that the writer loves you and will be returning soon to marry you. If you think the message is serious you can hardly ignore it, and it is not likely to leave you feeling neutral. Although further communication seems likely, and can be analyzed with reference to codes, sign transmission, and the like, the main problem thereafter is transactional. Does the content of the message delight or appall you? Is there or is there not an overlap of *EP*s regarding the transaction of marriage? If there is, what tactics or strategies (which may take the form of communications, true or false) will you use to make sure the transaction is completed? If you shrink from the thought of this marriage, what tactics or strategies can you use to prevent it from being given to you as a "gift"? Might perpetual pestering be used as a stress, to be relieved only if you agree to marriage?

Now the whole situation may eventually involve enough communications as transactions, transactions as communications, and other mixtures to fill a large book. (Many have been written about less.) The point is that to the extent that the problem is one of meaning it is communicational. To the extent that the interaction involves values (goods or bads, likes or dislikes) it is transactional. No part of the model of communication is found in the model of transaction, and vice versa. Although "interaction" is a useful abbreviation for "communication, or transaction, or some combination thereof," a major point of this volume is that we can never have more than low-level, largely empirical generalizations about interactions until the pure models are sharply separated. Once each is understood separately, their many combinations and mixtures can be dealt with. Some complex mixtures will always be "mushy ice" problems. In them many things are going on at the same time, with some of them unknown, some of the known ones unidentifiable, and some of the identifiable ones unmeasurable.

Finally, many real situations are ambiguous because the same overt behavior might result from very different system states. A gift may bespeak affection. Or it may be a softening-up strategy for a grand swindle later. The hostile shortening of an *EP* may represent dislike. But it could also be an attempt by someone fond of you to teach you more about yourself. An inaccurate statement to you by *A* may mean that he doesn't know any better. Or it may reflect an "honest" distortion of his detector by his selector, a deliberate attempt to misinform you, or his desire to activate your thinking processes.

Whenever different causes could produce the same behavioral effect, you cannot be sure which one caused it. Of the many possible consequences of this situation we will mention two. If a person is usually uncertain about other people's motives in their transactions with him he might become emotionally disturbed—an intrasystem result. An intersystem result is that large uncertainty about the motives of others increases the risks of dealing with them. These risks produce a general preference to deal with those one trusts—the topic of the next section.

Promises and trust

Trust helps make a society cohesive—a higher-level system instead of a mere aggregation of individuals. We have now come far enough to analyze trust, even though some aspects must wait till later.

Trust, unlike communication and transaction, is not a basic concept, but a combination of other things. One aspect of trust (Chapter 13) is simple reliability. I can "trust" something to happen if I am sure it always does—day follows night; water never runs uphill. My trust that the mailman will deliver my mail may no more be confidence in a person than is my trust that day will follow night.

Confidence is sometimes probabilistic. I trust that a wrapped package handed to me by the clerk actually contains what I bought because thus far my experience has never been otherwise.

In connection with transactions trust is confidence that the other party will actually deliver as promised. I trust the manager of my local garage to mount the tires I bought and give back my car, and he trusts me to pay. We will now examine the conditions under which a rational person will fulfill a promise, which is another way of describing the conditions under which he can be trusted in a transaction. We will first state the conditions of trust, then explore its meaning, and finally examine how this analysis applies to some less obvious situations.

Since a rational decision is one whose expected benefits equal or exceed its expected costs, a person will rationally keep a promise if the benefits of doing so will equal or exceed the costs. If costs exceed benefits, he will rationally not keep the promise. A's stake in keeping a promise is the value he will lose if he does *not* fulfill it. (For present purposes *stake* in a transaction means any valued thing, other than X or Y, access to which is contingent on fulfilling the promise.)

Obvious kinds of stakes are materials, titles, or money deposited by the promisor, which he will not get back unless he fulfills his promise. A watch placed with a pawnbroker, a car title placed with a bank, and a contractor's performance bond are all stakes, the loss of which may leave a promisor worse off if he does not fulfill his promise than if he does. In addition, civil courts and contract law subject a person to lawsuit and damages if he does not fulfill a contract, which is an explicit kind of promise.

Many more personal and subjective stakes parallel those of ordinary credit ratings. If a person fails to pay his bills he loses his credit rating, which means that his promises to pay are no longer accepted. Similarly, if one does not keep appointments, do the work he was hired to do, or generally do what he said he would, his promises lose credibility, and others will not do things for him on the basis of his promises. The express or implied promise to return favors pervades life, and if one's promises are not believed, his life can be difficult indeed. Because the credibility of promises has large potential benefit, it is generally rational to try to fulfill promises and to maintain this broad credit rating of life. The social pressures on those who do not keep promises are the semiformal parallel (Chapter 18) of court penalties.

Whereas the above stakes are external and intersystem, others may be intrasystem. If you have a strong sense that it is right, proper, and necessary to keep your promises, your failure to do so will set off negative valences inside you. One such valence is simple dissonance, which occurs when your overt acts do not match your inner patterns. A second is fear of such adverse consequences as retaliatory action or loss of reputation—a fear known as anxiety or guilt. Peace of mind and freedom from such unpleasant feelings are the stakes you may lose if you break a promise.

If the above are the reasons why promises are kept they are also the condition under which promises can be trusted—namely, when the promisor is believed to have an adequate stake. An overt stake, such as money, is asked when the promisor is *not* fully trusted. The stake for most of us most of the time is our desire to maintain credibility and approval. Since the passing stranger may have no such stake he often finds it difficult to get anything on the basis of a promise.

In our pure communicational analysis we paid no attention to the truth or falsity of a message, and examined only its transmission. Truth or falsity are transactional aspects of an interaction. In analyzing interactions, we can treat trust in truthfulness as logically parallel to trust in a promise. Instead of "I promise that I will later give you value in return for what you have just given me," we say or imply, "I promise that the information I now give you has the value of being truthful."

Here, too, the usual stake is credibility, along with the avoidance of dissonance, guilt, or anxiety. A person would rationally tell an untruth if the expected benefit of doing so exceeded its expected cost, with pangs of conscience and loss of credibility being counted among the costs. When loss of credibility is costly, deliberate lying would seem to reflect either stupidity or an unusually high positive time preference.

A short summary on consensus

We noted that successful communication *requires similarity* of concepts and that successful transaction *requires differences* in values. Either type of interaction, however, tends to *produce similarity* (reduce differences). Repeated communication brings people to similar concepts, in consensus by communication. Repeated transactions reduce discrepancies in valuations until, in a perfect market (consensus by transaction), all parties place the same relative valuations on goods. Thus, both types of social interaction reduce dissimilarities and make people more homogeneous—both increase the oneness, or unity, of interacting persons. However, similarity is not itself a social cement: ten thousand similar earthworms in a garden may still not constitute a society. The cohesive effects of similarity will be examined in connection with informal and semiformal organizations.

AGGREGATE POWER, CLASS, AND STATUS

Interpersonal power is the ability to get something wanted, and bargaining power is the ability to get it on good terms. The ability to acquire a Rolls-Royce therefore represents power. But acquiring ten Rolls-Royces reflects greater power than acquiring one, which represents greater power than getting a ten-year-old Volkswagen. Getting elected coroner represents greater power than being defeated, but less power than being elected governor. To get one person to act on a promise represents power. To get a million to act on it represents much greater power.

This section deals with the ability to get things of large rather than small total value. The total may consist of many things of small value, a few of large value, or some combination. This ability we call *aggregate power,* in contrast to the particular power to get one particular wanted thing. Whereas A's ability to get Y in a transaction is a measure of his particular power, his aggregate power is his ability to get $Y_1 + Y_2 + Y_3 + \ldots Y_n$, whether the successive Ys are the same or different.

Whereas particular power represents a flow of power in one transaction, aggregate power is a stock of power accumulated through previous transactions under circumstances in which the net inflows exceeded the net outflows. Since power in goods lies in being or having something wanted by others, large aggregate power lies in a stock of more things, or more intensely wanted things, than does small aggregate power. Furthermore, like water behind a dam, the stock is a potential that can be realized only by being allowed to flow out through transactions that use it. We will discuss accumulations of goods only, since the reader should easily be able to extend the rationale of using bads in a single transaction to using them as a basis for aggregate power. (For simplicity, "power" hereinafter will mean "aggregate power.")

Many kinds of power are transferable, and the easiest way to acquire a stock of power is by gift. Many prefer this method, but happen not to be in line to receive much from it. Since we have already discussed gifts, we will confine attention here to the process of accumulating power in the first place.

In simple money terms a stock grows if the expenditures flow is less than the income flow, and the difference is saved. If your income is $10,000 a year, and you save $1,000, in a mere thousand years you will be a millionaire. If you invest the saved stock productively, the accumulated stock will itself assist further accumulation by increasing the inflow. The most obvious, perhaps the only, way of making large and rapid accumulations is through successive transformations of assets (Boulding 1958), accomplished through a succession of collectively favorable transactions. If you can exchange one cow for five goats in one place, acquire one cow for four goats in a second place, then return to the first place and again get five goats for your cow, and if you can continue this process indefinitely you can accumulate one goat in each pair of transactions. By the end of four pairs of transactions you will have two cows, and so on ever upward.

The cows, of course, may age and die; the goats may run away; and

"I sold the cow for some beans; used the beans as collateral and bought tobacco warrants; unloaded the warrants and moved into hog futures, then land speculation and condominiums. . . ."

Reproduced from *Saturday Review,* © Lorenz, 1971.

the exchange ratios may become less favorable. Hunger or cold may force you to eat an occasional cow or wear the skin of an occasional goat. However, our interest here is not in the possible causes of failure to accumulate, even if failure is more likely than success. It is rather in the process, which is the same whether you succeed or fail.

In the illustration you "buy" cows for four goats each and "sell" them for five, the one goat being a profit. But in most cases one does not give up in a second transaction exactly the same thing he acquired in the first. More typically, he makes some transformation in between. He buys calves and corn, inserts the corn into the calves, and then sells them as steers. He acquires a shop, tools, and man-hours of hired labor, and sells the service of automobile repairs. In such cases the ability to accumulate depends on the ability to make productive transformations at one phase of the cycle. Though we will note their importance, such transformations are technological rather than social, and we will not detail them here. In any case, all large-scale transformations are made by organizations, not individuals. Organizations *are* social phenomena, to be examined later.

Power factors

The principle of accumulation through transactional inflows that exceed outflows applies most obviously to money, real estate, cows and goats, gold, and other material things that can be owned and transferred. These we call *material external power factors.* Such things as books one has written, paintings he has painted, recordings he has made, mentions of his name in print, or published pictures of him are also material external power factors. Either they can themselves be transacted or they have tactical or strategic effects on transactions. To illustrate the latter, the oftener one's name appears in print the larger (other things equal) will be the number of people who will generate *EP*s for some transactional relation with him—such as giving time, money, effort, or attention to hear him speak or see him perform. Power factors external to an individual can also be *nonmaterial,* in the form of system states of others. These include such things as his reputation, awareness of him, attitudes of friendship or loyalty toward him, and a sense of obligation to him.

In contrast are *internal power factors.* These are system states or characteristics of a person himself that give him power, such as knowledge, skill, strength, willpower, beauty, friendliness, courage, ruthlessness, or stubbornness. Internal power factors are not acquired directly by transactions, but by inheritance or learning. Transactions may assist them indirectly, however, as when one's knowledge and skill are improved by instruction, books, or equipment acquired from others. Actors, comedians, musicians, clowns, animal trainers, and other performing artists have this sort of power. The service of such performing skills can be sold simultaneously to audiences of thousands. However, the service of other skills, such as those of mechanics, physicians, architects, or lawyers, can be sold to only one or a few persons at a time. Only the former type is likely to provide a base for really large power. Hence we will attend to this kind of power at the celebrity level only. If others are willing to pay just to see you, because you are beautiful or freakish, your mere appearance is a pool of power. Along with information, appearance is a pattern that can be "given away" without diminishing the existing stock—a distinct advantage so far as it goes.[1] Perhaps the greatest capacity for multiplying power based on a personal skill occurs when a single action or performance can be duplicated and sold, as with books, recordings, or movies. Such reproduction has the advantage that, being external, it can be made without requiring the investment of additional time, energy, or skill by the creator, and can even continue after his skill has deteriorated.

External power factors are generally more reliable and durable than internal ones. Furthermore, there is no limit to the amount of them one can own. Hence large durable power usually rests on the ownership of land and its resources, factories, mines, railroads, and the like.

Influence is the ability to modify system states of others. We call it *intellectual influence* if it modifies their detector states, *moral influence* if it modifies their selector states. Influence can be translated into power only if it improves one's transactional relations, as by changing other parties' *EP*s. However, one's ideas may exert great influence without

---

[1] A material good, or a service that transforms, can be viewed as a matter-energy transfer, subject to the principle that what is transferred ceases to be where it was. Perception of oneself by others, like a communication to them, is a transfer of pattern, the source of which is not necessarily diminished by the transfer.

bringing him power to get anything in return. And although one's ideas may have influence for centuries, his power dies with him.

The accumulation of large quantities of power almost always requires investment, as in putting money into a business. Buying property, holding it while its price goes up, and then selling it is a pair of transactions similar to that of the cows and the goats, except that the two transactions are separated in time instead of place. In direct personal relations you may do favors for others, often without thinking of these favors as investments. These are gifts in open-end transactions, and normally produce some return obligation. If you get return favors of greater value to you than your costs of doing the initial favors, the pair of transactions has built an accumulation for you.

In politics even a small local office enables its occupant to do favors —arranging a bail bond, finding a lost welfare check, expediting the paving of a street. Votes are gained as more citizens know the officeholder's name and feel obligated to him, and his bargaining power within the town council tends to grow with the number of votes he can command outside it. More power means still more ability to do things that bring votes. These provide the base on which to run for higher office, and so on up the ladder.

At more mundane levels, a person who is sympathetic, understanding, able to give good advice, and willing to work hard gradually acquires power with others. This power often rests on nothing more than their willingness to seek and follow his advice.

Typically, there is a positive feedback relation between internal and external power factors. As the individual becomes better known, and as more people receive or seek favors from him, he achieves greater external power in the system states of others. At the same time his greater exposure and increased contacts give him greater skill in handling such relationships. The performing artist often finds that the greater his skill the oftener he is asked to perform and that the oftener he performs the greater his skill becomes.

Internal power factors have distinct limits. A person can possess only so much physical strength or skill, and it may peak early. However, a sports celebrity may shift his name and prestige to a restaurant, a nightclub, or an insurance business while his sports fame is still bright.

Organization coordinates the activities of many people, and can produce far greater results than can the actions of a single person. Hence, most large power is acquired through organization. As one moves up the ladder within organizations he directs more and more subordinates, and therein lies his larger power. Here, too, power is typically subject to positive feedback. The higher one's position the greater is his ability to provide favors, and the greater his ability to provide favors the more likely he is to rise still higher.

In addition to organization, other kinds of collective action can also enhance power. As has been noted in connection with transactions, a coalition among parties who are otherwise competitors can raise their power and bargaining power, whether through strikes, boycotts, conspiracy, "plowing under" excess chickens or corn, or other coordinated actions or coordinated refusals to act.

In all areas, and despite exceptions, it seems that aggregate power is self-aggravating. The more one has the easier it is to get still more. "To him that hath shall be given, and from him that hath not shall be taken away even that which he hath." Or, "Them as has gits." For this reason a society may remain viable only if it has mechanisms to reduce power at the top and raise it at the bottom.

A rationale of power and class

As noted (Chapter 9), one's power in transactions varies directly with his *EP.* To reverse the emphasis, persons with great power have longer *EP*s in dealing with others than do persons with little power. But one's power also varies directly with the other party's *EP.* For example, in Figure 14–1, *A* will have greater power as well as greater bargaining power in dealing with B_2 rather than with B_1. Given a choice, *A* will therefore prefer to deal with B_2. But since B_2 has greater power than B_1, this is another way of saying that *A* is better off dealing with a *B* of greater power than with a *B* of lesser power. As noted, B_2 is also the stronger competitor.

Figure 14–1

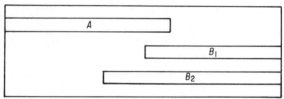

Hence people widely prefer to deal with those having greater, rather than lesser, power. If they can they tend to "deal upward," rather than downward or on the level. In everyday terms this means that if you want to get something important done you go to the top of the organization, not to the bottom or the middle. You go to the person with lots of money, not to the one who is struggling to make ends meet. This competition for their favor further enhances the power of those who already have it.

Status and status behavior

It is often convenient to lump similar people under a single name, and we will define a *class* as all persons of approximately equal aggregate power. Although money is not the only source or type of power, for most purposes we can think of a class as consisting of all people who have about the same amount of money. Levels based on money are nevertheless softened somewhat by other indicators of prestige, such as occupation, family name, political power, or outstanding accomplishment. The pattern of grouping people into different class levels is called *social stratification.*

The distribution of families into different income levels shows a J-shaped curve when plotted, as in Figure 14–2, curve *A*. It shows, for example, that the lowest fifth (quintile) of families received 5 percent (one twentieth) of total personal income in the United States. The lowest four-fifths (80 percent) together received 55 percent of the income, while the highest fifth of families received the remaining 45 percent. The dotted line shows an additional detail within the top quintile—namely, that the top 5 percent of families (95 to 100 on the horizontal scale) received almost 20 percent of the income (80.4 to 100 on the vertical scale). To use a simple contrast, the poorest 20 percent of families received 5 percent of the income while the richest 5 percent of families received 20 percent of the income, or 16 times as much on the average per family. Another study (Pechman and Okner 1974) that takes into account unrealized capital gains and other benefits that are available

Figure 14–2
DISTRIBUTION OF FAMILY PERSONAL INCOME AMONG
QUINTILES, UNITED STATES, 1962

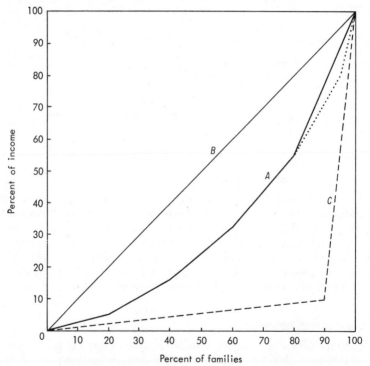

Key: Line *A* represents the actual distribution of income. Lines *B* and *C* are hypothetical reference lines. Line *B* represents complete equality of distribution. Line *C* represents extreme inequality, as if 90 percent of the families received only 10 percent of the total income and the other 10 percent of families received 90 percent of the income. The top 5 percent of families received 19.6 percent of the income.

Source: Bernard F. Haley, "Changes in the Distribution of Income in the United States," in James G. Scoville, ed, *Perspectives on Poverty and Income Distribution* (Lexington, Mass.: D. C. Heath and Company, 1971), p. 18.

largely to the wealthy shows somewhat greater inequality, as of 1966. Under that computation the 20 percent of American families with the lowest incomes received only 3.7 percent of the nation's income, while the top 5 percent of families received 22.1 percent of the income. The top 1 percent of families, all of whose incomes exceeded $56,667, received 10.5 percent of total income. The same study concluded that taxes make little difference in the distribution of income; all levels of income pay essentially the same percentage of their total income in taxes, except for the very rich and the very poor, who pay higher rates.

Income is obviously related to occupation, as shown in Table 14–1. There we can see that self-employed male professional and technical workers (such as architects, lawyers, and physicians) averaged over $17,-000 per year in 1971, service workers averaged only $5,500, and farm laborers less than $2,300. Wealth is distributed much more unevenly than income—though accurate data on ownership of money and property are much scarcer than those on incomes. It would seem that in 1956 in the United States about 25 percent of total wealth was owned by only about 0.5 to 1.0 percent of the adult population (Lampman 1959).

We have already given a basic explanation of why some people acquire more power than others—successive transactions, plus luck. In this section we are interested in behaviors that communicate one's class level to others, and in so doing serve to maintain, solidify, and possibly augment class differences.

We have seen that a transaction can communicate. Purchasing a

Table 14–1
MEDIAN MONEY INCOME OF PERSONS WITH INCOME, BY SEX AND OCCUPATION, UNITED STATES, 1971*

Occupation	Males	Females
All employed civilians	$ 8,371	$4,019
Professional, technical, and kindred workers	11,853	7,065
Self-employed	17,169	2,594
Salaried	11,571	7,203
Farmers and farm managers	4,627	1,602
Managers, officials, proprietors, except farm	12,412	5,900
Self-employed	9,433	3,623
Salaried	13,041	6,489
Clerical and kindred workers	8,426	4,726
Salesworkers	8,887	2,593
Craftsmen, foremen, and kindred workers	9,057	4,542
Operatives and kindred workers	7,275	4,036
Private household workers	000	849
Service workers, except private household	5,529	2,635
Farm laborers and foremen	2,274	940
Laborers, except farm and mine	4,847	3,318
Unemployed	3,763	1,892
In Armed Forces or not in labor force	2,444	1,350

* Covers persons 14 years old and over. Includes members of the Armed Forces living off post or with their families on post, but excludes all other Armed Forces; also excludes inmates of institutions.
Source: U.S. Bureau of Census, *Statistical Abstract of the United States, 1973* (94th ed., Washington: 1973), p. 334.

$250,000 yacht says, "I am rich," while looking hungrily at a hamburger and turning sadly away when told that it costs 80 cents says, "I am poor." Poor people cannot afford mansions, and few people will live in slums if they can afford not to. Hence one's address says something about his income. So do his clothes, his car, and numerous other things, though sometimes less reliably. Although a moderate income might permit an occasional $20 meal, regular visits to $50 restaurants bespeak wealth.

We have just seen why people tend to "deal upward," and the advantages of such behavior to those who are already "up." Since it is generally advantageous to have others competing for what one has, by the same token it is often advantageous to *appear* to have more power than one actually has—that is, to appear to belong in a higher class than one is actually in. To discuss this situation we will use the term *actual power* to refer to one's actual skills, strengths, money, formal authority in an organization, and the like. *Status* will refer to apparent or perceived power.[2] Depending on the circumstances, one's status may be greater or less than his actual power.

In the long run one's status will tend to approximate his actual power, since others will have ample opportunity to discover whether reality matches the appearance—though some marked discrepancies may last a long time. In the short run, however, others respond to one's status, not to his actual power. Status is the image of power, and people behave on the basis of their images. It is therefore status, not actual power, that brings others to compete for transactions with him. It will therefore often be seen as advantageous to make sure that one's actual power is converted into status and, perhaps even better, to raise one's status above his actual power.

Because of a desire for status people often behave in ways that sharpen class differences, as follows. Let us discuss three successive levels of class, *A, B,* and *C,* with *A* highest. For reasons already stated, *C*s will try to deal with *B*s if they can, rather than with other *C*s. But for the same reason that *C*s will seek to interact with *B*s, *B*s will seek to deal with *A*s, or at least with other *B*s. Hence a transaction of a *B* with a *C* may leave the impression that the *B* does not have enough power to deal with an *A,* or even with another *B.* To transact downward thus risks lowering one's status. If that result is expected, a *B* may refrain from relations with a *C,* even if the particular transaction would itself be advantageous to *B.*

---

[2] *Status* as used here resembles the semipopular version of Vance Packard's *The Status Seekers* (1959) or William H. Whyte, Jr.'s *The Organization Man* (1957), not the sociologist's concept of position and role. At the same time sociologists do clearly recognize rankings of statuses, as reflected in prestige and deference. The sociologist can perhaps most easily follow the usage here if he emphasizes the ranking aspect and deemphasizes role. *Prestige* will not do for the present purpose without redefinition, since it does not necessarily imply level of power. I could use *perceived power* or *apparent power,* but find those terms clumsy. Since (for those who use the term that way) "status always means position," it would seem to me that *position* alone would do, leaving *status* for some other usage. I have adopted it for this other usage because there is a concept here that needs a name and all the other available names seem even worse than this one.

*A*s will similarly be reluctant to deal with *B*s, even though the *B*s would be delighted. Since people generally seek to deal upward, but those above them are reluctant to deal downward, the net result is that no one has much choice but to deal mostly with others at his own level. Interacting mostly with others at one's own level is thus the normal experience of most people most of the time. It is an effect of class stratification. But by inhibiting interactions upward and downward between levels, such stratification hardens and sharpens the division of people into classes. The obvious exception is the world of business, where even the powerful will usually sell to anyone who can pay.

Other factors reinforce the effect. The upper-class woman is not interested in hearing how the poor woman saves 15 cents per meal by using scraps. Neither is the American slum dweller interested in knowing how to find tourist accommodations in London. For the rich merely to describe what they have been doing—which is the content of much conversation—is painful to the poverty-stricken listener and would seem dreadfully bad manners. What is more, if the rich do what they want while the poor do what they can, their paths seldom cross, except perhaps when the rich make purchases from the poor or hire them as servants.

Another factor helps separate classes. People who associate regularly cannot easily engage in unique transactions. Many of the transactions within continuing relationships are open ended and of the sort, "I'll do this favor for you without any explicit return now. But we understand that you will do an approximately equal favor for me should the occasion arise." Such favors are gifts at the moment they occur, in such forms as invitations to parties, experienced advice, and introductions to strategic people.

Suppose *A* gives favors that *B* cannot match—dinners that cost more than *B* can afford or professional advice at a level that *B* does not possess. If both sides expect reciprocity, then for *B* to return favors of obviously smaller value, or none at all, marks *B* as of lesser power and lowers his status.

The next step follows logically. If *B* cannot return the favors, one way to avoid loss of status is to avoid receiving them. But favors are nice to receive, so why would *B* want to refuse them except to avoid the obligation to reciprocate? For this reason, to refuse favors can also label one as of low status. *B*'s next step is to stay away from *A*s who might do him large favors, as by associating only with others of his own level. But that, too, marks *B* as of lower status.

Gifts have another role in connection with status. Because they are valued, nearly all goods are potential sources of power. A substantial gift therefore says that its giver has power to spare, and thus enhances his status. Distributed with good luck or good management, a series of gifts and favors may also be sound investments in obligations by others, which may increase power when the obligations are due to be paid off. At the moment of giving, *A*'s favor is exchanged for an "account receivable" from *B*—if use of the accountant's language will be pardoned. A particularly vivid account of the process is found in *The Godfather* (Puzo 1969). Gifts to charity may not build obligations for a return payoff, but they do demonstrate one's ability to give, and hence enhance status. Obvious wastefulness or "conspicuous consumption" can have the same effect. Other motives may, of course, reinforce either gift-giving or wastefulness.

Deference

As noted, if B cannot reciprocate A's favors he acquires inferior status. He can avoid this only by avoiding A—if A is inclined to continue giving favors. But if B prefers to receive the favors rather than to avoid lower status he may thank A more profusely than he would if he were A's equal. B may also communicate his lower status in other ways, such as bowing, doffing his hat, and calling A "Mister" while A calls him by his first name. Such behavior by B is deferential, and *deference* is behavior by B that symbolizes and acknowledges his lower status.

Status often becomes intrinsically rewarding, just as money does, and some therefore seek it for its own sake. Since deference says, "Your status is higher than mine," acts of deference by B can similarly be valued things to the A who receives them. Transactions can therefore occur in which A gives goods to B and B gives only deference in return.

From this point the plot thickens rapidly. If A insists, even subtly, on deferential behavior from B he may seem to be saying, "My status is insecure, and I can't afford to throw away opportunities to have it reinforced. So please support my status by deferential behavior." Oppositely, if A discourages deferential behavior by B he may seem to be saying, "My status is so secure that I don't need your deference to prop it up." Similarly, the new-rich or the merely well-to-do may engage in such conspicuous consumption as driving expensive cars and wearing fine clothes just to show they can afford them, whereas the established rich can drive older cars or wear older clothes if they like. The latter thereby enhance their status still further by demonstrating that they have so much status that they can throw away opportunities to display it. The differences in behaviors between people in different classes, and particularly those differences that make it difficult to interact easily and comfortably, are sometimes called *social distance.*

The above discussion deals with people who actually want status. Others do not, and feel uncomfortable unless they can conduct all their relationships as equals. The transactional behavior of such people must be diagnosed in the light of a different set of values.

In many areas of society signs of deference are firmly embedded in the norms, and many members of a given group will feel slighted if these signs are not used. The executive may be called Jim by his fellow executives, but subordinates will be expected to call him Mr. Jones. The clergyman expects to be called pastor or father, the physician doctor, and the college teacher professor or doctor. We address the president, senators, representatives, judges by title, seat them at the head table at banquets, put them first in processions, say respectful things when we introduce them, offer them chairs while others are left standing, rise when they enter the room, make sure others are quiet when they talk, go out of our way to get them to the airport on time, see that they are not kept waiting, and do scores of other things that signalize that they are not "ordinary." Those who refuse or forget to do these things are considered ill-mannered boors, and get crossed off the guest list. The armed forces have their own techniques for dealing with the private who doesn't salute or call the major "major," and few feel they have much to lose by calling the policeman "sir" when he stops them. The servant or caterer is called by his first name but uses Mr. or Mrs. in addressing the people being served. These things are done with remarkable uniformity, though not without exceptions.

Class and status symbols

We have seen why people interact mostly with others of their own class, and why it may be both instrumentally useful and intrinsically rewarding to have one's class recognized by others. By the same token it will often be found useful if members of one class can be readily identified. Such identifying marks are *status symbols,* and their use in many business and other organizations have been well described by Whyte (1957). They include such items as whether one has a reserved parking space, how close it is to his office, whether his office is private, whether he has a rug in his office or a key to the executive washroom, and how many secretaries he has. In some societies people in different classes wear different clothes, live in different areas, buy in different stores, have different numbers of servants, and sit in different sections of theaters. Money alone sometimes dictates the differences, as when the relatively rich sit downstairs at the opera, the middle incomes sit in the balcony, and the poor are not there at all. In other cases the differences are rigidly enforced by law or custom—as in the mandatory racial segregation of the Old South.

If people interact mainly with others of the same level, then merely to travel with a given group suggests that one belongs to it. Hence if one can associate with a group higher than his own he will tend to acquire their status. Consequently, people often "push themselves in" with higher-status groups and "drop names" of high-status people. But those above will tend to exclude the "intruder" to avoid his bringing down *their* status.

The kinds of status behaviors mentioned thus far are relatively "standard" or "establishment." Other groups that do not behave this way probably use different symbols and criteria of status, but still have status differences. Among some militants and street gangs the person who is more willing to use violence rates higher than the chickenhearted, and the top rating sometimes goes to the one who can take the largest doses of hard drugs. Among those who think of themselves as antistatus, the highest status may go to the ones most completely free of status behaviors. Although some hippie communities seem to achieve a status-free condition, it may be that some members are more highly regarded than others by virtue of such traits as greater dedication to the hippie culture, leadership capacity, or musicianship. It would be rare indeed in any group if some did not carry more weight than others in group decisions, in which case they have more power and presumably more status.

All in all it seems doubtful that any significant social group has existed very long without inner differences in power and status symbols, and animal societies often display such differences as well. (See, for example, Yerkes 1939; Stewart and Scott 1947; Crawford 1940; Greenberg 1947; Gregg 1942; Light 1942 and 1943; or Scott 1945.) What is more, competition for status *within* a given level may be the most intense kind—as in trying to be a notch above the family next door or the worker at the next bench. After all, others in the same class are the ones we really compete with and talk about, and who talk about us.

Summary on aggregate power, class, and status

We can summarize the rationale of class and status in the following steps.

1.   We first note the simple fact of differences in aggregate power, just as we note differences in height, weight, or hair color.

2.   Whereas height and hair color are biologically inherited, differences in power are the result of past behavior, particularly in successive transactions.

3.   Differences in power are perceived, and the images of those differences lead to differences in behavior both toward and by persons at different levels.

4.   Because one has more particular power in dealing with others with long (rather than short) EPs, and long EPs themselves represent greater power, one has more power when he makes transactions "upward" than when he "deals downward" or with others at his own level.

5.   But if those above also try to deal upward from *their* positions, the ones below may have no opportunity to do so. Thus if those at each level try to deal upward, but cannot, and refuse to deal downward, the result is relationships mainly with others at one's own level. (We again note most business dealings as exceptions.)

6.   Since one can respond only to his perceptions, any aspects of the above behaviors that do not depend on actual power follow the line of *perceived* aggregate power, or *status.* For many purposes it is therefore advantageous to achieve status that is above one's actual power. This result would seem to explain in part the widely observed tendency to seek status and to display its symbols. As communication, status can be false: status is roughly the aggregate-power parallel of tactics in bargaining power.

In closing, perhaps we should note one of the distinct virtues of selfish-indifferent transactions in goods, namely, that they are strictly voluntary. Under such transactions a person may be "poor but have his independence." Because strategic bads and gifts of goods can be imposed on a person without his prior consent both have the capacity to rob him of his independence.

part IV

Organizations: Social systems of multiple humans

In Part I we introduced the notion of system. In Part II we looked at the individual human as a system, including the way his detector, selector, and effector functions jointly produce and effectuate a decision within the system. In Part III we shifted from the individual as system to interactions between systems.

Any two or more systems which interact, however, also constitute a higher-level system. In Part III we nevertheless focused solely on the interactions, without attending to the higher-level system thus produced. We examined parts, interactions of parts, and the effects of interactions on the parts. But we ignored the ways in which the whole is more than the sum of its parts.

We now shift to the ways in which the whole *is* something more than its parts. These are the respects in which the parts and their interactions constitute a higher-level system, which can also be thought of as the *emergent* aspect of the relationship. Higher-level systems which consist of two or more persons will be called *organizations*. If the activities of these persons are consciously and explicitly coordinated toward some joint goal, their relationship is a *formal organization*. This is a *controlled system* of multiple humans, and can range in size and complexity from two persons jointly carrying a table to a major corporation or government. By contrast, if the activities of the parties are not explicitly directed toward some joint goal, the organization is informal or semiformal, depending on circumstances. *Informal organization* is an *uncontrolled system* of multiple humans, while *semiformal organization* is a *semicontrolled system*. Informal and semiformal organizations similarly run a wide gamut of sizes. To say that the parts of informal and semiformal organizations are not consciously coordinated does not mean that the system is chaotic. Many people engaging in transactions, each strictly minding his own business, constitute a market economic system that is orderly in many ways. They may also produce an orderly class structure or neighborhood.

To illustrate organizational types before going into detail, the people in an elevator are not an organization at all if they do not interact. If each tries to maximize the space around himself, the people will distribute themselves more or less evenly in the elevator. This would be a simple example of pure informal organization—the production of a clear non-random pattern through the purely self-oriented actions of individuals. If the elevator gets stuck, and by agreement A pushes a button while B stands on C's shoulders to open a trapdoor, we have simple formal organization—joint activity consciously coordinated toward a joint goal. If some individuals say things or use tones of voice designed to avoid panic and possible injury in the group, their behavior is semiformal organization—an attempt to have a desired effect on the whole, but without taking charge or consciously coordinating people's actions. Strictly speaking, *any* interaction of two or more persons constitutes an organization—since any two interacting components constitute a system, and any system whose components are persons is an organization. However, we do not view communication or transaction as organization, since there is normally no significant *joint* effect distinct from the effects on the parties themselves.

Just as we looked at pure transactions and pure communications, and then at the varieties in between, so we will look first at pure formal organization, next at pure informal organization, and then at the situations in between. Though nearly all real organizations are "impure," and fall along a continuous spectrum, they are mixtures, not compounds. To the extent that they are formal, the formal model helps us understand them. To the extent that they are informal, the informal model can be used. The "pure" models help produce good theory and clear concepts.

In deciding whether or not to view a given organization as formal, the best practical approach is to see whether it has detector, selector, and effector processes that operate for or on behalf of the organization as a whole. Is there some identifiable person or group who can make decisions more or less binding on others? Is there some meaningful sense in which the organization consciously directs its efforts toward a conscious goal? If so, it will probably be best to use the formal model to understand it. Otherwise not.

Like a spaceship or an individual human being, an organization consists of interacting components, the lowest-level components of an organization being persons. But whereas the component parts of a spaceship or the biological human interact in ways that involve such sciences as biology, chemistry, hydraulics, mechanics, and electricity, the interactions of people in an organization are all communications, transactions, or both. If two or more organizations interact, *their* interactions are also communications, transactions, or both. In short, if we focus on the organization as a unit, since it is a controlled system we use the intrasystem concepts of detector, selector, and effector. But if we focus on interactions of its parts, or on the interactions of the whole organization, we examine its communications and transactions. No matter how complex the organization, we can move up and down among its levels without needing any new or different science.

15

FORMAL ORGANIZATION: GENERAL THEORY

INTRODUCTION TO FORMAL ORGANIZATION

This is the first of two chapters on formal organization. After introducing the general concept, it moves to simple organization, trying to find the conditions under which people join, refrain from joining, or withdraw from organizations. Some of these conclusions help our later study of economic systems. We next identify the main kinds of relations of persons to complex organizations—for example, the roles of owners, bosses, workers, members, customers—and the main kinds of organizations. An understanding of these relations will help our later study of governments and economic systems. Finally we raise questions about who controls an organization and why, and how its decisions are made. These questions also apply to government as well as to many other organizations. The next chapter will examine more explicitly how an organization welds a batch of individuals into a team. Some concepts developed for formal organizations will be used later for understanding informal and semiformal organizations.

When is an organization?

If A gives up bread and receives cheese, while B gives up cheese and receives bread, the interaction is a transaction. If A gives up bread, B gives up cheese, and the two together produce cheese sandwiches, the interaction is an organization—a simple formal one, to be precise.[1] Or-

---

[1] To keep the distinction between formal and informal organization consistent with that between controlled and uncontrolled systems we use definitions slightly

ganization, however, does not eliminate transactional and communicational relations. Rather, it adds the new ingredient of jointness, or of joint effect, and we define *organization* as the relation of two or more persons in the production of joint effect. In formal organization the joint effect is explicit and intentional for at least one of the persons. In informal and semiformal organization the joint effect is either unintended or only partly or loosely intended—as we shall see later.

In this model formal organization exists whenever two or more persons jointly and deliberately do something they cannot do, or cannot do so well, separately. One person cannot run a railroad, carry a piano, play a string quartet, or make love. And although one might be able to carry a small table, help the poor, or worship God by himself, he may nevertheless find such activities more satisfactory or effective if he does them jointly with others—in formal organization. Sometimes the joint effect is transactional, as when two or more persons join to bargain collectively. Sometimes its purpose is communicational, as with a school, a broadcasting station, or two persons trying to teach karate to a third. Insofar as attention is focused on the jointness, however, the model of organization will help us to understand it. In any event, this book is interested in the *social*, not the technical, aspects of the joint activity. These aspects are essentially the same whether the objective is a joint communication, a joint transaction, or a joint transformation.

We noted that transaction involves two mutually contingent decisions: A decides to give up bread in return for cheese, and B decides to give up cheese in return for bread. But these are *two different decisions*. By contrast, a crucial aspect of organization is that A and B must agree on, or at least accept, a *single* decision binding on both. The bread and cheese must be used for sandwiches, not padding under the rug. Someone must decide whether the factory will produce airplanes, sausages, or both, and the decision must be binding on all who work there.

As with transaction, organization involves both cooperation and conflict. It is cooperative to the extent that more wants can be satisfied in total with it than without it. It is conflictual in that the less the inputs from and the greater the outputs to one member (other things equal) the greater must be the inputs from and the smaller the outputs to other members. Increasing the size of the pie is cooperative; dividing it up is conflictual.

By creating larger or better effects than can separate individuals, organizations enlarge *power*—which is the main reason for forming them. *Whose* power is enlarged will be examined later.

The next several chapters will deal with *voluntary organizations,* which the individual can join or leave, depending on how he sees their costs and benefits to himself. Such organizations are also *limited-purpose,* or *segmental,* in that they deal with only a limited segment or

---

different from those usually found in organization theory. In that theory *formal organization* would include only our *complex formal organizations.* Definitional consistency later requires us to use *semiformal organization* for much of the behavior that organization theory usually designates as informal. *Voluntary organization* is also somewhat broadened.

aspect of life. Later, families and governments will be our main examples of organizations that include involuntary memberships and a wide scope of purposes.

THE MODEL OF SIMPLE ORGANIZATION

If the function of organization is to do more or better of something together than two or more persons can do it separately, then the superiority of the joint effort over the sum of the separate efforts is the measure of the benefit from having the organization. Since the presumed purpose of joining an organization is to receive something valued, and relations based on values are transactions, the main relations between organizations and their members are transactional, albeit with communicational adjuncts. For the same reason that we started our study of transactions with easily counted units of value (commodities and money) we will use readily counted units for our beginning model of organization.

We start with a model that is simple enough for us to "see everything." Any or all of the transactions, communications, or their many mixtures described in Chapters 9 through 14 may go on inside simple organizations. We will not describe them again here, but will focus instead on the new relationships that are inescapably found in formal organization, and only there—relationships we need to know in connection with complex organizations, governments, and economic systems.

Equal skills and contributions

Our model of simple organization involves only a few persons, and we will start with two. As in the initial model of the transaction we will assume that the motivation of each party is selfish-indifferent, that the costs to each consist solely of his input contributions to the organization, that the benefits to each consist solely of his withdrawals of its outputs, that the organization has no fixed costs or investments, that there are only one or a few goals (limited purpose), and that only positive goods are involved. The logic is clearest when each individual can do something for himself, but when joint performance is more efficient or satisfactory.

Suppose that operating alone A and B could each catch 8 fish an hour, for a total of 16. Suppose further that if they fished together they could catch 24 fish an hour, or 12 each. The increase does not arise from extra effort or skill, but because the job is done more efficiently by two. It is obviously advantageous to both (a cooperative relationship) to fish as a team. The input contributed by each is his time and effort, and the output received by each is his share of the fish.

The situation is diagramed as a transaction in Figure 15–1. Each EP is the desire to work jointly rather than alone, and can be expressed in two ways. The extension of A's EP to 16 on the top scale means either (1) that A would be willing to give as much as (but no more than) 16 fish out of the joint catch in order to receive B's services in fishing jointly with him, or (2) that A would be willing to accept as few as the remaining 8 fish from *B* in return for his own services. Read from right to left on the bottom scale, *B*'s *EP* means the same as *A*'s.

An interesting aspect of the two-person simple organization is that employer and employee views coincide. If *A* views himself as the organization (the employer) he will be willing to pay *B* as much as, but no more than, 16 fish for his services, while retaining 8 for himself. If *A* views himself as an employee he will be willing to work for the organization (or for *B* as employer) in return for a "wage" of no fewer than 8 fish. (At a more subjective level, the consequences of "taking a mate" in marriage are the same for each party as "giving oneself"—unless the different wordings reflect different attitudes.)

This (or any other) simple organization is *terminable at will* (no commitments), which means that either party can leave it at any time without complications or loss. The organization as such owns no joint property, owes no joint debts, and (being selfish-indifferent) involves no ties

Figure 15–1

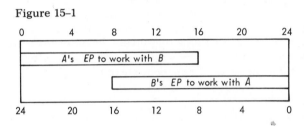

of sentiment or affection. Except for the benefit it produced while it operated, once the organization is dropped everything returns to where it was before. That is, neither party has any stake in the organization except to receive current benefits from it. By contrast, the more assets, liabilities, or both that the organization accumulates the harder it is to drop it, and the greater is someone's stake in continuing it. Also the more sharply will the employer and employee positions be distinguished—as we shall see.

If *A* and *B* are equally good bargainers, the catch will be divided 12–12 between them. If they are not, it may be divided on any terms between 16–8 and 8–16. Beyond those terms one party would be better off alone. That is, although the organization is cooperative by the amount it adds to productivity, transactional conflict can nevertheless occur over contributions of input or receipts of output. Regarding the extra output, we can say that the joint action is more productive, that organization adds to power, or (if we are careful not to personify it) that the organization contributes to output.

We have already seen the many variations of transactions, which may include generosity, hostility, friendship, bads, agents, and pleasure or displeasure in the process itself. All such variations can also occur in transactions about organization. Since their consequences are essentially the same in organization as out of it, we need not repeat them here.

Unequal skills and contributions

Suppose A develops a special skill in throwing a net while B catches it, and thereby raises the joint catch to 32. B, however, cannot learn this skill. Will A, who is its sole possessor, be able to command the whole increase of 8 for himself? Not under a selfish-indifferent relation. For even though it is wholly A's skill that brings the increase, A cannot use the skill alone. Hence he can still produce only 8 fish by himself, which amount remains the floor under his bargaining power. Given equal bargaining skill, the catch will still be divided equally, at 16–16. It is, of course, true that A has become more important to B than before. But B has also become more important to A, since A's new technique will not work without B's help. Given the interchangeability of the employer-employee positions, we can say either that the employer can capture part of the gain contributed by the employee, or that the employee can capture part of the gain contributed by the employer.

Historically both things have happened. Workers have often received wage increases when their productivity was raised by machines designed and paid for by employers, because their increased productivity made them more valuable to the employers. In other cases workers who increased their output by extra skill and effort have often received no reward—only an increase in expected output.

Competition

Let us now suppose that B_1 is lurking in the background. B_1 has been working with A_1, who does not have A's special skill with the net, and the two have been dividing their catch 12–12. Like B, B_1 could also catch 8 fish for himself, or contribute to a total catch of 32 if he worked with A and his new technique. Since B_1 has been receiving only 12 fish while working with A_1, he could improve his position by one unit if he worked with A for 13 instead. This arrangement would also improve A's position, by leaving him 19 fish instead of the 16 he has been getting by working with B. If B_1 made this offer, B could be forced to match it, or A would leave him for B_1. Given this competition among the Bs, if A continues to hold the monopoly on his special skill he can now capture some benefit from his superior skill.

More than two members—and marginalism

In the previous section we did not contemplate taking more than two into the organization. To illustrate our new problem, let us return to the original assumption that A and B could each catch 8 fish alone and 24 together, with equal division. If C were added to make a three-man team, the total output would rise to (say) 33. Could C receive 11, in an equal division? If not, how many could he get?

Because it occurs eventually in any organization as more and more producing members are added, we have illustrated diminishing marginal productivity. By this we mean that one *additional* unit of input (workers in this case) produces less *additional* output than did the previous unit of input, even though all of the workers use equal skill and effort. *Marginal* is a term widely used in economics, and refers to, as in Chapter 8, additional (or incremental) units of input and output, as contrasted to total or average input and output. That is, when *B* joined *A* he added 16 units to the total, whereas when *C* was added to *A and B* he added only 9 more units. Under a selfish-indifferent attitude *A* and *B* would not give *C* more than the 9 units he added. If they did, they would have less for themselves than before.

With more than two persons in the organization the employer and employee views are no longer interchangeable, for two reasons. First, to give one more unit to *C* would not take away one each from *A* and *B* but only half a unit. Second it makes a difference (1) whether we view *A* and *B* together as the organization trying to decide whether to hire *C,* or (2) whether we view *A* as the organization trying to decide whether to hire *B, C,* or both. In either case *C* would not be hired unless he worked for 9 units or less. Under the above conditions he would presumably accept 9, since 9 units would leave him one unit better off than if he worked alone.

But if *A* is the employer of both *B* and *C,* how will he feel about *B* once *C* has agreed to work for 9 units? Assuming selfishness, *A* will put *B* out of the organization unless *B* also agrees to work for 9. Why? If *A* continued to employ *B* at his previous wage of 12 units, *A* would have 12 left for himself. If he laid off *B,* the total catch would drop to 24, the amount produced by two persons. But *A* would pay *C* only 9, and have 15 for himself. In short, at a wage of 12 for *B, A* is three units better off without *B* than with him, and will eliminate him. In fact, if *A* were already employing *C* and paying him 9 units, *A* would not hire *B* for even as little as 10. If he did so, the total would again rise to 33. If he paid 9 to *C* and 10 to *B, A* would have 14 left for himself, which is one less than he got by doing without *B.* The reader can try other combinations for himself. But no matter how it is arranged, *A* will not employ *both B* and *C* unless *both* accept 9 units or less.

In this simple form we have previewed a fundamental principle of organization: that *no* employee (of a given type and ability) is worth more to his employer than the productive contribution of the *last one* added. The principle is known in economics as the marginal productivity theory of wages.

If all workers were employers, as in a producer cooperative, they would presumably seek the largest *average* return, which would occur above with two persons receiving 12 each. But thus far we have said nothing about who provides boats, nets, shoreline, fishing rights, or other inputs, all of which complicate the problem.

Indivisible outputs

Unlike the above instances, the results of some joint efforts are not divisible. After wife and husband jointly carry the table from the living room to the dining room, it cannot be in the dining room for the wife and in the living room for the husband. If the windows are clean they are clean for both, and the grass in the town square is either cut or not cut for all. Unlike the divisible catch of fish, an indivisible output is overtly the same for all. Here there can be bargaining only over inputs, and bargaining power is shifted toward the party who has a smaller desire for the joint output. Whether the product is an orderly living room, a well-trained dog, a continued marriage, a free society, or world peace, the party that wants it more has the lesser bargaining power and (other things equal) will make the larger contribution toward producing it.

Summary on simple organization

In the transaction, A gives up X and receives Y in return, while B gives up Y and receives X. In simple organization, A gives up X, B gives up Y, and both receive some Z, which is the product of their joint effort. In this respect organization resembles the transaction in services, in which the thing received by each party is not the same thing the other party gives up. However, organization does require both parties to work toward the same objective. The main features of the simple model are:

1.   People presumably form an organization to increase their productivity, and hence their power—given our broad definitions of productivity and power.

2.   One joins, refrains from joining, or leaves an organization by completing, not completing, or terminating a transaction of membership.

3.   In bargaining over contributions and withdrawals, the floor under one's bargaining power is his best alternative. The usual alternatives are to produce for oneself or to join some other organization.

4.   As with any other uncoerced transaction, no one will stay in an organization if he loses from doing so. Hence any voluntary organization is at least a zero-sum game, and will be positive-sum by the amount the joint product exceeds the sum of what the members could produce separately.

5.   When only two parties are involved, it does not matter whether one views himself as "the organization" deciding whether to add another member, or as an individual deciding whether to join the organization. Whatever the number of members, however, the organization's EP for adding another member is his added (marginal) contribution to its product.

As with transactions, it is easiest to illustrate the logic of organizations with simple, countable products. But people may go into organizations for companionship, emotional support, fun and games, to build an irrigation project, or to gain protection against natural enemies. As to details, to save space we simply say: "All the complications and variations already discussed in Chapters 9 through 14 also apply here." Our omission of the variations does not mean that reality is as simple as the model.

When all those complications are included, it is harder to decide whether an organization is worth belonging to than when the benefits are readily countable. But to the extent that one can sense some benefit and cost in joining a group (advantages and disadvantages), the above principles presumably apply. Emerson, for example, has found much the same kind of bargaining power factors determine whether children will or will not be admitted as participants in a game (Emerson 1962). Customs, habits, and social pressures will be dealt with later. Some looser situations—such as mobs, people in an elevator, and social gatherings—will be discussed in the next chapter.

MODEL OF COMPLEX ORGANIZATION

We will move in one leap from the simple model to more complex organization, leaving the reader to imagine various stages in between. A complex organization may or may not be incorporated—whether it be a business firm, a consumer cooperative, a church, a village, a ski club, a charity, or a mutual benefit association. Incorporation nevertheless has a trait that makes it an excellent illustration, and we will use it for our model. An incorporated organization is legally recognized as an entity in itself, independent of the individuals in it. Because all its components are replaceable, at least in theory, the corporation has a potentially permanent life.

The model: The parties and types of organizations

Complex organization differs from simple organization in several respects. (1) It has more than two persons. Among other things this fact makes a difference between employer and employee points of view. (2) It utilizes division of labor, both horizontally and vertically. The former means that different persons perform different tasks, and the latter means that some persons are supervisors and others are supervised—some are leaders and some followers. (3) Not all details of the relationship can be included in the major bargain of membership. This means that a member may be subject to decisions made after he has joined, which he may or may not like. (4) The structure of the organization is consciously designed by those in charge of it, who will be named the sponsors.

In simple organization the same persons decide what the organization is to do, provide the inputs, do the work, and receive the outputs. In complex organization these four functions are separable, and may be performed by different sets of persons, defined in our model as follows.

Sponsors: Those who determine whether or not the organization will exist and what it will do—e.g., whether it will make bubble gum, preach the gospel, or seek political control. In the pure case the goals, methods of operation, and structure of the organization are set by the sponsors. Formal organization is a controlled, or cybernetic, system, and the goals of the sponsors constitute the main level selector of the system. In this model the sponsors are those who actually perform these sponsor functions—the *real* sponsors. Often these are not the persons identified in the organization charter or letterhead—the *nominal* sponsors, whom we are not interested in here.

Staff: Those who do the organization's work, from janitor to president. ("Staff" in this context is not the same as in the frequent distinction between line and staff). "Staff member" is synonymous with "employee," and includes all executives as well as unpaid volunteer workers. Those sponsors who actively help direct the organization, along with those executives who are their close agents, are the *management,* or the *administration.* All members of the staff are direct or indirect agents of the sponsors.

Recipients: Those to, for, or at whom the output of the organization is directed: those who receive the output, whether commodity or service. In the kinds of organizations people pay to join, such as clubs, most members are likely to be recipients, not staff.

Factor suppliers: Those other than staff who provide inputs to the organization. Strictly speaking, the staff also provide inputs (time and effort) and are therefore factor suppliers. But because they are also members they require separate treatment.

Inputs and outputs can be described as either real or money flows. Real inputs are such things as raw materials, labor, supplies, power, fuel, machines, buildings, hired repair services, land space, and natural resources. Depending on the organization, outputs may be corn, houses, radios, stage shows, advertising, automobile repairs, medical care, social services, education, or sermons.

In most complex organizations (and in our model) the staff and suppliers are paid for their inputs. To the extent that they provide inputs without charge they share the sponsor role, for reasons to be seen. For this reason the main problems of staff and suppliers are the same for all the types of organization we will distinguish below. As Weber put it, members of the bureaucracy (staff) will serve any master. Although there are many reasons for distinguishing among churches, firms, armies, schools, families, governments, and so on, and many ways of classifying organizations, for the *social* analysis of organizations it seems most useful to distinguish four basic types. These will be distinguished on the basis of the allocation of costs and benefits between sponsors and recipients and of the kinds of transactions that take place between them.

The simple organization discussed earlier is cooperative; the jointness of its members' activities contributes to the welfare of each. We will continue to use the name *cooperative* if, instead of providing all the inputs and doing all the work themselves, the members purchase the supplies and hire a staff to do the work, while they themselves receive the outputs. This is the basic situation in a consumer cooperative, a church congregation, a club or professional association that serves only its members, or a democratic government. The same persons are both sponsors and recipients, who both bear the costs and receive the benefits of the organization—which relationship constitutes our definition of the cooperative organization. Because they bear the costs of the inputs only in order to receive the outputs, we assign the costs and benefits to them in their role as recipients.

The business firm is the chief example of a *profit organization*. Here the sponsors and the recipients are different persons: the sponsors set up and control the organization and the recipients are its customers. Outputs are sold to recipients in selfish-indifferent transactions. If the firm is successful, the receipts from sales are greater than the cost of producing the output. The difference is profit, which is the benefit produced by the organization and received by its sponsors. If things go badly, the profit will be negative—a loss, which will have to be borne by the sponsors. Since such an organization rarely seeks a loss, we will analyze it in terms of its profit objective.

The defining characteristics of the profit organization are (1) that its costs are borne by recipients and its benefits received by sponsors, and (2) that the transactions between the two are selfish. The resulting benefit to the recipients is incidental to the goals of the organization, in the same sense that in a selfish-indifferent transaction A does not care whether B is made better or worse off by it. In this case, if the sponsors are A, acting through their staff as agents, and the recipients are B, the benefit in question is that received by A in excess of what A pays out to staff and suppliers.

A *service organization* is one in which sponsors bear the costs and give the outputs as benefits to recipients in a generous transaction. Public or private charities and free public schools are examples.

Finally, there are *pressure organizations*. Here sponsors bear the costs and receive the benefits. If the sponsors are A, the outputs are provided to C in the hope or expectation that C will directly or indirectly alter his relation with B in some way that will improve the position of A in the A–B relation. A lobby sponsored by a utility company, A, for example, might exert pressure on a regulating commission, C, to get approval of a rate increase which would improve A's position relative to utility customers, Bs. Or the consumers might sponsor a lobby to get rates reduced, in which case the consumers are sponsoring a pressure organization. In these parallel examples the lobby is the pressure organization, the utility firms or the consumers are its sponsors, and the regulating commission is the recipient.

Such pressures can be very roundabout, as when utility companies employ an advertising company to influence the public to change its image of utilities so that citizens will write to their congressmen to put pressure on the regulating commission. The output of the pressure organization might have positive value to the recipients, as with useful information or samples of a product. In other cases the output might be essentially useless to them, and in still others it could be a bad rather than a good.[2]

---

[2] Although they come directly from Kuhn (1963 and 1974) the names of these four types of organizations partially parallel those of Blau and Scott (1962: 43). Basing their classification in turn partly on Simon, they list (1) mutual benefit, (2) business, (3) service, and (4) commonweal, depending on whether the main benefits of the organization go, respectively, to (1) the members or rank-and-file participants, (2) the owners or managers, (3) the "clients" outside but in regular contact with the organization, and (4) the public at large. For reasons that will

Figure 15–2
TYPES OF ORGANIZATIONS, BY ALLOCATION OF COSTS AND
BENEFITS AND BY TYPES OF TRANSACTIONS

Type	Costs	Benefits	Sponsor-recipient transaction
Cooperative	Recipients	Recipients	None (same persons)
Profit	Recipients	Sponsors	Selfish-indifferent
Service	Sponsors	Recipients	Generous
Pressure	Sponsors	Sponsors	Third-party strategies

The bases for classifying the four types of organizations are summarized in Figure 15–2, which shows for each type the allocation of costs and benefits as between sponsors and recipients, and the kind of transaction, if any, between them.

Many real organizations, perhaps most, are multiple types. A church, for example, is a cooperative in its relation to its own members, a service organization in its charitable work, a profit organization when it raises money through a rummage sale, and a pressure organization when it lobbies to retain tax exemption. A business firm is a profit organization in its basics, cooperative in its employees' bowling team or credit cooperative, service in its assistance to social agencies, and pressure in its lobbying or institutional advertising. A labor union is basically a pressure organization, designed to improve the position of its sponsors, the employees, in their relation with the employer. But it can be cooperative in its social events, service in helping the local community chest, and profit if it tries to raise money by selling embroidered union suits.

If most real organizations are mixtures, what is the point of the distinction? To answer by analogy, you are also a mixture. When you buy a car from a dealer the model of the selfish transaction would presumably apply, whereas when you help a sick friend the generous model would be more appropriate. It is the nature of the behavior, not the identity of the party, that determines what model we use.

The *social* analysis of an organization is concerned with the relationships of people, not with the nature of its output, which may be bird feeders, television repair, legislation, medical care, or belief in God. Hence we do not use categories like manufacturing, governmental, medical, or religious—which reflect types of outputs.

Evaluating the organization's performance

Depending on the type, it may be relatively easy or hard to tell whether an organization is doing its job well or badly. The evaluation is simplest in an incorporated business in a money economy, where both costs and

become clearer as we proceed, I think it more useful to classify the types of organizations by the type of transaction between two sets of parties rather than on the basis of the identities of the parties. That is, I consider it important to attend to the allocation of both costs *and* benefits rather than to the allocation of benefits alone.

benefits, and hence the difference between them, are measurable in money.[3] The larger the difference (profit) the better is the organization's performance.

Although the costs and benefits of a cooperative may be subjective in part, they are nevertheless measured within the value system of the same parties, who are simultaneously sponsors and recipients.

In a service organization the costs are borne by sponsors and the benefits accure to recipients. Since a recipient is apt to accept a gift whether or not he wants it very much, it is hard for sponsors to know how much benefit the gift creates, and whether the benefit equals its cost. What is more, the costs and benefits must be measured in the value systems of different parties, which comparison cannot really be made at all. That is, it is generally agreed that an interpersonal comparison of utility (Do you like coffee more than I like tea?) is not possible except under extremely limited circumstances that do not help with this problem. Although the transactions of the service organization *may* produce a large net benefit, like other generous transactions they can also bring a net loss to both giver and receiver. Hence the only sensible way to evaluate the service organization is to ask whether the sponsors believe or perceive the benefit to recipients to be equal to or greater than the cost to themselves. We might also ask whether the satisfaction the sponsors receive from giving is at least equal to their cost of doing so.

Evaluation of the pressure organization depends much on the case at hand. In some cases the organization might produce obvious results, positive or negative. In others the sponsors may never know whether the pressure left things better, worse, or unchanged. In short, profit and cooperative organizations are generally easier to evaluate than are service and pressure organizations. Needless to say, it may be hard to know whether *any* organization is performing well or poorly unless the sponsors have a pretty clear idea of their goals and objectives.

ORGANIZATIONAL DECISION AND CONTROL

In Chapters 6 and 7 we analyzed decisions as if they were being made by one person or by unanimous agreement within a group. Because organization requires the acceptance of a single decision by multiple persons, we must now move to the *social* level of decision making: how a decision can be reached among persons who have divergent views and goals.

For organizations we will raise this question at two levels. First, as among sponsors, staff, recipients, and suppliers, where does the control

---

[3] Actually, the amount of profit shown for any limited period depends greatly on some rather subjective aspects of cost accounting, such as the treatment of appreciation or depreciation and the allocation of fixed costs. Strictly speaking, it is only in the economist's model of the firm that benefits and costs consist solely of money. In real firms they take other forms, including the self-image of the executives or their concern as citizens over pollution. Even in real firms, however, the profit and loss statement is a useful first approximation measure of the organization's performance.

lie, and why? Second, within the controlling group (who turn out to be the sponsors), how is a decision reached if they disagree among themselves? Although we ask this second question about decisions among sponsors, we can apply its principles to *any* situation in which a number of persons must reach and accept the same decision.

The basis of sponsor control

We will open this discussion by an evasively circular statement that whichever persons do, in fact, control the organization will use it to implement *their* goals, and that those whose goals do, in fact, determine the organization's behavior are by definition the sponsors.

To many laymen it seems self-evident that the owners control a business "because they own it." However, ownership in turn is defined essentially as the right to control, and the layman's statement is no less circular. Often there is also uncertainty as to whether owners *do* control, and whether they *ought* to—the former a question in science and the latter in ethics. We will deal here only with the question of who *will* control, and why. We start with the simple model. Many complexities will be added later in connection with semiformal organization.

As among the four groups, the question of who will control can be answered by studying their transactional relations in more detail. The staff and suppliers provide their inputs on the basis of selfish transactions. If they are not paid they stop providing their inputs and the organization folds.

The question of control thus resolves into the question of who determines whether and how much, suppliers and staff will be paid, and in return for what contributions. It is the old story that who pays the piper calls the tune. In the pressure organization the sponsors provide the means to pay for inputs. In the cooperative the recipients provide the means; but they also double as sponsors. In the service organization the means are provided by contributors of money, materials, or work. In each case, if those who contribute the inputs (or the money to pay for them) cease to contribute, the organization ceases to exist. Hence they have the power to specify how their contributions are to be used as a condition of giving them. In this power lies control.

We have drawn the question in black-and-white terms. Once we have established that control lies with sponsors, the next question is, How much control do they exert? It must be answered partly in connection with the question of authority, which we will discuss shortly. But we can indicate here that this question, too, is subject to all the variations and complications of transactional and communicational analysis that we have already been through.

The profit organization is more complicated, because it is the only type whose costs are borne by recipients who are not also sponsors. Although the original sponsors pay its costs until the organization is under way, thereafter the costs are recovered through sales to recipients. The original investors, generally designated as the owners, then have no power to halt the organization by withholding contributions. In fact, the organization may even expand by reinvesting profits—again, without help from the original sponsors. This ability of the successful profit organization to avoid going back to the nominal sponsors for further contributions accounts for the widespread loss of stockholder control. Often referred to as "inside controlled," or as "separation of ownership and control," the sponsor function in such corporations has shifted to an essentially self-perpetuating group of directors and executives. As we define the terms, this group have *become* sponsors, not merely "taken control from" the sponsors.

Group decisions (among sponsors)

One of the most important questions in social science is how a decision is made by a group who disagree among themselves. In the framework of this book that question can arise only in connection with formal organization. Pure communication requires no decision at all—a decision could come up only in connection with transactional (valued) aspects of communication. Transaction requires two mutually contingent decisions. But as noted, these are different decisions, not the same decision. Unless persons work toward or are bound by a common goal (in which case they are part of a formal organization), there is never any occasion for two or more of them to reach or accept the same decision about anything. (Any interactions not subject to the same decision fall under informal and semiformal organization.) Hence a central question of formal organization is that of getting a decision among a group. Since people lower in an organization only do what they are told, or make individual decisions about their tasks, the question of group decisions arises only among sponsors, or among their agents in charge of the organization's subsystems. Hence we couch the question of group decisions as that of sponsor decisions.

Sponsor decisions also involve a fundamental question in social science. In our model of social man, motivation exists only in the selectors of individuals—in states of individual nervous systems. Strictly speaking, an organization has no motivations and no goals. Nevertheless there is coordinated action, and in formal organization it is consciously coordinated by the sponsors. Hence, whenever this volume speaks of goals or decisions of an organization *as a unit* it refers to those of the sponsors as reached through whatever decision processes they actually use (and as limited in practice by informal and semiformal behaviors of the staff, as will be seen later).

Of course, no problem of group decision exists when there is only one sponsor, as with an owner-manager of a small business; the problem arises only when there are multiple sponsors. A difficulty in analyzing large organizations is to discover who actually performs detector, selector, and effector functions—a matter well beyond the scope of this introduction. The group decision itself must be made by interaction, that is, by communication, transaction, or both. We now examine these as means of reaching *agreement.*

Agreement by communication and transaction. An attempt to reach agreement by communication would consist of argument and persuasion. If successful it alters detector or selector states of members till all agree on one alternative as the best. If some members of the family want to vacation in the mountains and others at the shore, they may discuss the matter till everyone agrees that the mountains are best. The decision is then unanimous.

If communication does not settle the problem, transaction may. Transaction, also known as compromise, means that some give up part of what they want in return for concessions from others. The terms of the compromise will be determined by the bargaining power factors discussed earlier, and one or many transactions may go into a settlement. If each person feels that others have made adequate compromises, agreement can again be unanimous. Thus, if persuasion does not bring everyone to agree on the mountains, the family may agree by trade-off to go to the mountains this year and the shore next year.

In decision by communication everyone gets what he wants, even if he first has to be persuaded to want it. Nobody gives up anything. By contrast, in decision by transaction each must give up some of what he wants and accept something less satisfactory instead. Thus, as between the two, decision by communication will be preferred.

Decision rules—and dominant coalitions. But if persuasion and trade-offs still leave disagreement, what next? Since we recognize only two kinds of interactions, and both have failed, we conclude that agreement is not possible. But to say that *agreement* is not possible does not mean a *decision* is not. It only means that some members will agree to the decision and others will not.

"As I understand it, if J. B. puts Henratty down, we acquire fifty-one per cent of their common stock at $12.75 per share, plus four seats on the board of directors. If Henratty puts J. B. down. . . ."

Courtesy of Vihan Shirvanian, in *Saturday Review*, April 3, 1971.

We can easily visualize this process under a *decision rule,* which is an advance understanding that when all cannot agree they will nevertheless accept a decision if it is reached through an accepted process. The process might be tossing a coin, consulting an arbitrator or an oracle, reading tea leaves, letting the chairman decide, or letting the leaders of the two main factions fight it out. A common decision rule is the vote, in which the majority get what they want and the minority do not.

A decision by ballot, whether majority or plurality, is one form of group decision by dominant coalition. A *dominant coalition* (not to be confused with a bargaining coalition) is a subgroup which supports a common position and holds more of the kind of power relevant to the decision than does any other subgroup. Where the vote is the unit of power, the largest bloc of votes wins. Where votes are proportionate to money invested, the largest bloc of money wins, as with corporate stockholders. A street gang is often ruled by the coalition that can beat up any challenging coalition. A person who can single-handedly beat up any collectivity willing to challenge him constitutes a one-man dominant "coalition"—if we may be allowed the definitional absurdity of a coalition of one. In the Norton Street gang (Whyte (1943) dominance lay with a group who were the best bowlers, fighters, and arguers. In some circumstances the coalition that can talk loudest, stay awake longest, or simply be most cussedly stubborn may carry the decision.

The kind of power "relevant to the group" will vary with the group and the circumstances. In an amateur theater group of 25 persons, 20 may like and 5 may dislike the director. But if the minority of five consists of the only four actors the patrons will pay to see and the only competent stagehand, and if those five will walk out if the present director is kept, the five are dominant in the relevant power and can get their new director—even if the vote is 20-to-5 against them. Sometimes a coalition can make itself dominant by simply taking or announcing an action or decision that is difficult for others to challenge or undo.

We have said that decision by communication (agreement) will be seen as more satisfactory than decision by transaction (trade-off). In the first everyone gets what he wants, and in the second everyone gets at least something in return for what he gives up. In a decision by dominant coalition, however, the winners win and the losers lose. That is, the losers not only do not get what they want. They do not even get any concessions for not getting what they want. Other things equal a decision by dominant coalition will be considered the least satisfactory. Thus among the three types, decision by communication is the most highly preferred and that by dominant coalition the least preferred. (March and Simon 1958: 129–31; Robinson and Majak 1967; Etzioni 1968: 371).

Dominance sometimes lies in a marginal amount of power. If a project requires $100,000, and $80,000 has already been collected or firmly committed, the person who can provide the remaining $20,000 may dominate some decisions about it. His power lies in the ability to withhold, which has been lost by those who are already committed.

And subcoalitions. This, however, is not the end of the story. A given coalition can become and remain dominant only if its own members

stick together in support of a single position. If its members do not initially agree among themselves about the position *they* want the coalition
to support, that decision is arrived at by the same process as is the main
decision. The members of the coalition make *their* decision by communication, transaction, or dominant subcoalition—and so on. Much of the
"art of politics" lies in knowing the hierarchical levels of a given coalition structure, and then through communications and transactions lin-
ing up the key people who can provide dominance at each level.

Decision processes within a coalition are the same whether it is dominant or not. A coalition may not know whether its members will stick
together, or whether it will be dominant even if they do, until the fight
is over.

Of the many intriguing questions about coalitions, we will mention
just two. Both revolve around the fact that the members of an effective
coalition must compromise some of their personal objectives to keep it
solid enough to win. One is the "employee" question of whether to leave
a nondominant coalition which closely represents one's views but has
little chance of winning to join another coalition whose position is less
attractive but is likely to win. The second is the "employer" question of
whether to induce more members into one's coalition so as to improve
its chance of winning, but at the cost of diluting its objectives or spreading its gains and thereby reducing the benefit of winning. The answers
to both questions are sometimes related to the power of a marginal contribution, discussed above. Those members whose support is unequivocally committed typically have less bargaining power than the marginal
(independent or swing) group who may make the difference between
winning and losing.

Political parties are conspicuous examples of coalition formation. The
problem is fundamentally the same, however, in corporations, clubs,
unions, churches, professional associations, and families. Many a child
learns the art of getting one parent into a coalition with himself against
the other parent, while parents may concentrate on keeping their own
coalition dominant over the children. A good analysis of coalitions is that
of Riker (1962).

Sponsor decisions and the paradox of voting (social choice)

Whether among legislatures, boards of directors, citizens, members of
a club, or union delegates to a convention the majority vote is probably
the most common single technique of making a group decision. Our
problem is still how decisions are made among sponsors, who in a formal
organization are most likely to be either the board of directors or a meeting of members. Again, the principle is the same regardless of the nature
or level of the group doing the voting, and we will talk of it in general
terms.

Because it is common in such circumstances to speak of a "group will"
or "public preference" it is important to know what relationship, if any,
exists between the wishes of the individual members and their collective
decision. We first note that a majority vote has a reasonably clear mean-

ing in a choice between two alternatives—the majority vote *is* the group preference (though the purist might insist on taking intensities of feelings into consideration as well). But when there are more than two alternatives, the meaning of "group preference" may be hazy indeed.

This can perhaps best be illustrated by the so-called *paradox of voting,* as in a group of 100 delegates to a convention who must choose among *X, Y,* and *Z.* The 100 consist of three subgroups, *a, b,* and *c.* The preference ordering of each subgroup can be read from left to right, so that *X Y Z* for subgroup *a* means that their first choice is *X,* their second choice *Y,* and their third choice *Z.* The preferences of the three subgroups appear as follows:

Subgroup	Percent	Preference ordering		
a	40	X	Y	Z
b	35	Y	Z	X
c	25	Z	X	Y
	100%			

In a straight vote in which each subgroup votes for its first choice, *X* will win with a clear plurality of 40 percent. *Y* will be second, with 35 percent, and *Z* last, with 25 percent. We therefore conclude that *X* is the choice of this group. But suppose we want an absolute majority, and conduct a runoff election between the top two candidates. Subgroups *a* and *c* prefer *X* to *Y,* and between them will give *X* 65 percent of the votes. Subgroup *b* prefer *Y* to *X,* and will give him 35 percent. *X* will win by nearly two-to-one, in an apparent demonstration that *X* is indeed the preferred alternative.

But let us look again. Subgroups *b* and *c* both prefer *Z* to *X,* while only *a* prefers *X* to *Z.* Therefore, if there had been a runoff between *X* and *Z,* *Z* would have won with a 60 percent majority. And this despite the fact that *Z* was lowest in the initial ballot. We now add the final confusing fact that if *Z* were to run against *Y,* *Y* would win by 75 percent to 25 percent.

In the language of preference theory, preferences are rational only if they are transitive. *Transitive* means that if you prefer *X* to *Y* and *Y* to *Z,* you will necessarily prefer *X* to *Z.* The trouble with group preferences

TRANSITIVITY

© Mel Lazarus. Reprinted by permission of Publishers-Hall Syndicate.

is that transitivity may or may not prevail. In the above case the whole group prefers X to Y (65 percent to 35 percent), Y to Z (75 to 25), and Z to X (60 to 40). The group preference is not transitive, even if the preference of every individual within it is transitive, and it is hard to know what the election really shows. Incidentally, proportional representation, while highly useful in some cases where multiple candidates are to be elected, is not applicable where only one is to be elected.

One procedure will produce one result, and if the group accepts that procedure as their decision rule they reach a conclusion. But a different decision rule might produce a different result. In that sense it is not very meaningful to speak of a group preference as existing independently of a particular technique for measuring it. There is only a collection of individual preferences. Not only have the people no voice; they have no message. Incidentally, the possible intransitivity of a voted ("political") choice contrasts with the generally transitive outcome of social decision making through the market process (Chapter 22).

The purpose of the discussion thus far is to demonstrate a *possible* result, by using a strong case. When the other three sets of preferences (X Z Y, Y X Z, and Z Y X) are also included, the outcome is more likely to be rational—that is, transitive.

If X, Y, and Z are policies rather than persons, there might be a half dozen subvariants of each. Some of the voters may prefer one of the variants of X to the version that actually got on the ballot. Furthermore, we have not measured the relative intensities of the preferences. To modify our original example, suppose that the voters in subgroups a and c prefer X to Y by a thin margin, and would almost as soon have Y as X. The voters in subgroup b, however, prefer Y to X with passion. Even if we have only a two-way election, leaving out Z, have we achieved a good measure of the group preference by selecting X? That is, does the weak preference of 65 percent for X more than compensate for the intense preference of 35 percent for Y? Straight majority elections always give the weak preference as much weight as the strong ones—one vote. But that does not mean that they measure the group preference better than other possible techniques, if as well.[4]

These complications reinforce our uncertainty about the meaning of "group preference" among the sponsors of an organization, or, on a larger scale, of the "public will." If there are three or more alternatives, the nature of the preference is highly uncertain, and different decision techniques will produce different results. If there are only two clear-cut alternatives, the vote will measure group preference clearly—if we ignore intensity of feelings. But if only two alternatives are presented, the most important decision may already have been made at the stage when

---

[4] In *The Measurement of Social Welfare* Rothenberg (1961) formalizes this approach. In a reasonably comprehensive discussion of the problem of formulating an optimum social welfare function he concludes, in effect, that whatever comes out of the social decision process *is* the social preference. If this seems to weasel out of the problem, one may be consoled or disconsolate, as befits his personality, to note that a voluminous literature on the subject of welfare functions has little better to offer, and a great deal worse.

other alternatives were eliminated from the ballot. An alternative *not* on the ballot might have defeated the winning one that *was* on. All in all, perhaps the only sensible approach is to adopt a decision rule that strikes people as generally sensible and then to stick to it knowing that even the best rule may not be very good.

A short note on group decisions

To review the three organizational decision techniques, communication and transaction are ways of achieving *agreement,* and each member gets what he agreed to. For the reasons stated, the members, and presumably a leader as well, will prefer agreement by communication to agreement by transaction. If both methods fail the dominant coalition gets what it wants, in a decision the remaining members have not agreed to. This method will presumably be the least satisfactory of the three.

In school or family, children often acquire idealized notions about group decisions. When they later learn how such decisions are actually made they are disillusioned, and tend to withdraw from the "whole messy business." It might be more sensible to teach them the real nature of organizational power at the outset. They could not then be disillusioned, because they had not first been illusioned. But then perhaps our schools teach unrealistic views about power because the holders of power prefer it that way. Or because social scientists have been slow in developing very good analyses of power.

16

FORMAL ORGANIZATION: STRUCTURE AND COORDINATION

STRUCTURE

Differentiation, coordination, and role

Most, perhaps all, systems operate through differentiation and coordination. Even protons and electrons behave differently, but their different behaviors are coordinated in a way that makes the atom a system.

Similarly in human organizations the work is accomplished as different subsystems are coordinated toward a joint result. The subsystems of an organization may be divisions, departments, bureaus, or individuals. Except for individuals, all subsystems of an organization are themselves organizations, or rather suborganizations. In organizations "differentiation" is widely known as division of labor. It is used for the obvious increase in efficiency that arises when people become specialists, concentrating on what they like and can do best, and avoiding the constant changes of task that arise when everyone tries to do everything. The overall process is one in which the outputs of one subsystem of an organization become inputs to another. If the various subsystems were not differentiated they would all have the same outputs, and there would be no point to feeding them into other identical subsystems as inputs. Coordination consists in determining which outputs of which subsystems flow as inputs to which other subsystems.

Each subsystem has a *role,* which is the image, concept, pattern, or blueprint of the subsystem and its function in the larger system. It is a pattern system. A role can also be described as a set of expectations about how a subsystem will behave in performing its tasks and in interacting with other subsystems. These expectations become internalized in the

DSE states of individuals—those persons in a given role and those in the other roles with which interactions occur. These inner patterns are then externalized (symboled) in actual behaviors. If the subsystem is a person (not a department or division) the personnel manager sees the role in terms of the job description plus the job specification—a statement of the tasks to be performed and the kind of person who is to perform them. In systems language (which can apply to departments or other suborganizations as well as to individuals) the role is a set of system states, actions, and boundaries, and includes the system's interactions with other system or nonsystem elements in or out of the organization. Thus a *role description* is a statement that identifies a subsystem, its boundaries, its functions, its system states, and its interactions with other systems or subsystems. A role description may be spelled out in writing, though in small and less formalized organizations it exists only in people's heads.[1]

In our model of pure formal organization all roles are determined by deliberate action of the sponsors or their agents. (We will deal later with the "impure" tendency of roles to "mold themselves.") The names of roles usually identify the basic kind of system involved: "waiter," for example, implies a person and "production department" a suborganization. The *structure of an organization* is its pattern described in terms of the names and roles of its subsystems. These are often arranged in a diagram (as in Figures 16–1 and 16–2) to make the structure more easily understood.[2]

Two problems of structure

It is well beyond the scope of an introduction, if not of present knowledge, to try to identify the "best" organizational structure—which depends on the organization's size, purpose, location, duration, available skills, environmental stability, and many other factors. We will nevertheless note two interesting questions about structure.

One is the degree of differentiation, also described as the degree of specialization or of division of labor. The greater the degree of differentiation, other things equal, the greater will be the number and variety of roles and the smaller will be the number of functions of each. When the medieval shoemaker did the whole job of making shoes, the job

---

[1] The use of terms in this section follows Kuhn (1974), and differs from some usages in organization theory and sociology. The language of existing disciplines was not designed to be coordinated with that of other disciplines, and if we want unified social science we must accept the cost of restructuring some concepts and terminology. My aim here is to assert the essential identity of the logic of subsystem function in organizational structure, whether the subsystem is a mother in a family, a medicine man in a tribe, a department in a corporation, a corporation in an economy, or a national government in a United Nations. Whether these *particular* changes are sensible is a matter beyond the scope of this volume.

[2] I have not used Miller's definition of structure (Miller 1971: 284) as "the arrangement of . . . subsystems and components in three-dimensional space at a given moment of time," since that definition implies an exclusively spatial boundary. It seems to me that for most purposes of organizations the functional or, occasionally, the analytical boundary is preferable.

required only one role, which incorporated many functions. In a modern shoe factory different persons cut soles, cut toe sections, cut sides, stitch uppers, polish, and so on. The whole job requires scores of differentiated but coordinated roles, with only one or two functions per role. An important result is that the greater the differentiation the greater is the necessary amount of overt coordinating activities, such as planning, scheduling, plant layout, materials handling, record keeping, personnel activities, and supervision.

A second structural problem concerns the degree of centralization of control. An automobile, for example, is a complicated system with many differentiated and coordinated parts. The organization that manufactures automobiles must therefore itself be highly coordinated from a central point, for otherwise the many parts will not get together in the proper sizes, shapes, locations, or sequences.

In marked contrast is an organization that produces many shapes and sizes of nuts, bolts, rivets, and screws that go to different customers for different purposes. Because the total output is a simple sum of parts, it makes little difference whether the division that makes eighth-inch bolts operates at the same rate as the division that makes quarter-inch wood screws. In short, the greater the degree to which the products of an organization are themselves coordinated systems, the greater must be the centralization of control in the organization that produces them.

Summary on structure

In its simplest terms the problem of structure has three aspects. One is to break the whole task of the organization into subtasks. The second is to design or decide on an appropriate subsystem to perform each subtask. These subsystems may be persons, departments, or other suborganizations. The third is to assign the various tasks to the various subsystems in such a way that among them the whole task of the organization will be accomplished. The outcome of the three is a description, blueprint, or image of the organization—its structure—in the form of a list of subsystems and a role description of each.

Instead of being consciously produced in one grand act of creative design, complex organizational structures are usually designed and modified gradually through experience (see Chapter 18), sometimes with the help of management consultants.

Having created the structure, the remaining tasks of organization are to find the people to fill the roles (recruitment), and to get them to do the work. We will not deal here with recruitment, but will assume that the persons have been located and selected, and go on from there.

INDUCTION, ROLE CHANGE, AND SOCIALIZATION

The people selected must both learn what they are to do in the organization and be motivated to do it (detector and selector), as discussed in this section and the next, respectively.

A person new to an organization may or may not know much about the role he is to fill. If he is an experienced specialist he may know a great deal about it before he starts. To some extent, however, he will learn his role gradually through experience. But to some extent he will also learn it through relatively straightforward communication, as from conversation, handbooks, or organization manuals. The manner in which a new occupant is made familiar with his role is called the *induction process,* or simply *induction.* (Induction is also often known as *indoctrination.*) since all roles interact to some degree with other roles, induction includes becoming familiar with the occupants and content of those other roles.

A ceremony or ritual is often useful for communicating to others, and for impressing on the memories of all concerned, that a new person now occupies a particular role. Such an induction ceremony can also perform part of the induction process, particularly getting to know other persons. If the new role occupant has large discretion in performing his role, as is the case with many administrators, he may use the occasion to indicate how he views his role. The inaugural address of the president may "set the tone" of his administration, and conversations over beer may reveal how the new director of research will run the laboratory. Whether or not one calls them a "ceremony," the new executive will want to make sure these communications take place.

Induction ceremonies can, of course, be dysfunctional if they fail to communicate the right things. In one way or another, however, the new role occupant must learn what is expected of him; those in other interacting roles must learn what he expects of them; and discrepancies in these expectations must be ironed out. With or without an explicit ceremony these parts of induction must take place.

More generally, whenever anyone changes roles, even if only to switch jobs within a department, the change may require some induction, and possibly a ceremony. These are known as "role change ceremonies." For many circumstances, particularly in primitive societies, we call them "rites of passage." Some ceremonies mark the ending rather than the beginning of a role, as with graduation, retirement, or funeral. Whether such ceremonies are useful again depends on circumstances. The retirement ceremony may help everyone remember that "Joe is no longer with us, so don't send him any more nasty memos." The funeral ceremony may help change others' images of Jack from live and active to permanently absent. Those who "just can't believe he's gone" may especially need such a ceremony.

Although all societies use many such rituals, we know remarkably little about whether they are worth their cost. Some research might therefore be useful to determine whether they are generally childish and primitive or essential social cement. (They might just possibly be both.) We might guess that they are more useful where people depend on oral rather than written communication, and more useful with respect to emotional and attitudinal relations, such as patriotism and sense of solidarity, than with logical and analytical ones, such as research or running a spaceship.

The inductee must learn not only his own role, the roles of various others, and the mutual expectations about their interactions. He must also learn what sanctions may be applied to induce him to perform as expected, and the conditions under which he may be expelled if he does not conform. All these are parts of what the sociologist calls *socialization,* and we will see more of this process later in connection with semiformal organization. Induction into a structure of roles is one of the two main vehicles for converting a batch of individuals into a coordinated team—i.e., an organization. At a wider level it is the learning and performing of his roles that ties an individual to a society, and collectively makes the society a system instead of a mere aggregation of individuals. Induction is supplemented by authority, which motivates each person to do these things.

In this section we have focused on the way the organization is divided into differentiated subsystems whose activities are coordinated to produce an overall result. In a general way that kind of question was dealt with by the older, or "classical," organization theory. The "newer" theory deals with the way individuals are motivated to do these things—with the so-called human side of organization. That kind of problem is dealt with in the next section.

AUTHORITY, MOTIVES, AND COORDINATION

The individual as subsystem

The components of an automobile interact to produce a particular result because they were consciously designed to. The parts of biological organisms were "designed" by the evolutionary process. In both cases the subsystems have no "choice" about their roles, and generally have no life or function and make no sense except as components of their respective systems.

By contrast, we are now focusing on complex organizations, such as corporations, churches, governments, trade associations, and unions. Here each member has a life and goals that exist quite independently of his role in the organization. A central question of sponsors then is, How do we motivate persons who have little or no inherent sponsor interest to perform the roles of the organization? That is, How do we induce these individuals in their own right to convert themselves into subsystems of the organization?

The transactional base of authority

The answer lies in authority, which is a particular kind of transaction within an organization. The individual completes a transaction of affiliation, or major bargain, with the organization. In it the organization says implicitly or explicitly: "We will contribute toward your goals (namely, give you pay and possible other satisfactions) if you will contribute toward ours (namely, do work that we want done)." In this transaction the work can be described in only a general way—typing, assembling, computer programming, selling, or accounting. Since all details cannot be specified at the time of hiring, one is hired with the understanding that details of his work will be spelled out from time to time by the organization. Within limits stated in the job description, one agrees to accept and perform instructions. If he performs satisfactorily he stays and is paid. If not, he is discharged. In a relation between persons at two different levels the one who holds authority is the *superior* or *supervisor,* and the one subject to it is the *subordinate* or the person *supervised.*

Authority is the ability of a superior to grant or withhold rewards or punishments (goods or bads) for the subordinate's performance or non-performance of instructions. In the formal model the authority goes with the superior's role, and can be exercised by anyone who occupies it. Although an instruction is a communication from the superior, and must be understood to be effective, we will focus on the transactional aspects of authority. Rewards and punishments used by authority are called *sanctions.* The rewards are pay, praise, friendship, promotion, security, or other benefits. Although families and governments may use bads, the punishments are generally the simple withholding of rewards. Often criticism, threat of discharge, or icy relationships are negative enough to qualify as punishments.

Several situations may be identified. If the superior has no sanctions to apply, he *lacks authority.* If he has sanctions, but they are not strong enough to induce a satisfactory response, his authority is *ineffective.* If the sanctions do induce the appropriate response they are, of course, *effective.*

Some rewards are provided by the supervisor himself, as with praise or relaxed, friendly relationships. Others, such as pay and promotion, come from the organization's resources, not the supervisor's, and depend on his position and role in the organization. The authority relationship, however, is the main way the organization harnesses the energies of staff members toward its own goals. We will return to that theme after a short detour.

On legitimacy

Suppose you are hired as a typist, and that after a year of satisfactory performance you are instructed to scrub the washroom. Or that you are hired as a design engineer and are later instructed to go out on the road as a troubleshooting repairman. Unless you are fearful or naive you will probably reply, "But that's not what I was hired for." In organizational language, you consider the instruction illegitimate. A *legitimate instruction* is one that falls within the terms of the major bargain. An *illegitimate instruction* falls outside of and violates the major bargain.

The logic of authority is that sanctions may be applied to a subordinate who refuses to comply with a legitimate instruction, and such refusal is called *insubordination.* Since insubordination is a violation of the major bargain by the subordinate it is generally construed to release the organization from its side of the bargain. That is, insubordination justifies discharge—although the subordinate may receive a lesser penalty if he agrees to accept subsequent instructions.

If a superior repeatedly gives an order that is not legitimate under the original understanding, and if the employee regularly accepts and performs it, then the major bargain has implicitly been changed. In the reverse direction, it is also changed if a legitimate instruction is repeatedly ignored and the subordinate is not disciplined. In legal jargon, there has been a "meeting of the minds" on terms that differ from the original agreement. The "minds meet" most clearly when both sides obviously know what is happening and neither side contests it.

The problem of the preceding paragraph is important in many continuing relationships, including marriages, whose terms "just grow" instead of being explicitly agreed on. It is also important in formal relationships when the major bargain is not revised periodically to reflect the march of reality. Here we can say either (1) that *legitimate* authority is *accepted* authority (reflecting a strong contemporary tendency in organizational and political sciences), or (2) that the major bargain *is* what the parties *do*. We will merely mention but not diagnose further the special cases on board a ship or plane, where the captain is effectually the head of a small, temporary, authoritarian government.

Transactional authority as hierarchical coordination

Let us now look at authority as a coordinating process, assuming that legitimacy is not in question. We will illustrate with an organization, such as a corporation or charity, whose sponsors have elected a board of directors, which in turn selects some top officer or officers over whom the board exercises direct authority. The board also makes a top officer (say, the president) responsible for carrying out its instructions, *responsibility* being the position of the person over whom authority is exercised. The president's responsibility (like anyone else's) lies in the fact that sanctions can be applied to him if he does not satisfactorily carry out instructions.

But the president cannot do everything, so he selects and makes a major bargain with subordinates. His authority and their responsibility then appear as follows.

Let us assume a transactional relation across three levels of hierarchy, A, B, and C, with A highest. A exercises authority over B, and agrees to provide rewards to C when B certifies that C has satisfactorily carried out instructions from B under an authority relation of B over C. Here A has *delegated authority* to B. Under these circumstances there has also been a delegation of responsibility from B to C, under which C is responsible to B to do work for which B is in turn responsible to A.[3] In a many-layered organization C exercises authority over D, who exercises authority over E, and so on. Thus authority, exercised through transactions

---

[3] Some authors insist that although authority can be delegated, responsibility cannot, since B is still responsible to A for C's work. While this is true enough in an overall sense, I consider it quibbling. At any given moment C is responsible to B for work assigned by B, and it seems sensible to view both the responsibility and the authority as having been passed down one level.

Drawing by Charles Addams; © 1972 The New Yorker Magazine, Inc.

between successive levels of hierarchy, ties all of the staff to the goals of the sponsors.

Authority in information

Things, however, are seldom that simple. To think of only two levels, not all of *B*'s instructions need come to him from *A*. If *A* is plant superintendent and *B* is a foreman, *B* may get instructions about personnel relations in his department from the personnel manager, about manufacturing processes from the chief engineer, and about record keeping from the head accountant. Relations of this sort may be explicit, in that *A* does not say to *B*, "Do as I say," but, "With respect to your personnel procedures, do as the personnel manager advises," and so on.

Under that kind of instruction *A*'s authority over *B* might seem to remain intact, and we might say that *B* is getting his instructions indirectly from *A*, via the personnel manager and other specialists. The force of this argument is diluted, however, by the fact that only the

Figure 16–1
THE "TREE" TYPE OF ORGANIZATION CHART

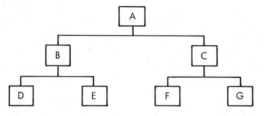

specialists who gave *B* the advice may be able to evaluate whether *B* is acting on it satisfactorily. If *A* asks for and accepts their evaluations, it is the specialists who are exercising authority over *B* in these matters, even if the formal decisions about *B* are made by *A*.

But the specialists also hold an even more direct authority. The continued availability of their advice is valuable to *B*. If they observe that *B* does not follow their advice they will not be inclined to provide more of it. Although their advice may not be thought of explicitly as instruction, their ability to stop the flow of this advice if it is not followed fills our definition of authority. To keep our model straight, however, let us note that it is not the act of communicating that provides the authority, but the transactional fact that the communicated information has *value*.

"Traditional" organization theory recognized no authority except that of one's immediate superior. Work flowed up and instructions and sanctions down. An organizational structure was therefore diagramed as an inverted tree, with all authority in one person at the top, which was divided and subdivided as it went down the scale. The preceding section on "authority as hierarchical coordination" describes its logic in pure form. A diagram of it appears in Figure 16–1. To change our cast of

Figure 16–2
THE MATRIX CHART OF ORGANIZATION STRUCTURE

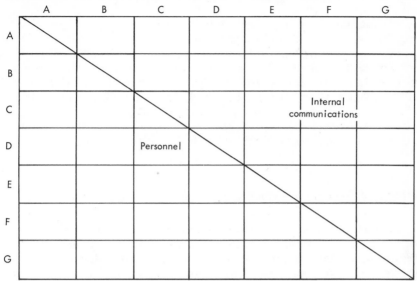

characters, *A* is the top authority, such as president. *B* and *C* are vice presidents responsible to *A*. *D* and *E* are (say) department heads responsible to *B*, while *F* and *G* are heads of two other departments responsible to *C*. This kind of chart can be extended downward to cover all levels in a given organization.

The more contemporary view that authority can lie in many places is better diagramed as a matrix, as in Figure 16–2. Everyone worth listing appears on both the horizontal and vertical scales—both rows and columns. The name of a person's position at the top of a column indicates his role of giving information, while its appearance at the left of a row indicates his role of receiving it. Since a person receiving information may also be expected to report back what he did about it, giving such a report is indicated by the row position while receiving it is indicated by the column position. That is, when a role is named at the head of a column it is acting as a superior, or authority-exercising, role. When it is named in a row it is acting in a subordinate, or authority-receiving, role.

For example, the cell in row *D*, column *C* is labeled "personnel." This means that *D* receives advice about personnel problems from *C*, and also reports back to *C* regarding his personnel actions. *C* (whom we have implicitly identified as a specialist in personnel) may need help from *F*, a communications expert, in getting his personnel messages across. The matrix cell for row *C*, column *F* thus indicates that *C* receives advice from and reports back to *F* about his (*C*'s) communications of personnel information. In a completed matrix some cells would be vacant and others might contain several items. To be logically complete, the total set of job descriptions should include all relationships shown in the matrix.

Although any real organization will have many more lines of communication and advice than could conceivably be diagramed, including secondhand or thirdhand information passed on at cocktail parties or around the water cooler, the matrix is clearly a better description of what goes on than is the tree chart. The tree diagram is nevertheless useful in identifying who will probably carry dominant weight in decisions about raises, promotions, discipline, or discharges. In fact, managers who think in terms of a tree diagram are often forced by the realities to behave with the greater flexibility reflected in the matrix.

Other coordinating transactions

Staff members engage in many transactions that are directly essential to an organization's work. For example, on November 1 a salesman dashes up to the production manager of a manufacturing firm and asks breathlessly, "Can you turn out ten thousand uptight phlogistons by May 15? Because if you can, I can land a half million dollar order." Here the salesman and the production manager are both indirect agents of the sponsors of the same organization. Each wants to look good to his principal, so as to justify a pay increase, promotion, or other rewards. The salesman is also an agent for the customer in dealing with the production department. What are the main ingredients in the ensuing transaction?

The ultimate decision will presumably have to be made by a superior of both the salesman and the production manager—perhaps the president or the plant manager. However, if the salesman and the production manager can work out a mutually satisfactory arrangement that does not seriously upset other aspects of the organization, the higher official is likely to accept it.

Promotability for the production manager depends on his ability to produce. His desire to accept the order therefore constitutes part of his effective preference (EP) in dealing with the salesman. If he enjoys seeing his department busy, or thinks the order might justify some new equipment, these motives add to his EP. His EP is shortened to the extent that he thinks the delivery date is unrealistic, since he can get the salesman, the company, the customer, and himself into trouble if he promises delivery and then fails. Knowing that things can go wrong, he prefers a cushion, as by promising July 1 delivery if reasonable luck would allow it by May 15. There are thus opposite tugs at his EP, which is lengthened by his desire to help get the order and shortened by his fear of not meeting his commitment.

In any case, the production manager will normally make his promise contingent on his receiving raw materials by certain dates. The salesman will thereupon dash breathlessly to the purchasing department in search of promises about dates for materials. Unless the prospective customer's dates are loose, the chances are that the expectations of customer, production, and purchasing will not all match the first time around. There will follow a series of letters, phone calls, and conferences, through which some compromise will be reached.

As anyone who has worked in a large corporation knows, all this is the merest beginning of the complications. We nevertheless again see communication and transaction as the techniques of interaction among the parts in doing the organization's own work. Chamberlain (1955) provides much more detail about the interrelated bargains throughout an organization than we can include here.

ORGANIZATION AS A CONTROLLED SYSTEM

As a controlled system, the formal organization has some DSE functions acting on behalf of the whole unit. Having examined some questions about coordinating the parts so as to perform the effector function, let us now look at the detector and selector functions of the whole organization.

The traditional individual proprietorship is a business firm of one person plus employees. As owner and active operator the proprietor is simultaneously both the sole sponsor and the whole management. In the simplest form of individual proprietorship his employees are "paid to do what I tell you, not to think for yourselves." The proprietor alone collects and processes the information for the organization's decisions. And his goals alone go into its decisions. Both the detector and selector functions thus reside in the proprietor, while the effector functions are divided among his staff.

As an organization grows, complexities arise apace. The top executive of a large corporation cannot personally receive and digest all the incoming information needed for the sponsor function. Such information must be gathered, summarized, and interpreted by numerous subordinates. If the subordinates pass on interpretations or inferences instead of raw data, they may actually play an important part in the decision, even though they have no formal decision making authority. March and Simon (1958) call this process "uncertainty absorption," and it inescapably occurs in any large organization. Unless the top executive is to suffer overload, most information must be stopped before it reaches him. So while he may need to know about the cost and location of a proposed new plant he cannot afford the time and effort to keep informed about the price of typewriter paper and the daily report on sick leaves. Normally, much of the information about any particular subsystem that is relevant to the management will be assembled and forwarded by that subsystem itself. The management, of course, will need independent checks on such information, since otherwise "only good news flows up."

Just as sponsor-level information is dispersed in a large organization, so, to a certain extent, is sponsor motivation. In fact it is often difficult to know exactly what motives of which persons *are* the determining factors of decisions on behalf of the whole organization. The goals of the organization may, of course, be spelled out in its charter or handbook—as to make money, heal the ailing poor, or glorify God. But to have effect the stated goals of the organization must become motives of individuals, and if the top decision makers can raise their pay, power, or prestige by manipulating company stocks, healing the rich, or glorifying the king the organization's stated goals may be neglected. The same kind of problem also exists at lower levels: if the subordinate can do better for himself by filching company property and flattering the boss than by doing his job well, it is his motives, not the suborganization's goals, that prevail.

On the other hand individuals at lower levels often hold what are essentially sponsor goals for their subunits, even if they do not care about overall goals. The production manager may get great satisfaction from having his machines operate smoothly, efficiently, and on schedule, and the head of purchasing may feel good when his knowledge and bargaining skills with suppliers bring prompt, low-cost delivery of even the most difficult items ordered through his department. On a smaller scale, even if the team loses, the third runner on the relay team may want to do his best, and feel that the team *would* have won if everyone else had done as well. Sponsor goals held by a staff member at any level increase his *EP* for membership in the organization. As such their general effect (other things equal) will be to increase the power but decrease the bargaining power of the individual, while increasing both for the organization in its relations with him.

Despite these complications there is a fairly standard relationship through which goals of the whole organization are translated into goals of successively lower units, sometimes couched as the difference between policy and implementation. To start at the top, the sponsors deal primarily with goals and first-level implementation. They decide *what* they want accomplished and specify the broad subgoals toward achieving it. Those broad subgoals are means of implementation—the *how* of achieving the main goals. When passed downward, a subgoal is again a statement of *what* is to be accomplished at the next lower level. The *what* is passed down another level, which subdivides it into instrumental *hows,* which become *whats* to a still lower level. That is, the means (implementation) at one level become the ends (policy) for the level below.

STATICS, DYNAMICS, AND THE MANAGERIAL FUNCTION

Let us suppose that an organization operates in a relatively unchanging environment. Inputs are routinely available at essentially unchanging cost. Recipients do not change much in numbers or traits. The organization has been operating long enough for reasonably efficient staff performance to be routine, and all important bugs have been worked out of the organizational structure. In conjunction with appropriate lower-level executives, a personnel department replaces and inducts new employees as necessary.

Under such circumstances the organization should be able to function indefinitely without top management. If each subsystem simply continues to perform its specified role, receiving inputs of materials and information, processing them, and releasing outputs, the work of the organization could continue regularly and successfully. Within its routine performance every subsystem would include techniques for detecting and responding homeostatically to moderate deviations in inputs, outputs, or internal processing. So long as subsystem deviations remained small, every other subsystem could accommodate to them. For example, in the automobile assembly plant if all the parts arrive about on schedule, if absenteeism falls within the rate for which substitutes are routinely available, if sales are steady, and if the transportation companies pick up finished cars before they fill the storage yards, no high-level executive need issue instructions to the assembly division. It is fully able to make all its own decisions.

Few organizations exist in such stable environments, and if they did the measure of really successful top managers would be that they could disappear for months without anyone's noticing. Instead, events that exceed the range of homeostatic responses built into subsystem roles keep cropping up, and are the occasions when higher management is needed. The organization's structure may then need to be changed, as by adding, modifying, or eliminating roles. Or role occupancy may be altered, as by transferring or replacing key individuals.

NONEMPLOYEE MEMBERSHIPS (mostly in cooperatives)

The discussion of organizational membership has focused thus far on the employee. Do the preceding generalizations about employment apply to other kinds of membership relationships as well? Except for some memberships that are too loose to analyze, the answer is yes. For this section we may think mostly of cooperative organizations, such as clubs, professional associations, and labor unions.

Any formal organization will have some charter, constitution, or bylaws, either written or embodied in practice. This "document" will normally specify the purpose (goals) and structure (roles) of the organization as well as its decision rules. The role description for the member typically takes the form of rules, which are simultaneously standing "instructions" as to what he may or may not do. These rules may, for example, state how many meetings he must attend, what work or money he must contribute, whether or not he can vote or be an officer, and whether or not he may belong to another organization with a conflicting purpose. Other parts of the role description will indicate how or when the member may use certain facilities of the organization—for example, requiring that each member must clean up after using the camera club's darkroom, or stating that he may not push others underwater in the swim club. The sanctions may be a fine, increased dues, denial of access to facilities, or expulsion from membership. Such a relationship constitutes authority, since it grants or withholds rewards or punishments for the member's performance or nonperformance of the "instructions."

Thus, although membership relationships appear in sharpest form in the employer-employee relationship, the same general principles also apply to other formal organizations. Looser organizations will be examined in the next two chapters.

17

INFORMAL
ORGANIZATION—
AND ECOLOGY

The last two chapters have dealt with one end of the spectrum of organization—the pure formal organization, which in this model acts as a consciously coordinated unit toward some explicit goal or goals. In this chapter we shift to the other end of the spectrum—-the pure informal organization. In such organizations each controlled subsystem acts only toward its *own* goals, with no deliberate joint action, and no concern at all about the overall result for the larger social system. The next chapter deals with the more typical mixed and intermediate conditions.

Because human beings are such confoundedly complicated critters they can never feel confident that any of their actions are truly devoid of broader concern. To circumvent those nagging doubts we will bypass human communities for the moment, and start with the ecological community of the biologist—the ecological system, or ecosystem—as our prototype, or paradigm. Here we feel reasonably confident that the bacteria working away in the fallen oak do not intend or desire to help convert it into topsoil, and that the deer does not know or care that its excrement helps fertilize that soil. We feel even surer that individual plants do not deliberately modify their behaviors to help produce a better ecological system. Each plant or animal behaves as its own nature dictates, in a given environmental setting, and the overall result falls where it falls.

The ensuing result is very definitely a system, something more than the mere sum of its parts, which often behaves in surprisingly precise and predictable ways. But the system has no sponsors, no manager, no internal decision processes, no authority-responsibility relationships, and no questions of legitimacy or discipline. (Those concepts were defined earlier.) In particular, it has no goal as a unit. It has a structure, however, which is sometimes remarkably clear and self-preserving. Once we have identified some principles of ecosystems without humans, we will see whether they also apply to the informal organization of human beings, which are often studied under the heading of *human ecology* (see Hawley 1950).

THE ECOLOGICAL MODEL

To word it in a way that may be useful to both the biological and the human ecologist, and hence help tie the two sciences together, we can define an *ecological system* as any uncontrolled system at least some of whose components are controlled systems. To the biologist the whole ecosystem includes such nonliving components (uncontrolled systems) as streams, atmosphere, light, and soil, along with living components (controlled systems) in the form of plants and animals. However, for certain purposes we can attend solely to interactions of living components, such as bees and flowers. We can ignore the nonliving ones, in much the same spirit that we attended to the human beings in the formal organization but ignored its buildings and machines. In that context we can define an ecological system simply as the uncontrolled interactions of controlled systems, or as an uncontrolled system of controlled subsystems. Such uncontrolled interactions are the focus of the social scientist's main interest in ecological systems.

Structure and membership in ecosystems

The boundaries of any particular ecosystem, like those of any other system, are set by the observer in light of his interest. A given ecosystem might thus consist of a pond, a field or forest, the large animals within a forest, a "balanced" fishbowl, the Mississippi Basin, the Pacific Ocean, or the entire land-water-air surface of the earth.

As with formal organization the *structure* of an ecosystem is defined and described in terms of its subsystems and their roles. Let us think of a wooded valley. Its subsystems can be identified in broad categories, such as trees, ferns, mammals, insects, and bacteria. Or they could be subdivided into species, as mammals are divided into deer, wolves, and rabbits. For some purposes they might even be divided into individual specimens, or counts of specimens. The *roles* are what each subsystem does, particularly its interactions with other subsystems. Squirrels help keep down the number of oaks or pines by eating their seeds, but also help propagate them by burying some seeds they never dig up. Bees pollinate flowers, wolves eat rabbits, and bacteria decompose dead plants and animals. Each subsystem pursues its own goals in its own way.

The structure of the ecosystem is not designed by sponsors, but "just happens." No selection and placement office seeks out new role occupants, which simply are born there or wander in. There are no induction processes, the newborn of most species being left unceremoniously on their own from the moment they arrive. Although parental care and

By permission of John Hart and Field Enterprises Inc.

some training of the young by higher animal species is a modest form of induction, it is done in the interest of the subsystem, not the whole system.

We are interested in the ecosystem (and in informal organization) because it enables us to see how interactions that are entirely without central control or central goals can nevertheless produce structures and functions that are intricately detailed, self-maintaining, and self-reproducing. With thousands of species of insects or bacteria alone in a single ecosystem it is not possible to deal with all details. Our goal here is to grasp the central logic of a fantastically complicated system in which "everything depends on everything else" (Boulding 1970: 24).

Differentiation and coordination

As in the molecule and formal organization, the wholeness of the ecosystem involves differentiation and coordination. Except for extremely simple plants, all living things can survive only among other living things. The general relation is that outputs of one subsystem become inputs to other subsystems—the "output" of one species sometimes meaning that it is eaten by another. To illustrate, most plants grow best in soil that contains decayed remains of earlier plants and animals. Directly or indirectly animals survive only by eating plants—directly, by eating the plants themselves; indirectly, by eating other animals that have eaten plants.

Relationships between two species can be cooperative, or *symbiotic* (living together), as when bees get food from flowers and simultaneously pollinate them. Symbiosis is a sort of low-level transaction, in which the parties exchange goods but do not negotiate terms. Relationships can be conflictual, as in the competition of wolves and hawks to eat rabbits, or in the rabbits' efforts to escape. Unlike the formal organization, which can plan and control its subsystems, the differences in behavior among species in an ecosystem reflect the slow evolutionary fitting of each species to its living and nonliving environment. Since the behaviors of a species are essentially the same as its role, and are for the most part inborn, changes in the structure of ecosystems come from changes in the mix of species, not from "training" or from inducting members into new roles.

An *ecological niche* is the biologist's term for role in the ecosystem— such as the disposal of dead animals by vultures or the reduction of insect populations by birds. There are usually fewer niches than species, because numerous species often perform essentially the same function. Leaves and grasses are eaten by *herbivores,* which include horses, cattle, goats, sheep, rabbits, deer, elk, buffalo, moose, and caribou. All in turn may constitute food for *carnivores,* meat-eating animals, such as wolves, coyotes, tigers, and bobcats.

Because no part is planned or directed on behalf of the whole, there is no meaningful sense in which a whole ecosystem can interact as a unit with another ecosystem. The ecosystem of the forest floor cannot interact as a unit with that of the timberline above it, or with that of another forest floor beyond the mountain. However, subsystems of one ecosystem may interact with subsystems of another, as when birds migrate or fish eat food washed from the land.

EQUILIBRIUM IN ECOSYSTEMS

The question of how an uncontrolled system can develop and maintain intricate, yet stable, relationships can be expressed, How can so many different interacting species develop and maintain an equilibrium? And, relatedly, Is an ecosystem really uncontrolled? A simple analogy helps clarify both problems.

Water poured into a bowl will promptly settle to a smooth, level surface, and will always return promptly to that same position following a disturbance. Three Ping-Pong balls in a round-bottomed bowl will reliably form a triangle. They can be carefully arranged in a straight line but will promptly return to the triangular formation if jostled. Seven balls will form a remarkably stable hexagon, and be very difficult to change much even by vigorous jiggling.

These systems regularly produce the *same* equilibrium following disturbance, so long as the amount of water or the number of balls is unchanged. If the quantity of either is changed, the system has no device for producing the same equilibrium as before. As in the example in Chapter 3, the uncontrolled pond will always return to the same level without controls so long as the inflow is constant. But if the inflow is changed, the pond will reach a different equilibrium. Unlike the controlled system it cannot maintain the same equilibrium in the face of changed inputs.

The basics of ecological equilibrium can be seen seen in a subsystem of two species, one predator and one prey. If rabbits are the main food of wolves, then the greater the rabbit population the greater will be the number of wolves (direct variation) and the greater the number of wolves the smaller will be the number of uneaten rabbits (inverse variation). With one direct and one inverse relationship an equilibrium is possible, and is often established. Or the relationships may oscillate around an equilibrium. Then an initial increase of rabbits will be followed by an increase of wolves, who have more food. But more wolves will eat more rabbits, whose numbers will then decline till the number of wolves is small enough to allow the rabbits to increase again—and so on.

But too many rabbits may overeat the grass on which they feed, and the number of rabbits will then decline till more grass grows. The equilibrium between wolves and rabbits thus depends in turn on that between rabbits and grass. If we can understand both one equilibrium and its interdependency with another equilibrium we have the key to the whole—an equilibrium of subequilibriums of sub-subequilibriums, and so on, simple in principle, fantastically complex in fact.

Moving vs. steady state equilibrium

An ecosystem may be in balance in the sense described just above. Yet the position of that balance may shift over the years, as some species increase and others decline. Over centuries and millennia the species themselves may undergo evolutionary change, while ice ages and mountain ranges come and go. Because of their parallelism to social ecology we will be concerned here only with shorter-run changes among existing species, particularly the distinction between a moving equilibrium (ecological succession) and a final, steady state, climax equilibrium.

To illustrate the moving equilibrium, the hillside behind my house was once vineyard and later pasture. Much of it is now an impassable jungle of honeysuckle, grape, and blackberry, which choke out most small trees. Trees of modest size nevertheless dot the area. As they grow the trees will eventually shade out the shrubs and vines (my biologist friends tell me), and the ground level will then be open and walkable. Unfortunately this transition may take a hundred years, which is more than standard mortality tables allot me. Justifying the activity as exercise, I meanwhile assist the clearing with chain saw and mower, and the open space brings a profusion of wild flowers. Were this area not too civilized for deer, they would help keep down the shrubs and vines.

Left undisturbed, the hillside would eventually reach *climax,* dominated by oaks, hickories, and maples. Meanwhile it is going through *ecological succession,* in which the quantities of each species change gradually over the decades. Once climax is reached, the equilibrium remains unchanged indefinitely. Even if the area were seriously disturbed, as by fire or lumbering, if it were then left alone it would again return eventually to the *same* climax equilibrium of oaks, hickories, and maples.

If the system reliably returns to the *same* equilibrium, does it not qualify as controlled? No. In the long run the main inputs to this system are temperature, rainfall, and soil nutrients. The system returns to the *same* equilibrium despite even severe disturbance for the same reason as did the uncontrolled pond of Chapter 3: the basic inputs remain unchanged. If both the temperature and the rainfall were to rise substantially and permanently, the system would change to something like the tropical rain forest of the Amazon Valley. If the temperature rose and the rainfall dropped, the system would shift to desert like that of southern Texas and Nevada, while if the temperature dropped and the rainfall remained unchanged it would become a forest of evergreens. If the whole hillside were cut bare and rains washed the surface back to bare rock, there would be no soil nutrients left to sustain new growth, and (as environmentalists point out) the area might never return to forest. Because the system returns to the *same* equilibrium only if its main inputs do not change much, we classify it as uncontrolled.

A well-established ecosystem may nevertheless be very tough. A very old forest constitutes much of its own environment. It does not depend on original soil, since its nutrition lies in the organic layer deposited by thousands of years of prior life. If rainfall declines, this soft earth holds the smaller amount so well that the decline may not matter. If temperature changes, the dense cover is an insulating blanket that keeps things warm or cool. Does this situation not qualify as controlled?

No. All we have said is that such a system is hard to disturb, but that its self-preserving quality does not also include the ability to return to its prior state once it *is* strongly disturbed and after its basic inputs have changed. When in doubt, if the observer can identify some kind of detector, selector, and effector processes that operate on behalf of the system as a whole he will probably do well to consider it controlled. Otherwise not. Miller (1965: 222) suggests that an identifiable "decider" is the crucial subsystem whose absence means that the system is not a living one, and hence (in his context) not controlled. Unless we are to leap from biology to theology, I know of no subsystem in the stream or forest that processes information on behalf of the whole system, has goals for the whole system, or engages in directed behavior for the whole system. Since our analysis of controlled systems focuses on their DSE functions, we cannot use that analysis if we cannot locate those functions.

Stability and redundancy

To move to a different problem of equilibrium, ecologists suggest that the greater the number and variety of species within a given niche the greater is the probable stability of the whole system. To illustrate, a blight killed all native chestnut trees in the United States in the 1920s. For a decade or so thereafter bare skeletons of chestnuts studded the woods. But in the forest oaks, maples, beeches, hickories, and some other species perform about the same biological and chemical functions as chestnuts. Since the chestnuts were usually scattered among other species, those other species shortly filled the gaps, with little effect on the whole system. Had chestnuts been the only large deciduous trees, the system would have changed dramatically, perhaps to forests of evergreens or fields of grasses and shrubs.

To generalize, the greater the redundancy in any one subsystem role the less likely is the whole system to fail or falter through failure of any one type of subsystem. That is, the greater the number and variety of subsystem types, and the greater the ease of making substitutions, the greater is the stability of the whole system. As noted earlier, a given system may go on indefinitely if all its components are replaceable. Adequate redundancy means an abundance of replacements and longer life.

Is equilibrium self-preserving?

Another generalization from ecology is that a system in equilibrium is apparently more resistant to change, more "self-preserving," than one not in equilibrium (Poore 1964: 217). The reason seems simple. For a system to continue very long in equilibrium means that each species has satisfactorily adapted to its environment. And since the environment of any one species consists of all other species, those other species must also be satisfactorily adapted to *their* environments. In short, any one satisfactorily adapted species simultaneously constitutes a part of the satisfactory environment for all other species. If each species is stable, other species that depend on it can also be stable, and all are secure.

Once this equilibrium has been reached, the system can go on indefinitely if every subsystem just keeps doing what it has been doing all along. But we also said something similar about formal organization—that once all subsystems are properly designed and all roles are mutually accommodated, the top managers can go off bear hunting in Alaska and no one will notice. This similarity provides a theoretical link between controlled and uncontrolled systems as well as between biological and social systems.

The important difference is that if something dramatic happens in the formal organization, the executives can be called back from Alaska—to restore balance, restructure the organization, or replace some components. The ecosystem has no executives to call back. It may eventually regain balance or develop a new structure. But any such results arise from interactions among parts, and may or may not "improve" the whole system. The structure of the pure formal organization is the conscious creation of its sponsors. The structure of the ecological system "just happens."

The tremendous learning capacity of human beings also gives formal organizations a flexibility not possible in ecosystems. By retraining an employee, or by replacing, say, a hydraulics engineer with a civil engineer, the organization in effect deliberately acquires a "new species." By contrast, new species come into an ecosystem only through chance wandering or slow evolution.

INFORMAL ORGANIZATION

This chapter is about the informal organizations of human beings, in which each controlled subsystem (person, club, corporation) pursues its own self-interest and none does anything about the overall result. We have taken a long but indispensable detour into ecosystems. Its purpose is to see that controlled subsystems (bees, ferns, wolves) can interact in ways that produce a very stable and orderly main system (the ecosystem), even though each subsystem pursues only its own goals in its own ways, even though no subsystem remotely comprehends or appreciates the whole system, and even though there is no sponsor or manager. It is precisely because individual humans do have some sense of the whole, which might create some doubts about the model, that we looked at a system in which we are quite sure no species or specimen plans or directs the whole. We will shortly apply to human ecology some principles from biological ecology.

In the model of informal organization people may engage in generous and hostile transactions and may care about the whole system, so long as these things reflect impulses or goals of the individual, and do not lead him into attempts to modify the larger system. To illustrate, I may *care* about the price of gasoline, and may, according to my needs and budget, increase or decrease my purchases as the price falls or rises. But unless I modify my purchases *in order to affect* the supply or price, my behavior is strictly informal. I and some friends may boycott a particular dealer or chain of dealers that has displeased us, but the action is still informal. There is no sharp line dividing such actions from those of the semiformal organization of the next chapter. However, to keep the nature and theory of informal organization clear, when in doubt we should think only of narrowly oriented actions that show no concern about the whole system—like those of the rabbits in the forest.

If people at a cocktail party or a beer bash produce some deliberate joint effect (such as moving a piano or planning the next party) they are a simple, temporary formal organization. If they merely interact through individually oriented communications or transactions they remain informal. If several individuals isolate the notorious nasty drunk so as to keep the party pleasant, their behavior is semiformal.

A mob tearing down goalposts after a football game would classify as a simple cooperative formal organization. The people create a deliberate joint effect. All participants are simultaneously sponsors (who want the goalposts down) and recipients of their shared result. Coordination is achieved mainly by mutual perception of one another's actions, perhaps assisted by instructions from self-appointed leaders. The "mob" style of organization could also bring productive results where little coordination is needed—as with many people building an emergency floodwall of sandbags. To classify a riot we would need to know whether its actions were consciously planned (formal organization) or the simple sum of separate actions by similarly motivated individuals (temporary if dramatic informal organization).

We have used the above examples to clarify some borderline instances. The study of informal organization (or human ecology) deals mainly with systems involving many more people. And instead of attending to people's interactions as such, the study of informal organization is interested in the systemness of the result, or the way in which there is a joint effect that is clearly distinct from the sum of the parts. As in the forest, even though the behavior of every plant and animal is directed solely toward its own goals, all are interdependent, and most could not even survive unless most of the others were also there.

Even when there is no interaction or explicit interdependence, a collective effect of many people doing the same thing is often different from the sum of their individual effects. For example, if one person lets his house deteriorate, the result is a shabby house; if many do the same, the result is neighborhood blight. If one rich man marries one rich woman, the result is a very rich couple; if most rich people do the same, the result is a hereditary wealthy class. In each case the whole is more than and distinct from the sum of the parts and, like the ecosystem, may be remarkably self-preserving. The whole is a societal structure, in which each part is intended by someone but the whole is intended by no one.

The cumulative effect is sometimes speeded by positive feedback. After a certain number of houses start to deteriorate, other owners may conclude that the whole neighborhood is going down, and each may then refrain from maintaining his own house.

Ecological principles in informal organization

The ecological system may warn us against oversimplification and overcomplexification. As to oversimplification, the way all the denizens of the wood contribute directly or indirectly to producing topsoil out of their collective remains is an extremely complicated causal chain, and we must not think that the reality is simple just because the basic theory is. So are many of the social situations described below, and nothing short of tracing many of their details will provide much real understanding of the individual case.

As to overcomplexification, the loss of power and bargaining power in "dealing downward" (Chapter 14) could alone lead the rich to marry mainly the rich, and leave only the poor for the poor to marry. If so, we might overcomplexify if we offered less simple explanations, such as a conspiracy to hold on to money, a desire to perpetuate a ruling class, or a social need for a hereditary elite. According to the *rule of parsimony,* we should avoid the more complicated explanation if a simpler one will do.

We have seen that in the forest the most important part of the environment of any one species is the other species among which it lives. So, too, the most important part of the environment of any human being is the other persons among whom he lives. In the forest the roles of each species are determined mainly by inheritance. In the pure model of formal organization they are determined by the sponsors. In pure informal organization the roles "just happen" as a result of interactions. But once a given role has happened, the behavior of the person in it is part of the environment in which other persons live and to which they respond.

Once a number of persons occupy a given role, such as father, sister, priest, hunter, or shoemaker, that role becomes part of the environment of many persons. In due time these roles become identified and are given names. Also in due time, in much the same way that each of us learns different behaviors toward rocks, chairs, and oranges, without necessarily attending to *which* rock or chair or orange we are dealing with, so do we learn different behaviors toward persons in different roles, without much regard to *which person* occupies that role. A role becomes a set of *expected behaviors* in the minds of persons who deal with anyone in it, and in turn helps induce each person in the role to behave as expected, in part because others will experience dissonance and possible hostility if their expectations are not met. Although the semiformal sanctions described in the next chapter greatly assist these processes, expectations alone can serve as wholly informal means to help standardize and sometimes rigidly preserve role patterns that originally "just happened." We have already seen some of the pressures toward following such expectations (Chapter 13, "Social Benefits of Norms"). Thus does even pure informal organization acquire a structure.

If the rich consciously view themselves as a ruling class and deliberately seek to maintain the class they constitute a semiformal organization, and might even formalize some aspects of it. But to discern whether the informal model is sufficient we simply ask, (1) Why would one rich person prefer to marry another rich person? and (2) Is this motivation likely to occur in most rich persons? If the first answer is sensible and the second affirmative, we have *an* explanation of a hereditary wealthy class—a theory of it. Whether this theory is valid can be told only by comparing it with the facts. That involves the much trickier problem of empirically testing the theory.[1]

It seems probable that most, perhaps all, of the generalizations stated above about equilibrium in ecosystems also apply to informal social systems. The predator-prey relation has social parallels in that if any group, Bs, receive outputs from another group, As, the Bs must not press too hard on the As, or the pressure may destroy the source. (The tax collector must not take so much that he bankrupts the taxpayer, and the husband must not make so many demands that his wife leaves him.) The notion of a general equilibrium of numerous subequilibriums has a clear parallel in economics, as we shall see. The moving equilibrium appears in places almost too numerous to mention, but certainly includes population increase, industrial growth, and changes in social structure. To illustrate the first, the old and the young may achieve a balanced allocation of duties in a stable society. If the population then starts to grow rapidly, there will be relatively more young than old. This new ratio will require a reallocation of duties—more infant care by adults and more chores for early teenagers. This allocation can itself reach an equilibrium, but it will be different from the previous one. A partial parallel of a climax equilibrium is found in closed, relatively primitive societies, in which for centuries there may be little or no pressure to change anything.

The stabilizing effect of redundancy and ready substitutability clearly operates in social systems. An area with only one source of energy faces immediate crisis if its supply is interrupted. But if oil, coal, natural gas, manufactured gas, and electricity are available, and can be interchanged on short notice, a stoppage of one fuel creates inconvenience but not crisis. If the mother is the only person available in a family to care for the young children, her sickness brings immediate crisis. But if there are

---

[1] As we observed in connection with transactions, a model may involve more assumptions than meet the eye. Similarly, the above model of informal organization assumes certain things about tax laws, legal inheritance, freedom to own and invest, absence of revolution, and so on.

also aunts, cousins, grandparents, and helpful neighbors who can step in to do the job, the situation again is inconvenience, not crisis.

Uncontrolled social systems, like ecosystems, can return to a previous pattern after disturbance. For example, if all the hereditary rich in a nation were "liquidated," the particular set of people who constituted that class would be gone. But unless the society's rules about ownership, inheritance, or marriage were changed, a new set of rich would probably arise and perpetuate itself by the same processes as did the first one.

We have observed that one ecosystem could not interact as a unit with another, and the same thing seems to hold true for informal organizations. Two corporations (controlled systems) can interact as units by buying and selling, and two governments (also controlled systems) can interact by making treaties or war. But as regards uncontrolled systems the whole American economy cannot interact as a unit with the whole British economy, nor can the American class structure interact as a unit with the American demographic structure. Parts may interact, as when an American importer buys woolens from a British mill. Or one system may be part of the environment of another and hence influence what happens in it, as the distribution of income within the class structure influences birthrates and hence the demographic structure. In neither case, however, does one whole uncontrolled system act on the other whole uncontrolled system.

Finally, the generalization that an ecosystem in equilibrium is resistant to change also seems to hold true for social systems. Equilibrium in a social system would presumably mean a condition in which the system is balanced well enough so that the needs of all parts are being adequately met. One dimension nevertheless differs as between informal organization and ecosystem. For the ecosystem "adequately met" means merely that a given number of each species can live and reproduce. For the informal organization it means that people *perceive* that their needs are adequately met, according to whatever standards they have come to accept. Because humans have a vastly greater ability than forest creatures to understand and evaluate their situation, stability in informal organization would continue only if both the overt conditions *and* the expectations of each subgroup remained the same. By the same token, a change in either the conditions or the expectations of any significant subgroup in a society might constitute imbalance and set off change in the larger system. Except for societies that are both primitive and isolated it is unlikely that any particular equilibrium will last very long, and in open societies disequilibrium and change are more probable than stable states. This does not mean that the study of equilibrium is not useful, since to identify the conditions for stability implicitly identifies the conditions for instability and change.

Some areas of informal behavior

We will not propose that the social patterns discussed in this section are, in fact, wholly informal, but rather that they behave as if they were largely so.

Much of the content and process of culture is informal. Eight-year-olds do not teach hopscotch to seven-year-olds in order to preserve the game in our culture. They teach it because they want someone to play with, or because the seven-year-olds have pestered them to be taught. Parents teach their children to talk or to shoot an arrow so the children can do these things, not to improve the social order. Most inventors invent and painters paint for self-expression, fun, prestige, or income, not to make the society better. When people do these self-oriented things they nevertheless transmit and add to the body of culture.

Historically the size and growth rate of a population were determined informally. Before reliable birth control a family accepted as many children as were born. Now the family may regulate the number it wants. Number of children thus becomes a controlled variable within the family, while the birthrate for the whole society nevertheless remains uncontrolled. Because of the "population crisis" some governments have recently attempted to alter birthrates (formal organization) and some families are voluntarily having fewer children than they might like so as to help stabilize the population (semiformal organization). Aside from such recent formal and semiformal modifications, such demographic factors as the size of the population, its rate of change, the number of persons in each age group, and the number in each religious or ethnic group are uncontrolled variables within informal organization.

If each person simply tries to earn as much as he can, the resulting structures of economic classes and social stratification are produced informally. If each family moves into the neighborhood it likes and can afford, the residential pattern is informal—although racial patterns of residence may contain powerful semiformal elements (resistance to "blockbusting") or formal ones ("Jim Crow" laws). Without zoning, the location of residences, stores, offices, and factories is informal. Although the building of a highway system is inescapably formal, the patterns of traffic movements on it are informal. These informal behaviors are human ecology in action.

The market economy

The market system is a major subsystem of commercial or industrial societies that produce and distribute exchangeable goods. Although three whole chapters are devoted to it later, it is mentioned here because it is one area of social organization to which informal organization theory has been consciously and explicitly applied (though not under that name), at least since Adam Smith's *Wealth of Nations* (1776). The theory of a market system, sometimes loosely identified as capitalism or laissez-faire, explicitly assumes that every businessman, consumer, banker, worker, and investor will pursue his own self-interest exclusively. All he could accomplish by trying to act in the public interest would be to foul up the system (according to the theory). That too is the only result government intervention could have (according to the pure theory). However, the government might intervene to prevent monopoly, regulate the money supply, or prohibit coercive transactions. Such restrictions on coercion in an otherwise uncontrolled system led to its early description as "anarchy plus a constable."

Because economists make highly simplified assumptions about the information and motivation (detector and selector) of the actors in their system, they are able to build a neat science about market systems—as in Chapter 22. Reality nevertheless differs from these hypothetical conditions in important ways—as seen in Chapter 23. Furthermore, some nations do not use the market system—as described in Chapter 24.

CONCLUDING NOTES

We have examined ecological systems, or at least some of the logic of such systems, because they are probably by far the best example we have of interactions which, with no central controls whatsoever and with no thought by the individual member of the system about the overall consequences of its acts, produce a coordinated result that is conspicuously greater than the sum of the parts. It is a system wholly without a general manager or sponsors. Despite its total lack of control at the whole-system level it nevertheless contains many goal-oriented, controlled subsystems. The ecosystem demonstrates (I hope) that one does not have to be either maudlin or a mystic to believe in the emergence of nonmanaged but highly ordered relationships.

Given this prototype, we can conceive of ordered and often quite stable structured relationships among humans that depend only on the fortuitous consequences of many self-oriented behaviors. This does not mean that controls are wholly absent from any real organization. It does mean that some order and continuity *can* exist without them.

Despite many deviations in practice, the theory or principle of a market system is that of a pure informal organization, or uncontrolled social system. A large volume of economic theory has been made possible because of simplistic assumptions about information and motivation on the part of the market system's controlled subsystems. However, it seems unlikely that comparable bodies of clear theory can be built for other informal aspects of social organization, mainly because no such simple assumptions are feasible for a theory of other uncontrolled systems. To illustrate, despite exceptions it is not too unrealistic to assume that most people who go into business do so mainly to make money, and that most of them prefer more of it to less. There are no equally realistic simple and widely applicable assumptions about why people marry, whom they marry, why they like certain schools or neighborhoods, why they do or do not live with their relatives, and so on.

All we can say in general about informal organizations is that what happens happens. If the system reaches an equilibrium, the equilibrium's nature and level are those that happen to balance the forces within it. If the forces change, so will the equilibrium position. Not only are there no sponsors and no general manager (Copeland 1958). There are not even any reformers or revolutionaries, no reactionaries or social foot-draggers. In *pure* informal organization there is not even someone who would deliberately spindle or mutilate his computerized telephone bill for the simple joy of fouling up the system, since such action would be semiformal.

We have not thereby abandoned our previous analysis. The humans in the informal system do pursue self-interest, based on their DSE states, which are translated into actions through decisions. They continue to interact with others through communications, transactions, and organizations. Of all the things we have discussed in previous chapters, the only thing they do *not* do is tailor their behavior toward the welfare of the larger society—in those areas subject to informal organizational analysis. Some of the more potent results of informal organization are reinforced by semiformal processes. Most "social" (as contrasted to economic or political) interactions are semiformal, including social parties, spontaneous demonstrations, and rap sessions. Discussion of all these things is therefore postponed till the next chapter, where we will also discuss in more detail the self-maintaining nature of many informal and semiformal organizations.

18

SEMIFORMAL ORGANIZATION

Human societies almost certainly used informal and semiformal organizational relations long before they developed formal ones. Once developed and understood, however, formal organization, with its conscious coordination of parts working toward a joint goal, helps sharpen such concepts as role, structure, authority, and sub- and supersystem. We have found these concepts to be useful in understanding informal organization as well, and will make further use of them here.

We now move from the two polar cases to the ones in between. But whereas there are only two "pure" theoretical polar cases, each clear and reasonably simple in concept, there is no limit to the possible variety of intermediate cases. To understand any intermediate type (and virtually all real organizations are intermediate) one can nevertheless ask, To what extent and in what respects does it behave like pure formal organization? Like pure informal? The intermediate cases can be viewed as mixtures of the two basic types, and hence as understandable in terms of those two sets of principles and concepts.

While recognizing any number of possible intermediate conditions, we will focus on only two, as we approach a middle ground from opposite ends. However formal a real organization may be it nevertheless contains many elements that are not formalized. Approached from this side, semiformal organization lies in the informal aspects of formal organization. And however informal a real organization, some people within it probably modify their behavior so as to have some effect on the overall result. Approached from this side, semiformal organization lies in the formal (or formalizing) aspects of informal organization. Thus "Informal within Formal" and "Formalizing Elements in Informal Organization" are the two headings under which we will approach semiformal organization.

INFORMAL WITHIN FORMAL

In the model of pure formal organization we view the individual as a cog in the organizational machine, behaving only as instructed by sponsors, and motivated to perform through sanctions of the authority relationship. In the model of pure informal organization the individual pursues his own goals exclusively, while any larger organizational result simply *happens*. To understand the intermediate conditions we need to look briefly at the difference between a human being as part of an organization and any other kind of subsystem.

A carburetor makes sense only as a subsystem of an engine, a liver only as a subsystem of an animal, and each belongs to only one main larger system. By contrast, each human being is very much a system in his own right, in addition to being a subsystem of numerous larger systems, often moving rapidly from one to another. The older, or "classical," organization theory, particularly that originated by Frederick W. Taylor about the turn of the century, focused on fitting the human subsystem into a coordinated total system. It concentrated on what we view here as the strictly formal aspects of organization. Although not completely abandoning that aspect of organization, the newer theory dates mainly from about World War II. Roethlisberger and Dickson (1939) and Simon (1947) paid much attention to the psychological and social characteristics of the organization member, and the ways in which the individual is not fully transformed into a mere subsystem. Bennis (1962: 270) expressed this distinction as one between the "technological, rationalized procedures" aspect, which views the employee as a factor of production, and the "human factors" aspect, which views the human as a system in his own right.

In the family and in close friendships one interacts along many dimensions, involving his loves, hates, fears, worries, and hopes as well as his health, recreation, car, house, clothes, spouse, and debts. In the purely formal aspects of his relation with a formal organization the individual interacts only in terms of his job—his instructions and his successes and failures in performing them. Yet people who work in the same shop or office, or who are members of the same club or professional association, do not cease to be whole humans. The formal organization's work puts them in positions in which they necessarily interact. As they then come to know one another, their interactions extend in many directions, and start to resemble those of friendships or even of family. These interactions often include some loose coalition function, as members move toward a common position in their attitudes toward superiors or subordinates about task assignments, work loads, rewards, programs, or other aspects of the organization.

Because the formal organization uses only a limited segment of the whole human it would not normally want to formalize all aspects of its members' behavior even if it could. And because the members remain whole humans the organization could not formalize all aspects of their behavior even if it wanted to. Hence nonformalized behaviors—not directed by the management—are a standard part of any formal organization.

To say that the individual remains a whole person, and is not merely a cog, is itself an important statement about formal organization. But that is only the beginning. As we have known since the famous studies of workers in the Bank Wiring Room of Western Electric's Hawthorne plant (Roethlisberger and Dickson 1939), the employees of an organization are also their own society, and in the large organization are a collection of many societies. That is, the employees constitute an organization of their own, often in ways that are quite independent of the formal organization they belong to.

In most discussion of formal organization such relationships among employees are called informal organization. In this volume we use *informal* only for interactions in a larger society beyond the scope and effect of face-to-face relationships, and give the name *semiformal* to these informal-within-formal relationships. It is because people may care and know about the effects of their behaviors on the group, and perhaps modify their behaviors accordingly, that they cannot exist in the ecological relation of pure informality. In that respect they also resemble those efforts to modify some larger social entity, such as a nation, that we here call the formal aspects of informal organization.

Informal modifications of roles and authority

Semiformal organizational relations often come about through informal modifications of roles and authority. As to the former, for a routine task like putting pickle jars into cartons individual differences in role performance may not matter much. But in many other jobs individual style, intelligence, or energy may make a great difference. Since roles are interdependent, for an individual to modify his own role means that the role of every person with whom he interacts will also be somewhat modified. An aggressive, empire-building middle-level executive fashions a very different role than does a nonaggressive middle-level executive, and every role with whose occupants he interacts is modified when its occupants accept or resist his empire building. Even roles two or three stages removed from the empire builder may be modified indirectly. In these respects the structure of the organization is not what the sponsors prescribe, but what the members make it through unprescribed behavior.

Even authority, the major device for tying the individual to the goals of the organization, can be significantly modified by informal behaviors. For example, since raises and promotions come from organizational superiors, staff members often hesitate to ask their bosses questions about their job for fear that they will look stupid—particularly if they already asked the question and forgot the answer. They will often go to a knowledgeable fellow employee instead, who may be flattered to be asked. But if he observes that his advice is not followed he will be reluctant to give it the next time. Since his advice is about doing the job it constitutes in a very real sense an "instruction" about the organization's work. And since he can grant or withhold his valued advice, depending on whether his "instructions" have been followed, he is exercising authority, as defined.

Because such relations involve the organization's work, they are not strictly informal. But because sponsors or their agents do not plan them or provide these particular rewards, neither are they strictly formal. Hence we view them as semiformal. This kind of semiformal authority is almost inescapable, and the wise management will work with it rather than fight or ignore it.

Informal modifications of the major bargain

In many respects the terms of the major bargain are not spelled out in the agreement itself, but are hammered out in daily living. Of the innumerable possibilities we will illustrate just one. The amount of work done in a given time is of intense interest to both employees and management. In relatively routine jobs time and motion study can determine with reasonable accuracy how much work a person can do—such as soldering eight joints per minute or sorting 3,000 letters per hour. In such situations management may successfully hold employees to an "objectively reasonable" quota of work.

But in the many jobs where such objective standards are not available, attitudes and habits developed by the individual or by group norms can be very important in determining how much work will be done, instead of chatting, taking coffee breaks, or girl watching. Negative attitudes will produce a hostile shrinkage of effective preference in the authority transaction, and employees may then give as little work as they can get away with. Favorable attitudes extend the *EP*s, and more work is done. Such attitudes are often thought of as "morale." Like those discussed above, such aspects of the organization are considered semiformal because they deal with its work, but are not determined by the sponsors or explicitly negotiated with them.

A strong consensus in favor of "taking it easy" may be difficult for management to overcome (Mathewson 1931). Each individual can truthfully say that no one else works harder, and in the absence of objective standards it may be difficult to demonstrate that a reasonable amount of work is *not* being done. Unless the entire group is discharged, new employees will pick up the existing norms through induction into the informal group. Although management is not totally helpless, the problem is not necessarily easy, and a frontal assault is not necessarily the best attack.

Pure informal goals within formal organization

Even less formal are behaviors within the formal organization that are directed wholly toward goals of the members. These reflect that each individual's role in the organization is only one aspect of his life. It is a "segmental" relationship—as the sociologist puts it. People converse at the water cooler, the janitor runs a betting pool, the former pharmacist's mate doles out free medical advice, and acquaintances made at work lead to dating and mating.

Because such activities have nothing to do directly with the formal organization, but nevertheless tie its members together, they fall somewhere between completely formal and completely informal.

FORMALIZING ELEMENTS IN INFORMAL ORGANIZATION

When we approach semiformal organization from the informal end, perhaps the best way to describe it is to say that it is something like formal organization, only looser. In it are certain elements of authority, responsibility, induction, structure, sponsor function, and awareness of joint action that parallel those elements in formal organization. But they are looser in that there are often no conscious decisions about these elements or behaviors, that no clear boundaries exist between sponsors and staff, and that organizational activities are diffused among the members. In these respects the general nature of semiformal organization is the same whether it occurs inside or outside of formal organization. Despite exceptions, as a general rule we can say that an organization is formal if it has a charter, constitution, or bylaws; if it has specified officers with titles; and if it keeps minutes of its meetings. Otherwise it is informal, semiformal, or not an organization.

A friendship or a group of children playing games are an example of small-scale semiformal organization. A group of persons separately trying to influence their congressman are not an organization. But a group who loosely agree to coordinate the timing or content of their letters are a semiformal organization. In a general way many interactions among the people in a nation other than those that constitute its government or its economy, and that are not themselves formal organizations, are semiformal.

Friendship as an example

Let us start with a simple case. You meet someone on several occasions and gradually become friends, going places and doing things together. As you come to like each other you develop an implicit major bargain: We are friends, and will do things for and with each other from time to time. If you become closer, the bargain may expand to an understanding that each will routinely inform the other of his plans. The implicit major bargain of a friendship also normally includes an understanding that although negotiations and arguments over terms will be avoided in most cases, each of you is obliged in due time to reciprocate contributions or favors by the other, so that case-to-case differences will average out. If your income or other capacities are very different, you may balance subjective sacrifice rather than overt contributions. And if one of you gets real satisfaction, or perhaps avoids a sense of guilt, by helping the other, the subjective aspects of the relation may still balance even if the overt ones are one-sided.

Thus far most of what has happened between you is that you behave as friends. Our society has a general concept of "friendship," and of behaviors appropriate to the role of "friend." If the other violates the expectations that go with that role you may voice your disapproval with: "But I thought we were friends!"

In addition to your general role as friends, you may develop roles that are specific to yourselves, and are at least implicitly recognized. If you go places your friend normally provides the transportation (because you have no car) and you provide refreshments. Knowing more about the local town, your friend usually suggests what to do. But being older and more self-confident, you initiate most of the conversations. As these and other roles become more clearly defined, your expectations about each other are more reliably filled, as each follows the expectations attached to his role. You become more comfortable with each other, in part for the same kind of reason that you become more comfortable after you have driven a particular car long enough to know exactly what to expect of it.

© King Features Syndicate, by Dix Browne, January 2, 1974.

At first you may have cared only about the costs and benefits of particular interactions, such as talking, walking, or listening to music together. In due time, however, you have come to care about the relationship itself, which has now become an entity above and beyond any one interaction. You then find yourself modifying your behavior in particular interactions in such a way as to affect the continuing relationship. Even if unconsciously, you stop thinking of yourself solely as a system-in-your-own-right and start seeing yourself as a subsystem in a two-person continuing relationship. As soon as you start thinking and caring about the relationship rather than about particular interactions, but do not formalize it, you are viewing the situation (in present language) as a small semiformal organization. We have noted some aspects of its major bargain. You have developed differentiated roles, thereby creating a structure, and these roles are coordinated to produce an overall result. Here we can identify some of the elements of formal organization, such as structure and major bargain. But the relationship remains informal to the degree that these elements develop in a relatively haphazard way, rather than being consciously designed by some sponsors of the organization as a unit to serve their ends.

Some introductory notes

In the above example of friendship we focused on a particular relationship and examined several of the organizational elements within it. For a more comprehensive view we will now focus instead on various organizational elements one at a time as they may appear in a wide variety of relationships, of which we can mention only a small sampling. The general logic is much the same, however, whether you go out of your way today to influence tomorrow's relationship with your friend or the next century's solution of air pollution. Although the term *group* is normally applied to persons who interact on a face-to-face basis and know one another as individuals, we will apply it more loosely in the remainder of this section to a collection of friends, a neighborhood, the adherents of a particular religion, a whole society, or any other collectivity around which beliefs or actions happen to be oriented.

Some elements in the semiformal organization may be concentrated in a few persons, as is especially the case with leadership. Others may be diffused across more or less the whole group.

Leadership as semiformal sponsor function

In the model of pure formal organization the sponsors and their agents determine its goals and structure, subdivide the tasks and decisions among the parts, plan the coordination of the parts, instruct the various subsystems, and exercise the authority which elicits their performance.

Leadership is the semiformal version of the same thing. Just as semiformal organization is like formal organization, only looser, leadership is like the sponsor function, only looser. Whereas in formal organization the sponsors themselves initiate the organization, specify the roles, and select the staff, in semiformal organization there is typically no clear distinction between sponsors and staff.

Often some group sense that they have some common goal, and think that coordinated action might be useful. On his own initiative or at the prodding of others, someone may make suggestions about clarifying goals, about steps necessary to achieve them, about subdividing the tasks among group members, and about coordinating their actions. Because his suggestions seem more sensible than others, or perhaps because he talks with more confidence, the rest of the group accept them. When both he and the others recognize this role and reliably behave in accordance with it, this person has become the leader. The same process often occurs to a significant degree within nominally formal organizations, but our interest here is mainly in the nature of the process rather than its location.

The sanctions available for the leader's semiformal authority lie mainly within himself, not in stocks of rewards that he can draw out of the organization, as such. His authority lies in his ability to reward the other members (followers) with such things as praise, the hope or actuality of successful accomplishment, and the continued use of his talents. Or he can punish them with criticism, predictions of failure if they do not do their part, or threats to withdraw if they disregard his advice. If the group are already strongly motivated, his contribution may be simply to suggest techniques or to guide group decisions. If they are not already motivated, his main function may be to inspire hope and courage.

We have introduced the term *leadership* in connection with semiformal organization. We did not need it for formal organization, since the notion of sponsor function was adequate. There is no place for it in pure informal organization, which has no explicitly coordinated action. Having introduced the term here to describe the sponsor function that "just grows" in a group—that is achieved, not ascribed—we can note that the term is widely used in connection with "official" leaders in complex formal organizations. However, to say that someone in a supervisory role is a "good leader" is merely to commend the job he is doing as an agent for the sponsors. Similarly, a "poor leader" in a formal organization is one who lacks the ability to do his job well. We might also say that a good formal leader successfully utilizes the semiformal relationships within the formal. Either way, it is a sponsor type of function. Leadership, of course, can also occur in simple formal organization.

Content and skills of leadership. Leadership can be divided among persons, either by parceling out its functions or by letting each leader perform some part of each function. In the former case one leader might formulate goals, a second subdivide tasks, a third motivate the group, and a fourth keep them congenial. When an organization has many, large, overlapping, and possibly conflicting goals, as with a national government, perhaps the most important leadership function is to clarify and set priorities among goals, while using authority mainly to hold together the coalition necessary to keep him in office.

Effective leadership generally requires two distinct kinds of skills. The first is technical ability in the methods of achieving the goal: knowing how to climb the mountain, design the car, win the election, capture the enemy bunker, or rebuild the slum. The second is the social and psychological skills required to exercise authority, by communicating the goals and motivating those who are to perform them. When the tasks and the persons are unusual, leadership is properly thought of as an art, not a science—for reasons detailed in Chapter 26. Certain aspects of both task performance and human interaction can nevertheless be studied systematically, and to that extent leadership can also be a science. Whether as science or art, it involves the dual ingredients of knowing how to do the job and of getting others to do it.

Beliefs and codes as semiformal sponsor goals

It is rare for anyone to grow up without acquiring values about his society and notions of how it ought to operate—which is why we detoured into ecological systems for our model of informal organization. For an understanding of semiformal organization it does not matter whether one believes that war is the worst evil or that to die in battle is the highest good. It does not matter whether he believes that government should prohibit all "dirty" literature or that it should allow the hardest core pornography to circulate freely. What matters is that he *have some be-*

liefs about and sense of responsibility toward the larger society and that he sometimes modify his behavior from a pure self-orientation to help effectuate his social beliefs.

One can, of course, help implement his beliefs through voting or holding office. Such actions, however, are part of the formal organization of government, and our interest in the semiformal centers on more individualistic behaviors. To the extent that an individual has some beliefs about what the whole society or some sizable subsystem of it should do, or how it should operate, he reflects a sponsorlike interest in it. To think and act in behalf of the whole system, not merely in his own behalf, is what we mean by the sponsor interest and role.

Such beliefs may arise from or be embodied in moral codes, as in a belief that everyone need but follow the Ten Commandments, the Sermon on the Mount, or the golden rule to produce a good society. Others may see the protection of property rights, the Bill of Rights, the dedicated pursuit of self-interest under a free enterprise system, or some other ideology as the best roads to a good society. Still others may focus on functional subsystems of the society, such as the farmers, trade unionists, the family, the church; and others may focus on some issue, such as war, the environment, abortion, prison reform, or alcoholism. Such sponsorlike interest can be very specific, as with a desire to clean up local streets or eliminate neighborhood rats. No sharp line divides such interest in the general good from the self-interest of the individual. Our point is simply that an interest extending beyond the individual or his close associates to some general good is a sponsorlike interest in the larger group, and can be construed as sponsor goals in semiformal organization. These sponsorlike goals lead people in turn to exercise semiformal authority, as we will see shortly.

Norms and expectations as semiformal instructions

In the model of formal organization a superior explicitly tells the subordinate what to do. In the pure model, norms are not involved in the present sense, although we could say that any instruction that is formally legitimate is also "normal" in that context. Semiformal organization operates on the basis of expectations rather than instructions, although the child may sometimes need formal instructions to know what is expected. One expects the extended hand to be taken in a handshake. For the most part he expects a favor to be followed by a thank-you; the flag to be treated with respect; the audience to applaud when the speaker is finished; the boy to marry the girl he made pregnant; the doctor to heal and the teacher to teach; the priest to profess belief, not atheism; and parents to care for their children.

Such expectations (images) about behaviors are known by sociologists as *norms* (Chapter 13), and *normative behaviors* are those that conform to them. Normative behaviors are usually felt to be right and proper, and nonnormative ones wrong. Some norms, of course, may differ from one society or subsociety to another, and are not necessarily the same even for all the members of the same family. Others are widely and deeply held, such as the expectation that no one will appear naked in public and that everyone will show loyalty to his immediate friends and family. The more rigid and deeply ingrained the norm the less likely one is to be aware of it.

The simple efficiency of uniformity also supports normative expectations, as in having everyone drive on the same side of the road. Habits save much time and decision making in the individual. When the habits of two or more persons must mesh, the gains in time and efficiency from sticking to expected behaviors can be far greater. Otherwise each person would try to adjust his behavior to what he thinks the other will do, while the second adjusts to what he thinks the first will do, and so on. The obvious advantages of uniformity often overshadow the question of whether the uniform procedure is itself very good. Since attempted improvement will produce nonuniformity till everyone gets used to it, the simple efficiency of having everyone follow expected patterns is often a potent self-maintaining force. The way students settle into the same unassigned seats in a classroom is an interesting example. When the normative behaviors are not inherently very sensible, the newcomers, notably the young, typically challenge them. Old-timers may agree that the norms are not sensible, but be unenthusiastic about changing ingrained habits.

Norms typically become internalized as system states of the individual. You do not consciously debate whether to dress before you go outdoors, any more than the experienced driver consciously decides to press the brake pedal to stop the car. Once norms become internalized patterns of this sort, the overt behavior follows the norms because it symbols the inner ones. Despite occasional "streaking," the norm against public nakedness is so deeply ingrained that many persons are almost frantic if they are suddenly exposed. A lesser dissonant feeling accompanies the violation of less important norms. Expressed as detector and selector states, the individual who has internalized the norms of his culture perceives and values things the way others around him do. His behavior conforms because the inner patterns symbolized by that behavior already conform.

Many norms belong to specific roles. Although to some extent each individual molds the role he occupies, the reverse effect is usually stronger—the role molds its occupant. Teacher and student do not behave differently because they are different kinds of persons but because one occupies the role of teacher and the other that of student. Popes and parishioners, presidents and citizens, males and females behave as they do largely because of the roles they occupy. Even if the liberation movement should remove all strictly normative differences between male and female roles in some societies, such differences have been nearly universal in the past and will long continue in many places.

Social pressures as semiformal authority and responsibility

If norms are expectations and expectations are a society's semiformal instructions to its members, the next question is that of enforcement.

What kinds of sanctions does the society use to see that its instructions are followed? We can first identify *conformity* as the semiformal equivalent of "following society's instructions." Nonconformity is the violation of those instructions, or semiformal insubordination.

In semiformal organization, as in formal, authority is exercised by rewarding conformity and punishing nonconformity. But whereas in formal organization these sanctions are applied only to legitimate instructions and by clearly identified agents of the sponsors, in semiformal organization they are applied somewhat unpredictably by those individuals who happen to feel a strong enough sponsor interest in the larger group to do something about it. The sanctions consist of *social pressures,* which are generous extensions or hostile contractions of *EPs* to individuals in return for their conformity or nonconformity to norms.[1]

If others can exercise authority over you by granting or withholding the rewards that go with their approval or disapproval, you are by the same token responsible to them, or to the society in general, for conforming. Furthermore, if a given group accepts a set of norms, those norms become part of the major bargain about what behavior is acceptable within the group. Expectations that the norms will be followed are thus semiformally "legitimate," and so are the semiformal rewards or punishments meted out to conformists and nonconformists.

Sometimes the authority of social pressures is loose and uncertain. If you are surly when you ask directions of a local resident, he may nevertheless give you correct information. Or he may decide to "teach you a lesson" by sending you miles out of your way. When you realize what has happened, the experience may teach politeness quite as effectively as formal discipline from a boss or a parent. If the wrong information reflected mere annoyance rather than his desire to reform you, its effect in molding you toward conformity with the code of politeness is nevertheless much the same. When expectations are highly uniform and sanctions for violations are reliable they can structure your social behavior as strictly as the existing network of roads structures your decisions about where to drive your car. And when similar things are being done by and to nearly all of us they create a structure (a pattern system) in human behavior that covers the length and breadth of the society.

Subtle sanctions, such as making one feel guilty or obligated, are often more effective than crude and obvious ones. In general, to reward approved, conforming behaviors by smiles and favors is more effective than

---

[1] The reader already conversant with social science, and particularly the sociologist, may need to remind himself from time to time that the discussion here deals with *models* of formality, informality, and semiformality. The models are designed to isolate the logic of different kinds of relationships, not to describe what goes on in any particular real organization. In any real organization of significant size a bit of everything is apt to be going on all the time, and our examination of only one kind of relationship at a time is meant to facilitate understanding, not to imply that reality is less complex than it is. Only by first getting the separate models clear can we later approach reality more closely by assembling parts of the models into a more complex whole. At least that is the way this volume is constructed.

to punish disapproved behaviors by frowns and hostility, as the latter often generate a reciprocal hostility and a desire *not* to conform.

Semiformal authority is often made formal by enacting it into law. Then fine or imprisonment supplement or replace the semiformal frowns, criticism, or boycott. Conversely, certain behaviors may be subject to semiformal sanctions merely because they are illegal, even if the behaviors do not violate any significant norms.

Role conflict. The biological or mechanical subsystem, such as a liver or a transmission, is normally a subsystem of only one larger system, and has neither consciousness nor conscience. But a human being is a subsystem of numerous formal, semiformal, or informal organizations, performing different kinds of roles in them. Often the same person occupies several different roles in the same organization. To illustrate both relationships, a woman may be simultaneously the president of the PTA, a member of a civic club, the chief fund raiser for a church, and a buyer for a department store; while she is also a mother, sister, wife, and daughter within a family unit.

Almost any set of roles can conflict, in the general sense that all make demands on limited time and resources. But sometimes they also have incompatible norms. The person who occupies multiple roles may thus be subject to *role conflict*, in which behavior expected in one role is frowned upon or prohibited in another.

We dress, speak, and behave differently in church than in a shop or the army. For the most part we learn the behavior appropriate to each role, and shift behavior as we move from one role to another. Dissonance may arise, however, when two roles intersect. When the clergyman becomes an army chaplain, does he use the language and mannerisms of the church or of the army? Is the answer the same in the base chapel as in the field hospital or on the battlefield? Can the same person learn to discipline his son successfully shortly after being his playmate? How does he keep one relationship from confusing the other? When the graduate assistant is simultaneously student and teacher, does he follow the norms of student or of teacher?

Role conflicts are especially difficult if they involve moral values or basic norms. In the role of parent or church member one may believe in and practice great fairness, integrity, and generosity. But in his role as bargaining agent, political boss, or advertiser the same person may use misrepresentation and hostile pressures. He may be a faithful husband at home, but not at a convention. Such an individual probably suffers least inner dissonance if he can isolate these conflicting situations, both in fact and in his head. The conflict deepens when roles intersect. They may intersect in fact if his companions at the convention become friends of his wife and children, and many "situation comedies" revolve around the often grotesque efforts to keep two incompatible roles apart. If the two roles intersect in his head, he may feel alternate twinges of conscience (Why can't I behave as strictly at the convention as at home?) and disappointment (Why can't I behave as freely at home as at the convention?).

Children encounter distressing role conflicts if behavior virtually demanded by the norms of classmates and other peer groups is denounced and punished at home—and vice versa. These conflicts can be very difficult if the child is unable to avoid either group, or even to avoid having each know about the other. If a child's family teach him independence and self-reliance while school allows no room for judgment, he may come to think of school as a prison. Other children may find school stimulating as compared to a barren, hostile home life, and experience role conflict if parents or friends scoff at school as "sissy stuff."

Handling role conflict. One way to soften role conflict is to drop one of the conflicting roles, as by avoiding conventions or leaving school. A second is to avoid intersections, by mentally or factually separating the conflicting roles. A variant of this technique is to continue both roles, but to accept only one of them as right and proper while nevertheless going through the motions of the other. A third method is to modify the roles so that the remaining inconsistency is not bothersome. A fourth is insubordination (or rebellion), as when one fully accepts one role, but insists on performing the second according to the standards and behavior of the first. The husband behaves at the convention as he does at home, or vice versa. The teenager behaves among friends as he does at home, or he brings his friends home and behaves with them there as he does elsewhere, even if his parents disapprove. A fifth possibility is to retreat from the source of the conflict.

One may, of course, feel more a "whole person" if he can avoid inconsistent roles. One complaint of the "youth revolt" is the alleged hypocrisy of a person who accepts inconsistent roles, or of the society that expects him to. However, it seems unlikely that any large society can avoid conflicts completely, although sustained effort might reduce them. Besides, many persons would find total role consistency boring and inflexible.

Even pure formal organization roles may conflict, as with the salesman whose efforts to please the customer may displease the production foreman, or vice versa. Anyone who exercises delegated authority is both an agent for his superiors in trying to get work out of his subordinates and for his subordinates in trying to get his superiors to relieve the pressure. Strictly speaking, this conflict occurs *within* the role since the single role of supervisor includes interactions with superiors and subordinates—with those above him and those below him.

In short, role conflict is the semiformal equivalent of having two or more bosses who give you conflicting instructions, and any of whom may discipline you if you do not follow *his* instructions.

Myth and ritual as part of semiformal induction

In pure formal organization the newcomer is introduced to his job by his job description, his contract of employment, the organization manual, or explicit instructions. He learns about the nature and goals of the organization through briefing sessions or house organs. He learns about the other persons he must interact with through description or by introduction.

A group in a club or office also induct new members to make them familiar with its ideals, goals, sense of loyalty, methods of operation, philosophy of life, and the "kind of people we are." Those who are already members tell the newcomers anecdotes about the group's past history, its leaders, its internal conflicts and cooperative relations, and its relations with outsiders. Depending on its size and continuity, the group may put on skits or dramas, give awards to meritorious members or leaders, stage parades or rallies, conduct discussions, hold competitions, or do a dozen other things that reflect its goals and philosophy. On a larger scale, most holidays celebrate some event or person symbolizing the larger group's view of what is important or good, and ritualistic speeches, parades, bonfires, or dances may symbolize their beliefs more explicitly. The myths of ancient Greece and Rome, of the Indians of North and South America, of the Eskimos, and of the Chinese exemplify the ways in which such tales reveal a group's concepts of good and evil. Since the bad guys and the good guys are readily identifiable in most fairy tales, these help children to visualize the group's abstract values. Much history as taught in public schools is part of a folklore that supports the group's self-image, as can readily be seen by comparing accounts of the Revolutionary War in American and British schoolbooks, or of the French and Indian War in American and Canadian schoolbooks. Songs often supplement the above, as with "Dixie," "The Eyes of Texas Are Upon You," or "We Shall Overcome." For a century or more the "darky" songs helped solidify and define the whites' view of blacks in the United States, while "spirituals" reflected the blacks' view of things. Artworks may show Washington crossing the Delaware or the Mexican peasants toiling under the whip of of the landowner.

We have mentioned only a few of the many ways in which a group semiformally communicates its views and attitudes to new members, and in the process refreshes and renews them in its older members. The general effect is a feeling that "we are a group. We are fine, honorable, and courageous people while our enemies are dishonorable and cowardly, and so are many other outsiders. We will stick together to defend and maintain our honor and our greatness." This kind of communication is often supplemented by group authority, as outlined above. Thus does the semiformal organization induct its new members, and try to convert them from systems in their own right into subsystems of the group, and to sketch into their images the boundaries between in-group and out-group. It is "like formal induction, only looser."

SOCIAL STRATIFICATION

In the preceding section we looked at processes and relationships. Organizations also create structures, consciously directed in the case of formal organizations and wholly undirected in the case of informal organizations. Semiformal organizations also produce social structures, and individuals or subgroups sometimes consciously seek to assist or preserve them. We will examine two aspects of such social structures that seem to be reasonably universal, stratification in this section and ethnic groupings in the next.

Stratification means that people fall into different levels of aggregate power, status, or both. Formal organization explcitly creates such differences when it assigns persons to fill roles that carry different levels of authority and responsibility in the management hierarchy. Normally we do not call such hierarchical differences "stratification" unless power in a formal organization carries over into the looser society outside. Stratification can occur through wholly informal processes. But it is usually assisted by certain semiformal actions, which is why we deal with it here. The most obvious bases for stratification are differences in wealth and income. Many societies, including our own, include people at all levels from abject poverty to fabulous luxury. To the former price is the main barrier to getting the things they want, and to the latter price is no barrier at all. Though most of us fall somewhere in between, the extremes dramatize the point. In smaller and simpler societies, as among tribes of American Indians, though discrepancies in wealth are sometimes small or nonexistent, types of power other than wealth differ from person to person.

The variety of bases for class and status

In Chapter 14 we defined a *class* as a collection of people of approximately equal aggregate power, and *status* as apparent, or perceived, aggregate power, noting also how power can be built and accumulated. We spoke of power that resides in a resource base of material external power factors, such as money, land, buildings, machinery, cattle, paintings, and jewels. We noted that power can also be based on nonmaterial factors, such as skill, personality, and publicity.

Differences in class level appear within subsocieties as well as within the society as a whole. In contemporary United States these subsocieties include café and theater society, artists and musicians, athletes, political figures, academic and intellectual circles, the executive hierarchy of large organizations, and the underworld of gambling and crime. Within a religious organization or among kings who claim to rule by divine right, different levels of power may be based on the apparent number of steps between oneself and God. Furthermore, a whole structure of class stratification may exist independently within each major religious group (Protestants, Jews, Catholics), within each ethnic and racial group (black, Puerto Rican, Italian, Irish), or perhaps within an industry group (automobiles, clothing, advertising).

In traditional societies (which designation includes most preindustrial ones) power was largely *ascribed*—a person had power because he occupied a role to which the society assigned power. Furthermore, the individual typically was born into the family or class that was accorded power. Ascribed power is far less important in industrial societies (Lenski 1966: 410). There power is more customarily *achieved,* which means that the individual gets power through his own efforts—though gift, inheritance, theft, or luck may assist him substantially. To the extent that power is based on internal power factors, such as skills or knowledge, it must be achieved, as there is no way to transfer these things directly.

Status is more transferable than actual power, as when such names as Roosevelt, Kennedy, Taft, or Adlai Stevenson propel the son farther or faster in politics than would his merits alone. Elsewhere the names Rockefeller or Du Pont, Fonda or Sinatra help open many doors.

Although internal power factors must be achieved, it helps if one's parents also have them. If the parent is a successful politician or businessman, the child learns much from his talk and experiences about the care and feeding of political or corporate power. Living among those who exercise power also promotes an ease in dealing with it that may be more important than knowledge. More generally, if the parents are educated and competent, the child probably grows up among books, magazines, and thoughtful conversation, with dictionary and encyclopedia readily available. If the parents have none of these things, the child, despite school, may find it slow and frustrating to learn to acquire information from the printed page.

One is not necessarily stuck at the same level as his parents. In the United States about 34 percent of sons cross to the other side of the line between manual and nonmanual work from the position occupied by their fathers. There is more upward than downward movement across that line, mainly because of the growth in the overall proportion of nonmanual jobs (Lenski 1966: 411–12). Such mobility is largely a function of industrialization, not (as is often thought) a reflection of unusual opportunities in the United States (Lipset and Bendix 1959: 17–28). In general the children in large families have less chance of doing well economically (Blau and Duncan 1967: 411; Belmont and Marolla 1973: 1096–1101). It is nevertheless true that most people who work with their hands had parents who worked with their hands, while most people at executive and professional levels had executives and professionals for parents. Throughout the history of the world the rich come mainly from rich parents, the poor from poor parents, and middle-income people from middle-income parents. What is more, the rich marry mainly the rich, leaving only the poor for the poor to marry. This fact tends to keep large chunks of power intact, and adds a positive feedback accentuation of the discrepancies.

In summary we can note three things. First, many external power factors can be transferred by transaction, and many internal ones by communication. Second, parents are more likely to make both kinds of cross-generation transfers to their own children than to the children of others. Third, because of its positive feedback nature, power is difficult to accumulate rapidly for those who start at a low level. As a result, and despite many exceptions, the amount of power any individual will have depends heavily on the amount possessed by his parents.

To people raised in a society with obvious differences in power, those differences tend to be accepted as *normal,* along with sunsets and taxes. Those in the poor part of town observe that those in the rich part live in different kinds of houses, dress differently, have servants, attend opera, and go away for the summer. Furthermore, roles and behaviors are interrelated. A person learns to behave in a certain way because he occupies a certain role, and "being upper class" is a different role than "being lower class." Once such behaviors and expectations are acquired they tend to keep people "at their own level" even when they are moved into quite different situations. For example, even when a military draft takes people from all levels, the education, speech, and self-assurance of upper-class people make them much more likely to be selected for positions as officers. Thus upper-class role behaviors tend to keep people in upper-class roles.

Class as semiformal organization

In Chapter 14 we saw why people at a given level of power interact mainly with others at that same level. In addition, status is relative, and one's status is higher if that of others is lower. Since high status is enhanced if only a few people hold it, there is potential advantage in keeping down the numbers at one's own level. Hence those people who want to enhance their status level will share the desire to keep newcomers out. One means of discouraging those who try to move upward is to call them pushy, climbers, ambitious, name-droppers, and other nasty names. Since status rubs off on associates, to defend the reputation and status of others in one's own group also indirectly defends oneself.

Despite exceptions in persons who consider status seeking vicious or silly, class behavior to many is real and for keeps. Who gets invited to what parties, wears which clothes, stays in which hotels, or marries whose daughter, are matters that command detailed attention among those conscious of status. Nor do such matters concern only the rich. At all levels in virtually all nations and societies status revolves around such questions as who owns more cattle, more acres, or a bigger hut; who has more beads or healthier children; who lives on which side of the tracks or on which floor of the apartment house; who earns a dollar more an hour or supervises more people; who gets a new car every year; and so on ad nauseam.

Whenever people consciously or unconsciously make it more difficult for those below to rise to their own level they are performing a sponsor-like function that converts social stratification from informal to semiformal organization. Sometimes, as when the old-line wealthy of a small town are challenged by "upstart newcomers," the former coordinate their actions against the challengers so explicitly as to make stratification virtually a formal organization.

Elites. The term *elite* is widely used in sociology and political science. As we use it here, the term can mean the same as "upper class." The elite thus include those at the top of their fields, be they musicians, authors, bankers, baseball players, comedians, philosophers, industrialists, generals, politicians, or cardinals. One way to identify the elite is to ask people, "What three or four persons do you consider tops in your field?"

If and when such a group exists, the "ruling elite," or "power structure," are those among the elite who make the important decisions in a society—the dominant coalition who have more power than any competing coalition. To illustrate, in a modest-sized town this coalition might consist of the leading banker, the leading industrialist, the newspaper publisher, and the largest landowner. By a consistent hostile stance toward persons who need money, jobs, publicity, or land, they can among them make life difficult indeed for anyone who challenges any one of them. Such a coalition may be very "tight" even if each member merely acts on his own perception of his own interest; although conscious coordination may occur, the elite group can continue intact without it. In addition, some carefully undenied rumors that these "big shots" have vast holdings elsewhere, and some strategically exaggerated reports of how they "clobbered" some earlier competitors, may add an awe that makes them seem more unchallengeable than they really are.

The power of such a coalition may nevertheless erode (1) if its resource base disappears (the industrialist loses out to distant competition or the landowner's land wears out); (2) if the interests of its members cease to coincide (the industrialist want to keep out new industry that will bid up wages, but the landowner wants it in to bid up land); or (3) if an independent new power arises (a small local farmer strikes oil or a national corporation establishes a local branch).

The principle is the same for larger units, including nations. But as the cast of characters grows, coalitions are harder to trace and less likely to be tight or stable. Even as the small-town landowner may desert the old local coalition to side with a large new outside-controlled industry, so may a power center in a large nation switch its allegiances. And whereas in the small local coalition of three or four it is easy for each to know what the others are doing, in a larger city those with substantial power may number from 30 or 40 to hundreds. These larger numbers vastly increase the communicational and subcoalitional problems, not to mention the diversity of interest to be compromised. Even in the moderate-sized city of New Haven, Polsby (1963) found numerous centers of power that differed and shifted from one kind of question to another.

For the United States as a whole, for most localities within it, and for advanced industrial nations, no simple statement seems possible about who forms coalitions with whom or for what purposes (Rose 1967), and farm, labor, business, and political blocs switch coalitions from time to time. It is easy for the extremist of left or right to assert that the country is in the iron grip of the military-industrial complex or of the communists—and either *may* be right. But hard evidence, as contrasted to a plausible-sounding assertion, is not easy to find.

On the other hand the power structure of a nonindustrialized nation may consist of a dominant coalition as tight and stable as that of the small town. Acting in conjunction with some local power sources, the United Fruit Corporation in Central America, the oil companies in the Middle East and Venezuela, the rubber interests in Indonesia, and copper and aluminum firms in central Africa have at one time or another held strong coalitional positions.

Caste. Whereas class stratification is typically informal organization with occasional semiformal adjuncts, caste is a highly formal set of class distinctions. As long found in India it was supported by the formal authority of government and by semiformal authority so massive and pervasive as to be almost inescapable. Now outlawed for more than 20 years, it nevertheless continues widely under semiformal authority in many rural areas. The mobility and relative anonymity of the city make it harder to enforce the caste patterns there.

In addition to its ethnic aspects (see below) racial separation in the United States long had many traits of a caste system, legally enforced in the South. For example, "untouchability" between a white female and a black male was enforced with a rigor resembling that separating castes in India. Precisely because that relationship was (is) viewed with horror by many whites, dating and marriage that violate the taboo dramatically communicate a couple's rejection of the caste concept. Paralleling some caste behavior in India, in the American South the white could treat the black with friendliness and affection if the circumstances did not suggest equality. The black could come into the white's house as a servant but not as a guest, while the black servant could be a guest at the white's wedding only if he wore the servant's uniform. Also as in India, to outlaw castelike behaviors does not necessarily stop them.

GROUPINGS BY CULTURE

In addition to grouping by class differences, people also tend to group by cultural traits. One such grouping is ethnic, involving people of the same race or nationality. New York City, the great melting pot, has sections of Irish, Jews, Italian, Poles, blacks, Chinese, Puerto Ricans, Armenians, and so on. Other large cities differ only by having fewer groups with fewer members. Some ethnic clusterings are rural, among them being the Pennsylvania Dutch (in Ohio and Indiana as well as Pennsylvania), the Scandinavians in Minnesota, the Italians and the Japanese in California, and the Mexicans in the Southwest. Among many others, a second kind of cultural grouping involves political and social point of view, in which conservatives associate mostly with conservatives, liberals with liberals, and hippies with hippies. Why do people associate so regularly with others "of their own kind"?

Language problems are one obvious reason. An immigrant unfamiliar with the language of his new country is so helpless that the urge to live among others of the same language is compelling. Hence new immi-

Courtesy of Washington Star Syndicate, Inc., by Brickman, December 12, 1970.

grants settle mainly in communities with prior immigrants who speak the same language. Movements out of the ethnic community come largely from the second generation, who learn the new language as children, along with those first-generation immigrants who have come to feel comfortable with it.

The whole of a culture is potentially part of its speech, and to really "talk American" nowadays one must know about Woodstock, the Kennedy assassinations, Kent State, Vietnam, the Bay of Pigs, and Watergate. Humor also makes little sense to those familiar with the language alone. In short, to know the language without the culture is enough to travel with. But only among others who share his culture can one really express his thoughts and feelings. Furthermore, one's credibility declines if he tells the conservative Catholic that he strongly approves abortion on demand, or the liberal student that the National Guard should have shot another dozen students at Kent State.

As to transactions, when one is selling among others of his own culture he knows what they typically like and are willing to pay; among strangers he may lose by asking too much or too little. Group factors are also strong. Whereas the hippie may be accepted among hippies, among "straights" he may be treated as inferior and suspect. All of this is a long story, which we cannot even introduce properly. Its point is simply that one's life is generally pleasanter and less complicated among others who share his ethnic and cultural patterns.

The small tribal society

Since we have used the formal model as the basis for understanding semiformal organization, it is interesting to examine relatively simple societies which have not themselves developed very complex formal organizations. In tribal societies, such as those of the Hopi Indians, the Eskimos, and tribal villages of Africa, Latin America, and the South Seas, patterns of formal, semiformal, and informal organization merge more or less indistinguishably. In the tribal village everyone knows everyone else, and may at some time deal directly with everyone. There is thus no strictly informal organizations, since there is no "larger society" beyond the circle of one's own relationships.

By the same token, to offend everyone you know is to offend the whole society. You cannot then drop existing contacts and start over with a new set, and social pressures are powerful because they are inescapable. They can, in fact, be so effective that some tribal societies have no formal government or enforcement procedures, and are sometimes at a loss about how to handle a really recalcitrant individual. Furthermore, since everyone can estimate at least roughly the effects of his own behavior on the whole society and its feedback effects on himself, everyone has a potentially strong sponsor interest in the whole society. Under our present definitions the tribal village is normally a cooperative, in which everyone is simultaneously sponsor, staff, and recipient.

We have noted that under stable circumstances an organization may operate indefinitely without top management if every member merely continues to perform his subsystem role and if new recruits are routinely inducted into existing roles. In the absence of war, natural catastrophe, or large contact with other cultures this is the typical situation in many tribal societies. The rudimentary character of their formal government indicates that much of the time there is little for the top executives to do. Because unusual circumstances do occur occasionally most such societies nevertheless have some formal mechanism for dealing with them, as by the chief, a council of elders, or a meeting of the whole community.

19

GOVERNMENT: IN GENERAL, FOR PROFIT, FOR IDEOLOGY

INTRODUCTION

What comes to mind when one hears the term *government?* The capitol building in Washington or Cheyenne? The taxes on gasoline and beer? The FBI catching criminals or the police "busting" hippies? The will of the people, the might of Hitler, red tape, social security, and questions of constitutionality? Government, of course, is all these things and many more.

What kinds of things or situations are governments? The national governments of the United States and Kenya certainly qualify. But is the United Nations a government? The International Red Cross? A "student government" or a university senate? A king is a head of government. But is the chief of an Indian tribe with a thousand members? Does it make any difference whether he can enforce his decisions, or simply state them and hope that other members of the tribe will carry them out? If we want to consider that tribal chief as a head of government, then what about the chief of a tribe of only fifty? The head of an extended family of twenty?

The world displays marked differences in forms of governmental and social organization, and in the quality of life under them. Barring a return to extremely simple, nonindustrial life, at or near caveman level, however, certain fundamentals of organization and power nevertheless suggest that the important question is not *whether* there will be a government, but what it will be like. Nothing in the analysis that follows tells what kind of government will be established under what circumstances,

277

or whether its sponsors will consist of 1, 50, or 100 percent of the people. It merely describes some general problems of government.

In this area of social science, as in many others, the customary language, with loose and varied meanings, has grown with the human race, and only recently (as history goes) have social scientists attempted to refine our understandings by giving precise definitions to things. We will state our definition of *government* as the formal organization of a whole society, and then leave it temporarily to look at some other preliminary questions.

POSSIBLE ORIGINS OF GOVERNMENT

Unlike artifacts, such as Stone Age hatchets or bowls, sociofacts, such as governments, leave no remains for archaeologists to dig up. So whereas we have pretty clear ideas of the tools, crocks, and dwellings used by early man, we have no records of governments until man started to leave written records, at least on stone. There are reasons to believe that governments in the sense we now know them first arose in the fertile valleys of the Middle East as collective attempts to develop irrigation.

Because examples resembling these efforts still spring up around us, we can speculate that governments had either or both of two main orgins. One has its primitive prototype among the lower animals, where it is common for the dominant male to monopolize some batch of females. He gets what he wants by denying others what *they* want, his dominance being based on physical strength. Urban gangs sometimes behave similarly, the "boss" being the member who can beat up or otherwise outfight any other member, or who can gather around him a coalition that can beat any other coalition. The underground government or kangaroo court of some jails, orphan homes, and mental hospitals sometimes follows similar principles. As noted earlier, the leader may be selected by some proxy contest—perhaps as when the one who can run fastest, drink the most beer, or outwit the cops most often. On a larger scale, the ruler in a given area may simply be the one who has come to the top by brains, brawn, favors, friends, or leadershp. If he uses his position for his own benefit, as by commanding taxes, tribute, favors, gifts, services, and deference, this type of government may be considered a profit organization. Since people will presumably not give up valuable things voluntarily, such a ruler will have to back up his demands with force.

The obvious alternative is for people to band together to *prevent* such profiteering, in a coalition of the weak against the strong. More particularly if people dislike transactions that use violence they might designate a committee to act as a coalition to prevent anyone else from using violence. Such a coalition would constitute a police force, and could be a simple government whose overall result is an orderly society. If the same persons are collectively both sponsors and recipients of such order, this relationship is a cooperative.

People could similarly act cooperatively to produce other joint results, such as defending themselves against a common enemy or constructing an irrigation project.

Service or pressure organizations seem unlikely as types of government. As to the former, if the main motive of a group is to provide gifts to others, they will not need to organize a government to do it. And as to the latter, for a government based on one fraction of the population there is no point in exerting pressure against the remaining fraction except to extract benefits from them—which would qualify the government as a profit organization. In short, service or pressure organizations make sense as parts or subsystems of a society, but not as forms of organization for the whole society. Whether governments first started as profit organizations, as cooperative organizations, as some of each, or by some quite different method, we do not know.

THE ORGANIZATIONAL NATURE OF GOVERNMENT

We have defined government as the formal organization of a whole society. All but very small and simple governments are necessarily subdivided and sub-subdivided, mostly on either a geographic or a functional basis. In the United States geographic subdivisions take such forms as states, counties, townships, boroughs, and cities. Functional subdivisions take such forms as a Department of Defense, a Bureau of Indian Affairs, a public utilities commission, or a police department. Geographic subdivisions are also generally considered governments in their own right, but we will here view them solely as subdivisions—which they are, since their rights and powers are subject to the national constitution and laws. Having noted these important subdivisions, we will nevertheless deal with the basics of government in connection with the national level alone.

To say that a government is the formal organization of a *whole society* involves possible circularity, since there is no convenient way of defining a whole society except as that unit subject to a single sovereign government. We will not get totally out of this impasse, though our later definition of "sovereignty" will help. For present purposes a "whole society" is a nation, which is bounded by its geographical borders—for reasons discussed in Kuhn (1963: 543).

To define government as a formal organization means that we already know quite a lot about it—if we paid attention to Chapters 15 and 16. We have already identified the basic types of formal organizations, and have seen that cooperative and profit organizations seem feasible as types of governments. We know about the distinctions among sponsors, staff, recipients, and factor suppliers, which we also need in connection with governments. We have observed the communicational and transactional relations among parts, particularly the distinction between the major bargain of affiliation and subsidiary bargains over details, while noting the power and bargaining power effects between them. Importantly, we have observed the nature of authority and the related legitimacy, and the ways in which communication, transaction, and dominant coalition are the possible decision techniques. For reasons elaborated below, questions of legitimacy and dominant coalition are more significant in government than elsewhere. Questions of structure, role, responsibility, centralization, and other matters that can arise in connection with *any* organization also arise in governments.

We have indicated that "whole society" in the definition of government refers to everything within the geographic boundaries of a nation. "Whole" also means that the government is a supersystem relative to any individuals or to other social systems in the nation. An informal economy, corporations, clubs, churches, private schools, and the various semiformal social systems are all subsystems within the whole society. The government is not itself the whole society, which includes all the subsystems just mentioned, and many more. Most relationships among the subsystems are informal or semiformal. Government is the only *formal* organization that encompasses and has authority over all the subsystems, as amplified below in connection with the potential all-purpose nature of government.

On public goods

In Chapter 11 we introduced the term *shared value,* as something that is the same for all members of some group, whether any particular member wants it or not. At the level of government we refer to such shared values as "public goods." They contrast with private goods, such as jelly or automobiles, which every individual may acquire as much or as little of as he wishes to and can afford. But one person cannot have a large army for his nation while his neighbor has a small one, or live in an economy of stable prices while his neighbor lives under inflation.

The important characteristic of public goods (or bads, such as pollution) is that there can be only a single decision about them, which is binding on everybody whether he is affected beneficially, adversely, or not at all.

If the government produces a public good that costs money, even the citizen who bitterly opposes it helps pay for it. The distinction between private and public goods is closely related to the parallel distinction between the market (economic) and the coalitional (political) processes by which a society makes decisions about them, as we shall see.[1]

There are many kinds of mixed and intermediate cases of public and private goods. For example, if no one can fish in a particular lake unless he pays a fee, access to fishing there is a private good, whether the lake is owned by a private developer or a government. It is "private," in that anyone who wants the use of it pays and receives it, and anyone who does not want it does not pay and does without—as with jelly or movies. Although there are many other interesting questions about public and private goods, our interest in this chapter is centered on the decisional process mentioned above: whether the decision about a particular good is made by the market process or the coalitional process.

---

[1] Economists and political scientists disagree as to the precise nature and boundaries of their respective disciplines. The present distinction reflects the particular framework of this volume, though not necessarily the views of economists and political scientists.

The special characteristics of government

Knowledge of organizations in general is only part of the story, and this chapter will focus on special or unique traits in which government differs from other organizations.

Mutually involuntary membership. In the major bargain in formal organization we noted that an individual will join if he perceives his benefits of belonging to equal or exceed his costs. The organization similarly accepts him if *its* benefits from having him as a member equal or exceed *its* costs. If either side finds continued membership disadvantageous he (it) can terminate the relationship by resignation or suspension. The terms of membership may limit the termination—as by requiring 30 days' notice, a formal hearing, or settlement of unfulfilled obligations. There may also be practical constraints to resigning or expelling—all of which are nevertheless some kind of costs and benefits. Such organizations are *voluntary* because, subject to reservations like those just cited, both the making and the continuance of the relationship are based on the *mutual consent of both parties.* Importantly, a person can totally avoid the authority of a voluntary organization by staying or getting out. The ultimate "punishment" that either side can inflict on the other is to terminate the relationship.

By contrast, a person living under a government is subject to its laws and regulations whether he consents to them or not. Now a foreigner traveling or residing in a nation voluntarily accepts its jurisdiction when he enters. And since the government could presumably have prevented his entry if it cared to, it can also be said to have accepted him voluntarily. Despite possible other complications we will consider foreign travel and residence as examples of a voluntary organizational relationship. Naturalization of an immigrant is also mutually voluntary, again despite possible complications.

Many citizens may leave a nation if they find it sufficiently unsatisfactory, and if another nation will accept them. Large-scale migrations sometimes occur, the massive immigration into the United States till about 1920 being a notable example. However, a central fact of government is that for most people and most governments most of the time, a people are stuck with their own government and it is stuck with them. With minor exceptions, a person born into a nation is automatically a citizen. Certainly he is subject to its laws, its courts, its police, and its taxes, and he has been given no choice as to whether he will accept that government. The government, too, has had no choice as to whether it will accept him as a citizen. This mutually involuntary membership relation between individual and organization is the first special characteristic of government.

Legitimate use of force. In general a government is the only agency within a nation which may legally and legitimately use force to coerce acceptance of its authority. Such coercive power is delegated to special subgroups, such as the police and the national guard, and to other law enforcement bodies, such as the courts, the Secret Service, the customs service, the narcotics squad, and jailkeepers. Parents, teachers, and others responsible for the young may be allowed limited use of force, as may some private guards, and force may generally be used in self-defense. Despite these exceptions, we càn best understand the main problem if we focus on a model of government in which it alone may legitimately use force to implement its authority.

This trait is related to the first. In voluntary organizations if social pressures and lesser penalties do not work the ultimate sanction is separation: resignation or expulsion. Since government cannot expel the citizen who insubordinately rejects its instructions, if all other methods fail it has no further recourse but the more compelling sanction of force. Such force is particularly imperative to stop the citizen who himself uses force against others.

Sovereignty. *Sovereignty* is defined here as the authority position of an organization (or possibly of an individual such as a king) which is not a member of any higher-level organization whose authority over *it* includes the legitimate use of force against it or its members. A sovereign government can join a higher-level organization and agree to accept its authority. The United States, for example, belongs to such organizations as the Universal Postal Union, the World Bank, and subdivisions of the United Nations. However, such membership is like that in voluntary organizations, not like the citizens' relation to their government, since the sovereign government can withdraw from such organizations if it perceives the costs of membership to exceed its benefits. One consequence of sovereignty is that a citizen or other party has no agency above his government to which he can appeal its decisions; the top level of a sovereign government ends the line of enforceable appeals.

A functional subdivision of a government, such as the Federal Trade Commission or the Department of Agriculture, is not sovereign, since it is subject to the coercive authority of the president, the Congress, or the courts. Neither is a geographic subdivision, such as a state, county, or city. The last time that relationship was openly challenged in the United States it was confirmed by a massive coercive act, the Civil War. If it makes some people feel good to refer to their subdivision as a "sovereign state," we need not stop their fun. But saying does not make it so.

Potential all-purpose function. Every real government is limited in what it can do for or to its citizens. Certain things are not possible, at least under existing technology or costs. The government of an under-developed nation cannot suddenly provide high-paid jobs for all its citizens in mass production industry, since there is no such industry and no feasible means of creating it. Nor, if it is small and weak, can the government provide a military victory over a large and powerful enemy in the enemy's home territory. A government may be unable to do other things because it cannot prevent all violations of the law. For example, although the Russian government is not wholly unwilling to use harsh methods, it has not been able to hold down the production and consumption of vodka. Although they have been limited, prostitution and gambling have almost never been successfully abolished by any government, and no large society has ever prevented all murders or robberies.

Despite these practical limitations all the things listed above certainly fall within the *province* of government, or of what people might agree among themselves to do or to avoid. What, then, if anything, is no business of government? Of any government, anywhere, at any time in history?

For our model we will think of a government with potentially unlimited scope. By this we mean that there is nothing in the realm of human affairs to which a government might not in some way respond. Let it be clear that we are *not* speaking of *our* government *now,* and any reader could make a long list of things he would not want our government to do. We are speaking instead of the general notion of government, as it has ever behaved or ever will—all feudal governments, dictatorial governments, primitive governments, oriental and occidental governments, ancient and modern governments, church-dominated and atheist governments, not to mention Orwellian ones. Among all actual or possible types it is hard to imagine any matter that some government might not see fit to act upon, that no government ever has acted upon, or that people might not wish to do something about. However, cooperative governments will presumably be the most limited in their scope and powers.

To illustrate further, we might agree that we do not want a government to invade privacy by collecting embarrassing information about people and then publicizing it if they criticize the president or the police. It does not follow, however, that the government should never do anything *about* privacy. In fact, to refrain from invasions of privacy is an action or policy *about* privacy. In addition, we might ask government to see that other agencies, such as credit bureaus or firms that prepare income taxes, do not sell personal information. More broadly, individuals or private organizations can harm one another in numerous ways. Whenever government officials do *not* act in such cases, the effect is to support or allow that private harm.

The point is that inactions in a government can be quite as important as actions in determining the structure, behavior, and livability of a society. Deliberately to refrain from acting on an issue is a policy on that issue, and a policy of inaction produces a different society than a policy of action. Since all a government's actions plus all its inactions encompass all possible actions, we will conclude that the sum of a government's active and inactive postures covers potentially all areas. When we add that there are few things that no real government anywhere has ever tried to do or deal with, our model of government as potentially unlimited in scope and purpose is basically sensible.[2]

CONSEQUENCES OF GOVERNMENT'S SPECIAL CHARACTERISTICS

Consequences to the individual

Although many people can leave a country they do not like, it is rarely feasible for more than a minor fraction to do so, and dictatorial governments may not let their people out. Hence, although there are exceptions,

---

[2] This list of special characteristics of government is adapted from similar lists found in Kuhn (1963) and Easton (1965).

the general problem of citizens' relations with government is essentially the same as if they cannot leave. If the individual cannot avoid the jurisdiction of a government when he feels its costs to him exceeds its benefits, and if the scope of government is potentially limitless, he cannot escape its effect. (The family partially shares these special traits.) Whereas the citizen who is not a member of the American Legion or the Penn Central Railroad can ignore its rules regarding members, if he thus ignores the rules of government he is subject to fine or imprisonment.

To clarify, let us note that no formal organization except government can impose these forceful penalties. Some can fine members, but there are two important differences between a fine levied by (say) a club and a fine levied by government. First, every member voluntarily accepted the rule about fines, either when he joined the club or when he failed to withdraw after the rule was adopted. By contrast a citizen may never have voluntarily accepted the rule that he must pay a fine if he drives too fast. Second, if the member chooses not to pay the fine, the voluntary formal organization can throw him out. But it cannot arrest him or seize his property to force him to pay. It is, of course, true that if a member has made certain commitments to the organization, it may sue him and collect. But it is then the government acting through the courts, not the voluntary organization, that applies the coercion. The social pressures that enforce cultural norms can also be pervasive. But like voluntary organizations, they too cannot fine or imprison the person who does not conform.

Given their inability to escape government, sensible citizens will find it imperative to have rules that limit the government's power. Among many other things, they will want assurance that they can be punished by government only if they have violated a valid law, and not merely because they have displeased some official—in a government of laws, not of men. They will want assurance that their property can be taken only for a valid public purpose, such as a park or a highway, and with fair compensation—not at the whim of a mayor or policeman for his personal use. Perhaps above all else they will want to make sure that the power of government is used only to enforce valid laws and not to keep particular individuals in power. In short, if the citizen cannot escape the power of government he will want assurance that its power is restricted by certain clear rules. The citizen will also presumably want a voice in determining what laws are passed and how they are enforced.

The rules about governmental powers and decision processes are generally known as a constitution, which may be written in a single document, spelled out in practice, or developed by some combination of these two methods. For the moment we will identify a *constitution* as the major bargain between a government and its sponsors. The function and content of constitutions will be discussed in more detail later.

Consequences to the government

A government also faces problems arising from its special characteristics. Persons in policymaking positions, such as legislators, may be forced to take a stand on virtually any issue at all. If you ask your congressman to introduce a bill allowing only the Irish to wear green on Saint Patrick's Day, he may ignore your letter. Ignoring it is an implicit position: "Your proposal has so little merit that I won't dignify it with a reply." Had he thought your proposal worthwhile he would presumably have done something about it.

The courts face a similar situation. Instead of asking your legislator to introduce a bill, you might file suit asking a court to enjoin your non-Irish neighbors from wearing green on the hallowed day. The judge would presumably dismiss your suit. But dismissal is a position. Similarly, if you ask the police to make your neighbor silence his dog or stop painting his house purple, by acting or not acting (or possibly by merely promising to act) the police unavoidably take a stand.

More broadly, a government may be forced to take cognizance of all demands made upon it. And whereas the voluntary organization can say, "If you don't like it here, go back where you came from," the government is stuck because its citizens *are* where they came from.

This relationship leads to the question of *revolt,* which is a sustained and repeated rejection of authority, particularly when undertaken collectively. There is basically no point to revolt within strictly voluntary organizations, for if someone is strongly displeased he can quit. But if a person can neither escape an organization nor change it enough to make it acceptable to him, revolt may seem to be his only remedy.

Except for the symbolic and publicity value of civil disobedience, there is no point to revolting against the government, however, unless one has enough counterforce to win. In a national showdown the outcome will normally depend on whether the army supports the government or the rebels, and on a local basis the alignment of the police may be decisive. Thus, if a government is to remain in stable control it must maintain a coalition of force so obviously dominant that no one will challenge it. In addition, perhaps the most promising way to avoid revolt is to govern so well that few citizens would want it.

If those in power suspect revolt, it might seem simplest to crush it early. But that approach has its own dangers. If such moves are overstrong, citizens heretofore sympathetic to the government might conclude that the government is as repressive as the rebels claim, and join them. As with the double edge of concession (Chapter 10), there is also a double edge of not conceding. The government can err by applying bads when goods would bring agreement, or by relying entirely on goods when only bads would work.

Because the citizen cannot escape government, the problem of revolt is sharpest there. However, the alternatives to being in a particular voluntary organization sometimes seem so bad that the member feels trapped. The logic of revolt is then much the same as with government. Workers for a company which is the only significant employer in an area—as with the remote mining or logging outfit or the large textile manufacturer in the small town—may face this kind of situation. An ingredient of the "student revolt" of the late 60s was that some students believed that a college education was both indispensable and abominably bad. The problem is sharper in the public schools, where students are compelled to attend. Children's membership in the family is similarly involuntary and may create similar problems. The conditions for revolt lie in the perceived unavailability of *either* significant improvement *or* alternatives, since either alone can relieve the pressure.

Some feel impelled to revolt for revolt's sake, and are likely to provide, or to seek to provide, its leadership. Unless the overt conditions lend credibility to their views, however, it is unlikely that they will command significant continued support, since most people prefer legitimate, orderly change.

Induction and indoctrination

We observed in Chapter 15 that some induction process normally accompanies a person's entrance into membership, to help fit him into his role, which includes acceptance of the organization's authority. Under the inescapable authority of government conflict will be least and the relation smoothest if citizens perceive acceptance of the government's authority to be to their advantage. This does not mean that every law or regulation need be to the citizen's advantage, any more than that every instruction an employee receives from his boss will be. It means rather that overall and on the average the citizen will find conformity to governmental authority advantageous.

Here, however, lies a difficulty of evaluation—a problem discussed in Chapter 15. The citizen may observe dozens or hundreds of voluntary organizations at first hand, possibly joining and leaving some of them several times. He can also talk to their members. He thus has a chance to evaluate whether particular organizations are worth belonging to. But the nature of sovereignty subjects him to only one sovereign government. If he lives in a large country he may have little opportunity to talk to citizens of other nations to find how well they like their governments, and thus to judge his own government.

Those who support a government will want to induct and indoctrinate its members so that they will accept its authority. The methods are varied, but the main ones are simple and reliable. For one, support of the government is labeled "patriotic" and opposition "unpatriotic." (We are speaking of the system, not the persons in power—though officials sometimes want citizens to believe that opposition to *them* is unpatriotic.) Through formal and semiformal organization citizens are given to understand that patriotism is good and unpatriotism bad. The attempt often succeeds so well that even rebels insist that they are "fundamentally patriotic."

A second induction device is the public schools. Paid for and operated through government processes, these are usually oriented strongly toward accepting those processes. A dilemma here is expressed by some social studies teachers, who feel that it is not their business to indoctrinate, but also feel that they should teach "good citizenship," which implies accepting the government's authority and working within the system.

The felt need for induction and indoctrination, or "political socialization," is not dependent on the philosophy or policies of any one government, but on the nature of organization in general and of government in particular. Even when rebels overthrow a government, as soon as they are in power they too induct and indoctrinate, and for the same reasons, in support of *their* government. In fact, *any* organization not suicidally inclined will use induction procedures to teach new members their roles. A central feature of those roles is to accept the authority and decision rules of the organization.

WHAT DO GOVERNMENTS DO? ORGANIZATIONAL AND COALITIONAL FUNCTIONS

The basic nature of organization is that it produces a joint effect which is more than the sum of its parts. Unlike informal organization, formal organization produces joint effects consciously and explicitly. Although it often produces unintended effects as well, we will focus on the intended effects of government.

The main function of coalition is to shift the location of power, by having some parties join together against others. Within the present framework it seems useful to classify all activities of government under the two headings, organizational and coalitional. The organizational function produces goods. The coalitional function allocates power, often but not always by taking sides in conflicts. We will indicate why these two functions encompass all government activities. Many real cases are mixed or ambiguous, and we will deal with them as best we can.

Producing goods: The organizational function

Whenever government joins the efforts of two or more persons to produce some good, whether a commodity or a service, it is performing the function of formal organization. The most basic service for any government is to provide for the public safety, as through national defense against external force and police protection against internal force. The provision of parks, highways, waterways, a system of justice, a monetary supply, an educational system, postal service, hospitals, streets, sewage and water systems, traffic controls, social security, sanitation and public health services, and garbage collection are all examples of goods produced by governments. A government can produce and sell strictly private goods, such as tractors and light bulbs. Since a later chapter is devoted to public (that is, governmental) production of private goods, an activity usually viewed as socialism in some form, we will confine attention here to the narrower governmental function: the public production of public goods. (A market system engages in the private production of private goods.)

Sometimes the same governmental activity may be considered either a public good or an allocation of power, depending on the level at which we view it. For example, a system of courts and justice is a public good if viewed at the level of the whole society, or the *macro* level. But as we will see in the next section, the courts allocate power as between in-dividuals, that is, at the *micro* level. Public schools are similarly a public good at the macro level, but a device to raise the power of individuals at the micro level. Although the production of goods is a highly important function of government, it is also easily understood, and does not require further explanation.

Allocating power: The coalitional function

Raising power. The second major function of government is the coali-tional one of allocating power. This is done in two main ways. One is to try to increase the power of citizens or their organizations. We have seen in Chapter 6 that intrasystem power is based on the ability to make transformations, taken in conjunction with certain environmental re-sources. The individual's ability to make transformations is largely de-termined by his skill and knowledge (effector and detector functions), and by his motivation (selector) to acquire and use them. Education in its broadest sense, including public schools, Job Corps training, adult education, and rehabilitation of the handicapped, is directed toward rais-ing the power of individuals. So are health care and the prevention or cure of drug addiction.

Government may also try to raise the transformational power of its citizens by increasing, or preventing the deterioration of, the resources available to them. Reclaiming or irrigating land, growing or protecting forests, stocking streams and lakes with fish, and maintaining the quan-tity or quality of water all help to raise the citizens' productive power. To the important degree that transportation assists the productive proc-ess, highways, airports, bridges, and waterways also help raise produc-tivity.

It is almost inconceivable that any of these activities or facilities could increase power equally and simultaneously for all segments of the popu-lation. Even though they may be directed toward helping some without necessarily hurting others, they nevertheless produce some reallocation of power, at least in the short run. Hence we classify them as part of the coalitional function of reallocating power. The longer-run reallocational consequences, however, are not so clear. In fact, we noted in Chapters 9 and 14 that in the transactional relation an increase in the power of A may actually raise the power of B. So even if B must initially pay some of the cost of A's improvement he may also benefit from it later.

Shifting power. By contrast, a second way in which government allo-cates power is by straightforwardly shifting it: that is, by increasing the power of one party and reducing that of another. The most obvious in-stance is a transfer of money (known in economics as a transfer pay-ment), as by collecting it in taxes from one segment of the population and giving it to another segment. Such action also falls under the head-ing of the service aspect of government, as in providing welfare pay-ments to poor mothers and subsidies to rich farmers. (Or should we say subsidies to poor mothers and welfare payments to rich farmers?) To illustrate mixed cases, although we have listed public education as a public good, it also contains substantial transfer elements, since school taxes are collected from essentially the whole population and are spent only on those who have children.

Another way for the government to shift power directly is to join a coalition with one party against another. The regulatory activity of government is of this sort. For example, when the police stop a purse snatcher they are joining a coalition with the victim against the thief. If the Environmental Protection Agency stops the discharge of wastes into air or water it is forming a coalition with the victims of pollution against the polluters. If the Federal Trade Commission prohibits false advertising it is joining a coalition with customers against certain sellers. When a court enforces a contract it is joining a coalition with the party who performed his half of the contract against the party who did not. When the courts convict and sentence a criminal they are joining a coalition with the victims and potential victims of crimes against the criminal. In regulating utility rates, the Public Utilities Commission is joining with the buyers against the sellers of electricity.

The above examples illustrate the nature of the coalitional function. But things do not always work as planned. Police sometimes join a coalition with the underworld to protect stealing or gambling. Judges sometimes enforce their prejudices rather than the law, and it is a commonplace that utilities commissions often protect the companies from the public rather than the reverse. Either way, however, the government joins a coalition with one side against the other. Especially under profit dictatorships (see below) government often helps the strong against the weak—the landowner against the peasant, the industrialist against the unorganized worker.

Since government has a monopoly of legal force, since it can use that force to enforce its regulations, and since force normally holds greater power than any positive goods, the government theoretically has the ability to make any coalition it joins a dominant one. If this result always occurred in fact, it would mean that every time the government took your side in a dispute you would win.

Life is not that simple. There are many reasons why the government's support may not help much and its opposition may not hurt. Enforcement requires people, money, and materials, and a government may make a regulation to please one group and then not enforce it to please another. Enforcement is often hampered for lack of facts. Who stole the TV? Who dumped oil into the bay? What are the actual costs of providing electricity? Sometimes the victim may find it easier not to bring charges or appear in court. Despite such reservations regulations often do materially shift power.

This allocation of power is an area in which inactions by government are important. If the victim asks protection against the thief, the user of water asks help against the polluter, and the defrauded customer asks legal redress, and if the government does nothing, its inactions have a great impact on the society. For government not to act on some problem is in effect to assign it to informal and semiformal processes, and to legitimize them.

To our question, "What do governments do?" the summary answer is that governments, be they democratic or dictatorial, produce goods and allocate power.

WHO'S IN CHARGE HERE? (or, take me to your leader)

Governments have many names. Democracy, dictatorship, monarchy, oligarchy, plutocracy, authoritarianism, totalitarianism, and theocracy are some of the best known. All have certain things in common, and all show some differences. The most obvious thing all governments have in common—if we are speaking of a reasonably large and complex society—is a substantial batch of people who run them. These people are often called the *bureaucrats* and are here called the *staff.* They are the people who make governmental decisions and carry them out. To illustrate, the "staff" of our federal government includes all elected officers (president, vice president, and the members of Congress), all appointed executive level policymakers and administrators (Cabinet members, presidential staff, heads of government agencies, etc.), and all hired employees in all branches and departments. As with top executives of *any* formal organization, many elected officials and higher-level appointed ones are simultaneously sponsor representatives and staff.

Although in a dictatorship one person may make all final decisions he does not run the government single-handed. Just below him he requires from a handful to several scores of people to provide him information, including summaries of possible courses of action and the probable consequences of each. He may receive their advice orally or in writing, may see them singly or in groups, and may or may not argue with or question them. Even if one person "makes" all the important decisions, however, he is not necessarily "in charge." Since his time and attention are limited, he is partly at the mercy of those who advise and inform him—a group sometimes known as the "palace guard." Although the sensible ruler or chief executive will acquire information his advisers did not intend to give him, he still faces the possibility that if, by accident or design, they do not inform him of certain things, he is trapped. In particular, the executive who wants his information condensed to two-page memos will find that many real decisions are being made by the writers of the memos.

Information processing limitations

Although the president or prime minister of a democracy can eventually be replaced, so long as he is formally authorized to make certain decisions his position is in some respects not very different from the dictator's. The brain needs time to digest information, and the executive's time is limited. All decisions are only partly informed, which means that they are partly uninformed. These same limitations on time require the top executive to delegate many decisions, often relatively important ones, to subordinates. We will illustrate one facet of the problem.

We noted in Chapter 14 that one has more power in dealing with those of greater power than with those of lesser power. Since the top person in government probably holds the highest personal power in most nations, the number of persons who want appointments with him is almost endless. Unless their requests are screened at some lower level, the top executive would spend so much time deciding whom to see that he would have no time actually to see anyone. But the subordinate who says no to most requests for appointments also decides what kinds of information and pressure get through to the boss. To some it seemed that a part of President Nixon's difficulties arose from delegating this function so completely to subordinates that he almost became their prisoner.

Communicational limitations, and nets

In short, top decisions are made by the collective effort of some group that is large enough to process information crucial to those decisions. Communicational constraints, however, limit the size of this group. Because matters are interrelated, even if the president's subordinates specialize on different problems, they must communicate with one another and/or with the president.

But even as potential visitors must be limited, so must the number of communications among the president's advisers. The size of the "intimate group" at the top level is thus limited to the number who can engage in significant mutual communication, while also leaving themselves time to communicate with persons outside the group. If the president chooses to talk to them separately and to minimize their contacts with one another, this limit lies in the time and energy he has to see them.

Figure 19–1

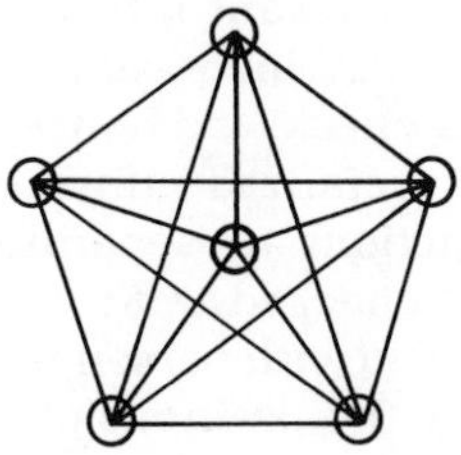

There now exists a substantial literature about communication nets. The present discussion barely opens the topic, and will mention only two polar cases. If we assume for simplicity five advisers to the president, who is at the center, the condition in which everybody talks to everybody else is the all-channel network, with 15 connections (Figure 19–1). The condition in which every adviser talks only to the president is known as the wheel, with only 5 connections (Figure 19–2). In a simple sense the wheel is the most efficient net, if we assume that the person at the hub

Figure 19-2

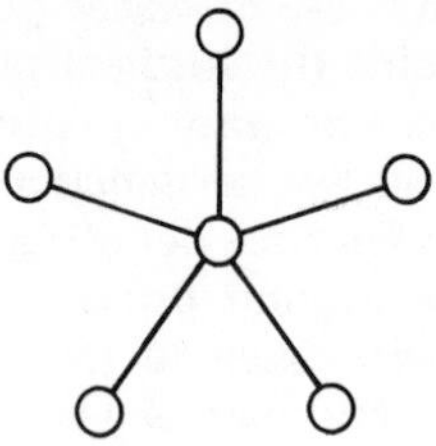

has unlimited, essentially instantaneous, and highly accurate information processing capacity—or at least enough capacity to process all the information required throughout the net. The unrealism of that assumption for top-level executive jobs is the main reason for using multiple channels. President Nixon's initial defense in the Watergate and related affairs, translated into this language, was that his subordinates used a more or less all-channel network, but left him out of it.

To restate the problem, decisions on different subjects are interrelated. For example, since farmers make loans, the person making decisions about credit must consider their effects on problems in agriculture, which are tied to foreign trade, which involves international politics, and so on. Hence a subordinate dealing with one kind of problem cannot make decisions in isolation; his proposed actions must be cross-checked with those who make decisions on other subjects. But cross-checking takes time, and the amount of time required for any given cross-check depends on how fast decision makers can communicate. In practical terms, this means the speed with which they can write, talk, show, think, read, listen, or watch. To increase the total number of persons involved will increase the amount of relevant information that can be acquired and understood. But it will also increase the number of other persons with whom each must cross-check, and hence reduce the amount of time each has left for his own specialized information.

When governmental functions are separated, as in the United States, each decision must be cross-checked and coordinated not only with decisions on other matters, but also with person in other divisions. A successful president needs to know the positions of the majority and minority leaders in both houses of Congress, of important committee chairmen, of potential rivals in the next election, of governors, of the chairman of his political party, and possibly of Supreme Court justices—and this is only the beginning of the list. The length of the list merely emphasizes the largeness of the demands on communication time compared with the limited supply of it.

Somewhere between the increased number of subordinates that increases the amount of necessary information and the decreased number that increases the completeness of cross-checking) there presumably lies some optimum. There is no magic formula for finding this number, which depends in part on both the persons and the decisions.

Summary on information processing and communications

All in all, perhaps the single most important determinant of the decision making structure of government (or any large organization) is the information processing and communicational capacity of the persons who run it, taken in conjunction with the types and sources of information needed. The human can handle fantastic quantities of information in uncoded form (sound waves, light waves, odors, etc.), the quantities often ranging into billions of bits of information per second. In coded form, however, he can process only about 20 to 30 bits per second, and nearly all information significant for decisions comes in coded form. Computers of course, vastly extend the amount of data that can be analyzed and help to make decision makers better informed. But as noted in Chapter 8, the most important aspects of decisions often lie outside the realm of neat rules, and can hardly be handled even by computers— for example, hunches about how others will respond to a certain decision. In any event, answers given by computers are limited by the assumptions made by their programmers. Often only the top decision makers are experienced enough to say what those assumptions should be, and if they know the right assumptions the answer is often clear without the computer! Hence no matter how much information and understanding are available among the people in a nation, factors of this sort seriously limit the amount that can be brought to bear on top-level decisions.

Planning, programming, and budgeting systems (PPBS)

The above somewhat dismal conclusion would certainly be challenged by students and advocates of systematic decision techniques. PPBS is the designation for a widely discussed approach to systematic decision making in government. It gathers detailed information about the existing state of affairs and scans the available alternative responses. It evaluates the costs and benefits—human and social as well as monetary—of each response, using explicit criteria.

In its most complete form it includes estimates of upper and lower limits on both costs and benefits, and makes multiple estimates as they would appear under different sets of value judgments. With this information it is possible to identify an optimal choice, or at least to narrow the range to two or three potentially best ones. PPBS also includes steps for implementing a decision, in terms of both actions and finances. Fully implemented PPBS not only goes about a particular decision systematically, it also analyzes each activity of a department in combination with all of its other activities, in light of their separate and total effects. By 1965, PPBS approaches had been adopted in about twenty departments or divisions of the federal government. It was perhaps psychologically unfortunate that the method was first adopted by the Department of Defense and declined in impact when Secretary MacNamara left, since its potential value may well be greater elsewhere.

As far as they go, PPBS and other systematic decision procedures are all to the good, and one may hope they will eventually improve the quality of society's decisions. Any systematic decision process is valid, however, only within the values and assumptions on which it is based, and establishing those values and assumptions is often more important than the calculations made within them. Yet systematic decision processes provide discouragingly little advice about how to establish those assumptions. Furthermore, persons in important posts may find that a "sound" decision in a particular area does not serve their purposes. For example, instead of being used as a basis for policy, in recent years carefully prepared reports by presidential commissions on drug abuse, student unrest, racial tensions, pornography, population, and violence on television have been ignored, bypassed, or severely castigated at top governmental levels, particularly by Presidents Johnson and Nixon. That is, the criteria applied in the "systematic" decision process by the commissions have not been the same as the values applied by the president. Furthermore, the criteria relevant to a decision at one level of the government hierarchy may not be at all relevant at a different level, even if the values of the persons at the different levels are otherwise similar. In any case, what is to be done if a highly "rational" decision recommended by PPBS is thoroughly disliked by the president, Congress, or most of the voters?

To tie this discussion to that of the several preceding pages, the informational and communicational limitations on decision making are basically the same at any level of the organization. They are both more obvious and more crucial at the top.

* * *

The answer to the question, "Who's in charge here?" is thus "A network of top decision makers" (see Deutsch 1963). Whether this group is large or small, sharply or loosely defined, open or closed to changes in membership, and so on will depend in part on the persons involved. The characteristics of the network will undoubtedly be influenced by the overall type of government, and we generally assume that the head of a democracy will necessarily make contact with persons in many important posts. Yet if he is so inclined a dictator might consult many advisers, while the head of a democratic nation may consult only a few.

What about transactions?

What has happened to transactions in this emphasis on communication and information? The answer is that transactions have a great deal to do with the *content* of the communications and decisions. At the moment we are not dealing with content, but only with the number of persons who can sensibly make top-level decisions, which number seems to be determined mainly by informational criteria. A problem which looks somewhat similar, and which *is* transactional, concerns the size of the dominant coalition, which we will discuss shortly.

THE PROFIT GOVERNMENT: WHICH SERVES ITS OWN ENDS

In a profit organization costs are paid by the recipients and benefits are received by the sponsors. Recipients pay the costs through a selfish transaction in which they give the organization some value in return for receiving its outputs. Business firms are obvious examples, in trying to sell something for more than it cost.

Business firms are studied by economists, and governments by political scientists. Since specialists tend to assume that nothing in other fields can be of much use to them, they typically talk and read little about one another's fields. It is thus not surprising that they fail to notice similarities—as that both political scientists and economists study some aspects of organizations. Or that both firms and governments sometimes give people a good bargain and sometimes "exploit" them, the latter by collecting much more for services than they cost and pocketing the difference. Although conventional social science does not notice it, there are similarities between the model of the profit firm and certain governments.

We have noted that a government could be started by a group who use force or other bads to extract goods from the rest of the populace. The outputs of the organization are these bads, the general citizenry are the recipients of them, and the sponsors are those who give top-level sponsor instructions to the staff and get the loot. A profit dictatorship uses the government's monopoly of force for the benefit of those who run the government, although it may also provide many normal governmental services, "selling" them to the public at a price well in excess of their cost. Some governmental services are private goods that can be "sold" directly, as with fees, permits, or licenses. The government might also sell material goods, such as public lands, alcoholic beverages, and salt.

Some state and local governments have been run as rather straight profit organizations through American history. In such cases roads or public buildings have been constructed at taxpayer expense and greatly inflated prices. The private contractors have made large profits, which they shared with the public officials who awarded the contracts. In fact, any large and complex government finds it difficult to avoid all graft of this sort. Some governments use such practices openly, and citizens know they will not receive public services unless officials are "tipped." Thus a government need not be dictatorial to be a profit organization. Rather, the desire for profit may be a dominant motive for running a dictatorship—subject to discussion of the ideological dictatorship below—and we will discuss it first in those terms.

Since it must hold dominant force the dictatorship's coalition must include the army. This means including one or more generals in the top group, buying the support of one or more generals, or both. A typical pattern in Latin America is for a general to use his control of the army to make himself dictator. While he is salting away deposits in Swiss banks, his necessary attention to the whole of government leaves him less in touch with the army itself. In due time some new general solidifies his control of the army and ousts the existing dictator. If lucky, the latter gets out in time to retire in luxury abroad.

Such a dictatorial coalition typically includes powerful groups other than the army, such as landowners or industrialists. The government gets the support of these groups by favoring the rich over the poor through laws, regulations, tax provisions, court decisions, and police actions. Examples of such measures are low taxes on land, industry, or banks, but high sales taxes on commodities bought by the poor, and ungraduated income taxes with small personal deductions, or massive tax evasions by the rich. Other examples are failure to enact such things as safety or sanitary regulations, welfare programs, public education, and employer liability for work-connected injuries. Courts and police who promptly evict families for failing to pay rent but take no action against landlords who fail to repair dwellings are other examples—of a type, incidentally, not uncommon in the United States.

In such a profit government the sponsors consist of the top government officials and the landowners or industrialists who support them. If landowner or industrialist groups are split among themselves, the sponsors consist of that dominant coalition of these groups which support the government, or at least do not actively oppose it. The staff consist of all government employees, including the police, armed forces, courts, and top levels of the staff. For reasons we need not detail here, it seems likely that unless some sponsors themselves occupy key posts they will lack the information and the transactional leverage to keep control. The recipients are the rest of the population.

Who's out and who's in?—the question of optimum coalition size

Control rests with the dominant coalition. But who will be in it and who will not? The basic problem of coalition size is the same for any type of government. But the logic of coalition formation is more easily visible in a profit dictatorship because its benefits to its sponsors, being something like those of a business firm, are more clearly defined than are those of some other types of government.

Whatever the power base of the dominant coalition, the more parties included in it the surer it is of winning. But the more who are in it the greater is the number among whom the loot must be divided, and the smaller the number from whom it can be extracted. For a gang of thieves there is no point in expanding till there is no one left to steal from! And as to policies, as the coalition seeks to take in more groups so as to raise its strength it will have to make more compromises to attract the additional groups. Since the costs rise and the benefits decline for the dominant core as the coalition expands, there must exist some equilibrium size that will maximize the payoffs—presumably the smallest coalition that is safely dominant (see Riker 1962). Who and how many must be included depends on the situation.

THE IDEOLOGICAL, OR TRANSITIONAL, DICTATORSHIP

Not all dictatorships are run for personal aggrandizement. Some have been started with at least the alleged purpose of reforming the society. The French and Russian revolutions would be major examples, and since World War II some underdeveloped nations have instituted rather dictatorial governments, allegedly to facilitate rapid industrialization. The ideologies involved usually assert that the people will freely support the new regime once it has made reforms and that dictatorial controls will then cease. Because of this rationale we may refer to such dictatorships as *transitional,* even if their later history does not always bear out the claims.

Equilibrium of costs and benefits

Although real cases are much more complex, to analyze some basics of a dictatorship not (yet) widely accepted by its people we can substitute the sponsors' goal of moving toward a new society for that of bringing them power and privilege. Even if the leaders focus only on the size and speed of their reforms, they will often find that after some point the costs of more or faster change will rise, for at least two reasons, while the benefits fall. The costs may rise, first, because the greater the change the more will the public have to be retrained, remotivated, and shifted from accustomed habits, all of which require increased time, effort, money, and confusion. Second, while people may accept some upsets without too much protest, as the upsets increase so may their resistance.

As to benefits, if the government first makes the changes that bring greatest benefit, then additional changes will be of lesser benefit. A reform or revolutionary government thus faces a decision about how fast to institute changes, in light of the probable increasing costs and diminishing benefits of additional speed.

On the other hand, at least for a time there may be an upward reinforcing feedback, in which minor success generates enthusiasm for larger changes, and so on. Or there may be a downward reinforcing feedback if, as in Uganda in the early 1970s, the government's efforts to consolidate its power lead it to eliminate the most skilled and productive segments of its population, and further depress the condition of a people who already disliked their government. A transitional government thus faces difficult decisions, often not knowing whether a particular policy will assist change, increase resistance to it, or produce stability in the process of change.

Coalition size and ideological purity

Despite difference in goals, with regard to the size of the ruling coalition an ideological government faces the same problem as does a straight profit dictatorship. The more numerous and varied the subgroups in the coalition the more stable it will be, but at the cost of diluting its ideological goals. Noncentrist groups in a democracy face a similar problem, as illustrated in the United States by the communists, socialists, American Nazi Party, John Birch Society, Black Panthers, Students for a Democratic Society, Young Americans for Freedom, and the Students for Constitutional Government. Only if they remain small can they retain and clarify their ideological purity. Only by diluting their ideology to appeal to more people can they increase their numbers to carry more weight. Zigzagging between ideological purity and wider popularity is a central theme of political movements not close to center. Parties at the center do not face this problem, since they are wedded to immediate victory, not ideology. The operating goal of a noncentrist ideology most of the time is not to become the dominant group, but rather to have enough power to give dominance to some other group if they decide to support it. In that role even a small minority, if cohesive, can sometimes wield substantial influence.

Ideological goals, freedom, and power

A transition dictatorship is likely to show an important difference from the profit dictatorship. If it is firmly in control the profit dictatorship can be reasonably lenient with its subjects. In fact, the more prosperous they are the more the government can extract from them. The profit dictator can allow freedom of religion, habeas corpus and trial by jury in ordinary crimes, reasonable compensation for private property taken by the state—in fact, a wide range of constitutional freedoms so long as the public does not direct them toward toppling the regime. The dictator is not really trying to change people's lives, but merely to get from them more than he spends on them.

By contrast, because the transition dictator wants to change the society radically, he may find it necessary to alter many details of life. Since family and church are important transmitters of culture, the transition dictatorship may attack or subvert the church and transfer the training of children from the home to the public nursery, while making an independent church or the traditional family seem treasonous. Because many controls can easily be violated under relative privacy, their enforcement requires spies and informers. And because cross-examination of witnesses would identify the informers, the right to confront one's accusers must also be denied. Thus may a dictatorship allegedly seeking the people's welfare be worse than one that merely exploits them. A dictatorship which thus tries to control vast detail of the nation's life is referred to as *totalitarian*.

This point raises another. Despite the above reservations it is conceivable that a nation might achieve some important objective much sooner if it temporarily gave its government dictatorial powers. Such a proposal is not necessarily ridiculous, since strong democracies like the United States and Great Britain have allowed their governments near-dictatorial powers during major wars. The nasty question nevertheless remains: How can a people assuredly get rid of a dictatorship once its job is done? Since the dictatorship possesses the means to prevent the people from taking back control, dare the people risk giving up control in the first place? The Soviet Union is a sobering example. For although there have been significant relaxations since the death of Stalin, the freedoms of the Russian people are still thin and uncertain almost 60 years after their revolution.

Gradual restoration of freedoms may be possible, but is subject to "threshold" effects. Just as citizens cannot give up more than a certain amount of freedom without losing their ability to defend the rest of it, so too is a dictator unable to give them back more than a certain amount without restoring their ability to seize the rest of it. The Russians apparently think they approached too close to that threshold in the late 1960s, when they curtailed some newfound freedoms, as reflected in their later expulsion of Solzhenytsin and their confinement of other dissidents in mental hospitals. The Czechs crossed that threshold in 1967, and quickly found Russian troops there to push them back.

A dictator faces a problem generally parallel with that of anyone in a position of power. Whatever his goal, from the most self-centered or sadistic to the most altruistic and humanitarian, if he wants to advance it he must hold power—which means to achieve and stay in office. Whatever the goal of having power, primary attention must always go toward getting and keeping it. But to retain power one must sometimes pursue policies contrary to the purposes he wants it for. A leader may want relaxed international relations, but find that nothing will solidify his support except a tense international scene. He may sincerely want lower taxes, but find that he can get elected only if he promises benefits that require higher ones. When the power objective and policy objectives conflict, the former will normally take priority. Not necessarily, however, since one could say, "If that's what I must do to hold power, it's not worth it"—as did Barry Goldwater in the 1964 presidential election.

20

COOPERATIVE GOVERNMENT: THE SPECIAL PROBLEMS OF DEMOCRACY

Democracy is variously described as rule of the people; government by consent of the governed; government of, by, and for the people; or self-government. Actually it is more complicated and less responsive than these idealistic phrases imply. Fundamentally, the problem of democratic government is that of a large, multipurpose cooperative organization whose sponsors hold a variety of conflicting views about both methods and goals as detailed in Chapter 15.

We will define *democracy* as a cooperative government in which essentially all adult citizens are sponsors. "Essentially all" means that some special categories, such as inmates of prisons or mental hospitals, might be denied a sponsor role. We will leave unanswered the question of how many other categories, such as nonproperty owners, slaves, or females, might also be denied the sponsor role without disqualifying the nation as a democracy.

SPONSORS, STAFF, AND RECIPIENTS

Having made the above reservations, for convenience we will speak as if all adult citizens were sponsors, and exercised their sponsor role most explicitly through voting. In democratic government, as in any other cooperative, the same persons collectively are both sponsors and recipients. This is the sense in which government can be both *by* and *for* the people. In what sense it is *of* them is less clear.

As to the staff, Articles I, II, and III of the Constitution of the United States formally divide the powers of the government respectively into legislative, executive, and judicial. Although the Constitution refers to "powers," and it has been popular to speak of "branches," it is analyti-

300

cally more sensible to think of three *functions,* any of which may be performed in some degree by any person or "branch" of the government. In our model of organization the legislative function encompasses the sponsor-staff relation and the executive function the staff-recipient relation.

Figure 20–1 shows these two relationships between the citizenry and the government organization. The left-hand arrow going from *Public* to *Government* indicates the flow of instructions from the public, acting in their role as sponsors, to the government staff, telling them what the public wants the government to do. In a broad sense these constitute the legislative function. Most activities of government constitute feedbacks of some sort from the government to the public, in which people are recipients of services or restrictions. These are indicated by the right-hand arrow, which shows the flow of activities from the government staff to the public in their role as recipients. This staff-recipient relation constitutes the executive function, in which policies formulated by the gov-

Figure 20–1
TWO MAIN RELATIONS BETWEEN THE PUBLIC AND
GOVERNMENT

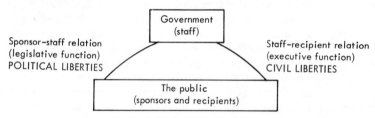

ernment staff in response to the public's sponsor role are now "executed" back on the public. Anyone who prefers can reverse the two boxes to show the people "over" the government.

In the most obvious sense Congress performs a legislative function when it passes a law that establishes policy, and the president performs an executive function when he appoints subordinates and instructs them to carry it out. However, the president exercises legislative functions when he recommends legislation to Congress, and also when he or his subordinates clarify details or ambiguities of a law while implementing it. Conversely, Congress performs executive functions when it establishes an administrative body, such as the Federal Trade Commission, or when it asks members of the president's Cabinet to testify about enforcement of existing laws. For those executive positions which the president can fill only with the advice and consent of the Senate, the Senate shares the executive function of selecting executive officers. (We will come to the judicial function later.)

The parliamentary system vs. separation of powers

The American Constitution was written largely by persons who feared strong centralized government. Its division of government among three "powers" reflected a desire to decentralize power through "checks and balances." By contrast, the British have been more interested in "responsibility." Their prime minister is both the chief executive and the head of the party responsible for legislation. If he puts his weight behind an important piece of legislation and it does not pass the Parliament, its rejection is considered a vote of no confidence. He must then either resign or call a general election to determine whether the public supports his party or the opposition. Under this arrangement the executive cannot blame the legislature or vice versa, since the prime minister and his party are responsible for both.

There is little point in debating which system is "better," since each is tied too closely to the history and temperament of its people to permit easy generalizations. However, given recent complaints about the growing power and secrecy of the presidency, the adoption of one part of the British practice might be useful—having the president appear before Congress from time to time for unrestricted questioning in the same way as the British prime minister appears before the House of Commons.

To return to the main point, the sponsor-staff and the staff-recipient relations are conceptually distinct. No matter what the form or structure of government, both functions must be performed. Incidentally, in the dictatorship the two are not likely to be confused, since the sponsors are a relatively small group while the recipients are the whole population. Under dictatorship the staff-recipient relation involves the same two sets of people as in a democracy—the government personnel and the people. The sponsor-staff relation is utterly different, however, and consists of the ways in which the landowners, industrialists, generals, or the church ·—depending on the country in question—convey their desires to the government staff about what they would like the government to do. In a single-party totalitarian regime the effective sponsors of government are the top leaders of the party, and the sponsor-staff relation consists of the instructions from the party to the top government officials.

Political liberties vs. civil liberties

Figure 20–1 has the label "Political Liberties" attached to the sponsor-staff relation, and the label "Civil Liberties" attached to the staff-recipient relation, in an attempt to make explicit what is often implicit or unclear. "Political liberty" here means the people's freedom to engage in activities related to exercising and maintaining their role as sponsors.

By permission of John Hart and Field Enterprises Inc.

This means mainly learning about alternatives, formulating their desires about them, and communicating them to the government staff. Instances of political liberty include the citizens' right to know what is going on in the government, to vote, to nominate or become candidates, to form and contribute to political parties, to lobby, and to campaign for candidates or policies. Political liberties concern the citizen's ability to influence his government's policies.

Civil liberties deal with things government may *not* do to citizens in the staff-recipient relation. Examples in America are that the government may not interfere with a citizen's free exercise of religion, find him guilty of a crime without a trial before a jury of his peers, hold him for excessive bail, treat him as guilty until he has been so proved, search his person or premises without a warrant, force him to testify against himself, quarter troops in his house without his consent, or take his property for public use without just compensation.

Freedom of speech, press, and assembly are important to both political and civil liberties. Without these freedoms citizens would have difficulty learning about and evaluating their government's actions, policies, and officials. They could not cast informed ballots or otherwise know how to exert their sponsor controls. But citizens want freedom to speak, write, and meet for many purposes other than to influence government. Hence freedom from restriction on such actions is a civil as well as a political liberty. In fact, almost any freedom listed above could have some relevance to either relationship. For example, we have listed freedom from excessive bail and the right to be considered innocent till proved guilty as civil liberties. But for a government to hold its political opponents in jail without bail or trial would destroy their exercise of sponsor function, and hence their political liberty as well. The problem is not to debate whether some particular freedom is civil or political, but rather to understand both aspects.

In Chapter 11 we identified freedom as absence of costs. The freedoms listed above, all found in the Bill of Rights of the American Constitution, identify costs the government may not impose upon citizens (e.g., excessive bail or taking property without compensation), or activities that citizens may engage in without having a penalty (cost) imposed by government (e.g., the exercise of freedom of the press or of religion).

Incidentally, the rights specified in the Bill of Rights are unqualified, in two respects. First, the Constitution does not say, for example, that a publisher shall have freedom of the press if he exercises it responsibly, or that a citizen is free to choose his religion if he selects a sensible one. The publisher has the constitutional right to say irresponsible things, and the citizen to select nonsensical religions. This does not mean that persons are freed of other consequences. An irresponsible publisher can be sued for libel or lose credibility and readers, and the individual risks the wrath of his fellows or perhaps of God when he chooses his religion. The Constitution means merely that the *government* may not impose costs (penalties) on citizens who engage in constitutionally protected activities.

The second respect in which these rights are unqualified is that they do not depend on majority support. In theory the government may not deprive a person of a constitutional right even if the Congress or the citizens voted unanimously to do so, unless they first amended the Constitution. The Founding Fathers were vividly aware that without such protection the majority in a wave of anger might vote away their own freedom in order to "get" somebody who momentarily upset them.

Because these rights cannot constitutionally be taken away by even an overwhelming majority, they are sometimes thought of as "minority rights." But at least insofar as political liberties are concerned, they can also be viewed as a longer-run protection of majority rights. To protect the rights of the minority at the moment is to say to the majority now in power: "You may not use your majority support *now* to change the rules in such a way as to hold your majority forever. The majority of today may not silence the potential majority of tomorrow."

ON LEGITIMACY AND MAJOR BARGAINS

In the early 13th century a group of English barons did not like the way King John was ruling, after which a series of military skirmishes demonstrated that they had the power to oust him. In 1215 on the plains of Runnymede, near London, King John signed the Magna Charta. This was an explicit agreement that these subjects would voluntarily accept King John's authority if he in turn would behave in certain ways acceptable to them. Much of the Magna Charta dealt with local and transitory matters, such as castle guards, royal forests, and fiefs. But other items concerned matters of lasting importance, such as seizures of property, coerced confessions, guilt determined by one's peers, and freedom to travel abroad.

Somewhat similarly, the people living in America in 1789, acting through elected representatives, explicitly accepted the Constitution and the authority of the new government it established. Subject to qualifications discussed below, the source of the government's authority, and of its legitimacy, was clear in both cases; those subject to the authority had voluntarily agreed to accept it. The authority relation was incorporated in a contract, a parallel to the way one accepts the authority of his employer when he takes a job or the authority of some other organization when he becomes a member. As in Chapter 16, *legitimate* authority is *accepted* authority, and the authority of the government in each case was explicitly accepted by those subject to it.

Can any government be wholly legitimate?

The obvious qualification to this neat description is that, even though this major bargain was explicitly accepted by a particular decision making apparatus, acting on behalf of the subjects, by no means every individual personally accepted it. Some individuals bitterly opposed it, and would have rejected it if they could. Should we nevertheless consider the new government's authority legitimate over *them?* If we do not weasel on our definition that authority is legitimate only when it is accepted, the answer is necessarily no. Then can any government's authority be wholly legitimate? Again the answer is no, except possibly at the moment the government is initially formed, and then only if it is accepted unanimously—a theoretically possible but highly improbable case.

We thus say that for all practical purposes, no government's authority can ever be wholly legitimate. However, we will handle this question as we have several others by shifting from an absolute criterion to a relative one. We have said, for example, that there is no such thing as perfectly accurate perception or communication, and that the only sensible question is whether these are good enough for the purpose at hand. We will similarly say that there is no such thing as a perfectly legitimate (totally accepted) government, and that the only sensible question is whether a government is well enough accepted to govern satisfactorily.

The conditions for adequate legitimacy can be clarified if we look at the voluntary organization, whose authority is legitimate over every member who voluntarily stays in, and whose individual members do stay in if they perceive its benefits to equal or exceed its costs to them. If a citizen sees the benefits of his government to exceed its costs he *would* stay in even if he *could* withdraw (which he normally cannot do). The condition of adequate legitimacy may thus be thought of as that in which most citizens feel no restraint from the compulsory quality of their membership because they do not want to escape it, and in which those who would want to get out but cannot create no significant problem. However, for one particular question below (the judicial function), we will consider the government's authority legitimate over every individual if it is accepted as legitimate by most.

Some miscellaneous bases of authority and legitimacy

With the Magna Charta and the United States Constitution particular people explicitly accepted particular authority. More often in history the authority of a government is seized by someone, or "just grows." In such cases the people may "accept" the government because they see no alternative. If their acceptance is grudging, interspersed with covert or overt sabotage, and if many people expect to replace the government the first chance they get, the government is not legitimate in their eyes.

By contrast, even if the people dislike their government, but nevertheless believe "It's the best we'll get for a while, so we may as well try to make it work," they are treating it as legitimate. No sharp line divides legitimacy from illegitimacy. As a state of consent, legitimacy depends on how people feel about it.

Rulers sometimes gain legitimacy by asserting that they have received the right to rule from some higher authority. Historically the most impressive alleged source of such authority has been God, as in the so-called divine right of kings. An advantage to a ruler who claims this status is that a potential competitor will be hard put to find a higher authority to back *him*. A second advantage is that if the people accept the religion they may find it hard to disprove the king's claim. This technique works best for the king if the church also supports it, thus seeming to confirm the thesis that God, in fact, supports the king. The church may also convey the impression that if the king fails to punish the disloyal or disobedient, God may later do it for him. If the people also believe that no violation will escape God's notice, the system is nearly foolproof—in theory.

In some societies authority is allegedly derived through inheritance. The son, or at least the oldest one, inherits his father's lands, business, or money. Typically he also follows his father's occupation. If the sons of farmers become farmers, the sons of carpenters become carpenters, and the sons of lawyers become lawyers, what is more natural than for the sons of kings to become kings? If anyone questioned the relation, the king could see that he was set straight. Straight, that is, to prison or the gallows.

Another source of authority is awe, some of which infects most of us. To the peasant in rags the sheer notion of a "house" with 150 rooms, scores of servants, a vast supply of ornate clothing, a jewel-studded crown, and a voice that commands with no doubt that it will be obeyed —all these things leave him aghast. They are so different from his own experience that he readily sees those who rule as a different breed, no more questioning their power than he does that of the tides or thunderstorms. A ruler with a flair for pageantry can do great things with this approach.

Most governments seek to elicit some awe, and a certain awe about the sheer hugeness of some governments is available without asking. For some years a refusal to believe that something so awesomely huge could possibly be a mistake probably contributed to support of the Vietnam war by many Americans who might otherwise have opposed it. Both those in power and those trying to unseat them typically try to enlist awe in their support, and awe often assists political novices whose rise is so rapid as to provoke it.

As a side aspect of awe, all but the most hardened cynic stops in wonder at the magnificent cathedral, mosque, or castle. One is dumbfounded at its size and complexity, and the skill, patience, and untold man-hours consumed in its making. Every man's sense of his own potential leaps to know that humans can do such things, even if he is personally humbled in their presence. A nation that does large things stirs a similar sense of accomplishment, even if its citizens are uncertain whether some grand things it does ought to be done at all. Sheer power may generate awe that will support legitimacy, even if it also generates fear.

BUT WHERE ARE THE JUDGES?

We have identified the sponsor-staff and staff-recipient relations as legislative and executive functions, respectively. But what about the judiciary? What do the judges do?

Rights vs. interests

To gain certain insights about law and the courts we must take certain logical steps. We have defined legitimacy as an aspect of authority: legitimate authority is authority that was accepted in the major bargain. Let us now try extending the meaning of "legitimacy" to encompass the carrying out of *any* bargain or promise between parties. To clarify, let us first distinguish rights from interests.

An *interest* is something a party wants but has no enforceable way of getting. A *right* is something that he has an enforceable promise of getting, whether he happens to want it or not. To illustrate, when a union and management are bargaining, the union has an interest in getting wages raised and the company has an interest in keeping them down. But neither has any enforceable right. However, as soon as they reach agreement and sign a contract, the union members have an enforceable, right to the wage rate stated in the contract and the company has the right to pay no more than those rates. The contract is the major bargain, and the payment of wages to an individual in return for his work is a transaction subsidiary to it. Similarly, if retired persons urge Congress to raise social security benefits, they have an interest in getting them raised, but no right to get them raised. But once Congress has passed a law raising the rates, each retired person has an enforceable right to the larger amount. If there were no law, constitutional provision, or judicial precedent, a publisher might have only an interest in freedom of the press. But if the Constitution specifies it and the courts enforce it, the publisher has the right to a free press. A man may have an intriguing interest in a lady's bank account. But it may take a wedding ceremony and associated law to give him any right to it.

What is right is legitimate

Within this meaning we can say that a right coincides with what is legitimate under the circumstances. (The excitable reader is reminded that many technical terms of social science float around in general usage with a variety of meanings. Hence before anyone takes exception to this statement, let him be sure he is using "right" and "legitimate" as defined herein.)[1]

In civil law. Let us look first at a simple civil suit. A landlord raises the rent. The tenant refuses to pay. The landlord seeks to have the court evict the tenant. The tenant argues that he has a year's lease with the landlord's promise of a fixed rental, and hence a right to stay at the old rent. The landlord insists that he only said he *expected* to keep the rent unchanged for a year, but never *promised* to.

The function of the court is to discover, if it can, what the parties *agreed* to, and to enforce that agreement. Clearly written contracts are handy, since they are so tangible. The main question, however, is not so much whether the agreement was put in writing as whether there *was* an agreement. Was there a "meeting of minds" on a clearly understood set of terms of the transaction?

A clearly worded lease with witnesses to both signatures will settle the

---

[1] In this connection the reader might consult Deutsch's suggestion that the legitimate is the just (Deutsch, 1971) and my suggestion that justice is the application of consensus terms to particular situations (Kuhn 1963: 696).

question. A scribbled note with the landlord's initials saying, "Rent not to be raised 1 year," will also probably settle it, especially if the landlord acknowledges his initials. Even without anything in writing, if the tenant says, "Don't you remember in the hallway when I told you how broke I was and you said, 'OK, you can have it at $150 for a year?'" and the landlord answers, "I couldn't say for sure that I didn't," the judge or jury may conclude that the landlord had, in fact, agreed. Without evidence of such a promise, however, the landlord has the right to raise the rent, and the tenant has no right to the original rates.

Now suppose that the landlord did not agree to keep the rent at $150, but that a law freezing rents was passed. In what sense, if any, is a question of legitimacy involved? Both landlord and tenant have accepted the authority of the government as legitimate. Hence the major bargain under which they operate is not solely their contract, but also a higher-level agreement between both of them and the government. Under that higher agreement the tenant has an enforceable right to his apartment at $150 and the landlord has a right to receive at least that much.

This is not necessarily the end of the road. The landlord might claim that the government had no constitutional right to pass the law. If the courts uphold the law as constitutional, the landlord could not raise the rent. If the courts declare the law unconstitutional, the rent can go up.

In short, people's right to do what they like, alone or with others, is subject to the authority of the government so long as the government itself acts within the authority granted it by the people in their major bargain, the Constitution.

In criminal law.   Criminal law shows a parallel logic, as with a citizen being tried for robbery. The law prohibiting robbery is undoubtedly constitutional. Implicitly at least, every citizen has agreed to obey constitutional laws, and to accept the government's use of force to penalize him if he breaks them. Anyone who violates the law thus violates the first half of this agreement with the government and gives it the right to punish him. Hence, in arresting, trying, and jailing him if guilty, the courts are settling questions of rights and legitimacy. The other half of this agreement is that one may *not* be punished if he fulfills his half of the bargain by obeying the law.

Let us return to our basic logic. Law dates back some thousands of years, and substantial theorizing and philosophizing about it are not much younger. By contrast, organization theory is only about a century old, and has taken marked turns in recent decades in such writers as Barnard (1938) and Simon (1947). To describe the rationale of law and government in the language of organization theory may therefore sound strange. And until someone with broad legal training makes extensive cross-comparisons between this and the legal way of saying things, it is difficult to say how good a description this is of the law and the judicial function. It nevertheless seems a concise and logical way of describing them, and of raising some fundamental questions about them. And if the function of the judiciary is to decide questions of legitimacy, not policy, it is presumably desirable to make judges as independent as possible of any responsibility to those who have interests in policy, whether they be members of the government staff or sponsor citizens. The practicalities are not as clear as the model, however, since, as we have already noted, the functions of government are not uniquely separated among the branches.

Our description may also sound very different from many firsthand experiences with the police, courts, or jails. This does not necessarily mean that something is wrong with this description of law, but merely that practice often varies widely from *any* general theory.

Legitimacy and the oath of office

An important link in the chain of legitimacy is the oath of office, in which elected and certain appointed government officials swear to support and defend the Constitution. When they do so, the major bargain between people and government is brought to bear, not merely on government as an overall entity, but on the individual officeholder. It is the people's way of saying: "We have agreed to obey the government if it limits its power in certain ways and does not violate our rights. To implement that agreement we will not let you exercise the powers of government unless you personally agree to be bound by those limitations."

Any government official who knowingly violates the Constitution, any policeman who knowingly enters a house without a warrant when no crime is in progress, or any legislator who votes for a law knowing beyond reasonable doubt that it is unconstitutional, is (in this model) guilty of insubordination. He is deliberately violating a basic instruction from the sponsors—an instruction, furthermore, that he has by oath already personally accepted. Under normal organizational logic deliberate insubordination is unquestioned grounds for immediate removal, regardless of a person's qualifications or successes.

We have noted that under stress the people sometimes seem ready to vote their freedoms away in order to "get" some group that has angered them. Not only may they refrain from seeking impeachment of the insubordinate official, but instead they may strongly support him while denouncing the courts for defending the Constitution. The logic suggests that if the people value their Constitution and their freedoms they should give insubordination in government the same no-nonsense attention that business managers give it among employees. It is cause for immediate removal, without regard to the quality of the employee's performance on the job.

This section describes the pure logic of the oath and of legitimacy. The due process method of removing officials is spelled out in the impeachment clauses of the Constitution—though citizens are always free to request or encourage resignation. In providing for the impeachment and conviction of a president for "treason, bribery, or other high crimes or misdemeanors," the Constitution is perhaps not as explicit as it might be about violations of the oath of office through the abuse of constitutional power, but by means that do not necessarily fall within the stated grounds for removal. In practice the norms often permit members of government to violate the Constitution, as in numerous police searches without warrants, and in the complete absence of penalties for legislators who knowingly vote for unconstitutional legislation in the hope that the courts will later throw it out.

Freedom can be troublesome in either dictatorship or democracy. The danger in a dictatorship is that the people will get so much freedom that they will use it to seize more. The danger in a democracy is that the people will get so much freedom that they will vote it away. Perhaps some wiser age will resolve these dilemmas.

HOW THE PUBLIC INSTRUCTS GOVERNMENT: THE SPONSOR-STAFF RELATION

The stockholders are the sponsors of a corporation. On one fundamental issue those sponsors are likely to be unanimous, or nearly so. They prefer larger profits to smaller ones. The rest is detail, to be studied and decided by experts. If the corporation does badly, stockholders are more likely to sell their stock than to try to improve management. Despite the many important questions that may arise in implementing the goal, the corporation is fundamentally a single-purpose organization—to make money.

This condition contrasts starkly with the potentially all-purpose nature of government. Some citizens want higher tariffs, more schools, controls on pornography, larger welfare payments, tight controls on pollution, or elimination of billboards, while others want the opposite. Often the individual faces conflicts within himself, like the textile worker who wants tariffs on textiles to keep his income up but cheap imports to keep his expenditures down. A central problem of democratic government is: How, out of this welter of confusing and conflicting goals, do the citizen sponsors decide what to instruct their government to do?

The Chapter 15 discussion of the paradox of voting indicates that the people can have a clear voice in a vote between two mutually exclusive alternatives. But if they must express their individual preferences among three or more alternatives, there often is no such thing as a "group preference" or "public will." True, a particular decision process will produce a particular result. But a different, equally sensible decision process might produce a very different result. If so, which result reflects the wishes of the electorate? Since there is no real answer to that question, seemingly the only sensible procedure is for the people to agree on some decision rule and process that strikes them as generally fair, and then to accept the decisions it yields.

The two- (or few-) party system

The above procedure is essentially what the people have adopted in the United States and, with variation, in other democratic nations, without necessarily being aware of the logic behind it. Let us examine the two-party system, approximately as it operates in the United States, as a technique for measuring the public's preferences and for passing them on to the government staff as instructions.

In the first place, it is possible to put an issue on the ballot, in a referendum. If the issue is stated with only two clear alternatives, the public can make an unambiguous choice. There is always the reservation, however, that the alternative the public most wanted did not appear on the ballot at all. Referendums are used from time to time at local and state levels, but are not part of our national decision process. Public decision making at the national level, and most of it at state and local levels, is made through votes for persons. Now many votes for persons are cast on the basis of "personality," including the religious or ethnic background of the candidate. To keep complications to a minimum we will include as "issues" such questions as whether the candidate is black or white, Catholic or non-Catholic, handsome or unappealing, trustworthy or deceitful. For the moment we will also assume that a candidate cares only about getting elected, not about implementing his own convictions, and that he takes a position on every issue. Of the many possible problems, we will deal with the candidate's selection of a platform (1) within a political spectrum and (2) as among several explicit issues. We will deal later with a political party, as distinct from a candidate.

The snuggle-up approach to the political spectrum

In a certain sense the electorate can be lined up along a political spectrum, from the radical left (for example, the Communist party) through the center to reactionary right (for example, the American Nazi party). Other things equal, voters are likely to be distributed in approximately a normal curve, with most voters at or near the center and smaller numbers toward the extremes, as in Figure 20-2. A is the leftist candidate, and B the rightist. A announces his position first, which falls at X. The logical move for B is then to announce his position as falling at Y. That is, B "snuggles up" as close as he can to A while yet remaining far enough away to be distinguishably to the right of A. B will then get all the votes to the right of Y, plus (we will assume arbitrarily) half the votes between X and Y. These constitute a majority, and B will win. True, the extreme right will be unhappy about B's position, but they will hardly gain by shifting to A. The logic is the same, of course, if B selects his position first, and takes it somewhere to the right of center, in which case

Figure 20-2
DIAGRAM OF A NORMALLY DISTRIBUTED ELECTORATE

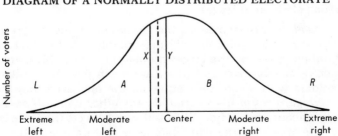

A snuggles up just a little to the left of him. This line of reasoning is based on Downs (1957).

What if *B* takes his position first, about at *Y?* If *A* insists on maintaining an image as a leftist he is stuck with a loss. But if he is not concerned about his left-right image he can take a stance just to the right of *Y,* while nevertheless remaining a little left of center, and win.

Real elections, of course, are much more complicated. Among other things, few voters fall at the same spot on the spectrum on all issues: the same person might take a rightist view on economic matters and a leftist view on the race issue. In addition, not all issues fall neatly in the left-right orientation. Is it leftist or rightist to be in favor of stable prices, freedom of religion, or good local transportation? What is more, many citizens do not base their vote on issues at all, but on the party, religion, or other trait of the candidate, or on some vague impulse. Despite such complications one conclusion seems safe. Voters often yearn to have one candidate take a clear liberal stance and the other an equally clear conservative one "so the voters will have a real choice." When this happens it must be viewed as an accident, not a normal outcome of political logic.

Two recent instances illustrate the process. In 1964 candidate Barry Goldwater took a clear conservative position well to the right of center, abandoning the whole center and all of the left to Lyndon Johnson, who won by an overwhelming majority. George McGovern lost even more decisively in 1972 by taking positions identified in the public mind as considerably left of center, leaving the whole center as well as the right to Richard Nixon. Although there were other contributing factors to the outcome in both cases, the basics seem clear.

If the people near the center are willing to swing their votes (as contrasted to giving consistent support to a particular party), they have large bargaining power in their "ability to grant or withhold" votes. Usually the voters to the left of the leftist candidate have no realistic choice, nor do those to the right of the rightist candidate. Since their votes are "in the bag," and cannot be withheld as leverage for concessions, their bargaining power is weak. The strong bargaining position of voters nearer the center is another way of explaining the urge of candidates to "snuggle up" near the middle. The recent rapid rise in the numbers of independent, noncommitted voters may require more candidates to be more sensitive to more people than before—if other forces do not cancel out the effect.

The coalition platform of issues

How a coalition wins—or tries to. If all issues in an election are of about equal importance to a voter, he will presumably vote for the candidate with whom he agrees on the larger number of issues. But many voters are guided by *strong issues,* by which we mean that they will vote for that candidate with whom they agree on the one issue they consider important, regardless of his position on any other issues. If such voters feel strongly about the candidate himself, according to the same logic we can treat the appeal of the candidate as if it were one of the "strong issues."

It goes without saying that if all issues are equally strong, a candidate may win if his platform takes a stand on each separate issue that is favored by a majority. He may also win if one issue is strong for most of the electorate, and he takes the majority position on it. It is often not recognized, however, that if different issues are strong to different groups, a candidate can win by taking a minority position on every issue. Suppose that to one third of a candidate's electorate, Group *G*, strict limitations on abortion are a strong issue, while the other two thirds of his electorate weakly prefer abortion on demand. A different third of his electorate, Group *H*, want vigorous efforts to reduce armaments, and to them this is a strong issue. The remaining two thirds weakly want more arms, not less. Suppose that the candidate now takes a clear stand against abortion and for arms reduction, even though each position is favored by only a third of the voters. His opponent meanwhile adopts the majority positions on both issues—for unrestricted abortion and more armaments. When the ballots are counted, our candidate will get *all* the votes of Groups *G* and *H*, or a two-thirds majority. He has built a *coalition of minorities* and won. The process is the same whether the voters are coldly logical or emotionally impulsive in their feelings about strong and weak issues.

To carry the logic further, if an electoral district contains subgroups, each with its own strong issue, a candidate could win by taking a series of positions, no one of which is supported by more than (say) 10 percent of the voters. For example, if he gets *all* the votes from *each* of six strongly committed 10 percent minorities he wins a resounding victory.

Again, reality is more complicated than this example. For one thing, actual minorities are not so conveniently bounded, so united in their views, or so assuredly strong on an issue as the example suggests. For another, to simplify the example we assumed that the candidate's opponent did not follow the same strategy. If he did, many new complications arise, which we need not go into here. There is no easy formula by which a candidate can plug into a set of voter views and extract a sure victory, particularly if some offhand remark during a campaign convinces people that he doesn't really mean what he says, or is an unstable personality. The central point remains that if a candidate wants a winning platform he had better attend to the relative intensity of feelings about issues, rather than simply count noses.

What have the voters told the winners?

For convenience we have noted how a candidate builds a winning coalition. Our underlying question is the reverse, however: How does the public decide what it wants and instruct government officials to do it? The general presumption of elections is that a candidate, if elected, is to carry out the platform on which he campaigned. And despite some well-founded cynicism about the subject, many candidates do make a reasonably serious attempt to do so—though under the doctrine of sunk costs and benefits the elected official may well look more toward the next election than toward the one just past. Let us nevertheless examine the winning candidate's platform as a set of instructions from voters.

If his platform took majority stands on issues, things are simple. But what if his victory was based wholly on a coalition of minorities? In that case the voters have "instructed" him to carry out a set of actions, every one of which is opposed by a majority. What is more, if he *should* follow the majority wishes on every issue (and if the voters are consistent, informed, and sensible, which they may not be) he would be defeated in the next election by the same coalition of minorities that elected him in the first place, whose votes would say, "You didn't do what we asked."

Although we have only scratched the surface we have nevertheless made clear that there is seldom a clear "public will" which a conscientious official can discern and implement. Students, politicians, or voters interested in making democracy work must understand the actual process of selecting officials, since the content of voters' instructions to government cannot be separated from the process of expressing it. Hence except on isolated issues we can rarely say with confidence, "The public *wants* so-and-so." We can only say, "Through such and such a procedure the public *has selected* so-and-so." Perhaps if the public held fewer wispy illusions about the "public will" and the government's supposed obligation to know and obey it, and understood more about the results that different decision processes actually produce, our citizenry might become more effective sponsors. At best, however, the relation between individual preferences and the actual social choice will be uncertain.[2]

The alert reader will have noted an assumption that underlies the above discussion—that the government *ought,* if it could, do what the people want. This assumption is not universally accepted, even within democracies. Perhaps we should recall Winston Churchill's suggestion that democracy is the worst form of government—except for all the others that were ever invented. Or Hutchins' characterization of the University of Chicago as not very good; merely the best that there was.

MORE ON POLITICAL PARTIES

A *political party* is a coalition of office seekers and their supporters who seek to increase their power over government decisions. Although political parties are a relatively new social invention, dating back only about 300 years (Loewenstein 1957: 57), once invented their uses became obvious. First, the likelihood of getting elected is enhanced if various office seekers coordinate their money-raising and campaigning activities. Second, once a number of people have been elected to various offices, their likelihood of successful action is greater if they work together. Third, for people who do not think for themselves a party is a vast information-economizing device: all they need remember is the name of the party they support. The party is thus a device both for acquiring

---

[2] In this connection see Arrow (1951) and Rothenberg (1961). The image of government taught in some civics courses constitutes dishonest merchandising about on a par with that for some over-the-counter drugs. If such courses would teach more about the nature of power and the politics of group decisions, and less about the "public will" and the "public good," we might hope to have a more effective citizenry.

power and for exercising it. Since it coordinates the efforts of two or more persons toward a joint result a political party is also an organization. We will continue to think of it as a coalition, however, since that is its main function, although (as noted in Chapter 15) most internal and some external activities of the coalition follow the organizational model.

The main function of the party is to put together a winning coalition, following the logic described above for a candidate. In addition to having a broader base and more persons to study issues, raise money, and conduct campaigns, the party also has greater flexibility in forming coalitions than does a single candidate. For example, personality may be an issue—and it is often a strong one—but no one candidate can be black, white, and yellow; Catholic, Jewish, and Protestant; conservative, center, and liberal. But the party's total slate of candidates can be. And often is—something for everybody.

Intraparty decisions

Candidates and platform. Why does a party reach the decisions it does on policies and candidates? According to the definition, a political party consists of those who want to be in office and those supporters who want them to be. Each office seeker has two main roles. First, as a citizen he is one of the sponsor group. In this role he presumably has ideas of his own about how his government ought to be run. These may be self-oriented, such as wanting farm subsidies because he owns a large farm, or public-oriented, such as wanting pollution controls. He may even vote for pollution controls in the public interest despite the fact that he owns a factory whose costs will rise as a result. Second, in his role as a member of the government staff he will (if elected) receive salary, prestige, power, and a stepping-stone toward other advantages and advancements.

Perhaps the best model for analyzing the elected official's position is that of principal and agent, as in Chapter 11. He is, in fact, a double agent, an agent both for the voters who elected him and for the party that nominated and financed him. What is more, since he does not know which citizens voted, or how, he is also an agent for those who voted against him, or who did not vote. He thus faces potentially conflicting transactional relations. His bargain with the voters is essentially: "If you vote for me, I will try to do what you have asked." His bargain with the party is: "If you nominate and finance me, I will do what will strengthen the party." If the two commitments coincide, fine. However, if what is good for the party is not good for the voters, he must let his conscience or his estimate of the probable consequences be his guide. If he wants to remain in politics he will attend to transactions that will build his own future power. In short, he is an agent for at least two sets of principals, while also having both a general and a personal sponsor interest. If it is sometimes hard for him to decide what to do, or for the voter to predict what he will do, the reason is clear. The ambiguities and internal conflicts in the elected official's position arise from the number of roles he occupies—and we have not even mentioned the multiple roles he may occupy within the government itself.

Hence to the question, "How does the party make internal decisions?" the first part of the answer is that it attends carefully to the wishes and positions both of the voters and of those already in office. The latter have both the power of office and a demonstrated ability to command votes. Both factors give them bargaining power with the party. The vote-getting ability is particularly important, since the party's influence on government decisions is weak if its candidates are not elected.

Money and workers. A second part of the answer is that the party cannot run without money. Hence its platform and slate of candidates must be drawn so as to induce a flow of funds. If the wishes of heavy contributors conflict directly with those of candidates who are strong vote getters, all concerned face some difficult choices. To raise the money shall the strong candidate be withdrawn or his platform changed? Shall the potential contributor insist on the platform or candidate he wants, even if that means risking the election? If the party is financed by numerous small contributors, this particular problem is eased considerably—which is the basis for the recent provision that contributions up to $50

© 1962 and © 1971 Walt Kelly. Courtesy Publishers-Hall Syndicate.

may be deducted from taxable income, and further suggestions for limitations on contributions or public financing of campaigns. Such proposals, however, are not without serious risks of their own.

Third, the party needs workers, particularly volunteers, in large numbers during campaigns. Like candidates, these volunteers have many motives, including both the general welfare and their personal welfare as housewives, lawyers, contractors, union leaders, or journalists. Some party workers are union or corporate executives who, while they technically work for the party as individuals, know that some political work is expected as part of their jobs. Through such persons some party expenses, as for telephoning or duplicating, are picked up wittingly or unwittingly by corporations and unions, particularly at the local level. Despite exceptions, corporate members appear most frequently in the Republican party and union members in the Democratic party.

Among the participants in party politics decisions are made by the processes identified in Chapter 15. Agreements are reached in part by the persuasive method of communication. Transactions produce further agreement through trade-off compromises. "Okay, I'll give you the money, and I'll accept your fair-haired candidate—but only if he softens that holier-than-thou plank of his about corporate influence in politics." If these two methods still leave questions unsettled, the dominant coalition within the party wins and the others lose. The dominant coalition will consist of some combination of money, media coverage, popular issues or candidates, powerful political friends, experience, and so on. Whatever collection of people holds more power than any other collection, and sticks together, will carry the day.

Coalitions: Main and sub

Government follows the pattern of other organizations, in that its decisions are made ultimately by a dominant coalition, whose decisions are made by a dominant subcoalition, and so on. Where there is tight party discipline, as in England, the party that wins an election constitutes the dominant coalition within government at that moment. The party makes its decisions on the basis of a dominant coalition within *it*, often determined at a party caucus. Some constituents within the party are themselves interest groups, such as consumers, importers, unions, manufacturers, or farmers. Each interest group may itself reflect the dominant coalition within it, which in turn may represent dominant coalitions within particular firms, unions, etc. The decisions that come out of this process reflect the structure and membership of a hierarchy of coalitions. Viewed in this light, the science of politics lies in learning how various kinds of coalition structures operate and interact, and the art of politics lies in learning a particular coalition structure extremely well. When things work well, the science helps the art, and vice versa.

In single-party governments, such as those of Russia and present-day Chile, the same party is always the dominant coalition, and runs the government. However, this fact does not prevent shifts in the dominant subcoalition which controls decisions of the party. To illustrate, the "Kremlinologist" students of the one-party Russian government give much attention to the shifting fortunes of various subcoalitions as they jockey for dominance.

Some nations, such as France, Italy, and Denmark have many parties, none of which is likely to win a majority in the legislature. In this case a government is formed—that is, a group of top governmental officials are selected—by a dominant coalition of parties. The decisions for the nation are then made by any collection of parties that can both consitute a majority and stick together. The decision making power in a government thus lies either in a coalition of parties (if no one party wins a majority) or in a party that consists of a coalition of interests. Either way, the process of forming and keeping a dominant coalition is the basic process by which governmental decisions are made. Decision by communication or transaction works mainly within coalitions, rather than at the final decision level.

The United States is perhaps best described as a multiparty system in two-party clothing. Party discipline is not strict. At times it is almost nonexistent, as Democrats vote for bills sponsored by the Republican party, and vice versa. In fact, it sometimes looks as if each member of Congress were his own party!

ON LEGISLATURES AND THINGS

A legislature displays the decision process of the whole society in microcosm, and is a sort of expanded version of a corporation board of directors. Like any other organization, a legislature makes its decisions by communication, transaction, or dominant coalition. An obvious difference between a legislature and both a corporate board and a public electorate is that of numbers. A board is so small that every member can talk; an electorate is so large that it is impossible for all members to talk; and the usual legislature is somewhere in between. The second difference is that of interest. A corporate board has the relatively single-minded goal of making money, and its decisions are mainly about means. An electorate has conflicting goals about an almost limitless variety of issues, and its decisions often involve ends. As agents for a disparate and conflicting electorate, a legislature also has many conflicting goals. It is more cohesive than the electorate, however, in that all or most of its members know one another personally, all operate under the same set of rules, and each understands the relation between another's behavior and his desire to be reelected.

As to the content of their communications, transactions, and coalitions, in Congress a senator or representative must give attention to at least three main interests: those of the nation, those of his local constituents, and those of himself and his reelection. The three occasionally coincide, but often they do not. The overall decision processes of balancing the interests among legislators when each is also doing an internal balancing act is all but impossible to trace in any real situation. Among all the things we might discuss we will focus on the difference between *compatible issues,* in which both of two proposals can be passed, and *incompatible issues,* in which passage of one means defeat of the other.

Within the limits of the total budget many bills for expenditures are compatible and subject to transactions, known more colorfully as back scratching or pork-barreling. Although the representative from Seattle may have only passing interest in a new national park in western Pennsylvania, and the representative from Pittsburgh may have even less interest in improved navigation in Puget Sound, a transaction is easily arranged in which "I'll vote for your bill if you vote for mine."

The allocation of costs and benefits favors this result. The voters in western Pennsylvania will be very displeased if their representative votes against their new national park, for if they get it they will receive all the benefit but pay only one district's fraction of the cost. They will be only mildly displeased if their representative also supports navigation for Puget Sound, for although they get none of the benefit they also pay only a fraction of the cost. As between the two, for them the park is a relatively strong issue and Puget Sound a relatively weak one. Hence the Pennsylvania representative will not hesitate to incur his electorate's mild displeasure over his vote for Puget Sound in return for the Seattle representative's vote for Pennsylvania's park. Since the logic is the same for all legislators, such deals are readily consummated.

By contrast, if Texans want a more militant policy toward China and

New Yorkers want less militancy, both cannot get what they want. We similarly cannot have a lower tariff on cheese to please Californians and a higher one to please Wisconsonians. Here tradeoffs are more difficult and decisions by dominant coalition more likely.

There are innumerable interactions between the legislature and the executive, the House and the Senate, Congress and the governors, and so on. These are mainly power relationships, which can be analyzed through our model of transactions. Here as well as elsewhere, power depends on who wants what and how much, and what he is willing and able to give for it.

SOME CONCLUDING NOTES

Voters have many different and conflicting interests concerning a vast variety of matters. Whether their interests are narrowly selfish or broadly humanitarian does not matter for the decision process. To have influence, voters must join others of similar interest, which means to choose a party. But each party is a coalition which includes some interests a particular voter agrees with and some he does not. Even within his own party some of his interests are therefore diluted, compromised, or rejected. Hence, even if his party wins and implements its platform, the member's transaction in supporting the party will bring about some things he wants and some he does not.

If there are many parties, the voter may find one that pleases him all around. But because it represents a very special point of view that party cannot command a majority. Those of its representatives who are elected may join with other parties to form a ruling coalition. But in doing so, they must accept many compromises not wanted by the voters who elected them. Or they can refuse those compromises, remain among the "outs," and get little or nothing their supporters want.

The coalition process has been emphasized because among the many divergent interests that bear on a government communication and transaction often fail to produce a decision. Hence coalitions and hierarchies of coalitions are the main technique for making governmental decisions. For this introductory discussion we have not said much about the particular interest groups or the interminable cross-relations that are possible among them—as indicated in Chapter 11. The process is extremely complicated, which is why, despite exceptions, the winners are generally those with much political experience who give great attention to detail.

Precisely what the relation is between the decisions thus reached and the wishes of the public is impossible to say, and there is no way of knowing what the public wants except as it is reflected through a particular decision process. We thus face the disconcertingly circular conclusion that the public gets what it wants because what it gets is our only palpable measure of what it wants. It is easy to say that an opinion poll shows majority support or opposition to some government action, and that the people are or are not getting what they want. The difficulty is that such a poll reflects sentiment on issues taken one at a time. Every issue has logical connections and power connections with other issues.

And whereas the public might strongly support a particular action when viewed alone, it might reject it as part of some larger package.

Nevertheless, to say that we cannot *know* the relation between public wishes and government actions under democratic processes is not to say that there *is* no relation, that a dictatorship could do as well, or that a government cannot at times and in certain ways be very responsive. The practicing politician who must face periodic elections knows only too well that he must keep tuned to the moods of the public, or politically he will soon be a very dead duck indeed.

We will rest our discussion of political decision making for the moment, and return to it briefly later as a contrast to the market process.

21
GOVERNMENT: INTERSYSTEM AND GLOBAL

Why do nations go to war, while states, parishes, corporations, and Rotary Clubs do not? If individuals, corporations, or townships can settle disputes in courts, why not nations? If individuals can learn to trust one another, why must nations be so suspicious? Does some aggressive human impulse make wars inevitable?

We recognize that governments are supersystems relative to individuals and their many other organizations. But a government is also a *party* when it acts more or less as a unit. As such it is subject to the same analysis of communications, transactions, and organizational memberships as any other party. To understand relations among governments we therefore use the same models as before; only the parties are different.

COMMUNICATIONS BETWEEN NATIONS

To what extent do special conditions of communications between national governments or across national borders make the relations of nations different from the relations of such parties as individuals or corporations?

Cost factors

The average distance, and hence the average cost of communications, is greater between nations than within them. As these things go, this means that communications between nations will be fewer and briefer than communications within them. The amount of difference, however, depends on particulars. In Europe few points in different countries are as far apart as New York and Los Angeles, and New York is far closer to Montreal than to Seattle. Postal, telephone, and telegraph rates are important here. The fact that they frequently rise when messages cross national borders discourages the untold thousands of messages that are the web of daily living from going into other nations. This communicational cost works toward keeping nations much more internally oriented than they otherwise would be. However, for really important messages between governments these costs are not significant.

Language factors

Languages often differ between nations. The importance of this factor also depends on circumstances and the level of the communicators. It may create little difficulty in Europe, where most educated people know two or more languages, and there is often someone near at hand who can translate. There are nevertheless few Italians who know Swedish, and vice versa. Communications between individuals in the two countries are thus unlikely to occur unless the communications are important enough to justify getting an interpreter. The same conclusion applies more strongly for areas where the people customarily learn only one language. Language is thus a distinct barrier to close and detailed relationships across national boundaries.

For relations between governments, or between business firms handling large volumes of trade, language differences are more likely to be a minor hurdle than a major obstacle. Translators can be hired. Documents can be drawn up in two languages in parallel columns. Deliberate redundancy can minimize misunderstandings—as by sending the same message couched in several different sets of words, so that a possible misunderstanding over one version will be caught in another. In important matters the parties have repeated conversations of the sort: "If I understand you correctly, you are proposing so-and-so. Have I got that straight?" We will deal later with cases where the parties may not *want* their messages to be clear—which is a different problem.

Cultural factors

The cultures of two nations may differ dramatically. Since a given message can be interpreted only in the light of the conceptual sets in people's heads, and those conceptual sets differ, misunderstandings are possible. So is offending the representative of another nation by remarks that are innocent in one's own culture but insulting in his. Nonverbal behaviors may also communicate unintended messages. Arabs, and some Europeans, typically talk with their faces less than a foot apart, while Americans typically leave two feet or more. In a conversation between an American and an Arab, as the Arab keeps moving closer and the American keeps backing off the Arab will think the American unfriendly and the American will think the Arab "pushy." An American may consider a Brazilian evasive if he will not talk business after several brief pleasantries, while the Brazilian will think the American ill-mannered for presuming to talk business the first day the two have met.

Such misunderstandings may occasionally cause difficulty. But important negotiations between nations take days, weeks, or years, again with great redundancy. And they are not likely to be influenced very much by face-to-face contacts in which ordinary citizens of different nations come to know and understand each other better.

Transactional factors

Any careful observer of international negotiations has noted the cryptic nature of many diplomatic messages. If the Kremlin issues a statement about some aspect of relations with the West, diplomats in every Western capital start analyzing it. What did Kosygin mean by "unrestricted" access to Berlin when last year he talked of "unimpeded" access? Do the two words mean the same? Or is he signaling a shift in position?

Diplomatic language is often exceedingly roundabout and subject to multiple interpretations. Although this fact complicates communication, the main problem is transactional. A nation usually has no problem in making its meaning clear *if it wants to*. Kosygin could say easily enough, "I intended 'unrestricted' to have a different meaning from 'unimpeded,' and the difference is as follows. . . ." Much diplomatic communication constitutes tactics in transactions, and the usual purpose of tactics is to mislead or conceal, not to inform.

Ambiguous language is often a means by which nation *A* makes a tentative concession to see how nation *B* will respond. If *B* responds favorably, *A* can acknowledge more explicitly that it actually meant what *B* interpreted it to mean. If *B* responds unfavorably, *A* can withdraw without losing face by simply asserting that the later language meant the same as the earlier. Such ambiguity is a deliberate transactional gambit, not a communicational problem at all in the strict sense.

INTERNATIONAL TRANSACTIONS

Transactions in goods

Nongovernmental (subsystem) transactions. Transactions across national boundaries occur at many levels. When importers buy and exporters sell, they face tariffs, quotas, customs, sanitary regulations, and multiple currencies in addition to internal transactional problems. If a private American firm trades with a government-owned Russian enterprise, the governments may also become involved. And when an American oil company negotiates with a powerful oil-owning Arabian sheik, we approach the making of American foreign policy by a private firm.

Tourists spend money abroad, immigrants send remittances to their native countries, and American corporations buy farms, forests, and factories all over the world. These and many other kinds of transactions take place between subsystems of different nations.

Governmental (main system) transactions. Our primary interest here is in transactions between governments. A socialized government may buy and sell goods on its own account, just as private corporations do. So may profit dictatorships. Governments can also negotiate concerning the conditions under which their subsystems transact, as by establishing currency values, specifying the duration of foreign travel, protecting citizens abroad, or determining the ratios of local employees in foreign-owned factories. In such cases the subsystems are the principals and governments their agents, but with the complication that the agents hold sovereign authority over the principals.

In general, however, governments act as agents for their sponsors, and the international relations of a democratic government are supposedly conducted in the interests of the people. With respect to "national security," however, it is not always easy to draw a line between the interests of government and those of its citizens. For if citizens want their nation to remain independent, then under certain rather common circumstances the defense of a government may be difficult to distinguish from the defense of national independence. Defense of a government, however, is not the same as defending the reputation or tenure of any particular official.

Transactions in bads: Armaments, wars, security

Security and sovereignty. "National security" is an elusive concept, and both brave deeds and monstrous crimes have been committed in its name. At base, however, the term refers to a nation's assured ability to remain sovereign—to avoid coming under the coerced authority of another government. On a day-to-day basis "security" also refers to freedom from probable challenge to the nation's power base.

A conspicuous recent lack of security occurred in Czechoslovakia in 1967. The Russian government then sent its troops into Prague without the consent of the Czech people or their government, and gradually replaced the Czech officials with other Czechoslovoks more satisfactory to the Russians. A fuzzier case was the intervention of American troops in the Dominican Republic in 1965—"fuzzier" because the foreign troops took sides between internal rivals rather than upset a legitimate and popular government.

Let us now look at the implications of sovereignty on transactions among nations. In the initial model of transactions Assumption *i* reads:

> The transaction is unique, and stands solely on its own merits. Neither party considers its possible effect on any other transaction with anybody over anything, or considers the possible alternative of dealing with someone else.

Among other things this assumption means that neither party considers that the transaction may be illegal, and hence lead to an additional transaction with government in the form of punishment. The model of transactions in bads also assumed that the effective preferences of the parties toward stress or threat reflected their own desires only, ignoring possible intervention by higher authority. In short, in the model the parties had "sovereign control" over their transactions. We have subsequently seen that such parties are not sovereign, and that formal and semiformal authority may modify their transactions.

Now, however, we are looking at transactions between parties that *are* sovereign. To an important extent they can and do constrain themselves by treaties and common sense. But when those constraints are inadequate, they can rape, plunder, burn, and murder their transactional opponents with no higher legitimate force to stop them. They can form coalitions, in the hope that the coalitions will be strong enough to deter any other nation or coalition from starting anything, or to defeat it if it does. But these too are subsystem arrangements among themselves, not a higher-level legitimate force. Although the social disadvantages of bads (Chapter 10) are at least as great for nations as for lesser parties, the world society has not yet produced any organization able to outlaw force between governments by itself possessing obviously superior force. There were profound hopes after World War I that the League of Nations would rise to that status, and after World War II that the United Nations would. Although the United Nations has performed "peacekeeping" functions of this sort on several occasions for small nations, it seems unlikely that it will achieve such global authority in the foreseeable future.

Sovereign systems sometimes join or merge into larger sovereign systems through positive goods transactions, as when the thirteen American states after the Revolution voluntarily merged to form the United States. However, nations more typically lose their independence through military action by other nations.

Individual sovereignty vs. national sovereignty. When the sheriff and marshal in the western movie are unwilling or unable to implement the police function, individuals are effectually sovereign. But whereas the shoot-out in the typical western totally eliminates some parties, a battle between nations merely reorders their power or authority. Japan and Germany surrendered unconditionally in World War II, but are hardly dead. Although the sovereign power in each for some time resided in the occupation forces, those forces have been long gone from Japan, and the troops still left in West Germany are there because the Bonn government wants them. Whether for nations or for individuals in westerns, the way to maintain independence is to stay strong, be alert, join a coalition, and weaken the potential enemy.

The westerns should make clear that being sovereign does not mean one can do anything he likes. A sovereign person or nation lives among other sovereign persons or nations, and if a sovereign unit is weak in transactions it may be forced to give other sovereign units much in return for little. To be sovereign does not mean to be free of power exercised by others, which at times can make one nation seem to have almost no power at all. It merely means being free of force exercised legitimately by a higher-level formal organization.

Some principles and complications of threat systems

Following Boulding (1966), we use the term *threat system* to refer to the set of relations between nations based on bads, even though those relations also include stress. The general theory of such relations is that of using bads as transactional strategies. A war is a mutual stress. Decisions about each step are made unilaterally, in light of each party's perceived ability to produce some effect on the other. The actual fighting is a pretransactional stress: an attempt to effect negatively valued transformations on the other party so as to lengthen his effective preference for relief of the stress. The total cost of the stress to one party, B, consists of the disutility of the stress imposed on B by A, plus the costs of resisting A's efforts while simultaneously trying to impose counterstress on A. The processes of imposing or resisting these negatively valued transformations are technical, not social; it is the *values* created by these transformations that provide the basis for social analysis.

A war ends under one of two main circumstances. The first is the transformational condition of physical blockage. Nation B surrenders unconditionally out of physical incapacity to stop A from doing anything it wants. This relationship is not transactional, since B's wishes have nothing to do with the outcome. Whether A is harsh and vindictive or gentle and generous depends on the kind of future relationship A wants with B, not on what B is willing to concede at the moment.

The second end to a war is the transactional, negotiated settlement, which can occur when EPs overlap at some moment short of unconditional surrender. The components of the EPs are mainly the following, recalling that A's EP is AY minus AX and that B's is BX minus BY. AY_1 consists of A's desire for positively valued concessions from B, such as freer trade, open waterways, or the cession of some territory. AY_2 is A's desire for relief of the stress of continued war. AX consists of the costs to A of making positively valued concessions that B may make a condition of stopping the war. BX and BY are logically parallel to AY and AX. In a variation of the negotiated settlement the war gradually peters out, in which case the conditions that actually prevail as the war fades away constitute an implicit agreement.

A war is normally preceded by threats. Except to note their catastrophic consequences there is little to be added about threats by nations beyond the discussion in Chapter 10. The general caution against making threats unless one has carefully assessed their possible consequences is nevertheless more poignant here than with lesser threats.

The tribal traits of the international community

In Chapter 18 we noted that an important trait of a tribal society is that everyone knows and interacts with everyone else and that no one can fully escape the consequences of his past behavior by disappearing to live somewhere else. As measured by the number of interacting parties, the world's 143 or so nations are a community of about the size of a modest tribal society, with the complication that any significant interaction between any two of them is visible to the other 141. This fact has many ramifications, and we will illustrate one.

In such a community no significant transaction can be unique. Because of A and B's visibility, the terms on which a war or other large transaction is settled between them have potential repercussions on each nation's relationships with every other nation, as well as on their future relationships with each other. A difficulty of certain international disputes is that each party feels that it must calculate the effects of the settlement on its relations with many other nations, as when the settlement terms of one war reveal something about a nation's ability (effective aspect) and willingness (preference aspect) to fight for its goals. Because of this communicational effect, or "face," a nation may fight longer than its immediate goal justifies for fear of impairing the credibility of its subsequent threats. Since defeat may suggest incompetent leadership in entering or fighting the war, personal vanity may also extend the war.

Much the same can be said of union-management relations. The main drift of union-management contracts is determined in a group of large companies and unions whose numbers are also of small tribal size and whose settlements have tribal visibility. And since a strike is a mutual stress, the meanings of AX, AY, BX, and BY in a strike essentially parallel those for a war.

Peace without world government? Short of sovereign international government war may nevertheless be avoided in several situations. One is that the opponents are so evenly matched that neither will start a war for fear of losing. A second is that the opponents are so unevenly matched that the weaker has no chance of winning, and the stronger has such a good bargaining position in lesser transactions that it sees nothing to gain by fighting. A third such situation is that the idea of "winning" a nuclear war seems patently ridiculous.

Difficulties nevertheless arise as part of the instability of threat relations (Chapter 10). Even if the power of A and B is evenly matched at one moment, the situation is seldom static, as each may strive for an edge over the other. If A thinks it has pulled ahead of B it may initiate a preemptive strike before B catches up, not because A wants any positive thing from B but merely to keep B from getting strong enough to beat A. A need not even think that B wants anything affirmative from A; merely that B wants to be strong enough to avoid being defeated by A.

Stability based on the relative weakness of one side often works well. For example, the United States could easily defeat Mexico, Canada, or both. But since neither poses a potential threat, there is no reason for a preemptive strike. Since the United States can profitably trade with both without the costs of governing them, and since in a larger war both would be either American allies or neutrals, the United States has neither economic nor security need for military conquest.

Between superpowers, however, inequality is less likely to be stable. By a single alliance with a secondary power the weaker side might overnight become the stronger. Under modern world conditions a successful preemptive strike by a superpower while it was ahead might put it well on the way toward becoming a single world government—which may be the only feasible way to achieve one. But the remaining nations will hardly like the prospect, and nuclear weapons vastly increase the risks of the preemptive strike.

Often one nation has conquered another to get such things as land space, minerals, or ports. Regarding positive goods the colonial period of the 18th and 19th centuries has generally convinced both practitioners and observers that the costs of colonies far exceed their benefits, and that the potential benefits of colonies can be acquired more cheaply through trade and economic exploitation.

But if wars are not fought for goods, then wars, armaments, and threats of wars have no *ends.* They are concerned solely with *means* —with one nation's maintaining the means to prevent another nation from utilizing *its* means. Viewed from almost any perspective, such a relationship is incredibly stupid. Unfortunately, to know that does not automatically tell us what is wise, or how to make the transition to it. A difficulty is that so long as there is a competition in violence the cost of being stronger than necessary usually seems smaller than the cost of not being strong enough. An arms race is a positive feedback relationship, and to change it from an upward to a downward movement requires trust, to which we now turn.

A short disquisition on promises and trust

We have examined the general principle (Chapter 14) that a promise will be kept if the value of the stake lost by not keeping it is greater than the cost of keeping it. A major problem between opposing nations is that it is so confoundedly difficult to find a large enough stake. Although there are many people whose integrity in personal relationships is unimpeachable, who would not lie to save his country? What other nation would risk *its* survival on the assumption that he would not lie? And if by telling a lie a leader could put his nation a large step ahead of an opponent, would his own people condemn him for doing so? Or would they laugh at the other country for being so gullible? The sad fact of international politics is that it would be stupid for any nation to risk anything important on an opponent leader's promise. Although some Americans observe cynically that the Russians or Chinese will not keep a promise unless it is in their interest to do so, those nations obviously feel the same way about us. Essentially all international relations involving significant power are in fact conducted on that basis.

Rights and interests between nations

But since courts settle disputes, why not those between major nations? As noted in Chapter 20, whereas courts decide questions of rights, not interests, most questions between nations involve interests, not rights.

It is possible, for example, that two superpowers could contractually agree to limit armaments. If one nation alleged a violation it would apparently have the the *right* under that contract to penalize the violator or to require him to stop, and a world court could logically decide the case. But as defined, a right is not a right unless it is enforceable, and how is the violation to be stopped if the court's order is ignored? What can the international court do to enforce compliance by a superpower?

To examine a parallel, unions and managements regularly arbitrate questions of rights (such as the amount of an employee's seniority) by agreeing in advance to be bound by the decision of an arbitrator and to accept enforcement of his decision by the courts. But few agree to binding arbitration of interests (such as a change in average pay). Why? Because to do so is to give an outside party the power to bankrupt the company if his award is too high or to disrupt the union and discredit its leaders if the award is too low. Both sides normally want the freedom to accept or reject any major terms they must live with. Nations similarly refuse to adjudicate questions that may affect their survival.

ON INTERNATIONAL ORGANIZATIONS

We have indicated that a sovereign nation can join a higher-level organization and accept its authority without losing its own sovereignty, so long as it can withdraw whenever the cost of accepting the authority exceeds the benefit. But is it not possible for all nations to cede sovereignty to an international government, such as the United Nations, and to accept the UN's legitimate force in international affairs? Of course it is possible, just as the thirteen former colonies ceded their sovereignty to the United States, and as the governments of Europe could, if they chose, form a United States of Europe. The question is not whether it is possible but whether it is probable.

In Article 42 of its charter the United Nations already has peacekeeping powers, which include authority to send troops into trouble spots. But two things keep the UN less than sovereign. First, the troops sent by the UN are not its own. They are the troops of its member nations, and unless the member nations provide such troops the UN has none. Further, the UN must depend for financing on what are essentially voluntary contributions from member governments. In these respects the United Nations resembles the government of the American colonies under the Articles of Confederation.

The second nonsovereign aspect is that under Article 27 any permanent member of the Security Council can veto any action regarding a dispute to which it is not itself a party. Since each major power has allies on the council this means, for example, that Great Britain could veto any action against the United States and China could veto any against Russia. Since allies would probably stick together it seems unlikely that any forceful disciplinary action against a major nation could pass the council. Neither the United States nor Russia would join the UN without this right of veto. Because of the above two items the UN cannot constrain any warfare involving major powers.

POWER POLITICS AND IDEOLOGY

A model of pure power politics is nonideological, and asks solely about relative power positions. It does not raise questions of morality, legitimacy (except insofar as legitimacy may affect internal power), honesty, democracy, or left-right political orientation. The United States, for example, could during World War II be allied simultaneously with the dictatorial communist Russians and the democratic capitalistic British against the fascist Germans and the feudal Japanese. In the late 1960s the United States could be allied simultaneously with fascist Spain and Greece, democratic part-socialist Britain, and communist Yugoslavia to build a power bloc against the communist Russians. The question is not whether nation A approves the morals or ideology of nation B, but whether B will support A in a showdown, and with how much power. "Politics makes strange bedfellows" is surprising only to those who do not see it in terms of power.

By contrast a pure ideological model of international politics would call for supporting only other governments with the same ideological view as one's own. Such a model suffers from obvious difficulties. A single election or coup could switch a nation's ideology overnight (as with Chile in 1973), yet leave its power position basically unchanged.

Furthermore, is a nation's ideology measured by what it says or by what it does? If a nation, for example, professes communist goals but actually operates a capitalistic market system on an extended "interim" basis, what ideological label does one attach to it? Some people view a government's seizure of property as left-wing radicalism. But if a government seizes the private property of a landed aristocracy and divides it up to produce competitive private enterprise farmers, as has been partly the case in Kenya, what ideology does the government represent? If a government initiates new industrial firms and later sells them to private enterprise, as has been done in Turkey, is such activity socialist or capitalist? And what are the American government's large loans to Penn Central Railroad and Lockheed Aircraft?

As between a power position and an ideological position things can become dreadfully confused if policymakers are not sure which they are pursuing, in what proportions, or why. For example, some of the American difficulty in Southeast Asia seemed to reflect confusion as to whether American policy was directed toward keeping South Vietnam ideologically noncommunist, toward maintaining the American power position in the area, or toward an assumption that American power depended on maintaining the noncommunist status of South Vietnam.

As with individuals the strictly selfish-indifferent model of international transactions can nevertheless be modified by friendliness or animosity, which may be based on ideological views. Some people in capitalistic countries simply do not want to do business with any communist country, no matter how much the refusal may hurt themselves. Hatreds similarly make things difficult in Africa, the Middle East, Ireland, and between Bangladesh and Pakistan. Hence we cannot choose totally between pure power on the one hand and likes and dislikes on the other, since likes and dislikes modify EPs and hence are themselves power factors.

ON NATIONS, NATIONALISM, AND PATRIOTISM

What is the appropriate unit for a nation?

The Soviet Union covers approximately 8.6 million square miles and Monaco six tenths of a square mile. Canada has 3.8 million square miles, mainland China 3.7 million, and the United States 3.7 million. Israel has about 8,000, Belgium about 12,000, and Lebanon about 4,000. The United States has one official language, Canada two, and Switzerland three. Although Russian is the dominant language of the Soviet Union, millions of its people do not speak it and dozens of different languages are in everyday use. India lists 15 "principal" languages, with Hindi "official." The United States combines black and white races, and much of Latin America is made up of native Indians, blacks of African origin, and white Europeans, with many Orientals added in recent decades. Many countries have a single predominant religion. Yet multiple religions are common, as with Buddhists and Mohammedans in India, Buddhists and Christians in Vietnam, and Christians and Jews in the United States and Europe.

The boundaries of nations are sometimes obvious barriers, such as mountain ranges or oceans. But they may also be arbitrary lines, like much of the boundary between the United States and Canada. Rivers and lakes that serve as boundaries raise the interesting question of whether water is a barrier or a link.

Some nations are relatively self-sufficient, like the United States and Russia; others are almost totally dependent on trade, like Japan and Great Britain. Some have a national identity that dates back several thousand years, like China, Greece, and Egypt; others are brand-new, like Qatar, Bahrain, and Bhutan. Old nations often have new governments, as with China, India, and Egypt; while a relatively new nation may have a relatively old government—that is, a government which has not undergone basic constitutional change. As history goes the United States is relatively new but now has one of the oldest governments (Deutsch 1970, p. 226). Most people in the world over 30 do not live under the same political regime into which they were born (ibid.).

What, then, makes a nation? What ties its people together? Statistically a common currency is the most frequent unit of identity, since few if any nations have more than one currency, and rarely do two or more nations use the same monetary unit. The most notable exception are a group of small, new African nations which use the franc CFA (Communauté Financiére Africaine). However, a common currency is probably a result, not a cause, of nationhood.

It is often suggested that a people constitute a nation when they "feel" like a nation. This may be so, but merely pushes the question back a step: Why does some particular collection of people feel like a nation? To this we can give another unsatisfactory answer: because they are or have been one. So why have they become a nation?

To preview later discussion, when it comes to explaining why some area and its people constitute a nation, perhaps the only available answer is: that's the way it happened. (A fuller discussion of this seemingly cavalier explanation appears in Chapters 26 and 27.) To state the problem more broadly, if *any* complex system continues to exist and function for very long, system analysis suggests that certain forces in the behavior of the system themselves create conditions that favor its continuance. Let us examine how such self-preserving forces may operate in the case of a nation.

If some leaders manage to establish a stable government, whether by persuasion or coercion, that government molds its subjects into a going system. It creates a common currency, a common system of law and courts, a common defense, and acceptance of a common authority. Simply by continuing for a time to *be* a sovereign entity to which a collection of people must look for changes in their laws, it forces them to work out communicational, transactional, and coalitional procedures for influencing or resisting the decisions binding on all, in a self-reinforcing feedback.

Sovereignty also is a highly visible and sharply bounded entity, which maps help us to conceptualize. The formal concreteness of a government provides a more explicit focus, with which one can identify more easily, than do such relatively amorphous semiformal organizations as ethnic group, class, and religion. For example, the government of India can join the United Nations, sign treaties, and raise an army; but Hinduism or the caste system cannot. Through government the people in an area can act as a comprehensive unit, which is something no class, caste, racial group, or religion can do, unless it too first organizes as a government. People with a common culture are more likely to form a government than are those with disparate cultures. However, even if quite different peoples have been pulled into a common government, that fact itself sets in motion certain cohesive forces. A government is often the only organization of which everyone in an area is a member, and thus provides a common tie. A government also creates much of the environment in which it operates. Although the same could be said of an ecological system or informal organization, unlike them a government exercises so many kinds of power that it can deliberately alter the society in ways that improve its own ability to survive. Once established, this power and control usually become decisive, even if challenged on occasion by internal or external rivals.

Cohesion does not always occur, however, and the pressure for disparate groups to work under the same government may generate more animosity than if they remained separate. History provides many cases—conspicuous recent examples include the Irish, the Pakistanis, and the South Africans.

National patriotism

"I am a _____." If you were at an international conference that included every type and category of person and were asked, "What are you?" what would be the first word you would fill into the blank? Most people would name their country. This does not mean that some would not name some other category, such as physician, Buddhist, or revolutionary. But the typical person would probably assume that his nationality is his best first approximation identification. This ability of one's nation to identify him is one reason for feeling a sense of identity with it. Whether traveling abroad or merely ruminating at home, one rightly suspects that the glories or shames of his country, its power or weakness, somehow reflect on himself. Furthermore, government is the only kind of organization nearly everyone will understand, since it is the only kind nearly everyone belongs to. It is also the only organization one is inescapably attached to, in the sense discussed in Chapter 19.

According to Chapter 14, to raise the status of some group is to raise the status of each of its members. Hence to keep the image of one's government great and glorious is to enhance one's own image. Now modesty about oneself is widely considered a virtue. Hence one cannot safely brag about himself. He is nevertheless freer to brag about his country, since most of its accomplishments are not his own. And whereas if one deprecates his personal achievements he raises the relative status of others, if he credibly deprecates his country he lowers the status of his fellows. And as to oneself, it is not merely that one fears that others will think less of him if his country is criticized. He may think less of himself. If he supports a policy, for someone else to criticize that policy is to criticize him. The strength of this effect is probably related inversely to the strength of one's personal status. The person whose status is high is less threatened by criticism of his country than is the person whose country is his only source of pride.

Many children go through a stage when it seems important that "my daddy can lick your daddy." Instead of outgrowing this attitude, many people simply transfer it to "my country can lick your country."

The strength of nationalism seems to have been growing apace in recent centuries. In the second half of the 20th century it has perhaps "gone just about as fer as it can go." Given the present high jealousy of national sovereignty, it would seem that any important international movement for some time will have to work *through* nations, not *around* them. Even communists now generally seem to give top loyalty to their national communist organizations, and there is certainly no formally organized sovereign power of "international communism."

Much confused thinking arises when people "reify" analytical pattern systems by talking as if they were acting systems. Western jargon often says, "Communism does this," while Eastern jargon says, "Capitalist imperialism does that." Whether in Moscow, Bogota, Cairo, London, or Washington governments or their agents are acting systems which *do* things, including signing treaties and dispatching troops. But "communism" and "imperialism" are mental constructs, or analytic systems. They have no substance and do nothing, albeit they are constructs that strongly affect people's actions. Perhaps because of this ghostlike quality, to say that "communism does this" or "imperialism does that" is somehow more frightening than to say that Russian officials have done this or American officials have done that. Being vaguer, such phrases are also more useful as propaganda.

DOES HUMAN NATURE MAKE WAR INEVITABLE?

We will not pretend to answer this question, but will merely rephrase it in the present models.

Our model of man identifies mainly processes, not content. It indicates *how* man learns concepts and makes perceptions, *how* he builds a complex of secondary motives on a small package of primary ones, and *how* he learns motor skills. The model does not specify *what* he learns, which depends mainly on his experience, which is molded by his culture.

Perceptions and feedback

If a people are taught to perceive that certain other peoples are "after them" and must be killed if they themselves are to survive, this "reality" will become part of their perceived opportunity set. A people reared with the world view that "they will kill us if we don't kill them first" will seek preemptive wars against "them." On the other hand, a people brought up to believe that "if we don't bother them they won't bother us" will perceive a "reality" in which being peaceful is the best self-defense. Both perceptions are equally in accord with "human nature."

Each such behavior is subject to positive feedback. In the first case if people *A* do make preemptive strikes against people *B* from time to time, the *B*s will learn that the only way to save their own skin is to strike the *A*s first. Such behavior will provide feedback to the *A*s that they were right in the first place. On the other hand, if the *A*s leave the *B*s alone until and unless the *B*s attack, the *B*s will perceive that they are safe so long as they keep their hands off the *A*s. This feedback to the *A*s confirms their original perception that they will be safe so long as they leave the *B*s alone.

The vast difference in consequences does not lie in "human nature," but in social and perceptual structures. We indicated earlier why it is difficult for powerful nations to shift into the second pattern from the first. But that difficulty also lies in the transactional and perceptual structure of the relationship, not in some immutable human nature.

Another instance of positive feedback has been observed in the cold war between the United States and Russia since World War II. Each nation contains both doves and hawks. A period of dovish behavior by either nation gradually raises the visibility and credibility of doves in the other, while the hawks in either tend to ascend following a period of hawkish behavior in the other.

Inborn urges vs. learning

In the selector of our model we included biological urges, such as the urge for food or sex, and the emotions of love, fear, anger, and frustration. Whereas in other animals many of the related responses are essentially instinctive and highly specific, in the higher apes and man they are increasingly diffuse and unspecific. That is, in man the specific response is determined by learning, by accounting for all the circumstances of the situation, and is not invariant for any particular circumstances. Someone is hungry. But whether he will be overjoyed or nauseated at an offering of stewed cat depends on his training. Many a male feels a compelling urge to seize an attractive female. But overtly he may be embarrassed even to be seen looking at her breasts or thighs. Even the housebroken dog shows a marked difference between impulse and behavior, and the trained Seeing Eye dog can walk past food when hungry, or past a female in heat without missing a step.

We do, of course, have crimes of passion, including some that stem from anger and frustration. Whether frustration will be aroused, however, depends on learned expectations. If I expect my mower to start on the first pull I am frustrated if it takes ten. But if I expect it to take twenty pulls I am delighted when it starts on the tenth. The sheik with a harem may show frustrated rage if he receives no sexual attention for several days. In other societies a husband may go without intercourse during his wife's entire pregnancy and six months thereafter, and display no overt frustration, since in his society that relation is "normal." Under slavery one may accept insults as part of the nature of things, while under other norms an insult calls for a duel to the death. The *inner mechanisms* for frustration and anger are part of human nature. But what triggers them is not.

To return to our main point, modern warfare is not conducted on impulse, but only through a complex of coldly calcualted decisions. The typical soldier does not shoot because he hates the enemy. It is more probable that he hates the enemy (if he does) because his army's propaganda apparatus has deliberately trained him to. In an industrial society anger is more a consequence than a cause of war.

An animal urge for space?

It is sometimes argued that an urge for "living space" provides an inescapable drive to war. The argument may or may not cite the "territorial imperative" (Ardrey 1966) evidenced in many mammals and birds. Whether one feels an urge for more space depends on whether he feels crowded, which for humans is almost totally a matter of learning. Depending on what he is used to, one person may feel crowded if his nearest neighbor is closer than five miles, while someone else does not feel crowded in the same apartment building with five thousand others. Is crowding a function of the number of others who live within ten feet, ten yards, ten blocks, ten miles, or the same nation?

A sense of crowding is related to privacy. Yet the least privacy may occur in a spacious small town and the most in a densely packed city. As the Japanese know so well, space is not a matter of square feet in a room or garden, but of the size and arrangement of what is in it. What has "human nature" and a "need for space" got to do with it? Nothing. There must, of course, be space to grow food. But that is because plants need space, not because humans do, and if food is imported the space may be in another country.

A sense of crowding may also be a function of time and interaction rather than space. You may feel crowded if it takes you 15 minutes to get out of your parking lot, and not at all crowded with the same number of cars if bigger exits get you out in one minute.

Much more could be added. But it should be clear that there is no simple connection between a given human emotion and overt behavior. If a man can temper the close-at-hand impulse to seize food or female because of trained habit, or the learned knowledge that the action will make him worse off, he can also constrain an impulse to shoot some alleged enemy of his country, whom he will probably not even dislike until someone tells him to. Although fighting a foreign invader may seem a simple case, it is advanced social learning, not impulse, that makes one think he would be worse off under the invaders. In France and Denmark during World War II some citizens cooperated with the invading Germans and some resisted them. As between "Fight the invader" and "If you can't lick 'em, join 'em," which represents "human nature"? In some societies, including the Eskimo, warfare never occurs (Honigmann 1959: 506).

A central point of social science is that culturally learned behaviors condition our responses in powerful and detailed ways. With war as with many other things, much behavior that we consider "natural" and "instinctive" is really the internalized tribal voice that we have heard since birth. Some human behavior may even be rational! But more of that in the chapter on culture.

22

THE MARKET ECONOMY

INTRODUCTION

Occasionally one of the rods that holds a felt hammer in our piano breaks. This wooden rod, about an eighth inch in diameter, is glued into a round hole in another small piece of wood, to which is glued the felt hammer that strikes the strings. No rod, no hammer movement, no sound. To put in a new rod the piano tuner (who doubles as repairman) must first squeeze out the remains of the glued-in old one. To do this he uses a tool specially designed to do this particular job very efficiently. But except by chance it has no possible other use.

The glue that holds this wooden rod is different from the glues that hold the label on a bottle of olives, the laminations in a sheet of plywood, or the insoles in a pair of shoes. Furthermore, some of those glues have been developed after long and painful experimentation so that they will do one job very well.

A modern industrial economy turns out millions upon millions of different parts, products, and services. Obviously we do not use as many man-hours or as much material to produce piano-hammer-rod-removers as we do to produce automobiles or food. But who makes the decision? How? How do we make sure that the total amount of steel produced will be enough to make all the desired automobiles plus piano-hammer-rod-removers plus all other steel products, and that we will not have huge piles of steel left over? The same question can be repeated for every basic material, every finished product, and every semifinished component.

If more steel is being produced than is required, how is this fact detected, and who is motivated to reduce output? If too little steel is being

337

produced, how is that fact detected, and who is motivated to produce more? In short, where in the system are the detectors and selectors that constitute its control mechanisms? Among the millions of products and the billions of parts and ingredients that go into them (including labor), how does it happen that everything comes out more or less even? Although the total number of decisions about detail is so vast as to boggle the mind, somehow things *do* come out reasonably well. What is more, things readjust rather quickly to rather large disturbances of the system, such as the energy crisis, even if the readjusted situation is in some ways less pleasant than before.

A conceptually simple but practically very difficult way to coordinate all the parts is to use a central coordinating agency, or planning bureau. This is a formal organization, also known as the bureaucracy approach. A polar extreme is pure informal organization, or market approach, which is conceptually more difficult but probably easier in practice. In informal organization, each low-level controlled subsystem chooses its own behavior in light of its own goals and perceived advantage. The total "decision" for the whole society is the unplanned and uncontrolled outcome of all these actions and interactions. Although no such thing as a pure controlled or a pure uncontrolled system has ever existed or ever will, the former is roughly exemplified by Russia and the latter by the United States. The study of such systems is known as economics, and the system itself is called an economy, or economic system. In this and the next chapter we will discuss uncontrolled economic systems, also known as market systems or decentralized economic systems. In Chapter 24 we will deal with controlled economic systems, sometimes known also as "command" economies or centralized economic systems. The former are also widely referred to as capitalist and the latter as socialist or communist. Because "centralized" and "decentralized," or "market" and "command" seem clearer descriptions, and because capitalist and communist have varied and emotionally charged meanings, we will use the more neutral terms. We will discuss the relatively pure types first and then go into complications and mixtures.

THE MARKET ECONOMY

A and *B* are neighbors. Each wants both potatoes and shoes. There are two main ways to get them. First, each can spend part of his time and effort growing potatoes and part making shoes. Second, *A* could spend all his time growing potatoes while *B* spent all his time making shoes, after which *A* would exchange (say) half of his potatoes for half of *B*'s shoes. In the first case *A* and *B* are independent producing and consuming systems. In the second case *A* and *B* together constitute a social system, within which they interact.

In the Introduction to Part IV we noted that any communication or transaction between two parties constitutes a higher-level system in the form of an informal organization, of which each of the two parties is a component subsystem. But we also noted that for the study of the communication or transaction itself we would ignore the higher-level system and focus on the interaction. We now move to that higher-level system, and at the same time shift attention from the interaction of two parties to the total set of such interactions among all the persons in a whole society. The interactions studied by economics are primarily selfish transactions in marketable goods, and a market system is the whole uncontrolled system consisting of such transactions, along with the associated transformations and communications.

In our initial model of the transaction we assumed that the necessary communications take place but did not explicitly discuss them. We likewise took for granted that the automobile had been produced, but did not discuss how. The economist's study of market systems similarly focuses on the transactional aspects of interactions and ignores or plays down the communicational and transformational aspects. But since a transaction consists of a pair of mutually contingent decisions, economics does attend to the cost/benefit positions of the parties that lead them to make those decisions.

Our earlier discussion of transactions included exchanges of both highly personal and highly impersonal goods. Affection and respect illustrate the former, whose values are strongly related to the particular persons involved. A cubic yard of concrete or an ounce of gold illustrate the latter, whose value is dependent solely on the nature of the items themselves. Goods whose value to the receiver is the same regardless of who provides them are *marketable goods,* or readily exchangeable goods. The study of markets deals with marketable goods, not with highly personal ones. It also deals with private goods, even though governments may be either sellers or buyers of some private goods. Pure uncontrolled market systems are also known as laissez-faire economies, in which government lets individuals do as they please in producing, buying, and selling marketable goods. Government nevertheless does outlaw force, violence, and theft in these private transactions, which means that market systems deal in goods, not bads—hence the early description of a market system as "anarchy plus a constable." Government also enforces promises between transacting parties, as by deciding law suits for breach of contract. This self-oriented activity by individuals and firms which nevertheless produces an intricately coordinated overall system is the respect in which a market economy is the logical parallel of an ecological system.

The study of a market system is thus seen as the study of the uncontrolled social system which consists of the network of selfish transactions in private marketable goods, in which promises to deliver (notably including promises to pay) are legally enforceable. Because of the net effect of this set of transactions, along with the associated transformations which produce the goods that are exchanged, the market system can also be described as the social system through which humans satisfy their wants for exchangeable goods from the resources provided by nature—which is the more traditional definition of an economic system.

From Robinson Crusoe to markets

The beginning of this section implied that there can be no market unless there is first division of labor, or specialization. If everyone produced everything he wanted and only what he wanted, there would be no basis for trade. Only when one person produces more of one thing and less of something else than he wants will he wish to give up some of what he has in return for something that someone else has. A market system thus involves the same basic principle of differentiation and coordination that we have observed in other kinds of systems. Specialization is the differentiation and trade the coordination.

In a figurative sense even a person living entirely alone, Robinson Crusoe style, specializes, in that he spends part of his time in providing food, part in building shelter, and so on. But in the stricter sense, he does not specialize, since everything he has he has produced (or collected) for himself. All known societies, however, show specialization within the family. Some is inescapable in that young children cannot hunt, fish, weave, or cook, but may pick berries or carry corn. Even in very simple societies there is division of labor between men and women, with the males typically doing hunting and the females preparing food and caring for children. A craft-level economy may show specialization among families, with some doing dairying while others do weaving, carpentering, baking, and the like, after which they exchange their outputs.

In more complex societies much production is done in business firms.

"But this is my livelihood!"

Drawing by Stan Hunt; © 1974 The New Yorker Magazine, Inc.

Here, too, there is division of labor, in which some persons (in, say, a clothing factory) cut while others sew, design, sell, buy, sweep, repair machinery, type, ship, or keep books. There is specialization among firms, in which some produce steel, some clothing, some TV repairs, some motion pictures, some piano-hammer-rod-removers, and so on. On a larger geographic scale there is also specialization by region or nation. Thus some areas grow corn and cattle, others forests, others produce light manufactured products, others heavy products like steel and automobiles, and so on.

The most important change in social organization that distinguishes modern industrial society from simple tribal society is that production has shifted from households to business firms, or enterprises. In tribal societies, as well as feudal ones, both production and consumption occur within the family group. In an industrial society, however, production is carried on by separate organizations—enterprises—while consumption activities remain within the family. Several important things happen in the transition.

For one thing, people cease to work for themselves and work for someone else. For another, transactions shift from a barter to a money basis, in which each person works for money, and then uses it to buy things he wants. Third, when one works for someone else he becomes dependent on others, both for a job and for the goods he consumes. Fourth, the individual worker becomes a small cog in the productive machine. Fifth, the people who own and manage enterprises generally come to have much more wealth and power than those who work for them. Sixth, the family changes, since when people do their main work outside of it they have less time for contacts within it. Seventh, there is a shift from personal relationships between people who know each other to the highly impersonal interactions of the market, while generous and hostile relationships largely give way to selfish-indifferent ones.

Along with other details this kind of change has been described by Polanyi (1944), who called it the Great Transformation. Some of today's youth dislike the consequences, and through communes and other arrangements seek more personal relationships. Others find the simpler life dull and economically much less efficient.

Having briefly sketched the change from nonmarket to market relationships, we now examine the latter.

Firms as coordinators

A firm is a formal profit organization, whose sponsors' goal is to purchase inputs from factor suppliers, transform them into goods (commodities or services), and sell those goods as outputs to recipient customers for an amount greater than the cost of the inputs. The difference between the receipts from customers and the payments to factor suppliers is the profit, which goes to the sponsors. Receipt of that profit is the goal of the sponsors and the purpose of forming and operating the organization. If the income from the sale of output is less than the costs of inputs, the profit is negative, a loss, which must somehow be absorbed by the sponsors. As noted (Chapter 15), factor suppliers provide the inputs through selfish transactions and will stop providing them if they are not paid for. If the sponsors cannot get the money to pay factor suppliers, the firm will eventually close for lack of inputs. By making decisions about these things, firms perform the principal coordinating function of a market system, as detailed below.

"Profit," incidentally, refers solely to this positive or negative difference between the values of outputs and inputs. The wages or salaries paid to staff are income to employees but are not profits. The desire to receive a wage is an *income motive,* not a profit motive, and is essentially the same whether one works for a private profit firm, a government, a nonprofit private organization, or a socialist enterprise. Similarly, the desire for income by factor suppliers who lend money or rent out their land or buildings is not a profit motive. The *profit motive,* by contrast, applies solely to the sponsors of firms, which are found mainly in market economies. Partial market economies are sometimes found within basically socialized nations, as in black markets, handicrafts, and some of the agricultural production in the Soviet Union.

A firm almost never sells exactly the same things it buys. Manufacturing firms buy materials, labor, and other ingredients and transform them into finished products. They might be thought of as selling mainly the service of transforming inputs into outputs. A repair shop buys such things as labor and replacement parts and sells the service of repair. Although a retailer sells the same physical items he buys he is also selling such services as warehousing, breaking bulk, and displaying merchandise.

If the market value of inputs to a firm is $8 and the market value of its outputs is $10, the firm can be said to have created $2 in value in the process of converting inputs into outputs. Conversely, if a firm converts $8 worth of inputs into $6 worth of outputs it has destroyed $2 of value. Thus in seeking to make a profit, a firm seeks to create value rather than to destroy it. Who receives this value cannot be answered easily, though generally if the firm is a monopoly it will get most of it, while under competition consumers will get most of it.

We noted (Chapter 17) that an ecological system is the prototype model of informal organization. In ecological language, the dominant species in the economic forest are firms, households, banks, and governments —all controlled subsystems. For the moment we will deal only with households and firms. A household (or spending unit) is the rough equivalent of a family, although it can consist of a smaller unit, such as a single individual, or of a larger unit, such as an orphanage. It is normally a collection of persons who pool their incomes and expenditures and who live in the same premises.

All persons in a market economy are members of some household. In that capacity they provide factor inputs to firms by selling the use of their labor, their money, or their property. In return they receive income from firms. Households that are sponsors (owners) of firms may also receive profits. With the money thus received, households purchase outputs of firms in the form of consumer goods. For this introductory discussion we will omit transactions between firms, such as sales by a steel company to an automobile manufacturer or of cloth by a weaving mill to a clothing factory. We will also omit direct sales from one household to another, as in the case of a household servant, or of a home gardener selling surplus tomatoes to his neighbor.

The dual relation of households and firms

The dual relation between citizens and government has a parallel in a dual relation between households and firms. We diagram the relation as follows.

Figure 22–1
RELATIONS BETWEEN HOUSEHOLDS AND FIRMS

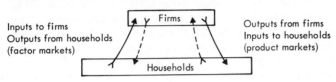

Inputs to firms
Outputs from households
(factor markets)

Outputs from firms
Inputs to households
(product markets)

The solid arrows represent the flow of goods. The broken arrows represent the opposite flow of the money that pays for them. The left-hand flow represents the total set of transactions through which factor suppliers provide inputs to firms. These transactions collectively constitute factor markets. The right-hand flow represents the total set of transactions through which the goods produced by firms become inputs to households. Collectively these constitute product markets.

Two differences should be noted between this economic relation and the political one between citizens and government. First, whereas nearly all citizens may be sponsors of government, only a relatively few households are sponsors (or at least active sponsors) of firms. Second, whereas the flows of goods from firms to their recipients consist of private goods transferred through individually agreed-upon transactions, those from government to citizens are largely public goods not individually agreed upon, and are paid for involuntarily through taxes. Furthermore, in product markets the flow of any one good is tied explicitly to payment for that good by its recipient, whereas with government the relation between good and payment is not usually explicit. If the two are explicitly related, as when households are charged a sewage fee, the government is behaving like a firm, albeit a monopoly.

To envisage the central role of firms in a market economy let us return for a moment to a lone household, pioneer style. Its decisions about what to produce are almost indistinguishable from its decisions about what to consume, since the household will presumably decide to produce only those things that it wants to consume.

In a market economy the household does not make direct decisions about what to produce. Instead it decides to sell its productive services to a firm, regardless of whether that firm produces anything the household wants. The household then makes decisions about consumption when it spends the money it earned by selling its productive services.

A market economy thus separates decisions about production and consumption within the *individual* household. But firms then coordinate these decisions for the collectivity of *all* households. Firms look at all households to see what the households will buy in their role as consumers, and attempt to produce what they (the firms) can sell to the households. Firms also look at households to see what the households can provide in their role of factor suppliers, and then buy from households the factors with which to produce what households will buy.

The manager of each firm must deal with the question: Will households (in their role as consumers) pay me enough for a good I produce to enable me to pay the price that households (in thir role as factor suppliers) must be paid for producing it?

One result of the market is both an expansion and a contraction of choices to households. The expansion is that each household has available a far wider choice of occupations and consumer goods than if it tried to produce everything for itself. The contraction is that when one works for someone else he loses much discretion as to when, how much, and how hard he will work.

In performing this coordinating function, firms occupy a unique position. To contrast it with that of households, when a person in a household decides to sell his labor he must compare the objective benefit in the form of money received with the subjective costs in time, effort, acceptance of authority, and so on, of holding the job. Similarly, when a householder decides to buy a good he must compare the objective money cost with the subjective benefit in satisfaction received. In both cases the overall decision is essentially subjective because the evaluation of one of the two things compared is subjective.

By contrast, the firm can compare the objective benefit of money received for its outputs with the objective cost of money paid for its inputs. If a firm cannot make sensible decisions when its costs and benefits are both measurable in the one-dimensional, cardinally quantifiable units of money, it is difficult to imagine how or when sensible decisions can be made. No other person or organization occupies such a position, and it is no accident that decision theory arose from the economic theory of the firm. More precisely, decision theory reflects the theoretical model of the firm, which considers only those costs or benefits that *are* measurable in money. Real firms, of course, have other costs and benefits, including pride, risk, a sense of accomplishment, friendships, and the prestige of executives.

The above relations can be summarized as follows:

Consumers:	Benefits	Subjective	(satisfaction in goods purchased)
	Costs	Objective	(money paid for goods)
Firms:	Benefits	Objective	(money received from sales)
	Costs	Objective	(money paid for factors)
Factor suppliers:	Benefits	Objective	(money wage received)
	Costs	Subjective	(time, effort, sweat, risk, discipline, etc.)

THE NETWORK OF MUTUALLY CONTINGENT DECISIONS

The initial model of transactions explains how a ratio of exchange is established between two parties. A market is an aggregation of competitive[1] transactions, and establishes a ratio of exchange as among a large number of buyers and sellers of some product. In a money economy this ratio of exchange is its money price. Product markets establish the prices at which firms sell their outputs to households, while factor markets establish the prices at which households sell their outputs to firms. The profit of a firm is based on the difference between the prices of its inputs and its outputs. Similarly the "profit" of a household (its standard of living or economic welfare) depends on the prices it receives for its factor outputs compared to the prices it pays for its product inputs. Since product prices are generally the same for households of different incomes, the transactions which determine the market prices of factors thus determine the relative real incomes of different households. That is, when factor markets determine that the executive will earn $25 an hour and the auto worker $5 they are determining who will get how much of the total output of the economic system. By the same token, factor markets distribute or allocate the total real income of a nation among its households, and determine who is poor, rich, or in between. This is another way of describing FOR WHOM the products are produced.

Product markets determine the prices of products. Firms then compare the prices they receive for a product with the costs of producing it. If the cost exceeds the selling price, they will eventually stop producing it. If the selling price exceeds the cost, they will continue to produce it, or possibly increase production. This process thus determines WHAT is produced.

Products can be made using different combinations of factors. A ditch can be dug with pick and shovel, using relatively little equipment and much labor. Or it can be dug with a trenching machine, using relatively much equipment and little labor. Automobile bodies can be made of steel, fiberglass, or aluminum; milk can be distributed in glass, plastic, or paper containers; and a television set can be put together by one person at a bench or by several dozen on an assembly line. What factors firms use determine HOW products are produced.

Whereas in a simple nonexchange economy these questions of WHAT, HOW, and FOR WHOM are answered separately within each household, in a market economy they are answered by the interaction of all firms and households, the households acting in both their producer and consumer roles. The exchange ratio, or EXCHANGE PRICE, of products is determined in product markets, as we have seen. WHAT, HOW MUCH, HOW, FOR WHOM, and AT WHAT PRICE are fundamental questions in any economy, and we have indicated how they are decided in a market economy.

Total and particular incomes

In a nonmarket economy the real income of each household consists of the total set of goods produced by the household, which output depends on its productive power (Chapter 14). A whole market economy behaves

---

[1] "Competitive" here means the same as defined in Chapter 11, not the economist's model of perfect competition.

something like a household in this respect. We could also say that a household that does not engage in transactions is itself a whole economy.

For a large market economy let us imagine that everything it produces, services as well as commodities, is thrown onto a huge heap. The size of the heap depends on the productive power of the people, including their equipment and knowledge, taken in conjunction with the available natural resources. The total real income of the people consists of this heap of produced goods; their total income *is* their output. This amount divided by the number of persons is the average, or per capita, income.

The heap is not distributed equally, however, in two senses. First, people do not all want the same things. If A wants rat traps but no ski boots while B wants ski boots but no rat traps, A and B receive a different product mix. The only way to measure which one gets *more* is to put money prices on each item, and if two households get the same total money value from the pile, we say they have received equal real icomes. The second type of inequality is that different households receive different total amounts of value, reflecting differences in the prices they receive for the factors they provide, differences in the quantities they provide, or both.

According to the theory of market systems each household is allowed to take from the heap a total value equal to the value it has contributed. If so, the logic is basically the same in a market as in a nonmarket system: the amount of goods available to a family is equal to the amount it produces. But the amount is also subject to the complication of measuring the contribution of a person who works on one specalized job. How much is contributed to the heap by the person who tightens bolt #572 on an automobile assembly line or who interviews applicants for jobs?

Again the answer is simple in theory, as described in Chapter 15 under the heading "More than two members—and marginalism." The contribution of one person in a complex organization is measured by taking him away and observing how much the total output goes down. If one person does not make a noticeable difference, take away ten, a hundred, or a thousand and divide the loss of product by the number of persons removed. Conversely, a person's contribution could be measured by adding him and observing how much the total product goes up. Either way, in the economist's language the payment to a given factor tends to equal its marginal productivity, and in a broad way a market economy does work this way.

Quantities and prices of particular products (supply and demand)

A transaction involves two mutually contingent decisions: A's decision that he would prefer Y to X and B's decision that he would prefer X to Y. When we shift attention to a whole network of transactions in a market, these decisions become questions of quantity: how much money to give for a given factor or product, and how many units to buy, make, or sell.

As the household (acting as consumer) acquires more units of any particular good, the utility of successive units goes down and the cost

Figure 22–2
COSTS AND BENEFITS TO THE CONSUMER OF VARIOUS
COMBINATIONS OF HAMBURGERS AND OTHER GOODS

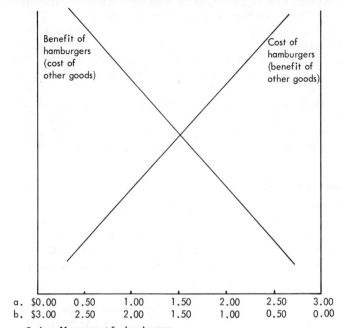

Scale a: Money spent for hamburgers.
Scale b: Money left for other goods.

goes up, as illustrated for hamburgers and milkshakes in Figure 8–1. In
a money economy we illustrate the same principle with one good, hamburgers, and money. Until money is spent it represents a potential claim
on any goods that might be purchased with it. As the consumer spends
more money on hamburgers he has less left for other things, as shown
in Figure 22–2. The rising cost curve for hamburgers does not mean a
higher money price for additional hamburgers, but rather the sacrifice
of more units of other things, whose marginal value rises as he receives
fewer of them.

Because consumers receive diminishing utility from larger quantities
of any given good they will be willing to purchase larger quantities only
at lower prices. Three other factors add to the effect. First, at high prices
only the relatively rich will buy, whereas at low prices the poor can also
buy. Second, at high prices only those with intense desires for a good will
buy it, whereas at low prices it will also be bought by those with weaker
desires. And third, at high prices consumers will seek substitute goods,
whereas at low prices they will not bother.

For all these reasons consumers collectively will buy more of a good
at lower prices than at higher prices. This relationship between the price
of a good and the quantity people will buy is the *demand* for that good,
and is a *demand curve* when plotted on a graph. As seen through the eyes

of sellers, firms can sell more of their output only at lower prices. As with the consumer, the firm thus receives a smaller and smaller benefit from each additional unit. If any one firm does not face this situation, the sum of all firms which produce that good do face it.

On the cost side the firm will find that as it increases output its total costs per unit will typically fall for a while as its fixed costs are spread over more units. But beyond some point the costs of additional units will rise as the firm tries to squeeze out more units, mainly (though not solely) because of diminishing productivity.

Hence the firm also faces decreasing marginal benefits and increasing marginal costs as it handles larger quantities. Its most profitable position is at the point where marginal cost and marginal benefit (revenue) are equal—again, for reasons spelled out in Chapter 8.

And of particular factors

As between firms and households a similar pair of contingent decisions occurs in factor markets. To use labor as an example, both individually and collectively households will find declining utility from extra income as they provide more man-hours of work. And as they do so they will have fewer hours left for rest and recreation, the sacrifice of which will be increasingly costly.

Firms that buy labor will find the benefit of additional units going down, because of diminishing productivity and possibly because they will have to lower the price of the product to sell the larger output. The cost of successive units will go up, partly because greater expenditures for labor will leave the firms less money for the purchase of other factors, and partly because they will have to pay successively higher prices for the more reluctantly supplied labor. With some complications unique to each the same rationale also applies to the other factor inputs, land and capital investment.

Thus in both factor and product markets the buyers will take larger quantities only at lower prices, while the sellers will provide larger quantities only at higher prices. When these collective decisions, or willingnesses, to buy and sell are plotted they are supply and demand curves, as in Figure 22–3. Price, which is the measure of value in a price system,

Figure 22–3
A SUPPLY AND DEMAND CURVE FOR A PRODUCT
OR FACTOR

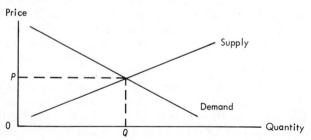

is shown on the vertical scale, and quantity on the horizontal, as in Chapter 8. Given this set of willingnesses to buy and sell, the quantity actually bought and sold will be that at Q, while the price will be that at P. The supply curve represents what sellers are willing to do, and the demand curve represents what buyers are willing to do. The intersection is the only thing *both* are willing to do: the only point which is mutually satisfactory, and on which collective agreement can be reached. Directly or indirectly, all demand curves represent benefits and all supply curves represent costs.

Why equilibrium?

In Figure 22–4 we can see what would happen if either the price or the quantity happened to fall at some point other than this intersection. Every point on a demand curve represents both a quantity (read on the horizontal axis) and a price (read on the vertical axis). Any point on that line represents the quantity that customers would be willing to purchase at that price. Any point on a supply curve similarly represents the quantity that firms would be willing to offer for sale at that price. Now let us see what would happen if either the price or the quantity happened to be set at some point other than the intersection. Suppose, for example, the price happened to be set at level P_2. We can see from the points where the P_2 line intersects the demand and supply curves that at this price consumers would be willing to buy only the quantity Q_1, whereas sellers would offer Q_2. The quantity represented by the distance between Q_1 and

Figure 22–4
PRICES AND QUANTITIES AT OTHER THAN THE
EQUILIBRIUM LEVEL

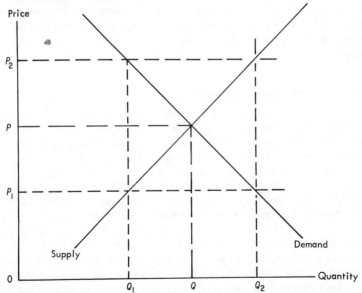

Q_2 would be offered for sale but remain unsold, exerting a downward pressure on prices, in response to which sellers would reduce the quantity offered for sale.

Suppose instead that the price happened to be set at P_1. At this price only the quantity Q_1 would be offered for sale, but customers would be seeking to buy the quantity Q_2. All units offered would be bought, and customers would still be looking for more. They would bid up the price, which would induce additional output by sellers. As between the two situations, any price above P would exert a downward pressure on the price and any price below P would exert an upward pressure on it. At that price everyone willing to buy would be able to do so and everyone willing to sell would also be able to do so. Since at P there is no pressure for change, that is the equilibrium price.

What would happen if the quantity happened to fall above or below the equilibrium? Suppose quantity Q_1 happened to be produced. At this quantity sellers would be willing to sell for price P_1, while buyers would be willing to pay P_2, and the discrepancy would exert an upward pressure on price. If the quantity happened to fall at Q_2, sellers would not be willing to sell for less than P_2, while buyers would not be willing to pay more than P_1, and the discrepancy would exert a downward pressure on both price and quantity. Again, only at quantity Q would there be no pressure for a change. As Boulding (1958) put it, at this point anyone with the will to change things lacks the power and anyone with the power lacks the will. Anyone with the preference half of an EP lacks the effective half, and vice versa.

Importantly, this uncontrolled relationship is self-correcting. No central authority need detect a discrepancy between quantity supplied and quantity demanded, and issue orders to correct it. By pushing down prices, the presence of unsold units induces sellers to produce less and buyers to buy more, thus removing the discrepancy. The presence of unmet consumer desires pushes the price up, which induces sellers to produce more and buyers to buy less, again tending to remove the discrepancy.

From *EP*s to supply and demand

A market is an aggregation of transactions, which we analyzed initially in terms of effective preferences. We started to show a connection between *EP*s of particular transactions and market supply and demand in Chapter 11 when we dealt with competition among several *B*s dealing with a single *A*. To describe a market we need only add multiple *A*s to the multiple *B*s. These are shown in Figure 22–5, with all *EP*s arranged in order from the shortest to the longest. As usual, the *A*s are customers and the *B*s sellers. The product is a particular style of black-and-white television set, all units of which are sufficiently similar that no customer cares which one he buys. Prices are marked across the top. Customer *A*-18 shows a willingness to pay only $55. His *EP* may be short because he has only a low desire for the set, because he has little money, or because he already has two other sets and (under diminishing utility)

Figure 22–5
FROM *EP*S TO SUPPLY AND DEMAND

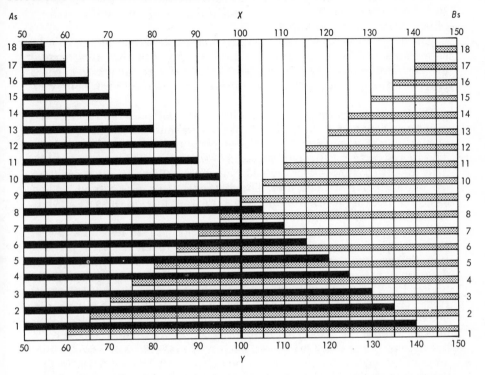

will buy a third only at a low price. The longer *EP*s represent successively
larger amounts of money (the effective aspect) or successively stronger
desires (the preference aspect) of either the same or different people.

Seller *B*-18 will not accept less than $145, presumably because he is
a high-cost producer and would lose money if he sold for less. The longer
*EP*s of the *B*s represent successively lower-cost producers, ending with
B-1, who is willing to sell for only $60.

A-18 could not get a TV set, since he will pay no more than $55, and
no seller will accept less than $60. However, if by chance *A*-17 happened
to get together with *B*-1, a sale would be possible at $60. Similarly, if
A-1 happened to get together with *B*-17, a sale would be possible at $140.
But if all buyers and sellers observe all other buyers and sellers, the
*EP*s on both sides will shorten to or toward the best alternative available
on the other side—as noted in Chapter 11.

After some jockeying in which the low numbered *A*s discover that they
can actually get TV sets for less than they are willing to pay and the
low-numbered *B*s discover that they can actually sell TV sets for prices
higher than they are willing to accept, the price would stabilize at $100
and ten units would be sold. All the *A*s above *A*-10 would have to do
without TV sets, and all the *B*s above *B*-10 would stop producing. In short,

if we draw a line connecting the tips of all the *EP*s of the *A*s we have a demand curve, while a line connecting the tips of all the *EP*s of the *B*s is a supply curve. The two intersect at a price of $100 and a quantity of ten, which is the equilibrium.[2]

The above illustration said nothing about the length of time, and may have sounded like a one-shot situation. To think of this as a normal market we need merely assume that the *EP*s of both buyers and sellers represent the number who would appear in the market each hour, day, week, or other period.

Earlier in the chapter we raised the question about who receives the difference between the values of the inputs and outputs of a firm. We can now answer this question somewhat better with the help of Figure 22–5. The *EP*s of buyers 1 through 8 extend beyond the market price of $100. This means that those eight would have been willing to pay more than the market price, if necessary. The distances their *EP*s extend beyond $100 is a measure of their subjective gain from buying the sets at $100, and is known as *consumer surplus.*

Subject to some complications we need not go into here, the lowest price at which a firm will be willing to sell a product is its cost of production, and we will assume that the limits of the *EP*s of sellers in this diagram represent their costs. All sellers (*B*s) with the number 10 or higher have costs of production that are higher than the market price. Hence they will not produce, and presumably will go out of business in due time. *B*-9 shows costs just equal to his price received, and he will take neither a profit nor a loss. All remaining *B*s from 8 on down show costs lower than the market price, and each will make a profit equal to the amount by which his own *EP* extends to the left beyond $100. In this arbitrarily symmetrical diagram the total "surplus" received by consumers equals the total profit received by producers. The profit to each producer represents the amount by which he is able to produce at lower cost (i.e., more efficiently) than the competitor whose costs just equal the market price, and may also be thought of as his reward for doing so.[3]

Decision by dollar ballots

The market process is often said to make decisions by dollar ballots. Every time a consumer spends money for any good he is casting a ballot

---

[2] The alert reader will have noted that in this diagram the price is on the horizontal and the quantity on the vertical axis, which is the reverse of the supply and demand curves presented above. This fact creates no problem. Whichever way the axes are arranged, the demand curve slopes downward and the supply curve upward, since the former is an inverse relation between quantity and price and the latter is a direct relation. For those who wish to make the connection more explicit, it is only necessary to reverse the positions of buyers and sellers on the diagram, drawing the scale of prices to read from right to left, and then turn the diagram 90 degrees clockwise.

[3] The reader may note that we are merely describing the nature and consequences of the market process; we are not passing ethical judgment on it. We are also assuming competitive factor markets, in which all firms pay the same price for inputs, which is the basis for saying that a lower cost of production represents superior efficiency.

"Whenever I'm in the dumps, I just sit back and think of my hundred and fifty million dollars."

Drawing by Whitney Darrow, Jr.; © 1973 The New Yorker Magazine, Inc.

in favor of having it produced, and the more dollars he spends on it the more ballots he casts. The ballots are counted on the cash registers of sellers, who are thereby both instructed and motivated to produce more. Goods that consumers want less have fewer or no ballots cast for them, and sellers are thereby instructed and motivated to curtail producing them.

This process conveys much more information about people's desires than does political decision making. Whereas a voter marks no more than a dozen to a score of Xs on ballots within a year, he casts dollar ballots day in and day out, often expressing more preferences in a day than his political ballots express in a year. This is not to suggest that we could substitute dollar ballots for political ones, since the latter deal with public goods.

Nevertheless, the fact that each person can experience the direct consequences of his dollar ballots while the consequences of his political ballot are often indirect and remote probably places a bias (perhaps unwarranted) in favor of private and against public goods. However, the rich cast more ballots in the market than do the poor, while rich and poor cast one ballot per person in the political decision process. Perhaps it is not unexpected therefore that the rich typically preach social salvation through the market while the poor show more confidence in salvation through government. Like many other problems, this is also subject to mixtures, as when the poor use their political ballots to reallocate dollars and the rich use their dollars to modify the direction and effects of political ballots.

We have also noted that social decisons made through the voting process are often intransitive, and hence in a sense irrational (Chapter 15). We can now amplify our previous statement that social decisions made through the market process are, by contrast, transitive, and hence more rational. By this we mean simply that if the market value of a ton of wheat is greater than that of a ton of corn, which is greater than that of a ton of cement, we can then conclude with certainty that a ton of wheat has greater value than a ton of cement. We have already shown how and why the market values of items do represent a social decision, which reflects the individual values both of those who provide the factors of production and of those who want the products. We also indicated in Chapter 15 that group decisions made through transaction are more acceptable, other things equal, than those made through a dominant coalition. Perhaps that same greater acceptability applies as well at this much larger level, at which the market process is the transactional one and the political process the coalitional. This general conclusion is, however, subject to important reservations about market systems detailed in the next chapter.

SOME AGGREGATE ASPECTS OF MARKETS (MACROECONOMICS)

Thus far we have have not dealt with the whole of a market economy, but only with subsystems of it: firms and households. In the preceding section we looked at supply and demand for a particular product. This includes all sellers of the same product, who together constitute a larger system known as an industry, which is an uncontrolled system if it is competitive. Certain other problems, however, concern the total of all firms, all households, and all industries. These are aggregative problems, and are studied under the heading *macroeconomics,* in contrast to the heading *microeconomics,* which is given to the study of the subsystems. Under the heading of macroeconomics we will look briefly at two problems, money and employment.

Money

Although it came into use through an evolutionary process, in light of our present knowledge we can define *money* as anything readily acceptable as a medium of exchange. This medium of exchange, like the medium in a communication, goes *between* some beginning and ending point. To illustrate, if in a particular exchange A gives up a goat in return for wheat because he wants the wheat, the wheat is not acting as a medium of exchange. But if he accepts wheat for his goat when he does not want wheat, but because he will later exchange the wheat for shoes, he is treating the wheat as a medium—it goes *between* giving up the goat and receiving the shoes. If people generally accept wheat for what they give up, because they know they can later exchange it for something else, wheat is *readily acceptable.* Being both a medium and readily acceptable, wheat then constitutes money.

This relation can be stated in more general transactional form. In a nonmoney transaction A gives X to B in return for Y. In a money transaction A gives X to B in return for M, a medium of exchange, after which A gives M to C in return for Y. The barter exchange of X for Y is more direct, and is satisfactory in a society with few goods. The indirect exchange of X for M and then M for Y is vastly more flexible when a society has many goods. For example, if my car is not functioning well, I might have difficulty finding someone who would be willing to give me a rebuilt carburetor in exchange for some instruction in unified social science, and then finding someone else who would install the carburetor in return for similar instruction. A "double coincidence of wants" is the traditional language for the conditions necessary for a barter exchange.

Over the centuries many substances have been used for money. We now know, however, that something need not have value in itself to perform this function. Money is merely a bookkeeping device. In our age of checking accounts and credit cards most money consists of nothing more than numbers on the books or magnetic tapes of banks. Two illustrations will suffice.

We tried above to visualize the economic process in terms of a heap of goods. One way to understand money is to imagine that everyone who makes a contribution to this heap is given a receipt indicating the value of his contribution. When he wants some of those goods for himself he presents his receipt and is allowed to withdraw an amount of goods equal in value to what he contributed. If we imagine a manager of this heap, the receipt he gives is his promise that in return for value received he will give an equivalent value when requested by any holder of the receipt.

As a second illustration, at one point two of my sons had borrowed money from me. During that period one of them needed a car and the other wanted to sell one. The second offered it to the first for $150. "But I haven't got any money just now," said the first. Said the second, "I'll subtract $150 from what I owe Dad, and you add $150 to what you owe him." Presto, the car changed hands and was paid for—in money! The vast bulk of money now in use in the United States and other industrial nations similarly consists of promises to pay, or credit. The main difference is that it is the credit of banks and governments. Their credit ratings, unlike my sons', are good enough to be "readily acceptable," and thus qualify as money.

The use of credit as money takes numerous forms. The following scenario represents the nature and origins of the vast majority of money now in use in market economies. A bank makes a loan to a customer, if it is confident he will repay. The customer gives the bank his promissory note. The bank gives the cutomer a deposit credit for the amount of the loan, the deposit credit being the bank's promise to pay the amount of the deposit to the customer or to someone designated by him. The customer then writes checks against this deposit. These checks are next deposited by the people who receive them, and the bank's promise to pay is transferred from the account of the original borrower to the accounts of the people who were paid by the checks. The typical borrowing of money from a bank is an exchange of the bank's promise to pay for the customer's promise to pay. Because of its higher credit rating the bank's promise to pay is readily accepted, whereas the customer's is not. In borrowing from the bank, the customer has exchanged his lower credit rating for the bank's higher credit rating, thus raising his promise to pay to a level of acceptability that qualifies it as money. For similar reasons, if a government is reliable its promise to pay also constitutes money.

The supply of money is thus potentially unlimited. Banks collectively can increase it by making more loans, with the reservation that no one bank can increase its loans proportionally faster than other banks or it will shortly be in trouble—for reasons we need not detail here. A national government can increase it by printing paper money, which is non-interest-bearing promissory notes. (The United States used to issue some paper money redeemable in gold or silver. It no longer does, gold certificates having been made unredeemable and taken out of circulation in 1935, and silver certificates having been withdrawn during the 1960s.) A national government also has other techniques for creating money, principally by using its treasury department like a bank. Because unlimited money would create unlimited inflation, governments use various devices to limit banks in creating money, which we also need not discuss here.

Does the quantity of money matter? Or its speed?

The main problem that arises from possible increases in the amount of money can be readily visualized if we return to our first illustration of the nature of money—as receipts for goods deposited on the national heap. To avoid large numbers let us assume that $100 worth of goods in total has been deposited on the heap. Let us also assume that for some reason $200 worth of receipts has been given to those who provided these goods. When the latter come for their shares they would take away the entire pile for $100 and still have $100 worth of receipts for which there is nothing left to take. Since the receipts are of no value except as claims for goods on the heap, holders of the receipts would begin to offer more than a dollar's worth of receipts for each dollar's worth of goods. Things would come out even in this case only if they offered an average of two dollar's worth of receipts for every original dollar's worth of goods. Conversely, if only $50 worth of receipts were for some reason given in return for the deposit of $100 worth of goods, people would redeem all their claims and still leave $50 worth of goods on the heap. In this case things would come out even only if the entire heap were given in return for the $50.

The first situation represents the equivalent of doubling the supply of money while the quantity of goods remains unchanged. The result is that the price of everything would double, which is the same as saying that the value of money has declined by half. This situation can also be described as 100 percent inflation or the "50-cent dollar." On the other hand, if the quantity of money changes by the same relative amount as does the quantity of goods, there is no change in the value of money. Hence to avoid a decline in prices we need a steady increase in the quantity of money as the output of goods increases.

An important complication is that money changes hands repeatedly. Just as a 50-passenger bus can move 100 passengers if it makes two trips a day and 500 passengers if it makes ten trips, so can a given amount of money do more "money work" if it changes hands more often. The number of times money changes hands during a given period (usually figured as a year) is called its *velocity,* and the *effective quantity* in circulation is the actual quantity (or stock) multiplied by its velocity (or flow rate). A rise or fall in the velocity of money thus has the same effect as a rise or fall in its quantity. As in physics, the effective force exerted by a given body depends on both its mass and its velocity.

Inflation and deflation: Nature and effects

Despite complications, the value of money changes basically because of a change in the effective quantity of money relative to the quantity of goods to be exchanged. Other causes may initiate a change in the value of money, but unless a change in the ratio of goods and money is eventually produced, the effect will probably not be permanent.

Except for some difficulties of bookkeeping changes in the value of money would be of no consequence if everything changed simultaneously. For example, if all prices suddenly doubled but at the same moment you also had twice as much money as before, you would be neither better nor worse off. But if you sell something in return for money, and if the value of money declines by 50 percent (the general level of prices doubles) before you have spent the money, you suffer a loss equal to the amount of money you held during that period of change. For example, if you have saved $200 for a TV set, and the price of the set rises to $400 before you buy it, you have lost $200 of value, measured at the new price level.

The effect is the same if you hold a claim payable to you in money. Suppose you sold the TV set to someone who promised to pay you a month hence. During the month all prices double. The TV set is now worth $400. But at the end of the month he will pay you only $200 for it, and you will have lost half the value of the set. In short, if prices double between the time a debt is contracted and the time it is paid, the debtor has to pay only half as much effective value as he received and the creditor receives only half as much effective value as he gave. If prices were to be cut in half during the same period, the gain and loss would be reversed. Changes in the value of money thus redistribute real income.

A theoretical way of avoiding this result would be to have all money obligations change by the same amount as the price level. For example, the person who bought your TV set would have agreed that if prices doubled during the month he would pay you twice as many dollars ($400) and that if prices dropped by 50 percent you would accept half as many dollars ($100). Such arrangements might be feasible for some relatively long-term loans, but would be impossibly complicated for small, short-term loans. Installment loans would be particularly confusing, since the amount of the installment payment might have to change every month during rapid price changes. Even so, such arrangements would be equitable only if all wages, salaries, rents, insurance premiums, and other obligations were also to change at the same rate as the price level. Since it does not seem feasible to put everything under such "escalator" clauses, changes in the value of money will unavoidably bring discriminatory shifts of value between payers and receivers of money, and between debtors and creditors.

Changes in price level, which mean changes in the overall value of money and which at the retail level are measured by the Consumer Price Index, are not to be confused with changes in the price of particular goods. In the former case the relative value of all goods remains unchanged. If a particular automobile was worth a thousand bushels of wheat before the change in price level it is still worth a thousand bushels after the change, because the money prices of wheat and of automobiles have changed by the same percentage amount. By contrast, if the price of wheat were $2 to begin with and then dropped to $1, while the price of cars and everything else remained unchanged, the car would now be worth 2000 bushels of wheat. That is a change in the price (of wheat) but not in the price level, and not in the overall value of money. To illustrate both, between 1930 and 1970 the prices of things in general roughly quadrupled, while the price of chewing gum remained unchanged at a nickel a pack. We can then say that the *money price* of chewing gum remained unchanged, that the *price level* rose to four times its previous level, and that the *real price* of chewing gum dropped by 75 percent—the last statement meaning that in 1970 one had to give only a fourth as much of other goods in exchange for chewing gum as had been the case in 1930. This remarkable instance of price stability finally gave way, though chewing gum's subsequent rise of about 40 percent still leaves it with a decline in real price of more than 50 percent since 1930.

Because we buy and sell nearly everything for money we tend to think of money as important in itself. It nevertheless is only a bookkeeping device for handling a vast complex of promises that result from discrepancies in time and parties between the two halves of transactional relations. It is a highly flexible method of keeping track of those who have given goods but have not yet received equivalent value in return.

Ideally money should be neutral between those two groups. However, if the money itself changes in value it is not neutral, and gives a benefit to one group at the expense of another. A time lag between receipt and payment constitutes credit (or debt, depending on whose eyes are looking at it). We have already seen that most money in industrial societies takes the form of credit instruments, or promises to pay. This is sensible, since the central function of money is the credit function. The main distinction between money and credit in actual use is that some credit is so widely acceptable that we consider it explicitly as money, whereas the acceptability of other credit requires investigation of the promisor's credit rating.

Unemployment

In a simple nonmarket economy, each household produces for itself. When it wants goods in its consumer role it activates its producer role to create them. If members of the household are not busy producing goods, it is because they prefer rest, recreation, or other activity. They presumably know that they can have the fruits of work only if they work, and that if they work more they can have more. Time spent not working can hardly be considered "unemployment," however, since anyone who wants to produce more goods can do so. Despite exceptions (like an Eskimo with no tools or materials who is caught in an igloo by an impenetrable blizzard), in most cases there is something productive to be done if one wants to do it.

Although the producer and consumer aspects of the household are separated in a market economy, there is no necessary reason why the same overall logic must be different for a whole economy than for a single household. If people wanted more goods they could work more, and if they wanted less goods they could work less. No one willing and able to work would be without work unless he preferred to do without income.

Unfortunately the separation of the consumer and producer roles into separate product and factor markets allows discrepancies to occur. Although these discrepancies are potentially temporary and correctable, what is "temporary" to society may be intolerably long for the individual. We will identify two principal types of unemployment, generally known as structural and aggregate.

Structural unemployment is a mismatch between supply and demand in factor markets. The main types of mismatch are occupational and geographic, and the two often go together. For example, consumers may be demanding color TV sets and TV comedians, which require assemblers in New Jersey and comedians in New York. But the persons looking for jobs may be lettuce pickers in Salinas County and economists in Berkeley. To bring about a match either the people or the industry must move geographically, and the people must learn new occupations. (Some people think of economists as comedians, but of a different sort than is expected by TV viewers.) Structural unemployment is presumably temporary, in that old jobs have disappeared and new ones have appeared. But the people who held the old jobs have not yet made the necessary occupational or geographic adjustment. However, particular people who happen to have been left without work may not find the unemployment temporary at all. Some may not be able to make the adjustment, particularly if they are well along in years. Others may not be able to afford the geographic move and the costs of supporting themselves during retraining. Some may not know about the new opportunities. Still others, such as Appalachian coal miners, may be tied to their location by their families, way of life, or love of their ancestral lands.

A related but less difficult version of lag is *frictional unemployment*. If a firm goes bankrupt, closes a plant, shifts to a new product, or changes methods of production it may permanently lay off employees. Even if other jobs using the same skills are already available in the same area, it takes time to learn where the other jobs are, to be interviewed for them, to make decisions, and to get started. Or a person may leave a job voluntarily and take weeks or months to find another that is satisfactory. Unless an economy were in absolutely steady state equilibrium—which is neither possible nor desirable—changes of this sort will always occur, with some persons being temporarily out of work during the readjustment. Since this kind of unemployment can never be totally eliminated, and we estimate that a minimum of 3 to 4 percent of the work force will be in this transitional process at any one time, we think of that level as "full employment." This view, interestingly enough, is taken even more strongly by the Russians, who do not consider a person unemployed during the period between his being "reduced" out of one plant and his starting in another.

Aggregate unemployment is a different matter. Although it may be complicated by structural factors, this is a condition in which there are simply not enough jobs for everyone who wants work, even if everyone were to move to the proper places and be properly trained. To understand this problem we must first look at a basic identity between cost and income. It was implicit above that debt and credit are the same thing looked at through different eyes. If I sign a note promising to pay you $1,000 a year hence, the note constitutes $1,000 of debt to me and $1,000 of credit to you. There is no possible way for the total amount of debt to be different from the total amount of credit. Nor is it possible for the total amount of debt passed on to the next generation to be different from the total amount of credit passed on. (If only the pessimists who keep worrying about the stupendous national debt the next generation will inherit could shift to a note of optimism, they could start rejoicing instead about the stupendous credit on which the next generation can collect.)

Similarly every time money changes hands it constitutes cost to the person who gives it and income to the person who receives it. Total costs and total incomes cannot differ, because they too are the same thing viewed through different eyes. This means that when a given output of goods is produced in an economy, and the factors which produced them are paid (including profits to the enterpriser), there is necessarily put into circulation enough money income to purchase everything produced at a price that will cover its cost. "We've overproduced: people don't have enough money to buy it all" is not a proper diagnosis. People necessarily have enough money to buy everything that is produced, since it cannot be produced without giving them the money. If they are not paid very much, the cost of production is not very much; but the payments to factors cannot help being enough to purchase the total output at a price that will cover the cost. If output is increased far enough to put everybody to work, the cost of the extra production necessarily generates the extra income with which to buy it.

The problem is not whether people *can* buy everything that is produced, but whether they *will,* which depends a great deal (though not solely) on expectations. If people expect their incomes to go down or be uncertain in the period ahead they may cut spending and keep their money. If people sew cash into mattresses, carry larger amounts in their wallets, or increase the balances in their checking accounts, goods may then go unsold even though enough money is available to buy them. If people stop borrowing from banks and repay loans instead, they not merely keep money out of circulation; they reduce the total stock of money, since most money consists of credit. For any or all of these reasons the total output may not be sold. In that case firms will reduce production and employees will be laid off.

Conversely, if people are taking money out of their mattresses, wallets, or checking accounts, and if they are borrowing more from banks than they are repaying, the amount of money spent will be more than enough to purchase all the goods produced. Firms will then increase their orders and take on more employees. If the economy should already be operating at full employment, however, the increased spending will induce a rise in prices instead of a further rise in employment and output. Even if there is perfect balance between production and consumption, however, there is no assurance that the balance will occur at a level of full employment. That is another story too long to go into here.

Macro vs. micro effects: Some possible conflicts

Before we go into some other aspects of aggregate employment, let us note an important difference between looking at the micro and the macro aspects of a market system. In the micro view we look at only one product at a time. We assume that the change in one small segment of the economy is too small to have a noticeable effect on the total system, so we ignore the total. Under this view a reduction in price of some product will induce more sales of that product, and increase employment in the firms and the industry that produce it. This is a stimulating effect.

But suppose we simultaneously reduce the prices in enough products to make a significant difference in the total—the macro effect. Now we must give attention to the fact that a reduction in selling price is also a reduction in the total incomes of the people who make and sell things. With reduced incomes they will have less money to spend; they will buy fewer products; and the result will be to reduce employment. The micro and macro effects of a price reduction may thus be precisely opposite, the one tending to increase employment and the other to decrease it. Similarly, a reduction in wages in an industry may enable it to reduce the price of its products, increase its sales, and increase its employment. But the macro effect is that the reduced wages constitute reduced purchasing power in the economy, with reduced total sales, and reduced employment. Unfortunately there is no easy way to predict which of the two consequences will dominate. Needless to say, unions typically emphasize the macro effect, arguing that higher wages will provide more purchasing power, which will mean more sales of goods, more production, and more jobs. Employers typically emphasize the micro effect, arguing that higher wages will force them to charge higher prices, which will lead to fewer sales, less production, and fewer jobs. This is another illustration of the fact that the whole system follows a different logic than do its separate subsystems.

A second important distinction between the micro and macro levels concerns the tendency to stability. We have already observed that an imbalance at the micro level tends to set in motion forces that will correct it. Too high a price for TV sets encourages output and discourages purchases, both of which exert a downward, self-correcting influence on the price. By contrast, imbalances at the macro level tend to be self-aggravating, not self-correcting. If prices start moving upward, people are likely to try to buy quickly before they go higher. The result is that the increased sales push prices still higher. Higher prices induce increases in wages to match them, which higher wages justify still higher prices, and so on. In the reverse direction, a downward movement in prices may induce people to hold off their purchases until prices go down still further. The ensuing reduction in sales then causes the prices to go down still further, and so on. Union contracts, minimum wage legislation, and a general belief by managements that wage reductions hurt morale tend to keep wages from going down. A downward pressure in this area is therefore more likely to take the form of layoffs and unemployment than of reduced wage rates. Several other factors also have a self-aggravating effect, which we need not go into here.

Some implications for policy

This difference between micro and macro behavior has important repercussions on policy. Since micro-level behavior shows a tendency to be self-correcting, it makes sense to refrain from governmental controls of such things. Controls, it can be asserted, only prevent the situation from correcting itself. But since a disequilibrium at the macro level tends to make itself worse, it makes sense to say that controls may be introduced to help restore equilibrium. Except during wartime, and until the

Nixon wage-price freeze introduced in 1971 and ended in 1974, we have been reluctant to apply governmental controls directly to supply and demand conditions except in unusual cases—notably agriculture. In contrast to these limited uses of micro controls we have used governmental controls at the macro level regularly ever since World War II.

Macro controls are of two main types. One is directed toward control of the money supply, and its use is referred to as *monetary policy.* A variety of different operations are available to the government for this purpose, but all seek directly or indirectly to increase or decrease the effective money supply.

The second main type of macro control is called *fiscal* policy. This has to do with the finances of the federal government itself. The federal government has two sources of money inflows: taxes and borrowing. Its two parallel outflows are spending and debt repayment. If spending equals taxation, the government neither borrows nor repays debt. If the government spends more than it collects in taxes it borrows the difference. Borrowing by the government constitutes an increase in the money supply, just as does private borrowing, only typically in bigger chunks. Government borrowing also affects bank reserves and enables banks to engage in increased private lending, in a sort of double-barreled effect. We need not go into the details here, if we are simply aware that a given amount of borrowing by the federal government can have a larger stimulating effect than an equal amount of private borrowing.

Conversely, if the government receives more in taxes than it spends, the difference goes to repay government debt, with the effect of reducing money and slowing the economy. Though essentially correct as far as it goes, the above description of monetary and fiscal policy is considerably oversimplified. If the realities were not more complicated than this, we could achieve nearly stable prices and nearly full employment rather consistently, simply by having the government introduce the appropriate monetary or fiscal moves at the appropriate time. We said "nearly" stable prices and "nearly" full employment advisedly. The general belief of economists for several decades has been that if the economy were stimulated enough to bring full employment it would also undergo some inflation. If it were relaxed enough to keep prices steady it would show significant unemployment. The distressingly high levels of both inflation *and* unemployment of the early 1970s left economists puzzled and sent them scurrying for new explanations.

A NOTE ON INTERNATIONAL TRADE

The principles of transactions in Chapters 9, 10, and 11 are the same across national boundaries as within them. So are the processes by which someone can accumulate money by a series of transactions in different markets. International trade, however, is complicated by tariffs, quotas, differences in money units, and differences in laws and customs. We will focus first on some domestic transactions that lay the groundwork for the international, and then move to the international ones.

We have noted that the execution and terms of a transaction depend on the value of each of two things to each of two parties, labeled *AX, AY, BX,* and *BY* (Chapter 9). In transactions across national boundaries we focus on differences in objective valuations within the two nations, rather than on subjective evaluations of particular parties. Four valuations are still involved: in this case the value of each of two commodities in each of two places.

The principles: Ignoring money

We can clarify the principle within a nation. Suppose that in Florida it costs the same to grow either apples or oranges. Based on cost, if both were grown in Florida they would exchange at a ratio of one apple for one orange. In Maine apples can also be grown rather easily, but oranges can be grown only in hothouses. If in Maine it costs 20 times as much to produce an orange as an apple, and if exchange ratios were based solely on the cost of producing both items locally, in Maine the exchange ratio would be 20 apples for one orange.

Now let us look at the process of accumulating wealth (Chapter 14), for simplicity disregarding shipping costs, time delays, spoilage, and related factors. The opportunity is obviously ripe for some enterprising Down Easter to take apples from Maine to Florida. For each apple he can acquire an orange. He then takes the oranges back to Maine, where he can get 20 apples for every orange. If he takes the 20 apples to Florida, exchanges them for 20 oranges, which he then reexchanges for 400 apples in Maine, and so on, he can shortly build himself quite an accumulation.

As elsewhere, the greater the discrepancy in relative values the greater is the gain from trade. If the relative values were two-to-one in Maine and one-to-one in Florida, our enterpriser could multiply his stock by 2 on each round trip, instead of by 20. If the ratio were the same in both places, he could make no gain at all.

A point badly misunderstood by amateurs is that it makes no difference to trade, as such, what the *absolute* costs are of producing either fruit in either place. For the same reason it makes no difference whether wage rates are equal in the two states or are dramatically different. The only thing required for profitable trade is a difference in *relative* values, or ratios, in the two places.

It is intuitively obvious that if the good people of Maine want oranges they had better not try to grow them at home. They had better grow apples instead and ship them to Florida. What is not so obvious, but can be seen with a little figuring, is that if the equally good people of Florida want apples they can get more of them by growing oranges and shipping them to Maine than by growing apples at home.

To be explicit, if a person in Florida wants an apple, he could grow it for the same cost as he could grow an orange. But if he grew an orange and shipped it to Maine he could have twenty apples for the same cost. In the economist's language Maine has a *comparative advantage* in growing apples and Florida a comparative advantage in growing oranges. Under these conditions it would be sensible for Florida to specialize in oranges and to import its apples from Maine, even if the absolute cost of growing an apple in Florida were less than in Maine. To borrow language from Gresham's law (which we will not go into here), Florida can drive orange growing out of Maine and Maine can drive apple growing out of Florida. (Question: Why can a stenographer who knows no engineering do all the typing for an engineer, even if the engineer is the better typist?) (Note on Women's Lib: The question did not specify the sex of either party. Did the reader?)

It is, of course, not necessary that the northward shipment of oranges be done by the same persons as do the southward shipping of apples. All that is required for a gain to both areas is that oranges go north and apples south.

After enough of both fruits have moved, the supply of apples in Maine will go down (because apples have been shipped out) and the supply of oranges will go up, leading to a decline in the relative value of oranges and a rise in that of apples. Meanwhile the relative value of apples will go down in Florida and the value of oranges will go up. The flow in both directions will stabilize when apples and oranges have reached the same relative values in both places—or more precisely, when the difference in values is no greater than shipping costs.

Nothing said so far about this trade depends on whether the two areas are in the same or different nations or on the same or different currencies. The problem is simply one of different areas with different relative costs of producing different goods. Such differences in production costs may be based on climate, soil, mineral deposits, forests, topography, labor skills, or available capital.

The principles: Money added

The above example focused directly on the exchange of goods and ignored money. If the exchange were made in money and the amount of money involved were very small compared to the total amount used in each place, the general principles stated above would be unaffected. But if the amount of money involved became large enough, a complication would be added, even if the basic principles remained the same. To illustrate the effect of a large dollar volume of trade, let us assume that apples and oranges are the only products of Maine and Florida, and that both states use the same money. The money cost of growing apples and oranges is equal in Florida, at a nickel each. Apples cost five cents to grow in Maine, and oranges a dollar.

Obviously the people of Florida will grow their own oranges *and* apples, since neither can be bought more cheaply from Maine. The people of Maine will grow their own apples, and will buy their oranges from Florida. But only for a while! Money will be flowing from Maine to Florida to pay for the oranges, but none will be flowing back. If Maine has an outflow of money and an inflow of goods, a rise in the ratio of goods to money (which is the same as a fall in the ratio of money to goods) will bring a decline in the price level. The price of apples might then decline to, say, three cents and the price of oranges to sixty.

Meanwhile the money flowing into Florida while goods are flowing out will produce a rise in all prices in Florida. Even under Florida's initial one-to-one ratio the price of apples and oranges would both rise to, say, eight cents each. The result? In money terms it is still cheaper for Maineites to buy oranges from Florida than to grow them at home, although the advantage is now smaller. But Floridians can now buy apples from Maine for less than half the cost of growing them at home—that is, for three cents instead of eight.

Whether the exchange is done by barter or by money, if the *ratios* of the production costs of two commodities—not their absolute costs—differ between two places, there is a basis for a *mutually* profitable trade. The principle is a simple extension to geographic areas of the most basic principle of transactions: if A and B differ in their *relative* desires for X and Y, there is a basis for trade. Conversely, no matter how different their absolute intensity of desires, there is no basis for trade if their relative desires are the same.

Relatives are not everything

Before leaving beautiful Maine and Florida let us look at differences in absolute costs. Suppose it takes one man-minute to produce either an apple or an orange in Florida. But it takes two man-minutes to produce an apple in Maine and forty man-minutes to produce an orange. We will assume that there are no other costs of production, in which case Florida has an obvious absolute advantage in producing both fruits. Although it is mutually advantageous to trade, there nevertheless will be a difference in economic well-being between the two places. By spending one man-minute producing an orange, the Floridian can command the output of the two man-minutes that it took the Maineite to produce one apple. Conversely, the Maineite would have to give two minutes' worth of his output to command one minute's worth of the Floridian's output. We will not trace the intermediate steps of the reasoning, but it is intuitively clear that the people of Florida will have higher real incomes than the people of Maine—unless Maine has an absolute advantage in producing something else, such as skiing.

If people move, another equalizing force will eventually set in. As the number of people in Florida increase relative to the fixed amount of land, after some point Florida will experience diminishing productivity per person. The decrease in the ratio of people to land in Maine will produce a reverse effect there. Eventually the output per person may become equal in the two places, and migration may cease. We are, of course, ignoring other factors, such as Maineites who can't stand the flatness and year-round-sameness of Florida, or Floridians who take a dim view of snow and rockbound coasts.

In short, the simple principles of transactions have an inexorable logic that rears its head whenever exchange is possible. Multiple (as contrasted to unique) transactions between two parties or places show equilibrating feedback, as follows:

The greater the differences in values the greater the trade.

The greater the trade the smaller the differences in values.

We finally go abroad

None of the basics change if the areas are different nations with different currencies, though many practical complications arise. Let us look at two countries, the United States and England, and two commodities, wheat and shoes. Because of wide land spaces the United States finds it relatively inexpensive to grow wheat. England by contrast is cramped for space and finds it relatively expensive. The conditions for making shoes are about equal in both countries.

Because of the ease of growing wheat in the United States wheat is relatively cheaper than shoes (as compared to England). Let us say that in the United States a pair of simple sport shoes costs $10 to produce while a bushel of wheat costs $2, with a resulting exchange ratio of five bushels of wheat for one pair of shoes. Because wheat is relatively more valuable in England the bushel of wheat costs £1 while the comparable pair of shoes costs £4, an exchange ratio of four bushels per pair. The logic is the same as with apples and oranges. But this time we will put it in the standard form for a transaction, in Figure 22–6. Because of the relative prices in the United States, Americans would give as much as five bushels of wheat for a pair of shoes. The *EP* for the United States thus extends to five. The English on the other hand would accept as little as four bushels for their shoes, so their *EP* is shown at four. An exchange is then possible on any terms between four and five bushels per pair.

What would happen if we explored the possibility of trade in the other direction? The above diagram is couched as a possible purchase of shoes to be paid for with wheat, which shows what the buyer, the United States, would pay and what the seller, England, would accept. Figure 22–7 shows the outcome if the United States takes the role of a buyer of wheat from England, to be paid for with shoes. The prices now take the form of fractions—the fraction of a pair of shoes that Americans would be willing to give for a bushel of wheat, and the fraction the British would be

Figure 22–6

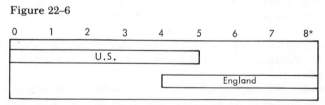

* This scale represents the value of a pair of shoes expressed in terms of bushels of wheat.

Figure 22–7

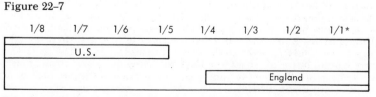

* This scale represents the value of a bushel of wheat expressed in terms of pairs of shoes.

willing to accept. Because one can get a bushel of wheat in the United States for a fifth of a pair of shoes, Americans will be willing to give no more than a fifth of a pair for a bushel of wheat from England. But since a Briton could get a fourth of a pair for his bushel of wheat at home he will accept no less than that amount. The two *EP*s do not overlap, and the transaction will not take place.[4]

Complications concerning currencies. We will deal briefly with one additional complication of international trade, a difference in money units—in this case the dollar and the pound. We start with the same situation as existed between Maine and Florida—that if Maine bought from Florida while Florida bought nothing from Maine, there would be a net flow of money from Maine to Florida. The English, being English, want to be paid in British pounds. An American who has dollars and wants to buy from a Briton in pounds must go through two steps instead of one. First he must buy British pounds with his dollars, and then he must pay the seller with the pounds. He can buy the pounds from any bank in the United States or Great Britain that deals in foreign exchange, or from a variety of other dealers in foreign currencies. Let us say he has bought a pair of English shoes for £4. He inquires and finds that the exchange rate between the two currencies is 2.5 to 1. That is, he must pay $2.5 for each British pound—the actual rate during much of the period since World War II. He pays $10 for the £4 and the £4 for his English shoes.

If the trade is one-sided, as suggested in our example, many Americans will be buying pounds and paying for them in dollars, while few English will be buying dollars and paying for them in pounds. In the foreign exchange markets there then exists a heavy demand for pounds. But there is no supply because Britons want to use their money to buy British goods, not American goods, and hence are not trying to buy dollars. Given a large demand and a small supply, the price of pounds goes up. Depending on the size of the discrepancy, the price of a pound will rise. To take a conveniently large and round figure, suppose the value of the pound doubles, to $5. The pair of shoes still costs £4. But an American must now pay $20 for the £4, and the effect to the American is the same as if British shoes had risen to £8 under the old exchange rate. Americans who formerly found British shoes a good buy now find them too expensive and stop buying.

The position of the British relative to buying American goods is reversed. The bushel of American wheat at $2 cost the Briton £0.8 under the original exchange rate of $2.5 to the pound. But that same Briton can now get $5 for each pound, which means that the bushel of American

---

[4] Anyone interested in playing with the diagrams further can put England in the position of buyer, diagramed from the left, and the United States in the position of seller, diagramed from the right. In Figure 22–6 the English *EP* for shoes from the United States would extend only to four bushels of wheat, while that of the United States would come in from the right to five, and there would be no overlap. If we similarly reversed the two countries in Figure 22–7, with England as the potential buyer of wheat, the English *EP* would extend to one fourth and the United States *EP* to one fifth, showing an overlap and the purchase of American wheat with English shoes.

wheat now costs him only £0.4. Altogether the price of British goods has doubled for Americans and the price of American goods has been halved for the British. So Americans stop buying British, and Britons start buying American. Next there will be many Britons trying to buy American dollars with their pounds and few Americans trying to buy pounds with dollars . . . and the reader can finish the story.

Numerous complications can make life miserable (or exciting) in international trade, and one had better be familiar with them before he pretends to understand real problems in this area. One of the most important is that there are distinct advantages for international traders if the ratios of national currencies remain stable for extended periods, for reasons essentially the same as those that hold for debtors and creditors with regard to price level. Various devices are available to keep exchange ratios stable despite short-term imbalances in trade. But if an imbalance is both severe and long-continued, the ratios must eventually give—as the United States acknowledged when President Nixon announced in 1971 that the dollar would be allowed to "float," that is, to reach an exchange ratio determined by the international supply and demand for dollars.

A QUICK SUMMARY

Our prototype model of a market system is an ecological system, defined as an uncontrolled interaction of controlled subsystems. The controlled subsystems in a market economy are households, firms, and banks, with governments also playing an important role in some aspects of the economy. The whole market economy is the uncontrolled main system, and each industry (if competitive) is an uncontrolled intermediate-level system. The field of economics contains highly developed analyses of the conditions of equilibrium within each type and level of system and between levels of systems, most of which are well beyond the scope of this text. This analysis nevertheless indicates that for a social system to be uncontrolled does not mean that it is haphazard or unpredictable. In dealing with particular products, we find strong reason to believe that equilibrium tendencies prevail—i.e., at the micro level. At the macro level, by contrast, certain movements away from an equilibrium tend to be self-aggravating, which fact justifies controlled intervention to restore balance, usually in the form of government action.

We introduced the concept of a market system by saying that it is the total set of transformations and selfish transactions in readily exchangeable goods. Whenever there is an overlap of EPs in a transaction, both parties benefit—equally if the terms are set at the midpoint of the overlap and unequally if they fall toward one side. If a competitive market system works according to its theory it does two main things. First, it makes all transformations (in exchangeable goods) for which the value of the outputs equals or exceeds the value of the inputs, and refrains from making those for which the inputs are worth more than outputs. The consequence is that every productive transformation is made and every destructive one avoided. By definition of the terms greater potential for satisfying wants occurs at this point than at any other.

Second, every transaction in which there is an overlap of *EP*s takes place, and every transaction in which the *EP*s do not meet does not take place. Again by definition of the terms the maximum of satisfaction is created when these conditions are fulfilled. These two aspects provide strong logical support for the market process. A third prong of support is that this seeming best of all possible worlds is achieved by purely selfish action—no one need face a conflict between each party's selfish interest and the social good. Adam Smith's "invisible hand" will lead his selfish interest to do what is best for society, and the logic extends across national boundaries.

This chapter has sketched only the basic rationale of an uncontrolled market system. The next chapter will deal with two main reservations. The first is that some important considerations for human welfare are left out. Even if the economic system worked perfectly according to its theory, since it is only one subsystem of the whole society, nonmarket forces from other subsystems might be needed to supplement or modify it for the best overall results. That is, optimization of the economic subsystem is not necessarily its own best position in light of the total needs of the whole society. The second reservation is that even within its own domain the economic subsystem by no means operates according to its theory, and its actual results may be wide of the conclusions stated above.

23

ECONOMY: SOME
LIMITATIONS
OF MARKET SYSTEMS

The preceding chapter described some of the most general aspects of a market system, an informal organization that tends to reach an equilibrium that balances inflows and outflows of factors, products, and money.

Other things equal, people will pay more for things they want intensely than for things they want only mildly. Suppliers will provide more of the things for which people will pay much than of those things for which they will pay little. The system thus is induced more strongly to satisfy wants for things intensely desired than for things only mildly desired. Furthermore, firms will be better off if they can use less expensive materials and methods for producing than if they use more expensive ones, and will be induced to do so. Together these tendencies mean that (to the extent that they work according to the theory) the system will provide at the lowest possible cost those things that people want most. The result will be to satisfy people's wants to the maximum possible degree.

That sounds like a highly commendable result. The purpose of this chapter is to sketch briefly some reasons why there is no such thing as a pure market system, some practical shortcomings of actual market systems, and some of the things a market system could not do even if it operated "perfectly." We will deal with this last problem first.

THINGS EVEN A PERFECT MARKET SYSTEM CANNOT DO

If this heading sounds self-contradictory, all it means is that even a perfect automobile cannot fly and that even a perfect TV set is not good to swim in.

Markets cannot handle nonmarket transactions

Since a market system deals with selfish transactions in marketable goods, even if it operates perfectly it cannot make decisions about generous transactions, such as charities, subsidies, grants, gifts, and free education. Nor can it handle hostile transactions using bads, such as wars, theft, or extortion, although it may affect such transactions indirectly, as by establishing the prices of war materials and gifts or the resale value of stolen goods. A market system also cannot make decisions about such nonmarketable goods as affection, respect, truth, beauty, knowledge, and morals.

If some businessman insists that he is not "selfish-indifferent," but is genuinely interested in the satisfaction of his customers, we need not quarrel. Some "nonselfish" behavior may be fully consistent with a profit-maximizing model if we simply note that investment in customer goodwill may be just as sensible a route to increased profit as is investment in plant, research, or employee morale.

Public goods

Since a market system deals in private goods it cannot make decisions about public goods, such as defense, justice, highways, national parks, and governmental regulation. Nor can it make decisions about the relative amounts of private and public goods that a nation will have. That is, on the basis of public decisions the government collects taxes and hires employees, and the private sector is what is left over. In 1971 as measured by money expended, government (federal, state, and local) accounted for somewhat under a third of the total economy, at $311 billion (excluding Social Security) out of a gross national product of slightly over one trillion dollars. As measured by number of employees, however, government constituted about 15 percent of the economy, with about 13 million employees out of a total labor force of 87 million. The difference represents the fact that the government purchases large quantities of goods, such as military equipment, buildings, and highways, from private manufacturers and contractors.

Absence of bads

Although a market system can provide goods it offers no way by which people can buy the absence of bads. For example, although an individual can buy an automobile or a can of fish bait he cannot through the market process buy the absence of air pollution produced by other people's automobiles or of water pollution produced by other people's factories. Nor, if he finds billboards unpleasant, is there any market process by which he can purchase their absence.

The absence of bads is essentially a public good, since it is the same for those who want it as for those who do not, and the same for those who are willing to pay to eliminate it as for those who are not. Like other public goods, the absence of bads can be brought about only by government action, not by the market. On a more limited scale one might nevertheless buy the absence of litter in his front yard by paying to have it picked up and he might buy quiet at night by paying the boy next door to turn down his electric guitar after 2:00 A.M.

Rules about markets

The market process cannot make the rules by which it operates, such as private property and contracts. Every market system has rules about allowable monopoly, even if there is merely a rule not to restrict monopoly—an important type of inaction by government. The system may also have rules about fraud, misrepresentation, or product safety. These rules are made and enforced by government, and could not be produced and sold as private goods.

Maximization of satisfaction

Economists tend to insist that a perfectly operating market system allocates productive factors in such a way as to produce the largest possible satisfaction for a people, adding the value judgment that any nonequilibrium position of the system *mal*allocates resources. There is no known way of testing whether this is actually so, but two conspicuous reservations need to be stated, one affecting consumption and one production.

As to consumption, since a perfect market responds equally and impersonally to anyone's offer of a given amount of money, with fine impartiality it as readily produces the twentieth suit of clothes for the rich man as the first suit for the poor man. Unless the twentieth suit for Mr. Rich brings as much satisfaction as the first suit for Mr. Poor—about which one may be skeptical indeed—even "perfect" operation of the system cannot maximize satisfaction for the whole people.

As to production, market systems produce highly unequal incomes. The very low ones probably leave many people far less productive than they would be if they earned more. Higher incomes might lead to better training, greater ability to cope with the large and small crises of life, better health, and stronger motivation to get and hold jobs. If so, a different distribution of income might well lead indirectly to greater productivity, a larger total income, and a larger satisfaction of wants.

Similar problems arise as between rich and poor nations. Rich nations tend to attract physicians, engineers, scientists, and other professionals out of underdeveloped countries that desperately need them—in the "brain drain." Meat, fish, fish meal, and peanuts that are desperately needed to supplement the protein-poor diets in underdeveloped countries are also drained off to the rich, developed countries, the fish meal and peanuts being used mainly for animal feed. In these and other ways the operations of markets between nations may retard increases in productivity in those areas where they are most needed. On the other hand, private investments by firms from the developed nations can help raise productivity in underdeveloped ones by introducing capital and modern technology that could not possibly be afforded by the underdeveloped nations. This too is a complex problem which we can only raise. But it is far from self-evident that free market exchanges between developed and underdeveloped nations produce the largest satisfaction for the whole global system.

There is also a monumental value assumption in any market system—namely, that people ought to get what they want if they can pay for it. The system does not contemplate that it might be good for one's soul to be denied some fruits of his labor or to receive more than he produces. It is a valid scientific judgment that the sum of all goods received by all people cannot exceed the total all of them have produced. But that each should receive income in proportion to his productive contribution is a value judgment, not a scientific one.

Macro-level problems

The alleged virtues of an unmanaged market system are mainly those at the microeconomic level. At the macro level, by contrast, although we are thus far not too sure of the precise relations between the two levels, we nevertheless feel reasonably confident that full employment, stable prices, and rapid economic growth are not fully compatible. Until we know the payoffs among these three conditions we cannot tell what combination would be best. Furthermore, to formulate policy toward them we would have to assign them priorities—a subjective and tricky problem. For example, how much unemployment would we accept to keep inflation within 2 percent a year? How much inflation will we accept to keep growth up to 3 percent?[1] In any event the market mechanism itself has no way of answering these questions.

To amplify one aspect of these macro-level problems, the costs of unemployment are not merely those of lost production and income—which for every one percent of unemployment in the United States amount to about 14 billion man-hours per year, or $42 billion in wages at a modest $3 per hour. A major obstacle to prison reform is that putting prisoners at productive work at regular wages—which is perhaps their best preparation for a return to normal life—raises outcries from "free" labor of "unfair competition from convict labor." Retraining and relocation of rural or urban poor is relatively easy if employers everywhere are ready to snatch up every available worker because they are shorthanded. By contrast, the best programs will not help much if no jobs are available for people who move or complete retraining. Majority resistance to minority entry into skilled jobs could be much less if the former felt no threat to their own jobs or income. Workers and management in an industry subject to competition from imports pursue tariffs or other restrictive trade policies more vigorously when there is heavy unemployment. Public willingness to finance schools, hospitals, parks, or improved public services drops dramatically when unemployment rises. Some problems of international peace might be eased if we were confident that

---

[1] Economists use a diagram known as a Phillips curve to chart the relationship between unemployment and inflation. While they are reasonably sure there *is* such a relationship, the precise location and slope of the curve are much disputed.

we could cut the production of military goods without producing massive unemployment. The human misery and psychological disorganization that afflict many unemployed are only two of the many other outcomes of unemployment, whose total social costs can be appalling. The point is not that unemployment and its attendant costs necessarily come with a market system. The point is that the market system cannot itself "decide" what constitutes the preferred mix as among unemployment, inflation, and growth, and may need to be supplemented by nonmarket controls if unemployment is to be kept within acceptable levels.

Conservation

The market system can bring natural resources into use, as by cutting forests, mining coal, drilling wells for water and oil, or setting up recreation facilities. The system itself, however, has no way of *not* using resources. If an area is covered with redwood trees that make valuable lumber, the market system has no feasible mechanism for protecting them. The system can respond actively and cut redwoods if even a fraction of one percent of the population want the lumber. It is also true that by not buying redwood lumber an individual can register his dollar ballots against cutting redwoods. But whereas an affirmative dollar vote of only a small fraction of the population can destroy the trees, the market would require a nearly unanimous negative dollar vote to save them. Someone with money and dedication can, of course, buy up lands where these trees grow and set them aside, as has been done with some redwood groves in California. However, actions of this kind are essentially gifts to the society, and fall outside the market relationship, as such. Much the same can be said for the preservation of any other species, or of wilderness.

A semantic note

For those who are sensitive about these matters, the above points are not necessarily "criticisms"—unless it is a criticism of an oak to state that it does not produce apples. Having first clarified what market systems can do, we are now indicating what they cannot do. If decisions are to be made on these matters they must be made by some technique other than the market. If they are to be made at all, decisions about levels of unemployment and inflation, about preserving wilderness areas, or about stopping such bads as pollution will probably have to be made by government. Government may nevertheless operate through the market process to effectuate some of its decisions, as by taxing pollutants, subsidizing cleanup techniques, or making purchases that will increase employment.

SOME PRACTICAL LIMITATIONS AND MODIFICATIONS OF MARKETS

Competition and monopoly

The theory of a market system assumes that any profitable business will attract new competitors, and that such competition will keep prices down and quality up. In business as elsewhere, power tends to show positive feedback—power begets power. If one firm grows much larger than its competitors, even if for the socially laudable reason that it is doing a better job, it may then have enough resources to drive its competitors out of business, in part by vastly outdistancing them in advertising. Once it has achieved monopoly, or merely enough dominance to intimidate competitors, it can raise prices and reduce quality, while leaving consumers largely helpless. The same firm might then use its resources to buy a large chunk of some other industry, and thus dominate two industries. Our theory of a market system assumes that each firm is in only one industry, and we also need to know much more than we now do about both the theoretical and the practical consequences of large conglomerates that are simultaneously in several industries, particularly if the same conglomerate is dominant in more than one.

By the late 19th century the United States was faced with trusts in whiskey, steel, tobacco, petroleum, sugar, and several other industries. In each of those industries one firm, or several in close cooperation, exercised control, either by owning the entire industry or by being so overwhelmingly large that no challenger dared to be really competitive. The Sherman Antitrust Act of 1890 was presumably intended to prevent such monopolies. How successful it has been is a matter of dispute, and we are long overdue for a full-scale public debate about the degree of concentration of ownership and control within the American economy. The last comprehensive public discussion accompanied investigations by the Temporary National Economic Committee (TNEC) of the United States Senate in the early 1940s.

Mergers, which usually mean the absorption of smaller companies by larger ones, are the main route to economic concentration, and have occurred in three main waves. In most of the past 75 years between 100 and 200 firms have disappeared by merger each year. But a thousand disappeared by merger in 1898, 800 to 1,200 each year from 1926 through 1929, and over 800 each year since 1958, with over 2,000 in 1968 alone. (Blair 1972: 258) Conspicuous were numerous acquisitions by petroleum companies. Even more conspicuous were the new conglomerates, eight of which alone acquired among them over 50 other companies per year from 1961 through 1968, their acquisitions being scattered over a wide variety of industries (ibid.: 285). Along with the general idea of a governmental hands-off policy, we must therefore recognize that unless government acts to prevent concentration the essential competitive aspect of the market system may contain a built-in self-destruct button that might be pushed, not by the communists or the New Left, but by General Motors, ITT, and Litton Industries.

At the same time, some industries are "natural" monopolies, with fixed costs so large that it would be extremely wasteful to set up competing facilities. Obvious examples are the public utilities, since it would be a near impossibility for a city to have a dozen sets of power lines, telephone lines, water pipes, gas mains, storm sewers, and sanitary sewers. In fact, in some cities the pipes under the streets are so crowded that it is next to impossible to have even one set of each. We accept monopoly in these services, and add regulating commissions which are supposed to substitute for the force of competition. It is a commonplace (and not without justification) to suggest that regulating commissions are often "captured" by the industry they regulate, and tend to protect the industry from the public rather than the reverse—as with many state public utilities commissions or the Federal Communications Commission.

Involuntary subsidy via implicit costs—the case of the family farm

If there is overproduction of a given commodity its price will fall, and inefficient firms that cannot produce at the lower price will stop producing. This is the expectation of theory, and enough thousands of firms actually fail every year to support the expectation.

In theory a business firm is viewed as an entity in itself, whose accounts record its receipts from product sales and its expenditures for factor inputs. As noted, if those who provide factor inputs are not paid the firm will have to stop operating.

If a firm is incorporated, payments for all factors are explicit. A family firm, however, may not clearly distinguish between household and firm. The family's money is the company's money, and vice versa, legally and often psychologically. Let us look at a family farm whose owner says, "I'm doing pretty well. I made a profit of $20,000 out of this farm last year." What he actually means is that sales of his products brought in $20,000 more in cash than he paid out for seed, fertilizer, repairs, gasoline, and other current expenses. He owns his land and equipment and works the farm largely with his own labor, plus some seasonal hired hands. He is a competent worker and manager. Let us see how he might fare if all his costs had to be paid for explicitly.

A competent farm manager–worker nowadays can command a salary of (say) $20,000. Let us therefore assume that he could have earned that much in salary if he had taken a job elsewhere as a farm manager. If he had chosen to rent out his farm he could have received $5,000 a year for the use of the land. He has $50,000 worth of equipment, which amount, if invested elsewhere at 8 percent, would have returned $4,000. Thus if he had viewed his business as a separate entity, and had paid market prices for the land, labor, and investment that he himself provided, his total costs would have been $29,000, in addition to the cash costs of seed, etc. Far from making a profit of $20,000, the farm viewed as a firm lost $9,000. The factors could not have been paid, and the farm would eventually have been forced out of business.

But the farmer is not likely to force himself into bankruptcy to pay himself the going rates for his own labor, land, or invested capital. He may, in fact, be happy in the belief that he is running a successful business, and there is no need to disillusion him. Nevertheless, by accepting less than the going market prices for his own factor contributions, he is subsidizing the purchasers of his product by charging them less than its real cost of production. *He* is making money, in his capacity as worker, investor, and landowner, but only by accepting $9,000 less than these factors would command elsewhere. The *farm* is losing money by transforming $29,000 worth of inputs into $20,000 worth of outputs. (For strict accuracy, we should add the costs of seed, etc., to both income and outgo. To do so would increase both figures but not change the $9,000 difference between them.)

Because it is subsidized by its owner this farm violates the general market principle that any firm will cease to produce if the price of its output in the long run does not cover its cost of production. This is one reason why special legislation was passed to assist farmers. Originally intended to help the really poor, substantial payments now go to huge corporate farms that are quite able to take care of themselves.

Two additional problems of the farming industry are the unpredictability of weather and some intractable traits of biological products. As to the latter, if the tractor or fertilizer factory is unable to sell all its output, it can shut down for a month. The equivalent for the farmer would be to stop feeding the chickens or cultivating the beans for a month, and then to resume when the market picks up!

Nonprice competition

Market theory assumes that the effect of competition is to keep prices down and quality up. In recent decades, however, much competition has changed. If a producer wants to sell more, instead of reducing the price he may spend money to induce people to buy, as by advertising, contests, fancier packages, trading stamps, or expensive display racks. Since the consumer of these products pays their entire costs he thus pays the cost of inducing himself to buy. Sometimes the additional volume of sales permits offsetting reductions in production costs, particularly for newly introduced products. In other cases no such savings are possible because adequate volume has long since been achieved, as with many drugs and cosmetics. The result is that with toothpaste, for example, a quarter to a third of the retail price goes for advertising. A study in Great Britain concluded that promotion of their brands by Procter & Gamble and Unilever amounted to about 25 percent of the retail price (*Business Week,* 4/29/67: 50), and the Federal Trade Commission in the United States found that 40 percent of the gross receipts of the Vitasafe company (vitamin tablets) went for advertising (*Nation,* 11/28/66: 579). Prescription drugs also show vast discrepancies between suppliers who advertise heavily and those who do not. In one extreme case the price of 1,000 prednisone tablets was $7.95 for a little-advertised brand and $169.98 for the brand of one of the heaviest advertisers. The quality of both brands was reported to be identical (Burack 1967). Putting 10 cents worth of cosmetic in a 15-cent bottle and selling the product for $5 is not uncommon, to the tune of advertising which implies that one's social life in general and his sex life in particular will be dead without it. A substantial fraction of the price of breakfast cereals also goes for advertising. As Sen. Estes Kefauver put it, "The consumer pays for his own brainwashing." Further, prime time television advertising is so dominated by the giant firms that it is nearly impossible for even quite large competitors to buy any prime time at all (Blair 1972: 313 ff.).

By permission of John Hart and Field Enterprises Inc.

Advertising can, of course, perform highly useful functions. In an age that offers thousands of consumer products with dozens of variations of each, advertising can inform people of what is available, where, when, and at what price. It could also tell the consumer what the product can or cannot do. Not to know that a product exists, or how to get it, means to do without it. In a complex society information about products is indispensable to their use, and the discipline of economics may be derelict in giving little attention to information flows in markets.

In other cases advertising can be useless to the whole system, a sheer waste. To an important extent it is subject to positive feedback, in that some advertising by one firm puts its competitors under pressure to do the same, and so on in a self-escalating cycle in which the net effect of some advertising is merely to nullify the effect of other advertising. Some merely induces consumers to change brands, without increasing total sales or providing useful information. Gasoline seems a case in point, since few people would drive without gasoline if they did not see it advertised, and most advertising of gasoline is remarkably devoid of useful information. In fact, gasoline companies have fought vigorously to avoid disclosing one piece of information that *would* be useful—the octane rating.

Advertising also raises the question of a possible reversal of the master-servant relationship. According to market theory the consumer is master. It is up to firms, as servants, to learn what consumers want and to produce it for them. Consumer wants are the goals, and the system is the means. Without necessarily recognizing the implications, many proponents of advertising self-consciously reverse the two. As they see it, the system produces a mountainous flow of goods. Advertising must make people want those goods. Otherwise they will not buy enough and the system will collapse. In this view the system is the end, consumer wants are the means, while Madison Avenue and its clients are the partial American equivalent of a central planning bureaucracy.

External costs and benefits

In a market system (as in other organizations) some costs or benefits of its decisions fall outside the decision making unit. A beautiful yard or an attractive house can bring satisfaction to neighbors as well as to the owner, and an eyesore can bring them costs. If the owner beautifies his yard he bears all the cost, but his neighbors get some of the benefit. If he lets it deteriorate he saves maintenance costs, but his neighbors share the cost of ugliness. A picturesque covered bridge may delight artists, photographers, and tourists for hundreds of miles around, who thus share its benefits. But if the entire cost of maintaining it must be paid by the sparsely populated, poverty-stricken township in which it is located, whose citizens are neither artists nor photographers, the benefit to *them* may be nearly zero, and they may replace it with a concrete slab.

Similarly, firms in a market system often impose external costs on outside parties which the firms might reduce considerably if they had to accept those costs themselves. If the electric generating plant that pours out sulfurous smoke had to pay all the costs of extra cleaning, painting, deteriorated health, or esthetic loss brought about by its smoke it might find it cheaper to reduce the discharge. But because the company does not pay those external costs it may allow the smoke to continue unless it is forced by law to stop. Other companies, however, have accepted pollution control voluntarily as a normal and proper cost of production. They have internalized the costs.

A different kind of external cost arises when a firm closes a plant, and is most evident in a small community. The firm may conclude, for example, that it will save a million dollars if it closes the plant and leaves town. But if there are no other major employers and the town is not attractive to other firms the townspeople may lose $5 million in moving costs and reduced property values, for a net loss of $4 million to the whole economy.

Firms can also create external benefits. To reverse the preceding illustration, a firm may move into a sparsely settled area for its natural resources. By bringing in employees to operate the plant, it may provide enough population to justify opening other opportunities that would otherwise not have been worth the effort, such as damming a stream for recreation. Many firms landscape and beautify areas around their facilities, and thereby increase the value of other properties and improve the neighborhood's appearance.

Another external benefit often arises when firms train employees, only to have them leave soon for better-paying jobs elsewhere. Even if the benefit exceeds the cost to that firm, an external benefit accrues to the trained employees and to the wider community that uses their skills.

To generalize, a decision may be made by a subsystem on the ground that the benefit exceeds the cost *to that subsystem.* This fact, however, provides no assurance that the decision will also provide a net benefit to the whole of some larger system of which it is a component. Nor is there any simple way of knowing how large a supersystem ought to be taken into consideration.

In connection with decision making we noted that everyone faces "bounded rationality," and that we can never know more than a fraction of the information potentially relevant to any decision. It is often difficult enough to know the costs and benefits of a decision for one's own subsystem. To suggest that each decision consider all potential effects to some indefinite number of larger systems would paralyze any social system.

Our policy should not aim at eliminating all external costs—an impossible task—but at reaching sensible decisions about acceptable and unacceptable types and levels of external costs. In the unacceptable cases we need to devise mechanisms for making external costs internal to the decision making unit.

Some miscellaneous items

We will identify briefly several other types of complications of market systems, particularly as currently found in the United States. One is "fair trade" pricing and the related fixed markup, which provide by contract or custom that all retailers either charge the same price for a given good or sell at the same markup over the wholesale price. The result is anticompetitive, in that efficient retailers have no way to undercut the prices of inefficient ones. This in turn results in an excessive number of retail outlets which squeeze one another's profits, not by the socially useful method of lowering prices, but by the socially wasteful method of dividing up the total business into so many small pieces that few units are large enough for real efficiency. Gasoline stations (at least before the shortage) and small retail stores are examples.

Second, "free" television is a peculiar phenomenon for a market economy, a basic tenet of which is that the consumer does not get any good he does not pay for through a purchase transaction. Perhaps more accurately described as "private socialism," commercially sponsored programs are paid for as part of the purchase price by the consumers of the products advertised, not by the recipients of the programs. The purchaser of toothpaste, cereal, autos, or other advertised products is in effect assessed a private sales tax to support TV programs, whether or not he likes or watches them. In ancient Rome free circuses for the populace, with violence aplenty, were provided by government. Those of 20th century America are provided by industry. In either case the populace pays, probably with little understanding of what it costs them and without being asked whether they would rather spend the money for something else. (This paragraph is intended solely to contrast commercial TV with the theory of a market system. It takes no position on the much broader question of whether some other arrangement would, in fact, be superior, all things considered.)

Third, the plowback of corporate profits into the firm that earned them is widely accepted as proper and natural. By contrast, according to market theory all profits are to be paid to the households that provide the investment. Those households will decide whether to spend the profits or to save and reinvest them. If they decide to reinvest they will presumably put this money where it promises the largest return, which may or may not be the corporation that earned it. A plowback of profits thus destroys this freedom of choice to the households that own the corporations. Since the pay, power, and prestige of corporate officers tend to vary directly with the size of their corporation, those officers must be presumed to have a biased view, or at least a conflict of interest, in making this decision. The situation is related to our observation in Chapter 15 that the profit organization is the only type that may operate indefinitely without further contributions, and hence without real control, from the original sponsors.

Fourth, even without considering interlocking directorates or other connections, a number of our largest corporations represent monumental aggregations of financial power. The budget of General Motors, for example, has been the sixth largest of any formal organization on earth. Although it is clearly exceeded by the national governmental budgets of the United States, Russia, and China, it is only slightly smaller than those of Great Britain and France. Without attempting to assess whether the effect is benign, malign, or neutral, we may nevertheless note that to direct the flow of some $40 billion a year is to exert very substantial effects on the political, economic, and social health of the nation. Furthermore, General Motors (like other large corporations) has large operations abroad, sometimes in locations that make an American corporation a dominant economic and political force in a relatively small nation. Substantial fractions of the most progressive and influential industries even in France and Britain are now owned by American corporations. Heavy purchases of these foreign business assets during the past decade have also contributed to America's adverse balance of payments, and have thereby had numerous other repercussions. Western economists (in my opinion) have given relatively too much attention to the economic system as an allocator of resources and far too little to it as an allocator of power. There is also the interesting question of whether and in what ways we should consider a corporation "private" if it is owned by a half million people, handles more money than most national governments, and can do business as an entity only because government laws and charter grant it the power to do so. There is also the interesting question of what the legal status of a corporation would be if in its own name it bought back all shares of its own stock—that is, if the corporation completely owned itself—a question raised by the fact that some 5 to 10 percent of stock trading during a period in 1973 was by corporations doing precisely that (*Newsweek,* 5/21/73: 15).

Fifth, an interesting development of recent decades is "consumerism." The term covers various consumer protection activities by government, by consumer testing agencies such as Consumers' Union, and by "activist" organizations, such as those of Ralph Nader or Common Cause. Such organizations and activities, to the extent that they make consumers better informed about the merits and limitations of the things they buy, presumably conform to and support the basic logic of the market system, whose theory assumes that people can, in fact, evaluate the merits of alternative goods. Wherever or to the extent that there is a conflict between meaningless or misleading advertising on the one hand and accurate consumer information on the other, it is the former that is properly labeled as "antimarket." "Consumer" information or pressures can also, of course, be biased, misdirected, or misunderstood, and produce anticonsumer effects. If carefully done, however, government intervention for consumer protection can join antitrust policy as a nonmarket activity designed to improve the market process.

A sixth question is how to handle an industry that seems essential but that cannot be operated privately for a profit. Despite their profitability before the days of the automobile, mass transportation passenger facilities now seem feasible in most places only if they are owned or subsidized by government. Coal mining in Britain occupies a similar position.

Finally, although developed market systems are reasonably competent in bringing higher real incomes to workers, in themselves they have not done well in providing economic security. Protection against the economic hazards of illness, accident, unemployment, and old age have come mainly through governmental action, in such forms as medical insurance, compulsory workmen's compensation, unemployment benefits, and social security pensions. Although there are now many excellent private programs in these areas in the United States, particularly those negotiated by unions, most of them are feasible only because they supplement public plans rather than substitute for them. A perennial difficulty of purely private approaches to economic security is that the persons most in need of such programs are least likely to be covered by them. Successful private plans require relatively long and continuous employment, preferably with the same firm, and the most needy are precisely those who lack such continuous association.

CONCLUSION

This chapter has attended to (1) things market systems by their very nature cannot do and (2) respects in which our actual market system deviates from the theory of market systems. We have noted that it is not necessarily a criticism of a system to identify things it cannot do, any more than it is a criticism of steel to say that it does not float. Nor is it necessarily a criticism to say that some aspect of the actual market economy is not like its theory. It is not even necessarily a criticism of the whole system to say that some part of it is useless or wasteful (like some advertising), since waste is one form of redundancy, and redundancy may be the most reliable way of keeping the whole system viable. This discussion is also not intended as a defense of any of the practices described, but is simply a way of saying that to evaluate any of them is a very difficult task, which must be done with knowledge of their larger system effects as well as their direct effects, and in light of their long-run as well as their short-run consequences. The plowback of profits, for example, might be very good for the system *and* contrary to its theory, or vice versa.

We must not forget that the purpose of theory is to help explain reality, not to mold it, and perhaps we should be at least mildly upset at people who, when they observe a discrepancy between theory and reality, want to modify the reality to conform to the theory rather than the reverse. We regularly hear people in socialist societies complaining of "rightist deviation" or "creeping capitalism" and those in capitalist nations complaining of "leftist deviation" or "creeping socialism." To the extent that they are expressing real convictions rather than expedient slogans such people are measuring certain pieces of reality by their consistency with mental models rather than by the desirability or undesirability of their actual consequences. It is easy to say that certain practices do not conform with the theory. But to know whether the economy or the society is better or worse off as a result is not at all easy. We have spelled out some of these deviations both to help clarify the theory and to identify areas in which reality is not like the theory.

We may close by noting that although the market system is the most conspicuous part of the informal organization of our society, and certainly the most intricately interconnected part, it is by no means the whole of it. Whereas the market system is concerned with profit organizations and the parties they interact with, the society also displays a generous and varied collection of cooperative, service, and pressure organizations. Although some of these overlap into the semiformal category in wanting to "improve the society," many are directed forthrightly toward the welfare of their own members or of clearly and narrowly defined groups of outsiders. Since cooperatives that produce and sell marketable goods are properly considered part of the market system, the vast multiplicity of clubs, societies, fraternal orders, unions, churches, and private social agencies are all nonmarket parts of the informal organization. In any event, neither the market system nor the whole of the informal and semiformal organization can conceivably constitute the whole of the social decision making process in a complex, industrial society. We do, however, get much better sciences of both economics and sociology if we separate the market interactions from the social ones for purposes of analysis.

24

VARIETIES OF ECONOMIC SYSTEMS

INTRODUCTION: DEVELOPMENT VS. CENTRALIZATION

Economic systems come in a bewildering variety, and it would hardly exaggerate to suggest that there are as many types as there are nations. The most important distinctions among them can nevertheless be described along two main axes, the degree of development and the degree of centralization. We will first identify the two axes, and then concentrate on the second.

The development axis

Although actual economies show a continuum, degrees of development are customarily divided into undeveloped, underdeveloped, and developed. For most purposes "industrialized" could be substituted for "developed." Undeveloped economies are illustrated by tribal societies, such as the original American Indians, the Australian Bushmen, and numerous African tribes. Tribal societies live primarily by hunting and fishing, use little or no agriculture or domesticated animals, and have few if any market exchanges.

Underdeveloped countries are represented by most of Central and South America, Turkey and Egypt, and nearly all of Asia, including India. These are characterized by simple crop growing, animal husbandry, handicrafts, some light manufacturing, shops and markets, and possibly mining. Some heavy industry may be included, such as steel and cement, and one or more highly developed large cities, such as Mexico City, Caracas, Nairobi, Singapore, and Bombay. The remainder of such nations are relatively primitive, and their major pockets of advanced industry are likely to be subsidiaries of foreign firms—or were before being expropriated. Fairly extensive market exchanges are used in such countries.

Developed nations make extensive use of modern techniques and mass production in nearly all aspects of their economies, including agriculture, and have large capital investments in productive equipment. The United States and Canada, Western Europe (with some reservations about Spain and Portugal), Russia, Israel, East Germany, Japan, Australia, and New Zealand represent developed nations. Most of the communist bloc of eastern Europe fall somewhere between underdeveloped and developed. These are broad labels, however, and there is as yet no completely developed nation. Even in the United States some Indian reservations are undeveloped, while Appalachia and some sections of the South are underdeveloped. Huge portions of the Soviet Union are underdeveloped, if not undeveloped, as in Azerbaidzhan, Kazakh, Uzbek, and Central Siberia.

The centralization axis: Formal vs. informal organization

Degree of centralization is related in part, but only in part, to the distinction between socialized, or public, and nonsocialized, or private, economies. Russia is the prime example of a centralized socialized economy. Pre-World War II Germany and present-day Japan exemplify rather centralized private economies, dominated by a few cartels and financial combines. Yugoslavia is a distinctly decentralized socialized economy, in that the major industries are owned by the government, but are allowed considerable autonomy at the plant or enterprise level. The United States is the prime example of a generally decentralized private economy, despite reservations about dominance by some large concentrations of capital.

Despite complications, the main distinction among economic systems, and the main focus of controversy about them, revolves around the question of whether the overall social system for producing and distributing marketable goods should be formal or informal. When government takes on the task of producing and distributing marketable goods it thereby makes a formal organization of the economy. That arrangement is generally known as socialism.

The production of nonmarketable goods by government can also be thought of as the public production of public goods, while the production of marketable goods by a market system can be thought of as the private production of private goods. Viewed in this context, a socialized economy constitutes public production of private goods.

Socialization appears in many forms and degrees. Chicago, Cleveland, San Francisco, and other cities have public ownership and control of their local transit facilities, while many communities publicly operate their water and sewage systems. Canada and most European countries have nationalized their railroads, and the United States has partially done so through Amtrak and massive financial assistance.

Public operation of schools and the postal service is virtually universal. Although Great Britain and Sweden are sometimes referred to as "socialist," each has actually nationalized only a few industries and operates a basically market system overall. Because of the vast welter of arrangements in different nations we will focus on Russia's full-fledged, centrally controlled, government-owned and -operated formal economy.

It will be noted that the chapter on the market economy was not a description of the American economy, but rather an analysis of the nature and logic of the transactional interactions of its parts, and the way those uncontrolled interactions produce "decisions" for the whole system, after the fashion of an ecosystem. In this chapter we similarly will not *describe* the Soviet system. Rather we will focus on certain aspects of its decision making processes, particularly emphasizing some differences between socialist theory and Soviet practice, and some points that are often argued about a socialist system by attackers and defenders of market systems. That is, in part we will discuss the Soviet socialist system, and in part certain questions about socialist systems that are argued in nonsocialist ones.

MOTIVES AND ALLOCATIONS

A much-debated, and often misrepresented, question is whether socialist systems abandon self-interest, and can be successful only if people are generous and public-spirited. Must people give freely of their productive inputs even if they are not personally rewarded, and must they exercise self-restraint by not taking more than their fair share of the outputs of the system? The quick answer is, No more so than do the 15 percent of the American work force, including professors in public universities, who are employees of government. But there is more to the question, which this section will explore.

Scriptures vs. reality

We will first dispel a naive notion that a socialist system throws aside rewards for initiative, hard work, and skill, and divides things up equally, while depending on dedication to the common good to induce people to work. True, a long-standing socialist doctrine has been, "From each according to his ability; to each according to his need," which would have the above effect. And the ritual dogma of the Soviets still proclaims that the state will wither away and each will work for the common good.

The Soviets have not officially thrown out this idea. But so far as we can see—and Soviet officials speak frankly about it—that approach is dead. They do not use it or expect their system ever to move toward it. Now viewing their ideology mainly as a religion, some Soviet spokesmen indicate that the Marxist-Leninist "scriptures" describe actual economic behavior in Russia about as accurately as the New Testament describes that in America.

Income vs. profit motives

Chapter 22 distinguished profit motive from income motive. The Soviets use steeply graduated income incentives. For production workers piece rates are used much more than in the United States, and often include bonuses that rise more rapidly than an individual's output. Workers with high levels of manual skill are paid relatively more, compared to unskilled workers, than in the United States. Better housing, longer vacations, and other material rewards go to outstanding workers. These are all income motives, but not the profit motive.

Actual production is done and managed in enterprise units, such as a farm, coal mine, steel plant, clothing factory, or railroad. Enterprise managers do not receive profits, as such. But expenditures and receipts are recorded for each enterprise, and the difference is recognized as profit. Managers have increasing freedom to plow this profit back into their enterprises. Since the manager's salary is related to the size of his enterprise, he benefits personally from this plowback. Soviet managers also receive a larger bonus for making a larger profit, much as do many American executives. The Soviet manager tends to push efficiency, since he has little opportunity to increase profit through new products, price policy, or aggressive selling.

The criterion of need

Appeals to the general welfare are not absent. Much Soviet art, literature, and official propaganda is dedicated to the proposition that all men are created eager to help the system. The people find this very dreary, even as Americans find repetitive, hard-sell TV commercials. Though not convinced that much good comes of this approach, the planners continue it, perhaps for want of something better.

Because the criterion of need still appears in assorted socialist literature, and is relevant to service organizations in a market economy, we will attend to it in more detail than is justified by the Soviet Union's limited use of it. To the extent that a person is motivated to work for the common good, his effort is directed toward needs—of the whole society, or of others less able to produce. Individual need is relatively clear at the biological level: one needs so much food, clothing, shelter, sanitation, and medical care to maintain health. He may also need certain education for his job, which encompasses subneeds for books, pencils, drawings, and so on.

Beyond health and education, however, "need" ceases to have much meaning. One needs transportation to work. But in a private car or a subway? He needs food. But need it be tender beef rather than equally nutritious horsemeat or cat meat? He needs water. But need it be running water? Both hot and cold?

And so the list could go on. The point is simply that beyond health and education need is not measurable, and we have no choice but to stop dealing with needs and to deal with wants. But wants are matters of tastes, preferences, and expectations. Proposals for income based on need appeal to the poor nations, and to the poor in more affluent nations. But however sensible it may seem for the underdeveloped nation or the urban ghetto, it sounds flat and incongruous to talk of income based on need for middle-class suburbia. "Workers of the world unite; you have nothing to lose but your outboard motors," as Boulding once observed, will hardly draw workers to revolt. Above real poverty what a person "needs" usually turns out to be about a third more than he has.

A related note on equality

Egalitarianism is related to need, but is not necessarily the same. Strictly applied it would provide equal incomes for all, and more loosely applied it would pull down large incomes and raise small ones.

Strict equality would drastically limit freedom. Everyone would receive the average income. Anyone who wanted more, and wanted to work harder for it, would be unable to get more. If we assume that social pressures would induce everyone to contribute as much as he could, people would similarly lose the freedom to work less and receive less. This difficulty cannot be resolved by allowing each to work as many

"If God hadn't wanted there to be poor people, He would have made us rich people more generous."

Drawing by Dana Fradon; © 1973 The New Yorker Magazine, Inc.

hours as he likes at identical rates per hour. Does the hotel night clerk who reads magazines most of his time on duty "work" the same amount of time as the maid who makes beds for the same number of hours? What about managerial and professional workers, who are on annual salary because it is not possible to tell which of their activities are work and which are not?

The notion of equality dissolves across geographic areas. As between cold and warm areas, for example, are the incomes of two people equal if they receive the same amount of money? Or only if the one in the colder climate gets paid extra for heating? If the person in the cold region gets extra pay for heat, should the one in the hot region get extra pay for air conditioning? Should those in between get both? How do we "equalize" incomes between the small town where everyone walks to work in 5 minutes and the large city where getting to work takes 40 minutes and 75 cents carfare? What is "equality" between the town that cannot support one movie house and the city that offers more entertainment events than one can possibly attend, or between the relative cost of skiing in Florida and Maine? Does the beefeater in cattle country receive the "same" real income in food as the fisheater by the sea?

These paragraphs indicate why, whatever their ideology, the Soviets continue differential incomes based on rank, skill, and productivity, much as in market systems. Money incomes are apparently not as discrepant in Russia as in the United States, though government-provided amenities make actual living styles more discrepant than money incomes. Because of the bureaucratic structure of Russia it seems likely that upper-class people wield more power than do their counterparts in the United States, even if they have less money of their own. That is, the Russian bureaucrats make decisions that directly affect the welfare and mode of life of millions of people, because the government exerts so many direct controls. However, it is not easy to know how to compare power in this sense.

Some earlier discussions seem relevant here. A person with something valued has greater power and bargaining power than a person without much of value (Chapters 9, 10, and 14). Superior skills and knowledge are valuable, and hence give extra power to those who possess them—in organization (Chapter 15) as well as out of it. Although it is conceivable that a society could be created in which individuals would refrain from using this power, that result seems more likely in a small close-knit tribal community than in the formal, semiformal, or informal aspects of a large and relatively impersonal industrial society. Hence there is a general expectation, even if not an inevitability, that those of greater "merit" will also receive greater pay and other rewards. And despite many exceptions, those with greater "merit" tend to be those with greater formal education. (In this connection one might see Bell's (1973) discussion of "meritocracy.")

Distribution by wants

To distribute on the basis of wants leaves a hopeless snarl. Among family and friends it is possible to know what people like, and to make valid interpersonal comparisons of utility. One may say with confidence, for example, that Jim likes rock music much more than Joe does, or even that Joe likes baseball more than Jim likes rock. Within the close circle it may therefore be possible to distribute goods sensibly on the basis of wants.

Any attempt to expand distribution-by-want beyond such primary groups entails different requirements about information and motivation. Those who would allocate goods among a nation of hundreds of millions —or even in a town of ten thousand—could learn what people want only by asking them. If each person were then given whatever he asked for, anyone who took more than his share would impose only a small cost on any other individual but receive a great benefit to himself. Given these payoffs, it seems most improbable that everyone would behave "properly." It would require nearly unanimous self-restraint to make such a system work, since if only one tenth of one percent were "hogs" they could wreck the system by making themselves billionaires. Moreover, the larger the fraction of the population who exercise self-restraint the greater are the potential payoffs for those who do not.

Of course, a limit could be placed on how much each person received. But each would probably then ask for his limit, and a shift would then have to be made to some other criterion, such as need, productive contribution, or equality.

What about *some* free goods?

To give each person what he says he wants is to make goods free for the asking. Although we have just said discouraging things about such a technique as applied to *all* goods, the problem is not the same if only a few goods are free.

Free material goods.   Pencils and paper might seem likely candidates for free distribution. One can use only a limited amount of these things, and there is no use in taking more than one wants, because they just get in the way. Carelessness might produce some wastage, but the costs of both are low, and no great harm is done. Further exploration, however, reveals that the problem is not that simple. I have found, for example, that old newspapers stacked inside grocery bags make excellent land fill. They rot in a few years if thinly covered with soil. Grass will grow on such fill immediately, and shrubs by the second year. The resulting soil is organic and free of stones.[1]

Packaged reams of new paper stack more neatly and require less cover dirt. If paper were thus available in unlimited quantities for the asking,

---

[1] I hesitate to mention this use of old paper for two reasons. First, one person unfortunately tried it in some areas subject to runoff, which promptly washed away the soil covering and left an unsightly mess. Second, widespread use of this practice would undercut the recycling of paper. On this second score I calm my conscience as follows. The collection of paper for recycling is most feasible in the cities, where most people have no land to fill, or in the suburbs, where most lots are already finish-graded. In the country the choice is not between recycling old paper and putting it into the ground, but between putting it into the ground (which is a kind of recycling) and burning it. If I discover abuses of this information I will omit it from the second edition—if there is still enough paper to print one.

new paper would do better than old. We will leave it to the reader's imagination to figure out other uses for writing paper if there were no charge for it. The reader can also start imagining the uses of ordinary wood pencils. For a start, they make excellent small kindling wood, playthings for children, and row-markers in the garden. The Soviets on at least one occasion ran into this substitution difficulty. They decided to provide bread at a price far below the cost of producing it—on the assumption that people would not abuse this near-gift. After all, everybody needs bread, and there is only so much bread one can eat, so why charge for it? It was shortly discovered that people in small towns were feeding it to cattle, in place of far less costly hay and unprocessed grain. Instead of reverting sensibly to a cost-based price of bread, they made it illegal to keep cattle in towns (Volin 1959: 18). We will also let the reader figure out some uses for automobiles if they were free for the asking.

Free services. The above problems arise out of the substitutability of material goods. By contrast let us look at a service—local passenger transportation. Would it be feasible to allow passengers to ride free on subways, street cars, or buses, with the cost borne out of the public treasury? Possibly so, and some very capitalist American cities are seriously considering it. Unlike paper and pencils, street transportation cannot be converted into some other use. True, some people might at first ride just to convince themselves that they could. But the cost in time and trouble would deter most people from going where they did not want to go just because they could ride free. The very poor might use these vehicles as shelter, but one might hope society could provide something better. Even for children transit vehicles are hardly exciting for very long. Although (in the language of a later chapter) the above simulation may have omitted some crucial variable, free transit is not obviously unfeasible.

Since services are generally not easy to transmute into unintended uses, free education, band concerts, ice skating, public lectures, or even lunches consumed on the premises seem generally feasible. Medical and health services that are free (or nearly so) of charge for particular treatments have been operated successfully in many nations, including numerous prepaid group practice plans in the United States. (We are speaking only of certain aspects of administrative feasibility, not necessarily of desirability, of free access to these services.)

On "free" goods and choice

In the above cases we do not mean that the goods are free of production costs, but merely that no explicit charge is made for them. The costs are born collectively, as by taxes or flat fees. In group medical practice, for example, each member pays a periodic flat fee, but pays no explicit charge when medical care is received.

Since consumers collectively must directly or indirectly pay the costs of what they receive, to provide a good free of explicit charge necessarily reduces individual choice. Let us illustrate with housing. To some people nice housing is important, and they would willingly skimp on other things to have spacious, pleasant quarters. To others housing means only a place to eat and sleep. They would willingly accept cramped quarters and use the money thus saved for other things. But if housing is free, one cannot get more or pleasanter space by offering to pay more. Nor can he have more of other things if he accepts cheaper housing.

It is possible, of course, to give people a choice, allowing those who accept poorer housing to have more of other goods and those who want better housing to have less of other goods. Such an arrangement, however, is merely a clumsy way of charging a higher price for better housing. For what is a "higher price" except an arrangement that leaves one less able to acquire alternative goods? Some years ago the Russians held out the promise of free housing, but they apparently have not gone through with it.

Free television—which Americans *have* gone through with—involves the same limitation on choice. As noted in Chapter 23, every time I buy a tube of toothpaste, an automobile, or a breakfast cereal I pay part of the cost of the TV programs sponsored by the sellers of those products, even if I consider their programs abominable. Furthermore, by not watching a given program, I cannot save any money with which to buy alternative goods. Nor, if television is free, can I encourage programs more to my liking by offering to help pay for them.

This lack of dollar ballot influence contrasts with the situation for movies or stage plays. Every time I go to a movie and cast my dollar ballots I encourage production of more movies of that type. Every movie I do not attend casts my ballots against it, so to speak, and leaves the price of its ticket available to me for buying other things. The cash registers of movie houses record every dollar ballot, and movie producers count them carefully.

By contrast, I do not pay for the commercially sponsored TV shows I watch by buying tickets, but by buying the products the shows advertise. Since it is the traits of those products, along with my preferences about them, that determine whether I spend my money on them, I have no way of registering my dollar ballots for or against their TV shows. In fact, if consumers generally *did* buy (say) cars on the merits of the TV shows sponsored by auto manufacturers, rather than on the merits of the cars, they would grossly distort the market process and seriously undermine its logical support. Barring such distortion, those who like a product but dislike its TV programs have no way of registering that dislike through the market process.

To count viewers or fan letters for particular TV shows, and to provide the kinds of programs that draw the largest audiences, is a basically political, not market, process. It is like taking a vote on automobiles and then producing only those preferred by the majority. The great strength of the market process as contrasted to the political is that it responds to both majority *and* minority wants—both beer *and* champagne—so long as the minority are willing to pay the possibly higher costs. The use of an essentially political, ballot-type technique for selecting TV shows is one reason why free TV was referred to in the preceding chapter as "private socialism." Whether for free housing in Russia or free TV in the United States, "there's no free lunch," and "free" distribution of goods that have significant production costs entails an inescapable loss of consumer choice.

This loss of freedom applies in principle to free public education, free local transportation, and free medicine. The loss of freedom is perhaps least in connection with medical care, since the amount of this service one uses is determined mainly by the state of his body, not of his preferences. The loss of choice is nevertheless definite in free transit and free education. In weighing how much social benefit justifies how much loss of freedom, it is not easy to formulate criteria. The very poor lose little freedom, since they have too little money to make significant choices. It might nevertheless seem sensible to consider (1) whether the free service benefits those who do not use it as well as those who do, and (2) whether the service is important enough to justify taxing those who can afford it to help provide the service for those who cannot.

Free local transportation probably meets the first criterion, since the person who drives benefits from having others in the subways instead of crowding the streets. Education and medical care are justified primarily on the second criterion. However, to the extent that medical care for one prevents the spread of disease to others it also qualifies under the first criterion. So does education to the extent that an increase in the power of one helps raise the power of others (Chapter 9).

To summarize this section, we are suggesting that to appraise some system for allocating economic goods among a people, and for relating or not relating receipts of goods to contributions toward producing them, it would be useful to look at the transactional relations involved, and that capitalist or socialist doctrine may not help much. For education and biological basics, need may be a feasible criterion of distribution. In fact, and however much they may fail in practice, capitalist as well as socialist countries widely accept in principle that no one should starve or freeze, or go without education or medical care, for lack of money. Possibly excepting those used immediately and on the premises, it does not seem feasible to make material goods free; though numerous services might feasibly be free—both without regard to ideology. Equal incomes, and to a lesser extent free goods, involve a dramatic reduction of individual choice. The effect of distribution systems on incentive and ability to work, and hence on output and real income, is less obvious, however, and we will not state firm conclusions about it. That question is related to the handling of land and capital (rather than merely rewards for labor), and hence cannot be evaluated independently.

WHAT IS PLANNABLE?

Some public goods, such as national defense, can obviously be incorporated into the formal organization of government and planned from a central point. Some nonmarketable ones, such as affection, obviously cannot be planned, and must be left to informal organization. In between these extremes are goods that may or may not feasibly be planned, depending on the goods and the circumstances.

If an underdeveloped nation is to be industrialized it will have to build a balanced variety of producer goods industries, such as electric power, oil, chemicals, steel, trucks, generators, railroads, and construction. Some consumer goods are also necessary to keep an industrial population going, such as food, clothing, shelter, and transportation to work. Education, medical care, and other "investments in human capital" might also be considered essential to industrialization.

For such a package of basic goods necessary for production it is feasible to plan quantities of production reasonably well from a central point. By this we mean that any one industry requires outputs of other industries, in the sense that the steel industry requires buildings and cranes and the transportation industry requires trucks, roads, locomotives, and rails. To compute all of these mutually interacting demands may be complicated in detail but is logically simple. For such items decisions about what to produce do not depend on consumer preferences, but on technical characteristics of the industries and their products. Subject to some later qualifications about values it is logically feasible to plan a nation's basic industrial output. Whether personalities and practical politics will allow it to be done sensibly is a different matter.

In all-out war, when all other considerations are subordinated to the objective of winning, a similar logic prevails. Normally democratic, capitalist nations like the United States and Great Britain used detailed central controls during World War II. Manpower, land, materials, tools, and buildings were all allocated in the United States by the War Production Board, at prices determined by the Office of Price Administration. Amazingly high levels of production were achieved under this centralized planning.

When a single overriding goal dominates, and when components of the total output are related by technical characteristics rather than by values, a strong case can be made for central planning. By contrast, if the main goal is to produce consumer goods the logic differs dramatically. A complex industrial economy has no real choice but to pay its people in money. But if so, the system may as well let people spend it for what they like, and then produce what people buy and stop producing what they do not buy. If the people buy only portable radios, there is no point in continuing to produce cabinet models to be stacked unsold in warehouses.

To judge by their words and deeds it has taken the Russians about 50 years since their revolution to recognize that, no matter how dedicated one is in principle to central planning, there is no sense in trying to plan consumer goods. Their recognition has taken the form of telling some factories to take some of their orders from the department stores instead of the planning office. This does not mean that the planning office does nothing about consumer goods, as it must still allocate manpower, materials, tools, and power to the consumer goods factories. These allocations, however, are based increasingly on predictions of what consumers will buy and decreasingly on instructions about what they should have.

All this does not mean that there is no role for government ownership or control as seen by those who prefer it. If the government actually provides top managerial controls, it is presumably easy to see that attention is directed toward safety, workability, reliability, and low pollution potential of products and processes and away from sales gimmicks. Other considerations, however, apparently affect the system, and Russians have many complaints about the poor quality and inadequate quantities of consumer products.

ON EVALUATING MANAGERS

In earlier chapters we observed that a key problem of formal organization is to get staff members to pursue the organization's goals instead of their own. The means is the authority structure, which rewards those who perform its instructions well and penalizes those who do not. Before good performance can be rewarded, it is first necessary to measure it. For many routine jobs this can be done by a simple count of output. For executives and managers, however, quality of performance may be difficult to measure, yet be tremendously more important to overall performance of the system. How can it be known whether a manager is doing a good job, so he can be rewarded or promoted accordingly?

Perhaps every role in every society has certain criteria for allotting "points" to its occupants. For students it is grades. For teachers it may be publications or popularity. For police it is the ratio of arrests to crimes committed, for defense attorneys the percentage of clients acquitted, and for prosecuting attorneys the percentage of defendants convicted. For the sales department it is volume of sales, for the production department it is volume of output, and for the top managers it is profit.

For successful managers of socialized enterprises the central planners provide such rewards as praise, increased responsibilities, larger salaries, more employees, bigger budgets, and promotion into larger enterprises or even into the planning bureau. What kinds of behavior or results by the manager provide the "points" that determine whether he will get the rewards?

The planners are obviously interested in production. If they have planned a 10 percent increase in output and the manager achieves 10 or 12, all is well. But suppose that in the push for quantity the scrap rate, spoilage rate, and cost per unit also go up. The planners award points for the rise in output but frown at the rise in waste. The planners then open a campaign to reduce scrap. They then find that quality goes down, because the managers use defective parts instead of scrapping them. The planners next emphasize quality. It goes up. But it does so because managers use more man-hours inspecting and repairing components, with the result that labor costs skyrocket. The planners next campaign to keep labor costs down—and so on and on. Each shift of emphasis says at least implicitly: "Increase your points in the direction now emphasized, and you will receive rewards."

The measure of quantity may itself be uncertain in some products. One story from Russia—possibly apocryphal, but nevertheless representative of actual problems—concerns corrugated steel roofing. Since sheets of roofing come in various sizes, the simplest common measure is weight. Tons of roofing thus became the measure of output. The planners instituted a drive for increased output. The producers started rolling thicker sheets, too thick, in fact, to be usable. The number of tons rose dramatically. But the number of sheets went down. The planners then shifted the measure from tons to square meters. Presto, the managers thereupon rolled the sheets much thinner, so thin, in fact, that they crumpled easily and quickly rusted through. But their "output" (and points) went up spectacularly.

Of the many additional complications we will mention just one. If faulty output from one enterprise becomes an input to another, the planners have difficulty knowing whether the managers of the second enterprise are doing poorly if *their* output is faulty. Suppose the planners complain that farms are not producing enough. The farm managers reply, "Those no-good tractors keep breaking down, and the fertilizer you ordered for us has only a third of the specified nitrogen." When the planners complain to the tractor factory, its manager says, "How can I turn out decent tractors? The engine blocks keep cracking because the steel they send us has too much sulfur in it. The generators from the electric equipment industry won't last three weeks. And the petroleum refineries make such poor lubricating oil that the bearings are shot in six months. Besides, we had to substitute copper tubing for bronze bushings because the bushing plant was two months behind." Is the manager of the tractor plant incompetent because his product is so bad? Or is he doing magnificently well, all things considered?

The planners might hire enough inspectors to determine whether the tractors are bad because of poor inputs or because of faulty performance in the tractor factory. Even so, problems remain. For example, if quality can be raised to acceptable levels by a 25 percent reduction in quantity, what are the payoffs between quantity and quality? Between expedited delivery at high cost and slower delivery at lower cost? Between low labor costs with high scrap rates and high labor cost with low scrap rates?

Evaluation in monopoly

Chester Barnard, for years a chief executive of New Jersey Bell Telephone Company and a noted writer about the managerial process (Barnard 1938, 1948), once complained that the difficulty with running a monopoly is that one has only technical, not economic, criteria for evaluating its management. One can count the new telephones installed, the cost of setting a telephone pole, or the average time required to complete a long-distance call. A 10 percent annual improvement in each of these measures might sound good. But under monopoly how can one know whether or not more competent managers might have improved them by 20 percent? The problem of evaluating managers in a centrally controlled economy shares important traits with that of evaluating the managers of a monopoly in a market economy—because a centralized planned economy *is* a monopoly. We will examine two aspects of the problem.

First is the problem of reducing a many-dimensioned measure to a single dimension. How can such varied aspects as quantity, quality, spoilage, speed of delivery, and cost be reduced to some single summary measure? In a complex economy the obvious common denominator is money. If one can figure the money cost of delayed delivery he thereby also knows the money value of prompt delivery. If he knows the money costs of repairs, wasted labor, and lost agricultural output resulting from faulty tractors he thereby knows the value of tractors without those faults.

If the farm manager knows the extra money value to him of a higher-quality tractor, it will be worth it to him to pay any additional amount up to that extra value to get a better tractor. If the farm manager is willing to pay 25 percent more for a quality tractor, the manager of the tractor factory then knows how much more *he* is justified in spending to raise the quality. Or if the farm manager figures he will lose 1,000 rubles' worth of output if his tractor is not delivered on time, we have a measure of how much extra expense is justified at the tractor factory to avoid late delivery.

During most of its history as a socialized economy the Soviet Union centrally specified in great detail which parts were to be produced in which factories, to which "customer" factories they were to be shipped, when, and at what price. Although the planners received persistent complaints about poor quality and slow delivery, because they were not close to the scene they had only the vaguest idea of the magnitude of the losses entailed, or how much cost would be justified to avoid them. Out of sheer desperation the managers have developed a large body of "fixers" (apparatchiks), whose function is to straighten out at the enterprise level the myriad pieces of detailed coordination that cannot be known, much less adjusted, at the planners' level.

For a decade or more the Russians have increasingly recognized that it might be more efficient to give more autonomy to enterprise managers. Perhaps more accurately we should say that the managers have been arguing for more autonomy for at least three decades, and that some understanding of its desirability is finally penetrating the planning bureaucracy.

Evaluation, autonomy, and profit

Even though all enterprises would remain government-owned, increased enterprise autonomy, or managerial discretion, would work as follows. The manager of each farm would be free to buy his tractors from any tractor factory, and to offer different prices for them, depending on how satisfactory he found them. If one tractor factory consistently turned out more reliable tractors or sold them at lower prices, its sales would go up and the sales of the others down. The manager of each tractor factory would similarly be free to determine where he would buy generators, steel, and other inputs, in reflection of their dependability, price, or promptness in delivery. Each enterprise manager could then estimate the payoffs as among quantity, quality, delivery, and cost and figure out which priorities among them would provide his plant with the largest excess of receipts over costs—the maximum profit.

As noted in Chapter 22, profit is more than a reward for enterprisers. At least in a stiffly price-competitive industry, an enterprise can make a large profit only by producing more efficiently than its competitors, and the managers of the profitable enterprises are thereby identified as the more competent. Under such competition, managerial competence is measured not only by ability to turn out a product, but also by the willingness of customers to buy it when known alternative sources are available. Because profit is the only measure of a manager's *overall* competence —as contrasted to his achievement of subgoals—the Soviets have been moving increasingly toward the use of a profit criterion for their enterprise managers, and toward more autonomy for them.

Interestingly, the use of profit as a measure of managerial competence is independent of ideology, and has been learned independently by those who control large enterprises in both the United States and Russia. To illustrate, although General Motors has the legal authority totally to control all its subdivisions from Detroit, it does not do so. Instead it has established relatively autonomous subsidiaries, the Chevrolet, Buick, Pontiac, Oldsmobile, and Cadillac divisions. In trying to sell cars, the Pontiac division, for example, competes just as much with the other divisions of General Motors as it does with Ford, Chrysler, American Motors, and the imports, and the central managers of General Motors use the profits of the divisions to evaluate their division managers. Managerially speaking, the Soviet economy is rather like an overgrown General Motors. Conversely, General Motors is a centrally planned partial economy, encompassing some 4 percent of the American economy. Though both General Motors and the Soviets have the authority to control everything from the center, both find some decentralization a useful managerial device. A fascinating question is whether the amount of decentralization that a planned economy discovers to provide the most efficient administration of the socialist system will closely resemble the amount of centralization that has evolved in market systems in the form of oligopolies and giant corporations.

Certain behaviors by an enterprise might, of course, increase its profits but not be socially useful, as with those based on monopoly or the sheer power of large size. Relatedly, American automobile manufacturers might have eliminated pollution and certain safety hazards much earlier, but did not because it was more profitable not to. The Russian use of either a profit criterion or a more limited criterion for rewarding their managers could produce similar results. In fact, Soviet enterprises have been no more concerned about pollution and product safety than have some American ones, presumably because the top party leaders gave higher priority to short-term increases in output than to longer-term protection of the environment, which led the planners to give more "points" to the managers for output than for environmental protection. Interestingly, workable controls of external costs may be essentially the same for both countries, in the form of direct governmental constraints on managers.

PRICES AND ALLOCATIONS OF FACTORS

Houses could be built on a given piece of land, corn could be grown on it, or it might be strip-mined for coal. To use the land for housing involves the opportunity cost of denying its use for corn or coal. That conclusion reflects physical and biological considerations, and is equally valid under socialist or capitalist organization. Under a competitive market system (with a few exceptions, such as churches), the land will be put to the use that commands the highest price. In market theory that use is also the one that will create the greatest value.

We observed that both decisions and transactions about things are based on values, not on quantities alone. In Russia all land is owned by the government, and no charge is made for its use by an enterprise. Suppose the manager of a state-owned farm says to the planners, "I think it would make sense to expand this farm to take in that plot," while the manager of a coal enterprise says, "I think this mining operation ought to be extended to include that plot." If the two managers cannot bid against each other for the plot (since land is provided to them free), how are the planners to know which use is the more productive? The rational approach is to inquire which is more valuable, corn or coal. But of what help are these prices to the planners when the prices of corn and coal are themselves set by the planners, somewhat arbitrarily and without regard to any cost for using the land?

A parallel situation arises in connection with capital funds, which are also provided to enterprises without charge. Out of a given stock of investable funds, how can the planners determine how much to apply to housing, corn, or coal?

The Soviets are aware that they have often made unsound decisions because they lack the valuations of land and capital on which sound decisions must be based. This does not mean they make obviously nonsensical decisions, such as shifting the land from corn to coal when coal is very plentiful and corn very scarce. But when the difference is less glaringly obvious, the decision becomes difficult indeed.[2] The difficulty arises from an error in Marxist doctrine, from which the Soviets are only beginning to extricate themselves. The Marxian labor theory of value asserted that all value is created by labor, and that labor alone should be compensated. Land is provided by nature, and capital is only congealed labor, Marx asserted. Now to say that land and invested capital should not be privately owned or provide private income is a value judgment, and anyone is entitled to his view about it. But to say that the use of land and capital have no cost is an analytical judgment, not a value judgment, about which Russian as well as Western economists conclude that Marx was wrong. The opportunity cost of using land for corn is that it cannot be used for coal. The same can be said for capital. Sound decision making requires that these costs be considered before land or capital is allocated, even if no payment is actually made for it. This difficulty of setting values in a totally planned economy is reflected in a classic remark of Stalin that cotton must be worth more than grain in Russia, because that is how it was on the world market (Grossman 1959: 62).

An interesting consequence of this analysis is a convergence of certain

---

[2] Things are actually much more complicated. The Soviets do have prices on things, in fact a whole series of different prices used for different purposes. But because of certain arbitrarinesses in those prices the underlying situation remains basically as described.

aspects of market and socialist thinking. The trend of contemporary socialists, unlike traditional ones, is somewhat as follows. Market logic is basically sound—they say. But capitalist nations are so encrusted with monopoly, entrenched position, advertising, tax shelters, external costs, and military-industrial collusion that the market system cannot work well. Not being encumbered with all this paraphernalia, socialists—they add—*can* make the market process work, possibly by first simulating it in a computer. East European members of the Soviet bloc tend toward this approach, and have developed some reasonably sophisticated models.

WHERE DO WE GO FROM HERE?

The previous section outlined some problems of a completely centralized economy, and the previous chapter examined some problems of a completely decentralized economy. No modern economy seems workable if it is wholly centralized or decentralized. In fact, one can hardly conceive of a *wholly* centralized system, in which, for example, the central planning bureau would determine whether Ivan the auto mechanic should use a socket wrench or a box wrench to tighten the bolts on an engine. In a market system it is incongruous to speak of "wholly decentralized" decisions by General Motors or ITT, and a leading economics text (Samuelson) consistently refers to the American economy as "mixed."

Unfortunately (in my view), vast effort has been dedicated to propagating ideologies, mainly of communism and capitalism, and it may be useful to examine the problem of economic centralization without ideological fixations.

Since there can be no such thing as a wholly controlled or a wholly uncontrolled system, the question is: What is the appropriate degree of centralized control for any particular time, place, or circumstance? More particularly, which *kinds* of decisions can most usefully be made on a centralized and which on a decentralized basis?

Some of the answers are unrelated to ideology. For example, certain decisions about public goods, such as a national highway system or freedom from air pollution, can be made effectively *only* on a centralized basis. So can decisions about such aggregative economic behaviors as rates of inflation, unemployment, or economic growth. Some persons are so dedicated to decentralism that they would leave inflation, unemployment, and economic growth wholly uncontrolled, whatever the consequences. However, virtually all liberals and most conservatives in the United States now accept (even if reluctantly) the need for governmental efforts to control at least inflation and unemployment. At the other extreme are decisions about obviously private consumer goods, such as peanut butter and shirts. Although decisions about these *can* be made centrally, it does not seem sensible to do so, and the Soviets are beginning to agree.

In short (and to skip some of the complications), if each nation could mold its decision structure toward practical workability instead of ideological dogma, and could assume that each other nation would do the same, we might remove much heat from the ideological conflict. In fact, many decisions *are* made on this basis, but unnecessary tension continues because of the ongoing preoccupation with ideology and related fears of international conflict.

Who's on first?

Marx predicted that nations would go through a cycle of capitalist industrialization. The rich would grow richer, the poor poorer (at least relatively), depressions successively worse, and capitalist control more concentrated. Finally the dispossessed workers would rise in revolt and seize the government, which would take over industry and establish a socialist state by and for workers. Two observations seem necessary.

First, Marxist economics deals with capitalism, not socialism. It tells how and why capitalist systems will collapse—in the Marxian view. It leads the oppressed people out of capitalist bondage to a peak overlooking the promised land of socialism. There it leaves them, without blueprints or instructions. Marx left no prescriptions about how to organize industry, how to decide what to produce, what to centralize or decentralize, how to select and evaluate managers, how to measure whether the system is doing well, or how to price products and factors. And, unlike Weber, Marx did not anticipate the bureaucratization of the planning process or the evolution of the planners themselves into a favored class who might block decentralization because it threatened their privileges. The "withering away of the state," which is essential for the transition to full communism, seems even less likely in Soviet Russia than in capitalist America.

Socialist economists have discovered that "capitalist" theory is not merely an analysis of a market system, but also a theory of rational decisions. As part of that theory appears in Chapters 7 and 8 it expresses the essence of rationality, whether by dictator, elected leader, business firm, socialist planner, parent, or consumer. Yet historically it is derived from the "capitalist" theory of the firm.

The second observation deals with the question, Which comes first, socialism or capitalism? When Marx lived, it seemed obvious that capitalism comes first. A hundred years after Marx the reverse seems more probable. Communism has little appeal in advanced industrial nations, but much appeal in the underdeveloped nations of Asia, Africa, and Latin America. If Russia and communist Eastern Europe are any sample, once basic industrialization has been achieved through central planning, and the economy shifts strongly toward consumer goods, central controls become rapidly less workable and "dollar ballots" more so.

In short, it now looks as if Marx had things reversed. The second half of the 20th century suggests that socialism is not what replaces a market system when the latter collapses, but rather that market techniques will dilute central planning once the single-minded, plannable goal of basic industrialization has been achieved. Perhaps more accurately, Marx anticipated a one-way movement and actual developments suggest a movement from both sides toward the center.

Indicative planning and conclusion

An interesting combination of centralized and decentralized controls exemplified in France, is called "indicative planning." Here representatives of government and industry sketch out the future of the economy. Their sketch consists in part of simple prediction and in part of a desired goal. This "indicated" future is then treated as a plan, to be implemented by voluntary, profit-oriented actions of firms. The plan identifies which industries and areas need to expand and which need to contract. The motivation to comply is that if the "indications" materialize firms will be best off if they have conformed. But any firm that thinks the plan wrong need not follow it. However, the government exercises much control over banks and credit, and the firm that conforms will find it easier to borrow. Because many important firms follow it, the plan tends to be self-fulfilling.

In a looser way the private predictions of major American industries have a similar self-fulfilling character, particularly those of the utilities which make at least rough plans for ten or more years ahead. Because the energy they provide is essential for other industries, the utilities' expansion makes possible the expansion of other industries, and their failure to expand would limit other industries. Predictions made by other basic industries, such as petroleum, steel, and transportation, have similar effects. In fact, the "energy crisis" that surfaced in 1973, and related difficulties, partly reflect certain inadequacies in private planning about petroleum refining capacity, compounded by inappropriate government regulations and research funding, and sharpened by a Middle East war. Because such private plans are not made by government they are neither "formal" nor "socialist." But, for example, because of the way utility companies are tied together across the country both physically and managerially, one would hesitate to call their decisions "decentralized." Nor, considering the long-range consequences of decisions in such large companies, and the care with which they often project the future, does it seem appropriate to call the American economy "wholly unplanned." Large investment banks also exercise a significant "planning" function when they grant or withhold credit from producing companies for large long-term expansions, and when they vote the large blocks of stock they own.

If there is some position on the scale of centralization-decentralization that would be optimum for any given nation, the problem is to locate and reach it. This seems a less dramatic but possibly more sensible approach than ideological warfare, which generates hate, fear, suspicion, and incredibly high costs. Under this approach a nation would not for the sake of dogma centralize what can be performed better by decentralized units. Nor would it dogmatically decentralize things that are better directed from the center. While joint Russian-American research in the Antarctic, the seas and outer space is all to the good, some joint investigation into what is feasibly centralized and what is not might be more to the point. We and they together still know remarkably little about this crucial aspect of organization theory at the level of the whole nation. Some people in both countries think it immoral even to ask the question.

25

THE FAMILY

We started our examination of organizations with the general discussion of pure formal organization. We then jumped to pure informal organization, after which we returned to the semiformal position in between. We then examined the most conspicuous example of formal organization, government, followed by the most conspicuous example of informal organization, a market economy. Orderly presentation calls next for an example of semiformal organization. But perhaps by nature of the species, there is no clean-cut example. Since the family has significant semiformal ingredients along with both formal and informal ones, and is very much worth examining in its own right, we look at it next.

Across time and space, families have come in many shapes and sizes. We will deal here solely with the nuclear family. In its simplest form this consists of an adult female, an adult male, and any offspring they may have. Typically the adults are married. But if there is continuity to their relationship, many of its social aspects are much the same whether they are married or not.

Like government, and unlike most other organizations (which are segmental), the family is potentially all-purpose. It deals with all, or potentially all, aspects of the person, rather than with merely one or a few aspects. At least for young children membership is not voluntary, and parents may legitimately use at least some force in their exercise of authority. We will trace some of the consequences later. Unlike government, however, the family is not sovereign. Nearly everywhere it is subject to some higher authority.

The nuclear family's crucial social role is to serve as the main communicator of information, or pattern, from one generation to the next.

The procreation of children transmits the genetic patterns developed through eons of biological evolution. And the rearing of children in the family transmits many of the cultural patterns developed through millennia of social evolution. The genetic patterns are almost totally resistant to change during the lifetime of an individual, and the cultural patterns learned deeply early in life can be highly resistant to change (Chapter 12). The adult pair first perform the biological function that produces the child and then (if they stay together) the socialization function that inducts the infant into the family and the larger society.

Most families are formed in response to urges and goals of the parties immediately involved. In responding to those urges and goals, they nevertheless perform the wider social function of transmitting genes and culture, even if the individuals have no understanding of this result and no intent to produce it. In this sense a family is a subsystem of an overall social system that is mainly informal, though with important semiformal ingredients.

The cultural and biological aspects are closely related, as we can observe by contrasting the parent-child relation of humans with those of fish, snakes, or insects. In the latter cases the young are totally on their own from the moment they are hatched. The parents do not feed, teach, or care for the young, which either take off promptly after their own food or starve. The human infant, by contrast, is dependent for years on parents or other adults for biological care and for most of his learning about his environment. The two factors are related. First, the infant's biological dependence does not allow him to leave his elders for many years, during which he learns their culture. Second, a society and a culture are necessary to provide for the child until he is old enough to be self-sufficient. Relatedly, since the human inherits no instinctive ability to produce or identify food, or to construct shelter, he must learn these things by living among others who know them. Long biological infancy and long social learning are the complementary halves of the relationship.

Families, incidentally, are essentially undifferentiated subsystems of a society, in that all families perform the same basic functions. If several families of a society are wiped out, the population is smaller, but no specialized function goes unperformed.

STRUCTURES AND FUNCTIONS OF FAMILIES

Like many other aspects of behavior, the functioning of the family is increasingly being examined to see if traditional ways of doing things are sensible. Much such examination now falls under the name of "liberation." It is not the function of this text to take a value position concerning any family form or any relationship of the sexes. Perhaps we can clarify most readily if we mention a theoretically possible but not-now-available situation, much like Huxley's *Brave New World*. In it all "natural" pregnancies are easily prevented. If a couple want their own children, an ovum is removed from the female and sperm from the male, the egg is fertilized in a hospital laboratory, and the fetus grows there in a glass jar until it is "born." The infant is bottle-fed after birth.

Under these circumstances sexual intercourse would perform only a pleasure-companionship function. Care of the child could be done by the father, mother, or such combination as they agreed on. Notably, the mother would be no more constrained by pregnancy, child care, or feeding than would the father. (Under the Supreme Court ruling of 1972 it would presumably be legal to discard the fetus during at least the first six months of its growth for any reason—as that it was deformed or of the "wrong" sex.) Biology would then not determine the roles and behaviors of husband and wife except as it affected such traits as the size, strength, intelligence, energy, health, or sex urge of particular individuals. The reader will understand that these two paragraphs are neither a prediction nor a recommendation. They are simply a way of clarifying certain relationships in a form that we might call the "completely liberated" model. Even without such medical developments, a couple who have only adopted children approximate that model, except that many norms (stereotypes) about male-female roles surround them in most places. Hence, while we use the model for certain purposes below, we must realistically deal mainly with the more traditional concept of the family as it actually appears in most places and has behaved through most of human history.

In its main characteristics a contemporary nuclear family with children is a complex, formal, cooperative organization with many functions. It is formal in that it is consciously created to meet certain goals of its members. It is also formal in that its structure is determined when tasks are consciously assigned to different persons, even if some tasks are rotated, or if the division of labor merely follows the norms of the culture. The family is cooperative in that the same persons are both sponsors and recipients, bearing the costs in their role as sponsors and receiving the benefits in their role as recipients. Unless a family has servants or slaves, its members are also the staff. When children arrive it is complex, in that it has three or more members, both a horizontal and a vertical division of labor, and an authority structure.

We will study the family according to the same procedure we used with government. Since a family is a formal organization, many general statements about it have already been made in Chapters 15 and 16. Our next move is to identify the salient respects in which families differ from the general model.

Some biological determinants

As we now find it, a family is different from other organizations in that certain aspects of its structure are biologically determined. There is no need for a couple to confer about who will be the father and who the mother. There is also a certain irreversibility between parents and children that no miracle of surgery can alter. That same biological difference also means that parents hold total dominance over the child so long as he is helpless, and partial dominance for some years thereafter. It also requires that many transactions between parents and children be overtly generous till the children are old enough to be productive. That relation might be described loosely as subjectively balanced from the beginning, in that even the new infant can "give" pleasure to the parents. However, at least during early infancy, this pleasure is "given" only in the loose sense that a sunset "gives" pleasure, and the parents' pleasure is more perceptual than transactional.

As to the number of children, the major biological limitations are that gestation takes three fourths of a year, that human babies normally come singly rather than in litters, that the female is fertile for about 25 to 30 years, that there may be long periods between births, and that bearing many children close together may debilitate the mother. Hence even without deliberate birth control a couple will produce no more than eight to a dozen children, not fifty or a hundred, and the number is usually smaller. Actually, some limitations on births are practiced in virtually all known societies, particularly industrial ones, even where religion disapproves them. Among others, the method may be as simple as late marriage, as in Ireland during the 19th century.

Economic and social factors

Despite those biological constraints the size and structure of the nuclear family are biologically free to vary in some respects. As to adult members, the nuclear family can consist of one male and one female (monogamy), one male and multiple females (polygyny), one female and multiple males (polyandry), or multiple males and females (group marriage). Polygamy is the general term for more than one mate, without specifying which sex is multiple. Although without formal names, at least two types of relationships seem frequent enough to be viewed as family forms. One is a continuing stable relation between one female and her offspring, with no adult male being regularly in the family. The second occurs when the male, female, or both have been married more than once, and the children are "his, hers, and theirs." (The movie "Divorce American Style" illustrates this relation among middle-class suburbanites.) "Swinging" groups are not a family form, but an arrangment for sexual relations outside the family. Homosexual pairs could constitute households, but not families as we use those terms here.

The above relationships are all considered types of nuclear family. By contrast, in some societies the *extended* family is standard practice, and *some* extended families occur within nearly all societies. The extended family simply means that the nuclear family does not live alone, but among a complex that includes grandparents, uncles, aunts, cousins, and in-laws in various combinations. Such group living includes significant pooling of incomes and expenditures (in a money economy) and of activities and facilities, particularly for food preparation and child care. An extended family differs from the kind of commune that spread in the United States and Europe during the 1960s, in that all members are related by blood or marriage. Extended families are most common in primitive, peasant, and rural societies. In modern Western cities they are likely to be found most frequently among people who have recently moved from rural areas, or among those forced together by inadequate income or poor health.

The monogamous family of one male and one female is the most common form, even in those societies which allow polygamy. Polyandry is almost nonexistent. It is found where conditions of life in the traditional family are so spare that it takes more than one male to work in conjunction with a female and her children to maintain the family. It also appears as a remedial arrangment in small societies where upon the death of a wife her sister may marry the widower while remaining married to her existing husband. In a parallel manner, polygyny may occur when a man takes his brother's wife upon the death of the brother. It also occurs in male-dominated societies when a man can "afford" multiple wives while other men cannot "afford" even one, as occurs among Arab sheiks. In that case multiple wives are a status symbol indicating wealth.

Formal group marriages, as contrasted to "swinging," are virtually unknown. Polygamous family forms are generally based more on economic and organizational factors than on sexual relationships, since the latter can be arranged without adding the extra partner to the regular family.

The one-to-one relationship of adults is the major family form among humans. This relationship contrasts with that of most other species of large mammals, where the dominant male holds a harem of females and leaves many other males without mates. The availability to humans of poisons, arrows, and guns largely eliminates dominance based on muscular strength, and the ability of humans to think and communicate allows mateless males to gang up on a male who might try to monopolize the females. The female also presumably prefers being the only wife to being one of several.

In nearly all industrial societies monogamy is now the only form of marriage allowed by law. Whether by law or social pressure, the family form in each society is determined mainly by cultural patterns. Around the norm of each society variations that reflect individual needs or preferences nevertheless occur, although with limits on variations that can be practiced openly.

In the discussion below we will concentrate mainly on the monogamous nuclear family: because it is the standard form in Western societies, because it is the most frequent form even in those societies which allow polygamy, and because nuclear units exist and show some characteristics of the type even when they are subsystems within an extended family.

The multipurpose aspect of the family

A family shows some of the same traits as a government. Like government, it is potentially all-purpose, and it is difficult to imagine any important function that the family has not somewhere, sometime engaged in. Because it is both all-purpose and small, the family deals with the whole person: his health, his food, his personality, his emotions, his friendships, and his loves. In this respect it differs from government which, while it potentially deals with any question about the society as a whole, does not deal with the whole individual in this sense. The sociologist describes this all-purpose aspect by saying that the family is *not segmental:* it does not deal with only one segment of the person, but with the whole of him. This all-purpose aspect nevertheless gives the family another trait which resembles that of government, namely, that its inactions may be as important as its actions. A decision *not* to do anything about the child's high fever, or high intelligence, or about the hole in the roof or the wayward child, may be quite as important as the decision *to* do something.

In two respects the relation of children to the family resembles that of citizen to government. The first is involuntary membership. The child does not choose to join the family, and has almost no choice about remaining in it until he is more or less grown up. The child is thus bound by the family decisions about many things, whether he agrees with them or not. Second, he is subject to the use of legitimate force by his parents. This force may include corporal punishment, and it certainly includes restrictions on freedom of movement or action—though the amount and types of such discipline vary greatly from society to society and family to family. These aspects of the relationship are basic to the power, bargaining power, and decision techniques within the family, which we will discuss below.

THE MARRIAGE BARGAIN

Why a major bargain?

The mutual attraction of male and female is powerful, and the relations between them go forward under many arrangements and circumstances, both socially approved and disapproved. Some are sexual encounters as desired and convenient, with no longer-run attachments at all. Some are series of relationships of indefinite duration, intense or casual, either in sequence or with two or more partners concurrently— simple organizations terminable-at-will when either party sees the costs to exceed the benefits. These and other kinds of relationships exist before, beside, after, or instead of marriage. Furthermore, in contemporary America about one in six first marriages turns out to be a temporary organization, being terminated by divorce (Leslie 1973: 581). Although transitory relationships are increasingly visible and accepted, and some sex outside of marriage has always been common among some fraction of the population, a reasonably durable relation between a given male and female is the expected and normal practice in all known societies. Why?

The motives are various. We will deal first with the desire for sexual relations, and later with other and more varied motives. In most animals except humans the sex urge is sporadic or cyclical. Typically the female is in heat and fertile only at short cyclical intervals, and the male becomes aroused only when the female is receptive. By contrast, humans display "continuous sexuality." This does not mean that the human is aroused all the time, but rather that neither arousability nor sexual relationships are confined to short, biologically determined intervals. In

"Alison, will you be my first wife?"

Drawing by Whitney Darrow, Jr.; © 1974 The New Yorker Magazine, Inc.

consequence the human tends to want more or less continuous or regular availability of *some* mate.

One arrangement for handling this situation is a continuing, exclusive relationship between a given pair. The opposite extreme is a "clearinghouse" to which any individual can go for a sexual relationship in the expectation that an acceptable mate will be available. An intermediate arrangement is to have relationships with a variety of other persons, under mutually agreeable circumstances, with or without significant emotional attachments. Other arrangements are also possible, and are found. These are sufficient to illustrate the general problem, although, with the variations noted, the first is the norm in all human societies. The second is a supplemental, largely one-sided arrangement found in virtually all large societies, in prostitution. Prostitution is approved or disapproved to varying degrees in different parts of the world, being illegal (but present) in most of the United States, but legal and regulated in some European and Asian countries. Nowhere, however, is prostitution or any other form of "clearinghouse" arrangement considered standard and basic, rather than supplemental. In fact, almost any except an ongoing, at least relatively exclusive, relationship between a pair is considered supplemental rather than basic. Why?

"I thought people had to be married for the magic to go out."

Drawing by Mahood; © 1972 The New Yorker Magazine, Inc.

At this point we are discussing a basic lifetime living style. Some other arrangements, especially by young people during their "experimental years" are discussed later in connection with dating and courtship. A continuing set of temporary relationships, "always changing before it gets boring," strikes some people as sensible and exciting. Those who are young, attractive, and popular would presumably respond more favorably to this life-style than those less well endowed by birth, experience, or temperament, as they would "win" more easily in this relatively competitive situation. But with passing years and decades most people are not likely to accept the continued cost in time, effort, gamesmanship, and uncertainty that a sequence of temporary relationships involves—as someone has suggested, it is like continually having to find a new cook. Those less attractive or energetic, or more interested in other activities would not like such perpetual competition even from the start. Even with the best of luck there would probably be gaps between relationships, sometimes long gaps, and they would probably increase in length as one got older.

Since a mating relationship must cover more or less the whole population, a form that works satisfactorily for only a minor fraction or for a limited age bracket is not likely to be the basic form. Although there can be many variations to meet individual needs, human societies are not likely to let such a regular and fundamental activity depend on uncertain, sporadic, and haphazard relationships. Other aspects of the problem involve the question of whether mating is a terminable-at-will organization, to which we now turn.

Is mating a terminable-at-will relationship?

An organization is fully terminable-at-will only if (1) no goods have been produced by and/or belong to the organization, as distinct from its individual members; (2) the organization has no debts or other obligations to others that will continue after the organization is dissolved; and (3) any goods jointly produced by or belonging to the organization can be divided among its members without significant loss of value.

Relations with a prostitute normally meet these conditions. So do some casual dating relations, short terms of living together, or relations based on close proximity (as when the two people having relations live in the same apartment building). But things are usually more complicated. Human societies have always had to face the possibility—which is still not unheard of despite modern contraceptive technology—that intercourse will produce children. Offspring obviously violate all three of the conditions for terminable-at-will organization stated above, and societies have not unreasonably insisted that people who produce children accept the joint responsibility of caring for them. If both parents develop strong emotional attachments to the child, and the child to them, separation involves intense emotional disruption, sometimes producing lifelong emotional damage to the child. Less dramatically, a couple who live together more than a few months are likely to acquire or make tangible goods whose disposition involves difficulties. Even without children or joint property, strong emotional attachments may arise that are not easily terminable. They may develop without regard to age or the length of the relationship, and are particularly difficult if highly unequal.

A pair of recent undergraduates illustrate such inequality. They lived together during their last year of college on the basis of "no commitments: we'll see how things go and then decide." The relationship worked out beautifully in all visible respects. As agreed, it was not discussed. As graduation approached, one of the pair assumed that if any two people could get along well, which they had demonstrated that they could, that they would marry shortly. After commencement the other said, "Be sure to let me know your address. We may want to keep in touch."

To a degree that differs greatly from person to person and from time to time in the same person, the sexual relation has strong psychological and social, as well as biological and neurological, components. By reason of culture or experience many persons have no desire for sex except with someone they love, and feel a lack of interest in or a revulsion toward other relations. Others can change partners easily and often. Even the latter, however, may become so attached to one partner as to lose all desire for anyone else, and feel distraught until the tie is made durable and perhaps exclusive. In short, even for persons who feel no moral or religious constraints, the intimate relations of mates often shift suddenly from terminable-at-will to terminable only at high emotional cost. To keep (or try to keep) that relationship exclusive reduces the risk that one partner will be emotionally damaged if the other shifts his emotional attachment to some third party on the basis of a sexual relationship there.

Some broader needs for closeness

A broader kind of tie, which may or may not have a sexual component, is the need for close, intimate companionship. It is the need to let down your hair to someone, in the confidence that the doubts and weaknesses you reveal about yourself will not later be used transactionally against you. It is the related need for comfort, support, and advice, and may include a need to give support rather than receive it. It is a need to care and be cared about, to many the essence of being human. When ill-health or other adversity strikes, there must be someone close enough to accept large inconvenience on one's behalf—the knowledge that there is someone else to whom you are the most important thing in the world. Because such needs are often so highly personal they can only be met by an intimate.

Some of these needs are easier to meet in an extended family, where someone is always there to care and help. Intimate ties are spread across more people. In some societies when one marries he makes an alliance, not with one person, but with the whole clan of the spouse. As noted in Chapter 17, a community of interacting systems is more stable if substitutes are readily available to fill any role that becomes vacant. This condition prevails much more in the extended than in the nuclear family. There the household contains not merely the spouse, but also uncles, aunts, in-laws, perhaps a grandmother who acts as psychologist, to advise, help, or commiserate when things go wrong, and to share joys when they go right. We have seen that in some societies the extended family automatically assigns a new spouse to replace one that died. With multiple ties of emotional and physical support it is less important whether the spouse himself is the most desired possible. In contrast to the extended family, one difficulty of an unconnected nuclear family is that each spouse is expected to fill more roles than some persons can handle. This contrast between nuclear and extended families has been simplified to make a point. Even in industrial societies with high mobility most nuclear families have relatives who assist in emergencies, and often live close enough to be part of a continuing, intimate group. In general, however, the more mobile and impersonal the larger society the greater is the need for a very dependable relationship with one's mate.

All this, of course, is not the whole story. But it does suggest why a continuing, often permanent commitment between a male and a female is the accepted norm in every major human society, even if not in every subsociety. The marriage contract performs the same essential function as any other contract. It provides a clear statement of at least some aspects of the major bargain, and significantly increases the stake of the parties in keeping their promise by exerting legal or social pressures if they do not. Various legal provisions about alimony, child care, and disposition of joint property in the event the marriage is terminated are all implicitly part of the marriage contract. As soon as children arrive, the terms on which a marriage is broken are no longer a concern of the husband and wife alone, but of the children and the rest of the society. In fact, in some respects the law is more concerned with whether a couple have produced children or own joint property than whether they are formally married. The wedding performs the double function of providing witnesses to the contract and of constituting a role-change ceremony. If it is also an occasion for conviviality, who should complain?

Content and terms of the major bargain

Because the bargain is normally expected to last a lifetime, and does much more often than not (see Table 25–1 and related discussion below), and because to most people it affects the quality of life far more than does any other transaction, its terms and content are highly important. We will examine three different sets of relationships. First are relations between husband and wife in the marriage itself. Second are transactional relations involving the children. Third are those between the unmarried male and female in the precommitment stages of dating and courtship.

The husband-wife transaction. In one sense one might assert that there is no question of "terms" in a wedding. It is "all of me for all of you"—and not necessarily in a possessive sense. Yet there are many details which it is appropriate to speak of as "terms," and which can therefore be analyzed as affecting power and bargaining power. In some societies a dowry is used, and in others a "bride-price." These payments may be made in money, land, cattle, shells, or something else valued in the society. Even if not usually viewed in that light, a dowry is a price paid by a girl's family for a husband and the "bride price" is a price paid by a boy's family for a wife. Depending on the circumstances, the price may be paid to the spouse or to the spouse's family.

These exchanges are viewed in various lights in different societies. A bride-price, sometimes called bridewealth, may be viewed as a token of respect to the bride's family, or as thanks for having produced and raised her. In some societies it is thought of as compensation to her family for

Table 25–1
NUMBER AND RATE OF FIRST MARRIAGES, DIVORCES, AND
REMARRIAGES: UNITED STATES, THREE-YEAR AVERAGES,
1921 TO 1971

	First marriages		Divorces		Remarriages	
Period	(thousands	rate*)	(thousands	rate†)	(thousands	rate‡)
1921–23	990	99	158	10	186	98
1924–26	992	95	177	11	200	99
1927–29	1,025	94	201	12	181	84
1930–32	919	81	183	10	138	61
1933–35	1,081	92	196	11	162	69
1936–38	1,183	98	243	13	201	83
1939–41	1,312	106	269	14	254	103
1942–44	1,247	108	360	17	354	139
1945–47	1,540	143	526	24	425	163
1948–50	1,326	134	397	17	360	135
1951–53	1,190	122	388	16	370	136
1954–56	1,182	120	379	15	353	129
1957–59	1,128	112	381	15	359	129
1960–62	1,177	116	407	16	372	133
1963–65	1,323	110	452	17	404	139
1966–68	1,488	110	535	20	463	150
1969–71	1,604	107	702	26	569	168

* First marriages per 1,000 single women 14 to 44 years old.
† Divorces per 1,000 married women 14 to 44 years old.
‡ Remarriages per 1,000 widowed and divorced women 14 to 54 years old.
Computed from National Center for Health Statistics, 1968, Tables 1–1 and 2–1, and 1971a, 1971b,
and 1972; United States Bureau of the Census, 1966, Table 3, and 1971a, 1971b, and 1972.
Source: Paul C. Glick and Arthur J. Norton, "Perspectives on the Recent Upturn in Divorce and
Remarriage," Demography, 10 (1973): 302.

the loss of her productive services, and in others it serves as a sort of
deposit-guarantee, to be returned to the husband or his family if the wife
leaves her husband or is considered unsatisfactory. (There is always
distortion in describing these practices in language not that of the peoples involved.) If we reverse the sexes, much the same kind of observations can be made about the dowry. Incidentally, although the term
dowry is sometimes used for a payment in either direction, anthropologists and sociologists most commonly refer to it as the payment from
female to male, and that usage is followed here. Although this factor
declines in importance in industrial societies with rising levels of universal education, in the long and broad view of the world marriages have
been most likely to occur between a pair whose families have about equal
wealth or status.

Many societies place a high premium on the bride's virginity, with a
large discount (in the form of having to accept a less prestigious husband) if she lacks this qualification. In some other societies, however, a
girl is not considered marriageable until pregnant. In no known society
is a premium placed on the virginity of the male.

Even aside from the family's wealth, there is a general tendency for husband and wife to be of about equal "value." A boy who is rich, intelligent, handsome, and personable does not normally marry a girl who is poor, stupid, homely, and socially awkward, or vice versa. The two need not match on any particular dimension. But shortage on one dimension will normally have to be made up in some others to produce an approximate equality of total worth. In cases of obvious discrepancy friends and family will say, "I wonder what he (she) sees in her (him)!" If the query is discreetly not put straight to the person who seems headed for a "marriage downward," he will probably hear hints about others who got "less than they deserved" in this important transaction, or who "threw themselves away" on some "worthless" partner. To the parents it is something like seeing an offspring with low income burdened with a $50,000 mortgage on a $10,000 house—a dreadfully bad bargain with long-lasting consequences. They can only hope he will be lucky enough to strike oil on the property—or whatever the appropriate phrase is for having an unlikely looking spouse turn out well.

For love or money. In the United States and some other areas there is a tradition of marrying "for love," with love often being interpreted as a romantic fixation something like being simultaneously "high" and hypnotized. Many other societies consider this an addlebrained criterion, and assume that a marriage built on no firmer a foundation has a low chance of success. There is, of course, no necessary contradiction between marrying for love and marrying for more "rational" reasons. The old dialogue illustrates it.

> *Daughter* (to wealthy parent). Daddy, should I marry for money or for love?
> *Father.* Of course you marry for love, my sweet. Just take care not to fall in love with any boy that doesn't have money.

The rationale of Chapter 14 indicates that in general people will fall in love with others of about their same level of power. They usually fall in love with someone they associate with regularly, and they mostly associate regularly with others of about their own level of power. If "love" involves more than sexual attraction it is likely to reflect similarities of tastes and values. Despite some initial fascination, the pacifist is likely to be "turned off" by a companion who would "drop the bomb on 'em, just to show 'em" and the hippie by someone who thinks money is all that matters—and vice versa. If love is not totally blind it may reflect factors that do indicate probable success in marriage.

In short, the power factors in the marriage bargain follow the same general rules as power factors in other transactions. Where dowry or bride-price prevails, the bargain is literally a question of "how much." Elsewhere, the question of "how much" is modified into a question of "who." Here the questions of matching are more qualitative, and there is no point to debating whether one partner's pleasure in reading mystery stories is "more" or "less" than the other's pleasure in skiing, or whether a dedication to art is quantitatively different from a dedication to rebuilding the slums.

Some other parts of the bargain. Some other possible ingredients of the major bargain are division of labor, authority, desired number of children, ground rules about sex, and child rearing. In many traditional societies these things need not be discussed, since both parties accept the norms of the prevailing culture. In a society where norms are changing, or allow much individual choice, the relationship is likely to be worked out in the give-and-take of living together, as both parties mature and undergo changes of values. Even if they do not explicitly discuss things before marriage, it is nevertheless helpful if each party has at least a general idea of what the other expects, which expectations become a sort of implicit bargain. Not everyone is flexible about his way of life, and even the flexible can bend only so far. For example, if he expects to earn all the money, make all the decisions about spending, have six children, have a family of strict churchgoers, take no responsibility for housework or child care, and be allowed an occasional affair "on the side"; if she expects to have her own career, have only two children, ignore religion, share all decisions and responsibilities, and allow no extramarital relations; and if these things are not ironed out in advance, the marriage is probably headed for the rocks. There may be sense in the tendency for people to write their own wedding ceremony, which is their contract, even if a vague one, and it will be interesting to see how such marriages turn out.

If these things are discussed in advance, several transactional results are possible. One is the absence of overlap of EPs, in which case the marriage transaction will not go through. A second is a marked discrepancy of EPs: A is desperate for a mate and sees no visible alternatives, while B has many alternatives and is not really interested in marriage. In this case A's EP is very long and B's short. Yet there may be an overlap, in which case an agreement will be reached mainly on B's terms. (We will not predict whether the marriage will work.) A third possibility is a strategic alteration of two initially short EPs. Conversations might suggest that neither party's expectations are sensible, and both may extend to an overlap about halfway between their starting points. Or one EP might grow a great deal to meet the initial position of the other, in a "conversion" of one party by the other. Many other combinations are also possible.

One of the devilishly difficult things about this aspect of courtship is that one, possibly both, of the parties may have only the haziest view of what will be important in marriage. Traits or behaviors that may seem vastly important before the marriage may turn out to be trivial after it, and vice versa. Plans may also turn out badly because of unexpected developments in such areas as health, income, deaths, or the reappearance of an "old flame."

On liberation and bargaining power.   Bargaining power, here as elsewhere, is closely related to available alternatives. In typical middle-class America during most of its history a girl would have been in a weak position indeed if she tried to bargain a prospective husband into allowing her to work while he stayed home full time doing the housework. If one prospect said no, she was unlikely to find someone else who would say yes. In a parallel manner, a male who nowadays tried to get a prospective American bride to agree to total male dominance, oriental style, would similarly find himself in a weak bargaining position because few females would accept such terms.

Assuming that she had found a man willing to marry her, a century ago a girl would have had no difficulty in getting him to agree to provide all her money income while she cared for the house and children. It was standard practice, and the male could not easily find a girl willing to work for money income. By contrast, if present trends continue, males willing to provide the whole money income for the family will become increasingly scarce. Females willing to do nothing but housework will also become scarce.

This shift in norms is not arbitrary, but reflects a change in underlying power factors. When there were eight children, when food preparation started with materials as they came from the soil or the flour mill, when all cleaning of floors or dishes or clothes was done by hand, when carpets were cleaned by broom and carpetbeater, and when clothing was hand-sewn at home, being "just a housewife" was more than a full-time occupation. Any woman who did it well was fully earning her way. Furthermore, when the man was working 60 or more hours a week he could not have much of a house unless there were someone there to keep it. Even without children, just "keeping a house" of moderate size was a substantial job.

Let us contrast the present situation, starting with a couple without children. What with vacuum cleaners, clothes washers, dryers, ready-made no-iron clothing, dishwashers, and automatic ovens, housekeeping alone is no longer a full-time occupation—short of spending ridiculous amounts of time in cleaning or cooking or refusing to use conveniences that our society provides. In fact, many available foods are so completely prepared that for those willing to eat them "cooking" consists of little more than changing their temperature. As a result, several ingredients of bargaining power have shifted dramatically. First, the male concludes that the female is not doing her share if she is "just a housewife." Second, with all the assistance of modern technology, taken in conjunction with a shorter workweek, a lone male can keep respectable living quarters for himself. Third, for the same reason that the male can make it on his own, so can the female who holds a job.

In short, because of the marked increase in productivity both in industry and in the household (even if the latter is an outgrowth of the former), what formerly took the joint strong efforts of two can now be done without superhuman effort by one. So whereas it formerly took two to "make a life," even without children, it now takes only one. For that particular purpose it did not particularly matter whether the two were of the same or different sexes. It nevertheless seemed sensible to combine the biological and the economic mates in a single package—particularly when the surrounding norms created difficulties for those who did it differently.

With the production side of the relationship dwindling in importance the content of the decision of whether or whom to marry shifts markedly. The male becomes less interested in the girl's qualifications as a home-maker, and the female becomes less interested in the boy's capacity to provide money, since each can do both. By elimination, interest shifts to the partner's qualifications as a companion, sexual and general. If companionship is the main criterion, the question moves in turn to whether marriage is a necessary condition for it, and whether marriage might, in fact, impede it. When combined with dependable birth control and a widespread conviction that one should help keep down the size of the population, the result is the increasing frequency of "singles" clubs and apartments and the emergence of a "singles" culture, including magazines directed to it. Its members have not "failed" to get married; they have deliberately chosen a different way of life, at least from age 20 to about 30 or 35, with sexual relations typically involving no more commitment than eating or going to the theater together. However, since this life-style, at least as it manifests itself at present, lasts only a little over a fifth of the average lifetime, its longer-run attraction probably cannot be assessed until those who are now trying it have lived out their normal span of three score and ten. The assessment must also note that thus far the probable losers in this kind of game—the poor, the unattractive, and the shy—are subtly but systematically excluded from singles communities (*Newsweek,* 7/16/73). We will not attempt to make the assessment here, but have already discussed some other elements that may make a close relationship terminable only with difficulty.

To use the contemporary term, there has been a marked *liberation* for both sexes, in an increased variety of available relationships. There is more freedom, in that the costs of some alternatives have greatly declined. All things considered, however, it seems that the liberation is not due to some new and inherently freer way of thinking, but rather that the liberation of both living and thinking is an outgrowth of the technology which makes the individual more self-sufficient as a householder and freer of unwanted children—the same technology, incidentally, that is so despised by some it has liberated.

It is nevertheless true that once changed thinking has been brought about by changes in underlying conditions, it can be seen that some of the newer forms could have been practiced under earlier conditions if the norms had been less rigid. Fifty years ago it would have taken a courageous couple indeed for her to hold a job while he cared for house and children. And because of the norms against females in business and the professions she would have had difficulty finding a good job. There must nevertheless have been many couples whose temperaments and skills would have produced a more satisfactory life if their roles had been reversed; but the society would not allow it. Increasingly it will, and thereby it accords an increase in freedom and power.

In the contemporary scene children obviously complicate the picture, though how much they do so may depend on the parties and the circumstances. In the United States and many other industrialized areas two children is increasingly becoming the normal expectation and fact. Spaced two or three years apart, they are close enough in age to be companions. If the mother holds a job till late in her first pregnancy and takes a job again when her second child enters kindergarten or first grade, she will be out of the work force only about eight years, rather than most of her adult life. Still further, if child care and housekeeping functions are fully shared by husband and wife and are supplemented by baby-sitters and child care centers, and if the wife's employer has flexible provisions for maternity leave, the wife may continue her job without significant interruption or abnormal strain.

Things are complicated further by conditions of middle-class suburbia, where it is often felt that till the children can drive themselves they must be ferried about for all kinds of classes, clubs and sports activities, and social events, in which parents are also expected to be "advisers." In that case housekeeping plus child care have much of the fulltime quality of earlier years, perhaps more.[1]

Some miscellaneous aspects of the husband-wife bargain. In the societies known to most readers of this book, the selection of a marriage partner is made by the persons to be married. In many societies the bargain is arranged by agents, mainly parents. Among traditional Arabs and Chinese, the bride and groom often did not meet until the wedding, and marriages were sometimes arranged for children not yet born. Such marriages were used to cement relations between families, not to please the parties. If the mate was not romantically pleasing, the husband was often allowed a mistress or a concubine. Being male dominated, these societies did not provide similar options for the wife.

All societies have rules about who may marry whom. Most forbid marriages below specified ages, the age in the United States being set by the states, with minima of 14 to 16 for girls with consent of the parents, and from 15 to 18 for boys. In tribal and peasant societies marriage often takes place so soon after puberty that there is no point to an age limitation.

All societies have rules about marriage of relatives, generally known as the incest taboo. Marriage (or intercourse) between brothers and sisters is almost universally forbidden, as is that between parent and child. Marriage of first cousins is forbidden in most places, and of second cousins in some places. The degree of restriction depends partly on the distribution of population, since in sparsely settled areas with poor transportation there may be few strictly nonrelatives within marrying distance.

Around the world, regulations about divorce also vary tremendously. These range from no divorce at all, as in some Catholic jurisdictions, to

---

[1] Before overemphasis on "women's liberation" goes too far for the good of either women or the society, it might be well to avoid being misled by some loaded terms. "Career" tends to carry glamorous implications, typically of professional or managerial work, while "housewife" sounds quite the reverse. In fact, however, many men's "careers" are decidedly routine, unstable, and unglamorous, whereas child care and household management, well done, require knowledge and creativity at a quite professional level. Since I am sure my motives will be suspect no matter how I phrase it, I will risk making a suggestion to men rather than women. Namely, refuse to accept responsibility for earning more than half the money income for the family; insist on doing at least half of all housework and child care; and insist that, if the total burden of work is fairly shared, whichever partner earns the money has no more right to control its use than does the other partner. If that arrangement does not fit the circumstances or personalities, let deviations from it be transacted on some reasonable basis.

divorce by mutual consent, or by "pink slip" handed by one partner to the other—again the latter by the male in male-dominated societies. In the United States the reasons for divorce have long been narrowly limited in most states, though no state any longer makes adultery the only grounds for divorce. Mental cruelty, felony, alcoholism, impotence, refusal of intercourse, and lack of support are also among the legal grounds for divorce in many states. As of 1973, 22 states permitted divorce by mutual consent—no-fault divorce. The law's refusal of divorces in some states expresses a moral sentiment with no significant effect on family stability, since rarely do a couple refused a divorce return to each other (DeWolf 1973). The data suggest that the rate of dissolved marriages—separations plus divorces—is rather unrelated to the laws about divorce. If people decide to separate they separate. If they decide thereafter to live with someone else they also often do that. The main difference made by the law is whether the new status of the parties is legally sanctioned. The law will also affect the status of their property.

Here we may note some long-term impacts of science. At least in the Western world, the natural sciences several hundred years ago completed the shift from authority (Aristotle or the Bible) as the source of knowledge to the experimental study of evidence. In the social and psychological sciences, by contrast, similar attitudes toward experimental study are not much over a hundred years old, and the shift is by no means complete. The result is ambivalence and conflict. Some feel that only religion and traditional morality are safe guides to conduct. Others look to experience and social experimentation, and notably take an experimental attitude toward sex and marriage. The older spirit is: "If something has always been considered wrong, prohibit it—until and unless the prohibition is proved to have serious adverse consequences." The newer spirit (often called "permissive" by those who dislike it) seems to be: "Until something is demonstrated to have adverse consequences, allow it, without regard to its status under some alleged authority." The traditionalist replies, "If it is wrong its consequences are necessarily adverse," to which the newer spirit rejoins, "But how can we tell without trying?"

On divorces. Statistics about divorce are often used loosely. To use an exaggerated illustration, four women are married. Three stay married for life. One is divorced, remarried, divorced, remarried, and again divorced. In total there have been six marriages and three divorces. In one sense it would be correct to say that one *marriage* in every two ends in divorce. But that statement fails to reveal that three fourths of the *women* who married were never divorced. A minority of repeatedly divorced persons makes the risk of a broken first marriage seem statistically greater than it actually is.

Actual rates of marriages, divorces, and remarriages have all been increasing in recent decades, as indicated in Table 25–1. Thus, although there is an increasing turnover in marriage partners, the single life during those decades was becoming rarer, not more frequent. In fact, the daughters born during the late 1930s (who were 30 to 34 years old in 1970) had the highest marriage rate on record. By 1970, 94.5 percent had married, and it was estimated that only 3 percent would remain unmarried for life (Glick and Norton 1973: 305). Furthermore, only about 2 percent of females recently entering their childbearing years want to have no children (Campbell, p. 110). If they do as planned, and do not have their children without marriage, this group of now-young women will set an all-time low level of those never married. Divorces, however, will be more common. Of those women in their late twenties and early thirties in 1971 it is estimated that 25 to 29 percent will eventually end their first marriage in divorce (Glick and Norton, 308)—though with a high likelihood of remarrying.

Reasons for these changes are complex and interrelated. For example, the mere fact that people live longer than they used to increases the likelihood both of marrying and of being divorced. In addition, such factors as Social Security, better health, higher incomes, and homes for the elderly reduce the need for a son or daughter to stay at home unmarried to care for the parents.

Divorces are not distributed equally across all groups. For example, divorce rates are lower for the more highly educated (Burgess and Cottrell 1939: 122, 271; Leslie 1973: 581). They are more than twice as great for men married before age 22 than for those married at a later age (28 percent versus 13 percent), with a comparable difference for women married before and after age 20 (27 versus 14 percent) (Leslie 1973: 588). Divorce rates are also higher for persons already divorced at least once than for those not previously divorced (ibid.: 581).

ON PARENTS AND CHILDREN

"The most important decision a child ever makes is his choice of parents." Unfortunately no one helps him with the choice. As to the parents, if they practice birth control they have some choice about the number and timing of their children. Despite interesting recent experiments they thus far cannot control the sex or possible abnormalities of their children. Nor can they bring on or avoid multiple births. If birth control is not used, the parents take what comes. The child's initial membership in the family is thus wholly involuntary for him and may or may not be voluntary for the parents. For the young child the parents are the government in which he is an involuntary citizen. At first it is wholly dictatorial, even if benevolent, although the authority of the dictators is limited by the inability of the infant either to receive or to execute instructions.

Adult culture and youth culture

In tribal and rural societies young people become productive at an early age. At four or five they do simple chores, and by ten to fourteen they do nearly adult work. Since few tasks require extended training, children join the adult work society early. They learn and accept its goals and values and copy its skills. The family produces most of what it needs, learning takes place by doing, and the same set of adults are simultaneously parents, teachers, and employers to the child. The child takes added responsibilities as his growing ability justifies them. His recreation consists of games, hunting, contests, or other activities with his peers, mostly within sight of adults.

This situation contrasts markedly with that which exists in present industrial nations, particularly the United States. To a degree that increases with the length of schooling, more young people spend more of their time with other youth. The consequence is a "youth culture." With the help of automobiles their routine social contacts are increasingly beyond the observation of their families, while money enough to travel often takes them far from parental supervision. The telephone, special publications for and by youth, and special TV programs put young people into increasing contact with one another and decreasing contact with their elders. Together these forces make for a separate youth culture.

This development involves a shift in the major bargain between offspring and parents. In preindustrial societies the bargain was: "You start producing for the family as soon as you are able. The family will make up the difference between what you consume and what you produce, though before you leave the family you should be carrying your own weight." This bargain was usually not stated because it was so obviously universal. In industrial societies before advanced formal education became widespread the bargain did not change much. The male youth was expected to take part-time jobs starting in his early teens, and to work full time by 16 to 18. To exaggerate for contrast, the major bargain today sometimes approaches the following extreme: "Your parents agree to support you through high school, college, and professional school till about age 25, paying all expenses of education, recreation, basic living, and possibly of your spouse if you marry. Our obligation is not reduced if you make no effort to earn income or to learn to support yourself within the industrial system from which we support you."

Many contemporary offspring do, of course, put themselves through college and graduate school (or marry someone who does) and end their dependency when they leave public school. As is typical with social changes, this one presumably generates more tension during the transition than after the new pattern is firmly established. Resentment is common among present-day parents who, as children under the old rules and parents under the new, feel shortchanged at both ends. The Great Depression exaggerated what would have been a substantial discrepancy in any event, and the man who had to leave school in 1935 at age 15 to help support his unemployed parents might show understandable resentment when in 1970 he was expected to help support his 25-year-old son in graduate school. Here, again, changes in the surrounding society often became translated into conflicts between persons within the family. Other parents, however, were happy to be able to give their children more than they themselves had received. Even the resentful parents often conformed because the shift in cultural norms lengthened their *EP*s by branding them as "not good parents" if they did not provide.

BEFORE THE KNOT IS TIED

Dating and courtship

If marriage is to be based on love and compatibility, prospective partners must get to know one another. In small societies this is no problem,
as all children in a village inescapably get to know one another. Among
the Spanish, whose tradition also covers most of Latin America, grown
girls are closely chaperoned, and are rarely left alone with a grown boy.
In many societies social contacts among teenagers are largely confined
to community parties which include adults. The practice of dating, in
which unsupervised couples may or may not engage in assorted erotic
activities, is largely an American invention, whose popularity is nevertheless spreading.

Dating is part of the socialization process, in which the individual
learns about others and how to get along with them, while it also provides
recreation and companionship. But as part of the search for a suitable
marriage partner it is relevant to family organization, which aspect we
discuss here.

A certain naive assumption infects some segments of the population:
that somewhere there exists *the* one person who is "just right for me,"
and that the task is to find that person. If they are the proper pair they
will fall madly in love. Otherwise they will not fall in love—at least not
true love. Each carries a sort of inner love thermometer; when the reading for both rises above a certain point they should marry. The only real
problem is to make sure the thermometer responds only to true love. This
test is met if the reading stays up for a reasonable period. If it drops in
a few months it is registering puppy love or infatuation, neither of which
is "true." Although this attitude is fairly widespread it does not seem to
require further diagnosis here.

Tactics and strategies in courtship. Although *courtship* sounds omi-
nously formal to many, we will use it simply to mean any dating relation
in which at least one of the two parties gives serious enough thought to
their possible marriage to modify his behavior in ways designed to increase the probability of marriage or to affect its terms. If one party is
courting (or is believed to be), restraining or thwarting actions by the
other are also part of courtship behavior. Courtship is a particular instance of tactics and strategies in a potential transaction. The X and Y
in this transaction are the persons themselves, not external goods, and
the transaction is one of affiliation in an organization that is normally
expected to last for life.

The tactical questions are basically the same as in other transactions:
what to reveal about oneself, when, and how to learn about the other. One
question of strategy is also reasonably standard: how to generate a strong
EP in the other party while holding one's own within manageable limits.
One problem of strategy is less standard—that a strong EP by the other
party can be a confounded nuisance if it is not reciprocated, and must
not be encouraged until one is sure one wants it.

Courtship is also unlike the simple unique transaction, where it is a matter of indifference to A whether B is pleased or displeased with the exchange, so long as A is pleased. A marriage transaction based on misrepresentations that leave either party seriously displeased can bring a mutual disaster. Despite exceptions, the marriage transaction typically places a premium on high candor at some point before it is completed. It does not follow, however, that complete frankness is necessarily desirable at the outset, since a trait of one party that may seem perfectly acceptable on fuller acquaintance might seem disqualifying if revealed too early. These are complicated and highly personal factors, and the ability of a given pair to avoid or survive errors about them may be a good test of marriageability.

Even for persons who reject the norms against extramarital sex, a marriage is nevertheless a highly exclusive relation in many respects. Hence many tactics and strategies of courtship probe and test the types and degrees of exclusivity that each expects and is committed to, and a developing courtship includes successive growth in the scope and intensity of that commitment.

One form of increased exclusivity is to spend more time together and less with possible competitors. A second is to reveal more information to each other than to others, particularly about things one might hesitate to publicize. A third is to increase physical intimacy with each other and reduce it with others.

In transactional language for exclusivity, marriage creates bilateral monopoly in certain aspects of life, and courtship is a movement from free competition toward such mutual monopoly. In this movement the question inescapably keeps coming back: "How can I be sure you care enough about me to justify letting myself come to care so much about you that I will be badly hurt if you back out?"

For each party an important protection of both emotional position and bargaining power lies in keeping alternatives open. To close off alternatives both communicates one's commitment and increases his vulnerability. For one to make more commitment than the other, and to communicate it, is to leave himself open to be "used." Any new step of commitment may thus leave a gnawing uncertainty whether one is thereby strengthening the relationship or making a fool of himself. This is another instance of the "double edge of concession" in transactions. Will a given concession satisfy the other party enough to induce a return concession? Or will it have an appeasement effect, branding the first party as weak, and leading the other to further demands but no concessions?

To summarize, starting from initial indifference about marriage, the courtship problem of each is to extend the other's *EP* without allowing his own to grow much faster. This is the strategic aspect. If one's own *EP* does grow too fast, his tactical move is to hide that fact. Such a tactic, however, may itself contain an important strategic ingredient. Other things equal, we tend to like others who like us, and the effect is still stronger with loving. Hence visibly to extend one's own *EP* in love and commitment may be the most effective way to extend the other's *EP*. Yet if this commitment is larger than the other person is ready to reciprocate it may shrink his *EP* through fear. The fact that there is no easy way to tell which will happen can be both intriguing and disquieting.

The strategy of "no games." It is easy to say, "We will be completely honest. No games." If this means that there will be no deliberate lies, misrepresentations, or concealments, it is entirely possible. If it means that no tactical or strategic elements of the sort described above are to enter the relationship, the promise is probably illusory. One of the devilishly complicated things about intimate relationships is that either to talk about the relationship or not to talk about it is itself part of the relationship. In the same sense that inaction in government and family may be as important as action, for a courting couple *not* to talk about their relationship is quite as important as *to* talk about it. Each decision to discuss or not discuss some aspect of the relationship has a strategic effect on it, even if the parties do not realize what it is. Not to think about it is also an important element of strategy.

To return briefly to the couple who parted at graduation, the vast discrepancy in their expectations could presumably have been avoided if they had discussed their relationship and feelings from time to time. But the basis of the relationship had been: "We are not going to make the mistake of getting into hassles every week over how we feel about each other, because that's a sure way to kill the whole thing." We thus conclude that either a couple in close relationship somehow communicate their feelings or they risk painful discrepancies in them. This is the sense in which a promise of "no games" is probably an illusion.

Sex and commitment

Polls and surveys make clear that the shift from traditional to experimental attitudes toward male and female roles in general and toward intercourse in particular is moving rapidly, and that data about how many people hold which attitudes may not be reliable for very long. On the other hand the "sexual revolution" is not really sudden, but a continuing development that has been under way steadily since the 1920s (Leslie 1973: 397). Here, as elsewhere, it may help clarify if we talk in terms of models rather than difficult-to-ascertain facts. We will talk first of the "liberated" model, and then of the traditional.

The liberated model. In the fully "liberated" model, sex is not inhibited by any feelings in either party of immorality, fear of pregnancy, or "appearances." Intercourse (when successful) is a highly pleasurable activity, to be engaged in as the desires and convenience of possible participants determine. (We are speaking here of the courtship situation, in which neither party is married or engaged.) However liberated intercourse may be, it nevertheless remains a transaction, and depends on two mutually contingent decisions. That is, unlike the satisfaction of eating (or of masturbation), which can be done at the pleasure and convenience of one party, here the desires and convenience of two are involved.

In the model, sex itself involves no commitment. To start with, it may be viewed as a unique transaction, with the greater bargaining power lying with the party with the lesser desire. That is, the party with the greater desire will accept the greater cost or make the greater concessions on details. A variation is that the person with the greater desire will say (perhaps implicitly, since these things are often not made explicit): "If you will give me sex, I will give you sex plus such and such." The "such and such" may be paying for the room, providing food or entertainment, gifts, or accepting greater inconvenience in the arrangement.

To go further, we can only mention the array of complications to which this, like any other transaction, is subject. Generosity might lead the less desirous party to go through with the relationship even if he does not then want it himself. Hostility would have an opposite effect. But because of the psychological components of intercourse, generosity or hostility might affect the ability (rather than merely the willingness) to complete the relationship successfully, or significantly affect its quality. As in other transactional relations, the party with the greater stake in continuing or repeating the relationship will (other things equal) have the lesser bargaining power in its details.

In short, "liberation" eliminates certain cultural and psychological constraints on sex, and lets people "do what they want." But it in no way eliminates the power and bargaining power effects of their wants (particularly if there are marked differences in wants), of liking or disliking, or of differences in the time range of their interests in one another. These are only the beginning of the potential complications. In contrast to the traditional model that follows, sex without commitment removes certain long-term problems of the relationship. But it still leaves many short-term ones, even if it changes their content. Furthermore, if sex is noncommittal, the commitment of one party to the other must take other forms. These include caring enough to be badly hurt if the relationship is broken, or investing time, money, or decisions about one's future into the future of the relationship.

The traditional model. The "traditional" model much more nearly represents the norms of most Western society during most of its history than does the liberated one. And despite the relaxation of many norms many people in America still accept the traditional standards. In addition, the traditional norms often exert some psychological effect on those who do not consciously accept them, as unconscious inhibitors; as challenges to demonstrate that one is, in fact, liberated; or both.

Under traditional norms of courtship, the decision about intercourse is a high-potential component of the commitment process itself. To focus this question let us assume for the model that the couple do not feel constrained by fear of pregnancy or disease, or by moral codes. For the moment we will also make a traditional assumption that the male wants sex, with or without love, and that the female wants it only as an expression of love.

If so, the stage is set for controversy. To him sex is intensely wanted but noncommittal. For her to resist seems to him a highly selfish act: "If you loved me at all you certainly would not frustrate me so." But his insistence on sex without committing himself seems to *her* to be selfish: "If you loved me you wouldn't keep asking." As she sees it, to grant sex prematurely denies her the opportunity to hold back this important symbol of her commitment until she is ready to give it freely. If she has had no previous sexual relations, an even greater symbolic value is involved. In the traditional model, when sex occurs, she wants it to say: "Now you know I am really yours. I am holding back nothing."

If she fears pregnancy or disease, if she thinks of sex-out-of-marriage as immoral, or if she prizes her virginity for additional reasons, the female will be much more reluctant than indicated above. Her bargaining power will rise, and she may make marriage, or at least firm engagement, the price of intercourse. As in other cases of shortened EPs, however, her greater bargaining power comes at increased risk of losing the transaction altogether, a risk that depends in part on the EPs of her competitors. On the other hand, if the male's attitudes about pregnancy, disease, morality, or virginity closely resemble hers, these factors provide no basis for differential bargaining power. Also, as with other transactions, one may have bargaining power but not use it for fear of spoiling other aspects of the relation.

Erotics and bargaining power: Liberated and traditional

Because it is intensely desired, sex has potentially high components of bargaining power. For the liberated model the essentials of that bargaining power have already been covered in this section. The complications of the traditional model involve more detail. Under that model, (which is exaggerated somewhat here to sharpen the distinction), if the male earned money and the female did not, he had many things to grant or withhold, and hence numerous bases for bargaining power. Assuming equal desires for companionship, she had only romantic and erotic satisfaction on which to base her bargaining power, and may have felt that she could not make much use of it unless she doled it out in tantalizingly small increments. The traditional method was to keep his hopes high but his accomplishment low, so that the move from kissing a hand to kissing a cheek seemed a glorious, mind-boggling advance. According to one tale the symbolism of Cupid is in the bow, not the arrow: Pull him toward you with one hand while you push him away with the other. To grant sex too early, or even a full-fledged kiss, thus might undercut her subsequent bargaining power (though it might also raise her bargaining power by further intensifying his desires). Revealing her EP made it difficult for her to retreat from any given salient once it had been breached. Traditionally the young female had great bargaining power in her ability to withhold the erotic satisfactions she could provide. The young male had none in denying sex to the female, who was not supposed to reveal any such desire. Shyness or social clumsiness could produce unexpected results. In the traditional model the parent's advice to their daughter, "Don't cheapen yourself," contained solid transactional logic. Needless to say, actual relations did not always follow the model.

Although sex is a more potent sign of commitment in the traditional than in the liberated model, this does not mean that it is everything. In fact, the absolute case of no-sex-till-married removes sex entirely from the realm of commitment in courtship. Thus in either the completely liberated or the completely prohibitive attitude toward premarital sex, commitment must lie in behaviors other than sex. These include the many aspects of personality, caring, competence, intelligence, and so on.

Dating as companionship and recreation

Dating can occur between a girl and a boy simply because they like doing the same things, enjoy each other's company, learn from each other, or find others dull. Sometimes there is a magnificent sense of well-being in just being together. Such a relationship can continue without reference to sex—even a good-night kiss—or to courtship. Those same nonsex ingredients may, of course, also accompany an ongoing sexual relationship. Whether the sex and nonsex aspects of the latter relationship will enhance or impede one another can be answered only in the individual case. The traditional model of more or less casual, noncourtship dating nevertheless has several interesting ingredients that are less likely in the liberated approach. They revolve around the expectation that the female would (by "nature" or culturally induced inhibitions) be reluctant about intercourse and the male tremendously eager. As noted, if she chooses to use her greater bargaining power in this multiple goods transaction she can say, "I will give you sex if you give me sex plus such and such." Or, "Not this time" may exploit bargaining power now in return for an implicit half-promise of future delivery. Like that of other promises, its value lies in its credibility.

In a community where people talk freely, as on some small-college campuses, status and reputation traditionally become involved. If a girl becomes known as a pushover, her bargaining power in this respect goes down considerably. Bargaining power lies in the will and ability to withhold, and once she acquires the reputation of not withholding her tactical reluctance loses credibility. Further, many people find the sexual relation more gratifying if the partner really cares about them. Since easy availability implies not caring, it reduces the value of the act itself, and further reduces bargaining power.

As perhaps reflected most strongly in the traditional fraternity bull session, no status as a sexual conquerer is accorded the man who "goes all the way" with the girl who accepts practically anyone. By contrast, status may result from only "a couple of good passes" at a girl who is both conspicuously desirable and reluctant. Since the latter girl can provide greater status than the former she herself acquires higher status and can attract higher-status boys. On the other hand, if her reputation is that "nobody can get *anywhere* with her," she also provides no status to her date, and can herself acquire low status if the attitude becomes, "Why bother to date *her?*" Cupid's bow can also recommend being "hard to get—but not too hard." Since a girl rarely acquires status by getting a male into bed with her, most of the above conclusions do not apply in reverse.

The traditional bull session typically had a late adolescent quality that exaggerated the importance of erotic exploits by focusing attention on them more sharply than reality justified, and by typically exaggerating actual accomplishments. With or without sex, girls who are fun, sensible, neat, reasonably attractive, and comfortable to be with are usually able to attract dates. Males are much more likely than females, however, to date persons of lower class than themselves, presumably because this enhances their bargaining power, while females accept this more exploitable position in the hope of making a "catch" (Leslie 1973: 390). In general men become more conservative about intercourse when they are in love, and women more liberal (ibid.: 392–93).

If both parties are away from home and do not expect future contacts, the relation is more like the initial model of the unique transaction. Its ingredients are nevertheless more complicated, involving such things as self-image and sense of competence. Furthermore, each glance, touch, or bit of conversation can be a transactional element in its own right, as it provides pleasure, humor, praise, embarrassment, or fear. Incidentally, we are not suggesting that the parties usually analyze these things as they go along, though some do. Relatedly, in some religious or ethnic groups a girl's reputation can be ruined unless she is very strict within her own group, while she can safely relax in her relations outside the group. One consequence is to strengthen the in-group-out-group stereotype, in which each group sees its own members as moral and the out-group's members as immoral—and has the data to prove it!

A short note on love and hate

A persistent problem in close emotional relationships shows a possible feedback sequence that deserves special mention:
The greater the love the greater the emotional dependence.
The greater the emotional dependence the less the bargaining power.
The less the bargaining power the greater the resentment.
The greater the resentment the less the love.
The nature of this sequence is apparently independent of whether the persons are married, and is related to the psychiatrists' suggestion that any love relationship also involves some anger.

Numerous strategies are used, mostly intuitive, to avoid being trapped in this sequence. A strategy for the first line is to keep one's love in check so as to avoid the resulting dependence. As to the second, there is no loss of bargaining power for either side if the emotional dependence of both sides is about equal. Regarding the third line, depending on one's culture and temperament, dependency may be enjoyed rather than resented. The final result can thus be avoided by avoiding any prior stage. There is also the possibility of equilibrium without breaking the cycle if we merely read from the last line back to a reversed first one: the less the love the less the emotional dependence. Although an equilibrium is thus possible, it may nevertheless occur at so unsatisfactory a level as to justify breaking off the relationship.

AUTHORITY AND DECISIONS IN THE FAMILY

The family represents an interesting interaction between system and environment. Untold numbers of decisions must be made within it. Shall we repair the roof this year or let it wait? What shall we name the new baby? Shall we put braces on Susie's teeth, or are they straight enough as they are? Should we have a dog, and if so what kind? When conscious decisions are made, their cost-benefit aspects are subject to the analysis of Chapters 7 and 8 and their group aspects to that of Chapter 15. Unconscious custom, habit, or the surrounding consensus may also either dictate the choice or specify who is to make it.

In traditional societies the role and decision structures of the family are determined by customs and norms. Who earns the living and who cares for the children, or who does the hunting and who the cooking, are no more open to debate than who is to be father, mother, and children. Because the cultural norms are internalized in each person, we say that such behavior is determined by culture, which means by communication, broadly defined.

Even if one does not personally accept the norms—he knows them but does not like them—he may follow them if the society allows no alternatives. In that case his conformity is transactionally determined. Also transactional are social pressures toward conformity. For example, suppose a father believes that for proper training he should spank his children every time they violate his instructions. If he lives in a community where this is common practice, no problem arises. But if his community considers spanking brutal, to be applied only to correct highly dangerous behavior, his neighbors and friends will express disapproval, his children will rebel because they are being treated worse than others, and he will find it more difficult to get along with other people.

In a small traditional society such pressures can be almost totally compelling. In a cosmopolitan society with a variety of subcultures one has more freedom. Even if he does something different from the way his immediate friends and acquaintances do it, he nevertheless can cite others who do it *his* way, which fact reinforces his confidence that he is sensible after all. The examples he cites to support his position may nevertheless be brushed off as out-group: "Oh, them! They're always doing stupid things."

SOME TRENDS

The family in Western society shows the same kind of trend found in other aspects of the society, namely, a gradual shift over decades and centuries from the influence of culture and traditional authority to that of rationality. Or perhaps we should say that the culture is gradually embodying an increasing component of rationality, or at least diversity. There is a decline in doing something because it is habitual or "right" and a rise in asking about possible alternatives and their consequences. There is an increasingly scientific attitude toward social structures and behaviors, even if many persons use "science" loosely.

We have already noted the changing role of the sexes, currently referred to as sexual equality or women's liberation. It means essentially identical rules for both sexes, since differences in size, strength, and procreative function seem destined to persist. The rules have been changing rapidly in recent years in industry and under law, which changes will have repercussions within the family. The federal Civil Rights Act of 1964 outlawed discrimination in employment or wages on account of sex, and "affirmative action" programs seek to implement equality. Although so basic a law requires time to take general effect, a wider variety of jobs for females has opened up, with the legal pressure in that direction being most direct in publicly financed jobs, including jobs in civil service and public universities. Among other consequences in the removal of "protective" legislation, such as that which prohibited women from lifting more than 25 pounds in a job or working at night. The Equal Rights Amendment to the Constitution (ERA), passed by the Congress in 1972 and awaiting full ratification as of 1974, would equalize all rules for the two sexes except those clearly based on biological and related functional differences. Perhaps the greatest difficulty growing from job holding by both spouses arises when one wants to accept an appealing job offer in a distant location, which means either that the other partner must also leave his job or that the couple must separate.

Sexual relations between unmarried couples, sometimes including living together, are now practiced more openly than in the past—though common-law marriages, in which a couple live together without formal marriage, have long occurred with moderate frequency in the lower socioeconomic groups. It is less clear whether the actual frequency (as contrasted to the visibility) of such sexual relations has increased very much, since the norm of no-sex-out-of-marriage has been widely violated in all periods that professed it. Similarly the recent increase in illegitimate births may reflect a decline in "shotgun" weddings rather than an increase in pregnancies incurred out of wedlock—again a possible decline in concealment rather than a change in sexual activity.

A conspicuous change in attitude is that of some official church groups. The former view was that sex has no legitimate, unsinful function except reproduction. The revised view is that sex may be accepted as a marital pleasure in its own right. Hence it may properly be viewed, if not as an end in itself, at least as a means to marital joy and solidarity. This view more nearly parallels our model of primary motives in Chapter 4—that the individual engages in sexual activity because it is pleasurable, while evolution has made it pleasurable so he will engage in it. In this view's most full-blown form "immorality" consists in being ignorant or irresponsible rather than "sinful" in the conventional theological sense. The "newer" views contrast most explicitly with the Victorian norms established about a century ago in the Western world. Although similar strict views about sex have occurred many times throughout history, relaxed views have also been common.

It seems likely that the decades ahead will witness a wider variety of overtly practiced "marital" relations than did the decades just past. Singles communities, deliberately childless marriages, swinging married couples, an expectation of successive marriages, and homosexual "marriages"—to judge from current trends—can be expected in larger numbers. It is also possible that the trend toward greater freedom and variety has already peaked, and that a reaction will shortly occur, perhaps paralleling the decline in readily available pornography after the Supreme

Court's 1973 decision on that subject. Certainly we will know more within a decade or two about the relative joys and frustrations of these varied life-styles than we do now, and can better estimate their future.

Meanwhile there is no indication that love is any less here to stay than sex, or that it will cease to draw couples into what they hope will be a lifetime relation. Furthermore, with a modest amount of sense and luck a couple's love and companionship may grow in depth and intensity with their years together. Even if the gestation of babies should take place in a jar, the evidence thus far is that the vast majority consider the raising of children in a family as a normal and expected part of life—to many, the essence of being human. These aspects of love, companionship, emotional support, child rearing, and the reliable attention of someone who deeply cares thus seem likely to continue the nuclear family as the basic norm of our society for the foreseeable future, while also allowing much more flexibility for those who prefer other ways, and whether or not religious faith keeps some in traditional paths.

part V

Focus on the unique—and on change

> For the poet a falling leaf is a simple thing . . .
>
> For the mathemetician it is appallingly complicated
> *Boulding* 1970: 100

This entire volume thus far has dealt with generalizations that are abstracted to some degree from time and place. Through Chapter 18 we dealt with broad generalizations. Starting with Chapter 19 we began to deal with particular kinds of organizations: governments, families, and economies. But we still dealt with general principles of these organizations, and spoke of particular instances only to help illustrate the principles.

In Part V we take an abrupt turn. In real life we must always deal with *particular things*—the Nebraska legislature, your Aunt Sally, your utilities company, or the flood of Japanese electronics imports—not with *kinds* of things or *principles* about them. To complete the above quotation from Boulding about the falling leaf: ". . . even today it is probably beyond his [the mathemetician's] reach to describe its dynamics explicitly." Science deals with and seeks to explain reality, sometimes with extraordinary success. But science is always an abstraction from reality, a partial view. The sum of many partial views is better than one, as in interdisciplinary research. Different disciplines are like different maps of the same area. One map may show highways, a second mountains and rivers, a third vegetation and crops, while still others show political boundaries, races and cultures, temperatures, income levels, rainfall, population density, or natural resources. All of them together provide much more information than any one map. Yet the total, while representing reality very well in certain respects, is still a most inadequate picture of it. Nor does it give the "feel" of places—whether they are beautiful or ugly, inspiring or depressing.

Furthermore, possibly excepting elemental particles, no two pieces of

435

reality are precisely alike. Science deals with similarities and uniformities from case to case. Dealing with the case-to-case differences and the complexities of the wholes will remain an art, not a science. This chapter will not solve this problem, but rather assert that it is insoluble. However, it will try to clarify the nature of the problem and suggest how to live with it. The remaining three chapters of this section will discuss three kinds of complex reality: social change, personality, and culture.

26

UNIQUENESS—AND SIMULATIONS

SIMILARITIES AND DIFFERENCES

Today I drove over the section of highway U.S. 52 between my home and Cincinnati for the 11,628th time, give or take several thousand. In certain respects this trip was like all other 11,627 trips. I started at my driveway, and passed Nine Mile Road, Eight Mile, Asbury, Five Mile, and the Coney Island entrance. It was like some, but not all other trips, in that it took between 12 and 13 minutes to arrive at the Little Miami River and that I slowed to watch removal of the old bridge. It was like no other trips in that the brake on my right front wheel grabbed at the Coney entrance, and a little boy waved to me from a 1968 Buick.

Any event is in some respects like *all* other events (all require time). In some respects it is like *some* other events. And in some respects it is like *no* other event. The same can be said of any person, any interaction, any object, any idea—in fact, of anything at all. Before focusing on differences, let us review the importance of similarities.

If event X always consists of subevents A, B, and C, in that order, then as soon as one knows he is dealing with X he can know that A will be followed by B, which will be followed by C. For example, event X is a dive from a diving board. In subevent A the diver jumps onto the end of the diving board, which bends downward. In subevent B the diver springs upward, assisted by the release of tension in the board. In subevent C the diver drops downward into the water.[1] If enough information is available

---

[1] Just as we said in Chapter 1 that a system is bounded by the interest and objective of the observer, not by nature, so is an event. For example, if someone prefers to consider the whole motion from diving board into the water as one single arclike event, one cannot say that such a dividing line is "wrong."

in subevent *A* to enable the observer to identify the main event as an example of event *X,* then he can know from previous experience that *B* and *C* will follow. That is, if by noting the bathing suit, water, and diving board, the observer can tell from the first-stage jump that the act he is witnessing is a dive, then he can reliably predict that the upward movement will be next, followed by the downward plunge into the water.

The prediction is not foolproof. The diver might slip. Or after the first stage he might bend his knees, absorb the upward thrust of the board, and not rise into the air at all. He might also go up, but come down onto the board again, to test it. The "prediction" (expectation) is therefore correct only if the whole event turns out to be an event of the type identified at the first step.

To the extent that one dive is like all other dives, one can know and predict something about it from knowledge of their similarities. This, basically, is the nature of all science—learning the reliable similarities among patterns so that one part of a pattern can be known from information about another part. But to the extent that dives are different (one is a jackknife and another a front somersault), knowledge about one provides no information about the other. The same is true if there are individual variations, as when Anna slides smoothly into the water on her first dive, but her legs slap the water on her second.

Thus far this volume has paid attention to the ways in which different instances of objects or events are alike, and most of the rest of the volume will do the same. The reason is simple and basic: similarities contain information that differences do not. Science tries to discover and report those things that are true for all, or nearly all, cases of a given type—that is, to abstract their similarities. By analogy, our attention above was on the three steps all dives have in common, not on the way Anna's calves slapped the water in her second dive. Those who have studied statistics may note that a coefficient of correlation is one way of stating the relative frequency with which two items are parts of the same pattern.

Our emphasis now shifts to the ways different instances are *not* alike—from the general and repeated to the specific and unique. It is often desperately important to know how a *particular* situation will turn out. But unlike maps and models, no two real situations are ever precisely alike, and science can give reliable answers only to the extent that they are alike. The main functions of this chapter are two: first, to spell out why science cannot give precise answers in the complexities of most real situations, and second, to show how science nevertheless can provide highly useful guidance in dealing with those situations, particularly through a rather recent technique known as the simulation.

As noted, science makes statements about models, which are valid for reality only to the extent that the case at hand is like the model. Since we can never be sure of that identity, no scientific statement will provide a wholly dependable prediction about the particular case—though in the physical sciences the relation between some models and reality is so close that we can place high confidence in our predictions. Intimate knowledge will help resolve the uncertainties, but will not necessarily do so for at least two reasons. First, a crucial detail may not be known—

for example, that the mistress of the premier of nation B is a spy for nation $C,$ and is dropping drugs into his nightcap brandy which make him benevolent by night but belligerent by day. Second, even knowledge of that detail would not necessarily predict its consequences. His belligerence might rub off on the rest of his cabinet and lead to a tougher foreign policy. Or it might make him seem less rational, and lead them to soften policy.

We should recall that the problem of uniqueness occurs not only in the behavioral sciences but in all complex systems. We noted in the appendix to Chapter 9 that even a seemingly simple principle like that of Archimedes requires many qualifications, and we cannot know the number or shapes of pieces into which a window will break when struck. Not only will present knowledge not tell us these things. Instead—and of the utmost importance—we consider them to be in principle unknowable.

A human personality, the sequence of experiences in a human life, or the total set of interpersonal relationships in a family or corporation, is many times more complicated than the shapes of broken glass. Hence precise knowledge of any of them is even more impossible—if we may speak of degrees of impossibility. Reliable predictions are, of course, possible in simple cases when we are sure of the detector, selector, and effector states of a person, and when a given motive is assuredly dominant. For example, the mentally normal, emotionally stable aware adult with unimpeded muscular faculties will step out of the path of an approaching locomotive. But note the qualifications we must state to make even this simple conclusion reasonably foolproof. In fact, in discussing such matters we tend to approach the circular and to say that the kind of person who will reliably step out of the path of an approaching locomotive will reliably step out of the path of an approaching locomotive. In any event, we have achieved predictability by reverting to a relatively simple model containing only a few variables, which we assume that we know.

THE COMPLEXITIES OF SOCIAL REALITY

> For want of a nail the shoe was lost.
>   For want of a shoe the horse was lost.
> For want of a horse the rider was lost.
>   For want of a rider the battle was lost.
> For want of the battle the kingdom was lost.
>   And all for the want of a horseshoe nail.

It may take a skilled psychoanalyst several hours a week for years to unravel enough of a person's past to discover the source of certain irrational fears. In *Ulysses* James Joyce takes nearly a thousand pages to describe some relatively "simple" events and thoughts of a single day. No description of any person's actions tells everything that is happening to his pulse, blood pressure, internal glands, stomach acid formation, or his neurons—and we have not even mentioned the molecular level of his subsystems. At the same time, precise description of events is the first step in making scientific generalizations about them.

It is, of course, not sensible to start with "for want of an atom the molecule was lost," and then to trace our way up in our effort to explain some momentous historical event. Yet it is true that a batch of faulty cells can mean a faulty liver, which can mean substandard performance by a whole person, under circumstances that produce serious social consequences. In 1066 the English and French stayed about even for a whole day. If a few English soldiers had been stronger or more courageous the battle of Hastings, and much of subsequent English and American history, might have turned out differently.

The traditional historian and descriptive political scientist, for example, are likely to insist that only by great attention to detail can one ever properly understand any event. Furthermore, these people think it important to understand particular events, in contrast to the principles, theories, and laws that intrigue the theoretical scientist. The difference partly parallels that between scientist and engineer. The scientist tries to formulate general principles, and the engineer tries to solve particular problems. The engineer employs such scientific principles as seem useful, but often adds generous doses of personal experience and intuition as well as great attention to detail. A possible bridge between the two approaches is the "simulation model" discussed below.

The potential complexity of "simple" situations

When you cash a check at a bank, open a conversation on the telephone, or engage in a thousand other interactions both your behavior and that of the other party are routinized by norms, and require little or no decision. Norms simplify much of life by narrowing all possible behaviors in any given situation to one or just a few. But real life faces more complexities and variety than norms can provide for, and leaves us uncertain about what to do. The vast variety of reality does not necessarily mean, however, that we also need a vast number of concepts or principles to understand it.

Let us take an example of a "simple" transactional relation. The categories of selfish-indifferent, generous, and hostile provide three alternatives. But one party can have one attitude while the other has a different one, as when A is generous and B selfish. Three possible attitudes by B for each of the three by A make nine combinations:

Case	A's attitude	B's attitude
1	Selfish	Selfish
2	Selfish	Generous
3	Selfish	Hostile
4	Generous	Selfish
5	Generous	Generous
6	Generous	Hostile
7	Hostile	Selfish
8	Hostile	Generous
9	Hostile	Hostile

The above list represents the possible *actual* situations. However, people often perceive incorrectly. For example, the situation may actually be that of Case 2, in which A is selfish and B generous. But A may mistakenly believe that he is generous and B hostile, as in Case 6. That is, A may believe that Case 6 prevails, although the situation is actually that of Case 2. For every *actual* one of the nine cases there are nine possible beliefs by A about what the case is, or 81 possible combinations of the actuality and A's beliefs. In addition, while it is actually Case 2 and A believes that it is Case 6, B may believe that it is Case 7. Thus for each of the 81 situations already stated, there are nine possible sets of beliefs by B, for a total of 729 combinations.

But this is only the beginning. People's interactions reflect not only their beliefs about what *is*, but also about what *ought* to be. Hence while the situation *is* Case 2, while A believes it is Case 6 and B believes it is Case 7, A may feel that it *ought to be* Case 5. For each of the 729 possible circumstances already identified, these nine possible alternatives that A might think ought to prevail bring our total possibilities to 6,561. For each of those there are nine additional possible alternatives which B thinks ought to prevail, for a total of 54,049. For each of those 54,049 situations there are nine additional sets of what A believes about B's beliefs, and another nine of what B believes about A's beliefs. We now have 54,049 $\times$ 9 $\times$ 9, or a total of 4,377,969 possibilities. Thus a "simple" transactional relationship might take any one of nearly 4.5 million alternative forms. The outcome of that particular transaction, and its effect on subsequent relations between those two parties may depend in important ways on which it is—using "is" at this point to include all the beliefs and attitudes as part of the "situation."

We can summarize the above alternatives as follows:

1. Actual situation...................................... 9
2. A's belief about actual situation...................... 9
3. B's belief about actual situation...................... 9
4. A's belief about what the situation ought to be 9
5. B's belief about what the situation ought to be 9
6. A's belief about B's belief about all of the above....... 9
7. B's belief about A's belief about all of the above....... 9

Total possible combinations of the above............. 9^7

Nine to the seventh power is almost 4.5 million, as stated.

Even this is only a start. We have not mentioned the strength of any of these items. To divide each into only three degrees of intensity, A might, for example, feel mildly generous, moderately generous, or very generous toward B. A might feel mildly confident, moderately confident, or highly confident that he has correctly estimated each of the items listed. We have also given no attention to A's or B's concern about the effect of the transaction on any additional parties, C and D, and the possible consequences to the relationship between C and D, A and C, A and D, B and C, or B and D. If we include only a few additional things of this sort we shortly find as many as 10^{30} different situations in a seeming "simple" interaction.

On the narrowing effect of norms

Fortunately in most relationships we do not have to scan the 4.5 million possibilities, much less the 10^{30} possible combinations. The actual relationships are often determined by norms, which call for a selfish-selfish relation in a commercial sale, a generous-selfish relation between a parent and a young child, and a generous-generous relation between established friends.

Norms, however, are associated with roles, which can be mixed or unclear. A mixed case occurred several years ago. My house needed painting. I was about to hire a commercial painter when one of my sons asked if he could have the job for the same amount. The money would help finance his forthcoming wedding trip to Mexico, and he would complete the job before the wedding. After discussing possible complications of a commercial relationship within the family, and spelling out carefully what the job included, we decided to go ahead on a "commercial" basis. His fiancée planned to help with some details.

Overall the relationship turned out to be amicable and (to the best of my knowledge to date) mutually satisfactory. It was not, however, without some potentially explosive components in the multiple-role relations. I will describe them solely as I saw them.

I wanted the job well done, and harbored a modest hope that my son would be somewhat more conscientious than the professional had been on a prior job. As a father I felt that I should emphasize the importance of conscientiously fulfilling obligations voluntarily assumed. I also experienced some temptations to relax the requirements when the days spent painting the metal roof turned hotter than they had any right to, and the work dragged into the final week before the wedding. There were also questions as to whether expecting full completion would seem to put pressure on the bride.

I can recall only a few of the many other questions that ran through my mind. Did my son *want* me to excuse him from some agreed-upon but unimportant details? Did he *expect* me to offer to excuse him? If I offered, would he accept, or would he insist on fulfilling his commitment? Did I perhaps expect (rather than merely hope) that he would be more conscientious than the commercial painter because it was the family house? Did he think that I expected more of him than of the commercial man? Or less? Did *he* feel obligated to do better than the professional, and did he think that I thought that he ought to feel thus obligated? Did his bride think that I ought to ease up, and might it sour the wedding if I didn't?

This instance illustrates that the many possible kinds of situations identified above are by no means unreal or overstated. True, norms greatly narrow the range of uncertainty in the "normal" case. But it is the many cases in life in which the norms and roles are mixed or ambiguous that cause the headaches.

As one authority put it:

> Family life is something like an iceberg. Most people are aware of only about one-tenth of what is actually going on—the tenth that they can see

and hear—and often they think that is all there is. Some suspect there may be more, but they don't know what it is and have no idea how to find out. Not knowing can set the family on a dangerous course. Just as a sailor's fate depends on knowing about the iceberg under the water, so a family's fate depends on understanding the feelings and needs and patterns that lie beneath everyday family events. (Satir 1972: 1)

THE SIMULATION MODEL

In connection with decisions (Chapter 8) we noted that any real situation is infinitely complex, and that the beginning of wisdom for decision makers is to recognize that they can deal with only a tiny fraction of what is potentially relevant. This chapter thus far has amplified that point, spelling out the vast number of complications and variations that can occur in even a "simple" social event. It emphasized the impossibility of ever really "knowing" an event, and the grave limitations of science in explaining or predicting the particular case. (The Senate Select Committee's Watergate hearings are in progress at the very moment I am writing this paragraph, and illustrate about as clearly as possible the extreme difficulty of knowing the particular case, especially when some of the principals have the soundest of transactional motives for obscuring it.)

Yet all of life, individual and social, is a sequence of particular events. Families can break up or nations go to war if the actors in the case are wrong about some detail of the complex reality. We thus face the dilemma that we cannot possibly know the reality, but that it is often desperately important that we do. How can we deal with this dilemma?

Perhaps the best short answer is that we can't, but that we do because we must—an approach best known by the British phrase as "muddling through." In another form the answer has already been stated in Chapter 5. We form images that in some ways correspond to reality and in some ways do not. An important respect in which all our images do *not* correspond to reality is that they are gross oversimplifications. This is true in the same sense that a road map omits all but a few details of reality.

Consider for a moment the law of gravity, Archimedes' principle, the proposition that one's bargaining power varies inversely with his own effective preference, and the generalization that the price of a product is determined by supply and demand. These generalizations are "maps" of certain kinds of events. "Maps" of events are typically drawn in the form of sentences, in contrast to the maps of objects which are drawn as lines on paper. Such maps display only the traits that all events of a given kind have in common. The law of falling bodies, for example, is not a map of the path and velocity of a particular baseball, falling through space, but a generalized map that describes the rate at which *anything* unimpeded will fall.

Objects are much easier to learn about than events. We can observe an object at leisure, dismantle it, cut it into cross-sectional or longitudinal views, or make transparent plastic models that show its insides and outsides simultaneously. For either very large things, such as the solar system, or very small things, such as atoms, we can construct table-sized models. The social scientist's parallel problem is to develop usable models of complex events. How, for example, can decision makers for a large city estimate the probable consequences of a decision, considering the number of inhabitants, their incomes, their spatial distribution, the kinds and locations of their jobs, the rate of growth of population, pollution rates, public transportation facilities, flows of goods and money, and so on? Is the quality of life doomed by the population explosion?

The basic logic of modeling a complex event is the same as that of making a road map. Out of the limitless possible details of a real geographic area the mapmaker selects those few traits that are important to him and ignores all the rest. In one respect his task is simple, in that he knows in advance what he needs to include and what he may leave out—namely, he includes information needed by drivers and omits information that they do not need. How do we apply this same logic to complex events?

In the model introduced in Chapter 5 the family planned to go to the beach: assuming that the car did not break down, the house did not burn, and so on. Let us add some details that might help in making the decision. "Let's go Saturday afternoon. We can spend the evening on the beach, and then have the whole day Sunday," suggests Tiny Tim. "Let's get there by six," says Big Bertha. "After supper we will still have two hours of sunshine." Agreed! So what time to leave? This is not a holiday weekend, so traffic will not be heavy. The trip is 120 miles, with 100 on two sections of freeway. A hundred minutes should handle that easily. In between is a 20-mile section through several towns. This will probably take 50 minutes, for a total of 2.5 hours. "Okay," says father. "We'll leave at 3:30." "Won't do," says Tim. "The golf tournament at Sandtrap will just be over, and the road will be mobbed." "An extra 20 minutes should do it," says mother. "So if we leave by 3:15 we'll make it," concludes Bertha.

Unlike the models of falling bodies or bargaining power, which can be applied to many different situations, this one applies to only a single case—a particular trip over particular highways through particular towns on a particular day with particular traffic conditions. To borrow language from the machine tool industry, the models we use to understand falling bodies and bargaining power are *general-purpose* models. This one, by contrast, is a *special-purpose* model, and will not help us to understand any problem but this one.

If next Saturday turns out to be like the model, the plans (and the predictions implicit in them) will be fulfilled. Each planned action will produce the anticipated result. Suppose, however, that a large barge bumps a bridge along the route, and the highway department orders the bridge closed. A six-mile bumper-to-bumper detour adds 50 minutes.

In contemporary jargon, a special-purpose model designed to help understand and make policy about some unique piece of reality is a *simulation model,* or simply a *simulation.* Its purpose is to simplify reality to a manageable level by focusing on some few conditions (or variables) that seem important, while disregarding all others. The understanding and prediction will be good if three conditions hold.

1. The model includes those variables which are, in fact, the main determinants of the outcome;
2. The measurements of those variables are accurate enough for the purpose at hand; and
3. The cause-effect consequences of each variable are adequately understood.

As to the first point, the original model of the trip to the beach seemed to include all important variables. If the bridge had been open, the decision about starting time, based on the model, would have been good. But because the model unwittingly omitted a crucial variable, the closed bridge, the prediction and action based on it turned out to be faulty. Second, aside from that omission, the family did have accurate enough measurements of the distance to be traveled, and of the feasible speeds in each section. Third, the family also understood the causal effect of distance and speed on the length of time required to make the trip. Had the family made errors in those respects as well, its overall prediction would have been subject to still further error. Such additional errors might, of course, either aggravate or offset the first one.

Simulations are used increasingly. San Francisco has simulation models of its metropolitan area, as have some other cities. With these simulations they predict the consequences of such varied things as migration of people, expansion or contraction of industries, a shift from property to income taxes, the extension of high-speed transit, or the effect on air pollution of a modified automobile exhaust system.

Under the third point above (cause-effect consequences) it is often necessary to design mutual causation and feedback into the simulation. For example, a change in the size of a city's population will affect the size of the tax base, which may affect the tax rate, which in turn may affect the size of the population by inducing migration. Or, the size of the population may affect the frequency of subway service, which will affect the number of people who will ride the subway, which will affect the level of air pollution, which may affect the number of people who will want to live there. To trace the mutual interactions of even a half dozen variables may require a sizable computer.

Deficiencies in any of the three points listed above can produce unsatisfactory results. Errors in the first, as by omitting a crucial variable, are probably both the most difficult to avoid and the most likely to be disastrous. In the second, by contrast, one at least knows *what* he is trying to measure, and may have a reasonably good idea whether he has or has not measured it accurately. If he has not measured it accurately he may at least have some idea how much inaccuracy he must allow for. As to the third point, one can also have a pretty good idea whether he does or does not know the nature of the effect to be produced by a given cause —and again can make allowance for his ignorance. The difficulty with the first point is that a really crucial item may be omitted for the simple reason that no one thought of it, or that there was no way of knowing about it. How much of an allowance, or what kind, should one make for a factor he has not even thought of?

The only way to evaluate a simulation is to try it. If the simulation predicts that recent a 10 percent increase in the city's tax rate will lead to a 2 percent decline in its population within five years, and the population actually declines by 2.5 percent within four years, the simulation is probably worth keeping, though perhaps in need of refining. But if the population goes up 6 percent, one would conclude that the simulation probably omitted some significant factor—a Point 1 error. The next step is to try to locate the missing variable(s) and add it (them) to the model. There is no guarantee that the correct one(s) can be found, and the only prescription is search and more trial. It is also possible that some variable(s) should be removed.

Because a multivariable simulation often provides a better "handle" on reality than do traditional scientific generalizations, it can also be a useful teaching device. If the simulation is reasonably good, a student can feed certain factors into it and observe the computed result. For example, in the simulation of a city he can assume, say, a 10 percent increase in property tax rates, and then compute the consequent changes in tax revenues, economic output, retail sales, population size, and migration of industry. A reasonably detailed simulation may also show the sequence of steps that lead to the eventual result. The student may thus get a clearer understanding about the way multiple forces interact in real cities than years of experience might provide.

Simulations can also take the form of games, in which opposing players seek to win. Among other widely used teaching devices are collective bargaining games. These specify a set of conditions about the company and the union. The "players" are union and management representatives, who negotiate a contract. The players must decide how much to demand or offer, when and whether to concede, whether to call or accept a strike, whether to arbitrate, and so on.

Whether formalized into a game, into a computer program, or into one's image of how to get from home to a vacation spot, a simulation is one name for the process of attempting to describe reality. As one author put it (Reitman 1965), "I think truth can be approached by simulation, and by simulation only"—an overbroad statement that nevertheless makes some sense if "truth" is taken to mean the particular, unique situation.

CONCLUSION

Science deals with the traits or behaviors that two or more things have in common. The study of the unique deals with the respects in which a given thing is different from all others. In that sense there can be no science of the unique. Science examines the particular event only to see if it follows some general principle. The study of the unique is to some degree interested in the event for its own sake.

Several sets of names are used to identify these two approaches. In a broad sense these are C. P. Snow's Two Cultures: the sciences and the humanities. In psychology they are the difference between the experimental and the clinical, and in sociology they are the difference between the broad generalization and the case study. In broad language introduced more recently, abstracting a principle from particular cases and stating it without regard to them is *nomothetic* study, whereas explaining a particular situation in light of its own unique details is *idiographic.* The distinction between an established science and an art is also pertinent, even if the process by which the science initially developed was itself very much an art. In any complex situation, at least in human affairs, no amount of knowledge of science will prescribe a proper response, which must come from the "feel" and "intuition" of those intimately familiar with the case. Science is a help, but it alone is not enough. The physician is most likely to be successful if he combines scientific knowledge about diseases and drugs with knowledge of the particular patient's history and peculiarities. Literature and drama are humanistic, in that they focus on particular circumstances, often in great detail. Many historians do the same. Poetry is humanistic in being an extraordinarily personal response to some idea or situation. In one respect feelings are always humanistic, in that they are private, whereas science deals with what is publicly observable. We are not thereby precluded, however, from formulating scientific generalizations about either the causes or the consequences of feelings.

The gap between the two poles is not unbridgeable. In fact, they are inexorably tied together, in at least two ways. First is the fact that any scientific generalization about reality is an abstraction, and an abstraction is abstracted from something. Those "somethings" are real events, any of which taken by itself is a complex, unique occurrence. Second, unique humanistic events are typically described in words, not formulas or diagrams. Except for proper names, however, semantic words represent abstractions of some traits or behaviors that two or more pieces of reality have in common. Hence every word used to describe a "unique" event inescapably proclaims its similarity to other events. Even the word *unique* applied to a particular event identifies a trait it shares with other events—uniqueness.

All this is a long story, and we have barely opened it. The distinction between the two worlds is not a question about reality, but about how a particular observer looks at it. Since every event is in some respects like all others, some others, and no others, the observer may look at whichever aspects he chooses. Literary taboos nevertheless help keep the two worlds apart. With the major exception of a few terms from psychology and psychiatry, it is considered stylistically bad for the novelist, playwright, or poet to use scientific terms from psychology or social science, even though much of what he describes falls within their subject matter areas. I am not suggesting that the practice be changed, but merely note that the scientific cost of literary style may be high indeed. So would be the literary cost of scientific style in literature. In fact, adequate scientific language is simply not available for describing much of the subject matter of literature. The gap would be closed if science developed to the point where all the content of literature *could* be redescribed adequately, if boringly, in scientific language. We do not foresee the day. That is another way of describing the limitations of science in dealing with the details of particular events, which limitations we will return to in a different context in the concluding chapter.

27

SOCIAL CHANGE

There is nothing permanent but change.

Plus ça change, plus c'est même chose.

MEANING AND TYPES OF CHANGE

Most of this book deals with cross-sectional, or static, analysis. This is
the question of how systems behave, assuming that they already exist
and have certain traits. In this chapter we shift to developmental analysis, or change. This is the question of how systems come into existence
or acquire certain traits to begin with. But first, what do we mean by
change? What are the forms or types of change?

Change depends on what you look at

In some ways you are not the same as you were five minutes ago. Some
red blood cells have died and been replaced. Some brain cells are gone
forever, and your hair is slightly longer. In other ways you are the same
as you were at birth: your head is still attached to your neck, and your
genes carry the same genetic program. "My, how you've changed!"
means you are still the *same* person, or it would make no sense. In some
respects Egypt is the same country it was 6,000 years ago, while in other
respects it has changed since last week.

A friend had a small boat. The seats wore out, and he replaced them.
Next went the rudder. Later came a new motor, and then a new hull.
Eventually no original part remained. He wanted to know: Is it the same
boat?

The problem of change returns us to observations about systems in
Chapter 2. Whether something is a system depends in large part on
whether we choose to view it as one. In connection with the unique in

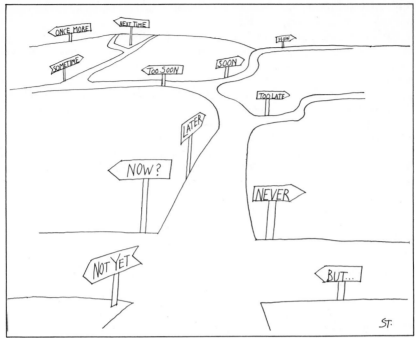

Drawing by Steinberg; © 1973 The New Yorker Magazine, Inc.

Chapter 26 we similarly said that whether two things are considered the same or different depends on what aspect we are looking at. Like beauty, same or different, changed or unchanged, are in the eye of the beholder. We do not mean that the reality makes no difference, any more than we would say about beauty that there is no difference between a forest and a dump. We merely mean that if two people disagree about whether something has changed they must say which aspects they have in mind. Kaufman (1971: 114) suggests that after enough parts of an organization have been replaced the original should be pronounced dead. We respond: It all depends on what you have in mind.

Change depends on patterns and levels

Pattern vs. substance. The shape of Niagara Falls can be stable for years despite a change of water every three seconds. The pattern of a corporation, government, or church can continue despite a complete turnover of personnel, and the pattern of your fingerprint is stable even though every skin cell in it has been replaced many times. Conversely, the pattern of desert sands may change with every shifting wind, yet the substance may be much the same for centuries. A first thing we need to know about change is whether we are interested in the pattern or the substance. For the most part social scientists are interested in pattern—

the structures of a society and its culture and the relationships of its roles, not the particular people who make it up.

Structure vs. process. A related though not identical distinction is that between structure and process. Perhaps the best way to say it is that components may change while the whole system remains the same. This is another version of the idea that a system is more than the sum of its parts, and that the continued sameness of the system lies in *similarity* of parts and their relationships, not in their being literally the *same* parts. That is why the parts can be replaced (your cells or the employees of a corporation) and still leave it the *same* system. Whether something has changed may thus depend on which system level we have in mind. At the level of your cells you have changed dramatically in the past month, while at the level of your whole body you have probably not changed enough to notice. Similarly, an employee may be injured and leave his job. But if it is filled by someone else, the organization may be considered unchanged. On the other hand, the larger system may change while the lower level one goes on. The independent motel may join a chain, which is later merged into a larger chain, which dissolves and leaves the motel independent again, while nothing much happens to the motel, its employees, or its operation. In short, supersystems may change while their subsystems remain intact, or vice versa.

When subsystems change and the supersystem does not, we may think of structure and process. In this view the whole *you* that remains unchanged is the structure, while the birth and death of your cells, the movements of food through your system, and all the other things going on inside you are process. Every subsystem within you also has *its* structure, whose internal changes are *its* process. In addition, changes in the whole you are process for the social systems of which you are only a subsystem.

Process may be a continuing steady state—water flows over Niagara, employees and officials flow through a government, lipstick and laxatives flow through a drug store. Or process may be cyclical—day follows night, spending increases before Christmas, a president is elected every four years. If a cycle is eliminated, the result is a steady state equilibrium. For our purposes we will not consider something as social change unless the structure (pattern) changes; ongoing process is considered steady state, and not change.

Growth and proportions

One form of change is growth. But most growth is more complicated than mere increase in size. The simplest growth is an increase in size, without change in structure, process, or system level. The delta of a river grows as more silt is deposited, and a population grows as births exceed deaths. Either can also be reversed—shrinkage, or negative growth.

Most growth, however, involves changes in proportion. As a tree gets larger its leaves increase in number but not in size, and an organization grows by taking in more people, not bigger ones. In an organization, other things equal, the number of people who coordinate the work of others rises faster than the total number. To illustrate, if one person were required to coordinate each five subordinates, each five supervisors would require a still higher person to coordinate *them,* and so on. However, this effect is often more than offset by other factors. Some horror movies notwithstanding, if an ant were to grow to the size of an elephant its weight (a cubic function of size) would increase almost 2 million times, while its strength (a squared function of size) would increase only about 60 thousand times. It then could not even carry its own weight, much less many times its weight.

As Boulding noted, anything that grows indefinitely will eventually occupy the entire universe. Most instances of growth start slowly, accelerate through a rapid growth, and then taper off toward some maximum. Such growth takes an S-shaped curve, as in Figure 27–1. The new human multiplies thousands of times in size from conception till birth, multiplies only four to six times in length from age one to age 15 or 20, and

Figure 27–1

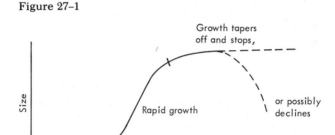

then stops growing. The territory of the United States grew slowly for a time, expanded rapidly during the early 19th century, then stabilized after adding Arizona and New Mexico early in the 20th century. Corporations, industries, plant and animal populations, cities, organisms, personal power, and political movements show similar growth curves—albeit with variations, including possible decline or disappearance. Growth curves reflect proportions: population grows relative to the available resources, a corporation grows relative to the size of its market.

Critical mass: The thin line between enough and too much

Up to a certain number the cars on a highway move freely. Additional ones slow the traffic, and still more virtually halt it. Up to a certain size a brain shows very limited learning. But starting at about a thousand cubic centimeters the brain can handle vast new levels of complexity—roughly those that distinguish humans from other animals. Up to a certain size a body of uranium emits radiation. Above that size it produces an atomic explosion. Up to a certain level tension improves your ability to take an exam—it "keys you up." But a higher level is an overload that "freezes" performance. The general principle is that over a wide range a small change brings only a proportionately small effect. But at some point an additional small change may cross some critical level, beyond which it produces dramatic large changes. These are problems of *thresholds,* or *critical mass,* and two pressing problems of our age, population and pollution, may be examples. Thresholds may operate in both directions. If a little additional pollution might make things disastrously worse, then in the reverse direction it would be nonsensical to spend vast sums to eliminate a pollutant completely if a slight reduction would bring it below the threshold level where natural processes would dispose of it. Some problems of international, marital, and political peace are those of keeping tensions below some critical level.

To combine two points, when things change size (1) they rarely change by the same amount in all dimensions and (2) they may cross a threshold and bring a wholly disproportionate result. An important social problem mentioned earlier may also be viewed in terms of thresholds—if people lose more than a certain amount of freedom they also lose the ability to defend the rest of it.

THE CAUSES OF CHANGE

The preceding section dealt with the meaning and types of change. We next examine its causes, starting with a caution that our knowledge of change is less assured than is our knowledge of static relationships. If a system is subject to deviation-correcting (negative) feedback it tends to keep returning itself to a previous condition. This is the steady state condition that we said is process, not change. By contrast, if the system is subject to deviation-amplifying (positive) feedback it continues to go farther and farther in a given direction, perhaps explosively. For example, a people become restive under a high-handed ruler. Instead of correctively softening his high-handedness, he represses the people even more, upon which they become still more rebellious, and so on till the relation explodes in armed revolt. There is then a new set of parts or relationships among parts—the alteration of structure that we consider change. In a broad sense we therefore say that the condition from which change arises is that of positive feedback (Maruyama 1963), or at least inadequate negative feedback. This is a very general statement, however, and will be tied to more specific conditions below. We call change *developmental* because it keeps moving for some time in the same direction, rather than return to where it started. Developmental change is *simple* if no change in system level is involved. Otherwise it constitutes *emergence* (if higher levels of system are added) or *decay* (if higher levels disappear).

Simple developmental change

Simple developmental change occurs whenever a second event, *B,* builds on the changed state of affairs produced by a preceding event, *A.*

This contrasts with a situation in which the effects of event A are dissipated or offset, and in which event B starts from the same base as did event A. For example, the Mississippi Delta undergoes developmental change, because each particle of silt deposited (event A) leaves a higher level on which the next particle is deposited (event B). By contrast, if the current that deposited particle B first carried away particle A, the delta would not accumulate. If I spend one chunk of money to purchase a dining room table I face new alternatives when I come to spend a second chunk—for two reasons. First, I no longer have the first chunk of money. Second, my desire for a table has disappeared. The situation is developmental in that the second spending spree starts from a different base than did the first. A tree gets bigger because this year's growth is added to last year's, in contrast to perennial flowers whose tops die off in the fall and start from ground level again the following spring. Historical change is developmental, in that situations never return to exactly where they were before. So long as national boundaries, governments, cultures, and languages keep changing, but without adding higher levels, the change is also simple.

Whether something is developmental change or merely cyclical process sometimes depends on how long we look at it. The cyclical move from day to night seems developmental if we look at it for only a few hours, and the same is true of seasonal change if we view it for only a few months. Cycles may also appear within long-run trends—seasonal cycles of temperature while the earth undergoes a long-term warming or cooling, or cycles of prosperity and depression while the economy goes through a long-term rise.

Much learning in an individual or a culture is simple developmental as we keep adding new ideas and information. So is the change in a language as it keeps adding new words. If there is an obvious change in level—as from grunts to spoken language, to writing, to printing—the change may be thought of as emergent (the topic of the next section). Perhaps simple developmental change can be thought of as simple irreversibility. A signed treaty may later be renounced; but the result is not the same as if it had never been signed. After a couple is divorced, their relation is not the same as if they had never married. If historians would focus on this question they might provide useful insights into the nature of irreversibility.

Prelude to emergence and decay

As elsewhere, pieces of reality often do not fit neatly into scientific categories. Often it is not easy to say for sure whether a given change is simple or emergent. There are nevertheless enough cases that *are* clearly emergent, and not simple, to enable us to make the distinction clear.

Systems come in hierarchies of levels. Under the static view we accept the hierarchies as given and examine the relations within them. As we now move to the dynamic view, however, we ask where the systems came from. Especially, how do higher-level systems appear where once there were only lower-level ones? Why do we sometimes find only lower-level systems where once there were higher-level ones? These are questions of emergence and decay, respectively. To answer them we borrow one principle from biology and another from physics. Because it is simpler, we start with the breakup of higher-level systems, or decay.

Decay of systems

As used here, *decay* is the process by which a system ceases to function as a unit, after which only its subsystems or its nonsystem components remain. It is also *disintegration,* in that the integrating forces that previously held the system together cease to do so. An example is the death of an organism, such as a dog. The first stage is that the central coordinating and integrating controls cease. The heart stops, and lack of oxygen then damages the brain (the main control system) so severely that it stops functioning. Thereafter no muscles can be moved and no information can be received through the senses. Without a brain the maintenance system of the dog may nevertheless be kept biologically alive by means of intravenous feeding and electrical stimulation of the heart. In this way many subsystems continue to function, including the lungs, liver, heart, and kidneys. But the dog is "like a vegetable," and cannot perform those integrated whole-system activities directed by the control system that make him a dog. The top-level system has decayed, but second and lower levels continue.

If intravenous feeding and heart stimulation are stopped, some second-level systems will go on for a while. Hair and nails may grow for a week or more, and molecular subsystems might continue to function for centuries.

Social systems can also disintegrate. If the children in a family are scattered and the parents divorced, the family no longer exists, but its human subsystems remain. Certain of its social subsystems might continue, such as father and son playing tennis or mother and daughter shopping together. The whole family might have Thanksgiving reunions, in a partial, temporary restoration of the family system.

History describes the disintegration of empires. But their people did not disintegrate, and some of their political subsystems, such as local governments, also remained. Nor did India, South Africa, and Canada disappear when they ceased being parts of the British Empire. Untold thousands of business firms, clubs, political parties, labor unions, towns, cooperatives, and national governments have gone out of existence.

Why do systems disintegrate? For one, they can be destroyed by external force, as when a swatter descends on a fly or an invading army tears up a nation. Centrally coordinated systems may be disintegrated by destroying the control center alone, as with a bullet through the brain or the enemy's seizure of a nation's leaders. The system may break up if outputs exceed inputs, as when a corporation goes bankrupt or an animal starves.

People are held together in an organization by certain cohesive or integrative forces, which in this framework are communications and transactions. If these decline or disappear, so will the organization. (For those who want to know where it goes, it goes to the same place waves go when the ocean is still, which is also where a hole goes when it is filled with dirt. Unlike matter and energy, patterns *can* be created and destroyed.)

Decay and replaceable parts. Any acting system not at rest undergoes wear, tear, and possible injury. If every component is replaceable, the system can continue indefinitely. But if significant parts are not replaceable, as they wear away or are injured the whole system eventually breaks down.

Humans can live only through regular replacement of cells as the cells die. Many specialized parts are not naturally replaced, as with eyes, whole organs, or whole bones. Nerve cells cannot be replaced naturally or artificially. Since many thousands of brain cells die every day, the brain (and its central coordinating function) has a finite life—of only several million days. In principle a corporation or a government could live indefinitely because every human and physical subsystem can be replaced over and over. Thus the essence of system preservation is replaceable parts. "Replaceable" also means "interchangeable": the new parts must be enough like the old to fit and to perform the same function. If the new parts do perform the function, but somewhat differently, the system may change instead of dying. Serious physical damage (such as a fatal auto accident) both destroys too many parts to be replaced and eliminates the central coordinating controls of the brain. A fire that ruined much of an organization's equipment and destroyed all of its files could "kill" the organization.

Most systems will run down without inputs of energy. They must also release outputs of energy, or it will accumulate and destroy them. If matter is used up, as a furniture factory uses up wood, the system must also be open for inputs and outputs of matter. The solar system is a conspicuous exception. Since there is no friction in the movements of the planets, they do not require new pushes to keep going. The internal structures of atoms behave similarly. All social and biological systems, however, must be open to inputs and outputs.

Entropy. The second law of thermodynamics is often cited in connection with the decay of systems. This law has its original meaning in physics, in connection with heat. Broadened to apply to many kinds of systems, the law says that all closed systems are subject to loss of differentiation. This loss of differences is called *entropy,* and the process is *entropic.* An increase in differences is negentropic. One social phenomenon that reflects this tendency is that members of a group who associate often with one another and seldom with outsiders become more alike in their perceptions, values, and behaviors. Thus relatively closed, isolated societies tend to become very homogeneous (to show little variation) and to continue nearly unchanged for centuries. Since any system depends on differentiation of parts, if entropy goes too far the system can no longer operate. Although in a broad sense all decay is entropic, at least for the present we will continue to think of several different causes of decay, as above.

Emergence in real systems—and evolution

Emergence is the process by which higher-level systems arise—the opposite of decay. Hence it is negentropic.[1] Atoms interact to form molecules. All living things in an area interact to form an ecological system on which all depend. Two people join to form a family, and a larger number form a corporation. Thirteen states join to form a national government. Someone connects one system, a steam engine, into another system, a wagon, and forms a higher-level system, a locomotive. Is there any general principle by which higher-level systems arise?

More explicitly, emergence is *not* the simple copying or repetition of an existing type of system. That is a form of communication. When a present-day couple marry they simply repeat an organizational form they observed elsewhere, as do those who form clubs, partnerships, governments, or lobbies. Although it is incredibly complex, information about every biological detail of the adult was already in his genes, and biological growth and maturation from a single fertilized cell is also communicational, in the broad sense.

The central idea of emergence is not in replication of an existing type of system, but in bringing a new kind of higher-level system into existence in the first place—the *first* marriage or the *first* corporation. However, if five different societies independently invent the wheel, rather than copy it from one another, that is also emergent. An emergent system can first appear as a real system: the solar system, a river system, living organisms, ecological systems. Emergence can also take place first in images in the brain: someone thinks up a new machine or type of organization and then tries it out. He may then observe the external form, revise his inner image, and so on (Chapter 6).

Whether emergence happens first externally in a real system or internally in a brain, its basic theory is inelegant but simple: It just happens. More precisely, it happens under conditions in which the new system does not promptly decay. Let us illustrate with the theory that the solar system originated from an explosion of the sun. Of the many blobs of substance thrown out from the sun, most fell back. Others flew on into outer space. But the direction and speed of just a few happened to put them in orbit. Where the gravitational force pulling them back just balanced the inertial force carrying them out, the sun and planet became a *self-preserving* system, which had *emerged* by *accident*. Only a tiny fraction of the blobs ever ended in orbit, which illustrates that it was *highly improbable* that any of them would do so.[2]

---

[1] It is confusing that entropy is a loss of differentiation and structure, while negative entropy (negentropy) is a gain—as in electrical theory, where the negative pole is where electrons are and the positive pole is where they aren't. In the case of entropy the confusion arises simply because the use of the term has been extended into areas not originally anticipated. This section leans heavily on Campbell (1962; 1965)—two excellent works.

[2] That a mass will stay in stable orbit is determined by gravity and inertia, not by accident; the accident lies in its having been projected into a stable combination of distance and velocity. That is the *random variation.* The fact that gravity and inertia together were such as to maintain that orbit is the *selective retention,* or *self-preserving,* aspect. These terms will be explained shortly.

Present theory of the origin of life follows the same pattern, but with a twist. Somewhere in masses of water, carbon, nitrogen, and other substances that boiled and bubbled for billions of years, the combination that makes up simple life happened. It was highly improbable, one chance in a billion billions. But if the conditions in which it *might* occur happen a billion billion times a billion billion, then (as the statistician puts it) the highly improbable becomes almost certain.

Like the solar system, elemental life happened. It too took a self-preserving form, but with the twist that it could also duplicate itself. If kept in an environment containing stores of its own ingredients, it could transform them into its own form—it could reproduce. However complex the reality, the principle is simple. The process by which those early simple forms of life moved on to produce the complex forms we now know, including man, was more of the same. Darwin learned that the process involves *mutation* and *selection,* and named it *evolution.* Mutation, or variation, is an accidental change—a slightly greener skin, a slightly longer snout, a somewhat larger brain. Most variations do not help survival, and many hinder it. But some do help. Those individuals with the favorable mutation are more likely to survive and reproduce. This means that the favorable variations produce relatively more of the next generation. Under fierce competition (survival of the fittest) during many generations the unfavorable traits disappear and the favorable ones dominate. In brief, a controlled system with survival value happened. But having happened, its consequences were thoroughly nonaccidental: the transformation of the earth by living creatures, including man.

Whyte (1965) indicates that most variations never see the light of day. Internal structural factors make them unworkable long before birth or hatching. Whereas Darwin emphasized external competition, Whyte suggests that overcoming the hurdle of internal structure may be more important. In either case the basic theory is still *variation* and *selection.*

Evolution occurs in social systems by the same logic. No social system can function very long without having something go wrong—"wrong" being one kind of variation or mutation. As we know, many important inventions were lucky accidents. Most social accidents, or variations, do not work, and people drop them. But some work better than the old ways, and are selectively retained. An accumulation of such retained variations can bring changes in social organization as conspicuous as the difference between the fish and the human.

If a variation occurs in a social subsystem, such as a family or a firm, external competition with similar subsystems may mainly determine whether it will survive. A variation that affects a whole social system may not face such external competition. In that case, only selective factors internal to the society will be relevant.

Emergence in the brain: Creativity

Mutation and selection can be described more explicitly as *random variation and selective retention,* or RVSR. When we move from biological evolution to another kind, the term random *generation* may be better, or RGSR. RVSR or RGSR are more accurate terms for "trial and error" and "adaptation." We noted earlier a distinction between external emergence in real systems and the internal emergence of images in a brain. We now move to the latter.

The beauty of emergence in the brain, popularly known as imagination or creativity, is that trials can be much faster and less costly than overt ones. By merely extending the process by which the youngster forms concepts, man can develop new theories in science, solve practical problems, invent new machines, or produce works of art. In each case the brain takes patterns already in it and puts them together in new combinations. Some combinations are obviously unworkable—like the idea of making an automobile body of jelly or planning a dance that requires performers to leap 30 feet[3]—and the brain quickly discards them. An idea that does not obviously fail inside the head can be reproduced and tested externally. On the basis of this external test the idea may be abandoned, retained, or improved. Mental RGSR can be consciously manipulated to increase efficiency, as by *search* and *scanning*, using repositories of information (such as libraries) and scanning devices (such as indexes, computers, and thinking).

More on RVSR. Some of the illustrations above did not deal with the emergence of higher-level systems. To clarify, in this theory random variation and selective retention is the *only* process by which new and higher-level systems emerge. However, RVSR can also bring simple changes at existing levels of a system—a new auto-body material or a more satisfactory family organization.

What survives depends not only on the new specimen but also on its environment. It may not be enough that a new organization is better. Unless it creeps in unnoticed it must also be seen as better for those who hold power and make decisions. Even if Russia would be better off with a capitalist economy, or the United States with a socialist one, vested interests in each country would prevent their adoption. In a male-dominated family a sensible proposal may not get far if father disap-

---

[3] As I was searching for illustrations I made an invention (whose merits I will not assess) by the very process I am describing. If you want a fancily decorated car, why not cover it with a print fabric, "glued" on and coated with clear brushing lacquer? If woven fabric could not be made smooth, a knit one or a patchwork certainly could. (I hold no interest in any textile or lacquer company, and disclaim responsiblity for any adverse consequences, such as the lacquer's loosening the paint.) I randomly generated the idea, but selectively retained it in verbal form only. Incidentally, "random" does not here carry the mathematician's implication of equally likely events—merely chance or accident. To avoid that confusion Campbell (1962) talks of "blind" rather than "random" variation. There are now some grounds to suspect that the brain may itself be specialized to perform the two phases of RGSR separately. It seems that the right brain may perform the function of making the loose, free-wheeling connections among things that we experience in fantasy and dreams—the random generation phase—while the left brain performs our logical functions—the selective retention of those combinations or connections that seem to correspond reasonably well with reality. If this suggestion is supported by further investigation we would conclude that, when it evolved the brain, the process of evolution produced a mechanism which has the capacity to perform the evolutionary process in a vastly speeded-up version.

proves. In informal or semiformal organizations, however, changes may occur without such conscious decision.

ENVIRONMENT AND CROSSBREEDING

We have not yet discussed the effect of environment on change. A social system has both a natural environment and an environment of other societies and cultures.

Every social system must be open for exchanges of inputs and outputs with its natural environment. Hence any change in the environment may induce changes in the system. Long-run changes in climate force peoples to migrate or adapt to the new conditions. Short-term drought or extreme cold can kill off plants and animals and force changes in behavior, some of which persist. Disease or famine can force new social relationships if they change the relative numbers of young and old people, or change the number of people relative to land space or other resources. Advanced societies alter their own natural environment (draining swamps, polluting air, using up petroleum reserves) and must then adapt to the environmental changes they themselves produced.

A population is itself an open system. People die and are replaced. Unless the socialization process is perfect, the replacements will be somewhat different. Accidents happen, and sometimes bring useful learning. Thus even a society completely out of contact with any other society experiences change in its interaction with its natural environment.

As to the social environment, immigration and travel may bring peoples of different cultures into contact, and provide variations from which new behaviors are selected. Historically the most progressive areas have been at crossroads of travel and mixtures of cultures. Here biological and cultural evolution are very different, because biological evolution requires a change in the genes whereas cultural evolution requires only a change in people's images. (For those familiar with the terms, biological evolution is Darwinian; cultural is Lamarckian.) For example, the brain can produce the idea of an elbekanpor—the result of crossbreeding an elephant with a bee and then crossbreeding *that* creature with the offspring of a kangaroo and a porpoise. There are no limits to the crossbreeding of images by the brain. By contrast, a living creature can breed biologically only within its own species, or across closely related ones, such as the crossing of the horse with the donkey to produce a mule. Thus for better or worse we get the equivalent of cultural elbekanpors. The Mexicans have joined Aztec, Spanish, and contemporary architectural styles to produce strikingly beautiful effects, and members of some contemporary American communes crossbreed such diverse ideological sources as the old frontier, the American Indian, Henry Thoreau, the Declaration of Independence, the Sermon on the Mount, and Karl Marx. Thus while biological evolution always takes many generations, and cultural evolution often does, culture *can* change greatly in a single generation.

Some sociologists emphasize stress and other disintegration (Lan-

decker 1951: 332) as causes of social change. Without necessarily disa-
greeing, the present model would state the problem differently. To say
that stress or disintegration *causes* change begs the question—it is like
saying a death was caused by a bullet, but without bothering to ask who
fired the gun, and why. True, once disintegration or stress has occurred
it may induce further change. But it also might just go on for a long time.
Accidental discoveries or cultural accumulation might also bring favorable change without first bringing stress or disintegration. (I see no reason why a cow's accidental wandering into a greener pasture, and even
fertilizing it to greater greenness, need be thought of as induced by stress
—and comparable happy changes occur for humans.) Emergence is also
an important form of social change, and it is an increase in integration,
not disintegration.

In short, an important—perhaps the most important—cause of social
change is people's responses to a change in the environment, even if the
environmental change has itself been brought about by prior action of
the people themselves.

CHANGE AND THE UNIQUE

In Chapter 9 we indicated that your intense desire for a particular
used car raises the bargaining power of the seller and reduces your own.
A low desire increases your bargaining power and lowers his. Each statement was preceded by an explicit or implicit *if.* The generalized scientific statement of such relationships is: If *A,* then *B.*

Note that we never said you *will* have an intense desire for the car,
nor tried to explain why you would or would not. And although we identified the effect of your desires on your bargaining power, we did not say
anything about the feedback effect of the completed transaction on your
subsequent desires. The reason is simple and fundamental. In the first
kind of statement we *assume* certain things. *Assuming* that you want the
car intensely, you *will* be willing to pay more than if you want it only
mildly. But we cannot even guess whether you *will* want the car intensely
unless we know a great deal about you: your background, immediate
situation, bank account, and personality. It is one thing to predict the
probable effects of a given feeling—*if you have it.* It is quite another
thing to suggest what will produce a given feeling in you. The first can
be handled with a simple and reasonably realistic *general* model of bargaining power. The second would require a very *specific* model of you
and the situation.

To illustrate, you have just finished a slow, carefully done drawing for
a class, and are viewing it proudly when your kid brother carelessly spills
his soft drink and ruins it. You may feel angry and want to push him right
through the wall. But maybe you just recently did something much worse
to someone else. You see the look of fright and remorse on his face,
remember how awful you felt, and say gently, "That's all right. Now that
I know how, I can do another one real quick." In short, our model can
help predict the effect of your anger on a transactional relation—*if you
feel angry.* It can help predict the effect of sympathy—*if you feel sym-*

pathy. But the model will not say anything about *which* you will feel.

Developmental change in the relation between you and your kid brother goes through a series of events—and we will confine our attention to transactions. A set of feelings in you and your brother leads to a given kind of transaction between you. The transaction leads to a next set of feelings, which leads to the next transaction, and so on. In this sequence our model (which is cross-sectional) helps explain one half of this set of relationships—the effect of generous, hostile, or indifferent feelings on the next transaction. It tells nothing about the effect of that transaction on the next set of feelings. But we cannot predict much about the development of the relationship over time unless we know *both* halves of this sequence of interactions. We have a science for every other step in the relationship; but we have no science for the equal number of steps in between. Hence we have no science for the whole sequence. Those in-between steps depend on who the parties are, what has happened to them recently, and many other very personal conditions. That is why the development of the relationship over a period of time depends on the unique circumstances of the case, and why we cannot make good scientific generalizations about it.

The preceding paragraph also applies the ongoing relationship between the Arabs and the Israelis, General Motors and Ford, every dating couple, the president and Congress, an elected official and the voters—in short, to every pair of parties who interact. The problem is complicated even further for social scientists by the fact that we cannot measure very accurately the strength of these feelings and of their effects on effective preferences. Nor is there much reason to believe we ever will. The above are reasons why we say that developmental change is unique and unpredictable—it all depends, and it goes where it goes.

The social science in previous chapters is largely useless for predicting the direction of change. Even so, it is still much better than no social science at all. (To know only that you must go in a general northeasterly direction to get to Boston from New York is not nearly so good as having a road map. But even that much knowledge will get you to Boston much quicker than if you thought you should go south or west. Where you get to also depends on where you start. "If I drive northeast, will I get to Boston?" can be answered only if I first know whether you are starting from New York or Bangor.) To guess even roughly where a society will go we must first know where it is and what it is like. We can be very sure the United States twenty years from now will be very different from the way Burma will be. To predict the future of either country we must know what it is now like and in what direction it is already moving.

Prediction, explanation, and control

We may want to understand the process of change to *explain* it, to *predict* what may happen in the future, or to *control* the course of events. Let us examine the idea of evolution in all three respects. We said that the evolutionary idea of RVSR is the only process that can account for emergent change, but that evolution can also bring simple change that does not involve higher-level systems. In its basic form evolution only *explains* change after it has occurred. From fossil remains we can describe where biological evolution *did* go, trace the variations that survived and those that did not, and perhaps identify the survival-favoring traits. But the theory provides no advance clues about where evolution *would* go, or will go in the future. Birds, whales, flowers, and oaks might or might not have happened, and birds are different because they developed from reptiles than if they had evolved from mammals, as bats did. Histories and archaeological remains similarly show how human societies *did* develop. But such knowledge gives us no theories that would enable us to predict those events if we had it to do over again—and most historians are wary about suggesting any such predictive theories.

If our main theory of change simply explains something after it has happened, does this mean that we cannot predict at all, except by sheer speculation? Not quite. In the simplest prediction we observe recent trends and then extrapolate where we will go if those trends continue. The difficulty is that trends slow down, speed up, or change course. And although all growth stops somewhere, we often cannot be sure where till it actually stops.

If we use evolutionary techniques in our thinking, the thinking also becomes a sort of predictor. In our heads we can try new combinations (intersections) of existing patterns—the random generation half of RGSR. For selective retention we ask which of those new combinations we think the society will accept and which not. If we have done this job well we may come up with a reasonably good prediction of social change. But often we cannot know of some development that will change things dramatically in unexpected ways, such as television or the atomic bomb. In that case our predictions will not be very good.

If we want to plan and control social change, rather than merely predict it, we start the same way. We begin by making in our heads (or our computers) new combinations or variations of patterns we already know. (We cannot combine or modify patterns we do *not* know.) From those new forms we select the ones we like, and then do what we can to see that they are the ones that actually happen and survive. The selected forms might include a city planning technique, an efficient system of rail passenger transportation, a prison reform, or a revamped educational system. We sometimes plan social structures unknowingly when we build physical facilities. In a dormitory the number of persons per room and the location of lounges and recreation areas will affect social relations among students. Social interactions are different in an apartment house near a shopping center than in an area where small shops are scattered among row houses. Vast changes in American society were brought about by people who thought they were only building automobiles and highways.

We have said that social change is unique, and also that the simulation model is a way of understanding the unique. We therefore can use simulation to help explain past change and predict or control the course of future change. A simulation is not really different from what we have just been describing about change. In a formal simulation we are merely more explicit about which variables we include or exclude, about measuring each as accurately as possible, and about the effects of each—as in Chapter 26.

There's always room at the top

There is one probable exception to our statement that change is unique, and hence not subject to reliable prediction. It does seem reasonable to predict that both real and conceptual systems evolve to higher and higher levels. The reason is simple. In due time all feasible variations of a given level of system tend to be tried, and the successful ones tend to survive. Hence any new specimens entering at existing levels go into niches already filled with successful competitors.

By contrast, a new system entering at a level above all others has no entrenched competitors, and more room for error—the first warriors to fight as a team against unorganized opponents, the first corporation competing with individual enterprises, the first national government among towns and principalities. Higher level does not assure success. It just makes failure less likely. (The dinosaur was not higher level than its competitors, just bigger.) Except for this general tendency toward higher levels the evolutionary model does not indicate whether change will go forward, backward, or sideways. (The barnacle is only one of the species that are now "lower" and simpler than they were in some earlier evolutionary stages.)

Change and nonchange

The processes of communication, transaction, and organization are basically the same whether they bring change or steady state. As Parsons (1966: 21) notes, "At the most general theoretical levels, there is no difference between processes which serve to maintain a system and those which serve to change it."[4] Under one circumstance or at one system level an interaction may have developmental effects; under another circumstance or at a different system level it may not.

---

[4] Parsons (1966: 22) also notes two steps in the process of change. Despite the difference in emphasis his *differentiation* and *integration* may correspond logically to the variation and retention aspects of the evolutionary model. Differentiation is certainly a form of variation. And a particular variation is more likely to be retained if it integrates into the remaining patterns of the society. At the same time we must note that we earlier referred to differentiation and coordination as two necessary ingredients of *any* system, whether or not it is undergoing change. That is, saying that hydrogen and oxygen must be both different and coordinated (integrated) if we are to have water is not the same as saying that differentiation and coordination are the *process* by which the two elements combine to form water. In evolutionary language we would say instead that the hydrogen and oxygen *happened* to come together (random variation) and that the bonding produced by their respective atomic structures held them tightly together (selective retention of the new system).

CONCLUSIONS

Societies and social scientists face a very real problem. Most social science, like most of this book, is static, or cross-sectional. But most real societies constantly change, and the changes are often what concern us most. Yet we conclude in this chapter that we do not have a very good science of social change, and probably never will. We have said that evolutionary theory is perhaps our best theory of emergence, and of much other social change as well. But evolutionary process is itself half-random—random variation and the conclusion that evolution goes where it goes.

But our social science is not therefore useless. Despite perpetual change every society also contains massive continuities (Chapter 29). Even as things are changing, we often find it important to understand what is happening as it happens. The static analysis helps us do that. It also helps us understand each step of social change as it occurs, and to know something about handling the next step—which is much better than no science at all. What social science cannot do is tell us much about the probable end result of a long sequence of steps. An overall evaluation of this limitation appears in the concluding chapter. Some additional aspects of change will also be dealt with under the heading of discontinuities in culture, in Chapter 29.

28
PERSONALITY

WHY STUDY PERSONALITY?

Everyone is interested in himself—what he is like and how he got that way. In part, that is what the study of personality is about, and it is interesting in its own right. Second, and as noted in Chapter 12 (Figure 12–2), the personality is a crucial link in the chain of culture—it contains the patterns internalized in persons which, when externalized, constitute the body of a culture. Third, and relatedly, the formation of each personality is part of the induction process which molds the potentially erratic individual into a subsystem of social organization. Fourth, each personality is unique; hence personality is an important example of studying the unique as part of the general techniques of social science. Finally, we have been studying acting systems up to this point, and personality is the first major pattern system we will study.

Most of our science—social, psychological, biological, and physical—is about acting systems. We have rather little science thus far about pattern systems. Indeed, the very idea of a pattern system in the sense of this book is not widely recognized. That is the main reason why this chapter on personality and the next one on culture, both pattern systems, have more description (as befits a young science) and fewer generalizations (which characterize better-developed sciences) than does most of the rest of the book.

THE NATURE OF PERSONALITY

A *personality* is the total set of inherited and learned detector, selector, and effector (DSE) states of a particular person, with emphasis on their relatively durable states and the way one personality differs from others. Let us look at the parts of this definition. By "relatively durable states" we do not mean whether you happened to be feeling joyous or depressed last week, but whether you are typically joyous or depressed. The emphasis on differences means that it would not tell us much about your personality to learn that you dislike drinking straight vinegar, since the same would be true for nearly everybody. However, if we learned that you drink a large glass of vinegar every morning for breakfast we would feel that we had a clue to something important about your personality.

All of your overt behavior is directed by your control (behavioral) system, which consists of the states of your DSE subsystems. The definition of personality therefore includes your overt behaviors, along with all your thoughts, perceptions, feelings, skills, attitudes, and likes and dislikes that produce those behaviors. Since your personality is defined in terms of your behavioral system, your body is not part of your personality, as such. However, your body (maintenance system) always accompanies your behavioral system, and often strongly influences your behavior. For example, your behavior and other people's responses to you will be different if you are strong or weak, large or small, ill or healthy, attractive or unattractive. Your body thus *influences* and helps mold your personality, yet is not part of it—much as very cold climates foster different personalities than do hot climates, though the coldness is not itself part of the personalities. However, to the extent that your physical appearance (posture, clothes, grooming) and state of health are subject to your own control, they reflect your personality.

You—a person—are an acting system. You are made of material, physical parts that act. Your personality is a pattern system. It does not have weight or occupy space. The distinction here parallels that made in Chapter 12 between the society as an acting system and the culture as a pattern system. The main questions about personality are: Where do those patterns come from? How are different parts of the pattern related to one another? And what effects do these patterns have on behavior? We will first look at the way the pattern system of personality is related to the pattern system of culture. And for anyone who might wonder about it, personality is not the same as the model of man. The model is very general and abstract; a personality is very individual and real.

The overlap of culture and personality

A large part of each personality is derived from the surrounding culture. But the two by no means coincide. The general relationship between culture and personality is diagramed in Figure 28–1. The large circle at the center represents some individual's total set of traits. These may be genetically determined, learned from personal experience, or learned from the culture. The ellipse labeled "Culture as Input" represents the whole of the culture around him. Area X is the portion never learned by this particular individual: constitutional law is part of our culture, but this person internalizes little of it. The remainder of that ellipse (A plus C) is the part of the culture that he does internalize. C is

Figure 28–1
THE OVERLAP OF CULTURE AND
PERSONALITY

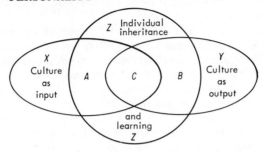

the internalized portion he also symbolizes externally, such as the beliefs he passes on to his children, the language he teaches them, or the way he designs his house or decorates his Christmas tree—if done according to patterns he himself learned from his culture.

Area B represents things this person has worked out for himself, and which, by externalizing them, he has made a part of the culture. For the ordinary individual this area is small, whereas for a noted artist, scientist, politician, or industrialist it could be quite large. Area A represents the part of the culture the individual has internalized but never externalizes in ways that are transmittable to others. For example, if the person is a woman she may learn the use of hair curlers from the culture. But if she never allows anyone else to see her in them, and never talks about them, she does not contribute this aspect of her behavior to the externalized culture. Area Y is that part of the overt culture produced or contributed by persons other than the one represented by the circle. Finally, the two areas marked Z represent the part of the individual's personality that he did not acquire from the culture, and that either is not externalized by him or is externalized but not observed by others. The relative sizes of the areas mean nothing, since we have no way to quantify different cultural patterns.

Even a perfectly transmitted culture does not produce identical personalities. For example, suppose a simple society included only farmers, priests, and chiefs. Although each would learn a little about the others, only farmers would learn all about farming, priests about religion, and chiefs about governing. If the circle represents a farmer, X would be the parts of the priest and chief roles the farmer did not learn, and Y would represent the cultural outputs contributed by the priest and chief but not by the farmer. The more complex the society the larger would be the X and Y areas relative to the circle.

By the same token a person's role provides part of his personality. Persons in different roles therefore have differences in personality, at least for those aspects of personality directly involved in the role. Since every culture incorporates a variety of roles peculiar to it, each culture unavoidably prescribes different personalities.

The variety of personality patterns

We have said that each personality is unique—that no two are alike. But if there are nearly 4 billion people in the world, is it really possible that no two are alike? Let us see.

People differ in sense of humor, intelligence, sensitivity, willpower, honesty, knowledge, and thousands of other traits. Each of these traits has subtraits. For example, writing humorous scripts, generating humor spontaneously, laughing at jokes, and laughing at one's own mistakes are quite different kinds of "sense of humor."

Suppose we try to describe personality in terms of a dozen traits, with ten degrees or variations of each. Although a mere dozen traits would vastly oversimplify the human personality, the combinations of ten different degrees of a dozen traits would produce a trillion (10^{12}) different personalities. Even two degrees (high or low) of each of twelve traits would produce over 4,000 (2^{12}) distinct types, and Allport and Odbert (1936) found almost 18,000 trait names in English. In short, there are enough potential types of personality for everyone to have one of his very own, with plenty to spare. By the same token it would be silly to try to have a separate name for each type, and we must make do with crude descriptions, such as "exciting" or "dull-but-hardworking." Such brief characterizations, however, give no idea whether the person likes music, is dependable, makes friends easily, shows racial prejudice, collects stamps, or is insensitive to criticism. Even "likes music" might mean listening to records, going to concerts, practicing alone, performing with a private group, or performing in public. It gives no idea about the *kinds* of music the person likes, or whether he cares about quality of performance or actually knows much about music. Only by citing very many different traits could a real personality be adequately described. Personality thus clearly displays the two main characteristics of uniqueness— the vast number of possible patterns and the impossibility of describing any one of them accurately in detail.

INDIVIDUAL CONTENT OF PERSONALITY

Figure 28–1 shows the parts of one's personality that he acquires from his culture (*A* plus *C*) and the parts that he does not (*B* plus *Z*). In trying to describe where and how a person gets his personality, we will examine the same two main sources, under the headings, "Individual Content of Personality" and "Social Content of Personality." In this section we discuss the former, first the effects of inheritance and then those of learning.

Inherited differences

Despite many similarities in biological inheritance no two persons inherit precisely the same equipment—though "identical" twins may be remarkably similar. People differ in size and shape, strengths, glandular activity, allergic sensitivities, susceptibility to disease, and tendencies to longevity—to mention only a few. These conditions often produce differences in behavior, as when glandular secretions make one person excitable and another relaxed. Primary motives may be strong in one person and weak in a second.

The effects of such differences are most obvious at the extremes, as with the defective body, or the damaged brain that can learn certain things only very slowly if at all. Even within a normal range, however, if people get off from different starting points, the cumulative effect of such differences over the years may be tremendous. For example, a person who starts life highly motivated is likely to work hard, and to succeed in many things. His success strengthens his motivation, and so on in an upward positive-feedback relation. The person less motivated to start with is more likely to fail. His failure further weakens his motivation, in a downward positive-feedback relation. Part of the concern for "disadvantaged children" is to get them "over the hump" and into an upward spiral that will increase their power.

Individual differences are often couched in terms of heredity versus environment, or nature versus nurture. Much of the argument is fruitless. There are obvious differences in sex, size, bone structure, hair color, color of skin, and shape of eyes among individuals and among races. But almost any personality can appear in connection with any set of physical characteristics—even if the female is unlikely to become a seductive sex symbol if she is squat and squarish or the male a football hero type if he is five feet tall and weighs 110 pounds. Tendencies toward artistic, mechanical, or mathematical genius sometimes seem to be inborn—though for some aspects of genius, and for intelligence in general, stimulating childhood surroundings must not be discounted, particularly if the stimulation starts early and continues to maturity.

A hotly debated issue is whether certain regularly observed differences in average IQ between whites and blacks is genetic or cultural, and whether the tests themselves contain cultural biases that favor whites. We will not go into the controversy here, because it takes a great deal of space even to pose the question accurately. It would be useful both for science and for social policy if we could get an authoritative answer to the question, since policy with respect to any problem presumably should be based squarely on the facts. There is also a sense, however, in which it does not matter. In most situations that count, we make decisions sensibly if we base them on the traits of the individual, not of his group. In hiring, for example, if a job applicant has the necessary skill, intelligence, and sense of responsibility he should not be rejected because others in his group lack these qualifications. If a job applicant does not have the necessary qualifications he should not be hired because other members of his group do have them. If decisions are made on the basis of the individual, the traits of other members of his group are irrelevant. (It is not sensible to reject a black with an IQ of 120 in favor of a white with an IQ of 110 on the alleged grounds that on the average whites have higher IQs.)

All of this is a rather unsatisfactory statement. There are undoubtedly differences in the quality of the equipment people inherit—in the brain, muscles, sensory processes, glands, and so on. But the consequences of those differences are not at all clear, and may be affected as much or more by the experiences of growing up than by the inborn traits themselves—except at the level of obvious incapacity. Thus even if there are differences in potential, they may be overshadowed by what is done with the potential. With those observations we move to surroundings and experiences as influences on personality.

Learned differences, and experience vs. environment

As to the effects of learning, we learn from experiences, not from some environmental package of things around us. Even in the same "environment" two people may have very different experiences and different learning.

No two persons deal with the same other persons. For two brothers, *A* is part of *B*'s environment while *B* is part of *A*'s environment. In addition, since every member of the family learns and changes, except for twins the behavior and attitudes of the parents when *B* is born are different than when *A* was born. The excitement is greatest for the first baby. Parents learn from the first child and treat the second differently. Between the first and second child grandmother may move in or father out. In these and many other ways the human environment is not the same for different children, even in the same family.

"Key" experiences often serve as threshold experiences, switching points, or traumatic events. Two brothers walk atop a fence. One is successful and gains self-confidence. The other catches his foot, has a nasty fall, and loses confidence. Because such small things sometimes have large consequences, we emphasize experience rather than environment. Some broad patterns of environment that *do* have substantial effects—such as racial group, income, and nationality—are part of the cultural content of personality, to be examined later.

On positive and negative feedback

What goes on inside the brain is unbelievably complicated. For that reason there is no simple relation between an experience and what we learn from it. For example, through recollections we still learn from an experience ten or twenty years after it happened. We will focus on one kind of complication.

In Chapter 5 we noted how imagination and fantasizing can take one's ideas farther and farther from reality, in a positive feedback relation. Contact with reality provides negative feedback that checks and corrects such deviations. If the negative feedback is inadequate, or is avoided, one's images may move farther and farther until the individual is significantly out of touch with reality—or psychotic.

We have noted the role of fear in this connection. If a person with an irrational fear of heights or of mice avoids them completely he thereby avoids the experiences that might remove the fear. In fact, merely to think repeatedly about something fearful may strengthen the fear. On one hand, the ability of human beings to make long chains of purely mental connections is the basis of creativity. But creativity may also produce flights from reality—which is why it is sometimes hard to tell a genius from a fool. It is also why some teachers feel uneasy with creative students.

The way we learn to avoid unpleasant acts also enables us to avoid unpleasant thoughts. Psychiatry reveals many examples, of which we will cite one type. It is pleasant to think of oneself as sensible, intelligent, and liked. To think the opposite is a threat to the self-image. If certain observations suggest that one is stupid or incompetent, he can avoid the pain of that conclusion by restructuring his image of reality to make himself look wise and competent. On public issues one can read only those views that support his own, or selectively forget opposing ones. He can conclude that the authors he agrees with are wise while opposing ones are uninformed.

Everyone shows this response to some extent. Perhaps it is a simple extension of our model of man—that we perceive only that for which a pattern already exists in our heads. A view we disagree with is one for which we have no pattern, or only an unclear one. To accept views we disagree with we must modify our concepts—a relatively slow and difficult process. To accept a view we already agree with is simple perception, swift and easy. Though we all to some extent pay attention to things that enhance our self-image and ignore those that threaten it, people differ widely in the strength of this tendency. A personality that readily learns from criticism is quite different from one that rejects all criticism as threatening.

A feeling of inadequacy generates fear: of failing in one's job or in his relations with others. In our model pleasantly valenced thoughts tend to take precedence over unpleasant ones. But if emotions are aroused, fear tends to dominate. Then fears of failure or ridicule may produce chronic depression, anxiety, or guilt. These feelings may lead in turn to refusing to take a job or a college course for fear of failing. Such feelings may also lead to self-punishment, or to attributing to others weaknesses or motives one refuses to acknowledge in himself. Positive feedback often operates, as when the more fearful one becomes the less able he is to perform, and the less well he performs the more fearful he becomes. However, a new activity or an unexpected success may start the spiral upward. Merely talking out the problem may also reverse it, and sometimes the downward reaction simply wears out. In any event, the different ways in which people respond to fears and uncertainties are important ingredients of their personalities.

Decisional aspects of personality

Some ways of making decisions are important parts of personality. A person with a strong positive time preference assigns high values to present satisfactions and low values to delayed ones. He will be reluctant to make investments, pay fixed costs, or avoid borrowing. A person with a strong negative time preference (willpower) denies himself present satisfactions so as to have more satisfactions in the future. One reason for the difference is the clarity of one's images of the future. If one does not have a very clear picture of what the future will be like he is not likely to sacrifice very much for it. Some engage in self-denial because their culture teaches it, as in the Puritan view that most pleasurable or self-indulgent things are sinful.

Some persons seem to understand intuitively that sunk costs should not be counted. They go on from where they are and let bygones be bygones. Others "just can't stand to let all that effort go to waste," and insist that costs already sunk must be "saved" by sinking still more. The public debates over the supersonic transport (SST) in 1970 are an example. Its supporters asked Congress to spend millions more so as not to waste the millions already spent developing the plane. When sunk costs include deaths, the appeal is stronger. "Our boys must not have died in vain" is an appeal that the sunk costs of their deaths require us to finish whatever they started, even if it was never worth starting. The attitude reflects a difference between objective and subjective rationality. Whereas objective rationality ignores sunk costs, subjectively we often value things in proportion to the costs expended rather than for the benefits expected—even though it's useless I treasure it because it cost so much! And there may be a simple reason. If we have incurred a large cost for something that turns out to provide a small benefit, it is obvious that we have made a serious mistake. If the costs cannot be hid, we still have a chance to avoid looking wrong if we can exaggerate the benefit so that it seems worth the cost. On this score the objectively rational person is often thought to be cold and unfeeling while the subjectively rational one seems impulsive and illogical.

Unless future decisions depend on knowing who made some error, persons who always want to know whose fault something was are irrationally preoccupied with sunk costs. (They may, of course, be trying to prove their own superiority—a result that does affect the future.)

The chapter on decisions noted that the information costs of assuring a "right" decision are sometimes larger than the loss from making a "wrong" one. As regards personality, some persons take a positive delight in carefully gathering all the facts about a particular decision. To them, making a careful decision is fun, not a cost. Others find careful calculations intensely frustrating, and the decision process very costly. Other things equal, the latter might be better off to make intuitive, impulsive decisions. Other things equal (which they usually aren't), the former may make the more sensible decisions. Decision theory thus provides a focus for studying certain aspects of personality—in the valuations a person puts on time preference, investment, fixed costs, sunk costs, and decision costs. An interesting aspect of personality—which must be studied in the individual case—is to learn what background and experiences produce which kinds of attitudes toward decision making.

SOCIAL CONTENT OF PERSONALITY

In the preceding section we looked at ways in which a personality is formed by forces that do not directly involve others. Some of these forces derive from biological inheritance and others from learning. We now move to the social content of personality, all of which is learned. The social content itself falls into two main parts. The first is the learning of patterns that already exist as part of one's culture, and are transferred rather directly to the individual—the cultural content of personality. The second part is patterns that the individual learns from his own experiences in interacting with others—the social-interactional content. To illustrate the difference the society may tell you not to tell lies—an attempted direct transfer of cultural content. Or you may learn not to tell lies because you were frightfully embarrassed when you were caught in one, and thereafter avoided lying, whether or not you were told not to lie. Although such learning from interactions might also be thought of as individual content, we will include it here because much of the cultural content (especially roles) is also learned in the interactions.

The cultural content of personality

In her *Sex and Temperament* Margaret Mead (1935) vividly describes the difference in personality types in different tribes. The Arapesh personality is typically mild, relaxed, easygoing, tolerant, and permissive. The Mundugumor personality is typically hard, aggressive, militant, eager to display strength and endurance of pain. Although the difference is one of degree, and each society includes individuals who do not conform to these norms, each society does cultivate its own norms, and enforces them by example and sanctions.

Personality also includes other culturally acquired traits (DSE states). To provide food a person in one society will learn to spear fish. In a second he will learn to hunt rabbits with bow and arrow, and in a third he will learn to earn money to buy food. If a tornado wipes out a village, the survivors in one society prostrate themselves before the gods; in a second they shake their fists at the sky; and in a third they ask the government for disaster relief. One society sprinkles dried frog legs on the sick man's chest; a second drains some of his blood; and a third gives him penicillin. Whichever of these behavioral patterns one learns, they become parts of personality.

More generally, all the things discussed in the next chapter as part of culture can become part of personality. Among other things each person occupies certain roles, and as father, shoemaker, teacher, priest, or servant he will incorporate into his personality behaviors assigned to his role. If a person belongs to a Jewish, Catholic, French-Canadian, Chicano, or black militant subculture, its traits too become part of his personality.

The social-interactional content of personality

In the course of living among others each person learns a great deal about others, about himself, and about interactions. With greater or lesser insight he learns many things about transactions, communications, and organizations. Some of the fundamentals are learned early, as with a student who said he had learned before he was three that occasional feigned reluctance to kiss his parents good-night could bring him many goodies. Almost every kindergarten child knows that tattling brings different transactional payoffs from teacher than from other children. Some persons learn some things about interactions, other persons learn other things, and some reach erroneous conclusions. These differences in what is learned produce different behaviors—hence different personalities.

The self-image: Process. In his interactions each person acquires a picture of himself—a self-image, ego-image, or sense of identity. An important part of the self-image is role. In the preceding section we discussed the portion of the role content prescribed by the society. We now shift to the aspects of role that one works out through interactions, and to one's self-image in relation to his role.

Recalling how inner images can be externalized, let us think first of externalizations that require skill, as when you make a table, draw a picture, or play a musical instrument. When you observe your product you learn something about your skill. Are you good, mediocre, or poor with the sketching pencil, woodworking tools, or piano? More broadly, to compare the result of *any* directed effort with your intention helps form your self-image of being competent, incompetent, or in between.

In your social behavior, if you observe that others are warm, cordial, and helpful toward you, you tend to build an image of yourself as friendly and likable. If others are cold, hostile, and withdrawn, you tend to build an image of yourself as not liked. If you try to be liked but find yourself unliked you tend to build an image of yourself as socially incompetent. These interactions hold many possible clues about other people's atti-

"I only growled at you because you looked as if you were going to growl at me. I'm sorry. I didn't realize I'd become so paranoid."

Drawing by Frascino; © 1973 The New Yorker Magazine, Inc.

tudes. When you talk, do others listen? Or do they glance around as if looking for something more interesting? In group discussion do others seek out your ideas, or always follow someone else's suggestions? Does your young niece run eagerly to greet you or shrink away? All these things are cues about yourself.

Although many pieces of your personality are derived from your culture, so long as you stay in your own culture you may not notice them. But when you get into a different culture—as when you travel—you notice that "those people" are different. At that point your self-image starts to include seeing yourself as a member of a particular society and culture. Your image of who you are now includes the group(s) to which you belong. *Seeing* yourself as an American, Catholic, Democrat, Bircher, hippie, etc., is more than just *being* one.

Social interactions add to the effect. Other persons have *their* images of an American, Catholic, etc., and respond to you accordingly—at least until they know you well personally. Hence you not only *are* a member of a group, but tend to be pushed into its patterns by others who treat you as one. Your role is molded not only by you, but by the concept in the minds of others of the group to which you belong. What is more, just as you form a self-image from the way others respond to you, so do you form an image of your group as you read that image in the behavior of others.

A difficulty is that cues are often ambiguous, that social reflections are often made by distortion mirrors, the distortions being the personalities of the other persons. For example, another person's coolness to you may reflect *his* personality, role, or culture rather than your own. Or it might be a bargaining tactic. A related complication is that if you do not like the reflection you may blame the mirror rather than yourself. Despite these reservations, in broad ways the responses of others do provide a sort of mirror image of yourself, and help mold your self-image. In fact, others are your only source of some kinds of information about yourself. Cooley (1902) perceptively coined the term "looking-glass self" to describe this source of self-image. Since it revolves around image transfers this problem is basically communicational. Cooley also noted how we approve or disapprove of these self-images, and then mold them (and hence our behavior) into patterns we ourselves approve. When our behavior fits our self-image, we feel good about ourselves, and we feel bad when our behavior violates our self-image. In a very real sense this is an exercise of inner authority, in which we reward or punish ourselves when we follow or violate our instructions to ourselves in the form of self-expectations.

Self-image: Content. Many of the dimensions of self-image involve a sense of power—not in the layman's sense (high position or wealth) but in all the forms discussed in earlier chapters. Intrapersonal power is the ability to do things for oneself. It hinges mainly on such detector and effector aspects as strength, skill, and knowledge; and on such selector states as desire to accomplish, tolerance for frustration, and willpower. It may also depend on such environmental conditions as available materials and reasonable weather.

As we have seen, interpersonal power (other than that involving bads) depends on being able to provide things wanted by others. The ability to make or do things for others thus constitutes power. So does the possession of information or understandings that make others seek one's advice or company. A "wish for worth" and a "desire to be useful" are thus layman's phrases for a desire for power. A desire to be liked nevertheless has important other dimensions, and is almost certain to become intrinsically rewarding, strongly and early in life. The reason is that the sense of being liked and loved is associated from birth with the pleasant feelings of being warm, fed, clean, and cuddled. Except for children raised without those affectionate relationships, the reward value of being liked and loved is likely to be so strongly conditioned so early in life that it becomes much like a powerful primary motive. Because it is a more universal currency than money it is also more likely to become intrinsically rewarding. However, just because being liked is often its own reward, we should not neglect its importance to interpersonal power—to which we now return.

We have noted how one's power rises with a generous extension of the other party's effective preference, which typically occurs when one is liked. When one is deeply loved, the extension may be tremendous, and virtually guarantees access to wanted things that belong to those who love him. A parallel shrinkage accompanies dislike or disapproval. Since being loved also contributes to being wanted, these two sources of power partially overlap.

To say that the desire to feel loved and wanted is also a desire for power does not mean that people actually think of it this way. In fact, many would feel uncomfortable to hear such feelings associated with the idea of power. Even in layman's language, however, almost anyone would feel frighteningly powerless if everyone around disliked him and he had nothing at all that they wanted.

Because power, as the ability to satisfy wants, is really a generalized concept of instrumentality, and because a person without any of it must literally do without food, clothing, and satisfying emotional relationships, perhaps the most important single ingredient in anyone's self-image is his view of his own power: (1) the ability to do things for himself; (2) the ability to do or to make things for which others will give something in exchange; and (3) being liked or loved by others. Because others also want to be loved, then to love others—perhaps merely to express affection—is a good for which they may give other goods in exchange.

Someone who stands high on all three types of power can feel secure. If he is high on one or both of the first two he might feel secure in material respects but insecure about his emotional relations. If he feels rich in affectional relations but poor on the other two scores he would be vulnerable if he should lose the affections of others. Jealousy includes the sense of lost power from a lover's transfer of affection. (Described in terms of the model of man, jealousy is not a separate emotion, but some combination of love, fear, and anger.) Anyone who sees himself as short on all three types of positive power will probably see bads (force, stealth, cheating, blackmail, theft, rape, threats) as his only source of power. The absence of positive power is not the only reason for using bads. Hostility may lead one to give bads as "gifts," or a sense of guilt may lead him to commit crime in an unconscious desire to be punished and relieve the guilt.

It is often useful not only to *have* power, but also to have status, or perceived power. Hence criticism, insults, nondeferential behavior ("Do that," instead of "Would you mind doing that?"), or other behavior by others that suggest lesser power also undercuts one's ego-image. Unless one is secure on other grounds, status-lowering actions by others will be resented, resisted, or avoided. Status is relative; hence one can sometimes raise his own status by undercutting that of others. The person who sees his own power as small therefore tends to be "touchy" about threats to his self-image, and to respond with counterattacks on the status of others. On the other hand we typically try to avoid saying things that will undercut other people's self-images, under the often-correct assumption that they would like us less otherwise. Polite language is supportive of status, and we use it for similar reasons.

"What will people think?" is the stated or unstated question that keeps many of us from doing all kinds of things. (I often feel like jumping over a trash can or swinging my leg up over a parking meter, and would do so if I were absolutely sure no one were looking. But I don't, even though none of the passersby know me, and I probably would not suffer any adverse consequences even if they did.) The desire to avoid having "generalized others" observe us in nonnormative, unconventional behavior is perhaps the most powerful force for conformity. We can guess that it is tied to the real, but often very exaggerated, fear of disapproval and the consequent loss of power.

The role content of personality: Identity

We hear a great deal nowadays about youth's identity crisis. Who am I? What am I doing here? Where am I going? Why should I bother?

Until induction and socialization are fully effective, all youth undergo some such questioning. However, during most of human history the young person understood at an early age—perhaps before he even thought about the question—that "who he was" was established by his family, and that he would probably go through life in the same career as his parent of the same sex. Traditional societies are still like that. In industrial or developing societies this is often not the case. In fact, the occupation of the child may not have existed when his parents were young, as with computer programmer or astronaut.

"Who am I?" means: "What role(s) am I now in and into what roles am I headed?" In systems language: "What kind of subsystem am I, what kind of functions am I to perform, and what are the supersystems of which I am a subsystem?" The child in the slow-moving society might not like to become a duke, peasant, soldier, or shoemaker like his father. But from an early age he knew where he was headed. However, when roles are changing rapidly, youth may be disoriented. Many avenues are open, and conflicts may arise about which one to follow.

A stable personality needs a clear sense of identity—a clear image of one's roles and acceptance of the values attached to them. Roles in transition produce inner conflict—about which roles to occupy and how to behave within them. That inner conflict and disorientation are then part of one's personality—perhaps bringing a sense of guilt for failing to fit prescribed roles or of anger at society for failing to provide more suitable roles.

"You think you're the only one around here with an identity crisis?"

Drawing by Carl Rose; © 1971 The New Yorker Magazine, Inc.

The worldwide "identity crisis" of contemporary youth is related to changing roles. Underdeveloped nations show a gap between rising expectations and static or deteriorating reality. There a youth may be torn between following the role of his parents and shifting to some dramatically different one, often poorly defined, that seems more modern. In America the Vietnam war, race tension, pollution, corporate power, Watergate, the energy crisis, and other pressing problems have caused many to doubt the sensibleness of such basic roles as those of corporations and governments, and to question the propriety of working within them. But corporations and government provide most of the jobs. Many thus face a conflict: they desperately need jobs but feel that the available jobs help foster an unsatisfactory society. One may also want to "blow the whistle" if he sees his corporate or government boss doing something immoral or illegal, but is afraid he will lose his job if he says anything. The "who am I?" complex means: "I haven't found the role(s) into which I can fit." When one identifies his role(s) he identifies himself.

When persons with different concepts of roles interact, a shift in the concepts of roles becomes conflicts between persons. Many a parent-child argument has revolved around the fact that the parent was raised in one culture and the child in a very different one. Expected behaviors about dress and grooming, the use of drugs, grades in school, or sex relationships have changed, and the cultural change often called the "generation gap" leads to conflicts between persons when those cultural differences are internalized in persons who have to interact.

Identity, role, and behavior

Like many other images, a self-image is not merely what is in the head but a determinant of what comes out of it—overt behavior symbols inner patterns. The little boy who enjoys playing with dolls is apt to be called a sissy. The little girl who enjoys wrestling may be told, "Little ladies don't wrestle." In due time each child learns two things. First is the role of boy or girl—how boys and girls are expected to behave. Second is knowledge of oneself: "I am a girl" or "I am a boy." After that one behaves like a girl because she has an image of herself as a girl—or like a boy because he has a self-image of being a boy. Later on, each person moves into more advanced roles: student, cheerleader, musician, employee, parent, auto mechanic, teacher, priest. In each case he behaves according to the role because he has an image of the role and an image of himself as an occupant of it. Similarly, the behavior of the child may resemble that of the parents because he knows what the parent is like and has heard people say, "He's just like his father" or "She's just like her mother." The child may then *be* like the parent because he has the self-image of being like the parent. One of the difficulties of rehabilitating criminals is that they may develop self-images as burglars, junkies, prostitutes, or smugglers.

The individual as subsystem vs. the individual as system-in-own-right

Another present-day identity problem is the resentment at being only a cog in a machine. The prisoner in the penitentiary and the corporate executive frustratedly struggling with a wrong charge against his credit card can both sense the futility of being only a number—of trying somewhere in an impenetrable maze to contact a human being who will listen and understand. (Each student may identify with either the prisoner or the executive.) As societies become more complexly industrialized, people increasingly *are* cogs in the machine and many increasingly resent it—though others do not. Since everyone is a subsystem of many organizations—formal, semiformal and informal—the question is, How much emphasis should be placed on my subsystem roles as compared to my being a system in my own right? "Corporation man" is one who gives his all for the company; "dedicated public servant" is his counterpart in government; while the "dedicated parent" holds back nothing from spouse and children. At the other extreme is the person who gives as little as he can get away with.

Which response will provide a more satisfactory life both reflects and molds the personality. One person most completely "finds himself" when he totally loses himself in the group, while another feels smothered by very much group involvement. "It's great, you never have to worry about anything" and "It's dreadful, you can never decide anything for yourself" are the reactions of two different personalities to military life. Often, however, the personality eventually conforms to the circumstances. Ten years in prison might destroy one's desire to make choices, while ten years of unrestricted choice could produce resentment at any restrictions at all.

In Nazi Germany the national system level was given top priority: people counted only as subsystems. Democratic nations reverse the emphasis: people are given top priority; government is important only as a means to serve them. In dictatorship the people have no rights except those accorded them by the government. In democracy (when it works right) the government has no rights except those accorded it by the people. Each government generates personalities that reflect its philosophy. Those personalities then tend to support the kind of government that fostered them.

Conformity and deviance as personality traits

Conformity or deviance are also ways in which different personalities respond to authority. The conformist accepts the subsystem role given to him by his society or his organizational superiors, and behaves like an individual-as-subsystem. The deviant insists on being a system-in-his-own-right, rejecting or seeking to modify the role—perhaps because he dislikes the role or dislikes being a subsystem. A feeling that one does not belong in *any* role is called alienation, well described about American youth by Keniston (1965). Its extreme form is sometimes thought of as *anomie,* a sense of almost complete detachment from any aspect of society. It is also viewed as normlessness, in that such a person does not accept the norms of any culture, subculture, or role.

There is no simple explanation of conformity or deviance. When and whether one accepts conformity or revolts against it is an important component of his personality—a component that has meaning only in the context of a structured society that expects certain behaviors.

PERSONALITY AS A PATTERN SYSTEM

A major function of this chapter is to examine the personality as a pattern system. Whereas in preceding sections of this chapter we looked at the relations of parts of a personality to inheritance and experience, now we look at the relations of the parts to one another. In Chapter 2 we noted that our main concern about pattern systems is "whether their parts are consistent or inconsistent with one another according to some kind of standards or criteria of some acting system." The acting system is the person, and the problem about personality as a pattern system is how consistent or inconsistent the person sees its parts to be. How much is he bothered by inconsistencies within himself, and what, if anything, does he do about them? One of the most interesting aspects of any person is his handling of inconsistencies. Inconsistencies are also often forms of conflict; how one handles them is an important measure of his emotional stability. The core of the question of patternness is whether a personality "hangs together" or is seemingly a disorganized batch of unrelated pieces.

Consistencies and inconsistencies of pattern

In ways we hardly understand at all, the brain shows two opposite tendencies. One is to connect very different things—a matter in which poets are specialists. From them we accept "love as deep as the ocean" without flinching, though the intensity of love is a degree of excitation, while the depth of the ocean is a simple linear measurement—in fact, to a point where the ocean is remarkably still. Here we accept as consistent things that might seem inconsistent if we think carefully about them.

The brain's opposite tendency is to keep apart things that are similar—of not accepting their consistency. For example, as an American studying German, it was immediately obvious to me when I learned the word that *Handschuh* (the German word for glove) is a "shoe for the hand." Yet a native German I talked to recently had never thought of the word in this way. And it never occurred to me until recently that *welfare* and *farewell* have the same root meanings. Because inconsistencies are more likely to be troublesome than unnoticed consistencies, we will focus on the former.

In his church a man may accept that all men are brothers and equally children of God, while from the Declaration of Independence he accepts that all men are created equal. Yet he may also believe that one American life is worth a hundred Orientals and never note the discrepancy. With great conviction one may recount how as a youngster he learned through his own mistakes, yet expect his own children to learn from their parents' advice.

We tend to think of a personality as integrated or organized if its parts are consistent in logic (detector) and values (selector), and as unintegrated or disorganized if its parts are inconsistent. Discrepancies like those of the preceding paragraph seem to reflect disorganization.

It might be gratifying if we could state some simple rule about these matters, such as that greater integration and organization make for a better personality or a happier life. The trouble is that reality is incredibly complex. If we change one element of a personality to make it consistent with a second, we may thereby make it inconsistent with some third element. Furthermore, although consistency has obvious merit in certain areas of logic and science, one may be skeptical about whether consistency is always or necessarily good.

For example, the parent who insists that he learned from experience seems inconsistent when he wants his own children to learn from precept. Yet he may also remember that some of his own learning experiences were very dangerous, and conclude that the knowledge gained from them was not really worth the risk. It may thus seem consistent with his present knowledge to steer his children away from those risks—though his children may not agree. One may also see universal brotherhood as a fine goal (preference function) but consider it an impractical base for real policies (not available within the opportunity function). In such cases it is not easy to say for sure whether the pieces of the personality are or are not consistent with one another. In fact, it is hard to imagine a wholly consistent personality, if only because one's culture is itself loaded with inconsistencies (Chapter 29) and each of us must live with them. Perhaps our most completely consistent personalities are in mental hospitals, precisely because they distort or ignore all potential inconsistencies. Some people are *dichotomizers*—a lesser form of distortion—who see everything as black or white, right or wrong. They cannot tolerate the ambiguities of life, much of which falls somewhere in between.

On handling inconsistencies

Inconsistency (in our model) is a pattern mismatch, generally unpleasant if recognized, and producing frustration if strong enough. Being unpleasant, it is something the system tends to reduce or avoid.

We tend to assume that the proper response to observed inconsistency is to study or think about it until we have resolved it. To a certain extent this is what all of us do, starting with the exploratory activities of early childhood. However, the number of potential inconsistencies is far greater than we can ever deal with. Even if we had the time and the brainpower we could not resolve them all, and much effort of many of our scientists is spent trying to resolve inconsistencies in science. Humans thus have to live with inconsistencies, and show a number of more or less standard responses to them—often called "defense mechanisms." Which of these responses an individual typically gives is an important dimension of his personality.

Perhaps the simplest response is the shrugged shoulder—a simple refusal to be bothered by the inconsistency. Whether or not this response is emotionally "healthy" depends on how regular it is and how serious are the inconsistencies thus shrugged off. A second device is the *logic-tight compartment*. One can vigorously dislike the growth of government regulation. Yet every time he sees something he dislikes he wants to "pass a law" to stop it. In principle he may oppose government subsidies, while as owner of a barge line he lobbies for government-built navigation dams. The potential list is endless, and covers the minutiae of life as well as public issues. These inconsistencies are possible because the individual so arranges his thinking that he does not consciously confront the two halves of the contradiction simultaneously. Each half is logically sealed off from the other.

Rationalization is another device, in which we substitute "good" or "plausible" explanations for real ones. If the barge owner is aware of his inconsistency he may rationalize it by arguing that dams and locks are public services, not subsidies, or that the dams are needed anyway for flood control. The student who is flunking may blame the teacher, the text, his health, the noisy dorms, or his part-time job.

Repression, projection, and displacement are variations of a third device for handling inconsistencies, especially those involving strong values or urges. For example, one's parent or spouse might be so frustrating at times that one might (at least for some purposes) wish him dead. But to wish someone dead is felt to be dreadfully shameful. Hence one does not allow the wish to rise to the conscious level, where it might shatter his self-image. However, it might come out in a dream, as follows. *A* hates his wife and unconsciously wishes she were dead. He dreams that someone tries to murder her, but that he (*A*) heroically saves her. The attempted murder, which even in the dream is attempted by someone else, reflects his unconscious *repressed* wish. *A*'s appearance as the rescuer reflects the role he thinks he *ought* to occupy. Dreams, incidentally, can provide crucial insights into one's personality when interpreted by someone skilled in such matters. Dream interpretation is no business for amateurs, however, and one must be wary of "standard" interpretations not based on intimate knowledge of the individual. We might also understand our normal thinking processes better if we gave more attention to dreams, as the brain is a much more freewheeling gadget than we give it credit for being.

Projection is related. If *A* wishes his father were dead but finds the wish inconsistent with his self-image, he may accuse his brother of trying to kill their father, or insist that some amorphous "they" are "trying to get him." Projection puts into someone else the urges one refuses to acknowledge in himself. Less dramatically, we often blame our own mistakes on others. *Displacement* shifts the form of an idea. In one reported case (Hinsie and Campbell 1969: 219) a person showed a morbid fear of gas escaping in his room, although repeated checks found none. Psychoanalysis revealed that the fear was a displaced wish for the death of his father.

A widely accepted way to handle inconsistencies is *faith*—as that some higher being or destiny resolves all seeming inconsistencies. A faith need not involve theology, as with the faith that war will disappear or that some new social order will triumph.

In Chapter 18 we discussed role conflict that arises when a person occupies multiple roles calling for different kinds of behavior. A role conflict is another form of pattern inconsistency, and any of the devices discussed above can be used as responses to it.

Of the many possible inconsistencies, those that show conflict between one's behavior and his self-image are likely to be the most troublesome, and are most likely to give rise to emotional problems. As noted earlier, many (though certainly not all) problems of self-image are related to one's concept of his power. In that sense many of the defense mechanisms used to bolster the self-image are really attempts to convince oneself that he is not without significant power.

Viewed as a problem in pattern systems, the question is how much inconsistency each individual finds tolerable—and whether he notices inconsistencies. Viewed as a problem in human values, the question is, Which parts of a pattern are modified and which are held intact in the effort to achieve consistency? The core of each person is his self-image, and in a conflict he will generally modify something else to maintain it. For it to slip too far is one of the causes of suicide.

THE SCIENCE OF PERSONALITY

Can there be a science of personality—considering that each personality is unique, and that we have questioned whether there can be a science of the unique? The answer is no—but yes. To understand a particular personality is an art, not a science—whether for the trained psychiatrist or for the untrained parent trying to learn what makes Joey tick.

In Chapter 12 we observed how we can describe a concept that does not have a name by intersecting other concepts that do have names. In that same way we can describe Joey's personality by saying that he is intelligent, somewhat phlegmatic, caustic, demanding, selfish, self-assured in social relations, open-minded and tolerant in intellectual matters, talented in art but a clod with music, and so on. We noted earlier that we can never fully describe any personality because it has too many dimensions. But we can narrow our range of ignorance about Joey by using the above kind of intersection of traits about him. And narrowing our ignorance is all we can do by any learning.

In Chapter 12 we noted that each of us learns much of the knowledge embodied in a culture when he learns its language. Similarly, merely to be able to use such terms as intelligent, phlegmatic, and selfish means that we have some knowledge about personalities. In fact, merely to divide personality into subparts is a step in the scientific study of it. And as with any other use of language, we can at least partly describe very different personalities with a single list of trait names, simply by intersecting them differently. Furthermore, to acknowledge that every personality is unique tells us how to go about trying to understand it—the simulation. The simulation does not try to encompass the whole personality, but to discover those few traits that dominate it and that best predict behavior. That is what a psychiatrist or clinical psychologist does in seeking to understand a patient—even if he does not call it a simulation. In studying a personality (or any other complex situation), it is likely that some few forces are more important than others, and the problem is to find them.

Because of the many ties between culture and personality, and because culture is also a pattern system, the discussion of personality merges into that of culture. That is the subject to which we turn next.

29

CULTURE

REVIEW AND INTRODUCTION

In this chapter we continue our focus on patternness, the unique, and change. In the preceding chapter we looked at personality as the pattern of the particular individual. In this chapter we look at culture—already defined as communicated, learned patterns—as the pattern of a particular society. Both personality and culture are the pattern systems according to which their corresponding acting systems act. Each is also unique—no two are alike. Perhaps even more than with personality, the science of patternness in culture remains largely at the descriptive stage. Anthropologists have given us excellent descriptions of the patterns of many cultures. Although various parts of a pattern are related in certain obvious ways noted below, we do not yet have a very good science about the causes or reliabilities of such relationships. Thus although we cannot say much by way of a science of relatedness, we will try to give some of the feel of relatedness through illustrations.

Whereas the noninherited aspects of personality are learned during a lifetime, a culture is produced or "learned" over many generations, and raises two questions: How is a given set of patterns cumulatively learned and modified during many generations, and how are those patterns acquired by any one generation? The second question was dealt with in Chapter 12, as a communicational process, often assisted by transactional sanctions. The first question concerns the origins of culture, discussed later in the chapter. This chapter also deals with the patternness of culture, shifting the emphasis from *how* each generation learns the culture to *what* it learns. This approach parallels our treatment of the individual—discussing *how* he learns in Chapters 4 and 5 and *what* he learns in Chapter 28. Because so much of what an individual learns comes from his cultural environment, we can also view culture as the human environment of humans.

Of the two phases of the cycle of culture (Figure 12–2) the internal phase relates to personality and the external phase to culture. Some parts of the external phase are durable, such as books in a library or the pyramids. These can be passed on without being externalized anew every generation: when books or buildings are lost and rediscovered centuries later they skip over many generations. Such leaps do not alter the basic internal-external cycle, whose external phase is the medium in a communication. Thus the body of culture exists either *in* human heads or *between* them. Although our interest in culture centers mainly on its externalized phase, the parts of culture that consist of habits and other behaviors of persons depend directly on their internalized phase.

THE CONTENT OF CULTURE

Since in the internal stage the patterns of culture consist of detector, selector, and effector states of people, we group the content of culture under those headings.

The image structure of a culture: Detector

In pure form the detector states deal with a society's concepts of what *is*—its conceptual structure. At its most formal level this consists of the society's science and its organized knowledge of arts and crafts, as reflected roughly in the courses in a university. We can lump much of the remaining detector content under folk wisdom. This is what "everybody knows," whether true or not: that hollow objects float, water runs downhill, and power corrupts. Primitive societies rely heavily on folk wisdom, some of it much like that of advanced societies, and some primitives have much valid knowledge of heavenly bodies, basic mechanics, and the medicinal effects of many substances.

The conceptual structure of primitives includes their magic—which is not to be confused with their religion. Magic typically involves human activity, and may or may not involve the gods. According to its "principles" your rain dance will bring rain just as surely as turning the ignition key will start your car. A failure does not prove you wrong. It merely means that some necessary condition was lacking—your battery was dead, or the cries of the warriors were not loud enough. People who use magic distinguish it from directly observable cause-effect science (Malinowski 1948), much as the scientifically naive American distinguishes the visible ball-breaks-window from the "magic" of television. The first *he* understands; only the "medicine man" understands the second.

Most religions include some cognitive explanations. The Book of Genesis tells how earth and man came into being, and most other religions, primitive or advanced, describe origins. Concepts of heaven, hell, purgatory, happy hunting ground, reincarnation, soul, gods, earth, and universe are often parts of religion. Although some of these are not subject to scientific testing they nevertheless deal with views of what *is*. Serving as a "cognitive safety net" (Wilson 1966: 476), "God did it" or "God understands" provides *some* explanation for those baffling gaps left by science.

In or out of its religion, each society also has explanations of its own origin. Several forms are common. One form dates the group from the time it fought its way out from the tyranny of some inferior person or group: the Jews' release from Egypt, the Americans from George III, or the Russians from the czars. The facts are usually fictionalized enough to show the in-group as brave, long-suffering, freedom-loving, generous, and wise, while those they escaped from are shortsighted, cowardly, stupid, and selfish. Each group's violence against their enemies was justified and righteous (otherwise whey would they have used it?), while violence against themselves was unjustified and barbarous (since how could their noble group have deserved such treatment?). Colonial Americans did double duty, heroically winning their freedom from both the tyrannical English and the bloodthirsty natives. Cattle rustlers and stagecoach robbers filled the folkloric gaps when the English and Indians wore thin. That people never tire of the story is attested daily by television. Other peoples trace their origins to a god, a great traveler, an animal, the descent of a star, or some other supernatural event.

Those portions of technology that involve *knowledge* (rather than physical equipment) are also part of the detector aspect of a culture. Along with those fields of knowledge that customarily go under the heading of "engineering," they also include such "human engineering" knowledge as personnel policies, applied psychology, the mutual adaptation between job and worker, public relations and advertising, and managerial techniques.

The value structure of a culture: Selector

The values within a culture seem limitless, and include a vast scope of likes and dislikes and of approved and disapproved behaviors. Whereas the detector deals with what *is*, much of the selector content of culture deals with the *oughts* of life—the good or bad in tastes and the morally or ethically right or wrong.

Westerners generally like to eat red meat and potatoes, while Easterners eat fish and rice. Dogmeat, catmeat, and horsemeat are disgusting to most dwellers north of the Rio Grande, but are widely eaten by the poor from there to Cape Horn. Western males wear tight trousers, while Easterners wear loose-fitting ones. Many Orientals sit on the floor, while Occidentals prefer chairs and sofas. Much interior decoration in the West is lush and crowded; most in Japan is sparse and lean. The American national sport is baseball (plus football and basketball), while England's is rugby and Mexico's jai alai. In these and many other ways most individuals come to like and enjoy what their society has accustomed them to.

Moral codes reflect more fundamental attitudes. According to the Old

488 Unified social science

Testament, the Ten Commandments were presented to Moses and carry the authority of God. The New Testament attributes many rules to Jesus, such as loving thy neighbor, giving to the poor, and not casting the first stone. Zen and Taoism state rules for proper living without ascribing them to a divinity: beauty and moral truth are within, and the way to find them is contemplation.

Each society has values about itself—the group's parallel of the individual's self-image. Typically this group self-image is that we are good, wise, the salt of the earth, while other people are inferior in character, beliefs, art, habits, dress, and cleanliness. In cosmopolitan societies (as in the United States, Western Europe, and Hong Kong and many other large cities) each subculture tends to develop a self-image of the group, as with the Italian, Greek, Jewish, Irish, Chicano, or Chinese communities. A great difficulty faced by American blacks is that slavery and its aftermath brought many to consider *themselves* inferior. The terms *black* and *Afro-American* have won favor in recent years because they help to avoid the present low-status implications of "Negro" and "colored." "I'm proud to be black" helps to achieve a customary sense of superiority, while courses in black culture reflect the need for pride and group identity.

In many societies values are attached to certain words, and often include mystical or magical values. Among the ancient Hebrews the sacred name for God, generally transliterated as "Yahweh" (Jehovah), was not to be spoken at all. In many circles God is spoken of only in hushed tones. In some cultures certain magic words are believed to produce effects (usually harmful) on others, even if the others do not hear them.

In English "four-letter words" share this magical property. Among those who accept those values, something evil is presumed to happen if these words are spoken. To print them is worse, and it is felt that even the child who hears these words regularly will come to some unspecified harm if he sees them in print. The magic is in the words, not their meanings, since there are other acceptable words with the same meanings. These taboos are strongest in the middle classes, to whom status is important. "Clean language" will not bring status to the lower classes anyway, and upper classes get theirs by other means. Many contemporary youth use the four-letter words to show that they reject middle-class values, and that their own morals involve the way people treat one another, not arbitrary customs of language.

The way the new generation learns the "dirtiness" of certain words illustrates how other traditional values are transmitted. The child learns to expect dismay or punishment from others when he uses a dirty word. The quick gasp, the shocked expression, or *"You* ought to be ash*aaaa*med!" may be followed by soap in the mouth. After enough repetitions the youngster himself starts to experience the same feelings he observes in others, perhaps strengthened by fears of disapproval and memories of punishment. Once fully conditioned, the individual himself feels uncomfortable about dirty words, and may try to get others to avoid using them. Even if he shows only a little tightening of facial muscles on hearing a dirty word, others observe it, know he feels uncomfortable, and avoid such words in his presence.

What is disapproved varies from culture to culture. The *methods* by which semiformal authority transmits attitudes are reasonably standard—by making the individual feel uneasy whenever he does, thinks about doing, or observes others doing things the culture disapproves. That uneasy feeling (a form of dissonance) is widely called conscience —"the voice of the tribe or group speaking from within" (White 1949).

It is not surprising that those aspects of moral codes that are arbitrary and conventional (such as dirty words) differ sharply from culture to culture. But even some fundamental aspects of person-to-person relationships are not so universal as many think. Even parents who believe that conscience is absolute or of divine origin recognize the influence of the group when they worry lest their children "travel with the wrong crowd."

Some aspects of law ignore this problem when they assume that every "normal" person can "tell right from wrong," regardless of his background. Actually, ideas of right and wrong are not born into human beings, but are learned from the culture. Although injuring members of one's own group is rather universally considered wrong (for obvious transactional reasons), many other ideas of right and wrong differ widely from culture to culture—this difference being known as *cultural relativism*. Even within the same main culture the rules differ among subcultures, often in connection with different roles.

When a person changes cultures (as contrasted to merely visiting a foreign land) he is likely to experience conflict. If he stays he may or may not change his code, or even his conscience. As examples of changes, a person trained to use "clean" words may soon learn to use dirty ones gracefully in that subculture known as the armed forces. Attitudes toward sex are not the same in the army as back home in the small town, and stealing clothing from the army, or anything from the enemy, does not twang the conscience like stealing from a neighbor. That morals are often looser away from home illustrates the role of conscience as the still, small voice that tells you someone who disapproves is looking. However, when the norms are really internalized they work when the only one looking is yourself.

Religion and emotions.   In addition to its conceptual and value aspects, religion deals with feelings and emotions. For birth, marriage, death, sickness, travail, and worry, religion and its priests strengthen, soften, redirect, or otherwise modify the related emotions. Some Western religions suggest during grief over death that the departed will someday rejoin those now left behind. Or religion may help purge grief by making it intense, visible, and shared, as in the wailing ceremonies of traditional Jews. In a different culture religion may transmute grief into ecstasy, by shouting, hysterical laughter, or trance, possibly assisted by drugs or erotic release. Others use religious dancing until the participants drop from exhaustion. In some cultures the powerful emotions thus raised are seen as the deity visiting the individual.

The external forms of culture, and effector

Any overt behavior and any material artifacts are symbols of internal patterns. In a broad sense any such externalizations, including those that basically involve concepts and values, can be considered "effectuations" of internal patterns. This section on external forms of culture therefore includes many items that reflect detector and selector states, rather than merely effectuational ones. The parts of the external culture that are most obviously effector instruments are plows, tools, machines, factories, railroads, and the like—the material forms of technology. Having mentioned them, we will now broaden our view to include all kinds of externalizations.

For a society with a written language, all its novels, poems, treatises, newspapers, journals, billboards, plays, and graffiti are part of its public culture. So are its films, photographs, paintings, sculpture, drawings, murals, etchings, tapestries, wallpapers, textile designs, and flower arrangements; its houses, barns, skyscrapers, factory buildings, bridges, mine shafts; broadcasting towers, outhouses, geodesic domes, lamps, rugs, flyswatters, and water meters—in short, any things made by man within a society, with particular emphasis on things that are widely found, are parts of its externalized culture.

Many sociofacts are conspicuous, such as governments, corporations, families, schools, and banks. Contracts, laws, deeds, guarantees, press conferences, patriotic speeches, funerals, conventions, family prayers, racial integration or segregation, trial by jury, and giving gifts at Christmas are all sociofacts. Many are so thoroughly ingrained that we scarcely think of them, such as shaking hands, driving on the right, or eating cereal for breakfast but not dinner. Following Sumner (1906) such widely found practices are known as *folkways*—if they are *expected* but no strong value judgments are attached to them. *Mores* (mo-'rays) are behaviors society feels so strongly about as to make them *required,* such as wearing clothes in public. Like habits in the individual, these uniformities are both restricting (because they narrow the range of behavior) and liberating (because their automaticity frees the mind for other matters).

Even seemingly unimportant behaviors may be rigidly controlled if a people believe they bring adverse consequences. Depending on the society, one may not mention a tribesman who has gone to war, eat a certain fish or meat, cook in an iron kettle after sundown, say incantations over the bed of his uncle, or wear the ceremonial headdress except during the ceremony. A child may be severely punished in many societies if he manipulates the genitals of himself, a friend, or an animal, or watches any act of copulation. The rule that a baseball sportscaster may not mention that a pitcher "has a no-hitter going" is rarely violated, and even most players will not mention it till later. To call these things superstitions does not reduce their rigidity.

RELATEDNESS: CULTURE AS A PATTERN SYSTEM

A pattern is a relationship of parts. Parts are related to one another *at the same time*—the anthropologist's *synchronic* view. They are also related *through time*—the *diachronic* view—in the way one stage of development follows another. In either relation the parts may fit, or match—in relationships we call *consistencies*. Misfits, or mismatches, are *inconsistencies*. Through time consistencies and inconsistencies may be thought of as *continuities* and *discontinuities*. A culture is still a pattern system even if it is loaded with inconsistencies, though it is probably more stable if it is more consistent. The patternness of a culture can be referred to as its relatedness, systemness, or configuration (Honigman 1959: 13). We will look first at relatedness at a given time, then at relatedness over time, and in each first at the consistencies and then at the inconsistencies.

Relatedness at a given time (static view)

Consistencies. Certain consistencies are inescapable, as with technology. An industrial society builds skyscrapers and airplanes; a primitive one makes one-story buildings and wooden carts. Skyscrapers and airplanes are consistent with the knowledge, skills, and equipment of an industrial society, but inconsistent with the knowledge, skills, and equipment of a tribal society. A society could not develop many serums and vaccines if its religion prevented (because inconsistent with) experimentation with animals. Increased attention to early toilet training is consistent with a society's shift from dirt to wooden floors (Honigman 1959: 14).

Since language incorporates a conceptual code, a people's views about many things are consistent with its language. And regarding values, one can hardly learn such words as monopoly, stench, freedom, prostitution, or honesty, without mentally attaching little tags of goodness or badness to each.

Emphasis on memorization is consistent with a primitive society without writing. Skills at information storage and retrieval are consistent with an advanced society that has books and libraries. The multitudes of cathedrals and religious paintings were consistent with dominance of the medieval church, while the formlessness of much drama and art is consistent with contemporary doubts about religion and society. American laws about sex and gambling are consistent with our remaining Puritan tradition, while constitutional freedoms are consistent with the English-American emphasis on individual liberty.

In American history the Protestant ethic's dictum that hard work is good for the soul meshed with a continent waiting to be subdued to produce rapid development—assisted by the view that nature was there to be exploited (defeated?). By contrast, the American Indians' view that nature was to be lived with harmoniously was consistent with *their* way of life. The English settlers' view of the invincibility of man and the Indians' view of the inviolability of nature thus fitted internally within the culture of each and contributed externally to dominance by the Europeans.

Inconsistencies. Consistency is probably even less possible for the whole culture than for the whole personality. For one thing, all but the simplest cultures include differing subcultures. Because of its "melting pot" history the United States includes Boston Catholics, Appalachian whites, Hopi Indians, Harlem Puerto Ricans, white Anglo-Saxon Protestants (WASPs), West Coast Japanese, Detroit Poles, upper middle-class blacks, Reform Jews, and midwestern farmers—to mention only a few. China and Russia include subcultures ranging from nomadic tribesmen to urban industrial workers.

A professed belief in the brotherhood of man did not prevent American whites from treating Indians and blacks in a most unbrotherly fashion. "Honesty is the best policy" does little to stop dishonest advertising. Many who profess devotion to education vote down taxes to finance it, while many who profess belief in freedom of dissent are intolerant of it in fact.

Folk wisdom is full of contradictions. "Absence makes the heart grow fonder" is accepted right along with "Out of sight, out of mind." "God will provide" comforts those who also believe that "the Lord helps those who help themselves." One says "Opposites attract" just after protesting cross-cultural marriage. "Everything that goes up must come down" is proclaimed by the same person who watches the launching of a spaceship to Mars and complains that prices never stop going up.

Consistencies and inconsistencies in the culture are connected to personality. Because of the continuous cycling of patterns between personality and culture—between their internal and external forms—it is difficult to separate the two. Because patterns from the culture become internalized in individuals, the consistencies and inconsistencies of the culture become consistencies and inconsistencies inside persons. Yet in the next stage the consistencies and inconsistencies in the culture can be said merely to reflect those inside people's heads. Whether change toward or away from consistency is more likely to start in the internal or the external phase is a matter beyond the scope of this book, if indeed we know.

The whole pattern of a culture is more than the sum of its parts.

Drawing by Niculae Asciu; © 1974 The New Yorker Magazine, Inc.

It is a matter also more appropriate for the subject of change than of culture, though the next section may provide some background for the topic.

Relatedness over time

To say that patterns are related over time is to say that they do or do not change. Change in culture is thus one particular instance of change, as discussed in Chapter 27. We will confine ourselves here to noting the nature and some examples of continuities and discontinuities. The continuities lie in the fact that most cultural patterns change slowly, and that over decades or centuries certain patterns persist in a culture. We may also observe changes, sometimes rapid—discontinuities or discrepancies through time.

The massive continuities. In Chapter 12 we noted that the transaction of selling a car could not take place without a great many things in the background, such as insurance, credit, engines, highways, and gasoline. Chapter 27 discussed the process of innovation, and hinted that new patterns are usually variations or combinations of existing patterns. To focus on the relatedness of cultural patterns to their "ancestor" patterns, we will look again at some background items in that used car deal. Where did they come from?

Our question does not refer to the origins of the physical things, but of their patterns or ideas. Some can be traced to particular people—the gasoline engine to Benz in 1885, the light bulb to Thomas Edison, or paving to McAdam. The ideas of money, titles, and recipts can be traced to the Egyptians several thousand years B.C.

Today's important ideas trace back—from hundreds of years to tens of thousands. The recent acceleration in the pace of change would itself have been impossible without many centuries of prior learning. Color television depended on black-and-white TV, which depended on radar, which depended on the radio, which depended on the telephone, which depended on the telegraph, which depended on electrical circuits, which depended on the battery, which depended on certain chemical discoveries, and so on. All of those developments depended on printing, which depended on writing, which depended on oral language. Automobiles are based on carriages, which are based on wheels—and so on.

Patterns that do not involve inventions can be particularly persistent—language, for example. Shakespeare's plays of 400 years ago are still largely understandable, and we must go back another 400 years to Chaucer to find English that seems more like a foreign language. The basic differences among Japanese, Tahitian, Mexican, and American meals are much the same now as they were a century ago. Games and art forms go on for generations, as with hopscotch, rope-skipping, and square dances. The basic differences between oriental and occidental music and dance are now much the same as five centuries ago, while many a Dixieite hates Yankees with the same purple passion as did his great-great-grandfather. Some of these continuities reflect the almost-genetic pattern transmissions of early childhood (Chapter 12), others reflect the natural environment (desert nomads and fur-clothed Eskimos), while still others reflect the entrenched power of privileged groups. These massive continuities are why the historian insists that one must know how a society behaved a decade or a century ago to understand its present behavior.

Importantly, the patterns of a culture must be in people's heads to be effective. If an industrialized people had all their equipment destroyed they could reproduce it in a decade or two. By contrast, if the equipment remained but the people were replaced by others with no technical knowledge, almost nothing could be done with the vast industrial machine. Though a few principles might be learned by tinkering, most of the equipment would soon rot away, leaving no knowledge of how it worked.

Some sharp, if partial, discontinuities.   It is also true, however, that rapid change does sometimes seem to dwarf the continuities. Due to the automobile American residential patterns have changed dramatically since 1920, while mass transportation underwent a downward spiral.

"Could you redefine those commandments so as to make them more meaningful to the youth of today?"

Drawing by W. Miller; © 1971 The New Yorker Magazine, Inc.

Since World War II, television has revolutionized entertainment, and with it the life-styles of children, retirees, and many in between. Television has also revolutionized education in some underdeveloped areas, where a few skilled teachers at a central point can bypass the slow training of teachers for each village. By silencing opponents and shifting child training from home to nursery, the contemporary Chinese have replaced centuries-old living patterns and loyalties by forms more compatible with communist organization—though the undercutting of ancestor worship and reverence for family got well started under Sun Yat-sen 50 years earlier. Whether a given social change is considered evolution or revolution may depend on whether the observer focuses on the dramatic surface changes or on the piece-by-piece changes of detail that precede or follow them.

A fusion of cultures can bring rapid cultural change, as in the Japanese merger of Eastern and Western cultures. South Vietnamese culture, both rural and urban, was rapidly altered in permanent ways by massive war and occupation.

Relatedness to natural and human constraints

Natural environment and human biology have pervasive impacts on culture. As to environment, there are no tribes or cities at the North or South poles, and no one can live in Antarctica without importing nearly everything. Deserts support only sparse populations, while arable lands are almost universally tilled. Heavy physical work is more common in temperate than in tropical zones. And despite the capabilities of modern technology one does not grow bananas in Maine, build hydroelectric plants in the Sahara, or put naval bases in South Dakota.

Behaviors which thus relate humans to environment are called *adaptive*—a word that deserves comment. Adaptive behavior is basically rational behavior—an improvement in the means-ends relationship. Some sociologists, anthropologists, and social psychologists hesitate to admit that societies are significantly rational—a sensible counter to the economists' overemphasis on rationality. By characterizing some behavior as adaptive, the sociologists et al. nevertheless indirectly acknowledge rationality. However, once a given behavior is established, the cultural process often keeps it going long after it has ceased to be adaptive—in "cultural lag." And that, after all, provides a basis for believing that many norms are not very rational. Each reader may take a rational stand on this issue at a point dictated by the norms of his culture!

In any culture some constraints are also inescapably imposed by the biology and psychology of man. Though the means are varied, all cultures must provide for births and deaths, eating, sleeping, procreating, keeping warm, keeping cool, and caring for the young and the infirm. All cultures must accommodate differences in temperament and strength, handle deviant personalities, and induct new members.

Because reality is so complex, any one culture can incorporate only a small fraction of all possible forms and combinations. As Benedict (1961: 21–22) put it, the identity (uniqueness) of each culture lies in its selection of some segments from an arc of potentialities. Expressed as pattern learning and perception, a given pattern can be identified only if the brain has formed and stored a relatively small number of patterns, which show significant differences between each pattern and the next most similar one. If every possible variation were included in a culture,

Figure 29–1

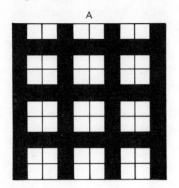

Figure 29–2

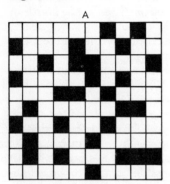
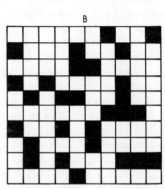

Note how easy it is to tell whether *A* and *B* are the same of different in Figure 29–1, where all black squares appear in ordered rows, as contrasted to the difficulty of telling the difference in Figure 29–2, where neither pattern is ordered. If all possible patterns were found in a given situation, one might have to compare every single cell of two squares to know whether they were the same or different.

it would be almost impossible to identify any one pattern—as illustrated in Figures 29–1 and 29–2. These are only a few of the ways in which a culture is constrained by the information processing limitations of the humans who create it. We will examine these constraints further in the concluding chapter.

CULTURAL RELATIVITY

Despite the above constraints on cultural content there is almost nothing not dictated by sheer biological necessity that all known cultures have in common. To follow some examples from White (1949), some believe in one god, some in many gods, and some in none. Killing animals is a sin in some cultures, a source of food in others, and sport for still others. Killing other humans is absolutely forbidden in some cultures, but is allowable under varying circumstances in others. Eating human flesh is disgusting beyond contemplation in most cultures, but a very special feast in several. Infants and the aged are tenderly cared for in most societies, but some are put out to die in others. Some cultures prescribe that the bride must be virgin, others don't really care, while still others consider her not marriageable until pregnant. Some cultures expect a husband to display jealous rage, possibly killing his wife or her lover, if the wife has intercourse with another male. Other cultures (the Eskimo) expect the husband to offer his wife to a male guest, and in many cultures sexual jealousy seems silly. Some cultures consider it a sin to be seen naked in public. Others use no clothing much of the time, and see erotic implications only in certain postures. For adult males to kiss on the mouth is blatantly homosexual in most Western cultures; in some Eastern ones it is merely the equivalent of handshaking.

Many people tend to think that much behavior reflects immutable "human nature." "It's instinctive" or "only human nature" to be jealous when your mate strays or to be nauseated at the thought of eating worms. The difficulty is that what is "human nature" in one culture is quite unhuman in others. Absolutes in morals and tastes are not readily found in real societies, though taboos against incest and killing other members of the in-group are nearly universal. (This and the preceding paragraph are based on White 1949: 152–55.)

The values attached to different norms vary tremendously. While Americans typically take a stern view of all killing not done in self-defense, they readily accept a wide range of responses—from indifference to massive retaliation—to the infidelity of a spouse. Similar variations appear in other cultures about other norms, and it is not easy to summarize them. Nor does our model of man tell us what to expect, since it insists that all behavior of interest to social science is learned, not biologically inherited.

When Darwin proposed the theory of biological evolution about a century ago, it became popular to suggest that moral codes also evolve. Under that view primitive societies would have primitive moral codes and advanced societies would have advanced ones. This hypothesis had to be discarded, as we subsequently discovered a wide range of codes at every level of development. For example, we find very strict, very loose, and intermediate sexual codes, in societies at every level from the most primitive to the most highly developed. Differences also exist within societies. Sexual codes may be strictest for the higher classes or the lower—for the priests, medicine men, rulers, or commoners. Except for increasing complexity of knowledge and technology, evolution goes where it goes, which may be forward, backward, or sideways (Chapter 27). Neither "human nature," cultural evolution, nor the analysis in preceding chapters seems to lead us into any one form of behavioral code—an important reason why every culture must be considered unique.

SOME CONCLUDING THOUGHTS ON CULTURE

The *process* of culture is communicational: it transmits patterns but does not originate them. Their *content* originates through processes discussed under the heading of social change, simple and emergent. Variations and change occur roughly in proportion to the openness of the society—cultural crossroads are particularly open. Temperate climates are more open than tropical or Arctic ones: the changing seasons force more varied behaviors. In addition, the tropics make variations less likely because the heat tends to lessen *all* behavior, while the Arctic environment is so demanding that it leaves little time or energy for experiment.

Rapid transportation and communication that now reach all corners of the globe hold both promise and threat for generating future variations and change. The promise is that almost any point on earth has access to almost any pattern found anywhere—every place is now a potential crossroads. The threat follows from the same facts. If every culture absorbs the patterns of every other culture, then every place will have the same culture, which is a conglomerate of all cultures. If so, the variations that arise through crossbreeding will cease. That day, however, is a long way off. Uniqueness will remain, and for many years the benefits of increased interaction are likely to outweigh the costs.

The body of culture similarly has both a broadening and a narrowing effect on the individual. The broadening effect is that an accumulated culture contains vastly more information than anyone could learn for himself. The narrowing effect is that any one culture contains only a small fraction of all known cultural patterns—it is a set of blinders. The blinders are not all disadvantage, however, since without them the youngster would face information overload and be very confused if he were raised amidst a limitless variety of patterns—according to the logic of Figure 29–1.

The culture is thus both a cleared path that makes it easy to travel through the forest and the uncleared thicket on both sides that makes it hard to go to places not on the path—the structure of roads with which we opened this volume. The more internally consistent the culture the clearer is the path and the denser the thicket. Internal consistency can also be viewed as an equilibrium tendency that helps make such a system self-preserving; the pattern match of inner consistency does not motivate thinking the way the dissonance of inconsistency does. A culture presumably could be self-preserving through its internal consistency even though it is significantly inconsistent with outer reality. We have not given this problem enough thought to identify an optimum level of consistency, if, indeed, there is such a thing. Or to say much about a science of pattern systems.

Any particular culture is unique and complex. To classify or describe cultures therefore presents much the same problems as do personalities. Some anthropologists—the specialists in studying cultures—have nevertheless done an excellent job of it.

The transmission of culture is communicational. The enforcement of it is transactional, carried out mainly by the semiformal authority of social pressures, reinforced at points by law and other formal organization. The greater the diversity within a given culture the less clear are the guides it provides to its members, the greater is the leeway it allows to try different ways, and the less is its authority in enforcing any given set of patterns.

part VI

Overview

30

SCOPE AND LIMITATIONS
OF SOCIAL ANALYSIS
AND OF SOCIAL SYSTEMS

From time to time through this volume we have raised questions about the nature of knowledge—about what we can know and how we can know it. Although our central concern was with social science, we sometimes used analogies with or illustrations from other sciences. This chapter will raise the question of what we can know again, but somewhat more comprehensively in light of all the parts of the volume. We will deal with that question in the first main part of this chapter, under the heading "What can we know about social systems?"

In the part that follows it we will raise a parallel question, "What can we do about social systems?" The question might also be appropriately phrased as, "What can we do *with* social systems?" Either wording indicates concern about our ability to use social systems as vehicles for achieving human goals.

WHAT CAN WE KNOW ABOUT SOCIAL SYSTEMS?

Facts, generalizations, and logic

"France has a larger population than Switzerland." "Switzerland has a larger population than Andorra." Each of these statements contains information of a particular sort about a particular social system or systems. Neither alone provides any other kind of information about any other social system. Assuming that we understand certain logical processes, we can nevertheless put the two pieces of information together to produce (deduce) new information: "France has a larger population than Andorra."

"Other things equal, sales of a given product in a given nation will vary directly with the size of its population." This statement says nothing about any particular social system. It is not a "fact" in the same sense that the previous statements are. It is a low-level generalization, which might have been learned by observation. It might also have been deduced by applying simple logic about quantities to a new situation, since the statement is a logical parallel of "Other things equal, it will take more paint to paint two houses than to paint one." One statement of fact can be combined with a generalization to produce a new conclusion, "Other things equal, I will be able to sell more wild rice in France than in Switzerland."

One needs to know a vast number of facts and low-level generalizations to make his way in this world, and he will behave like an utter idiot if he does not know them. But the trouble with facts is that there is no end to them, and the number of low-level generalizations is much larger than one cares to contemplate. For example, Berelson and Steiner (1964) have done a magnificent job of collecting and ordering several thousand empirical generalizations from the social and behavioral sciences. To illustrate, "The more flexible, better adjusted, and energetic the worker, the higher the job satisfaction" (ibid.: 411), and "Members of a group typically perceive the group's opinion to be closer to their own opinion than it actually is" (ibid.: 336). Each of these generalizations is useful for dealing with a particular, relatively narrow problem. But none of them are widely applicable. Nor do they individually or collectively give much of an idea of how a whole social system operates.

And back to models

By contrast, economists have taken a few simple assumptions of wide generality: that the owner of a business will seek larger rather than smaller profits, that consumers and factor suppliers will seek more satisfaction rather than less, that consumer goods are subject to diminishing utility, and that factors of production are subject to diminishing productivity. From these and a few other broad generalizations about behavior, used as assumptions, economists have constructed a model of a whole market system, and can make reasonably reliable predictions about some of its details when the model is joined with certain facts. For example: "A rise in the volume of money relative to the volume of goods produces a rise in prices (generalization). The volume of money has been rising while the volume of goods has not (factual observation). Therefore we can expect inflation (deduced conclusion)." As another example: "Of two substitutable inputs a profit-maximizing firm (which we assume all firms are) will use the less expensive. For generating electricity, strip-mined coal is cheaper than oil. Therefore electricity will be generated from coal rather than oil."

In a general way we can say that we can learn about reality from a model only to the extent that reality is like the model. That is so, but the learning we can achieve from a model may be broader than the statement suggests. Because of its well-developed theory let us illustrate again from economics. According to the model a single price for a given commodity will prevail in a market if (1) all units of the commodity are identical; (2) there are a large number of buyers and sellers; (3) all buyers and sellers have full information about the situation in the market; (4) no buyer or seller has any motives except to sell as high or buy as low as he can; (5) there are no transaction costs to the act of buying or selling (or the costs are equal for all buyers and for all sellers); (6) etc. If any of these conditions is violated in any particular market, then the price will not be uniform through the market. For example, if friendship or hostility enters a transaction, if one brand of refrigerator is different from another, if customer A does not know that the price of granulated sugar is a cent less in the store across town, if saving the penny is not worth the trip, if B can convince A that his sugar is sweeter than his competitors', etc., then discrepancies, not identity, of prices will prevail. In fact, the cases that are exactly like the model are remarkably few.

Models: Understanding, prediction, control

If few pieces of reality are like the model, does this mean the model is rarely of any use? Not at all. If the model is well thought out it is useful in explaining, in predicting, and possibly in controlling reality. Let us assume that we know that prices are not set and enforced by government or by collusion of sellers. Then as to explanation, if we find that prices of a commodity are equal, we can conclude that actual conditions approximate those of the model. If the prices are unequal, we can seek to find which conditions stated in the model do not prevail. If we find one such condition, we can then say that it "explains" or "causes" the inequality. If we find more than one, we can say that they jointly explain the inequality, though it may be hard to tell which explains how much or which type of inequality.

By similar logic we can use the model to predict. If all the conditions of the model prevail in fact, then prices will be equal throughout the market. If we find that one or more of the conditions of the model do not prevail we can predict that prices will not be equal. We can further predict that the magnitude of the inequality will be at least roughly proportional to the magnitude of the deviation of actual conditions from the model. Once we have a good model in which we have confidence, the presence of a cause explains the presence of the effect, and the absence of the cause explains the absence of the effect. In reverse, if we observe the absence of the effect we can infer the absence of the cause. In short, reality need not necessarily correspond to the model for the model to be useful. Sometimes predictions made from the model actually occur in reality by pure chance, under conditions where reality is wide of the assumptions of the model. There is no sure way to avoid such spurious explanations except persistent skepticism and continued checking.

As to control, if we want prices to be equal through a market we know a set of conditions we could create to make them so. If we want them to be unequal we also know what moves are available to produce *that* result.

Models: Natural and social science

The above relations of models to reality apply to the natural as well as the social sciences. For example, we can make precise statements about the speed and acceleration of a perfectly round and perfectly hard sphere rolling down a perfectly smooth and hard plane. But we cannot say much about an irregular boulder rolling down an irregular hillside. Depending on how its flat and rounded surfaces happen to contact the steep or shallow, soft or hard portions of the hillside, the boulder may roll in a reasonably straight line at increasing speed, may follow a lurching and meandering path, get stuck halfway down, or not roll at all. In fact, the only thing we can be sure of is that it will not roll uphill. Although that is not much, it is a great deal better than no knowledge at all. We can at least stand uphill from the boulder with confidence that it will not roll over on us.

Similarly the law of falling bodies states precisely how fast a rose petal would fall in a nonexistent vacuum, but not how fast it will fall in the real and gusty atmosphere. Since rose petals do not fall through vacuums in ordinary life, the physicist's law of falling bodies does not apply strictly to any real cases that concern us, of rose petals or of anything else. Except for man-made machines and equipment, most problems in life are like the mushy ice problem cited earlier.

All this gives rise to a reasonably sore point among social scientists. If you ask the physicist, "Where will that boulder go and how fast will it be traveling when it gets there?" or "Where and when will this feather land if I drop it out of this airplane?" he will answer, "Don't be silly. It is not possible to answer questions like that." If he wants to sound more erudite he might say, "There are too many variables involved in that situation, and I do not see any possible way of measuring them all in advance, and of computing their individual effects, much less of computing their combined effect."

If the physicist says, "Don't be silly, that's not an answerable question," his reputation does not suffer. Social scientists are legitimately miffed when they are asked questions that are incredibly more complex and then are thought incompetent if they cannot give precise answers or if their predictions are wrong. In any complex real situation precise prediction is not possible, whether in the physical, biological, psychological, or social sciences, or some combination thereof. This is a restatement in different context of the problem of uniqueness.

By "prediction" in this sense we mean reasoning to a conclusion from an understanding of prior conditions and their cause-effect relation. We do not mean a simple projection that the past will continue, in the sense that people with no knowledge of astronomy could accurately predict that night would follow day, or that people with no understanding of biology could predict that the infant would get larger as he got older.

Perhaps we need to soften our statement in connection with predicting that something as complex as a given spaceship will reach the moon. Even there, however, we should note that the basic determining factors are few, since for the basic computations about its flight the spaceship is a simple lump of a certain mass. Nothing about its internal complexities need be known to compute the amount of thrust required to give it a certain velocity and direction within the gravitational field of the earth, and later within the gravity of the moon. To make the journey "complex" in the sense we are speaking of here we might add such things as the gravitational pull of several passing meteors, the retarding effect of an interstellar dust storm, and significant fluctuations in the gravitational pull of the earth and the moon during the trip. Furthermore, something more than prediction is involved. Since the spaceship is itself a controlled system, measurements of its performance are made from time to time, and deviations corrected. We can marvel at the incredible complexity of the spaceship while yet noting its kindergarten simplicity compared to even a single living cell. In any event, most predictions about the spaceship's actually getting to the moon are not computed from knowledge of its components but from simple projection of past performance: previous ones did, so the next one probably will.

Models and laboratories

For the purpose of science, situations can be made uncomplex by two main methods. One is to construct a piece of reality that is itself simple, and is like the model we are trying to test. To study movement down an inclined plane we can actually make a steel ball and a steel slab that are round enough, flat enough, and hard enough so that their deviations from the perfect conditions of the model are so slight that they do not matter. We can then roll the ball down the slab and measure velocity and acceleration, to see if the theoretical statements are correct and to refine them if they are not. In many other instances it is also possible to create real laboratory conditions in which to measure and test generalizations.

A second way to make things uncomplex is a "laboratory of assumptions," which is another way of describing a theoretical model. Here we say, *if* the conditions are such and such, *then* so-and-so will follow. If the pull of gravity is known, and if a body falls unimpeded by atmosphere or by any other obstruction, then it will accelerate at the rate of 32 feet per second per second. A laboratory for falling bodies is harder to duplicate than one for the inclined plane, since it is dreadfully expensive to create a good vacuum big enough to test any significant distance of fall. Heavy, dense, streamlined bodies whose fall is little affected by atmosphere nevertheless provide a reasonably good test outside the vacuum chamber.

For social theories about large or long-lasting organizations or relationships it is out of the question to set up real laboratories. No one will create a whole government or corporation just to test some political or organizational theory. In fact we will not specify and control even one marriage or the total experiences of one child to test a social or psychological theory. Both our ethics and our inability to create wholly controlled social situations eliminate the possibility of such real social laboratories. In these respects the problem of social science is almost what the physicist's would be if he had to learn all the principles of gravity, electricity, mechanics, and hydraulics by studying the operation of a spaceship built on another planet, but without being allowed to take any of it apart, to push any buttons, or to feed into it any inputs on his own. On the other hand the social scientist is often a part of the systems he is studying, and has his own conscious awareness to help provide insights.

Small groups as laboratories

Small group research sometimes achieves at least partial laboratory conditions by setting up a temporary group more or less to specification by the researcher. He can determine the number and types of persons in the group, and by instruction or manipulation determine what goals the participants will pursue, what information they will receive, who can communicate with whom, and how each participant will be identified to the others. He can exert some detailed control by "planting" participants who, unknown to the others, act out carefully prepared roles.

If a small group goes on for some time, it is possible to trace many social processes in microcosm. These include the emergence of leadership, the formulation or modification of group goals, the increasing similarity in the use and meanings of words, the process of making collective decisions, the formation of cliques and coalitions, the division of labor for particular group tasks, the development of likes and dislikes based on similarities and dissimilarities in personality and values, the implementation of social pressures, and the emergence of status differences. Sound tapes and videotapes of the interactions can be analyzed in as much detail as the researcher wishes. A large volume of experimentation has by now been conducted in this area, and the literature describing it is a useful source of generalizations, many of which are reported by Hare (1962) and Berelson and Steiner (1964).

A family is another excellent microcosm for studying group behavior, particularly developmental changes—although detailed records cannot be made as easily for a family as in small group experiments. Because every member is learning, growing older, becoming more or less dependent, becoming ill and recovering, and developing outside contacts, a family cannot avoid developmental change. Regarding communications, each family develops some "inside" language, and even the slowest learner comes to realize that the way he handles transactions with other members of the family will affect his future relationships with them. Because members of families know they must continue to live together, and hence face the real and continuing consequences of their actions, behaviors within families are more "real" than those within laboratory small groups, and conclusions reached in the latter must be applied with greater caution than those reached in studies of the family.

The spectrum of knowledge

We now shift from the process of acquiring information about social behaviors to the form the information takes. It can take the form of generalizations, testable, verified, and useful for particular purposes. Yet, as Berelson and Steiner indicate (ibid.: 660), these are really "the stuff of theory; the material of which theories are built," and from which "higher order principles" might be derived. We have indicated that economics has a coordinated body of theory that covers much of its whole field, at both micro and macro levels. Other social sciences have no such coordinated theory, and it is suggested that some of the materials in this volume (and more particularly in Kuhn: 1974) provide at least some underpinnings for it.

More explicitly, this volume is an experiment in one kind of unified theory. It suggests that the "basic social science tools" constitute this broader social science theory. Its main ingredients are the intrasystem concepts of detector, selector, and effector functions, and the related intersystem interactions of communications, transactions, and organizations. The basic science about each may be thought of as a sort of minidiscipline. Each is "mini" only in that it seems feasible to give a respectable introduction to it in a chapter or two; there is presumably no limit to the detail that can be added. Each minidiscipline deals mainly with the pure case, as the pure detector function or the pure transaction. Although we often used real examples to illustrate these concepts, the main discussion of them deals with models rather than reality. Yet it is hoped that at many points the models are enough like real situations so that the reader will feel better able to understand, predict, and control real situations with the aid of these models than he would without that aid. The model of the transaction in Chapters 9 and 10, for example, should certainly provide insights into many of the reader's own interactions with others.

From the initial most-general-purpose models we move to more particular ones. Some of these are simple combinations of the ingredients of the initial models, as with the mutual effects of detector and selector on one another, the communicational aspects of transactions, and the transactional aspects of communications. Others involve the general concepts as they appear in more explicit circumstances. Authority, for example, is a special kind of transactional relation between superior and subordinate in a formal organization. Agreement by communication is a particular case of communications under circumstances when two or more participants in an organization must reach, or at least accept, a common decision. Transactions in a particular sequence give rise to an accumulation of aggregate power, and status is a perceived and communicated view of aggregate power. A constitution is an authority relation of citizens over government and ordinary law is an authority relation of government over citizens. Social stratification is a particular configuration of aggregate power. The social aspects of organization, as contrasted to its transformational ones, also involve transactions, communications, and their combinations within a particular context. Formal organization is one such context, informal is a second, and semiformal combines aspects of *those* two models.

This volume then went into several still more explicit types of organizations: government, the market economy, and the family. Each is sufficiently complex and widely enough found in the real world to justify a discipline in its own right. In fact, one can be a lifetime specialist in some subdivision of any of these, such as the parliamentary system of Britain, the traditional Chinese family, or the particulars of the market economy of Italy.

To diagram this structure of social knowledge, Figure 30–1 shows the basic social science tools to the left, real problems at the right, and disciplines in the middle circle. It uses only one circle to represent all disciplines, partly to keep the diagram uncluttered and partly to remain noncommittal as to what an appropriate list should be. This diagram also shows a stage between the basic tools and the disciplines, and another between the disciplines and real problems. There is no magic to the number of stages, which might be six or eight, or possibly only three or four.

Figure 30–1

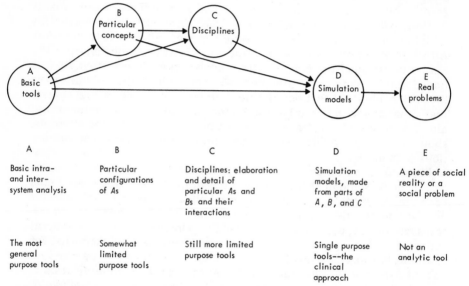

A	B	C	D	E
Basic intra- and inter- system analysis	Particular configurations of As	Disciplines: elaboration and detail of particular As and Bs and their interactions	Simulation models, made from parts of A, B, and C	A piece of social reality or a social problem
The most general purpose tools	Somewhat limited purpose tools	Still more limited purpose tools	Single purpose tools--the clinical approach	Not an analytic tool

Source: Kuhn 1974: 17.

The basic social science tools at *A* are the minidisciplines already identified: the intrasystem analysis of detector, selector, and effector, and the intersystem basics of communication, transaction, and organization. The model of social man is also part of this kit of tools at *A*. The particular configurations at *B* include such things as authority, agreement by communication, social stratification, the transactional aspects of communications, and similar items mentioned above. As somewhat specialized tools their advantage is that they do a particular job better than do the most-general-purpose tools, at the cost of being unable to do as many jobs. For example, the model of authority does a better job than does the general model of transactions in helping to understand the relation between boss and subordinate, or parent and child. But it is of no use in understanding the purchase of a used car or negotiations between the

United States and Russia over arms limitation, since in neither case are the parties operating within an authority relation under a major bargain.

Conventional vs. rearranged disciplines

Within this framework the "disciplines" at level C would presumably be partly the same as and partly different from those listed in Chapter 1. Economics as the study of market systems would certainly remain a discipline in this context. I would consider the general study of formal organization an important discipline in its own right, within which the study of government, the corporation, and the family would logically be subdisciplines. Incidentally, when we speak of disciplines and subdisciplines we are speaking of their logical relationships, not necessarily about their relative importance.

The study of social change might well be a discipline of its own, with history (or at least some aspects of it) as an important subdivision. The study of pattern systems could perhaps be considered a discipline, within which language might take its place beside culture and personality. Culture as a pattern system would presumably be studied mainly by anthropologists, personality by psychologists, psychiatrists, and social psychologists, and languages by students of linguistics. Human geographers would presumably act as specialists in the effect of space and location on social structures and behaviors, and in the idiographic interactions of all forces within some spatially defined area. Historians might be viewed as giving attention to the idiographic interactions of all forces on some particular event, particularly as viewed through time.

Sociology would seem to occupy a different spot. Although it has been described by one of its practitioners (Smelser 1963: 22) as a "sort of grab-bag of leftovers," I would tend to see it instead, along with its companion of social psychology, as encompassing the A and B levels in Figure 30–1. In that spot sociology would operate at a broader level of generality than the other disciplines, and would provide the basic tools underlying the other and more specialized disciplines. Thus viewed, it would not be the leftovers of other disciplines, but their underpinnings.

This scheme might give rise to other disciplines, depending both on the time and inclination of academicians and on the kinds of practical problems to be dealt with. I suppose my main complaints about the traditional division of disciplines are (1) that systems analysis, organization theory, social change, and pattern systems have not customarily been considered academic disciplines in their own right and (2) that sociology has not very well defined either its own content or its appropriate relation to other social science fields. On the latter score I do not expect that sociologists will take kindly to having their role defined by an economist, although the one I have assigned them actually puts them a goodly notch above the rest of us. (Our language in these matters is interesting, in that the *under*pinnings constitute a *higher* level of generality than do the *super*structures of knowledge.)

To move to the right side of the diagram, it is never possible to study a real problem, strictly speaking. We can study only a particular image or formulation of it, which is necessarily a vast oversimplification. For reasons described in Chapter 26, we call such an image a simulation model.

As indicated by the arrows in Figure 30–1, the basic tools can be used ("plugged into") the limited-purpose tools at level *B,* the disciplines at level *C,* or the simulation models at level *D.* The particular concepts at level *B* can feed into the disciplines or the simulations, and the disciplines can also feed into the simulations. We start with the broadest and most widely applicable concepts and propositions at the left and move successively toward narrower and more particular ones at the right. To speak of the extremes, whereas the basic concepts of communication and transaction can be applied to *any* interaction between *any* human beings at *any* time or place in history, a good, detailed simulation model cannot be applied to any problem except the one it was designed for. Although all simulations of, say, cities, might incorporate some common elements, the simulation for Chicago would include a different total set of elements with different weightings than would the simulation for Sioux City.

It would seem that the goal of social science must be eventually to encompass the entire spectrum of Figure 30–1. It is conceivable that we might develop a reasonably complete set of basics at level *A* and possibly enough slightly specialized tools at level *B* to satisfy us for a time. It is not conceivable that there could ever be a complete coverage at level *C,* the disciplines. At *D* the number of real situations to be studied is potentially infinte, and so too are the possible number of simulations. As we attempt to develop simulations for ever-new problems we may expect to discover gaps and discrepancies in the disciplines to their left. Hence we may assume that the quest for new or modified concepts will be permanent.

Image structures are the technology of knowledge. Like other technologies, they do some things well, some not so well, and others not at all. They are also subject to obsolescence as new technologies are developed. It is nevertheless true that certain technological basics, such as the wheel and the lever, show no sign of being displaced although invented thousands of years ago. They continue to be incorporated into ever new and higher-level configurations.

The distinction between factual judgments and value judgments, here couched as detector and selector functions, goes back over 2,000 years to Plato and Aristotle, and the ancient Greeks certainly recognized the overt execution of behavior that we here call the effector. When we now recognize these same three items as the logically irreducible ingredients of any adaptive system we may anticipate that the DSE trio has not only a long and distinguished history but probably a durable future as well. If so, it would seem sensible to use them in a fairly basic way in our science of adaptive systems. Being based on information, values, and overt effectuations, respectively, the intersystem parallels of communication, transaction, and organization seem to allow clearer analysis than does lumping these relationships (as sociologists have traditionally done) under the catchall heading of "interactions." Success in one kind of interaction, communication, depends on the degree of *similarity* between parties (in the detector, or cognitive dimension), and success in another kind of interaction, transaction, depends on the degree of *difference* between parties (in the selector, or value dimension). How we could expect good theory of interactions without separating them is therefore quite beyond me. Once the two have been separated, and the principles of each carefully stated, they can be recombined into as many arrangements as anyone desires—as discussed in "The Jointness and Separability of Communications and Transactions" (Chapter 14).

I have not taken much space to argue the merits of the present approach, but have simply used it and let the chips fall where they may. After some years of use, we can look again to see where they have fallen.

Society and a science of society

Social science is about society and social behavior. The components of societies are human beings, who are controlled systems. Like other controlled systems their behavior is determined in important part by their information about reality. In humans that information consists largely of concepts in the detector, most of which are learned from others. Increasingly our concepts of social reality (which for most of us most of the time is the most important part of our environment) comes out of social science. Whereas atoms, planets, and falling bodies do not study physics and possibly change their behavior as a result, human beings do study social science and psychology, and very probably behave differently in consequence. The behavioral sciences about humans thus face the disconcertingly circular possibility that people will behave as the science says because the science says they will. Although not enough people thus far study enough social science, and the conclusions of social science are not sufficiently standardized, to create much difficulty on this score, we certainly must consider the possibility that social behavior changes because it has been studied, and that the presence of social science may actually change the reality.

To understand a controlled system we must also examine its selector states, which in this case are man's values. As with man's concepts, it is not possible to ask about, analyze, and publicly report information about values without changing the values. The mere fact of discussing sex frankly and openly in newspapers and magazines, or in classes on sex education, changes attitudes toward sex. Publishing public opinion surveys or airing individuals' views about ex-convicts on television changes public opinion and public attitudes about ex-convicts. We presumably face a positive feedback relation here, in which the development of a science of human behavior changes the behavior of the subjects of the science. At this point it would be hazardous to guess when or whether this relationship will reach an equilibrium at which more social science will no longer produce further change in the social behavior it studies.

WHAT CAN WE DO ABOUT SOCIAL SYSTEMS?

Improvements in health followed the discovery that many diseases are caused by bacteria, as the discovery was implemented by sanitary water supplies, sewers, quarantines, vaccinations, and noninfected food. Improvements in transportation followed the scientific discoveries on which trains, planes, and automobiles are based, while radio and television vastly increased the speed of communication. Although some proposals about social organization were made at least two thousand years ago, social sciences that systematically formulate theories and test propositions about society on a wide scale are roughly a century old. Given their early floundering, we might even suggest that reasonably comprehensive systematic approaches to the study of social organizations are only about fifty years old.

The obvious question follows: Will social science bring the kind of dramatic improvements in social systems that other sciences have brought in health, transportation, and communication systems? To this question we can answer with high confidence: We do not yet know enough about social systems to answer the question. Hence we will not attempt to, but will instead raise some other questions and identify some kinds of information that we still need.

First, we may note a difference between the technology of social systems and that of some other systems. The technology of television, spaceships, and medicine, for example, is studied and decided upon by a relatively few specialists. Although they need not construct or operate these systems, they do design them more or less from top to bottom. To illustrate, although television communication requires thousands of people who can assemble or repair television sets, the rest of the population can use those sets without the vaguest notion of how they work. People are also protected by a sanitary water system whether or not they know anything about bacteria.

By contrast, there is great uncertainty about how much understanding of social technology must be possessed by how many members of a social system, and in what roles, to make the system work. Presumably someone in each family must know at least rudimentary things about family organization. But how many people need know much about the political system to make it work? How well must it work in order to "work"?

The internals of complex formal organization

Before we examine what a whole society might do to improve itself we will focus briefly on some questions of structure and behavior of complex formal organizations, which do most of the work of a modern society.

We must first distinguish bottom-up from top-down aspects of organizations. In one respect this is the difference between a cooperative organization, in which sponsors and recipients are the same persons, and other types of organization, notably profit, in which they are different persons. The bottom-up question is: How do multiple sponsors choose the goals and policies to pass on as instructions to the top executives? Whether the organization is cooperative, profit, service, or pressure, these decisions are made by communication, transaction, and dominant coalition, and that conclusion is equally valid for a national government, a local Kiwanis club, a trade union, or a corporation.[1]

Once the decision has been made by sponsors and passed on as instruction to top executives of any organization large enough to hire a substantial staff, the overall relationship is top-down—again regardless of the basic type of the organization. By "overall relationship" we mean at the minimum that if the sponsors have established the goal of the organization to be governing the city, manufacturing bulldozers, or improving conditions for migratory workers, the staff may not then use the organization to raise cattle, fight subversion, or sell insurance instead. Whatever the organization, if the staff do not do what they were hired to do, the sponsors presumably will fire them.

A question nevertheless remains as to how much autonomy the staff have in determining subgoals and details of organizational structure as a means of achieving the sponsor goals. This question parallels that raised at a larger level about the optimum amount of enterprise autonomy in the Soviet economy, and we will not try to answer it here. Relatedly, if employee participation in such decisions should come to be considered necessary for a "satisfactory life," much as pension and welfare plans did in recent decades, would life in the corporation be more satisfactory than it is now, and would the effectiveness of the organization rise or fall as a result? It would be interesting to see how many employees would find fulfillment in such participation, how many would find it simply an extra chore, and how many would say, "Just tell me what to do."

For some fifty years there has been a tendency in organizations to keep subdividing the work until each role is simple and routine. In recent years this tendency has been increasingly challenged on two fronts. One is that it is not really as efficient as had been assumed, because people will work harder on a job that allows more variety and individual judgment. Second, some argue that even if simplified jobs are more efficient they are also inhuman, and that we ought to have less efficiency and more humanity.

Again we will not try to answer this question, but will note several things. First, we have already suggested (Chapter 16) that the amount of allowable subsystem discretion depends on the degree of coordination in the organization's output. Second, the continued life of any system depends on replaceability of its parts, and the more routine an employee's job the easier it is to replace him. Third, if routinized jobs *are* more efficient, we must choose between shorter hours at a dull job and longer hours at a more rewarding one—if we want to maintain real income. Fourth, some people prefer an undemanding job that leaves them free to think or daydream. In short, it seems unlikely that some new

---

[1] One may suspect that when so many people for so many years have expressed hopes that "education" would bring the peaceful solution for many social ills one of the things they had in mind (translated into present language) was the achievement of consensus by communication.

organizational arrangement will soon be found that is both much more
efficient and much more humanly satisfying. We must also ask how
much of the alleged current dissatisfaction over routine work arises because it is now popular to believe that routine work is unsatisfactory.[2]

At the same time we still know rather little about the effectiveness of
different organizational structures, and it is difficult to believe that the
continuing serious study of that topic will not produce *some* significant
improvements.

This question is important to organizational planning. Planning presumably means increasing the central controls over the subsystems and
their operation. But if for some reason we decide that subsystems should
have increased autonomy we add to the difficulty of planning.

Broad-scale social planning

It would be an unimaginative soul indeed who could not list a dozen
ways in which he would like our society to be different. Depression,
pollution, crime, poverty, military expenditures, race conflict, and urban
problems are only a few of the items that come to mind. Could we and
should we engage in long-term social planning to solve these problems,
or at least to improve things significantly?

The answer is, "Yes, if . . . ," and the real question concerns the "ifs."
Such things can be done in a democratic society *if* there is a broad
consensus about both ends and means, and in broad social goals the ends
often seem less controversial than the means. Such things can be done
if the public wants a given result enough to finance it in the face of
conflicting demands on their money. The confoundedly difficult thing
about large social goals is that only rarely is there a consensus about
ends, means, and finances.

There is high agreement that we do not want depression and unemployment. But there is vast disagreement over whether the means lie in
more governmental activity or less, and whether the government, if it
acts, should use monetary policy, fiscal policy, or more direct controls.
If there is a conflict between full employment and stable prices, people
do not agree at all on the relative disadvantages of inflation and unemployment. Even if it were agreed that he government should stimulate
the economy with more money, there is sharp disagreement over
whether the money should be put into the income stream through corporations or through workers and the unemployed. There may be agreement that we do not want the poor to starve. But people disagree over
whether money payments will give the poor the courage to do more for
themselves or convert them into confirmed loafers.

Nearly everyone agrees that crime rates are too high. But some think
guns in the hands of the people are a cause of the problem, while others
think they are part of the cure. Some think prisoners must be treated

---

[2] As I have suggested elsewhere (Kuhn 1967: 381), a drastically shortened standard workweek might allow each person to hold two very different and complementary jobs.

© 1962 and © 1971 Walt Kelly. Courtesy Publishers-Hall Syndicate.

more like human beings so they will be fit to enter society when they are released, while other think "soft" treatment will encourage more crime. It is easy to agree that we want peace. But some think it comes through disarmament, while others think it comes only from having more armaments than the enemy. Furthermore, positions on these matters are often intensely and emotionally held, and may be based on religious faith as well. How, then, does one build a dominant coalition strong and enduring enough to make real progress?

Science, prediction, and planning. To shift to a different question, of what use is social science knowledge for solving these problems? Again there is no conclusive answer, but we can note some circumstances that affect the answer.

Our libraries contain a substantial literature about arms races, and the logic of transactions in bads might assist understanding. However, we cannot deal with disarmament only in general or in theory. We must deal with it in the unique context of Russia and the United States in the late 20th century, one nation nominally capitalist and one nominally communist, with different internal decision structures, different world views, and particular persons as leaders. A given posture by an American president must consider its effect on the next election, and the Soviet premier must similarly consider his power position in the Presidium. General knowledge of politics and bargaining strategies is essential. But so is vast familiarity with the particular situation—a detailed simulation. Such a simulation must assess the personalities and goals of leaders in both nations, and the way each perceives his own and his nation's situation—matters on which informed specialists may disagree. The science of transactions can say, "*If* the *EP*s of the parties are so-and-so, an agreement is possible on such and such terms." The question, however, is not about the principle, but whether the *EP*s *are* so-and-so. And how is one to know, when the science of transactions indicates that each party will presumably misrepresent his *EP*? In short, on the subject of disarmament we face only one instance of the problem, and a very complicated one to boot. The simulation is the appropriate tool, and the requirements for successful simulation are detailed knowledge, good intuition, much trial and error, and luck.

By contrast, let us look at social security and prison reform. Although we already have social security, the general questions about it are worth examining. If we were planning a social security program where none existed before, it would be possible to simulate the situation with reasonable confidence that the most crucial variables were included. It would be possible to know the size and age distribution of the population at the start, mortality rates, and similar data, and to compute how much each employee must contribute for how long to produce a given retirement income. If these later turned out to be wrong, the contribution rate, benefit rate, or both could be adjusted. The basic "science" involved concerns inflows, outflows, and the stock of money in the trust fund. Although the problem is more complicated than this description, the money costs and benefits of a social security program are basically knowable in advance. The question then is; Given these costs and benefits do we want the program? Within the realm of the possible, for this kind of problem we can accomplish pretty much what we want through social planning.

Prison reform is more difficult, because little about it is readily calculated. Whereas social security has the reasonably straightforward goal of providing income for retirement and other emergencies, we are thus far uncertain about the purpose of imprisonment. Is it to rehabilitate the offender, prevent him from committing other crimes while in jail, deter others by his example, or achieve transactional balance by inflicting a bad on the offender to balance the one he inflicted? Are these goals mutually consistent? Or, for example, might the goal of making the prisoner "pay his debt to society" conflict with the goal of rehabilitation? Is a desire that he "pay his debt" an irrational attachment to a sunk cost?

Prison reform nevertheless has one experimental advantage. Because there are many prisons, it is possible to try different approaches in different places and to observe the results. There is also the difficulty, however, that rehabilitation cannot succeed unless many employers hire ex-convicts and unless the other employees treat them decently. Prison reform thus seems more difficult than social security, since (1) we are not agreed on what we want prisons to do; (2) we are not sure what result a given kind of action will produce; and (3) success may depend on the attitudes of scattered millions of people rather than on those who directly operate the program. Thus, although our capacity for successful social action here rests on shakier grounds than with social security, our knowledge is nevertheless far ahead of our practice For decades we have known how to do much better than we do, and probably at much less money cost. But the social resistance is high, partly because of uncertainty and disagreement over objectives.

Whatever the intended reform, and whatever the social structure in which it occurs, it is important that the desired change be brought to bear explicitly on those who make the operating decisions. To return to a previous example, it is sometimes thought that because Soviet publicly owned enterprises are supposedly run "for the public good," while capitalist ones are run "for profit," the latter will be more likely to pollute. No such difference has shown up. For while capitalist enterprisers emphasize profit, the Soviet planners emphasize output. In neither place have operating managers typically been rewarded for avoiding pollution, and in neither case did they do much about it on their own initiative.

Only when the payoffs to managers are altered (as by fines and taxes in the United States and slower promotions in Russia) do managers make significant changes. In the United States the Sierra Club and other conservation societies have publicized pollution and "needled" corporations and governmental bodies into action. Because no such associations are allowed in Russia, concerned citizens' needling of the government is blunter and more diffuse (Goldman 1972). Interestingly, nongovernmental organizations (NGOs) are gradually coming to be recognized as a means by which concerned citizens and specialists can join in formulating policy and proposals, particularly at the international level, with a flexibility and efficiency that delegates of governments are denied by the politics of their constituencies.

Planning: Pieces, wholes, implementation. Although the heading of the this section is "Broad-Scale Social Planning," we have talked thus far about piecemeal reforms, and deliberately so. In light of the difficulties of building a reasonably good simulation of such relatively simple things as a city, or even its local transportation system, great skepticism is in order about the prospects of making a good enough simulation of a whole industrial society to serve as a feasible basis for controlled change. Whatever their overall structure, real societies focus mainly on those problems that happen to be urgent. "Urgent," however, is not merely a question of fact, but also of values and of communication. A problem is not "urgent" unless it is dramatically called to the attention of decision makers and they are motivated to respond.

Social and behavioral scientists have nevertheless been giving much attention recently to the "implementation of change," and to the role of the "change agent." Most such study attends to small-scale change: in a university, business firm, or neighborhood. How fruitful this developing knowledge will be, particularly in its possible application to such larger social units as an industry, a class, an ethnic group, or a nation, is still largely untested.

Even if they become successful as instruments, nothing about the techniques of change gives any hint about the appropriate content or goals of charge. Nor can the techniques of change be separated from the acceptability of goals. There are so many ways people can sabotage a program they disapprove that general acceptance of goals is indispensable. Such acceptance may be relatively simple in a limited-purpose voluntary organization, in which people would not be members unless they basically accepted its goals to begin with. For a national government strong consensus is rare except in obvious crisis.

CONCLUSION

In closing, let us again note the relation between Parts V and VI of this text and the rest of the volume. Most of this book is about basic social mechanics—the social equivalent of the wheel, lever, gear, and pulley. From there it moves to low-level combinations of these things—how a pulley belt can be attached to a wheel which is geared to a lever. In a few cases, as with government, the family, and the economy, it deals with particular kinds of social "machines" made from those components. But in an introductory text, and in light of the current state of knowledge about these things, it seemed more important to clarify how the more complicated social systems can be made out of such components than to elaborate the detail of particular systems—the latter a subject for specialists and advanced courses. Knowledge of components alone will not tell whether a particular complex system made of those components will work or how it can be improved. But—and this is important—the basic principles of the components are not necessarily challenged if a system constructed of them does not work.

In Chapters 26 and 27 we discussed the unique and change, indicating that our knowledge of these things is much more tentative than in some other areas, and suggesting that it may never be very good. It would be pleasant to think that the latter conclusion may some day be invalidated, but we should not count on it. Meanwhile we have identified some focal points in social structures and interactions that one might usefully consider before deciding whether or how to implement change. To do much to change social organizations we must first understand how they work. This text should help us understand the basics. About the more complex configurations and the dynamics of change we still have much to learn.

We have talked about the future of social science and social systems. What about the social science *student?* Where is he, and where does he go from here? First, if he takes no further courses in social science, we hope that this approach has given him a more comprehensive and usable introductory understanding of social systems and behaviors than he could get through any other single course. If he goes on into any one social science, it should be feasible for him to enter a second-level course rather than an introductory one—though this possibility will depend on

Drawing by Charles Addams; © 1974 The New Yorker Magazine, Inc.

the student, the instructor, the department, and the school. It is unlikely that he will find the "regular" social sciences using system concepts as much as this book does. However, with reasonable initiative and occasional references back to this text (or to Kuhn 1974, on which it is based) the student should be able to continue using the system concepts on his own. In any case, system analysis is rapidly becoming academically very respectable, and difficulties on this score may soon decline noticeably. Even if advanced study in the social science specialties does not explicitly use system concepts, the student should have a more comprehensive and workable understanding of many situations studied in the specialties because of his background in systems, communications, transactions, and organizations. The model of social man might even be a useful framework into which to fit the materials of advanced study in psychology.

BIBLIOGRAPHY

Ackoff, Russell L. "Systems, Organizations, and Interdisciplinary Research." *General Systems* 5 (1960): 1–8.

Allport, Gordon W., and Odbert, H. S. "Trait Names: A Psychological Study." *Psychological Monographs,* vol. 47, no. 211 (1936).

Ardrey, Robert. *The Territorial Imperative.* New York: Dell Publishing Co., 1966.

Arrow, Kenneth J. *Social Choice and Individual Values.* New York: John Wiley & Sons, 1951.

Ashby, W. Ross. *An Introduction to Cybernetics.* New York: John Wiley & Sons, 1958.

Barnard, Chester I. *The Functions of the Executive.* Cambridge, Mass.: Harvard University Press, 1938.

——. *Organization & Management.* Cambridge, Mass.: Harvard University Press, 1948.

Bell, Daniel. *The Coming of Post-Industrial Society.* New York: Basic Books, 1973.

Belmont, Lillian, and Marolla, Francis A. "Birth Order, Family Size, and Intelligence." *Science,* December 14, 1973, pp. 1096–1101.

Benedict, Ruth. *Patterns of Culture.* Boston: Houghton Mifflin, 1961. (Originally published by Houghton Mifflin in 1934).

Bennis, Warren G. "Towards a 'Truly' Scientific Management: The Concept of Organization Health." *General Systems* 7 (1962): 269–82.

Bennis, W. G. "A Funny Thing Happened on the Way to the Future." *American Psychologist* 25 (1970): 595–608.

Berelson, Bernard, and Steiner, Gary A. *Human Behavior: An Inventory of Scientific Findings.* New York: Harcourt, Brace & World, Inc., 1964.

Berrien, F. Kenneth. *General and Social Systems*. New Brunswick: Rutgers University Press, 1968.

Blair, John M. *Economic Concentration: Structure, Behavior, and Public Policy*. New York: Harcourt Brace Jovanovich, Inc., 1972.

Blau, Peter M., and Duncan, Otis D. *The American Occupational Structure*. New York: John Wiley & Sons, 1967.

Blau, Peter M., and Scott, W. Richard. *Formal Organizations*. San Francisco: Chandler Publishing Co., 1962.

Boulding, Kenneth. "Welfare Economics." *Survey of Contemporary Economics*, edited by Bernard J. Haley. Homewood, Ill.: Richard D. Irwin, Inc., 1952.

_____. *The Image*. Ann Arbor, Mich.: University of Michigan Press, 1956.

_____. *The Skills of the Economist*. Cleveland: Howard Allen, Inc., 1958.

_____. *The Impact of the Social Sciences*. New Brunswick: Rutgers University Press, 1966.

_____. "Economics as a Moral Science." *American Economic Review*, March 1969, pp. 1–12.

_____. *Economics as a Science*. New York: McGraw Hill Book Co., 1970.

Boulding, K. E., Kuhn, Alfred, and Senesh, Lawrence. *System Analysis and Its Use in the Classroom*. Boulder, Col.: Publication #157 of the Social Science Education Consortium, Inc., 1973.

Brehm, Jack W., and Cohen, Arthur R. *Explorations in Cognitive Dissonance*. New York: John Wiley & Sons, 1962.

Bruner, Jerome; Goodnow, Jacqueline; and Austin, George. *A Study of Thinking*. New York: John Wiley & Sons, 1956.

Burack, Richard. *The Handbook of Prescription Drugs*. New York: Pantheon Press, 1967.

Burgess, Ernest W., and Cottrell, Leonard S., Jr. *Predicting Success or Failure in Marriage*. New York: Prentice-Hall, 1939.

Campbell, Arthur T. "Three Generations of Parents." *Family Planning Perspectives* 5 (1973): 110.

Campbell, Donald T. "Blind Variation and Selective Retention in Creative Thought as in Other Knowledge Processes." *General Systems* 7 (1962): 57–70.

_____. "Variation and Selective Retention in Socio-Cultural Evolution." In *Social Change in Developing Areas,* edited by Herbert R. Barringer, George I. Blanksten, and Raymond W. Mack, pp. 19–49. Cambridge, Mass.: Schenkman Publishing Co., Inc., 1965.

Caplow, Theodore. *Two Against One: Coalitions in Triads*. Englewood Cliffs, N.J.: Prentice-Hall, 1968.

Cartter, Allan. *Theory of Wages and Employment*. Homewood, Ill.: Richard D. Irwin, Inc., 1959.

Chamberlain, Neil W. *A General Theory of Economic Process*. New York: Harper & Bros., 1955.

Cooley, Charles Horton. *Human Nature and the Social Order*. New York: Charles Scribner's Sons, 1902.

Copeland, Morris A. "Institutionalism and Welfare Economics." *American Economic Review*, March, 1958, pp. 1–17.

Crawford, M. P. "The Relation Between Social Dominance and the Menstrual Cycle in Female Chimpanzees." *Journal of Comparative Psychology* 30 (1940): 483–513.

Deutsch, Karl W. *The Nerves of Government.* New York: The Free Press, 1963.

———. *Politics and Government.* Boston: Houghton Mifflin Company, 1970.

———. "Integrative Processes in Nation States." Paper presented at University of Illinois, Urbana, unpublished, 1971.

DeWolf, Rose. "Myths of American Marriage." *The Nation,* April 23, 1973, p. 527.

Downs, Anthony. *An Economic Theory of Democracy.* New York: Harper & Bros., 1957.

Dunn, Edgar S. *Economic and Social Development: A Process of Social Learning.* Baltimore: Johns Hopkins Press, 1971.

Easton, David. *A Framework for Political Analysis.* Englewood Cliffs, N.J.: Prentice-Hall, Inc., 1965.

Emerson, Richard M. "Power-Dependence Relations." *American Sociological Review* 27, (February 1962): 31–41.

Etzioni, Amitai. "Basic Human Needs, Alienation, and Inauthenticity." *American Sociological Review* 33 (December 1968): 870–84.

Festinger, Leon. *A Theory of Cognitive Dissonance.* Evanston, Ill.: Row Peterson, 1957.

Glick, Paul C., and Norton, Arthur J. "Perspectives on the Recent Upturn in Divorce and Remarriage." *Demography* 10 (August, 1973): 301–14.

Goldman, Marshall I. *The Spoils of Progress: Environmental Pollution in the Soviet Union.* Cambridge, Mass.: MIT Press, 1972.

Gregg, R. E. "The Origin of Castes in Ants With Special Reference to *Pheidole morrisi* Forel." *Ecology* 23 (1942): 295–308.

Greenberg, B. "Some Relations Between Territory, Social Hierarchy, and Leadership in the Green Sunfish." *Physiological Zoology* 20 (1947): 267–99.

Grossman, Gregory. "Industrial Prices in the USSR." *American Economic Review,* May 1959, pp. 50–64.

Hare, A. *Handbook of Small Group Research.* New York: The Free Press of Glencoe, 1962.

Hawley, Amos H. *Human Ecology: A Theory of Community Structure.* New York: The Ronald Press Company, 1950.

Hebb, D. O. *The Organization of Behavior.* New York: John Wiley & Sons, 1949.

Hein, Piet. *Grooks.* Cambridge, Mass.: MIT Press, 1966.

Hinsie, Leland Earl, and Campbell, Robert Jean. *Psychiatric Dictionary.* 4th ed. New York: Oxford University Press, 1970.

Honigman, John J. *The World of Man.* New York: Harper & Bros., 1959.

Jourard, Sidney M. *Self-Disclosure: An Experimental Analysis of the Transparent Self.* New York: John Wiley & Sons, 1971a.

———. *The Transparent Self.* New York: Van Nostrand Reinhold Company, 1971b.

Kaufman, Herbert. *The Limits of Organizational Change.* University, Ala.: University of Alabama Press, 1971.

Keniston, Kenneth. *The Uncommitted—Alienated Youth in American Society.* New York: Harcourt, Brace & World, 1965.

Kuhn, Alfred. "Toward a Uniform Language of Information and Knowledge." *Synthese* 13 (June 1961): 127–53.

———. *The Study of Society: A Unified Approach.* Homewood, Ill.: Richard D. Irwin, Inc. and the Dorsey Press, 1963.

_____. *Labor: Institutions and Economics.* New York: Harcourt, Brace & World, 1967.

_____. *The Logic of Social Systems.* San Francisco: Jossey-Bass Publishers, 1974.

Kuhn, Thomas S. *The Structure of Scientific Revolutions.* 2d ed. Chicago: University of Chicago Press, 1970.

Laing, R. D. *knots.* New York: Pantheon Books (Random House), 1970.

Lampman, Robert J. "Changes in the Share of Wealth Held by the Top Wealth-Holders, 1922–1956." *Review of Economics and Statistics* 41 (November 1959). Reprinted in *Perspectives on Poverty and Income Distribution,* ed. by James G. Scoville. Lexington, Mass.: D. C. Heath & Co., 1971.

Landecker, Werner S. "Types of Integration and Their Measurement." *American Journal of Sociology* 56 (January 1951): 332–40.

Lenski, Gerhard F. *Power and Privilege: A Theory of Social Stratification.* New York: McGraw Hill, 1966.

Leslie, Gerald R. *The Family in Social Context.* New York: Oxford University Press, 1973.

Light, S. F. "The Determination of Caste of Social Insects." *Quarterly Review of Biology* 17 (1942): 312–26; 18 (1943): 46–63.

Lipset, Seymour Martin, and Bendix, Reinhard. *Social Mobility in Industrial Society.* Berkeley: University of California Press, 1959.

Little, I. M. D. *A Critique of Welfare Economics.* Oxford: Oxford University Press, 1949.

Loewenstein, Karl. *Political Power and the Governmental Process.* Chicago: University of Chicago Press, 1957.

McClelland, D. C. *Personality.* New York: Dryden Press, 1951.

Mack, Raymond W. "Theoretical and Substantive Biases in Sociological Research." *Interdisciplinary Relationships in the Social Sciences.* Edited by M. Sherif and C. W. Sherif. Chicago: Aldine Publishing Co., 1969.

Malinowski, Bronislaw. *Magic, Science, and Religion.* Glencoe, Ill.: The Free Press, 1948.

March, James G., and Simon, Herbert A. *Organizations.* New York: John Wiley & Sons, 1958.

Maruyama, Magoroh. "The Second Cybernetics: Deviation-Amplifying Mutual Causal Process." *American Scientist* 51 (1963). Reprinted in *Modern Systems Research for the Behavioral Scientist.* Edited by Walter Buckley. Chicago: Aldine Publishing Co., 1968.

Mathewson, Stanley B. *Restriction of Output Among Unorganized Workers.* New York: Viking, 1931. Reprinted, Carbondale, Ill.: Southern Illinois University Press, 1969 (paper).

Mead, Margaret. *Sex and Temperament.* New York: William Morrow & Co., 1935.

Meier, Richard L. *Developmental Planning.* New York: McGraw Hill, 1965.

Miller, James G. "Living Systems." *Behavioral Science* 10, nos. 3 and 4 (1965). Three articles.

_____. "The Nature of Living Systems." *Behavioral Science,* 16 (July, 1971). 1–182 (entire issue).

Morrissett, Irving. "The New Social Science Curricula." In *Concepts and Structure in the New Social Science Curricula,* ed. by Irving Morrissett. Boulder, Col.: Social Science Education Consortium, Inc., 1966.

Mowrer, Orval Hobart. *Learning Theory and the Symbolic Process.* New York: John Wiley & Sons, 1960.

Olds, James. "Psychological Mechanisms of Reward." In *Nebraska Symposium of Motivation,* edited by Marshall R. Jones. Lincoln: University of Nebraska Press, 1956.

Packard, Vance. *The Status Seekers.* New York: D. McKay Co., 1959.

Parsons, Talcott. *Societies: Evolutionary and Comparative Perspectives.* Englewood Cliffs, N.J.: Prentice-Hall, Inc., 1966.

Pechman, Joseph A., and Okner, Benjamin A. *How is the Tax Burden Shared?* Washington: The Brookings Institution, 1974.

Pepitone, Albert. *Attraction and Hostility.* New York: Atherton Press, 1964.

Polanyi, Karl. *The Great Transformation: The Political and Economic Origins of Our Time.* New York: Beacon Press, 1963. (Paper. Originally published 1944).

Polsby, Nelson W. *Community Power and Political Theory.* New Haven, Conn.: Yale University Press, 1963.

Poore, M. E. D. "Integration in the Plant Community." In *British Ecological Society Jubilee Symposium,* edited by A. MacFadyen and P. J. Newbould, a supplement to the *Journal of Ecology* 52 (1964).

Puzo, Mario. *The Godfather.* Greenwich, Conn.: Fawcett Publications, 1969 (paper).

Reitman, Walter. *Cognition and Thought.* New York: John Wiley & Sons, 1965.

Riker, William. *The Theory of Political Coalitions.* New Haven, Conn.: Yale University Press, 1962.

Robinson, James A., and Majak, R. Roger. "The Theory of Decision Making" edited by James C. Charlesworth in *Contemporary Political Analysis* (New York: Free Press, 1967): 175–88.

Rose, Arnold M. *The Power Structure: Political Process in American Life.* New York: Oxford University Press, 1967.

Rothenberg, Jerome. *The Measurement of Social Welfare.* Englewood Cliffs, N.J.: Prentice-Hall, Inc., 1961.

Roethlisberger, F. J., and Dickson, W. J. *Management and the Worker.* Cambridge, Mass.: Harvard University Press, 1939.

Russell, Bertrand. "Freedom and Government." In *Freedom, Its Meaning,* edited by Ruth Nanda Anshen. New York: Harcourt, Brace, Inc., 1940.

Samuelson, Paul A. *Economics.* 8th ed. New York: McGraw-Hill Book Co., 1970.

Satir, Virginia. *People Making.* Palo Alto, Calif.: Science & Behavioral Books, Inc., 1972.

Simon, Herbert. *Administrative Behavior.* New York: Macmillan Co., 1947.

Smelser, Neil J. *The Sociology of Economic Life.* Englewood Cliffs, N.J.: Prentice-Hall, Inc., 1963 (paper).

Stebbins, G. Ledyard. *Processes of Organic Evolution.* Englewood Cliffs, N.J.: Prentice-Hall, Inc., 1966.

Stewart, Jeannie C., and Scott, J. P. "Lack of Correlation Between Leadership and Dominance Relationships in a Herd of Goats." *Journal of Comparative Physiological Psychology* 40 (1947): 255–64.

Sumner, William Graham. *Folkways.* Boston: Ginn & Co., 1940. (Originally published 1906).

Taylor, Robert. *Introduction to Cultural Anthropology.* Rockleigh, N.J.: Allyn & Bacon, Inc., 1973.

Thibaut, J. W., and Kelley, H. H. *The Social Psychology of Groups.* New York: John Wiley & Sons, 1959.

Volin, Lazar. "Soviet Agriculture Under Krushchev." *American Economic Review,* May 1959: 15–32.

Walton, Richard E., and McKersie, Robert B. *A Behavioral Theory of Labor Negotiations.* New York: McGraw-Hill Book Co., 1965.

Watson, J. B., and Morgan, J. J. B. "Emotional Reactions and Psychological Experimentation." *American Journal of Psychology* 28 (1917): 163–74.

White, Leslie A. *The Science of Culture.* New York: Grove Press, 1949 (paper).

Whyte, Lancelot Law. *Internal Factors in Evolution.* London: Tavistock Publications, Ltd., 1965.

Whyte, William H., Jr. *The Organization Man.* Garden City, N.Y.: Doubleday & Co., 1957 (paper).

Wiener, Norbert. *Cybernetics.* Cambridge: Technology Press, 1948.

Wilson, Everett K. *Sociology: Rules, Roles, and Relationships.* Homewood, Ill.: The Dorsey Press, 1966.

Yerkes, R. M. "Dominance and Sexual Status in the Chimpanzee." *Quarterly Review of Biology* 14 (1930): 115–36.

index

INDEX

Family—*Cont.*
  biological determinants of, 406
  economic and social factors in, 407
  extended, 407
  multipurpose aspect of, 408
  nuclear, 404
  not segmental, 409
  as transmitter of culture, 165
  trends in, 431–33
Fear, 62
Feedback, 22, 36
  negative, 22, 25
  positive, 22–23, 25, 64
Festinger, Leon, 186
Final net benefit, defined, 87–88
Firms as coordinators, 343
Folkways, 490
Formal logic as syntax, 169
Formal organization, 208–41
  complex, 209, 215–41
  simple, 210–15
  simple temporary, 249
  structure of, 228–30
Fradon, Dana, 389
Free, goods, 83, 381
Freedom
  as egalitarian, 143
  and interpersonal costs, 143
  power and, 141–44, 298
  sense of, 144
Friendship, 188, 260–61
Frustration, 43, 68, 73, 176
  and war, 335
Function, 1–2
Functional boundaries of systems, 11
Future, 85

G

Game, 110
  in dating and courtship, 426
General Rule of decisions, 85–86
Generous transaction, 120–23
Genetic drift, 41
Geography, 2–3, 509
Gift, 196
  and status, 201
Glick, Paul C., 415, 422
Goals, 75
Goldman, Marshall I., 517
Goldwater, Barry, 299, 312
Good
  defined, 81
  free, 83, 381, 391
  public, 280
Government, 277–320
  all-purpose function of, 282
  coalitional function of, 288
  defined, 278
  functions of, 287

Government—*Cont.*
  induction into, 286
  organizational function of, 287
  origins of, 278
  special characteristics of, 281
  sponsor-staff relation in, 310
  world, 327
Greenberg, B., 204
Gregg, R. E., 204
Gresham's law, 365
Gross benefit, 87
Grossman, Gregory, 400
Group, 33, 262
  small, 506
Group decisions, 220–27
  by communication and transaction, 221
Group marriage, 407
Growth
  curve of, 451
  and proportions, 450
  simple, 450
Guilt, 192

H

Haley, Bernard F., 198
Hare, A. Paul, 506
Hart, John, 172–73, 244, 379
Hawley, Amos H., 243
Hebb, D. O., 54
Hein, Piet, 131
Hierarchy, 12, 234
Hinsie, Leland Earl, 483
History, 2–3, 509
Hoest, Bill, 126
Homeostasis, 15, 240
Honigmann, John J., 336, 491
Hostile transaction, 123, 125
Human
  ecology, 249
  nature, 34, 47, 497
  nature and war, 333–36
Hunt, Stan, 340
Huxley, Aldous, 405

I

Iconics, 69
Identification, problem of, 51
Identity, 477, 479
Ideology, 297
  power politics and, 329
Idiographic, 447
Image(s), 52–54, 56, 62
  consensus in, 175
  as cultural content, 486–87
  models as, 50
  transmission of, 165–68
Imagination, 45, 71, 470
Impeachment, 309

This book has been set in 9 and 8 point Primer, leaded 2 points. Part numbers and titles are 24 point (small) Helvetica. Chapter numbers are 30 point Helvetica Medium and chapter titles are 18 point Helvetica. The size of the type page is 27 × 46½ picas.

117981

DATE DUE